Nurturing Child and Adolescent Spirituality

Perspectives from the World's Religious Traditions

Nurturing Child and Adolescent Spirituality

Perspectives from the World's Religious Traditions

EDITED BY

KAREN MARIE YUST

AOSTRE N. JOHNSON

SANDY EISENBERG SASSO

EUGENE C. ROEHLKEPARTAIN

ROWMAN & LITTLEFIELD PUBLISHERS, INC.
Lanham • Boulder • New York • Oxford

ROWMAN & LITTLEFIELD PUBLISHERS, INC.

Published in the United States of America
by Rowman & Littlefield Publishers, Inc.
A wholly owned subsidiary of
The Rowman & Littlefield Publishing Group, Inc.
4501 Forbes Boulevard, Suite 200, Lanham, Maryland 20706
www.rowmanlittlefield.com

PO Box 317
Oxford
OX2 9RU, UK

British Library Cataloguing in Publication Information Available

Library of Congress Cataloging-in-Publication Data
Nurturing child and adolescent spirituality : perspectives from the world's
religious traditions / edited by Karen Marie Yust . . . [et al.].
p. cm.
Includes bibliographical references and index.
ISBN 0-7425-4462-1 (cloth : alk. paper)—ISBN 0-7425-4463-X (pbk. : alk. paper)
1. Children—Religious life.   2. Religious education of children.   3. Teenagers—Religious
life.   4. Religious education of teenagers.   I. Yust, Karen Marie. BL625.5.N87   2006
200'.83—dc22

                                                                    2005017569

Printed in the United States of America

♾ ™ The paper used in this publication meets the minimum requirements of American National
Standard for Information Sciences—Permanence of Paper for Printed Library Materials,
ANSI/NISO Z39.48–1992.

Contents

Editors' Preface   ix

Acknowledgments   xi

1   Traditional Wisdom: Creating Space for Religious Reflection on
Child and Adolescent Spirituality   1
*Karen Marie Yust, Aostre N. Johnson, Sandy Eisenberg Sasso,
and Eugene C. Roehlkepartain*

PART I. CHILDREN AND ADOLESCENTS IN MAJOR RELIGIOUS TRADITIONS   15

2   Awakening Latent Spirituality: Nurturing Children
in the Hindu Tradition   19
Vishal Agarwal

3   The Child as Compassionate Bodhisattva and as
Human Sufferer/Spiritual Seeker: Intertwined Buddhist Images   33
Yoshiharu Nakagawa

4   Learning to Be Righteous: A Jewish Theology of Childhood   43
Michael Shire

5   The Dignity and Complexity of Children:
Constructing Christian Theologies of Childhood   53
Marcia J. Bunge

6   Filling the Heart with the Love of God:
Islamic Perspectives on Spirituality in Childhood and Adolescence   69
Yetkin Yildirim

PART II. SPIRITUAL CHANGE AND RITES OF PASSAGE   81

7   Saintly Children: Roman Catholicism and the Nurture of Children   83
Adrian Gellel

 8   After a Child's First Dance with God: Accompanying Children
     on a Protestant Spiritual Journey   95
     Catherine Stonehouse

 9   In Right Relationship with God: Childhood Conversion
     in Evangelical Christian Traditions   108
     Kevin E. Lawson

10   From Naming to Initiation: Childhood and Adolescence
     in African Christian Spirituality   122
     Nicholas Otieno

11   The Child on Loan: The Pathway from Infancy through Adolescence
     in Islamic Studies   132
     Ruqayya Yasmine Khan

12   Entering the World, Entering Torah: Moving from the Natural
     to the Sacred in the Jewish Life Cycle   143
     Roberta Louis Goodman

13   Educating the Warrior: A Tibetan Buddhist Approach
     to Spiritual Growth   157
     Richard C. Brown

PART III. RITUALS AND PRACTICES TO NURTURE THE INNER LIFE   171

14   Young Minds, Youthful Buddhas: Developmental Rituals
     and Practices in Tibetan Buddhism   175
     The Dzogchen Ponlop Rinpoche

15   Narrative and Imagination: The Role of Texts and Storytelling
     in Nurturing Spirituality in Judaism   191
     Howard Schwartz

16   Sanctifying Time: A Jewish Perspective on Prayer, Holy Days,
     and Blessings in the Life of Children   199
     Shoshana Silberman

17   Schooling the Heart: Introducing Catholic Youth to the Meaning
     and Practice of Prayer   209
     Robin Maas

18   Sacred Celebrations: The Role of Festivals in Nurturing Hindu
     Children's Spirituality   223
     Melukote K. Sridhar

19   Reformed Spirits: Christian Practices in Presbyterian Preschools
     in South Korea and the United States   236
     Kathy Dawson and Shin-Kyung Park

PART IV. CONNECTING THE INNER LIFE WITH ETHICAL ACTION   249

20   A Way of Mind and Life: The Relationship of Adolescent
     Catholic Spirituality to Life Structure   253
     Michael Warren

21   Singing Hope and Practicing Justice: Adolescent Emancipatory
     Hope Embodied in the Life of Ruby Doris Smith   264
     Evelyn L. Parker

22   Repairing the World: The Place of Mitzvot
     in Children's Spiritual Lives   275
     Sherry H. Blumberg

23   Nurturing Young People's Spirituality as a Force for Social Change:
     A Bahá'í Perspective   285
     Lori M. Noguchi

24   Children and the Five Pillars of Islam: Practicing Spirituality
     in Daily Life   296
     Afeefa Syeed and Nusaybah Ritchie

25   Value-Creating Education: A Nichiren Buddhist Perspective   309
     Monte Joffee

PART V. WHO IS RESPONSIBLE FOR NURTURING SPIRITUALITY?   321

26   At Home with Faith and Family: A Protestant Christian Perspective   325
     Elizabeth F. Caldwell

27   Sunday School for Buddhists? Nurturing Spirituality in Children   338
     Sumi Loundon, Ilmee Hwansoo Kim, and Benny Liow

28   Personal Responsibility with Communal Support:
     The Spiritual Education of Muslim Children   352
     Pamela K. Taylor

29   Understanding Dharma, Performing Karma: Shared Responsibilities
     for Spiritual Grooming in Hindu Traditions   366
     Venkatakrishna B. V. Sastry

30   Transforming Bar/Bat Mitzvah: The Role of Family and Community   380
     Jeffrey K. Salkin

31   Teaching Correct Principles: Promoting Spiritual Strength
     in LDS Young People   394
     David C. Dollahite and Loren D. Marks

**PART VI. SOCIAL AND CULTURAL FORCES
          THAT SHAPE SPIRITUALITY**   409

32   Scarce Discourse: Exploring Gender, Sexuality, and Spirituality
     in Buddhism   411
     Rita M. Gross

33   Identity Jihads: The Multiple Strivings of American Muslim Youth   423
     Marcia Hermansen and Shabana Mir

34   Countering a Malforming Culture: Christian Theological Formation
     of Adolescents in North America   437
     Ellen T. Charry

35   Resistance and Resilience: Cultivating Christian Spiritual Practices
     among Brazilian Children and Youth   449
     Débora Barbosa Agra Junker

36   Spiritual Economies of Childhood: Christian Perspectives
     on Global Market Forces and Young People's Spirituality   458
     Joyce Ann Mercer

37   Born with a Knife in Their Hearts: Children and Political Conflict
     in the Middle East   472
     Arik Ascherman

Postscript: Expanding the Conversation   481

About the Editors   487

Contributors   489

Index   495

Editors' Preface

When we first began conceptualizing a book on the wisdom offered by religious traditions on spirituality in childhood and adolescence, we knew we had taken on a daunting task. How do you do justice to the wisdom of multiple religious traditions within a single volume—particularly on a "fuzzy" topic like spirituality? In a world with hundreds of religious traditions and thousands of variations within those traditions, where do you start? And where do you stop? How do you honor the specifics of diverse religious perspectives and cultures while also creating enough cohesion and structure to help the reader understand and enter the conversation?

It would have been easier to narrow the scope—focus on one or two traditions, stick with one continent, delve deeply into one or two questions, look at just childhood or just adolescence. However, we believed then—and believe even more firmly now—that our charge was to expand the vision and boundaries beyond our own comfort zones. By thinking expansively, we hoped to broaden the conversation in ways that introduced new voices, challenged assumptions, raised new questions, and broadened the base of knowledge and investment in this important domain of life.

So instead of picking between this or that, this is a book of "ands": Buddhism, Christianity, Hinduism, Islam, Judaism, and other religious traditions; North America and Africa, Asia, Europe, and Latin America; children and adolescents.

This approach did lead to making other choices that would allow us to create a publishable volume. We focused primarily on five major world religions (with selected voices from others), knowing that there are hundreds of other traditions and approaches that also have much to offer. And within these traditions, we could only include a few voices from each, being aware that we have only begun to introduce the richness of thought and perspective that has developed over the centuries. Our hope is that these chapters and this book stimulate additional dialogue and publications that push beyond these boundaries while also delving much more deeply into the specific themes that are only introduced here.

One other important choice merits further mention: This book is specifically and intentionally focused on theological or philosophical perspectives from within religious traditions. It does not seek to examine the wealth of insight and knowledge that is emerging in other settings and disciplines, including the social sciences (psychology, sociology, anthropology), education, philosophy, medicine, and others. As we articulate in the introduction, our intention is to create space for the religious traditions to find their voices around this issue so that they are not drowned out by other perspectives.

Furthermore, we developed this volume to complement a separate volume, *The Handbook of Spiritual Development in Childhood and Adolescence* (Roehlkepartain, King, Wagener, and Benson, 2006), which concentrates exclusively on social science perspectives on these issues. Together, these two books provide a strong, multidisciplinary foundation in religious studies and the social sciences for future scholarship and cross-discipline dialogue and integration.

Aside from differentiating the content of two complementary volumes, we also wanted to develop a book that is firmly grounded in the language and priorities of religious studies in hopes that disciplines of theology, textual studies, historical studies, philosophy of religion, and related areas will take more seriously the specific issues of child and adolescent spirituality. In doing so, we would hope that the book helps to stimulate explorations of whether and how religious communities are truly tapping their own wisdom and strengths in nurturing today's young people in a complex and changing world.

Undergirding both this book and the social science handbook has been a grant to Search Institute from the John Templeton Foundation, which focused on mapping the state of knowledge about child and adolescent spiritual development in both religious studies and the social sciences. This project is designed to set the stage for new waves of scholarship and dialogue within and across traditions, disciplines, and cultures that will enrich understanding and strengthen how the world's religious traditions, and others, understand and cultivate the spiritual lives of children and adolescents around the globe.

Reference

Roehlkepartain, Eugene C., Pamela E. King, Linda M. Wagener, and Peter L. Benson, eds. 2006. *The handbook of spiritual development in childhood and adolescence.* Thousand Oaks, Calif.: Sage.

Acknowledgments

Over the past two years, dozens of individuals have contributed to shaping this book. Without their guidance, recommendations, contributions, and support, we could never have completed such an undertaking.

First and foremost, we thank the forty-two scholars who wrote chapters for this volume. Coming from many traditions, perspectives, and nations, they invested tremendous energy and insight into their chapters, responding to the demanding expectations, pressing deadlines, and evolving process with grace and patience. We are honored that you chose to contribute to this work and to this field, and we are pleased to have come to know you through this process.

Less visible, but vitally important, are the dozens of unnamed individuals who offered recommendations along the way, helping us link with the networks, scholars, and resources needed to identify and bring together the authors. Your generosity of time and connections created the unseen web of relationships that ties this book together. Thank you.

The John Templeton Foundation, Philadelphia, Pennsylvania, made this book possible through its support of Search Institute's initiative to map the state of spiritual development. Thank you for your commitment to and investment in examining the spiritual domain of life. Particular thanks to Arthur Schwartz, who first identified the need for this volume and then has supported and encouraged us throughout its development.

We also wish to thank all of our work colleagues at our respective institutions, who tolerated our preoccupied minds, closed doors, and overflowing in-boxes. We especially thank those colleagues who have contributed to the development of this book.

At Christian Theological Seminary, where Karen Marie Yust was teaching during the development of this volume, we thank Joyce Krauser, who helped keep the project on track when needed. At Saint Michael's College, thanks to the Education Department faculty and staff, always a source of support, and to Edward Mahoney of the Edmundite Center for Faith and Culture for his ongoing encouragement. Special thanks to Sharon Hein for her tireless attention to detail and administrative assistance in her work with Sandy Sasso. Also to Dennis C. Sasso, Sandy's husband, for his thoughtful suggestions and insights throughout the creation of this collection. He has been an invaluable source of wisdom and encouragement.

At Search Institute, thanks go to Mary Byers, who guided the manuscript through copyediting; Sandra Longfellow, who assisted with library work, literature searches, and bibliographies; Brent Bolstrom and Katie Streit, who provided research assistance; Susan Herman, who not only provided administrative support but helped protect time for writing and editing; and Peter Benson, who provided insight, encouragement, and guidance throughout the process.

To Brian Romer, Stephen Driver, Maria denBoer, Michael Bifulco, and Carol Bifulco at Rowman and Littlefield: Thank you for seeing the potential in this project, for encouraging us amid the challenges, and for your careful attention to the project, ensuring that this book is of the highest quality.

Finally, we particularly appreciate our families for their support, encouragement, and patience throughout the process of developing this book: Brady Schutt and children David, Paula, and Michael; Aostre Johnson's mother, Ruth Fering Black, and daughter, NoorJehan Johnson; Dennis Sasso and children Debora, David, and Dana; and Jolene Roehlkepartain and children Micah and Linnea. You have nurtured our spirits and reminded us of what is important through it all. We are deeply grateful.

CHAPTER 1

Traditional Wisdom: Creating Space for Religious Reflection on Child and Adolescent Spirituality

Karen Marie Yust

Aostre N. Johnson

Sandy Eisenberg Sasso

Eugene C. Roehlkepartain

An Age of Spiritual Inquiry

Spirituality occupies a precarious place in our world. On the one hand, literally billions of people view spirituality as a source of meaning, purpose, direction, and devotion. From another perspective, people who claim to be spiritual or religious in some form or another express those commitments with attitudes of hostility or acts of violence. And from a third angle, many people have grown up in a world that, in the words of Rabbi Michael Lerner, "demeans and marginalizes spiritual consciousness and represents the advance of rationality and science as the moment in history when spiritual forces from the Dark Ages were finally replaced by the 'Enlightenment'" (Lerner 2000, 2).

Now add children and adolescents to the mix. Some are growing up in religiously dominated societies that are suddenly being infiltrated by Hollywood-style media, introducing them to competing and conflicting worldviews. Others are growing up in secular societies where religious affiliation is low and being religious is viewed as outmoded and irrelevant, or, in some cases, has been declared illegal. They may undertake a search for spiritual meaning seemingly independent of religious institutions. Still others are seeking a way to shape a religious and spiritual identity as new immigrants or a religious minority in a culture that does not seem to understand, value, or support their practices. How do they—and those who care for them—find their way?

At one level, the search should be easy. In some parts of the world, interest in spirituality appears to be pervasive. Mainstream magazines, celebrities, public figures, and other cultural icons have demonstrated interest in a myriad of dimensions of spirituality, from angelic encounters to Zen meditation. Organizations, books, and Web sites for the study of kabbalah abound. Religious sociologist Colleen McDannell notes that the number of Christian bookstores in the United States grew from 725 in 1965 to more than 7,000 thirty years later (McDannell 1995, 222). And one study reported by a British journalist found that during five years in the 1990s, the number of religious book titles grew by 83 percent, and books on New Age and the occult grew in number by 75 percent. At the same time, the number of chemistry and physics books fell by 27 percent (cited in Hartill 2000, 264).

Similarly, a March 2005 search on amazon.com revealed 12,789 books catalogued that contain the word *spiritual* in the title or description, with an additional 665 listings for popular and classical music identified as spiritual and another 592 listings for items that promote or invoke spirituality in homes, gardens, workplaces, and personal care (e.g., angel statuary, dreamcatchers, framed images of Mohandas Gandhi, meditation cushions, and infant christening bonnets, among many others). American restaurants lure customers with promises of a spiritual ambience: the Candle Café in New York City extols the spiritual experience of excellent vegetarian cuisine, while on the opposite coast, the Desert Fire restaurant in Redmond, Washington, celebrates the spiritual significance of the American Southwest in its decor and menu selections, and Tita's Hale Aina in San Francisco aims to create "a magical and spiritual haven" evoking the Hawaiian islands.[1] Partly in response to this popular interest, academic journals and conferences have emerged to examine questions of spirituality and its place in society. University and seminary courses explore spirituality as part of many disciplines, from medicine to education—not to mention theological and religious studies. Degree and certificate programs in spirituality and spiritual direction are marketed to persons with a desire to foster their own and others' spiritual awareness and practices.

Locating Children and Youth in the Discussion

Despite the popular buzz about spirituality, relatively little critical attention has focused on the spiritual lives of children and adolescents. Much of the literature on spirituality has focused instead on adults. Robert Wuthnow's groundbreaking sociological study, *After Heaven: Spirituality in America since the 1950s,* is composed entirely of interviews with adults (Wuthnow 1998). Some observers presume that the topic is only relevant to adults. Bill Easum, a prominent North American pastor and workshop leader, argues that mainstream Protestant congregations in the United States are declining in part because they do not understand twenty-first-century spirituality as an adult-centered phenomenon rather than a child-centered concern. He contends that Christian worship in emerging "Praise" and "Sensory" churches is rightly adult-oriented, whereas dying "Traditional" congregations lose their spiritual focus when they try to incorporate children into worship. Children, in his view, belong in "age-appropriate" educational settings where they can learn the "basics" of a Christian worldview in entertaining ways.[2] As a result of these types of studies and arguments, theories and practices regarding children's spirituality or the spiritual lives of youth are often either constructed as methods for laying foundations for future adult spiritual work or put forth as simple adaptations of approaches developed for adults.

When children or adolescents are considered, one of two emphases appears to dominate. In the field of education, the concern is with how the natural spirit of the child can be nurtured and enhanced through family and classroom practices from birth through higher education. The role of religious institutions may receive some attention, but the tendency is to define spirituality as a phenomenon distinct from religious identity. In religious disciplines, the primary focus seems to be socialization (or even indoctrination) into a particular adult form of spiritual awareness rather than attentiveness to the spiritual experiences of children and youth at whatever stage of life they are in. Stereotypes regarding children's capabilities and youth angst limit the types of spiritual nurture that adults believe will be effective in cultivating predetermined beliefs about and attitudes toward what is holy or divine. Left unaddressed, these assumptions contribute to the impoverishment of spirituality research, and, except in the work of noted psychiatrist Robert Coles (1990) and a handful of other, lesser known, scholars, the growing social scientific inquiry and popular discussion regarding spirituality remain relatively uninformed by the perspectives, questions, and wisdom of the world's children. Perhaps most significant, however, an important opportunity to enrich the lives of children and adolescents is being lost, set aside by most religious traditions and religious studies scholars as unworthy of critical attention.

Listening to the Wisdom of Religious Traditions

The world's religious traditions—Buddhism, Christianity, Hinduism, Islam, Judaism, and many others—have centuries of wisdom regarding the spiritual nurture of children and adolescents, manifested in their narratives, beliefs, and practices. This insight—rooted in diverse cultures, worldviews, belief systems, and experiences—has often been taken for granted or assumed within the traditions. Traditions have been passed from one generation to the next, with relatively little theological or philosophical reflection on the "why" behind the beliefs and practices. Furthermore, the traditions have rarely been in dialogue with each other about young people and their spiritual nurture.

As we enter this new millennium, however, three realities press for both articulation and dialogue. First, many religious traditions, particularly in the West, are struggling to shape the identity and life journey of the young in pluralistic cultures where shared assumptions, beliefs, and practices cannot be taken for granted.[3] Challenges of identity and continuity within faith traditions are salient and pressing, as young people grow up in communities and societies that do not necessarily share and reinforce and, in fact, often challenge and contradict their religious and spiritual beliefs and practices.

Second, in the midst of this growing pluralism and, in some cases, secularization of society (e.g., Inglehart et al. 2004), the world's religious traditions no longer have a "corner" on spirituality. In many parts of the world, a growing number of people describe themselves as "spiritual but not religious" (see Lippman & Keith 2006), and religion is often now viewed in contrast to (not facilitative of) spirituality (e.g., King 2001).

Finally, although the world has always been religiously diverse, ours is a time when the world's peoples and religions are intermingled through migration, media, and geopolitical engagement. This contact can breed—and sometimes has sparked—suspicion, mistrust, hatred, and violence. Or this contact can lead to—and sometimes has cultivated—new levels of dialogue and mutual understanding that not only deepen respect and cooperation but also provide the opportunity for each tradition to become more articulate and intentional about its own beliefs and practices.

The twenty-first century offers, therefore, a tremendous opportunity for a rigorous and creative exploration of religious perspectives regarding childhood and adolescent spirituality. However, within the limited domain of contemporary scholarly discussions on the spiritual lives of young people, there has not been adequate systematic attention to conceptualizing and understanding the philosophical and theological perspectives that the world's religious traditions might bring to the topic. With the exception of books that focus on children within specific religious traditions (e.g., Bunge 2001; Lundy 2001; Miller-McLemore 2003; Oppenheimer 1994; Silberman 1996; Stonehouse 1998; Tarazi 1995; Yust 2004), few currently available titles take both theological discourse and children's spiritual lives seriously. An analysis of sources catalogued in the ATLA Religion Database (1993–2003) illustrates the gap in the field. Of the 305,498 articles, books, and dissertations catalogued, only 2,705 include *child* as a key word, and only 977 use the key word *youth*. Furthermore, only 120 entries include key words of *child, youth,* and *spiritual*. Many of these entries are book reviews or are practice-oriented articles concerned with religious socialization ("passing on the faith/tradition"), not intentional explorations of religious or theological themes in relation to real children's lives. The wisdom of a specific religious community is generally relegated to perpetuating that tradition among the children of the faithful; it is not often explored by scholars for its interpretative usefulness as we talk about the shape of human societies, the challenges of creating just and caring relationships, and solving the global ecological crisis and the world's future.

Nurturing Scholarly Reflection

Those contemporary religious scholars who take an interest in childhood and adolescence often make space for this work by subsuming it into their specific discipline (e.g., theology, ethics, or religious education). They have had few forums for dialogue with and learning from others who focus on this age group. There are signs that this situation may be changing, however, and that a critical knowledge base regarding religious perspectives on spirituality in childhood and adolescence is emerging. The American Academy of Religion, the principal guild for scholars of religious studies in the United States and Canada, instituted an ongoing Childhood Studies and Religion consultation in 2003 that attracts approximately a hundred scholars a year from various religious traditions to its panel presentations and discussions. In 2002, Christian scholars and practitioners from Asia, Europe, Africa, South and North America launched a multi-year international exploration of the topic of "child theology" at a meeting in Penang, Malaysia (Collier 2002). And some sessions in education conferences, notably the annual Spirituality in Education event at Naropa University (since 1997), the biennial Education as Transformation conferences (since 1998), and workshops based on Quaker educator Parker Palmer's *The Courage to Teach* philosophy (for the past decade), focus on childhood and adolescent spirituality.

In addition, at least three new conferences on children's spirituality (one international and two within the United States) have been inaugurated since 2000 to bring scholars and practitioners together around issues of understanding and advancing spirituality among children and adolescents. The International Conference on Children's Spirituality, initiated by British researchers engaged in the Children's Worldview Project, has been promoting interdisciplinary conversations with scholars from around the world. The Children's Spirituality–Christian Perspectives conference is a distinctly evangelical Christian initiative begun in 2003, with some participation by mainstream Protestant Christian scholars (see Ratcliff 2005). The ChildSpirit Conference, also convened for the first time in 2003, takes a more humanistic approach to the topic while welcoming participants whose primary focus is spirituality as practiced within religious traditions.

STEERING THE CONVERSATION TO THEOLOGICAL AND PHILOSOPHICAL ISSUES

What some of these scholars are finding is that religious and theological assumptions are powerful in shaping the attitudes and practices of children and youth and of the adults who seek to nurture them. Christian Smith's 2002–3 National Survey of Youth and Religion (NSYR) in the United States helpfully expands on Robert Wuthnow's adult-centered survey of contemporary American spiritual practices by offering a parallel snapshot of youth spirituality. Smith has discovered that the teens in his study have a kind of faith he calls "Moralistic Therapeutic Deism" (see Smith 2005).[4] This adolescent spiritual perspective operates according to five principles:

1. A God exists who created and orders the world and watches over human life on earth.
2. God wants people to be good, nice, and fair to each other, as taught in the Bible and by most world religions.
3. The central goal of life is to be happy and to feel good about oneself.
4. God does not need to be particularly involved in one's life except when God is needed to resolve a problem.
5. Good people go to heaven when they die (Smith 2005, 162–63).

Such a perspective raises significant questions about religious anthropology, divine immanence and transcendence, soteriology, eschatology, good and evil, suffering and blessing, justice and mercy, and other religious and theological themes. Sustained, rigorous attention to how religious communities have traditionally interpreted these issues and how childhood and adolescent experiences contribute to or challenge these interpretations has the potential to significantly enrich and strengthen our understanding of the spiritual dimensions of young people's lives—and to challenge and shape the families, schools, congregations, communities, and institutions that nurture them.

LAUNCHING A NEW INITIATIVE

With this goal in mind and with support from the John Templeton Foundation, Search Institute launched (in 2003) a major international, interfaith initiative on spiritual development in childhood and adolescence. As part of this initiative, the institute is collaborating with other scholars to assess the state of religious/theological understanding (this volume) and social scientific understanding (see Roehlkepartain et al. 2006) of spiritual development in childhood and adolescence. By first drawing together insights, wisdom, and knowledge from multiple perspectives and disciplines, this initiative is envisioned as a multiyear major focus that seeks to stimulate interest and scholarship in this field across the coming decade.

Nurturing Child and Adolescent Spirituality: Perspectives from the World's Religious Traditions lays the intellectual foundations in religious studies for this ongoing initiative of research, scholarship, dialogue, and application. It seeks to introduce and facilitate a kind of conversation and reflection that responds to the realities of the new millennium. First, it invites scholars within each tradition to reflect on and articulate how their own tradition understands spirituality in childhood and adolescence. In doing so, it sets the stage for exploring how each tradition can tap its narratives, beliefs, and practices to cultivate the spiritual lives of its children and adolescents. Second, it gives voice to those traditions in ways that remind the broader community of scholars (social scientists, historians, educators) and practitioners that the religious traditions have a great deal to contribute to understanding and nurturing the spiritual lives of children and adolescents. Finally, it brings together voices from multiple traditions and cultures to articulate their own perspectives on key questions in ways that set the stage for respectful, thoughtful dialogue leading to greater understanding and respect.

Laying the Foundation for International and Interfaith Discussion

This book presents the voices of prominent religious scholars and practitioners who articulate how their traditions have approached major questions regarding spirituality in childhood and adolescence. It particularly examines the state of religious knowledge and theological reflection on spiritual development in childhood and adolescence in the world's five major religious traditions: Buddhism, Christianity, Hinduism, Islam, and Judaism. By creating a tapestry of wisdom and insight on the nature, processes, and practices of spirituality, the volume not only surveys current understandings of spiritual development but also invites reflection on helpful agendas for future dialogue and scholarship within and among traditions. Its goals are fourfold.

To establish a baseline of scholarship and knowledge regarding religious perspectives on childhood and adolescent spirituality. To provide a snapshot of the breadth and depth of this area of scholarship, the book is as comprehensive and inclusive as possible within the scope of a single volume. It seeks to balance harmony and dissonance across (and within) religious traditions, cultures, and contexts around the world. This attempt is hampered by the hegemony of North American perspectives, for much of the contemporary research linking childhood and adolescent spirituality with religious traditions grows out of recent studies in the United States. It is also limited by the predominantly Euro-Caucasian perspective of faculties and textbooks related to doctoral studies in religion and spirituality. Scholars from around the globe attend North American or European universities to study or work at home from Eurocentric resources translated into multiple languages for wider dissemination. We recognize that such dominance necessarily shapes the kinds of questions scholars ask about the spiritual beliefs and practices of children and youth and the types of research projects they construct for publication in refereed scholarly journals. Our goal, then, is to expand the width of the scholarly baseline through the inclusion of voices and perspectives that challenge or disrupt the often unconscious projection of American experiences onto the rest of humanity, even as we recognize the forcefulness of American interpretations in the discourse as it is now constructed.

To highlight the importance of spirituality as an area of intentional study and practice within religious and theological studies with children and adolescents. The primary emphasis of the volume is to establish the knowledge and theoretical base (beliefs, traditions, practices) for understanding the approaches taken to spirituality in childhood and adolescence within religious traditions. Essays also explore the implications of this knowledge base for informing and shaping spiritual formation practices in families, faith communities, educational institutions, and other settings in society. Although authors sometimes accent certain periods in childhood or adolescence, most address broadly the first two decades of life, offering the reader a sense of the unfolding trajectory of the spirituality of young people across time rather than focusing on distinct, predictable, or developmental stages disconnected from the larger picture of life from birth to approximately age twenty.

To bring together the insights of leading scholars from multiple disciplines, traditions, and continents to enrich knowledge and scholarship in this domain. The volume's contributors are scholars in various disciplines (spirituality, biblical/sacred text studies, theology, ethics, and religious education) within religious studies, as well as scholars in other academic fields with an interest in children, youth, and spirituality. Some of them are highly trained and experienced practitioners whose primary work is among children and youth rather than in the academy. Most come from the traditions of Buddhism, Christianity, Judaism, Islam, and Hinduism, but a few scholars come from lesser-studied traditions (Bahá'í, Latter-day Saints). While many contributors live and work in the United States or Canada, nine chapters offer perspectives from authors representing ten countries outside the North American continent: Japan, Great Britain, Malta, Kenya, Brazil, South Korea, China, Malaysia, Taiwan, and Israel. In this way, we hope to introduce readers to the rich foment of religious and theological discourse currently under way around the world in a time of increased globalization.

To model intentional dialogue across and among faith traditions about how spirituality is understood and nurtured in children and adolescents. The volume does not seek to reach consensus or to engage in debates among religious traditions. Rather, it emphasizes mutual learning and dialogue toward understanding. Authors have attempted to place themselves ideologically within their own religious tradition while remaining respectful of other traditions. They have tried to fairly represent some of the perspectives that exist among their tradition's "insiders" and to offer a self-critical assessment of their tradition's beliefs and practices, particularly when certain perspectives undermine respectful dialogue across traditions.

DEFINING SPIRITUALITY FOR INTERRELIGIOUS DIALOGUE

A primary challenge in developing this book has been setting boundaries around a term—*spirituality*—that is used in so many different ways by so many different people, traditions, disciplines, and cultures. While recognizing the importance of remaining open to multiple perspectives, we also recognized the importance of stating the definitional assumption for the book as a starting point for engaging authors in dialogue and for shaping the content of the volume. Thus, guiding this volume is the following working definition:

> Spirituality is the intrinsic human capacity for self-transcendence in which the individual participates in the sacred—something greater than the self. It propels the search for connectedness, meaning, purpose, and ethical responsibility. It is experienced, formed, shaped, and expressed through a wide range of religious narratives, beliefs, and practices, and is shaped by many influences in family, community, society, culture, and nature.

Contributors to this volume approach spirituality in childhood and adolescence differently, based both on their own religious tradition as well as the cultures and disciplines in which they live and work. Each author makes clear her or his own assumptions and definition of spirituality, particularly when that definition differs from the volume's working definition. Several assumptions or hypotheses in this definition merit further explication.

Spirituality is an intrinsic part of humanness. This definition asserts that being spiritual is part of being human; it is an intrinsic human capacity. Throughout history and across all societies, forms of spirituality have become part of human experience, and spirituality has remained a robust force in life for both individuals and societies, despite numerous predictions of its demise. That said, it is understood and manifested with great variety across cultures and religious traditions, as illustrated by the authors of this book.

Spirituality is related to but not defined by religion and faith. Our emphasis is on spirituality and spiritual nurture, not necessarily religious or faith development as that might be more narrowly understood. The accent is on one's connectedness (with others or the Other) and sense of meaning and purpose, rather than orthodoxy in belief or practice or religious knowledge, per se. This approach assumes that spirituality, as part of our humanness, may be cultivated both within and outside traditional religious frameworks. We recognize, however, that the lines are blurred between these concepts, and traditions—and authors within traditions—vary in their understanding of spirituality and its relationship to religion, faith, belief, and orthodoxy.

Spirituality involves growth and change. The editors of this volume understand spirituality as involving some sort of change—transformation, growth, maturation, ebb or flow—across childhood and adolescence. Although religious traditions understand this process very differently (based, in part, on their understanding of the nature of children and childhood), they each recognize and nurture that process, often with sophisticated rituals, rites of passage, education, and practices aimed at guiding, shaping, or unleashing a child or adolescent's spiritual life.

Spirituality must be an actively nurtured domain of life. Although the working definition understands spirituality to be part of every person's humanness, it also asserts that this capacity must be actively cultivated or nurtured for it to be fully realized. Indeed, one of the reasons the definition and book did not adopt the term *spiritual development* (which is being used elsewhere in the larger Search Institute initiative) is that development implies, for some, an inevitable or predictable process, as well as a presumption of growth from less to more. This approach seems to downplay the more mystical, relational, and divinely gifted understandings of spirituality our definition seeks to retain.

Spirituality is embedded in relationships and community. Some traditions have long viewed the religious community as the vessel for the spiritual, whereas many contemporary Western conceptualizations of spirituality see it primarily as an individual experience and phenomenon (Benson 2006; Mattis et al. 2006; Mbiti 1969). The definition used here emphasizes the role of communal narratives, beliefs, and practices in shaping spirituality, as well as broader forces in society and culture.

Spirituality is expressed in ethical behavior. Although spiritual practices are often perceived as focusing on the "inner life" or one's disciplines that emphasize experiencing, connecting to, or participating in the divine, the definition (and virtually all authors in this book) holds that a full understanding of spirituality should also be manifested in the "outer life" of ethical behavior and action. Thus, spirituality, when actively and intentionally nurtured, is a life-shaping force, not only for the individual but also for the larger community. Indeed, for many authors, the demarcation of inward and outward spirituality is a false dichotomy, as the two dimensions are integrally and dynamically linked.

Spirituality necessitates interdisciplinary study. As noted earlier, this volume specifically and intentionally focuses on theological and philosophical perspectives on spirituality within several of the world's religions. At the same time, the intent is to give voice to these theological perspectives so that they are more present in contemporary academic discussions of spirituality, which have tended in recent years to be dominated by social scientific and educational perspectives.

We encourage readers to engage with the editors and authors in the complex work of articulating one's definitional assumptions in ways that set the stage for thoughtful dialogue within and across religious traditions, as well as across the multiple disciplines of religious studies, theology, philosophy, and social sciences, all of which bring important perspectives and insights to our understanding of this vital dimension of life.

CORE QUESTIONS FOR EXPLORATION

The structure and flow of this book grew out of the working definition and the hypotheses that are embedded within it. For the editors, the definition raised a series of questions about how the world's religious traditions understand these issues. Thus, we organized the book around six sets of core questions:

1. *How do the world's religious traditions understand and view children and adolescents?* What is the nature of childhood and adolescence? What role do children and adolescents play in the tradition? How have religious/theological studies within traditions dealt with children and adolescents, both historically and currently?
2. *How do religious traditions understand the process of spirituality or self-transcendence in childhood and adolescence?* How is spirituality understood to be nourished or to grow within children and adolescents? How does spirituality change across the first two decades of life? What role do rites of passage play in both shaping and marking this process?
3. *What rituals and practices within religious tradition nurture the inner spiritual lives of children and adolescents?* What key rituals, holy days, or celebrations are emblematic of a tradition's approach? How are the narratives or stories of a tradition used to shape young people's spirituality? What individual and communal practices by young people are encouraged, nurtured, or taught to cultivate young people's spiritual lives?
4. *What rituals, practices, and obligations of the spiritual life guide young people to meaning, purpose, and ethical action?* How do traditions understand the relationship between spirituality and social/ethical obligations, including service and social action? How does spirituality relate to issues of vocation?
5. *To whom do the religious traditions assign responsibility for nurturing spirituality (connectedness, meaning, purpose, and ethical responsibility) in children and adolescents?* What do religious traditions expect from the community of faith, parents, peers, other adults, and other institutions in nurturing spirituality among children and adolescents?
6. *How do religious traditions view and address the social, policy, and cultural forces that influence child and adolescent spirituality?* How do major social, political, and cultural forces and dynamics influence and shape young people's spirituality? How do these forces affect how spirituality is nurtured among children and adolescents?

The diverse array of contributors who address these questions provides both a survey of major themes in the field across religious traditions and invites dialogue among scholars about different interpretations of and approaches to spirituality and spiritual nurture among children and youth, thus strengthening understanding and practice within and across multiple religious traditions.

Negotiating Similarities and Differences in Perspective

There are some fascinating similarities in the ways authors respond to the core questions posed, and some equally intriguing differences worthy of note. Many of the authors place at least some emphasis on interpreting spiritual texts important to their traditions in relation to talking about childhood and adolescent spirituality. Bible stories, rabbinic literature, the Qur'an, mythic tales, the Lotus Sutra, the writings of religious forebears, the Vedas, traditional sayings, the Upanishads, and other revered sources are used to shed light on traditional religious understandings and formation of childhood and adolescent spirituality. This similarity makes sense given the role that inspired texts play in the five major religions represented by the majority of the authors. Readers may wish to take note of the degree to which sacred texts or stories are given authority in relation to various topics and different traditions. Readers might also notice the surprisingly large number of stories and references to children and youth within the scriptures and writings of the world's religions. Several authors invite exploration of child saints or youthful actions on the part of founders, and these often hidden histories accentuate the importance of early spiritual experiences and practices in ways not typically emphasized in classical theological reflections.

Contributors have also tended to speak of children and youth as collectives (or ideal types), rather than as particular persons identified by specific racial/ethnic, gender, and socioeconomic characteristics. This is, in part, a by-product of the chapter page limit imposed by the editors: it is difficult enough to be one of the first to speak of a religious tradition's thinking in reference to an assigned set of questions in relatively few pages; to nuance that discussion further in terms of a thorough analysis of cultural factors affecting the tradition's children and youth would require much greater space and research. When cultural factors are concerns foremost in the minds of a religious group or, as in the chapters included in part VI, are orienting issues for the discussion, authors have tried to address the effects of varied social identity and status on spirituality and religious identity. The absence of this fuller discussion elsewhere requires the reader to hold in mind the need for greater exploration and critical nuance of these topics in future books and conversations.

A difference obscured during editing but worthy of mention here is the extent to which Christian authors tended initially to adopt a perspective that assumed they were talking with other Christians, reflecting (the editors surmise) their ready access to opportunities to discuss such topics in denominational or ecumenical contexts rather than interfaith settings and perhaps suggesting as well the unconscious hegemony of Christian beliefs and practices in religious studies circles. Authors from other traditions rarely adopted this "insider" voice, and the greater difficulty encountered by the editors in finding networks of scholars talking about children and youth—or even spirituality—in non-Christian traditions points to the lack of intrareligious conversations in which they might participate. Some Muslim authors elected to include an honorific title for Muhammad, believing that a true picture of their tradition's spirituality could not be constructed without the retention of this spiritual practice of respect for their prophet. Some Christian authors preferred to use masculine language for the deity and the historically familiar designations of "Old" and "New" Testament for the Christian scriptures, despite the problematic nature of this terminology, because they wished to represent the ways in which they communicate the beliefs and practices of their faith to their young. These varied commitments to particular forms of address and the blurring of distinctions between scholarly conventions and religious profession speak to the weight placed on orthodoxy and orthopraxis in the spiritual formation of children and youth. Thus, the editors' decision to adopt common language appropriate to a scholarly volume where that was acceptable to authors, while honoring the language choices of authors electing to use particular terms central to their belief systems, underscores the tensions inherent in respectful interfaith dialogue.

The assembled chapters also represent varied degrees of engagement in self-critical assessment of religious beliefs and practices regarding children and youth. As a rule, traditions already well known and accepted in North America, where many scholarly agendas are defined and cultural judgments intoned, are more comfortable engaging in public self-criticism. The assumption of goodwill on the part of the reader permits greater freedom to identify weaknesses in and contested interpretations of the tradition's beliefs and practices. Religious groups that already find themselves defending the legitimacy of their spiritual expression to a skeptical public are more hesitant to air internal disagreements or name problematic aspects of their beliefs and practices because such statements might be used to further denigrate their public status. They choose to offer their spiritual ideals without the accompaniment of internal dissonance in order to encourage public and scholarly acceptance of their place at the religious table. The editors are grateful for the large as well as small risks taken by authors, and hope that readers will approach each chapter with generosity as well as the critical eye that all scholarship merits.

Joining the Conversation

The forty-two authors and four editors already assembled as conversation partners through our participation in this book project welcome you, the reader, to the discussion. We hope that as you listen to the perspectives offered in these essays, you will begin to formulate your own responses to the issues raised and explored by persons influenced by similar religious traditions to those you know best, as well as by those whose perspectives have developed in unfamiliar religious or cultural contexts. While it is not necessary to read the book in any particular order, it may be helpful to begin with part I, as the essays there attempt to provide a broader overview of the five major religious traditions' thinking about children and youth than do the later chapters. You might choose to read sections as units so as to experience the tensions and interplay of pluralistic discourse around a more focused topic, or to follow one at a time through all the sections the contributions to the larger conversation offered by a particular religious tradition. Whatever your choices, we encourage you to imagine yourself sitting down with many other interested and interesting people to listen, question, affirm, prod, wonder, and exclaim as we seek together greater understanding and support of childhood and adolescent spirituality in a pluralistic, secularized, and global world society.

Notes

1. See www.candlecafe.com; http://www.amazon.com/exec/obidos/tg/detail/-/B0000637 MY/qid=1111502573/sr=1-1/ref=sr_1_1/02-2226981-8980057?v=glance; and http://www .sanfranciscomerchants.com/castro/titas/1.

2. Easum communicated these views as part of his "Dancing with Dinosaurs" presentation at a Metropolitan Boston Association of the Massachusetts Conference of the United Church of Christ annual meeting, March 6, 1999 (Karen Marie Yust, personal notes and conversation with Easum).

3. The award-winning 2003 Public Broadcasting System documentary, *What Do You Believe? American Teenagers, Spirituality and Freedom of Religion,* highlights the personal experiences of six adolescents of diverse religious traditions who are caught up in this struggle with their faith community. Three of the six (a Muslim, a Wiccan, and a Lakota Indian) speak explicitly of the tensions inherent in the interplay of particular religious identity and religious pluralism.

4. The NSYR represents 3,370 telephone surveys with English- and Spanish-speaking young people ages thirteen to seventeen.

References

Benson, Peter L. 2006. The science of child and adolescent spiritual development: Definitional, theoretical, and field-building challenges. In *The handbook of spiritual development in childhood and adolescence,* edited by Eugene C. Roehlkepartain, Pamela E. King, Linda M. Wagener, and Peter L. Benson, 484–97. Thousand Oaks, Calif.: Sage.

Bunge, Marcia J., ed. 2001. *The child in Christian thought.* Grand Rapids, Mich.: Eerdmans.

Coles, Robert. 1990. *The spiritual life of children.* Boston: Houghton Mifflin.

Collier, John. 2002. Report of the Penang Consultation on Child Theology, June 24–28, 2002. http://www.viva.org/tellme/resources/articles/gods_heart/penang.pdf (accessed March 28, 2005).

Hartill, Rosemary. 2000. Mind, body, spirit—the new millennial age? In *Spirituality and society in the new millennium,* edited by Ursula King, 261–74. Brighton, UK: Sussex Academic Press.

Inglehart, Ronald, Miguel Basáñez, Jaime Díez-Medrano, Loek Halman, and Ruud Luijkx, eds. 2004. *Human beliefs and values: A cross-cultural sourcebook based on the 1999–2002 values surveys.* Mexico City: Siglo XXI Editores.

King, Ursula. 2001. Introduction: Spirituality, society, and the millennium—Wasteland, wilderness, or new vision? In *Spirituality and society in the new millennium,* edited by Ursula King, 1–13. Brighton, UK: Sussex Academic Press.

Lerner, Michael. 2000. *Spirit matters.* Charlottesville, Va.: Hampton Roads.

Lippman, Laura H., and Julie D. Keith. 2006. The demographics of spirituality among youth: International perspectives. In *The handbook of spiritual development in childhood and adolescence,* edited by Eugene C. Roehlkepartain, Pamela E. King, Linda M. Wagener, and Peter L. Benson, 109–23. Thousand Oaks, Calif.: Sage.

Lundy, Robert J. 2001. *How we see God and why it matters: A multicultural view.* Springfield, Ill.: Charles C. Thomas.

Mattis, Jacqueline S., Muninder K. Ahluwalia, Sheri-Ann E. Cowie, and Aria M. Kirkland-Harris. 2006. Ethnicity, culture, and spiritual development. In *The handbook of spiritual development in childhood and adolescence*, edited by Eugene C. Roehlkepartain, Pamela E. King, Linda M. Wagener, and Peter L. Benson, 283–96. Thousand Oaks, Calif.: Sage.

Mbiti, John S. 1989. *African religions and philosophy.* 2nd ed. Oxford, UK: Heinemann.

McDannell, Colleen. 1992. *Material Christianity: Religion and popular culture in America.* New Haven, Conn.: Yale University Press.

Miller-McLemore, Bonnie J. 2003. *Let the children come: Reimagining childhood from a Christian perspective.* San Francisco: Jossey-Bass.

Oppenheimer, Helen. 1994. *Helping children find God.* Harrisburg, Pa.: Morehouse.

Ratcliff, Donald, ed. 2005. *Children's spirituality: Christian perspectives, research, and applications.* Eugene, Ore.: Cascade Books.

Roehlkepartain, Eugene C., Pamela E. King, Linda M. Wagener, and Peter L. Benson, eds. 2006. *The handbook of spiritual development in childhood and adolescence.* Thousand Oaks, Calif.: Sage.

Silberman, Shoshana. 1996. *Siddur Shema Yisrael: A siddur and a sourcebook for students and families.* New York: United Synagogue of Conservative Judaism.

Smith, Christian. 2005. *Soul searching: The religious and spiritual lives of American teenagers.* New York: Oxford University Press.

Stonehouse, Catherine. 1998. *Joining children on the spiritual journey.* Grand Rapids, Mich.: Baker Books.

Tarazi, Norma. 1995. *The child in Islam.* Burr Ridge, Ill.: American Trust Publications.

Wuthnow, Robert. 1998. *After heaven: Spirituality in America since the 1950s.* Berkeley and Los Angeles: University of California Press.

Yust, Karen Marie. 2004. *Real kids, real faith: Practices for nurturing children's spiritual lives.* San Francisco: Jossey-Bass.

PART I

CHILDREN AND ADOLESCENTS IN MAJOR RELIGIOUS TRADITIONS

How do the world's religious traditions understand and view children and adolescents? This question frames the chapters in part I of *Nurturing Child and Adolescent Spirituality: Perspectives from the World's Religious Traditions*. Authors intimately familiar with Hinduism, Buddhism, Judaism, Christianity, and Islam offer a broad look at how their faith traditions conceptually and practically relate to children and adolescents, both historically and in contemporary times. The five authors' reflections on the following more specific questions help turn our attention to the broader issue of how the tradition theorizes the *nature* of childhood and adolescence: Does the tradition have what we might call a *theology* or *philosophy* of childhood and adolescence and what is it? How has that theology or philosophy changed over time? What roles do children and adolescents play in the tradition conceptually? That is, how does the tradition use images and examples of young people to understand and explain its belief system? And what roles do children play practically? What is their place in the lived reality of the religion in terms of rituals and obligations?

Drawing on examples from the many forms of Hinduism, Vishal Agarwal demonstrates that the Hindu tradition contains a complex and vivid relationship with childhood and adolescence in terms of theology and practice. Both in historical and contemporary times, in all Hindu traditions, the One Supreme Being takes the forms of various children as gods and goddesses and objects of worship. The concept of the latent spirituality of children is key to Hindu theology. The understanding of karma and rebirth held by most Hindus leads to the idea that young children may be highly spiritually evolved. This idea is strengthened by a belief in the power of rituals to awaken spirituality in children and adolescents. Children and adolescents naturally participate in prayers and rituals at the family shrine and at public shrines, and they accompany their families on pilgrimages to holy places. Adherents also believe it is never too early for children to begin studying with a Guru or teacher who can help them develop powerful spirituality at a young age. Thus, it is not surprising that Hinduism is also replete with the theme of youthful saints and young Gurus who are held up as exemplars for adults.

In contrast, Yoshiharu Nakagawa states that the Buddhist tradition does not have a developed theology of childhood and adolescence. He goes on to suggest one, drawing from the life of the Buddha, historical information, and Buddhist theology. He tells us that the Buddha named his son, born as he was about to leave his palace to seek liberation for all human beings, "Rahula," which means "fetter" or "eclipse," symbolizing that staying with his child would be an impediment to his enlightenment journey. However, when his son was seven years old, the Buddha began educating him as a Buddhist practitioner, and Rahula became a monk at the age of twenty. This training seemed to set a precedent, as Buddhist monasteries in Asian countries typically accept children for serious study at about seven years of age. Nakagawa suggests that this practice illustrates two views of childhood, one of the child as an ordinary human being subject to suffering (the fundamental human condition) and the other as a being with the potential to become a "bodhisattva" or enlightened one. The Buddhist belief in rebirth, while not implying the continuation of an unchanging soul, does suggest that children are born with varying karma, the result of past actions in other lives, that allows one child to be more "enlightened" than another.

Michael Shire draws on biblical stories, rabbinic interpretations, and Jewish customs to offer a Jewish theology of childhood. He says that while classical historical Judaism does not have a developed literature about the nature of childhood, it is quite possible to infer such a theology from these abundant sources. He suggests that the "cherished status of children" in the Jewish tradition is emblematic of this theology. The child is understood as God's greatest gift to humanity and its hope for the future; the child's nature is seen as pure, innocent, and containing "a trace of divine beneficence." Moreover, the parent–child relationship symbolizes the special covenant between God and the people of Israel. Children are included in the life of the worshipping community; in fact, the major purpose of childhood is to learn to carry out God's commandments by entering the world of duty and religious obligation. Judaism strongly emphasizes the role of study and learning in order for children to understand and embody the moral obligations at the heart of the Jewish religion.

Marcia J. Bunge tells us that although Christianity has produced many writings about children, it "has not developed robust theologies of childhood" that might provide a sophisticated base for understanding, educating, and advocating for children and adolescents. She suggests that this limitation is changing, however, marked by a growing recognition of "the child" as a significant category within theology and religious studies. After reviewing the literature, Bunge suggests six key and sometimes conflicting perspectives on childhood that have already emerged from Christian scholarship: (1) children as innocent gifts of God and sources of joy; (2) children as inherently sinful creatures with the moral agency to take some responsibility; (3) children as developing human beings who depend on adults for nurture and guidance; (4) children as complete human beings made in the image of God and inherently worthy of dignity and respect; (5) children as models of faith and sources of revelation for adults; and (6) children as vulnerable victims of injustice, war, and disease. Bunge suggests ways in which these six perspectives can be developed to intensify both theological reflection and effective ministering to the needs of youth.

Yetkin Yildirim uses the Qur'an and writings on Prophet Muhammad as his sources for explicating a Muslim understanding of childhood and adolescence. The essential innocence of childhood and the understanding of children as "gifts from Allah" are key Islamic concepts. Following the examples of the Prophet, adults are held accountable for the mercy, love, respect, and trust with which they are asked to treat children. Adults are responsible for protecting the innocence of children and guiding them carefully to ensure that they learn and practice the fundamental teachings of Islam. To that end, children have been historically welcome to participate initially informally and later formally in the adult life of the community, joining in prayers, learning the Qur'an, and leading an ethical life. Yildirim proposes a specific model of education based on these traditional understandings that is appropriate for the contemporary world.

As can be seen from these summaries, the field of theologies of childhood and adolescence, while more developed in some religions than in others, is just beginning to emerge across all five traditions. Readers will note distinct similarities as well as notable differences in the way in which each religion understands the nature and place of childhood and adolescence. For example, all stress the importance of stages of development and of adult responsibility for future religious and spiritual maturity. While all hold some image of childhood purity and reflection of divinity, the degree varies as do conceptions of the potential of children to attain advanced spiritual understandings. The presence or absence of belief in rebirth or original sin contributes to these differences. It is striking that these chapters make few references to gender differences in their conceptions of the nature and place of childhood; this would be one fertile area for continuing scholarship. Overall, it is clear that these chapters are beginning to map out a broad terrain of the theology of childhood and adolescence, some of which will be elaborated in other sections of this volume—but much of which will depend on future scholarship to continue the explorations offered here.

CHAPTER 2

Awakening Latent Spirituality: Nurturing Children in the Hindu Tradition

Vishal Agarwal

Numerous factors go a long way in enabling Hindus to accept, appreciate, and even expect spirituality in children and adolescents: a rich corpus of sacred stories in classical Hindu texts depicting young devotees, or presenting divinity itself as a child or a teenager; the philosophies of rebirth, karma, and *samskaras* (rites of passage) that allow for and awaken latent spirituality "inherited" from previous lives; and finally the emphasis on devotion, meditation, scriptural learning, and intuitive knowledge in various spiritual traditions of Hinduism. This chapter explores how various strands of Hindu worship, philosophy, and practice perceive spirituality in children and adolescents.

Devotional Practices: Children of God, God as a Child

Approximately two thousand years ago, Hindu Dharma or classical Hinduism, as we know it today, began crystallizing. Worship of the One Supreme Being through icons, sacred symbols, and elaborate ceremonies and prayers was aligned among six traditions of worship—*Shaakta, Vaishnava, Shaiva, Ganapatya, Kaumaara,* and *Saura*. In all these traditions, which encompass practically all Hindus today, children and teenagers have a prominent presence. The texts pertaining to these traditions are the two epics (Ramayana and Mahabharata), eighteen major Puranas, several minor Puranas, and all literature derived from them.

SHAAKTA (WORSHIPPING THE DIVINE MOTHER)

The Devi has eight major forms according to tradition, and numerous rituals directed toward her involve worship (called *kanjaka-puja*) of prepubescent girls as manifestations of those eight forms.[1] Pilgrimages to several Devi shrines (such as Vaishno Devi in Jammu, India) are concluded with this ritual. In Nepal, a girl is periodically selected from a particular lineage and worshipped as a living goddess till she reaches puberty. In an annual ritual, she is taken out in a ceremonial procession in a chariot, which even the king participates in pulling (Regmi 1991).

VAISHNAVA (WORSHIPPING LORD VISHNU AND HIS CONSORT LAKSHMI)

Vishnu is generally worshipped as his two major incarnations (*avataras*), namely, Rama and Krishna. Hindu texts contain dozens of sacred stories narrating the childhood and teenage exploits of the two, especially of the latter.[2] Between 500 and 1000 C.E., Alvar saints composed numerous devotional songs in the Tamil language to celebrate the themes of the divine childhood.[3] This trend picked up all over the Indian subcontinent, and numerous saint-poets (e.g., Suradasa in Hindi) wrote thousands of devotional poems describing the wonderful pranks (*lila*) of child and teenaged Krishna. The doctrine of *vaatsalya bhakti*, with its strong Vaishnava associations, advocates loving God as a mother loves her child. Iconic representations of Krishna as a child ("the butter thief") are common, and elders often narrate stories of his escapades to children. Children are themselves often referred to in their homes as child Krishna or child Rama, and the "birthdays" (the days on which Lord Vishnu incarnated in these forms) are celebrated as major festivals. Nativity scenes of Krishna and Rama are depicted in households and temples. Icons depicting them as children are placed on a swing and lullabies sung to them. These rituals naturally appeal to children. Temples in Mathura and Ayodhya at the site of Krishna's and Rama's birth, respectively, are visited by millions of Hindu worshippers even today.

The Vaishnava tradition is also replete with the theme of young devotees who are held up as exemplars of true devotion. The story of Prahlada[4] relates that the prince was born to a powerful, evil, and atheist king named Hiranyakashipu. From his childhood, the virtuous prince was inclined toward worship and prayer. The atheist king, who considered himself superior to God, tried unsuccessfully to have his son killed several times. Finally, he unsheathed his own sword and challenged Prahlada to summon the Lord from a pillar in the palace if He really existed. Upon Prahlada's prayer, Lord Vishnu manifested as half-man, half-lion and killed the king. This inspiring story is often related to children and is the subject of numerous movies (e.g., the Hindi movie *Bhakta Prahlad*), plays (Sama 1998), and popular devotional opera texts (e.g., Tyagaraja 1965).[5] One of the major festivals (Holi) of Northern India is celebrated in memory of the event in which Holika, the evil sister of Hiranyakashipu, tries to incinerate Prahlada, but herself is burned to death through divine intervention.

Another interesting story is that of Prince Dhruva.[6] When he was five years old, he learned that he could not succeed his father on the throne because his mother was not the king's favorite wife. Enraged, Prince Dhruva determined to attain greater glory that was his own, not inherited, and he stomped out of the palace into the forest in search of it. There, he encountered the Seven Sages of Hindu tradition, who taught the child that nothing but worship of the Lord can grant the infinite glory that exceeds the power of kingship. The determined child started worshipping Lord Vishnu with dedication and perseverance, abandoning even food and drink, and the entire universe became ablaze with his spiritual splendor. Lord Vishnu manifested before his child devotee and said that he would become the Pole Star that never leaves its position in the sky, just as Dhruva did not deviate from the path of worship.

SHAIVA (WORSHIPPING SHIVA AND HIS WIFE PARVATI)

In this tradition, it is said that a childless couple prayed to Lord Shiva to grant them a son. He asked them to choose between a virtuous son who would live for a mere six-teen years, and a dunce with a long life. The parents opted for the former, and Markandeya was born. As the hour of death approached, Markandeya prayed to Lord Shiva to deliver him from death. When the Lord of Death came to ensnare the young man's soul, Lord Shiva intervened and granted immortality to the boy. The site of this miracle in Tirukkadavur (state of Tamil Nadu, India) has a temple that is visited by people praying for long life on their sixtieth and eightieth birthdays. Markandeya grew to become a great sage, and one of the eighteen major Puranas is named after him.

Another Shaivite saint, Jnanasambandhar, is said to have become spiritually enlight-ened exactly as Adi Shankaracharya, upon being suckled by Devi Parvati. He started com-posing his verses to Shiva even as a child and is considered one of the greatest saints of the Shaiva Siddhanta tradition. However, it is primarily in the next two traditions, after the two sons of Shiva, that we find the theme of a youthful God becomes really prominent.

GANAPATYA (WORSHIP OF GANESHA/GANAPATI, THE SON OF PARVATI AND SHIVA)

The very form of Ganapati as an elephant-headed deity appeals to children, who often have a personal icon of the deity in their homes. In fact, he is primarily worshipped as an adorable child, and tales of his childhood are often used as parables to inculcate virtues in children such as respect for elders. Most of the sacred stories in Hindu scrip-tures concerning him relate to his childhood and youth. One of the eight important shrines of the devotees of Ganapati, Sri Ballalesvara of Pali, commemorates the mani-festation of the deity to a child named Ballal, who constructed a rudimentary shrine for worship. So sincere was Ballal's devotion that it attracted other children his age, caus-ing great concern to their parents. Alarmed, the parents complained to Ballal's father, who destroyed the shrine and beat his son mercilessly. Lord Ganesh then manifested at the site and rewarded the devotion of his little worshipper (Grimes 1995, 119–22). A still-popular Marathi hymn celebrates how little children placed their hope in the lib-erating power of the deity.

KAUMAARA (SKANDA OR KUMARA, SON OF SHIVA)

The very alternate name "Kumara" of Shiva's second son, Skanda, indicates his youthful and perpetually celibate status.[7] The deity was worshipped over large parts of India till about fifteen centuries ago. Today, his worship is largely confined to the Indian state of Tamil Nadu, where he is more commonly called Murugan or Karttikeya. Skanda is said to have six heads and is normally depicted as a handsome youth or teenager. The longest major Purana is named after Skanda and has almost 82,000 verses.

SAURA

This mode of worship, which perceives the divine as Sun, is practically defunct in India, but it is worth mentioning that a twelve-year-old boy named Dharmapada played a pivotal role in the construction (1238–63 C.E.) of the exquisite Konarka temple (Swarup 1980) on the eastern coast of India, one of the four major shrines of the tradition. It is said that the twelve hundred artisans could not figure out how to get the spire in place. Dharmapada appeared and solved the problem, allowing for the completion of the structure.[8]

OTHER TRADITIONS

Other Hindu religious traditions that cannot be compartmentalized within the preceding six modes also have their versions of young deities or Gurus. For instance, Ayyappan,[9] whose temple atop the Sabrimala hill in the Indian state of Kerala draws millions of worshippers each year, is said to be a divine teenager who combined the powers of Shiva and Vishnu. In deference to his adolescent and celibate status, women are even today barred from entering the shrine. In the Sikh tradition, the eighth of the ten Gurus was Harkrishan. He was asked to be the spiritual leader of his community at the age of five and died of smallpox in Delhi three years later in 1664 (McLeod 1997, 41–42). In his memory, Sikhs have established a chain of schools in northern India where students are imparted secular as well as religious lessons.[10] As one would expect, Harkrishan serves as an inspiration to Sikh children.

The Philosophical Basis: Assumption of Latent Spirituality in Children

KARMA AND REBIRTH

Rebirth upon death is considered axiomatic in all streams of Hindu tradition. As a corollary, it is held that the residual "impressions" of karma performed in our previous lives are carried over, and can influence the way we think and act in our current life.[11] In the spiritual text Garbha Upanishad 3–4, a startling claim is made that in the ninth (lunar) month of pregnancy, the fetus is mature enough to recall its prior births:[12]

> [T]hen he remembers his earlier births and has a knowledge of his good and bad deeds:

> After I had thousands of times before lived in the mother's womb, I
> enjoyed many kinds of food, And drunk many a mother's breast. Born
> was I, died again and was continually born anew. What I did for my
> fellow-creatures, Work, good or bad. For that I must suffer alone; Those
> who enjoyed it, are gone. Alas! Sunk in the ocean of grief, I see no rem-
> edy. . . . If once I escape from mother's womb. I shall meditate on the
> Supreme Being.
> But then, when reaching at the opening of the genital organs, . . . he is hardly
> born, . . . then touched by the Vaisnava wind [i.e., the wind of the outer
> world as against the wind in the body], he can no more remember his births
> and deaths and has no knowledge any more of good and bad deeds.
> (Deussen 1980, 2:642–43; adapted slightly)

It is held that if the impressions from previous lives due to engagement in religious
and spiritual matters are strong, individuals may manifest strong spiritual urges at a
very young age, even without being motivated by external influences such as religious
friends, elders, or teachers. If the fetus can remember its prior births, and if it has
already reaped the fruit of all its karma, can it achieve spiritual realization while still in
the womb? Hindu scriptures seem to answer in the affirmative. The canonical Hindu
text Aitareya Upanishad 2.5–6 narrates the following account:

> "While I was in the womb, I knew all the births of the gods. A hundred
> strongholds made of steel guarded me. I burst out of it, with the swiftness of
> a hawk." Vamadeva spoke this verse even when he was lying in the womb.
> He, knowing thus and springing upward, when the body is dissolved,
> enjoyed all desires in that world of heaven and became immortal, yea,
> became (immortal). (Radhakrishnan 1995, 522)

PERSPECTIVES FROM HINDU MEDICAL TEXTS

Interestingly, the embryology and parturition sections of ancient Hindu medical
("Ayurvedic") texts [13] also argue in favor of the philosophy of rebirth from various perspectives[14] and then give a more "material" or concrete basis for the development of
and "retention" of spiritual traits in infants and children. According to these texts, life
commences immediately after conception, when the soul, enveloped by a "subtle body"
(which includes mind and subtle forms of sense organs, and impressions of karma of
previous lives), enters the fertilized egg.[15] In the third or the fourth month, the embryo
actually becomes "alive" or "conscious" but is not an individual yet because its own
experiences and feelings are dependent on those of the mother (and the feelings of the
fetus affect those of the mother, to some extent).[16] The exchange of emotions between
the mother and the embryo takes place through the umbilical cord, which is why the
texts urge that all the wishes and cravings of a pregnant woman must be fulfilled. In the
fifth month, the fetus is endowed with mind; in the sixth, with a sense of cognition.[17]
In other words, the personality of a child starts developing (over and above the personality inherited from prior births) in the embryonic state itself, and he or she does not
have to wait for physical birth to experience the sensations of the outer world. Popular

Hinduism advocates that the expectant mother listen to recitations of sacred texts and religious hymns to enhance virtue and spirituality in the growing embryo.

SAMSKARAS: RITUAL AWAKENING OF LATENT SPIRITUALITY IN CHILDREN

Normative codes of Dharma (Smritis and Kalpasutras) also emphasize, however, that in order to accelerate the process of "awakening" this latent spirituality in children, parents should perform numerous sacred rites of passage (samskaras) even before conception and till the children get married.[18] After being physically born, the child must undergo a second "spiritual birth" through these samskaras. Various texts prescribe more than a dozen samskaras that are performed before conception, after conception, after birth, in childhood, and in teenage years before marriage.[19] It is indeed doubtful whether all of these samskaras were ever performed for a majority of Hindus (Basham 1959, 160). Nonetheless, they are quite meaningful if examined closely. As an example, we may consider *upanayana*, which was the most important sacrament that formally initiated the spiritual and religious life of a child, and made him eligible to study the sacred texts and perform all kinds of Vedic rituals befitting a noble member of the society.[20] While the upanayana was ordinarily performed at the age of eight (Manusmriti 2.36) for a Brahmin boy, the parents had the liberty of advancing it to the age of five (2.37) if they desired their child to shine above others in knowledge and wisdom. The rite involved numerous related ceremonies such as investiture of a sacred thread (or girdle), a staff and a hide of black antelope, and ritual begging for food. The staff symbolized the authority of a student and the discipline that he would have to exercise over his thoughts, speech, and actions during the entire period of study. The sacred thread was made of three strands, which reminded him that he would have to discharge his three debts (toward elders/ancestors, toward ancient Sages, and toward the divinities). The hide symbolized spiritual luster. While taking the staff from his teacher, the student said: "This staff of mine, which has fallen from the sky to the ground, that I take again (or take properly) for a long life, for Vedic study and for holy luster" (Paraskara Grhyasutra 2.2.14).[21]

The staff was thus a reminder and a symbol of religious authority or discipline with which the teacher invests the student and motivated him to pursue his divinely ordained duty of studying the sacred texts before he got married.

OTHER IGNITERS OF THE SPARK OF SPIRITUALITY

It must be emphasized that the awakening of spirituality does not depend on samskaras or one's karma alone. In several Hindu traditions, divine intervention or the benevolence of a spiritual teacher—the Guru (literally the "remover of darkness of ignorance")—is also said to awaken this latent spirituality in youngsters. For instance, a verse of the hymn Saundaryalahari (Saraswati 2001) is taken to mean that when Adi Shankaracharya was an infant and was deprived of milk, Parvati took pity and manifested on earth to suckle him. Her milk caused an effulgence of spiritual wisdom in the infant, and he grew to become a great spiritual philosopher. Likewise, it is said that Totakacharya was a dullard as a child, but the grace of his Guru Shankaracharya made him proficient in spiritual wisdom.[22]

The net result of such core beliefs and traditions is that childhood and adolescent spirituality is considered "natural" or explicable by ordinary Hindus. This acceptance manifests as the presence of numerous child or teenage Gurus, Acharyas (teachers), and yogins in Hindu society. Acceptance of child and adolescent spirituality also implies, however, that parents often get concerned when their beloved child demonstrates spiritual inclinations. Instead of considering the child mentally ill, they try to bring him or her "back to the world" through early marriage or material comforts. Anandamayi Ma, a Hindu girl born in 1896 in Kheora (Bangladesh), was married at the age of thirteen, but her husband soon discovered to his dismay that she was always engrossed in spiritual matters. He became her first disciple, and she herself rose to become one of the most celebrated Hindu mystics of modern India (Johnsen 1994, 47–57). The influential and affluent parents of Sri Ma launched a frantic search to recover their sixteen-year-old daughter when she left her home to pursue her spiritual quests (28–46), but they were unsuccessful.

Practical Aspects of Engaging Youngsters in Religion and Spirituality

THE TEXTUAL BASES

The four Vedas, and secondarily the Brahmanas, Aranyakas, and Upanishads, are considered revealed texts by orthodox Hindus. In Rigveda 10.114.4, the seer (*Rishi*) observes divinity from nearby and likens it to the blissful vision of a child kissed by and kissing his mother. The impact of devotional hymns of sages on the divine is described as "caressing the child" (Rigveda 10.123.2d) or kissing the child (9.85.11c). Verse 8.69.8 urges that children should also pray to the deity Indra, who is a refuge like a mighty fortress. A long Vedic hymn[23] deals with the glory of a child who undergoes a "second spiritual birth" upon being initiated formally into a student's life by his teacher. Hinduism upholds that human beings (i.e., their inner selves) are essentially divine, and a verse declares that boys and girls (Atharvaveda 10.8.77ab) are all manifestations of that divinity. Youngsters are also credited with having played an important role in the teaching, revelation, and preservation of canonical Hindu texts and rituals. It is narrated that Shishu ("child") Angirasa taught the Vedas to his elders.[24] Since he surpassed them in knowledge, he addressed them as "children." The enraged elders approached divine beings (*devas*), who declared that they had been addressed appropriately because even a child who knows the Veda is an elder, whereas an elder who is ignorant of the scripture is like a child. Kumari ("young girl") Gandharva-Grhita is cited as an authority on the *agnihotra* ritual in a Vedic text.[25]

The Katha Upanishad, one of the ten major canonical revealed texts (*shruti*) of Hindu spirituality, consists of the instruction of Yama, Lord of Death, to a teenager named Nachiketa, who rejected the hypocritical ritualism of his father and chose to travel to the realm of death to learn the truth himself. Another text narrates the story of Satyakama Jabala, who did not hide the fact that he was the son of an unknown father upon approaching Sage Gautama for spiritual instruction.[26] Jabala risked being rejected by the Sage because one's lineage was considered an important criterion for gaining admission into renowned schools of learning. The Sage was so impressed with Jabala's honesty that he immediately performed the *upanayana* of the boy, who eventually rose to become a celebrated figure in Hinduism.[27] The injunction to include children in family and congregational prayers is maintained in later Hindu texts[28] as well as in modern Hindu practice.[29] To summarize, then, Hindu texts accept the immense spiritual potential of children and teenagers and advocate their involvement in Dharma.

PRACTICAL WAYS OF INVOLVING CHILDREN IN DHARMA

Most Hindu homes have a private shrine accessible to all members of the household, including children. Depending on the religiosity of the family, prayers are conducted by the entire family, and children are encouraged to participate in the ritual. In heavily attended congregational prayers in temples, parents are seen to lift their children above their shoulders so that they can also have a vision (*darshana*) of the divine icon that may be obscured by the crowd. Childless couples commonly seek divine intervention and often dedicate their subsequent progeny to the benevolent deity by naming them after the deity (*devata*). Such children are often taught by their parents to remain devoted to the devata throughout their lives. Another widely prevalent practice is to name one's child after a devata, which is not merely a constant reminder of divinity to the child, but is also believed to give spiritual merit to parents whenever they call out the name of their child (and the devata simultaneously). Pilgrimages form an important part of popular Hindu practice and are generally made by the entire family together. Newborn children are often taken on arduous pilgrimage to be blessed by the deity of the shrine.

Hindus celebrate dozens of festivals, and there is hardly a month in which there is no major religious festival. The associated celebrations provide a frequent and attractive opportunity to involve children in the spiritual and religious life of their elders. The entire story of Ramayana, for instance, is enacted by volunteers over a period of nine nights preceding the festival of Vijayadashmi in northern India. Many of the roles in the "monkey army" of Lord Rama and of the evil (but interesting) characters are often given to child or teenage actors. On the actual day of the festival, huge effigies of the big three evil brothers (King Ravana, Kumbakarna, and Meghanada) are stuffed with firecrackers and set aflame. This spectacle is naturally enjoyed by children, who are then told how evildoers meet the fate of these effigies. In southern parts of India, dolls are artistically displayed on this day and on other festivals with children as enthusiastic participants. The extremely rich corpus of supernatural sacred stories in Hindu texts ensures their easy adaptation to hugely popular contemporary comic book series (such as the Amar Chitra Katha), animated electronic versions,[30] and collections of parables meant for children.[31]

CHILDREN IN THE HINDU DIASPORA

Parents in the ten million-strong Hindu Diaspora face a unique situation because the surrounding environment is alien and non-Hindu.[32] Overall, Hindu parents in the West tend to stress the spiritual aspects of Hindu Dharma more than they do its cultural, ritual, and historical aspects. They adopt several ingenious means to inculcate Hindu values in their children. For instance, the Hindu deity Hanuman is often compared to Superman. Parents take their children frequently to India and visit pilgrim centers with them, and grandparents visiting from India or other traditional Hindu societies play a central role in transmission of Hindu teachings to the youngest generation. Parents are often known to buy several volumes of the Amar Chitra Katha series for their children. They also purchase videos of *Ramayana* and *Mahabharata*—two multi-episode TV serials based on religious Hindu epics that were telecast throughout India a few years ago. Local temples conduct special cultural programs during festivals in which children play a prominent role. Organizations such as Chinmaya Mission have started schools in various U.S. cities to impart a Hindu-centric education to children and also conduct summer camps and other short courses for Hindu youth. These camps teach yoga, basic Hindu values such as vegetarianism, Hindu modes of worship, spiritual teachings, and parables from Hindu scriptures.

The Child as Spiritual Guru and the Liberating Yogas

Hinduism has traditionally advocated three major overlapping Yogas, or paths that lead to liberation (*moksha*) from the cycle of births and deaths, in which emphasis is placed on one of the three major aspects of Hindu philosophy. For reasons discussed in this section, children and teenagers figure in all these three traditions, most prominently as enlightened souls and Gurus.

BHAKTI YOGA

This path entails loving devotion toward a Personal God worshipped in one of the six forms described at the beginning of this chapter (and more typically as Vishnu or Shiva) through prayers, repetition of His holy names, and ritual worship. Philosophical acumen and proficiency in meditation, which take time to develop, are less important. The examples of Prahlada, Markandeya, and other narratives in this tradition were listed earlier. These stories exalt innocent devotion to God above everything else, and make liberation accessible to even children and teenagers. Even today, it is not uncommon to come across spiritually gifted children leading a congregation in the chanting of hymns,[33] and the author has personally participated in one such event. Several prayers and hymns found in Hindu texts are ascribed to children.[34] Jnaneshvari, the oldest surviving commentary on the Gita in an Indian vernacular and also one of the most influential ones, was completed by its author, Sant Jnaneshvar, in 1290 C.E., when he was merely nineteen years old.[35] He and his siblings showed saintly qualities even as children, and today they are revered by millions of members of the Warkari sect of Hindus (Pradhan 1967, 13ff.). Numerous blockbuster movies have been made about the life of Sant Jnaneshvar, and he is conventionally portrayed as a teenager with an angelic smile.

JNANA YOGA

This path emphasizes that *moksha* results through adherence to spiritual philosophies combined with meditation and the renunciation of a worldly life. Jnana yogins focus on texts such as the Gita, Upanishads, and Brahmasutras. One of the longest Upanishads, the Brihadaranyaka Upanishad, has a passage (3.5.1) that seems to exalt some traits of a child while discussing the path of spirituality: "Therefore, let a brahamana, after he has done with his learning, desire to live as a child" (Radhakrishnan 1953, 221). This passage has been the subject of a prolonged discussion in the commentaries on Brahmasutra 3.4.47–50, which clarify that the sacred text does not mean that all wisdom and learning must be shunned in order to attain moksha. Rather, the text means that a learned man must become free of cunning, arrogance, sexual desires, and other such negative forces if he wishes to progress on the path of spirituality (Thibaut 1968, 2:322–25).

It would appear that the emphasis on mastery of abstruse philosophy and theology would prevent youngsters from becoming Jnana yogins. But, counterintuitively, some of the greatest exponents of this path have been teenagers. The epic Mahabharata 3.132–34 narrates the story of Ashtavakra, who while still in his mother's womb, spoke up to correct the errors in his father's recitation of Hindu scriptures. Enraged, his father, Kahor, cursed the child that he would be born with several physical deformities. Kahor, however, was defeated in a philosophical debate by Vandin, the court philosopher of King Janaka, and was therefore banished to the subterranean realm of Lord Varuna. When Ashtavakra turned twelve, he went to the court of Janaka and defeated Vandin in a philosophical debate, thereby freeing his father. The scintillating spiritual discourse on mystical intuition and the nature of reality given by the boy Ashtavakra to Janaka is recorded in a famous spiritual text named Ashtavakra Gita (Chinmayananda 1997).

The very revival of Hindu spiritual philosophy of Vedanta after setbacks caused by the rise of Buddhism in India is attributed to Adi Shankaracharya, a dynamic Hindu monk who lived only for a brief thirty-two years in the seventh to eighth century C.E. (Pande 1994, 52). Tradition states that his brilliant commentary on the Brahmasutras was completed by the age of sixteen (Bader 2000, 84). For the rest of his life, Adi Shankaracharya toured the entire Indian subcontinent, defeating rival scholars in philosophical debates and founding four major monasteries, which exist to this day. Three of these four monasteries recruit only lifelong celibates to succeed the reigning pontiffs. And typically, the pontiff uses his spiritual intuition to nominate a spiritually inclined boy for grooming to this post. Therefore, it is not uncommon even in modern times for these institutions to be headed by teenage monks, to whom millions of Hindus bow in respect.[36]

Significantly, the classical formulation of the four stages of life of a Hindu often assumes that one must pass through student, householder, and hermit stages before becoming a monk or an ascetic (*samnyasin*). But followers of this path who renounced the world as children or teenagers do not fail to cite the few scriptural passages that permit a young student to skip the householder and hermit stages before becoming wandering monks to follow the path of Jnana Yoga.[37] The influential school of Advaita Vedanta of Shankaracharya rejects the older notion that an intensive study of ritual treatises and performance of Vedic rites as a student or householder are prerequisites for acquiring spiritual knowledge. This idea has also promoted the practice of initiating children and teenagers into monkhood in Hindu communities.

KARMA YOGA AND RAJA YOGA

This path combines the eight-limbed system of Raja Yoga (meditation, spiritual exercises, etc.) with the performance of rituals and worldly duties with the goal but no expectation of any reward from the Supreme Being.[38] Celibacy is an important component of the Raja Yoga practice, and the loss of one's procreating fluids is said to result in spiritual impoverishment and in the degradation of one's physical health and intellect. Conversely, adherence to celibacy ensures a youthful vitality even though the follower of this path may be quite advanced in age. Naturally then, tradition considers the renowned practitioners of this path as ever-young celibates (*kumara* and *kumari* for men and women, respectively) who do not wither with age and always maintain the youthful appearance of adolescents. This applies to forms of the divine, such as Skanda, mentioned earlier, and to Sages and Seers as well. Prominent examples of the latter are the perpetually teenage four sons of Brahma (*Brahmakumaras*), each of whom is credited with religious texts or teachings recorded in texts authored by others.[39]

Hinduism lays great emphasis on respect for elders, and yet it does not reject or ignore that children too can be profoundly spiritual. Although learning and understanding typically come with age, the positive impressions of one's virtuous deeds done in previous lives, innocence, practice of celibacy, and sometimes even divine intervention can bridge the gap of age and transform a youngster into a spiritually and intellectually mature Guru of his elders. This is quite evident from examples of such Gurus who have played seminal roles in the development of Hinduism as it exists today by living as exemplary philosophers, devotees, scholars, and yogins.

Postscript: The author is a nondenominational, practicing Hindu with Vaishnava leanings, struggling to bring up his four-year-old son in the United States according to Hindu spiritual traditions.

Notes

1. This custom must be distinguished from the rare and now defunct (and illegal in India) practice of dedicating adult women as lifelong temple courtesans (*devadasis*), often leading to

their abuse. The ritual referred to in the text typically involves girls from one's own family or neighborhood whose role is over as soon as the rite is completed.

2. Bryant (2003) gives a recent rendering in English of the sacred story of Krishna as narrated in the Bhagavata Purana.

3. Some of these songs are translated in Narayanan (1994).

4. Vishnu Purana 1.16–20. I have used the popular edition with a Hindi translation by Gupta (2002).

5. The writer lived between 1767 and 1847 C.E. and is considered the greatest exponent of Carnatic music of India.

6. Vishnu Purana 1.11–12.

7. A comprehensive yet accessible compilation of the religious cults surrounding Ganesh and Skanda is contained in Mani (1990).

8. Information from http://www.geocities.com/bpatnaik_2000/konark-story.htm (accessed December 10, 2004).

9. The quasi-official Web site of the temple is http://www.ayyappa.com/Sabarimala.htm (accessed December 15, 2004).

10. Sikhism is today considered a separate religion.

11. The relationship between karma, rebirth, and individuality is treated admirably in Krishan (1997) and Näreaho (2002).

12. The text is typically dated to the early centuries of the first millennium. A similar statement is made in another passage, Nirukta 14.6, which is considered an interpolation in the original text that is dated to the sixth century B.C.E.

13. The primary texts are Charaka Samhita (Sharma and Dash 1976) and Sushruta Samhita (Atridev 1958), both of which are normally dated before 200 C.E.

14. Charaka Samhita, Sutrasthana 11.6–33. Sushruta Samhita, Sarirasthana 2.57 adds that individuals who have purified their minds with intensive study of scriptures start recollecting previous lives.

15. Charaka Samhita, Sarirasthana 4.8.

16. Susruta Samhita, Sarirasthana 3.18.

17. Susruta Samhita, Sarirasthana 3.30; Charaka Samhita, Sarirasthana 4.15–19.

18. Another important function of samskaras is to ward off birth defects and other childhood physical deformities and ailments. See, for instance, Manusmriti 2.27. For this text, I have referred to Olivelle (2004).

19. For the textual basis of these rites, see Deshpande (1936).

20. For a detailed description and significance of this sacrament, refer to Pandey (1969, 111–52). By and large, this rite has been maintained only among the Hindu priestly (Brahmin) communities, although scriptural backing for the eligibility of males (and even girls) of other sectors of Hindu societies is not entirely lacking. Hindu literature does give examples of non-Brahmin boys and girls having undergone this ceremony. The modern Hindu reformist sect Arya Samaj performs this rite for boys and girls of all Hindu communities today.

21. Bakre (1982, 197); my translation.

22. For details of his life, see my Web page at http://vishalagarwal.voiceofdharma.org/articles/acharyas/totakacharya.htm (accessed December 14, 2004).

23. Atharvaveda 11.5.1–26. Rigveda 10.109.5 declares that such a student becomes "the very limb of divine beings."

24. Manusmriti 2.150–53.

25. Aitareya Brahmana 2.9.

26. Chhandogya Upanishad 4.4.4–5.

27. Several Upanishads are named after him, and he is also apparently the codifier of the

Jabala school of Yajurveda. Chhandogya Upanishad itself states that Jabala acquired the knowledge of Supreme Being while tending his Guru's cows in the forest as a teenager, but nevertheless returned to Gautama to complete his education.

28. For instance, Matsya Purana 1.18.1–5 states that if a man visits the temple of Vishnu and listens to religious discourses *in the company* of his wife and children, he abides in heaven for a long time.

29. Huyler (1999) shows numerous photographs of Hindu children engaged in worship, rituals, and religious festivities.

30. A prominent example is the animated story *Ramayana,* produced by a joint Indo-American-Japanese venture named Nippon Ramayana. The DVD is being used by thousands of Hindu parents in the West to introduce the Hindu epic to their children.

31. An excellent example of one such book written by a non-Hindu is Clooney (1998). The author is a Jesuit priest.

32. Leonard (1997) reports: "Growing up in a predominantly Christian context and knowing little about the conflict and diversity that have characterized the history of Christianity, the children of Hindu immigrants look for a single unified tradition and a standard text or texts. The majority religion seems so monolithic and transparently simple that second generation Hindus want to be presented with one easy set of beliefs, analogous to Christianity and Islam (or so they think). To achieve this, the immigrants tend to emphasize beliefs only, not socio-religious practices, not the caste system, the village society, nor gendered practices or the daily interactions with fellow citizens of other religions" (122).

33. A Hindu nun and prominent contemporary politician named Uma Bharati owes her success in politics in no small measure to her reputation as a charismatic preacher of the Hindu devotional text Bhagavata Purana in her childhood.

34. An example of such a prayer supposedly composed by children is the Baalakrita Krishnastotra in the Brahmavaivarta Purana. The prayer in Sanskrit is available online at http://sanskrit.gde.to/all_pdf/baalakrishnastotra.pdf (accessed November 29, 2004).

35. The text is celebrated in both Bhakti Yoga and Jnana Yoga traditions and is the bedrock of modern Hinduism.

36. Swami Bharati Tirtha, the current pontiff of the Shringeri monastery, was initiated into monkhood as a teenager. All the pontiffs of the influential Kanchi Kamakoti monastery since 1885 have been nominated as successors in their teenage years.

37. Even Swami Dayanand Saraswati (1824–83), who founded the Hindu reform organization of Arya Samaj in 1875, and who rejected most Hindu texts as nonauthoritative, does not fail to cite Jabala Upanishad 4 in his works while dealing with the institution of Samnyasa. He himself fled his home at a young age the night before he was to be married and became a samnyasin. Adi Shankaracharya cites the texts of the Jabala school an unusual nine times in his commentary on Brahmasutras. Other commentators such as Ramanujacharya (who was a householder) either ignore Jabala texts or cite them much more rarely.

38. Raja Yoga is sometimes considered a separate path from Karma Yoga, and is quite strongly fused with Jnana Yoga.

39. For instance, the "no death" doctrine preached by Sanatsujaata in Mahabharata 5.42–45.

References

Atridev. 1968. *Susrutasamhita.* Delhi: Motilal Banarsidass. (In Hindi and Sanskrit)
Bader, Jonathan. 2000. *Conquest of the four quarters.* New Delhi: Aditya Prakashan.

Bakre, Mahadeva Ganghadhar (ed.). 1982. *Grihya-Sutra by Paraskar with five commentaries.* New Delhi: Munsihram Manoharlal.

Basham, A. L. 1959. *The wonder that was India.* New York: Grove Press.

Bryant, Edwin F. 2003. *Krishna: The beautiful legend of God.* London: Penguin.

Chinmayayanda, Swami. 1997. *Discourses on Astavakra Gita.* Mumbai: Central Chinmaya Mission Trust.

Clooney, Francis X., S.J. 1998. *Hindu wisdom for all God's children.* Maryknoll, N.Y.: Orbis.

Deshpande, Kamalabai Kelkar. 1936. *The child in ancient India.* Poona: Author.

Deussen, Paul. 1980. *Sixty Upanisads of the Veda.* Vol. 2. Translated by V. M. Bedekar and G. B. Palsule. New Delhi: Motilal Banarsidass.

Grimes, John. 1995. *Ganapat: Song of the self.* Albany: State University of New York Press.

Gupta, Manilal. 2002. *Sri Sri Vishnu Purana.* Gorakhpur: Geeta Press. (In Sanskrit and Hindi)

Huyler, Stephen P. 1999. *Meeting God: Elements of Hindu devotion.* New Haven, Conn.: Yale University Press.

Johnsen, Linda. 1994. *Daughters of the goddess.* St. Paul, Minn.: Yes International.

Krishan, Yuvraj. 1997. *The doctrine of karma.* New Delhi: Motilal Banarsidass.

Leonard, Karen Isaksen. 1997. *The South Asian Americans.* Westport, Conn.: Greenwood Press.

Mani, V. R. 1990. *The sons of Siva.* Delhi: Sharada Prakashan.

McLeod, Hew. 1997. *Sikhism.* London: Penguin.

Narayanan, Vasudha. 1994. *The vernacular Veda.* Columbia: University of South Carolina Press.

Näreaho, Leo. 2002. *Rebirth and personal identity.* Helsinki: Luther-Agricola-Society.

Olivelle, Patrick. 2004. *The law code of Manu.* Oxford: Oxford University Press.

Pande, G. C. 1994. *Life and thought of Sankaracarya.* New Delhi: Motilal Banarsidass.

Pandey, Raj Bali. 1969. *Hindu Samskaras.* New Delhi: Motilal Banarsidass.

Pradhan, V. G. 1967. *Jnaneshvari.* Translated from the Marathi. Vol. 1. London: Allen and Unwin.

Radhakrishnan, S. 1995. *The principal Upanishads.* New Delhi: HarperCollins.

Regmi, Jagadish C. 1991. *The kumari of Kathmandu.* Kathmandu: Heritage Research.

Sama, Balakrishna. 1998. *Prahlad.* Kathmandu: Royal Nepal Academy.

Saraswati, Chandrasekharendra. 2001. *Sri Samkara Bhagvatpadacharya's Saundaryalahari.* Mumbai: Bharatiya Vidya Bhavan.

Sharma, Ram Karan, and Vaidya Bhagwan Dash. 1976. *Agnivesa's Caraka Samhita. Text with English translation.* 2 vols. Varanasi: Chowkhamba Sanskrit Series Office.

Swarup, Bishan. 1980. *Konarka: The black pagoda of Orissa.* New Delhi: Ramanand Vidya Bhawan.

Thibaut, George. 1968. *The Vedanta-Sutras with the commentary of Sankaracarya.* Part 2. New Delhi: Motilal Banarsidass.

Tyagaraja, Swami. 1965. *Tyagaraja's Prahlada Bhakti Vijayam. Text of the opera with the songs in notation.* Tirupati: Sri Venkateswara University. (In Telugu)

CHAPTER 3

The Child as Compassionate Bodhisattva and as Human Sufferer/Spiritual Seeker: Intertwined Buddhist Images

Yoshiharu Nakagawa

Buddhism has spread to Asian countries and more recently all over the world as a religion of wisdom and compassion. In Buddhism's long history of twenty-five hundred years, Buddhist monasteries have served as educational and religious institutions to train practitioners; they have accepted children as novice monks and nuns. Also, since the beginning of the modern era, a great number of temples have established Buddhist-inspired schools for children and adolescents from the nursery to the university level. In their educational practices, a number of Buddhist teachers must have pondered childhood. Strangely enough, however, when we try to review Buddhism, we come to know that it has developed few distinctive ideas about the nature of childhood and child spirituality. Education has rather been a matter of everyday living to be dealt with in a practical way. Faced with relatively little information for our topic, this chapter will draw on a hermeneutic interpretation of relevant descriptions selected from Buddhist texts to highlight some of the Buddhist ideas of childhood in terms of spirituality.

The Buddha and His Son

The Buddha's life story is the starting point of our survey. Siddhattha Gotama (in Sanskrit, Siddhartha Gautama) was born in 563 B.C.E. as a son of King Suddhodana near the Himalayas. He was raised very carefully by his father with luxuries and elaborate entertainment so that he would not be tempted to abandon his destiny as the ruler of Sakiyan kingdom, for the prophecies were uncertain concerning whether he would succeed his father as king or leave the palace to become a spiritual master. In spite of his father's protection, Siddhattha came to know old age, disease, and death as unavoidable sufferings for all human beings. His encounters with these existential questions finally led him to forsake his royal environment to seek liberation from sufferings in an ascetic life. When he was about to leave his home at the age of twenty-nine, his wife, Yasodhara, gave birth to a son. He could not enjoy this news and gave his son the name

Rahula, meaning "fetter" or "eclipse." Without seeing his son, Siddhattha left to set out on his spiritual quest.

Siddhattha devoted six years to his ascetic exercises before his great enlightenment took place. At the age of thirty-five, Gotama attained a complete awakening and became the Buddha, or the awakened one. The original meaning of Buddhism comes from the Buddha's experience of awakening, or Buddhahood. Then he started his teaching activity and his *sangha* was formed, a monastic community of his disciples. The Buddha and his disciplines visited various places in India. His father, Suddhodana, asked him to visit his hometown, Kapilavatthu, to deliver his teachings and to meet his family. After seven years' absence the Buddha returned to his homeland, and many of his relatives became his disciples. Among them, his son, Rahula, draws our attention, for the Buddha's attitude toward him laid a basic orientation to children in the Buddhist tradition.

Rahula was then seven years old. Yasodhara brought her son to his father and let him ask his father to give him his property, according to tradition. Saddhatissa (1976, 53) describes the scene: "The Buddha made no reply, nor did he attempt to discourage the child. But as he walked he thought: 'He desires his father's wealth, but this is only a worldly thing, a source of trouble. I shall give him instead far greater wealth, the sevenfold noble wealth which I received at the foot of the Bodhi tree. Then he will be the possessor of an excellent inheritance.'" Eventually he ordained Rahula as a novice Buddhist monk. The Buddha's great disciples Sariputta and Moggallana mainly took care of Rahula as tutors, but the Buddha himself at times gave instructions for Rahula's spiritual development. Rahula was said to be an obedient and diligent practitioner. At the age of twenty, Rahula was ordained as a monk, and finally he became an *Arahat* (saint) (Schumann 1989, 123–24).

This story suggests that the Buddha thought that even a young boy of seven was in a position to become a Buddhist practitioner. However, this was another shock to King Suddhodana, who asked the Buddha not to ordain young children without the permission of their parents. The Buddha agreed to this request. Put differently, the Buddhist tradition recognized that children before seven years of age should stay with their parents to be raised with parental love and care and after that should be accepted in monasteries only with their parents' assent.

Although Buddhism has a doctrine of no-self or selflessness (*anatta*), it does not really mean that one should eliminate one's own ego. It is necessary for a child to develop a soundly functioning ego. Buddhism speaks against false beliefs and defenses formed around the ego, or false representations of the ego, that produce cravings, desires, and attachments, thereby causing suffering. Buddhist meditation enables us to see who we are without these false beliefs and representations. In this sense, it becomes possible for a child after the age of seven to start Buddhist meditative practice to work on the false representations of the ego.

Children at Buddhist Monasteries

The historical facts tell us that Buddhist monasteries in Asian countries have accepted young children's entry at about seven years of age. According to Harvey (1990, 220),

"From the age of seven or eight, a child can take the lower ordination, or 'going forth' (*pabbajja*), so as to become a *samanera* (female, *samaneri*): a 'little *samana*' or novice." Parents must give permission for a child's ordination. Full ordination is given to a person over twenty years of age, who becomes a monk (*bhikkhu*) or a nun (*bhikkhuni*).

After their first ordinations, children are to be raised and trained under the guidance of senior monks or nuns. The principal part of each child's monastic life consists of serving as an attendant to a monk or nun, who in turn acts as a personal teacher to the child. In Buddhism a child is always seen in relationship to an adult who is taking care of the child, just as a relationship between mother and child is grasped as a unit of being. A monk or nun has the responsibility to raise a particular child as if he or she were the child's parent; however, if the monk or nun becomes sick, for example, the attending child is expected to take care of him or her. So the relationship between an adult and a child is a reciprocal one. With senior monks or nuns, children participate in the monastic life that consists of religious practices, learning activities, and practical tasks for everyday living. A Buddhist community, having both children and adults of different ages, sometimes looks like an extended family that has members from several generations.

There is an essential teaching of the Buddha about the meditation practices of the Four Immeasurable Minds (*brahma-viharas*) to cultivate true love (Nhat Hanh 1999, 169–75; Salzberg 1995), which has been practiced widely in the Theravada (Path of the Elders) tradition of Buddhism in South and Southeast Asia, and this teaching has been applied to child rearing. The Four Immeasurable Minds are loving-kindness (*metta*), compassion (*karuna*), sympathetic joy (*mudita*), and equanimity (*upekkha*). In terms of child rearing, loving-kindness is to pray for health and happiness when a child is born; compassion is to embrace a child to relieve his or her sufferings such as pain, sorrow, fever, and hunger; sympathetic joy is to rejoice together that a child playfully explores the world with joy; equanimity is to observe in a nondiscriminating way that a grown-up child takes in all the kinds of experiences he or she encounters.

It is also important to understand that Buddhism has regarded child rearing as a spiritual practice for adults to develop the Four Immeasurable Minds within themselves. To take care of a child, adults need to work on themselves so as to transform the qualities of their minds, which constitutes the Buddhist practice. The sangha, or Buddhist community, is regarded as essential in Buddhist practice because the Buddha's teachings are transmitted only in such reciprocal relationships as those arising between children and adults or in later life in a strong relationship between a master and a disciple.

The Four Noble Truths

It is commonly known that at the heart of the Buddha's teachings are the Four Noble Truths. The First Noble Truth is the recognition of life as suffering (*dukkha*). The Second Noble Truth concerns the origin (*samudaya*) of suffering. It is craving and attachment to what is impermanent that causes suffering. The Third Noble Truth is about the cessation (*nirodha*) of suffering. The cessation is called *nibbana* (Sanskrit, *nirvana*), or "extinction of a fire," which is the ultimate goal of the Buddhist practice. Finally, the

Fourth Noble Truth refers to the path (*magga*) leading to the cessation, which is called the Noble Eightfold Path: right view, right thinking, right speech, right action, right livelihood, right diligence, right mindfulness, and right concentration. These moral, mental, and spiritual practices are central to the Buddhist way.

The Buddha's teachings centered on suffering and liberation from it. When the Buddha exposed the four truths, he claimed at first that birth, old age, disease, and death are suffering. This statement tells us that all aspects of human life are subject to suffering, and no one, not even a small child or a baby, can avoid suffering. Here Buddhism seems concerned not so much with the idea of developmental stages as with the fundamental human condition of suffering, regardless of age. A child is also a suffering being. But this is not merely a pessimistic view of childhood, for it is possible to cease suffering by practicing the Buddhist path.

The Child in the Cycle of Rebirths

Buddhism holds that any life-form is embedded in a continuity of existence over countless lifetimes. This is what Gotama realized in the first watch of his great enlightenment. "Then he turned his attention to the past, and he saw his and others' countless past lives stretching back over many eons and ages of the world" (Kohn 1994, 34). Buddhism views every life-form as emerging in the cycle of countless rebirths. A rebirth can take a different form such as a human, an animal, a hell being, a ghost, or a god, to be born in one of the six different realms. A small child may not be a totally new being with no trace of previous lives but an existence with the accumulation of a long history of lives. As Bernardo Bertolucci's film *Little Buddha* illustrates, Buddhism sees children as beings connected with a vast stream of life across countless rebirths.

Buddhism does not recognize any kind of permanent existence. Therefore, the Buddhist concept of rebirth does not imply that a permanent entity such as a soul survives across lives. Sogyal Rinpoche (1992) explains this distinction: "Most people take the word 'reincarnation' to imply there is some 'thing' that reincarnates, which travels from life to life. But in Buddhism we do not believe in an independent and unchanging entity like a soul or ego that survives the death of the body. What provides the continuity between lives is not an entity, we believe, but the ultimately subtlest level of consciousness" (90).

The Buddhist concept of rebirth is based on the idea of *karma*. What drives rebirth is the law of karma, that is, past actions. In his second watch, the Buddha came to know how karma works: "He saw beings being born and passing away in accordance with karma, the law of cause and effect" (Kohn 1994, 35). A new birth takes place as a fruit or an effect of certain kinds of past actions. This does not necessarily mean that a child is determined by causes, but he or she is conditioned in the sense that he or she is an heir to past actions. Therefore, environmental and external conditions play important roles for child development. Although a child is born into a certain family at a certain time, as a result of past actions, the parents, family, and society affect how the child is going to be formed in this lifetime.

The Buddha understood the karmic life as that from which we have to liberate ourselves. He realized this in his last stage of enlightenment. In his third watch, he saw the wheel of dependent arising beginning from ignorance to suffering and the way of liberation from the wheel. Having seen the last trace of ignorance, he thought: "I have attained the unborn. My liberation is unassailable. This is my last birth. There will now be no renewal of becoming" (Kohn 1994, 35). Thus, he attained nibbana. The core of Buddhist teachings lies in ultimately transcending the cycle of rebirths by spiritual enlightenment.

Buddha's Child as Metaphor

Mahayana (Great Vehicle) Buddhism has a similar view of childhood to earlier Buddhism discussed so far in this chapter. It is notable, however, that Mahayana Buddhism used the term *child* mostly as a metaphor to indicate different states of the mind. Although the metaphor does not refer to real children, it is indicative of child spirituality as conceived in Buddhism.

Mahayana emerged in northern India about 100 B.C.E. as a new movement of Buddhism, which later had major developments in northern and eastern Asia. During a long period of time, it created a large number of new sutras, or scriptures, including the Prajna-paramita Sutras (the Perfection of Wisdom Scriptures), the Vimalakirti Sutra, the Avatamsaka Sutra (the Flower Ornament Scripture), and the Saddharma-pundarika Sutra (the Lotus Sutra). These new sutras developed various forms of the Buddhist cosmology that described all-embracing universal Being in countless ways with cosmic images of the Buddhas (*tathagata* with different names, Amitabha, Virocana, and others) and the great Bodhisattvas (such as Maitreya, Avalokiteshvara, and Manjusri). Associated with these sutras, a variety of Mahayana schools developed, such as Madhyamika, Yogacara, Tathagata-garba, Hua-yen, Pure Land, Ch'an/Zen, and Tantra. The Buddhist thinkers of these schools explored philosophical conceptions of reality and consciousness, for instance, *sunyata* (Emptiness). Also, Mahayana highlighted the path of a bodhisattva in which one seeks wisdom (*prajna*) to attain perfect enlightenment and, at the same time, helps others toward their enlightenment by expedient means created in compassion (*karuna*).

Following are several examples of metaphorical images of children from the Mahayana texts. *The Lotus Sutra* (Watson 1993) has several parables describing children. A famous one (56–59) is a story about a very rich man and his sons. His big house was old and decaying, and it had only one gate. When a fire broke out in the house, his sons were still inside. Seeing the huge flames from outside, the rich man thought: "My sons are inside the burning house enjoying themselves and playing games, unaware, unknowing, without alarm or fear. The fire is closing in on them, suffering and pain threaten them, yet their minds have no sense of loathing or peril and they do not think of trying to escape!" (56). He called to his sons to come out at once, but the sons were absorbed in their own games. They had no alarm, no mind to leave the house, and even no idea of fire and danger. The man thought, "I must now invent some expedient means that will make it possible for the children to escape harm" (57). As he knew his sons' preferences for curious objects, he shouted to them that the playthings they liked—goatcarts, deercarts, and oxcarts—were outside the gate. Hearing their father's voice, the sons dashed out of the burning house safely.

In this story the sons mean ordinary people including both adults and children who are caught up in everyday business without no idea of suffering and liberation. The rich man signifies the Thus Come One (tathagata), namely, the Buddha in Mahayana conception. The burning house is nothing but our condition of being human in this world. But fortunately, ordinary people are children of the Thus Come One who will save them with great wisdom and compassion. "He is born into the threefold world, a burning house, rotten and old, in order to save living beings from the fires of birth, old age, sickness and death, care, suffering, stupidity, misunderstanding, and the three poisons; to teach and convert them and enable them to attain anuttara-samyak-sambodhi [perfect enlightenment]" (59). The text says that the Buddha or the Thus Come One is the "father" of ordinary people: "I am the father of living beings and I should rescue them from their sufferings and give them the joy of the measureless and boundless Buddha wisdom so that they may find their enjoyment in that" (59). The Buddha's children are those who will be rescued by expedient means the Buddha will create. It is true that childhood described in this context involves people's weakness or limitation in undertaking the spiritual path by their own initiatives, but it is at the same time paired with the father's parental care as seen in the Buddha's attitude toward Rahula.

Kukai's articulation of the human mind coincides with the image of childhood just mentioned. Kukai (774–835 C.E.), the founder of the Shingon school of Esoteric Buddhism in Japan, presented a ten-stage developmental scheme of the human mind in his major works, *The Ten Stages of the Development of Mind* and *The Precious Key to the Secret Treasury* (Hakeda 1972, 157–224):

1. The mind of lowly man, goatish in its desires;
2. The mind that is ignorant and childlike, yet abstemious;
3. The mind that is infantlike and fearless;
4. The mind that recognizes the existence of psychophysical constitutions only, not that of a permanent ego;
5. The mind freed from the seed of the cause of karma;
6. The Mahayana mind with sympathetic concern for others;
7. The mind that realizes that the mind is unborn;
8. The mind that is truly in harmony with the one way;
9. The profoundest esoteric Buddhist mind that is aware of its nonimmutable nature; and
10. The glorious mind, the most secret and sacred.

These stages illustrate a comprehensive view of the development of the Buddhist mind from the lowest to the highest stages. In this scheme, Kukai referred to "childlike" and "infantlike" minds in the second and third stages. According to Hakeda (1972, 69), the second stage of the mind is still ignorant like a child but ethical in the sense that the observance of social and Buddhist ethics is required to go beyond the first stage of animal being. The third stage of the mind has non-Buddhist hopes for rebirth in heaven, which is called "infantlike." These "childlike" and "infantlike" minds in the lower stages of development have to be seen in relation to the mind that takes care of them and helps foster their development, which is the compassionate "Mahayana mind" appearing at the sixth stage. Here is a caring relation between these minds, which is resonant with child rearing to be practiced in the meditations of the Four Immeasurable Minds.

The Child as Compassionate Bodhisattva

Childhood has two aspects. On the one hand, as we have seen, it demonstrates a state of the mind that remains in the lower stages of spiritual development; on the other, it reveals a higher state of becoming a bodhisattva. Watson (1993, 312–18) relays a parable that describes the aspect of bodhisattva found in certain children to support their parents' enlightenment. In the land of a cosmic Buddha named Cloud Thunder Sound Constellation King Flower Wisdom, the king, Wonderful Adornment, and his consort, Pure Virtue, had two sons, Pure Storehouse and Pure Eye. "These two sons possessed great supernatural powers, merit, virtue, and wisdom, and for a long time they had been practicing the way appropriate to a bodhisattva" (312). They wished to visit the Buddha to listen to what the Buddha was preaching, but their father had a non-Buddhist faith. Then they manifested supernatural powers to successfully influence their father. The sons said to him that the Buddha Cloud Thunder Sound Constellation King Flower Wisdom was their teacher. Hearing this, the father wanted to see this teacher. And their mother assented for the two sons to leave household life to meet the Buddha. Eventually the sons went with their parents and their attendants to the Buddha's abode. Listening to what the Buddha preached for the king and the queen, the king turned over his kingdom to his brother, and he himself, with his queen and two sons, renounced household life to practice the Buddhist path.

After attaining enlightenment, the king addressed the Buddha: "World-Honored One, these two sons of mine have carried out the Buddha's work, . . . enabling me to abide safely in the Buddha's Law, and permitting me to see the World-Honored One. These two sons have been good friends to me. They wished to awaken the good roots from my past existences and to enrich and benefit me, and for that reason they were born into my household" (Watson 1993, 316–17). The Buddha replied, "If good men and good women have planted good roots, and as a result in existence after existence have been able to gain good friends, then these good friends can do the Buddha's work, teaching, benefiting, delighting, and enabling them to enter anuttara-samyak-sambodhi" (317).

Although this is a parable, it demonstrates the possibility that a child can be a "good friend" to benefit another's spiritual development. This possibility cannot be denied, because in some cases children manifest higher spiritual qualities. Gotama Siddhattha himself was such a "gold child" who was determined to rescue other people. The bodhisattva image of children seems to represent a higher aspect of child spirituality.

The Child as Spiritual Seeker

Just as early Buddhism honored Rahula as a model of an obedient and diligent practitioner, Mahayana Buddhism described a young person as a spiritual seeker. We have two examples for this. One is a well-known story recounted in the last chapter of *The Flower Ornament Scripture* (Cleary 1993, 1135–1518). This source offers a comprehensive view of Mahayana Buddhism, and especially the last long chapter, "Entry into the Realm of Reality," illustrates the way of the bodhisattva through the story of a child named Sudhana. In the story, the great Bodhisattva Manjushri found a boy, Sudhana, in a city and expounded to him the teachings of the Buddha, causing him to set his mind on enlightenment. Induced by Manjushri to see people who would serve as spiritual benefactors, Sudhana undertook a journey of pilgrimage to meet fifty-three teachers. It is interesting to remark that these spiritual teachers included a wide variety of people and beings: monks, laypeople in marketplaces, night goddesses, mendicant, non-Buddhist Brahmin, boy, girl, kings, perfumer, mariner, goldsmith, householders, celestials, and bodhisattvas. This broad range emphasizes that his journey was made in an ordinary world. As background information, there are stories in early Buddhism about those kinds of people who came across the Buddha to join his path and to attain enlightenment. From each benefactor who embodied some form of knowledge, Sudhana learned lessons. Sudhana could not stay at any one place, for each one of them sent him onward so that he could progress along his spiritual path through the ten stages of the bodhisattva way. Sudhana had been a student during his pilgrimage, but in the later stages of his journey, he started teaching, for he undertook a great journey to become a compassionate bodhisattva benefiting others. In depicting the child Sudhana as a seeker, the story shows the possibility for ordinary people to become bodhisattvas in this world, starting in childhood.

Ch'an/Zen Buddhism provides another story of a young person in the *Ten Oxherding Pictures* (Suzuki 1960, 129–34), ascribed to the Ch'an master Kaku-an of the Sung dynasty in China, which articulates the gradual process of attaining enlightenment in a series of ten pictures with the following titles: Searching for the Ox; Seeing the Traces; Seeing the Ox; Catching the Ox; Herding the Ox; Coming Home on the Ox's Back; The Ox Forgotten; Leaving the Man Alone; The Ox and the Man Both Gone Out of Sight; Returning to the Origin, Back to the Source; and Entering the City with Bliss-Bestowing Hands.

The ten pictures illustrate how a young man makes his quest for enlightenment. The first seven stages portray his existential and spiritual search for the true self. The man symbolizes the ego, and the ox the true self, or the deeper level of the psyche. At the initial stage, he has a feeling of loss or existential vacuum. His present state becomes a question, and he is driven to begin a search for the true self. At the second stage, he learns to know spiritual teachings. Through the next three stages, he strives to see, catch, and herd the ox, meaning that the ego gradually comes to terms with the true self. At the sixth stage, which describes the ox coming home with him on its back, his struggle with the ox is over. The ego comes to function in the service of the true self. Psychologically, this is an attainment of individuation or self-actualization (Kawai 1996).

The sixth stage is not the goal. Here the ox brings him back to his "home." The existential search for the true self turns into a spiritual search for a true nature of reality. Next, in the "home" of the seventh picture, the ox disappears and the man alone sits serenely. The ego and the true self are so completely unified that only a genuine person arises. As the home is located in the midst of nature, this stage means an ecological harmony realized between the person and nature. The seventh stage, however, is not the final destination. In other words, the last three pictures represent what Zen really conveys.

At the eighth picture, there is nothing but an empty circle, which stands for sunyata (emptiness), a true nature of reality. The ninth picture describes nature, and the tenth picture the human world. These last two pictures show two phases of *tathata* (suchness), or a world emerged after sunyata experience. In seeking for true reality, the man realized sunyata, and then he returned to the ordinary world. But the world is now radically transformed, for all the false identifications disappear in sunyata. Emancipated from all kinds of false identification, including false representations of the ego, he comes to terms with the ordinary world in a most liberated way, which is meant by tathata. In this way, Zen sees a twofold direction of seeking and returning in the spiritual path.

The tenth picture particularly portrays an old man encountering a boy on the road. Having started from the first stage in his adolescence, the young man has undergone the whole process of enlightenment and returned to the marketplace as a compassionate bodhisattva (an old man), who can invite ordinary people to realize their Buddha nature. While the young man in the first stage reveals a spiritual potentiality, the old man in this final stage shows a spiritual maturity (Nakagawa 2000, 153–62).

The discussion in this chapter, drawing upon selected Buddhist stories, has revealed at least two facets of childhood. In one aspect, a child is an ordinary human being who is subjected to suffering as the fundamental human condition. But in another, a child is a being who is bestowed with the potential to practice the Buddhist path and to become a bodhisattva. From the Buddhist perspective, these seemingly opposite views of childhood capture a fuller range of being human in this world. Also in the Buddhist tradition, the relation between child and adult plays an essential role in which each of them benefits each other's spiritual development, for each one is a good friend on the path.

Note

I wish to express my special gratitude to Professor Tsuneyuki Akatsu, Mr. Vimala Inoue, and Ms. Ayako Shiotani, who kindly shared with me valuable resources for this chapter. Especially, I acknowledge a number of comments offered by Mr. Inoue, a Buddhist practitioner, which I have included in this work.

References

Cleary, Thomas, trans. 1993. *The flower ornament scripture: A translation of the Avatamsaka Sutra.* Boston: Shambhala.

Hakeda, Yoshito. 1972. *Kukai: Major works.* New York: Columbia University Press.

Harvey, Peter. 1990. *An introduction to Buddhism.* Cambridge, UK: Cambridge University Press.

Kawai, Hayao. 1996. *Buddhism and the art of psychotherapy.* College Station: Texas A & M University Press.

Kohn, Sherab Chödzin. 1994. *The awakened one: A life of the Buddha.* Boston: Shambhala.

Nakagawa, Yoshiharu. 2000. *Education for awakening: An eastern approach to holistic education.* Brandon, Vt.: Foundation for Educational Renewal.

Nhat Hanh, Thich. 1999. *The heart of the Buddha's teaching.* New York: Broadway Books.

Rinpoche, Sogyal. 1992. *The Tibetan book of living and dying.* San Francisco: Harper.

Saddhatissa, H. 1976. *The life of the Buddha.* London: Allen & Unwin.

Salzberg, Sharon. 1995. *Lovingkindness.* Boston: Shambhala.

Schumann, H. W. 1989. *The historical Buddha.* London: Penguin.

Suzuki, Daisetz T. 1960. *Manual of Zen Buddhism.* New York: Grove Press.

Watson, Burton, trans. 1993. *The lotus sutra.* New York: Columbia University Press.

CHAPTER 4

Learning to Be Righteous: A Jewish Theology of Childhood

Michael Shire

After three days of an inspection in a Jewish state school in the United Kingdom, the state inspector responsible for personal, social, and cultural development sat down with the Jewish denominational inspector to compare findings. They were specifically reflecting on "acts of worship" in the whole school assembly that they had both observed that morning and the Grace After Meals the previous day. The assembly had consisted of a brief Jewish morning worship service, mostly sung with a story on the theme of the reading of the Torah for that week in which children actively participated. There were also announcements and the giving out of certificates. The Grace After Meals had taken place in a classroom, led by two children after lunch.

The perspectives of the two inspectors were very different. The state inspector commented that she felt neither act of worship evidenced any spirituality. She felt the children were just repeating songs that they knew by heart and to which she did not feel they were connected. She liked the way the children participated, but it was noisy, not contemplative, and the children did not have the discipline of "shutting their eyes and listening to a prayer." She felt the Grace After Meals had cut too much into the afternoon lesson.

The Jewish denominational inspector's view was that there was a great deal of spirituality in the way in which the children sang and were engaged in these acts of worship. The singing was liturgical and meaningful, and students had urged teachers to choose them to be the leaders of the prayers. The children sang beautiful melodies, and after the last part of the morning service and the Grace After Meals there was a natural moment of silence before the teacher intervened with the next instruction. It was a pause to reflect on all the enthusiasm and spirit that had been engendered. When the children were asked why they pray after lunch, they were able to articulate very clearly that if you thank God for what you have eaten, "it's a way of knowing that God is looking after you" or "appreciating that we have enough food" or "saying thank you" and "thinking about God."

The two inspectors were looking at but not seeing the same things. Their assessments were colored by their own cultural and religious experiences, as well as the understandings of spirituality in the contexts with which they were familiar. Rebecca

Nye describes the need for a multidimensional characterization of spirituality that attends to each child's personal "signature" (Hay and Nye 1998, 99). Using a grounded theory technique, Nye explored the expressions of spirituality in young people rather than imposing a preconsidered characterization upon them. Through conversations demonstrating both religious and nonreligious themes and issues, she places young people's expressions of spirituality within the context of their own lives. The very act of listening to children describes that which makes meaning in their lives and helps them refine the language and expression of their own spirituality.

Judaism understands that the spiritual life of children is expressed through study of Torah (understood as all of Jewish learning), by participation in the ritual and prayer life of the community (*avoda*), and in righteous deeds and acts of loving-kindness (*gemilut hasadim*).

This chapter will provide a description and analysis of Jewish attitudes to childhood drawing upon biblical stories, rabbinic interpretations, and Jewish custom. An examination of *halacha* (Jewish law), *midrashim* (biblical interpretations), and *minhagim* (customs) relating to children will provide a number of views of childhood as an approach to a multifaceted Jewish theology of childhood.

The Blessing of Children and the Blessings Children Bestow

Children are considered a great gift in Judaism, and parenthood is considered a blessing. There are many and varied customs and ceremonies to introduce a child into the Jewish community. Although classical Judaism does not have an abundant theoretical literature about the nature of childhood itself, it is through rituals, legal traditions, and interpretative literature that we learn what Judaism teaches about the spirit of the child. Childhood itself is an important state of being in Judaism, signified both by the cherished status of children in the classical literature and by the child-parent relationship that epitomizes the way in which the human-divine relationship is understood. Childhood is a symbolic depiction reflecting the special covenant between God and the People of Israel, which is characterized as a parent-child relationship

Toward the end of the nineteenth century, Solomon Schechter wrote of the child in Jewish literature (Schechter [1896] 1938). Schechter describes the child at the knee as "a trace of divine beneficence and sanctifying sentiment" (282). For Schechter, Judaism always considered the child as the greatest blessing God could bestow on humanity and its absence as the greatest curse. Quoting Abraham: "O God, what can you give me, seeing I shall die childless . . . ?" (Genesis 15:2). Schechter quotes the kabbalistic tradition that thought of the man who died without posterity as one who had failed in his mission in this world so that he would have to return to fulfill his duty.

Not having children is considered a position of great despair, and many potentially barren women and bereft men in the Bible describe their desperate childless condition (Genesis 30:1; 1 Samuel 1:10). Children are therefore considered to have a special place in God's protection respecting their vulnerability and innocent righteousness:

Rabbi Judah said, see how beloved the little children are before God. When the Sanhedrin went into captivity, the *Shechinah*—God's indwelling presence did not go with them. The watchers of the priests went into captivity but the Shechinah did not go with them. But when the little children went into captivity, the Shechinah went with them. For it says in Lamentations: "Her children are gone into captivity" and immediately after, "From Zion her splendor is departed." (Lamentations Rabbah 1:33)

Here the comparison of two verses in the Book of Lamentations gives rise to this rabbinic concept of God's presence (cf. "splendor") accompanying children wherever they go. This notion is further illustrated in a classic passage from the midrash illuminating the incomparable status of the child in the very act of God's revelation:

When God was about to give the Torah to Israel, he asked them, will you accept my Torah? And they answered, we will. God said, give me surety that you will fulfill its ordinances. They said, let Abraham, Isaac, and Jacob be our pledges. God answered, but the patriarchs themselves need sureties. . . . Then Israel said, our children shall be our sureties. God said such as these pledges I will indeed accept. Straight away the Israelites brought their wives with their children, even infants at the breast, even babes yet unborn. And God gave them power of speech even to those yet in the womb. He said to them, I am about to give your parents the Torah. Will you pledge yourselves that they will fulfill it? They said, we pledge ourselves. Then God rehearsed command after command and to each in succession the children promised obedience. (Tanhuma Vayiggash)

The Talmud states that childhood is a garland of roses, while the prophet Malachi calls children "the seed of God" (Malachi 2:15). One rabbi states that the very breath of children is free of sin (Shabbat 119a), while the Jerusalem Talmud pronounces, "Better are the late fruits we ate in our childhood than the peaches we ate in our old age" (Jerusalem Talmud Peah 87:4). Children are regarded as the hope for the future in that they have been entrusted to parents as a divine gift.

A midrashic collection (Yalkut Proverbs 964) relates a heartbreaking story of children born to Bruria and Rabbi Meir, both second-century scholars. While Rabbi Meir is away in the study house on Shabbat, the babies tragically die. On returning home at the end of the Sabbath, Bruria asks him a seemingly theoretical question: "If someone lent you a precious possession and then asked for it back, would you willingly give it up?" Rabbi Meir, unaware of the fate of his children, responds by affirming that he would return the gift, since it is held in trust for the rightful owner. Bruria then reveals the news of the death of the children, gifts from God.

According to Ecclesiastes Rabbah 5, there are three partners in the creation of a child: mother, father, and God. Children are therefore a component of God's creation and not exclusive to the parents who bear and raise them. Indeed, the tradition postulates a prebirth existence whereby the unborn soul struggles with the notion of being born against its will. It says, up to now I have been holy and pure; do not bring me into contact with what is common and unclean! Two angels are said to take the unborn soul and show it the glory of the righteous ones who dwell there and the sufferings of the sinner. The unborn soul wants to remain pure and cherished, yet the soul knows that it must adapt to the human world of trial and struggle to fulfill God's purpose.

What is, then, the theological purpose of children in the scheme of creation? A famous story from the rabbinic tradition seeks to affirm the purity of God's realm while acknowledging the task of human beings as growing, learning creatures. Newborn children are therefore contrasted with angels and lowly beasts of the field:

> On the second day of creation, God created the angels with their innate goodness. Then God created beasts with animal instincts not knowing right or wrong. Since God was unhappy with these extremes, God created humanity who would combine characteristics of both angel and beast in order to have free will to follow his good or evil inclination. In order for free will to be truly exercised, the child is made to forget all that he or she has learned as an unborn soul. Before it enters the world, an angel strikes it on the upper lip and all knowledge and wisdom disappear. The ridge in the upper lip is the result of this stroke. (Seder Yezirat HaValad)

The mission of the child is to glorify the name of God on earth. "You shall be to me a kingdom of Priests" is understood literally in that every child is considered a predestined priest to be prepared to serve God and complete the work of creation.

Just as children are received as blessings, they, in turn, bless their own parents as well as the larger community as indicated in the concept of *zechut banim*—through the merits of the children, the parents deserve honor. Noah found favor in God's eyes on account of his children (Tanhumah Noah 2), and Abraham was said to have been saved from a midrashic furnace on account of his son (Genesis Rabbah 63:2).

There is a recognition of revelation in children's experience. Mary Elizabeth Moore (Moore 2004, 84) poses the view that children actually "incarnate God's kingdom" in a reading of the Gospel of Mark in which Jesus encourages the children to come to him, saying whoever does not receive the kingdom of God as a little child will never enter it (Mark 10:13–16). This concurs with the Jewish notion of the power of children to inherently reveal the presence of God for others. Such is the case with Moses as a baby in a basket, setting in motion God's plan for the liberation of the Hebrews from slavery (Exodus 1:15–22); or Isaiah's powerful image of a child herding the wild beasts and the infant playing by the viper's nest (Isaiah 11:1–9); or Joseph's dreams about his brothers (Genesis 47). The distinct nature of the spirituality of children in Judaism is therefore expressed as a purity of nature and a potential for the highest aspiration of holiness and goodness. Judaism cherishes children and childhood as perhaps the purest form of being created in God's image (*b'zelem elohim*)

Ritual and Moral Obligations

Children, being minors, are free from the performance of religious duties, but they are expected to honor father and mother (Exodus 20:12; Leviticus 19:3; Deuteronomy 5:16). There is no special command for children to love their parents. Children are required only to give them respect, which is construed by the Jerusalem Talmud as the simple payment of a debt for having brought them into the world. From investigation of attitudes in the Midrash based on biblical narratives of the childhood experiences of Joseph, Samuel, and David, we can see emerge a state of childhood, treasured for a special role. Biblical stories about children demonstrate their ability to see what others cannot, as in Joseph's dreams or Samuel's call in the Temple. Childhood is a state treasured in the young and one to be fostered even into adulthood. Invoking the prophet Elijah, harbinger of the Messiah, at the covenant of circumcision demonstrated that each boy had the potential to change the world and bring it to completion and perfection. Covenantal birth ceremonies for girls, many of which also acknowledge Elijah's presence, came later. The sublime notion of harmony and perfection as described by the prophet Isaiah incorporates a young child playing with a wolf and lamb, leopard and goat, and lion and calf at the end of days.

There is no single picture of the child in the Bible (Alexander 1999, 155), and the promotion of childhood to an elevated status in the aggadic (narrative) literature is balanced by the halachaic (legal) treatment of children as minors. In contrast to adults, minors do not have obligations or responsibilities. Halachaic restrictions are placed on what children can be obliged to do ritually. Children are treated differently within Jewish law and practice from adults, particularly in regard to obligations in the public domain.

There is a strong understanding, however, that the purpose of childhood is to carry out the Commandments and to learn to enter the world of religious duty. This understanding is not considered lightly, and it is applied from an early age so that as soon as a child is free from his mother's care, he is old enough to be under the obligation of dwelling in the sukkah (tabernacle) on Sukkot (the harvest festival of thanksgiving). If he knows how to wave a *lulav* (palm branch), he must wave one. If he understands the laws of tzitzit (knotted fringes on the prayer shawl) and tefillin (phylacteries, small leather boxes containing slips of paper on which are written scriptural passages) and can put them on, it is his father's duty to provide him with them. As soon as a child can speak, his father teaches him the Shema (the central affirmation of God's oneness), Torah, and Hebrew; otherwise it would be better had he not come into the world (Jerusalem Talmud Hagigah 1, 2). Females did not have the same ritual obligations and were taught laws related to the home and family purity. Over time in the non-Orthodox movements, women have assumed full participation in Jewish ritual life.

The child eventually comes to fuller obligation at the time of bar or bat mitzvah. Previously referred to in the literature as *katan* (also *monir, olal, taf, yonek,* and *tinnok*), the elementary-age child does not have responsibilities or obligations. Now the term *bachur* or *bachura* ("one who chooses") is used to describe the emerging adolescent.

How does this transformation come about, and what does it signify in understanding a theology of childhood? The Talmud Sanhedrin 91b teaches that the "evil inclination" (*yetzer ha'ra*) enters the child at birth, and thereby is an innocent creature guided by natural impulses. The yetzer ha'ra is understood as all the natural impulses, including ambition and drive, that when undirected or misdirected can result in sin.

The medieval philosopher Maimonides viewed the child as unaware of knowledge of good and evil so that parents have a fundamental obligation to instill the values that will lead a child to choose well while he or she is yet young. Therefore, children cannot fulfill the Commandments of whose moral rightness they have no comprehension. These early years are precisely to set children on the right moral path of life based on knowledge of the unique nature of children and their innate qualities and character. Tradition then holds that only at the time of b'nai mitzvah does the "moral inclination" (*yetzer hatov*) enter the soul (Ecclesiastes Rabbah 69). Now the adolescent is able to make a positive choice in carrying out the Commandments and becomes obligated to a greater or lesser extent depending on gender. The spiritual elements of the soul are in place to carry out the Jewish task of learning and living as an adult. Modern movements in Judaism have found the age of thirteen to be too young to make this kind of personal transformation and spiritual commitment; fearing that children will leave their formal Jewish education after becoming bar or bat mitzvah, they have extended formal learning and created confirmation ceremonies.

Study and Learning as Quintessential Childhood Activities

Great emphasis is placed on training children for religious observance and teaching them Torah. The second-century rabbi Judah ben Tema said that children should be taught Scripture at age five, Mishnah at ten, to fulfill the law at thirteen, and to study Talmud at fifteen (Mishnah Avot 5:21). Children, when minors, are free from the performance of religious duties, but learning starts at an early age. In Temple times, children even participated in the sabbatical reading of Deuteronomy by the king (Deuteronomy 31:10–12).

The vital role of learning in fulfilling the purpose of childhood and finally entering the adult world is richly described in Jewish literature. The elaborate ceremonies developed from early rabbinic times continue to this very day and reflect influences from all the cultures and countries in which Jews have lived. The traditional approach to learning was to start with the study of Leviticus and its sacrificial order. The rationale for this priority was that just as sacrifices are pure, so are children: "therefore let the pure learn about the pure" (Leviticus Rabbah 7:3). Children are seen as pure of heart and mind and therefore regarded as potential for ultimate service to God through the priesthood. This is echoed in the story of Samuel, who is indentured to the High Priest in the Temple by Hannah, his mother, in thanksgiving for his long-awaited birth. His innocence is emphasized by the fact that he is the only one who can hear God's call to him in the Temple. Only a child's receptivity has the ability to perceive God's presence and respond to a call for duty and lifetime service. As he grows and develops, Samuel becomes the paradigm for the child's potential as Priest and Prophet, teaching others through his wisdom and moral courage.

On the first Shabbat after a birth, all the children of the community would be taken to the newborn's house, where they would recite the Shema and the Ninety-first Psalm. This communal welcoming by the children was called *Shalom Zocher*—"peace for the boy." In premodern times the ceremony of *holikreish* emerged as an equivalent welcoming for girls.

Judaism's view of learning was therefore a means not just to train individuals but to educate them to be engaged in a higher purpose. Thus, the Hebrew word for education is *hinukh* ("dedication" or "commitment"). Knowledge of Torah does not necessarily lead to commitment or engagement or even continuity. Rather, a life of religious sensibility lived out in community with a sense of duty to others is a prerequisite for determining what knowledge is worth acquiring and what constitutes the vision of the good. For Judaism, education ultimately is essentially an ethical activity. Studying, practicing, and celebrating Torah are what lead to spiritual renewal and commitment to God's moral purpose for all.

This was the function of the educational system that emerged first in the circles of ancient Hebrew Priests and Prophets. In the second century C.E., a well-established schooling system existed in every town in Judea, formed by High Priest Yehoshua ben Gamla (Baba Batra 21a). However, parents have always been considered the primary educators of their own children through modeling positive religious attitudes and providing an enculturation of home and community. Boys were instructed in the tasks and duties of the Jewish male. Girls' education took place at home and was particularly geared toward their traditionally separate adult responsibilities. It was not customary for girls to attend school, but some rabbis did encourage the teaching of Torah to girls, which gave rise to some eminent female scholars of Judaism in the second century. In modern times most girls receive the same education as boys. In their turn, children were required to show respect for parents and teachers as specified in the Fifth Commandment.

Children as serious transgressors of Jewish law, however, are a source of discussion in the biblical and rabbinic literature (Deuteronomy 21). In the eyes of the rabbis, wayward children contradicted the normative view of childhood. Such rebelliousness was therefore construed as a violation of the values of piety and goodness. This attitude enjoins the Jewish family and community to aspire to the highest ideals of purity and holiness for each child, to encourage each child to become a mensch (the Yiddish term for a responsible and caring human being).

The Jewish notion of education derived from this is not instrumental in that it seeks to achieve something extrinsic to the learner; rather it is spiritual in that it puts forth God's vision of goodness for all (Alexander 2004). These are seen to be the ultimate aims of education that makes for a more human world and, by consequence, a more divine one.

Children learning and studying, therefore, are elevated to the highest esteem, and their teachers are perceived as the very guardians of the world in which they live and as security against evil:

> Yuda Nesiah sent Rabbi Hisda, Rabbi Assi, and Rabbi Ammi to traverse the cities of the land of Israel in order to appoint Bible and Mishnah teachers. They came to a city and they found no teacher of Bible or Mishnah. They said, bring us to the guardians of the city. So they brought them to the senators of the town. They said, are these the guardians of the town? They are the destroyers of the town. Who then, they asked, are the guardians of the town? They were told, the teachers of Bible and Mishnah. As it is said, unless God guards the city, its watchmen stay awake in vain (Psalm 127:1). (Pesikta de Rav Kahana Piska 15:5)

The Talmud states that the world depends on the breath of schoolchildren. The rabbis of the period even suggest that Jerusalem was destroyed because children did not attend school and loitered in the streets (Shabbat 119b). Abrogating the primacy of study led to the destruction of the whole people.

Yet the tradition also saw that every child was different and needed to be treated individually. Maimonides stated that the teacher should entice each child with things he will like in order to bring him to a love of learning, which the philosopher considered more important than learning itself. The nineteenth-century biblical commentator Samson Raphael Hirsch criticized Isaac and Rebecca for showing favoritism to one son over the other and for not following the dictum of Proverbs 22:6: "Educate each child according to its own way." For Hirsch, the nature of the child is not something to be broken, nor is character predetermined. Education takes into account the diversity of individuals while it fulfills its function of teaching a vision of the good.

The first Jewish teacher is in fact God, who in Genesis 12 teaches Abram and Sarai what is right and good. This teaching is called Torah and entails a vision of goodness dedicated to a divine moral purpose. Later, this Torah is given to a people liberated from oppression and slavery, demonstrating that this moral way of life requires a precondition of freedom and choice. "Teach them to your children," it states in Deuteronomy 6, recited twice a day in Jewish liturgy as the Shema prayer. Literally the Hebrew translates as "Impress upon them," since these ways lead to a moral life and a life of Torah.

Children as Symbolic of God's Relationship with the Children of Israel

Childhood is also seen as a symbolic depiction reflecting the special relationship between God and the People of Israel, which is characterized as a parent-child relationship. When Rabbi Akiva, a second-century rabbi living under Roman occupation in Judea, describes man's belovedness by virtue of being created in the image of God, he emphasizes the nature of the child-divine relationship:

> Beloved is Man, for he was created in the image of God. Beloved are the people of Israel, for they are called the children of God. Beloved are the People of Israel, for a precious tool was given to them with which the world was created. (Mishnah Avot 3:14)

Within humanity as a whole, the Jewish people occupy a special position as the "children of God." This love for children is enduring and eternal. Even when children cease to behave, they are still their parents' sons and daughters. Similarly, Israel's special position is one that does not change according to Israel's behavior. God's relationship with the people of Israel is compared to that of a parent and child; you are the children of the Eternal your God (Deuteronomy 14:1).

In Exodus 4:22, God tells Moses to say to Pharaoh that Israel is the "firstborn son." Israel is also called holy to God, the first fruits of God's harvest (Jeremiah 2:3). This implies both a special relationship and responsibility to live out Torah, the blueprint for Israel's mission to be a "light unto the nations."

Even though Israel is often depicted as failing in its duty to fulfill its mission, nevertheless its status as child is not questioned. This concept emphasizes the unconditional love of parents to children. As children are the fulfillment of their parents' hopes, so Israel is the crowning glory of God's creation.

The most prevalent use of children as exemplars in Jewish ritual is the Pesach Haggadah (the liturgy narrating the central Jewish story of the Exodus), in which the seder (Passover meal) cannot be conducted without a child asking the initial questions about the purpose of the evening meal and ritual. Nor can the seder be concluded without bargaining with a child for the return of the *afikoman* (hidden matzoh, unleavened bread). The Haggadah describes four types of children: wise, wicked, simple, and those who do not know how to ask. Each child is to be answered according to his own question and in line with his own attitude. Rosenak (2001), based on the Vilna Gaon, sees the four types as two pairs of opposites. The "wise child" is set opposite the "one who does not know" in his intellectual capacity. The simple and pure child who behaves uprightly is set opposite the wicked one in a moral capacity. There are therefore four examples of the relationship between learning and goodness. The "wise child" represents the combination of learned and good; the "wicked child," the learned but not good; the "simple and pure," not learned but good; and "the one who does not know," not learned and not able to distinguish good from bad. These categorizations therefore encompass all of the combinations of learning and moral religious identity. At Passover, the major Jewish festival of national and personal liberation, four types of children are used to symbolize how all Israel struggles with growing in wisdom and goodness.

Robert Coles (1990), in his interviews and observations of Jewish children, is sensitive to the personal signatures of children, but he also identifies a common trait of "righteous humility" that he feels marks a Jewish spirituality in children:

> In years of work with Jewish children, I have encountered such moments over and over again to the point that I feel it makes up an aspect of the righteousness those children keep espousing, describing, urging upon one another. At its best this is a righteousness that avoids the fatal deterioration of self-righteousness precisely because it is not accompanied by professed certainty. I know exactly what the Lord wants and why he wants it and anyone within my sight or sound of my voice had better take heed. On the contrary, as these four children kept reminding us all, "God doesn't let on all his plans but He'd like us to show we trust Him and the best way to do it, is by doing some good while we're here." An acknowledged uncertainty as an aspect of religious passion. (Coles 1990, 266)

These qualities as described in the ancient and modern views of Jewish childhood endure. The varying Jewish conceptions of childhood encompass a purity of the child with a powerful potential to grow in wisdom and goodness. Judaism understands childhood to be both formative and lifelong and indeed a paradigm for the holiness and moral purpose of life itself.

Note

I am grateful to my colleague Dr. Helena Miller for the anecdote with which I begin this chapter.

References

Alexander, Hanan A. 1999. A Jewish view of human learning. *International Journal of Children's Spirituality* 4(2):155–64.
———. 2004. *Spirituality and ethics in education: Philosophical, theological and radical perspectives.* Brighton, UK: Sussex Academic Press.
Alexander, Hanan A., and Shmuel Glick. 2003. The Judaic tradition. In *A companion to the philosophy of education,* edited by Randall Curren, 33–49. Oxford, UK: Blackwell.
Cohen, Arthur, and Paul Mendes-Flohr, eds. 1987. *Contemporary Jewish religious thought.* New York: Scribner.
Coles, Robert. 1990. *The spiritual life of children.* Boston: Houghton Mifflin.
Cooper, John. 1996. *The child in Jewish history.* Lanham, Md.: Jason Aronson.
Feldman, W. M. 1917. *The Jewish child: Its history, folklore, biology and sociology.* London: Bailliere, Tindall and Cox.
Hay, David, and Rebecca Nye. 1998. *The spirit of the child.* London: Fount.
Heschel, Abraham J. 1966. *The insecurity of freedom.* New York: Farrar, Straus and Giroux.
Hirsch, Samson Raphael. 1958–62. *The Pentateuch.* 7 vols. London: Judaica Press.
Kadushin, Max. 1938. *Organic thinking: A study in rabbinic thought.* New York: Jewish Theological Seminary.
Marcus, Ivan. 1966. *Rituals of childhood: Jewish acculturation in medieval Europe.* New Haven, Conn.: Yale University Press.
Matzner-Bekerman, Shoshana. 1984. *The Jewish child: Halakhic perspectives.* New York: Ktav.
Montefiore, Claude G., and Herbert Loewe. 1960. *Rabbinic anthology.* Philadelphia: Jewish Publication Society of America.
Moore, Mary Elizabeth. 2004. Walking with children toward hope: The long road to justice and reconciliation. In *Spirituality and ethics in education: Philosophical, theological and radical perspectives,* edited by Hanan Alexander, 83–97. Brighton, UK: Sussex Academic Press.
Rosenak, Michael. 2001. *Tree of life, tree of knowledge: Conversations with the Torah.* Boulder, Colo.: Westview Press.
Sasso, Sandy Eisenberg. 2001. When your children ask. In *Spiritual education. Cultural, religious and social difference: New perspectives for the 21st century,* edited by Jane Erricker, Cathy Ota, and Clive Erricker, 9–18. Brighton, UK: Sussex Academic Press.
Schechter, Solomon. [1896] 1938. *Studies in Judaism.* First series. Philadelphia: Jewish Publication Society of America.
Shire, Michael. 2003. Educating the spirit. In *Teaching about God and spirituality,* edited by Sherry H. Blumberg and Roberta Louis Goodman, 117–30. Denver: ARE.
Urbach, Efraim. 1987. *The sages: Their concepts and beliefs.* Cambridge, Mass.: Harvard University Press.

CHAPTER 5

The Dignity and Complexity of Children:Constructing Christian Theologies of Childhood

Marcia J. Bunge

Throughout the history of Christianity and today we see many examples of concern for and care of children. Christians have offered food and shelter to poor children and orphans. They have established schools and pediatric hospitals. They have worked for social and political policies that protect children and provide them with the resources they need to thrive. Christians have also always attended to the spiritual and moral development of children and sought ways to nurture it in the home and through religious education programs.

Although there are many instances of care and concern for children throughout the Christian tradition, and although Christians have written and thought about children, in general, the church has not developed robust theologies of childhood that acknowledge the needs and vulnerabilities of children, as well as the gifts and strengths they bring to families and communities. Contemporary theologians and ethicists, too, have neither struggled directly in their work with issues regarding children nor sought to articulate sound theological understandings of children. Certainly, theologians and ethicists have devoted significant attention to many issues related to children, such as abortion, human sexuality, gender relations, contraception, marriage, and the family. Yet even most studies on marriage and the family have neglected to include serious reflection on fundamental subjects regarding children, such as the nature and status of children; parental obligations to them; the role of church and state in protecting children and providing them with the resources they need to thrive; the role of children in religious communities; the moral and spiritual formation of children; the role of children in the faith maturation of adults; children's rights; and adoption.[1] Although some theologians in the past addressed issues regarding children, contemporary theologians and ethicists have tended to consider such issues "beneath" the work of serious scholars and theologians and as a fitting area of inquiry only for pastoral counselors and religious educators.

Furthermore, children have played a minor role in the way theologians and ethicists think about central theological themes or religious practices. For example, reflection on children rarely informs discourse on the nature of faith, language about God, or the task of the church. Even current theological reflection on human nature has been typically built on a narrow model of human beings as adults alone, ignoring both the development and full humanity of children. In addition, aside from discussing infant baptism or communion, theologians and ethicists devote little attention to children in serious reflection on religious rituals and practices, such as prayer, worship, or even hospitality.

Thus, theological discourse has been dominated by simplistic and ambivalent views of children that diminish their complexity and integrity, fostering narrow understandings of adult-child relationships. For example, some Christians today and in the past have perceived children mainly as innocent or spiritually wise, and they have thereby often underestimated adult responsibilities of teaching and guiding children and helping them develop morally and spiritually. Other Christians, however, have tended to view children primarily as sinful and in need of instruction, thereby narrowly restricting their view of adult-child relationships to instruction, discipline, and punishment, and neglecting the lessons that children can teach adults. These kinds of simplistic conceptions of children in the church inform and reflect other widely held perceptions about children also found in contemporary culture. As several scholars have now argued, we tend to depict infants and young children as pure and innocent beings whom we adore and teenagers as hidden and dark creatures whom we must fear. In cases of juvenile crime, we argue whether twelve- and thirteen-year-olds are victims of abuse or fully conscious criminals. Other scholars have also convincingly shown that in a consumer culture a "market mentality" molds our attitudes toward children (see Miller-McLemore 2003, 1–23, 88–94; Whitmore 1997). Thus, instead of seeing children as having inherent worth, we tend to view them as being commodities, consumers, and even economic burdens.

The lack of complex thinking about children in the church and the wider culture has also undermined the church's commitment to them and had serious consequences for children themselves. Although the church certainly has a long history of serving children, there are many ways in which it has treated them as truly "the least of these." This has been witnessed most blatantly in the sexual abuse cases within the Roman Catholic Church, when financial concerns, careers of priests, and the reputations of bishops or particular congregations have come before the safety and needs of children. Yet, Christian churches as a whole exhibit a lack of sophisticated understandings of children and our commitments to them in other, subtler ways.

For example, although there are certainly examples of sound religious education programs, many congregations offer weak religious education programs and fail to emphasize the importance of parents in faith development. The curricula of many programs are theologically weak and uninteresting to children, and they assume that children have no questions, ideas, or spiritual experiences. Programs for children and youth are often underfunded, and leaders for them are difficult to recruit and retain. Furthermore, there is little coordinated effort between the church and the home in terms of a child's spiritual formation. Many parents don't even know what their children are learning in Sunday school, nor are parents given the sense that they are primarily responsible for the faith formation of their children.

As a result, we find that many parents within the church fail to speak with their children about moral and spiritual matters and are neglecting to integrate practices into their everyday lives that nurture faith. This claim is confirmed by several recent studies by Search Institute and the Youth and Family Institute. For example, according to one study of eight thousand adolescents whose parents were members of congregations in eleven different Protestant and Catholic denominations, only 10 percent of these families discussed faith with any degree of regularity, and in 43 percent of the families, faith was never discussed (Strommen and Hardel 2000, 14).

Nor have national churches been consistent public advocates for children. On the one hand, mainline Protestant churches support legislation to protect children's health and safety, yet they hesitate to contribute significantly to public debates about strengthening families. Protestant evangelical and conservative churches, on the other hand, are more vocal in nationwide debates about marriage, divorce, and the family, participation that has been positive. However, these churches sometimes focus so narrowly on the rights of parents to raise and educate their own children without governmental intrusion that they do not adequately address the responsibilities of parents, church, and state to protect, educate, and support all children.

Christians can do much to overcome these simplistic views of children and thereby strengthen the church's commitment to them by retrieving a broader, richer, and more complex picture of children from the Bible and the Christian tradition. Although theologians within the Christian tradition have often expressed narrow and even destructive conceptions of children and childhood, there are six central ways of speaking about the nature of children within the Christian tradition that, when critically retrieved and held in tension, can broaden Christian understandings of children and strengthen the church's commitment to them. This chapter provides grounds for this claim by first reviewing significant developments regarding children and childhood in the areas of theology and religious studies that are providing the resources needed for strong theologies of childhood to emerge and revealing a wide range of attitudes and behaviors toward children in the Christian tradition; and then outlining six Christian perspectives on children that provide the foundation for strong Christian theologies of childhood.

Research on Children and Childhood in Religious Studies and Theology

Several recent developments in the academy underscore the growing recognition of "the child" as an important category of analysis within many disciplines, including theology and religious studies. These developments are creating the space for theologies of childhood to emerge. Furthermore, scholarship on childhood, especially in the areas of biblical studies and church history, is providing specific resources for theological and ethical reflection on children by offering a corrective to common perceptions about Christianity's view of children, and by exposing a wide range of perspectives and resources within the Christian tradition on children and childhood.

Although interest in issues regarding children is growing in many disciplines, until recently, most of the scholars in the areas of religious studies and theology who focused much attention at all on children were religious educators or practical theologians working on issues of the family.[2] This is now beginning to change, however. More scholars in the areas of pastoral care and practical theology are now writing directly about children.[3]

Additionally, some religious educators are revisiting fundamental assumptions about faith formation and religious education, recognizing that previous theories often excluded not only insights into child development but also sound theological understandings of children themselves.[4] Others are focusing more attention on the importance of spiritual formation in the home.[5] Educators and child psychologists, both inside and outside the church, are also exploring the complexities of children's spirituality.[6] Various not-for-profit institutes and projects are holding conferences or publishing manuscripts on the subject, attracting scholars and practitioners from a wide range of disciplines and religious communities.[7] Child psychologists are also raising provocative methodological questions about how to study or even define children's spirituality (Hay and Nye 1998).

Furthermore, scholars in a number of areas in religious studies and theology outside the fields of religious education, pastoral care, and child development are beginning to publish more work on children and childhood and finding more opportunities to present their work at professional meetings. For example, within the past six years alone, several journals in theology and religious studies, such as *Dialog, Interpretation, Conservative Judaism*, the *Jahrbuch für biblische Theologie, Christian Reflection, Living Pulpit, Sewanee Theological Review*, and *Theology Today* have published entire issues on the subject of children.[8] In addition, several dissertations and books have been written on views of childhood in various religious traditions.[9] These and other publications include contributions from scholars in theology, ethics, biblical studies, history, cultural studies, and comparative religions. The American Society of Church History, the Society of Christian Ethics, and the American Academy of Religion (AAR) have recently devoted a few sessions at their national meetings to the themes of children and childhood. Furthermore, in 2002 the Program Committee of the AAR approved a new program unit, the Childhood Studies and Religion Consultation, which is now providing a forum for a more focused and sustained interdisciplinary dialogue about children and religion.[10] Some new national projects also focusing on children and religion have been funded that are generating new discussions and research opportunities for theologians and scholars of religion.[11]

Much of this new work, especially in the areas of biblical studies and church history, is offering a corrective to common perceptions about Christianity's view of children and providing important resources for Christian theologians and ethicists who seek to construct vibrant theologies of childhood. Since little serious attention had been given to children in contemporary theology, assumptions about Christian perspectives on children and childhood have been shaped mainly by popular studies about the religious roots of child abuse or by historical studies that assumed that viewing children as sinful fosters inhumane treatment of them, whereas viewing them as innocent encourages their humane treatment. Some of the most familiar studies exposed what has been called a "poisonous pedagogy" in some past and present strains of European and American Protestantism.[12] This type of inhumane pedagogy stresses that children are sinful and defiant and that parents should therefore "break their wills" at a very early age by demanding absolute obedience from children and by harshly punishing them. Other histories of childhood did not focus on religious roots of child abuse, but they did assume that a "key" to greater sensitivity to children and a more humane treatment of them, which they claimed took place primarily in the eighteenth century, came from a decline in the belief of original sin and a rise in the notion of children as naturally good or innocent.[13]

Although there are appalling instances throughout the history of Christianity and in the church today of child neglect and abuse, as more scholars have been reexamining the Bible and the history of Christianity, they have found an astonishing and complex range of attitudes and behaviors toward children. For example, by using childhood as a lens to reexamine the past, historical theologians and historians have uncovered significant yet often ignored aspects of the ideas and practices of selected theologians and movements in the church, and they have discovered a wide variety of theological perspectives on the nature of children and our obligations to them.[14] These studies have provided a partial corrective to oversimplified assumptions about religious roots of child abuse and Christianity's views of children and uncovered assorted views on children's innocence, sinfulness, or potential for both good and evil. In addition, these studies have demonstrated that even notions of original sin and "breaking the will" are complex and do not automatically lead to the harsh punishment of children. Indeed, the idea of original sin, set within a particular larger theological framework, has in some cases fostered the more humane treatment of children, especially the poor. The German Pietist August Hermann Francke (1663–1727), for example, emphasized the breaking of a child's will and religious conversion, yet these notions, set within the context of Francke's broader theological framework, fostered his humane and compassionate treatment of children (Bunge 2001). Furthermore, his theology led him to express a deeper concern for poor children than did many of his "enlightened" contemporaries, including John Locke (1632–1704).

In addition to emerging historical studies, several new articles and books have also been published during the past decade that are disclosing a range of biblical perspectives on children.[15] Children are depicted in a host of ways in the Bible: not only as ignorant, capricious, and in need of instruction and discipline, but also as gifts of God, signs of God's blessing, and models of faith. The studies also show that children have played more complex and diverse roles in families, communities, and religious life than has often been assumed. Although at times powerless and marginal, they also influence many aspects of community life. Furthermore, they are called to honor and obey their parents yet sometimes also to deceive them or leave them behind. They are depicted as victims of injustice yet also agents of God. In addition, childhood is used metaphorically in a variety of positive and negative ways in the Bible.

Many of these biblical studies also highlight the striking and even radical ways in which Jesus spoke about and treated children.[16] At a time when children occupied a low position in society and abandonment was not a crime, the Gospels portray Jesus as blessing children, welcoming them, embracing them, touching them, healing them, laying his hands on them, and praying for them. He also rebukes those who turn them away and even lifts children up as models of faith and paradigms of the reign of God. "Let the little children come to me, and do not stop them; for it is to such as these that the kingdom of heaven belongs" (Matthew 19:14). Furthermore, he equates welcoming a child in his name to welcoming himself and the One who sent him.

These and other recent studies have already confirmed that the history of children and childhood in relation to Christianity as well as other religions is much more complex than previous literature has suggested and merits further investigation. Like all histories of childhood, these studies are showing that scholars cannot mark a date for the "discovery of childhood" or chart simple historical accounts from "regressive" to "progressive" approaches to children. Scholars also recognize that they must distinguish the history of childhood from the history of children, realizing that it is much easier to study adult conceptions of children than to find out how adults actually treated children or to uncover the ideas and experiences of children themselves. Scholars acknowledge that even memories of childhood written by adults raise a number of provocative questions: Do these memories accurately represent that adult's childhood experience? How much are adult memories of childhood shaped by assumptions of what that childhood should have been or questions posed by historians?[17]

Resources for Constructing Robust Theologies of Childhood

As research on children and childhood continues to emerge in all areas of theology and religious studies, and as biblical scholars and historians continue to mine resources from the Christian tradition, one way that Christian theologians and ethicists can develop complex understandings of children is by critically retrieving and holding in tension at least six important and almost paradoxical perspectives on children that scholars have already brought to light. I outline these six perspectives briefly here and have discussed them more fully elsewhere (Bunge 2003). They are also echoed in some of the excellent Christian theologies of childhood now being written. Bonnie Miller-McLemore (2003, xxiii), for example, emphasizes that children must be "fully respected as persons, valued as gifts, and viewed as agents." Building primarily on the Gospels and the work of the Protestant theologian Friedrich Schleiermacher (1768–1834), Dawn DeVries (2001, 161–62) criticizes an instrumental view of childhood, stressing that children have intrinsic worth and both rights and responsibilities that correspond to that worth.

Although these six perspectives and others are found within the Christian tradition, Christian theologians today and in the past have often viewed them in isolation from one another, resulting in narrow and destructive understandings of children and our obligations to them. Theologians have often focused on one or two such perspectives alone, failing to appreciate the range of Christian thinking regarding children and critically retrieving them into serious and full-blown theologies of childhood. Thus, even though the six perspectives outlined here are not exhaustive, they do remind theologians of the complexity and dignity of children and can help combat simplistic and distorted views of children in the church and the wider culture. Furthermore, these six perspectives, when held together instead of in isolation, can help guide emerging theologies of childhood and strengthen the church's commitment to children.

GIFTS OF GOD AND SOURCES OF JOY

The Bible and the Christian tradition often depict children as gifts of God and sources of joy who ultimately come from God and belong to God.[18] Whether biological or adopted, children are gifts not only to parents but also to the church and the community. They are members of a community from the start, and they play various and complex roles within it. In addition, they will grow up to be not only sons and daughters but also husbands, wives, friends, neighbors, and citizens. Viewing children as gifts of God to the whole community radically challenges common assumptions of them as "property" of parents, as consumers, or as "economic burdens" to the community.

Related to this notion that children are gifts and signs of God's blessing, the tradition speaks of them as sources of joy and pleasure. Here, too, there are many examples. Sarah rejoiced at the birth of her son, Isaac (Genesis 21:6–7). Even in his terror and anguish, Jeremiah recalls the story that news of his own birth once made his father, Hilkiah, "very glad" (Jeremiah 20:15). An angel promises Zechariah and Elizabeth that their child will bring them "joy and gladness" (Luke 1:14). In the Gospel of John, Jesus says, "When a woman is in labor, she has pain, because her hour has come. But when her child is born, she no longer remembers the anguish because of the joy of having brought a human being into the world" (John 16:20–21). Some parents in the past wanted children for reasons we do not always emphasize today, such as to perpetuate the nation or to ensure that someone would care for them in their old age. Nevertheless, there is a sense today, as there was in the past, that one of the great blessings of our interactions with children is simply the joy and pleasure we take in them.

SINFUL CREATURES AND MORAL AGENTS

The Christian tradition often describes children as sinful creatures and moral agents. "The whole nature" of children, John Calvin held, is a "seed of sin; thus it cannot be but hateful and abominable to God."[19] The German Pietist Johann Arndt (1555–1621) claimed that within children lay hidden "an evil root" of a poisonous tree and "an evil seed of the serpent" (1979, 34–35). The American colonial preacher Jonathan Edwards (1753–58) wrote that as innocent as even infants appear to be, "if they are out of Christ, they are not so in God's sight, but are young vipers, and are infinitely more hateful than vipers."[20] The view of children as sinful is based on interpretations of several biblical texts. For example, Genesis 8:21 states that every inclination of the human heart is "evil from youth," and Proverbs 22:15 claims that folly is "bound up in the heart" of children. The Psalms declare that "the wicked go astray from the womb; they err from their birth" (Psalm 51:5; 58:3). Paul writes that all people are "under the power of sin," and "there is no one who is righteous, not even one" (Romans 3:9–10; cf. 5:12).

On the surface, this way of thinking about children can seem negative and destructive, and as some historical studies have shown, viewing children exclusively as sinful has often warped Christian approaches to children and led in some cases to child abuse and even death. However, the notion that children are sinful is worth revisiting and critically retrieving. It can correct an equally simplistic and dangerous view of children as primarily pure and innocent beings who automatically love God and their neighbors. Such a view leaves no room for appreciating a child's own growing autonomy and accountability, and thereby the "innocent child" easily becomes a passive cipher for the hopes and fears of adults. Viewing children as sinful underscores two important points.

On the one hand, it recognizes that they are "born in a state of sin"; they live in a world that is not what it ought to be. Their parents are not perfectly loving and just; social institutions that support them, such as schools and governments, are not free from corruption; and the communities in which they live, no matter how safe, have elements of injustice and violence. On the other hand, viewing children as sinful recognizes that, as they develop, they commit "actual sins" and are moral agents who bear some degree of responsibility for their actions. They can act in ways that are self-centered, unjust, and harmful to themselves and others. This view of "actual sins" of children becomes distorted if theologians mistakenly equate a child's physical and emotional needs or early developmental stages with sin. However, when used cautiously and with attention to psychological insights into child development, it can also strengthen the awareness of a child's growing moral capacities and levels of accountability.

DEVELOPING BEINGS WHO NEED INSTRUCTION AND GUIDANCE

A third helpful and central perspective within the tradition is that children are developing beings who need instruction and guidance. Adults are to nurture, teach, and guide children, helping them develop intellectually, morally, emotionally, and spiritually. Several biblical passages speak about these responsibilities. Adults are to "train children in the right way" (Proverbs 22:6) and bring up children "in the discipline and instruction of the Lord" (Ephesians 6:4). Parents and caring adults are to tell children about God's faithfulness (Isaiah 38:19) and "the glorious deeds of the Lord" (Psalm 78:4b). They are to teach children the words of the law (Deuteronomy 11:18–19; 31:12–13), the love of God with the whole heart (Deuteronomy 6:5), and doing what is right, just, and fair (Genesis 18:19; Proverbs 2:9).

There are also many examples in the tradition of theologians who took seriously the spiritual formation and education of children. They encouraged adults to pass on the faith to the next generation and to help children develop particular skills, virtues, and habits that would enable them to cultivate friendships and contribute to the common good. For example, John Chrysostom, in the fourth century, wrote sermons on parenting and the duties of parents to nurture the faith of their children. He viewed the home itself as "a little church" and ranked parental neglect of children's needs and their spiritual formation among the gravest injustices (Guroian 2001, 64, 73). Luther and Calvin also wrote catechisms and religious education materials for parents to use in the home, and they emphasized the responsibility of parents to guide and to instruct their children in the faith.[21] In his popular book, *Christian Nurture,* Horace Bushnell, a nineteenth-century Congregational pastor and scholar, emphasized that parents are the primary agents of a child's spiritual formation, claiming, "Religion never penetrates life until it becomes domestic" (Bushnell [1861] 1994, 63).[22]

FULLY HUMAN AND MADE IN THE IMAGE OF GOD

Although children are developing, they are, at the same time, whole and complete human beings made in the image of God. Thus, they are worthy of human dignity and respect from the start. The basis of this claim is Genesis 1:27, which states that God made humankind, male and female, in God's image. It follows that children, like adults, possess the fullness of humanity. Regardless of race, gender, or class, they have intrinsic value. Although parents nurture them, they are not made in the image of their parents but in the greater image of God. The sense of the integrity of each person, including children, is also grounded in a view of God, who intimately knows the number of "even the hairs of your head" (Matthew 10:30), forms your "inward parts," and "knit" you together in the womb (Psalm 139:13).

The notion that children are fully human and made in the image of God has often been neglected in Christianity, and some parts of the tradition describe children as "animals," "beasts," "prerational," "preadults," "almost human," "not quite human," or "on their way to becoming human." Some theologians, however, have emphasized the full humanity of children, including infants. For example, Cyprian in the third century depicted infants as complete human beings. All people, regardless of age or character, are "alike and equal since they have been made once by God." All share a "divine and spiritual equality" and are able to receive God's grace and gifts. "For what is lacking," Cyprian wondered, to one who "has once been formed in the womb by the hands of God?"[23] The twentieth-century Catholic theologian Karl Rahner also asserts that children have value and dignity in their own right and are fully human from the beginning. Thus, he believes that we are to respect children from the beginning of life. We need to see them as a "sacred trust" to be nurtured and protected at every stage of their existence.[24]

MODELS OF FAITH AND SOURCES OF REVELATION

The New Testament depicts children in striking and even radical ways as moral witnesses, models of faith for adults, sources or vehicles of revelation, and representatives of Jesus. The gospel passages turn upside down common assumptions held in Jesus' time and our own: that children are to be seen but not heard and that their primary role is to learn from and obey adults. In contrast, these New Testament passages remind us that children can teach and challenge adults. They can prophesy and praise God. They can be vehicles of revelation, models of faith, and even paradigms for entering the reign of God. "Unless you change and become like children, you will never enter the kingdom of heaven," Jesus warns. "Whoever becomes humble like this child is the greatest in the kingdom of heaven. Whoever welcomes one such child in my name welcomes me" (Matthew 18:2–5). Viewing children as models for adults or vehicles of revelation does not mean that they are creatures who are "near angels," "closer to God," or "more spiritual" than adults. However, these passages and others do challenge adults to be receptive to the lessons and wisdom that children offer them, to honor children's questions and insights, and to recognize that children can positively influence the community and the moral and spiritual lives of adults.

Like the notion that children are fully human and made in the image of God, the idea that children can be teachers, bearers of revelation, or models of faith has not been emphasized and has often been completely neglected in the Christian tradition and among Christians today. Throughout the tradition and today, however, we do find theologians who have grappled seriously with these New Testament passages, forcing them to rethink their assumptions about children and exploring what adults learn from them. For example, Friedrich Schleiermacher emphasized that adults who want to enter the kingdom of God need to recover a childlike spirit. For him, this childlike spirit has many components that we can learn from children, such as "living fully in the present moment," being able to forgive others, or being flexible.[25]

ORPHANS, NEIGHBORS, AND STRANGERS IN NEED OF JUSTICE AND COMPASSION

There are many biblical passages and examples in the tradition that remind us that children are also orphans, neighbors, and strangers who need to be treated with justice and compassion. There are numerous biblical passages that explicitly command us to help widows and orphans—the most vulnerable in society.[26] The Bible depicts many ways in which children suffer and are the victims of war, disease, or injustice. In the New Testament, Jesus also healed children. These and other passages clearly show us that caring for children is part of seeking justice and loving the neighbor.

Although we cannot ignore the church's neglect and harm of children, Christians have also at times protected children and helped them to achieve wholeness, and there are many examples within the past and today of those who have taken seriously the situation of orphans and poor children. For example, Martin Luther and Phillip Melanchthon influenced positive policies and reforms in Germany for universal education that included girls and the poor. Francke attended to poor children in his community by building hospitals, schools, and orphanages to serve them and their families. Like Luther and Melanchthon, he also influenced positive educational policies and reforms in Germany so that all children could receive a good education. John Wesley, the founder of Methodism, is another strong example of a theologian who attended to the poor in concrete ways, and he inspired Methodists from his time to today to care for the poor and to establish a number of institutions and initiatives to serve them.

The Significance of Robust Christian Theologies of Childhood

When incorporated into theologies of childhood and held in tension, these six perspectives have tremendous implications for combating simplistic and destructive conceptions of children and strengthening the church's commitment to them. For example, when held in tension, these six ways of speaking about children could strengthen spiritual formation and religious education programs. If Christians see children as gifts of God and sources of joy, then they will include them in worship services as true participants and welcome them as full members of the church, and they will incorporate more joy and laughter into religious education at home and at church. Furthermore, if Christians see children as sinful and in need of instruction, then they will develop more substantial religious educational materials and programs for children in the church and create Christian education programs that emphasize the importance of the family in spiritual formation and faith development. They will also more readily cultivate the growing moral capacities and responsibilities of children in many other ways, such as by introducing them to good examples, mentors, and stories of service and compassion; including children in service projects and teaching them financial responsibility; and helping them discern their vocations and explore how they can best use their gifts and talents to contribute to the common good. Finally, if they believe, as Jesus did, that children can teach adults and be moral witnesses, models of faith, and sources of revelation, then they will listen more attentively to children and learn from them; structure religious education programs in ways that honor children's questions and insights; and recognize the importance of children in the faith journey and spiritual maturation of parents and other adults.

The six ways of speaking about children could also deepen theological and ethical reflection on children and inform strong Christian theologies of childhood. For example, if Christians see children as gifts of God and developing beings in need of instruction, then they will no longer see children as "belonging" to their parents, but rather as gifts to them as well as to the whole community. They will take more seriously their obligations to all children and strengthen theological and ethical reflection on the role of church and state in protecting children and on the responsibilities of parents. They will also begin to understand spiritual formation as a serious area of inquiry in all areas of theological and biblical studies—not just pastoral care or religious education. In these and other ways, the church could build strong theologies of childhood.

The six ways of speaking about children could help renew the church's commitment to serving and protecting all children. If the church viewed children as made in the image of God, as fully human, and as orphans, neighbors, and strangers in need of compassion and justice, then it would treat all children, regardless of age, race, class, or gender, with greater dignity and respect. Christians would no longer tolerate the abuse or harsh treatment of children, and they would warn against equating "discipline" with physical punishment. Furthermore, they would support local and federal legislation that addresses the needs of all children and families, such as fighting for a true living wage, parental leave policies, and strong educational programs for all children. The church would also promote governmental support of proper nutrition and adequate health care for children. Christians would attend to the needs of poor children in their communities and around the world, work more diligently to protect and serve all children in need, and become stronger and more creative advocates for children in our country and around the world.

There are many other implications of a complex and biblically informed understanding of children. A more vibrant view of children can combat simplistic and destructive conceptions of them and thereby strengthen the church's commitment to them in a number of areas. By appropriating a view of children that incorporates at least these six central perspectives found in the Bible and in tradition, all those within Christian communities can strengthen their efforts in spiritual formation and religious education; do what they can to facilitate stronger theologies of childhood in the church; and take up more wholeheartedly and responsibly the Christian call to love and care for all children.

Notes

1. As Todd David Whitmore has argued, "For the most part, church teaching simply admonishes the parents to educate their children in the faith and for children to obey their parents" (Whitmore, 1997).

2. Initial work on children was written primarily by ethicists and practical theologians within the context of studies on the family. See, e.g., Cahill and Mieth (1995), Cahill and Shannon (1988), Carr and Van Leeuwen (1996), Miller-McLemore (1994), Peters (1996), and Post (1994). Don Browning's Religion, Culture, and the Family project also challenged the leadership of mainline denominations to address familial issues and has supported a number of major studies in the area, including research projects on biblical views of the family, feminism and the family, and specific ethical issues that families face today. One of the central texts generated by the project is Browning et al. (1997).

3. See, e.g., Anderson and Johnson (1994), Couture (2000), Dawn (1997), Miller-McLemore (2003), and Stevenson-Moessner (2003).

4. See, e.g., Berryman (1991), Lillig (1998), Morgenthaler (1999), and Stonehouse (1998).

5. See, e.g., Garland (2003), Miller-McLemore (2002), Strommen and Hardel (2000), Thompson (1996), Wigger (2003), Wright (2003), and Yust (2004).

6. Some of the psychological studies on the spiritual lives of children that inform this debate include Cavalletti (1983), Coles (1990), Heller (1986), and Rizutto (1979).

7. For projects, conferences, and institutes focusing on children's spirituality, see, for example, the Children and WorldViews Project, which has sponsored an annual international conference since July 2000 and launched the International Journal of Children's Spirituality in 1996 (http://www.cwvp.com); the ChildSpirit Institute (http://childspirit.net); and the triannual conference "Children's Spirituality–Christian Perspectives" (http://childspirituality.org), which recently published several papers from its first conference, held in 2003, in Ratcliff (2004). Search Institute is also supporting a new project that explores scientific research and theological perspectives on children's spirituality. For more information, see http://www.search-institute.org.

8. Dialog 37 (Summer 1998); Interpretation 55, no. 2 (2001); Conservative Judaism 53, no. 4 (Summer 2001); Jahrbuch für biblische Theologie 17 (2002); Christian Reflection (July 2003); Living Pulpit 12, no. 4 (2003); Sewanee Theological Review 48, no. 1 (2004); and Theology Today 56, no. 4 (2000).

9. See, e.g., Coward and Cook (1996), Gil'adi (1992), Kinney (2003), Marcus (1998), and Ziolkowski (2001).

10. For information on the Childhood Studies and Religion Consultation and the AAR annual meeting, see the Web site of the AAR (http://aarweb.org).

11. The Center for the Interdisciplinary Study of Religion (CISR) at Emory University, for example, is sponsoring The Child in Law, Religion, and Society, a project directed by Martin Marty. I am also directing a new project titled The Child in Religion and Ethics, which aims to strengthen theological and ethical understandings of children and our obligations to them and to encourage course development on children and childhood in all areas of religious studies and theology.

12. See, e.g., Capps (1992, 1995), Greven (1991), Miller (1983). See also Greven (1977), in which he ties methods of child rearing to three distinctive religious "temperaments" he finds in the seventeenth and eighteenth centuries.

13. Herrmann (1988) states, for example, that the more loving care of children one finds in the eighteenth century could only take place once the "theological view" of children as weak and depraved was replaced by the "pedagogical view" of children as individuals with open futures

(12). See also Cunningham (1995, 61–62). Elsewhere, Cunningham recognizes the complexity of this particular period and admits that some thinkers who had the sternest views of chidren and saw them as "conceived and born in sin" could be "kind and loving in practice," and others "seemed able to perceive of children as both innocent and sinful" (1991, 47–49).

14. See, e.g., Bakke (2005), Bunge (2001), and Wood (1994). Significant foundations for these kinds of historical studies on children were laid in research that provided detailed analyses of many aspects of family life in the past, such as childbirth, motherhood, marriage, and divorce.

15. See, e.g., Carroll (2001), Fewell (2003), Gundry-Volf (2001), Mueller (1992), and the articles in a special issue titled *Gottes Kinder* published in volume 17 (2002) of the *Jahrbuch für biblische Theologie*.

16. Some of the most significant passages in the Gospels are Matthew 11:25, 18:1–5, 19:13–15, and 21:14–16; Mark 9:33–37 and 10:13–16; Luke 9:46–48 and 18:15–17.

17. For insightful discussions of these and other kinds of questions that can guide research in the history of childhood, see Hiner (1978), 15–16; Hiner and Hawes (1985), xx–xxii.

18. Many passages in the Bible speak of children as gifts of God or signs of God's blessing. For example, Leah, Jacob's first wife, speaks of her sixth son as a dowry, or wedding gift, presented by God (Genesis 30:20). Several passages indicate that parents who receive these precious gifts are being "remembered" by God (Genesis 30:22; 1 Samuel 1:11, 19) and given "good fortune" (Genesis 30:11). To be "fruitful"—have many children—is to receive God's blessing. The Psalmist says children are a "heritage" from the Lord and a "reward" (Psalm 127:3).

19. Calvin (1975), 97; quoted by Pitkin (2001), 167.

20. Edwards (1972), 394; quoted by Brekus (2001), 303.

21. For discussions of Luther and Calvin, see Strohl (2001), 134–59, and Pitkin (2001), 160–93.

22. For a full discussion of Bushnell, see Bendroth (2001).

23. Cyprian, Letter 64.3; in Donna (1964), 217–18. Although Cyprian is making strong claims for the spiritual and divine equality of children, he does not draw implications for their social equality.

24. See Rahner (1971). For an excellent discussion of Rahner's views on children and childhood see Hinsdale (2001), 406–45.

25. For in-depth discussions of Schleiermacher, see DeVries (2001a, 2001b).

26. See, e.g., Exodus 22:22–24; Deuteronomy 10:17–18 and 14:28–29.

References

Anderson, Herbert, and Susan B. W. Johnson. 1994. *Regarding children*. Louisville, Ky.: Westminster/John Knox Press.

Arndt, Johann. [1606–10] 1979. *True Christianity*. Translated by Peter Erb. New York: Paulist Press.

Bakke, O. M. 2005. *When children became people. The birth of childhood in early Christianity*. Translated by Brian P. McNeil. Minneapolis, Minn.: Fortress Press.

Bendroth, Margaret. 2001. Horace Bushnell's *Christian nurture*. In *The child in Christian thought*, edited by Marcia J. Bunge, 350–64. Grand Rapids, Mich.: Eerdmans.

Berryman, Jerome. 1991. *Godly play: An imaginative approach to religious education*. San Francisco: HarperSanFrancisco.

Brekus, Catherine A. 2001. Children of wrath, children of grace: Jonathan Edwards and the Puritan culture of child rearing. In *The child in Christian thought*, edited by Marcia J. Bunge, 300–328. Grand Rapids, Mich.: Eerdmans.

Browning, Don, Bonnie J. Miller-McLemore, Pamela D. Couture, K. Brynolf Lyon, and Robert M. Franklin. 1997. *From culture wars to common ground: Religion and the American family debate*. Louisville, Ky.: Westminster/John Knox Press.

Bunge, Marcia J. 2001. Education and the child in eighteenth-century German pietism: Perspectives from the work of A. H. Francke. In *The child in Christian thought*, edited by Marcia J. Bunge, 247–78. Grand Rapids, Mich.: Eerdmans.

———. 2003. A more vibrant theology of children. *Christian Reflection: A Series in Faith and Ethics* (Summer):11–19.

Cahill, Lisa Sowle, and Dietmar Mieth, eds. 1995. *Concilium*, no. 4.

Cahill, Lisa Sowle, and Thomas A. Shannon. 1988. *Religion and artificial reproduction*. New York: Crossroad.

Calvin, John. 1975. *Institutes of the Christian religion: 1536 edition*. Translated by Ford Lewis Battles. Grand Rapids, Mich.: Eerdmans.

Capps, Donald. 1992. Religion and child abuse: Perfect together. *Journal for the Scientific Study of Religion* 31:1–14.

———. 1995. *The child's song: The religious abuse of children*. Louisville, Ky.: Westminster/John Knox Press.

Carr, Ann, and Mary Stewart Van Leeuwen, eds. 1996. *Religion, feminism, and the family*. Louisville, Ky.: Westminster/John Knox Press.

Carroll, J. T. 2001. Children in the Bible. *Interpretation* 55 (April):121–34.

Cavalletti, Sofia. 1983. *The religious potential of the child*. New York: Paulist Press.

Coles, Robert. 1990. *The spiritual lives of children*. Boston: Houghton Mifflin.

Couture, Pamela. 2000. *Seeing children, seeing God: A practical theology of children and poverty*. Nashville, Tenn.: Abingdon.

Coward, Harold, and Philip Cook, eds. 1996. *Religious dimensions of child and family life: Reflections on the UN Convention on the Rights of the Child*. Waterloo, Ont., Canada: Wilfrid Laurier University Press.

Cunningham, Hugh. 1991. *Children of the poor: Representations of childhood since the seventeenth century*. Oxford: Blackwell.

———. 1995. *Children and childhood in western society since 1500*. New York: Longman.

Dawn, Marva. 1997. *Is it a lost cause? Having the heart of God for the church's children*. Grand Rapids, Mich.: Eerdmans.

DeVries, Dawn. 2001a. "Be converted and become as little children": Friedrich Schleiermacher on the religious significance of childhood. In *The child in Christian thought*, edited by Marcia J. Bunge, 300–328. Grand Rapids, Mich.: Eerdmans.

———. 2001b. Toward a theology of childhood. *Interpretation* 55 (2):160–73.

Donna, Sister Rose Bernard, trans. 1964. *Fathers of the church: Saint Cyprian, letters 1–81*. Washington, D.C.: Catholic University of America Press.

Edwards, Jonathan. [1742] 1972. Some thoughts concerning the present revival. In *The great awakening*, edited by C. C. Goen. New Haven, Conn.: Yale University Press.

Fewell, Danna Nolan. 2003. *The children of Israel: Reading the Bible for the sake of our children*. Nashville, Tenn.: Abingdon.

Garland, Diana R. 2003. *Sacred stories of ordinary families: Living the faith in daily life*. San Francisco: Jossey-Bass.

Gil'adi, Avner. 1992. *Children of Islam: Concepts of childhood in medieval Muslim society*. New York: St. Martin's Press.

Greven, Philip. 1977. *The Protestant temperament: Patterns of child-rearing, religious experience, and the self in early America*. New York: Knopf.

———. 1991. *Spare the child: The religious roots of punishment and the psychological impact of physical abuse.* New York: Knopf.

Gundry-Volf, Judith M. 2001. The least and the greatest: Children in the New Testament. In *The child in Christian thought,* edited by Marcia J. Bunge, 29–60. Grand Rapids, Mich.: Eerdmans.

Guroian, Vigen. 2001. The ecclesial family: John Chrysostom on parenthood and children. In *The child in Christian thought,* edited by M. J. Bunge, 61–77. Grand Rapids, Mich.: Eerdmans.

Hay, David, and Rebecca Nye. 1998. *The spirit of the child.* London: Fount.

Heller, David. 1986. *The children's God.* Chicago: University of Chicago Press.

Herrmann, Ulrich. 1988. Kind und Familie im 18. Jahrhundert. In *Das Kind im 18. Jahrhundert: Beiträge zur Socialgeschichte des Kindes,* edited by Johannes Oehme. Lübeck: Hansisches Verlagskontor H. Scheffler.

Hiner, N. Ray. 1978. The child in American historiography: Accomplishments and prospects. *Psychohistory Review* 7 (Summer):15–16.

Hiner, N. Ray, and Joseph M. Hawes, eds. 1985. *Growing up in America: Children in historical perspective.* Urbana: University of Illinois Press.

Hinsdale, Mary Ann. 2001. "Infinite openness to the infinite": Karl Rahner's contribution to modern Catholic thought on the child. In *The child in Christian thought,* edited by Marcia J. Bunge, 406–445. Grand Rapids, Mich.: Eerdmans.

Kinney, Anne Behnke. 2003. *Representations of childhood and youth in early China.* Stanford, Calif.: Stanford University Press.

Lillig, Tina. 1998. *The catechesis of the Good Shepherd in a parish setting.* Chicago: Liturgy Training Publications.

Marcus, Ivan G. 1998. *Rituals of childhood: Jewish acculturation in medieval Europe.* New Haven, Conn.: Yale University Press.

Miller, Alice. 1983. *For your own good: Hidden cruelty in child-rearng and the roots of violence.* Translated from the German by Hildegard Hannum and Hunter Hannum. New York: Noonday.

Miller-McLemore, Bonnie. 1994. *Also a mother: Work and family as theological dilemma.* Nashville, Tenn.: Abingdon.

———. 2002. Heard and seen: The challenge of religious formation in families. *Concilium,* no. 4:45–54.

———. 2003. *Let the children come: Reimagining childhood from a Christain perspective.* San Francisco: Jossey-Bass.

Morgenthaler, Shirley, ed. 1999. *Exploring children's spiritual formation.* River Forest, Ill.: Pillars Press/Concordia.

Mueller, Patrick. 1992. *In der Mitte der Gemeinde: Kinder im Neuen Testament.* Neukirchen-Vluyn: Neukirchener Verlag.

Peters, Ted. 1996. *For the love of children: Genetic technology and the future of the family.* Louisville, Ky.: Westminster/John Knox Press.

Pitkin, Barbara. 2001. "The heritage of the Lord": Children in the theology of John Calvin. In *The child in Christian thought,* edited by Marcia J. Bunge, 160–93. Grand Rapids, Mich.: Eerdmans.

Post, Stephen. 1994. *Spheres of love: Toward a new ethics of the family.* Dallas: Southern Methodist University Press.

Rahner, Karl. 1971. Ideas for a theology of childhood. In *Theological investigations,* volume 8, translated by David Bourke, 33–50. London: Darton, Longman & Todd.

Ratcliff, Donald, ed. 2004. *Children's spirituality: Christian perspectives, research, and applications.* Eugene, Oreg.: Cascade Books.

Rizutto, Ana-Maria. 1979. *The birth of the living God: A psychoanalytic study.* Chicago: University of Chicago Press.

Stevenson-Moessner, Jeanne. 2003. *The spirit of adoption: At home in God's family.* Louisville, Ky.: Westminster/John Knox Press.

Stonehouse, Catherine. 1998. *Joining children on the spiritual journey: Nurturing a life of faith.* Grand Rapids, Mich.: Baker Books.

Strohl, Jane E. 2001. The child in Luther's theology: "For what purpose do we older folks exist, other than to care for . . . the young?" In *The child in Christian thought,* edited by Marcia J. Bunge, 134–59. Grand Rapids, Mich.: Eerdmans.

Strommen, Merton P., and Richard Hardel. 2000. *Passing on the faith: A radical new model for youth and family ministry.* Winona, Minn.: St. Mary's Press.

Thompson, Marjorie. 1996. *Family, the forming center: A vision of the role of family in spiritual formation.* Nashville, Tenn.: Upper Room Books.

Whitmore, Todd David, with Tobias Winwright. 1997. Children: An undeveloped theme in Catholic teaching. In *The challenge of global stewardship: Roman Catholic responses,* edited by Maura A. Ryan and Todd David Whitmore, 161–85. Notre Dame, Ind.: University of Notre Dame Press.

Wigger, Bradley J. 2003. *The power of God at home: Nurturing our children in love and grace.* San Francisco: Jossey-Bass.

Wood, Diana, ed. 1994. *The church and childhood.* Oxford: Blackwell.

Wright, Wendy. 2003. *Seasons of a family's life: Cultivating the contemplative spirit at home.* San Francisco: Jossey-Bass.

Yust, Karen Marie. 2004. *Real kids, real faith: Practices for nurturing children's spiritual lives.* San Francisco: Jossey-Bass.

Ziolkowski, Eric Jozef. 2001. *Evil children in religion, literature, and art.* New York: Palgrave.

CHAPTER 6

Filling the Heart with the Love of God: Islamic Perspectives on Spirituality in Childhood and Adolescence

Yetkin Yildirim

This chapter reviews Islamic concepts on spirituality in childhood and adolescence and attempts to establish a baseline of scholarship and knowledge on these topics. It concentrates on historical and current understandings of spiritual development and contemporary educational concepts. Since the main sources of Islamic knowledge are the Qur'an and the Sunna (the prescribed way of life based on the teachings and practices of Prophet Muhammad),[1] the teachings on the subject are collected and summarized mainly from these sources.

According to Islamic teachings, spiritual education in childhood and adolescence is crucial for raising physically and mentally healthy people. As stated by the Islamic scholar Said Nursi, if children are not exposed to belief in God and spirituality at an early age, it will be much more difficult to settle belief and spirituality in their hearts in later years. The more children are exposed to a community observing religion the easier it will be for them to understand religion and spirituality later in life (Nursi 2002).

One of the main sources for understanding the concept of spirituality in childhood according to Islam is Prophet Muhammad's teachings. According to Islamic teachings, Prophet Muhammad is an example for humanity. Since the Prophet's conduct embodied Islam and the Qur'an, when his wife Aisha, may God be pleased with her, was asked about his conduct by Sa'id ibn Hisham, she answered: "Do you not read the Qur'an? His conduct is (the embodiment of) the Qur'an" (Saheeh-i Muslim, Chapter Musafirin).

Just as in other aspects of life, he was an example for his students on how to educate and treat children. His love for children is exemplified in the following story from one of his students:

> One day the Prophet was in one of the markets of Medina. He left (the market) and so did I. Then he asked thrice, "Where is the small (child)?" Then he said, "Call Al-Hasan bin 'Ali." So Al-Hasan bin 'Ali got up and started walking with a necklace (of beads) around his neck. The Prophet stretched

his hand out like this, and Al-Hasan did the same. The Prophet embraced him and said, "O Allah! I love him, so please love him and love those who love him." Since Allah's Apostle said that, nothing has been dearer to me than Al-Hasan. (Saheeh-i Bukhari, Book 24: Book Pertaining to Clothes and Decoration)

Islam teaches that every child is born sinless and is certain to gain paradise if he or she passes away before reaching puberty. Children are viewed as precious gifts from God and need to be taken care of and protected by their parents and their surrounding communities. The primary way for children to attain spiritual development is to observe the personal spiritual practices of adults in their surrounding communities. Therefore, Islam not only gives these people the responsibility for the spiritual well-being of children but also makes them accountable.

Spiritual development in adolescence concerns the time when young minds acquire the basic knowledge they will use their entire lives. Islamic scholars point out that spiritual development should accompany this basic knowledge. A good model of education proposes the mutual development of mind and spirit, where children are well educated in the sciences and also spiritually well nourished.

Spirituality in Islam

This section attempts to explain the concept of spirituality in Islam in relation to the daily lives and practices of Muslims and its role in the education of children and adolescents. Spirituality in Islam is based on the teachings of Prophet Muhammad and the interpretation of the Qur'an, and concentrates mostly on the spiritual dimension of Islamic teachings, trying to draw attention to the essence of man's being, the real nature of existence, and the inner dynamics of man and the cosmos.

Said Nursi states that the ultimate spiritual experience can be achieved by filling one's heart with the love of God, which requires belief in and knowledge of God (Nursi 2002). God is the source of all knowledge, and by knowing more, human beings draw closer to God (Husain and Ashraf 1979). Through the remembrance of God, faith and knowledge are supposed to be put into practice in all aspects of life. The spiritual advancement that contains the joy of the spirit and the satisfactions of the heart is possible only by means of this remembrance. The Qur'an states, "Those who believe, and whose hearts find satisfaction in the remembrance of Allah: for without doubt in the remembrance of Allah do hearts find satisfaction" (Qur'an 13:28).

The Qur'an and the tradition of Prophet Muhammad give detailed information about how to put the belief and knowledge of God into practice. Considering both the physical and spiritual existence of human beings, Islam dictates both bodily and spiritual rituals and exercises to achieve the ultimate spiritual experience. These rituals and exercises include regular worship, abstention from all major and minor sins, self-control, and a continuous struggle to resist the temptations of Satan and the carnal self. These practices are an integral part of spiritual development and cannot be separated from it.

In Islamic teachings, spirituality is an integral part of daily life. Only through spirituality does life find its essence and meaning. Regular practices, such as the five daily prayers, and other religious obligations, rituals, and exercises have a specific spiritual purpose. They aim to enable people to live at a high level of spirituality through self-purification and spiritual training. As the individual's spirituality grows through the development of universal values, such as sincerity and purity of intention, through the struggle with the self, and through the habits of prayer, self-control, and self-criticism, the veils over the inner dimension of existence are torn apart. As a result, one gains a strong conviction of the truth of all the principles of faith.

Through this training, people are educated to be able to observe spirituality in their lives. That is why religious practices and spirituality cannot be separated from one another; they should go hand in hand. Spirituality in Islam concentrates on the meaning of religious duties and other daily activities with special focus on how to make worship an inseparable dimension of man's existence and how to elevate man to approach to the rank of a universal, perfect human being (*insan-i kamil*) (Gülen 2004).

For children, the development of spirituality also goes hand in hand with, first, the awareness of and faith in God and then continues with the development of the religious practices that help strengthen this faith and further their spiritual improvement. The development of moral values also aids in the growth of spirituality. Thus, the development of spirituality cannot be separated from the religious, faith, and moral development of children as they grow. Each of these elements is part of the whole picture of a child's development into a Muslim.

General Concepts of Spirituality in Childhood and Adolescence

Age and maturity need to be taken into account when evaluating a child's spiritual level. Many Muslim scholars provide guidelines defining what subjects are adequate for children of various ages. For example, most children younger than seven years old are still in a stage at which they mimic adults, not really understanding the consequences of their actions (Gülen 2003). The age of seven, when they become more aware of themselves, is a good time for children to start going into deeper subjects in spiritual development.

Following the example of Prophet Muhammad, Said Nursi states that children need kindness and compassion. Since children are weak and powerless, their spirits can flourish best in knowing and experiencing a compassionate and powerful Creator. As human beings, they will certainly have far-reaching desires in their small hearts and large goals in their little heads. They will be able to deal with facing fears in later years through trust in God and surrender to God's guidance (Nursi 1997).

According to Islamic teachings, there is no difference between spiritual education for boys and girls. Although there may be gender differences present in Islamic societies today, these mainly originate from cultural issues and do not stem from Islamic teachings. In Islam, women and men are created equal and maintain that equality throughout their lives. Prophet Muhammad encouraged spiritual development of all believers regardless of sex.

GIVING MERCY AND LOVE AND TEACHING GRATITUDE

Mercy and love have a special place in Prophet Muhammad's teachings. To signify the importance of mercy in the spiritual development of children, Prophet Muhammad stated, "He is not of us who does not have mercy on young children, nor honor the elderly" (Tirmizi 1981). Some of the most important concepts in approaching children according to his teachings can be summarized as mercy, love, respect, and trust. There are many teachings related to us from Prophet Muhammad about the importance and the methods of showing this mercy and love to children, such as kissing babies and patting their heads.

His wife Aisha related the following example:

> One day a person from the desert came to Prophet Muhammad and said, "You are kissing children, but we traditionally don't kiss them." The Prophet replied, "What can I do if God removed mercy from your heart?" (Saheeh-i Bukhari, Book 73: Book of Good Manners; Saheeh-i Muslim, Book 30: Book Pertaining to the Excellent Qualities of the Holy Prophet)

Another example was explained by his daughter, Fatima:

> The Prophet came to Fatima's house and sat in the front yard. He asked, "Are there any children here?" Fatima's child (the Prophet's grandchild) came running toward him and hugged him. The Prophet kissed the child. (Saheeh-i Bukhari, Book 31: Book Pertaining to the Merits of the Companions)

Another instance is narrated from Jabir b. Samura:

> I prayed along with Allah's Messenger (may peace be upon him) the first prayer. He then went to his family and I also went along with him when he met some children (on the way). He began to pat the cheeks of each one of them. He also patted my cheek and I experienced a coolness or a fragrance of his hand as if it had been brought out from the scent bag of a perfumer. (Saheeh-I Muslim, Book 4: Book of Virtue)

Although his son stayed with a babysitter during the daytime, Prophet Muhammad visited him often (Ibin Hanbel 1982). During his visits he held his son, hugging and kissing him. He also emphasized the importance of having daughters: "He who is involved (in the responsibility) of (bringing up) daughters, and he accords benevolent treatment toward them, there would be protection for him against Hell-Fire" (Saheeh-i Muslim, Book 32: Book of Virtue).

He also showed mercy and love to youngsters from different religions. He emphasized the rights of neighbors, even those from different religions, treating them as we would treat our close relatives. For instance, he visited one of his Jewish neighbor's sons when he was sick (Saheeh-i Bukhari, Book 23: Funerals).

According to Islamic teachings, children are gifts of the All-Compassionate and Generous God. We should love and protect them with ultimate compassion and tenderness to ensure their healthy growth. Only in an environment where mercy exists can children feel secure. The best way to give them this sentiment completely is to teach them that God is The Most Merciful and The Most Compassionate and that He is the one who is protecting them from all evil and bad things.

A feeling of security is particularly important for the healthy spiritual development of the child. The child needs to feel love, trust, and confidence in God to grow as a spiritually healthy person. In order to become merciful, loving, trustworthy, and respectful adults, children need to experience a similar kind of environment during their upbringing. Teaching children to be thankful for everything they possess and receive is another aspect of healthy spiritual development. Children should be made aware that everything given to them is ultimately from God. With these teachings, the youngsters will grow into appreciative people who will be truly thankful in their hearts for even for the smallest favors.

PLAYING AND GAMES

In Islamic teachings it is emphasized to play with children, especially those younger than age seven. Prophet Muhammad placed a special importance on children's games; he sometimes even played with them. He encouraged parents to play with their children (Saheeh-i Muslim). He advised parents to teach youngsters sports such as swimming, running, and wrestling. His students related several examples of Prophet Muhammad's games and jokes with children (Saheeh-i Bukhari, Book 3: Book of Knowledge):

> The Prophet with some of his students was invited to a dinner. On the way they ran into his grandson Hussein, who was a very young child. He was playing with some other children. When they saw the kids, Prophet Muhammad went forward and opened his arms wide in order to embrace them, and the children started to run around in play. Then Prophet Muhammad ran after Hussein to join him in his game until he caught him. When he caught Hussein, he put one hand under his chin and one hand at the back of his neck and kissed him. (Taberani 1984)

Imam Ghazali also emphasizes the importance of playing in a child's life:

> It is advisable to let a child play and have fun after finishing his homework. This way he will unwind and rest from the exhaustion caused by school. If he is kept away from play and fun and asked to continuously study his heart will die, his brain will stop working, and work will become a heavy burden for him so that he starts looking for dishonest ways out of it. (Ulvan 1994)

PROTECTION

Children's spirituality is shaped by their surroundings. Starting with the immediate family at home, the environment at school, friends, and the extended family all play a role in the development of spirituality in childhood. In the teachings of Prophet Muhammad, it is very clear that every child is born with an ability to get close to God, but after that, based on his or her surroundings, he or she might fall away from God.

After a child's creation, everything has an effect on his or her spirituality. Even the occasional stop at the grocer, dry cleaner, or barbershop has its effect on the soul of a child. Therefore, it is essential that the environment to which the child is exposed should be chosen carefully. An imperfection that penetrates into the child's spirit could surface as a problem later in life. In Islamic teachings, it is primarily the parents' responsibility to protect a child against destructive environments.

Islamic scholars emphasize that every form of imperfection that the child absorbs places a black spot on his or her heart. Not solely indecent images or sounds, but even food that is not acquired through legitimate means (stolen or bought with money earned from unlawful acts) is believed to pollute the delicate spirit of a child (Gülen 2003).

Another source of impurity that children need protection against is people with licentious thoughts, immoral feelings, and sinful eyes. Protecting the child against these spiritual imperfections is considered a religious duty toward God.

Parents are responsible for creating an environment in which the child can learn about God. Prophet Muhammad stated that it is a duty of parents to give the child a fine education (Munavi 1974). If the parents' own spiritual lives are in order, if they are in constant remembrance of God, then the required environment can be established.

In today's busy world, parents should be particularly careful about their children's environment. Since parents often come home drained by their hectic day, they do not get to spend enough high-quality time with their children in terms of development. Children often fill their time with less beneficial pastimes, such as watching television, which may not provide programming that is aimed at properly shaping children's personalities. Aydinli (2004) argues that children who watch television have slower or limited analytic capabilities and become conditioned to be interested only in attractive, fast-moving figures. They often have difficulty even concentrating on their classes or schoolwork, since these things require prolonged attention and cannot hold their interest for very long. As discussed previously, the love and mercy that they will experience from their parents is key to the spiritual development of children. Therefore, in the modern world, parents are faced with more challenges in transferring spiritual values to their children.

PRAYER AND HAVING A PLACE IN THE MOSQUE

According to Islam, spirituality enters life through daily religious practices. Prophet Muhammad stated, "Prayer is the pillar supporting religion" (Munavi 1974). Prophet Muhammad also stated that one can experience the highest level of proximity to God during prostration in prayer (Ibin Hanbel 1982). From these sayings we can understand that the highest level of spirituality can be experienced during prayer.

Prayer is therefore very important for the development of spirituality in children. Young children are not expected to pray, but through observation of prayer conducted by parents and other adults in the community, children become accustomed to the practice and come to consider it a part of daily life. They can experience the spirituality of people praying and see them as examples. Children can observe the deeper aspects of spirituality, which are difficult to explain through simply lecturing, and can learn them by seeing their application. Consequently, the presence of children in places of prayer is greatly encouraged to help in their spiritual development. People praying in places of worship become role models for children.

Unfortunately, in modern times, lack of knowledge among adults in the area of Islamic education for children leads some to consider bringing children to the mosque as inappropriate (Gülen 2003). For adults, performing prayers with full concentration is important, and to achieve this focus, in general, people prefer silent, calm environments. The presence of children in places of worship can affect people's concentration, and they might feel uncomfortable. This is, however, in opposition to the teachings of the Prophet, who not only allowed children in the mosque but even assigned a special space for them to join the prayers (Saheeh-i Muslim, Book 4: Book of Prayers).

It is clear from the Prophet's teachings that he did not condone the removal of children from places of prayer, even if he was leading the congregational prayer. While praying, he often widened his stance so that children could pass through his legs in play. It is also reported that in some cases, children played by climbing on him when he was at the point of prostration. In one case, when he was at the point of prostration, a baby climbed on him, and although he was leading the prayer, he waited in that state until the baby climbed down (Ibin Hanbel 1982).

The Prophet allowed even infants to be present in places of prayer. He shortened the prayers for mothers to be able to assure their babies' needs. The Prophet said, "When I stand for prayer, I intend to prolong it, but on hearing the cries of a child, I cut it short, as I dislike troubling the child's mother" (Saheeh-i Muslim, Book 4: Book of Prayers). In some cases he held babies in his arms to be able to keep them in places of prayer when he was praying. He held them in his arms when he was standing and carefully placed them to his side when he was going to the stage of prostration.

Prophet Muhammad emphasized bringing both boys and girls to the mosque to pray. It is narrated that one day Prophet Muhammad came to the mosque carrying Umamah, his granddaughter, on his shoulder. While she was on his shoulder, Prophet Muhammad prayed at the mosque. When he bowed, he put her down and took her up when he got up. He kept on doing so until he finished his prayer (Saheeh-i Muslim, Book 4: Book of Prayers).

Adult religious studies are an important time period when people need extra concentration. In these cases, even when he was preaching, Prophet Muhammad did not seek to remove children from the congregation (Saheeh-i Bukhari, Book 57: Companions of the Prophet).

The aspect of having children in adults' places of worship is also important for the spiritual improvement of the adults themselves. In Islam, it is important to be able to live spiritually in every part of life. This goal can be achieved by learning how to be with God even in difficult times of our lives. Having children in places of prayer teaches us how to concentrate in our spirituality when disturbing factors exist.

Therefore, it is clear that keeping children away from places of worship during the daily prayers and sermons because of inappropriate behavior is completely against Islamic teachings. In the Islamic methodology of educating children, being an example is key for children to learn to appreciate the value of worship. Children can greatly benefit from the spiritual environment and learn to become active in their religious duties. Adults too can train themselves to concentrate on prayers in the presence of children, thus improving their ability to focus on their relationship with God even in distracting environments.

THE QUR'AN

The Qur'an, according to Islamic teachings, is the literal word of God. The Qur'an was sent to be read, understood, and acted upon, and, with its help, a state that will be full of peace and love would be established on God's earth. The Qur'an makes people reach the summit of spiritual glory. Reciting the Qur'an is one of the most important aspects of spiritual development.

As defined in the preceding sections, spiritual improvement is synonymous with getting closer to God. What better way to get closer to God than listening to His words? With this in mind, it is highly encouraged to expose children to a beautiful recitation of the Qur'an. *Beautiful* is the key word here since not all recitations come from the soul of the reader. There are a number of teachings from the Prophet regarding the way to recite the Qur'an, such as, "The most beautiful among people are those that recite the Qur'an, the ones that recite the Qur'an seriously and solemnly" (Darimi 1992).

It is very important to recite and listen to the Qur'an while feeling God's presence. A recitation that deep surely will have positive impacts on young spirits and will bring their spirituality to life in the same way rain brings life to plants.

SETTING A GOOD EXAMPLE

The most important tool in guiding a child in his or her spiritual journey is being a good example. If parents want their children to pray like them, they have to pray in the presence of the child in the most serious manner and be an ideal example. Similarly, if parents desire that their children's hearts not be polluted with inappropriate words, they should make sure that their children are not exposed to those words. Performing spiritually moving prayers in the presence of children has profound effects on them. Seeing parents in a state of elation during a devout prayer can open a child's soul and might lead him or her to ask questions and learn about the prayer being performed. Explaining the spiritual delights of prayers and rituals in this state would naturally penetrate deeper into the soul of the child. Trying to explain the effect of a spiritually fulfilling ritual that one has never experienced would not have a similar effect on the child.

Prophet Muhammad is the perfect example of how a human being can be elevated through the stations of spirituality. He is referred to as the "living Qur'an," since he perfectly exemplified the guidelines that God prescribed with His own words in the Qur'an. Following his example, Muslims are required to be transparent in their thoughts and actions. In other words, a Muslim should not think one way and act another; he should be the same inside and out (Ay 2002). Being consistent in this regard for children is important. Inconsistency between what one says and what one does can lead to deep wounds in the spiritual life of a child (Ulvan 1994).

Islam emphasizes the importance of a complete person. For example, a person might be spiritually healthy in all other respects, but if he is a miser it might pollute the perfect spirit. Therefore, it is important to teach a child the importance of sharing and having compassion for the needy. The suggested way of teaching this is, again, through example: if parents show mercy toward the needy and share their wealth with them, a child surely will grasp the importance of this behavior (Gülen 2003).

TEACHING FOR THE FUTURE

The teachings of the fourth caliph of Islam, Ali, point to yet another important subject regarding spiritual as well as physical development of the young: "Teach your children the etiquette and values of tomorrow, not the knowledge and culture of today because they are created to live in a time different from yours" (Gülen 2003). That is, we need to make sure not to become stuck in the past but always to look into the future when it comes to what we teach our children. The consequences of not following this teaching today are evident in the status of the Islamic world in that it lags behind the industrial Western world, especially when it comes to the material aspects of education.

COMBINING SPIRITUALITY IN EDUCATION

One of the most important ways in which children's spirituality can be affected is through education. Throughout childhood and especially adolescence, young minds acquire the basic knowledge that they are going to use in their entire lives. Many Islamic scholars emphasize that spiritual development should accompany this basic knowledge. For example, according to Said Nursi, focusing only on issues concerning the progress of civilization and materialism in adolescent education extinguishes children's spirits and destroys their moral values. Nursi further states that if man consisted only of a physical body and had no intellect, the materialistic principles that the modern world teaches to adolescents would give some worldly benefit in the form of some temporary childish amusement (Nursi 1997).

Based on these ideas born in the Turkish Islamic context, the Islamic scholar Fethullah Gülen and people inspired by his teachings have developed and put into practice an educational system that is an example of a way to add spirituality in modern education. This system, called the Golden Generation model, embeds strong spiritual motivations, combining the strengths of both Western and Islamic cultures. This model aims to cultivate students who possess scientific knowledge, spirituality, and deep ethical grounding (Yildirim and Kirmizialtin 2004).

Gülen argues that the main problems of this century, such as pollution, hunger, and the increasing erosion of moral values, are caused by the current materialistic worldview. This worldview stems from a lack of spirituality in adolescent education, which emphasizes the goal of material success and severely limits religion's influence in contemporary social life. Gülen's teachings carry the assumption that many major global problems such as environmental pollution are created by scientists who do not take responsibility for the consequences of their work (Agai 2003). To Gülen, harmony between humans and nature and an understanding among peoples will only be achieved when "the material and spiritual realms are reconciled" in the upbringing of young generations (Gülen 2000). Peace with nature, peace and justice in society, and personal integrity are possible only through integration of spirituality in one's life (Gülen 2000).

Unlike many modern secular educators who see religion as a "useless expenditure of time and at worst an obstacle to progress" (Michel 2003), Gülen's writings have pointed out that science and religion are perfectly compatible and must be combined for science to have meaning. Alternatively, the modern dichotomy between religion and science has resulted in some religious scholars rejecting modernity altogether (Gülen 1996a). The consolidation of different educational currents should result in a holistic system that trains individuals of "thought, action and inspiration" who are able to cope with the changing demands of the modern world (Gülen 1996b).

The Golden Generation model of education, which is practiced in many countries around the world, proposes a system that enables individuals to live spirituality while excelling in the modern world, emphasizing the compatibility of modern science with spirituality. This educational system stresses the education of a generation that is not only well educated in the sciences but also spiritually well nourished with the aim of bringing up people equipped with knowledge and moral values. Placing the responsibility of guidance in all areas upon the shoulders of teachers, schools should combine spiritual education with concrete training in the sciences (Gülen 1996b). Gülen argues that education that is founded on the universal values of honesty, hard work, harmony, and conscientious service, and is consistent in imparting these values to students, would create individuals who would work together to bring about peace and harmony, putting all their energy toward good works for the benefit of humankind (Agai 2003).

Concluding Observations

Spiritual education in childhood and adolescence is crucial in Islamic teachings. Childhood is an impressionable time, during which belief in God can be formed and a spiritual life can be more easily established. If a child is exposed to an environment in which spirituality has a strong presence, it will be easier to understand spirituality later in life and continue with religious practices.

Therefore, it is important that certain elements in a child's life be attended to in order to adequately develop spirituality. Children first must be shown mercy, love, respect, and trust, which are important concepts for all Muslims to understand and put into practice in their lives. Children will come to develop the qualities that they are exposed to in childhood and will learn to treat people in the way that they are treated. Although it is important to nurture the exuberant and joyful sides of children by playing games with them, children must be protected from scenes that can taint their hearts and minds with imperfections.

To nurture spirituality from childhood on into adulthood, Islamic practices must be emphasized throughout childhood. It is important to demonstrate the importance of prayer and be a good example for children to follow. By bringing children to places of worship during daily prayers and sermons, daily spiritual practices will become habitual for them. As the word of God, the Qur'an is the most important source of knowledge for Muslims. By hearing a profound recitation of the Qur'an, children can be affected in a positive way that impacts their spirits and inspires them to read the Qur'an throughout their lives.

A person's spiritual life is established from the earliest stages of childhood through the adolescent years. From the teachings of Prophet Muhammad, we know that every child is born with the capacity to know God and lead a spiritual life, but the correct influences are necessary to lead him or her down the correct path toward truth and not away from God. The current materialistic and individualistic world perspective poses many challenges to bringing up a spiritual person. An education that is equally committed to modern scientific knowledge as well as spiritual advancement is necessary to lead young people into a virtuous and spiritual existence.

Note

1. In any publication dealing with the Prophet Muhammad, his name or title is followed by the phrase "upon him be peace and blessings," to show our respect for him and because it is a religious requirement to do so. However, as this practice might be distracting to non-Muslim readers, these phrases do not appear in this chapter, on the understanding that they are assumed and that no disrespect is intended.

References

Agai, Bekim. 2003. The Gülen movement's Islamic ethic of education. In *Turkish Islam and the secular state: The Gülen movement*, edited by M. Hakan Yavuz and John L. Esposito, 48–98. Syracuse, N.Y.: Syracuse University Press.

Ay, Mehmet Emin. 2002. *Ideal Din Egitimi*. Istanbul: Bilge.

Aydinli, Hasan. 2004. The effect of television in the early years. *Fountain* 46:42–45.

Bukhari, Ebu Abdillah Muhammad Ismail. 1993. *Saheeh-i Bukhari, Mehmed Vehbi*. Translated from the Turkish. Istanbul: Ucdal.

Darimi, Ebu Muhammad Abdullah Abdurrahman. 1992. *Sunen*. Istanbul: Cahri.

Gülen, Fethullah. 1996a. *Criteria or lights of the way (Pearls of Wisdom)*. Vol. 1, 9th ed. Izmir, Turkey: The Light Publications.

———. 1996b. *Towards the lost paradise*. London: Truestar.

———. 2000. The necessity of interfaith dialogue: A Muslim perspective. *Fountain* 3:31: 4–9.

———. 2003. *Religious education of the child*. Somerset, N.J.: The Light Publications.

———. 2004. *Key concepts in the practice of Sufism II*. Somerset, N.J.: The Light Publications.

Husain, S. S., and S. A. Ashraf. 1979. *Crisis in Muslim education*. London: Hodder and Stoughton.

Ibin Hanbel, Ahmed. 1982. *Musned*. Istanbul: Ensar.

Michel, Thomas. 2003. Fethullah Gülen as educator. In *Turkish Islam and the secular state: The Gülen movement*, edited by M. Hakan Yavuz and John L. Esposito, 69–84. Syracuse, N.Y.: Syracuse University Press.

Munavi, Abdurrauf. [1396] 1974. *Feyzul Kadir*. Beirut: n.p.

Muslim, Ebu'l-Huseyin B. Haccac En-Nisaburi, Saheeh-i Muslim, el-camiu's-sahih, Istanbul, 1981.

Nursi, Said. 1997. *Letters*. Istanbul: Sozler.

———. 2002. *Existence and divine unity*. Rutherford, N.J.: The Light Publications.

Tabarani, Sulayman ibn Ahmad. 1984. *Al-Mu'jam al-kabir*. Baghdad: Wizarat al-Awqaf wa-al-Shu'un al-Diniyah.

Tirmizi, Muhammad Isa Sevre Musa. 1981. *Sunen*. Istanbul: Yunus Emre Publications.

Ulvan, Abdullah Nasih. 1994. *Islam'da Aile Egitimi*. Konya, Turkey: Uysal.

Yildirim, Yetkin, and Suphan Kirmizialtin. 2004. The golden generation: Integration of Muslim identity with the world through education. Paper read at annual meeting of the American Muslim Social Scientists, at George Mason University, Washington, D.C.

PART II

SPIRITUAL CHANGE AND RITES OF PASSAGE

Across religious traditions, it is through participation in religious life and ritual celebrations that children first experience and learn to give expression to their spiritual lives. Rituals and ceremonies are the markers along the life cycle that connect the private to the communal, the personal to the transcendent. How do different religious traditions understand the process of spirituality in childhood and adolescence? How can spirituality be nourished, and what changes take place across the first two decades of life? What role do rites of passage play in both marking and helping to shape the spiritual journey? These and related questions are addressed by the authors in this section.

This section is unique in that it contains four Christian perspectives. Adrian Gellel illuminates the history of Catholicism, which for centuries typically saw children as little adults, more concerned about what they would become than who they were. However, in the twentieth century, following the publication in 1910 of new rules that permitted children to participate in communion at age seven, an understanding grew of children as models of sanctity, as individuals called to be holy and capable of relationship with God. Gellel writes of the ways in which children are formed in faith by ritual, story, and liturgy and the importance of guidance from family, community, school, and lay organizations.

Catherine Stonehouse writes of the Protestant understanding of a grace that draws children to God as opposed to forces that pull them toward sin. The spiritual journey is relational, beginning with God's call and the human response. She suggests that children hear that call but lack the language to express it. Early experience in family and community, stories of faith, worship, and opportunities for service give children the language to name their experiences of the holy and provide them with the resources to develop their potential for relationship with God.

The evangelical church also sees spirituality as beginning with a gift of divine grace. However, Kevin E. Lawson highlights the differing views in this community regarding the sinful nature of children. Divergent views lead to a variety of methods of faith formation, ranging from conversionary to spiritual-nurture approaches, and to the need for further research regarding the spiritual experiences of children raised according to these different approaches.

Nicholas Otieno writes from the perspective of African Christian communities, which view children as the sacred custodians of the generational continuity of life, linking the ancestral spiritual world to the human community, both present and future. Otieno highlights the importance of rituals of naming and initiation into the community at puberty as ways to build communal solidarity and connect this world with the world of the spirit. The incursion of Western civilization and especially the catastrophe of the HIV/AIDS pandemic threaten to shatter this generational continuity and uproot traditional spiritual anchors.

Ruqayya Yasmine Khan and Roberta Louis Goodman, each from a different tradition, see children's souls as pure at birth. In Islam, Khan explains, children are seen as on loan from Allah in care of their parents who, along with the community, are responsible for bearing witness to God's presence in their lives. Narrative, worship, and ritual play pivotal roles in helping to make ordinary time and shape sacred space.

Goodman provides a glimpse of the Jewish perspective of spiritual life, which involves connection not only to God but also to community and heritage. Through life cycle rituals from birth through adolescence, children participate in and become the builders of the keystone moments of creation, revelation, and redemption.

The goal of spiritual development in Shambhala Buddhism is enlightenment, the realization of awakened "warrior mind" through the cultivation of fearlessness. Richard C. Brown explains that although Buddhism understands all human beings from birth as already embedded in Buddha nature and therefore basically good, it also recognizes the need of individuals to awaken to their true nature. Practices such as meditation and mindfulness help soften the natural ego development of children. A welcoming ceremony in infancy, an eight-year-old rite of passage, and a sixteen-year-old rite of warriorship introduce children into the community and the tradition's spiritual heritage, helping children move from dependence to independence to interdependence.

While traditions vary regarding the nature of children and some focus more on either individual faith or communal belonging, all these authors view children as spiritual beings able to connect to God. Practices differ, but in each case, family, community, and religious structure play important roles in nurturing the spiritual life. The religious traditions discussed in these chapters accentuate the power of rites of passage, sacred narrative, ritual practices, and service to others as ways of enriching the spiritual journey through childhood to adolescence.

Although these authors are generally positive about the ways in which religious traditions accompany children through the early years of life, most raise concerns about outside cultural influences, emphases on teaching doctrine, and the delivery of factual information about faith traditions that sometimes distract from attention to the spiritual lives of children.

CHAPTER 7

Saintly Children: Roman Catholicism and the Nurture of Children

Adrian Gellel

Many think that the Catholic Church is a monolithic reality led by a centralized, male-dominated, hierarchical organization. In the minds of many, the pope and the Roman Curia are the center of this large faith community. This is only partially true, however, since the institutional church is only part, albeit an important part, of the Catholic reality.

Catholicism is a widespread complex faith community comprising more than 17 percent of the world's population. It is a communion of some 2,800 local churches that recognize the primacy of the Church of Rome, served by more than 4,200 bishops, 404,500 priests, 848,500 religious women, and 428,000 catechists (Weigel 1999). It is thus a communion of different communities that have different cultures, languages, levels of adherence, liturgical rites, spiritual traditions, and, at times, even different emphases on doctrinal truths. It is a diversity that is united by the same creed coming from the apostles, the sacraments, and the apostolic succession of bishops who have the ministerial role of guiding and uniting the family of God (Catechism of the Catholic Church 1992, 815).

This chapter will be mainly concerned with the Roman Catholic Church that is predominantly Western in thought, theology, and ideology. More specifically, while speaking of general concepts and attitudes, the European Mediterranean countries will serve as the context for the illustration of the spiritual formation of Catholic children.

One of the central beliefs of Catholics is that God became human so that all may participate fully in divine life (2 Peter 1:4; Athanasius 1882, 54.3). Because humans are created in the image and likeness of God (Genesis 1:26), they have the ability to transcend the self. It is, however, because of the death and resurrection of Christ, and through the action of the Holy Spirit, that the baptized person is able to enter in communion with the persons of the Blessed Trinity. Thus, from a Catholic point of view, spirituality is the human capacity to move beyond the self in and through the relationship with others and God. The highest ideal for the Christian is to live in the presence of and in union with the Blessed Trinity (Downey 1997). Spirituality is seen as a personal growth to become more authentic in a complete self-transcendence in love (Kinerk 1981).

This openness to divine life is not exclusive to adults. Indeed, Christ indicates children as models for entering the kingdom of God (Matthew 19:14), and in their process of sanctification, adults are called to become as little children (Matthew 18:3). This does not mean that adults must be childish, but it is a call to be closer to the mystery of life and to live in a spirit of warm reception of the kingdom of God (Borriello 2002). Saint Theresa of Lisieux understood perfectly this mystery, and she taught that sanctity can only be achieved if one experiences and lives divine adoption by the Father, through Jesus, under the guidance of the Holy Spirit. Like children, everyone is called to feel little and powerless in order to truly feel the all-embracing Love of God (Teresa di Gesù Bambino 1997). This doctrine about childhood and the need to become like children has become so important in the life of the Roman Catholic Church that the pope declared the young Theresa, who died at the age of twenty-three, Doctor of the Universal Church (John Paul II 1979).

Unfortunately, although there is such a rich theological basis to support the notion of children's spirituality, it is only in comparatively recent times that the church has started to discover the spiritual potential of children. Many hold the prejudiced idea that children are not able to grasp spiritual and religious meanings. This was one of the reasons why, for centuries, the church did not declare nonmartyred children and adolescents as saints.

For centuries, children were perceived as little adults or adults in the making (Ariès 1962). The future, rather than the immediate present, is still considered by many to be the most important aspect of childhood. *Il-Quccija* (pronounced "uuchya"), a still popular Maltese social rite, is a clear illustration of this mentality. It is a custom among Maltese to invite relatives for the first birthday of their child. On this occasion the toddler is presented with an array of objects, such as red and blue pens, a calculator, and a rosary, each object symbolizing a profession. In the midst of the excitement of the relatives, the child is encouraged to choose an object that is thought to predict his or her future career.

Participation through the Sacraments

This preoccupation with the future has limited theological discourse and reflection on the child. Discourse has instead centered on the sacramental initiation of children. One should not be misled into thinking that the concern is more of a religious, rather than a spiritual, nature, since the spiritual is not divorced from the religious. Catholics believe the seven sacraments (baptism, Eucharist, confirmation, reconciliation, matrimony, holy orders, and anointing of the sick) to be vital actions efficacious for sanctification. Each sacrament is a gift that either elevates the human person to a new and higher dignity, making possible the intimate union with God, or develops and strengthens grace, thus bringing the human closer to the radiant love of God.

Baptism is the first among the sacraments necessary for becoming part of the Christian community. The practice of infant baptism is well documented from the second and third centuries C.E. Origen of Alexandria (185–253) claims that this practice came from the apostles. During the first centuries, when Christianity was in its infancy and initiation into the church included many converts from paganism, the church accepted candidates for baptism of any age. Various authors, among them Tertullian, objected to the baptism of infants because they claimed that the sacrament demands understanding and maturity. However, many church fathers and official church teachings defended the practice. By the sixth century, the prevailing custom became that Christians were baptized at birth and most of the candidates were infants (Turner 2000).

From a very early period there were two major lines of thought, both equally valid. In the first instance, there were those who defended the baptism of infants for purification purposes, especially from original sin. There were others who supported this practice on the ground that infants are models of spiritual innocence and that baptism strengthens the soul. In this regard Saint John Chrysostom claimed that baptism added to innocence by bestowing the gifts of sanctification, divine adoption, justice, and inheritance. Most important, he stated that through baptism infants become members of Christ and dwelling places for the Holy Spirit (Turner 2000).

Against those who claimed that baptism of infants only purifies from original sin and does not bestow grace, both Pope Innocent III in 1201 and the Council of Vienna (1311–12) reiterated that baptized infants are not only forgiven but also conferred the virtues and grace necessary for sanctification (Denzinger 1996, 780, 904). Unfortunately, the fear of the infant not deserving heaven in case of early death, rather than prospect of a complete spiritual life, prevailed in the mentality of many parents and religious persons.

In most cases, the spiritual and religious formation of children is tied to the visible sign of the sacraments of initiation (baptism, the Eucharist, and confirmation). By the ninth and tenth centuries, due to practical social reasons, the sacraments of the Eucharist and of confirmation were administered at a later stage in life. Various local church councils and chapters exhorted parents to form their children into Christian life (Braido 1991). In the eleventh century, Wulfstan II, archbishop of York, prescribed that parents should catechize their children and at least teach them the Lord's Prayer and the Creed before their First Communion (Turner 2000). In the East, Saint John Chrysostom was more explicit when stating that parents are duty bound to raise their children in the perfection of Christian life. For him, the virtuous life of parents counts nothing in front of God if they do not educate the child in godliness. Chrysostom was so adamant about his beliefs on childhood and on the duties of parenthood that he claimed that those who neglect the formation of their child are guilty of the gravest evil and injustice (Guroian 2001).

The requirement of the Fourth Lateran Council (1215) on those who are in the "age of discretion" to confess and receive Communion at least once a year was interpreted as an instruction to postpone the First Communion to the age of seven. Later praxis, however, put the decision about when the child should receive the First Communion at the discretion of the priest and the father of the child, normally between the ages of ten and fourteen (Gianetto 1986). The "age of discretion" was negatively understood as the age of capability of deceit and thus the age at which the child is able to commit sin. For almost eight centuries, most children were excluded from receiving the Blessed Sacrament until they reached their teens.

On the other hand, there was no restriction on the age of receiving the sacrament of confirmation. Many theologians, including Thomas Aquinas, were of the opinion that the sacraments should be received early during childhood so as to spiritually strengthen the person against the struggles of life. The double function of bestowing spiritual strength and the affirmation of a mature spiritual life was tied to the sacrament of confirmation. The latter meaning was the main reason behind the justification of conferring the sacrament at a more mature age. In the medieval period, few appreciated the significance of the sacrament of confirmation and, notwithstanding the various exhortations from local church councils, many chose not to celebrate it (Turner 2000).

During most of the second millennium of Christianity, spiritual formation, although mainly the responsibility of the parents, was also a collective responsibility of the parish community. The child was spiritually and religiously nourished by the entire community through catechesis, stories of saints, and the socioreligious customs that pervaded everyday life. The Confraternities of Christian Doctrine that arose in the sixteenth century are a clear example of the catechetical work of communities of priests and laypersons on behalf of children and adolescents. These confraternities were spurred by the prevalent moral neglect and pastoral needs of children and adolescents and by the catechetical fervor brought about by the Catholic Counter-Reformation (Braido 1991).

The devotion toward the Blessed Sacrament was probably behind the introduction of the ceremony of the First Holy Communion, which is still practiced in many Catholic parishes. In 1593, we have the first record of a ritualized ceremony in a country parish in France. Within a relatively short period the practice spread to most Catholic countries through grassroots movements. The ceremony began to be celebrated once a year, with adolescents wearing white garments, symbolizing baptismal imagery (Turner 2000). A catechetical program was developed to prepare children for this event. From this point onward the First Communion serves as a means to instill in children devotion toward the Blessed Sacrament and to form them religiously and spiritually. It also serves to move adults to a true devotion toward the real presence of Christ in the Eucharist.

A major shift in the lives of Catholics and in the spiritual life of children was made possible by the document *Quam Singulari,* approved by Pope Saint Pius X in 1910, which permitted children to receive communion at the age of seven (S. Congregatio de Sacramentis 1910). This decision brought considerable protests from French dioceses, where many feared that the formation program, which at times lasted four years, would be threatened. A typical program covered doctrine, educated to prayer, included retreats, and made genuine efforts to form children in Christian love. Since for the previous two centuries, the ritual of the First Holy Communion had also become an established social rite of passage to adulthood, it was feared that all the structure of Christian initiation would be shaken and children would no longer attend the catechetical program.

In response to the protesting bishops, the pope maintained, "There will be saints amongst children" (Borriello 2002). Indeed, these were prophetic words, for no other century had ever seen the opening of so many causes of canonization of young children and adolescents. By the end of the century, the church had proclaimed Domenico Savio, who died at the age of fifteen, as Saint, and declared Jacinta and Francisco Marto, who died at the ages of nine and ten, respectively, as Blessed. For the first time, the Universal Church could venerate, and pray to God through the intercession of, children. Indeed, after two millennia, the church was at last presented with children as concrete models of sanctity in the ordinary life.

Call to and Participation in Divine Life

Understanding the historical developments of formation and reception of the sacraments of initiation helps us understand the traditions and the present practices of Catholic communities. The Second Vatican Council, the movements and the theology that preceded it, and the life of the church after the Ecumenical Council are the main pivots around which the spiritual lives of whole generations of children and adolescents were formed during these past decades.

The Second Vatican Council affirmed that all disciples of Christ without any distinction are called to be holy and perfect as the Father who is in heaven (Vatican II 1965, 40). In no other century had the Catholic community better understood the unique spiritual call and life of children. Apart from increasing devotional practices toward saintly children, the church has understood how the wisdom of God is revealed to and lived by children. It has also discovered how these young disciples are uniquely called to actively participate in God's plan of salvation. This new understanding has prompted the church to continue to renew its formation practices and to adapt to the pastoral needs of children, especially through the reformation of the liturgy.

AT THE SCHOOL OF SAINTLY CHILDREN

Until a century ago it was unthinkable that children and adolescents could be included in the canon of saints and blessed. There seems to have been a certain perplexity with regard to the capability of younger members of the church to live to the full the perfection of Christian life. The issue was discussed for more than forty years, and it was only in 1981 that the Catholic Church accepted in principle that children of the age of seven and above could be considered for the process of canonization (Borriello 2002).

The church was aware that children and adolescents could give a heroic testimony to Christ through martyrdom. In this sense, it always used the stories of Saints Tarsicius, Pancras, and Agnes, all adolescent martyrs of early Christianity. These saints are presented as heroic models and are intended to instill a deep sense of personal adherence to God through specific virtues. For instance, legend narrates how Tarsicius, who is often purposely depicted as a young boy, was entrusted to sneak into Roman prisons and give the Eucharist to condemned Christians. His heroic determination not to surrender the consecrated Bread to a pagan mob and to die in order to defend the Eucharist is presented to young listeners as a means of instilling in them an understanding of the sacredness of the Blessed Sacrament and a sense of devotion to the Eucharist.

Giving one's life completely to God has always been seen as the highest ideal, even for a child. Various saints were "converted" or consecrated themselves completely to God from a very early age. For instance, Domenico Savio consecrated himself to God at the age of seven, whereas Catherine of Siena saw Jesus in a vision at the age of six. In this regard, Pius XII reiterated the theology of Thomas Aquinas that childhood is not an obstacle to sanctity and encouraged those entrusted with the formation of children to propose high objectives to the children under their care, and in doing so, sustain and accompany them with patience and love. Most of all, he recommended that children should frequently participate and receive Holy Communion and that formators should not put any obstacle to the action of God (Pius XII 1954).

EDUCATED IN THE WISDOM OF GOD

The latter advice can only be understood in the context that Catholics understand sanctity as a gift from God. It is only grace that attracts the person to God. The closer one gets to God, the more God's wisdom and inner peace is manifested. Christ thanked his Father for revealing His wisdom to mere children (Matthew 11:25). In everyday life, many parents and educators are witness to this wisdom that is so naturally expressed in innocence. The church has learned this truth through, amongst others, the lives of Blessed Francisco and Jacinta of Fatima, Saint Bernadette Soubirous of Lourdes, and Antonietta Meo, the six-year-old girl affectionately known as Nennolina. Whereas Bernadette, Francesco, and Jacinta were directly admitted to the wisdom of God through visions and instructions from Our Lady, the life of Nennolina shows how children can intuit and assimilate God's wisdom through an intimate relationship with God and through a virtuous life.

The wisdom and profound spirituality expressed by Nennolina (1930–37) astonish psychologists and theologians, for her faith was comparable to that of a mature person who had taken a long spiritual journey (Vanzan 1999). Nennolina prayed a lot and developed a personal, and intimate relationship with Jesus, God the Father, the Holy Spirit, Mary, and the Guardian Angel. Her individual relationship with the persons of the Blessed Trinity was possible because she perceived that humans have the seed of the divine in their being. It was this personal and individual relationship that led her to understand the individuality and action of each person of the Triune God (Del Genio 2000). It is indeed astounding that deep theological and spiritual themes find echo in a six-year-old child who had never read or studied the great mystics or theologians. Nennolina's profound spirituality, mainly manifested in her awareness of divine indwelling, was possible only because of her openness to the action of the Spirit, which was nurtured by the formation received from the family, parish, Catholic Action, and the Catholic school she attended.

FAMILY AND PARISH

Family and parish are the basis of children's spiritual and religious formation. They sustain and supplement each other in nurturing the child to live a perfect Christian life. The family is considered to be a "domestic church," where parents are the first heralds of faith (Vatican II 1965, 11). The institutional church insists on the obligations the family has in initiating and sustaining the Christian education of the child. In its formation, the family introduces the child to the concept and to a sense of God, equips the child with the language of prayer, and forms the moral conscience as well as the Christian sense of love as a reflection of the Love that exists among God the Father, the Son, and the Holy Spirit (Congregation for the Clergy 1997). This formation accompanies and precedes any other form of education (John Paul II 1979). The parish is equally important in the child's formation. Official documents state that the parish is a privileged place for formation (John Paul II 1979) in that it brings together and introduces its members to human differences and invites them to live in communion (Congregation for the Clergy 1997), which is one of the first fruits of the Spirit.

Besides the theological significance of the family and the parish it is understandable that the child cannot practically become knowledgeable of God and spiritually nurtured unless there is a supporting faith community. Unfortunately, the changing religious situation in many European countries is making it more difficult for the child to acquire the spiritual language that has been developed and passed on from generation to generation. Many European families, who may profess themselves to be Catholic but do not participate in the liturgy or parish life, are indifferent or at least at a loss when it comes to educating their children in the Catholic faith. This poses great limitations on the spiritual formation of children. On the other hand, many parishes feel helpless in the face of the apparent apathy of many families concerning religion. This has led many Catholics to be more concerned with doctrinal truths than with education to prayer and with educating children to build a personal relationship with God. In the mentality of many Westerners, but especially Europeans, the cognitive comes before the affective.

Nonetheless, human limitations are not a restriction for the Spirit. Indeed, the Second Vatican Council has brought with it a rejuvenation in many parts of the church and has promoted the institution of many lay organizations, including the Focolare movement, the Catholic Charismatic Renewal, and the Neocatechumenal Way. These organizations, together with an increasing surge of new and diverse Catholic spiritualities, have sustained the lives of many parishes and practicing families. These lay movements have been a source of tangible community in the increasingly anonymous cities. Through their distinctive spirituality they form whole families in faith, apostolate, prayer, contemplation, or ascetics. Children and adolescents are offered the possibility to participate in the community or to develop their faith through these associations.

CHILDREN AS MINISTERS

These associations, together with the parish and the Catholic school, offer practical means to practice the fundamental commandment of the love of neighbor. One cannot claim to love God and at the same time hate one's neighbor (1 John 4:20). This principle of love of neighbor has been translated into charitable action and in giving oneself to others. In Catholic spirituality, giving oneself to others in complete love is believed to be a privileged way to arrive at a union with God. Catholics fervently believe that if one resides in love, one resides in God (1 John 4:16). Love is not an abstract feeling; it is a concrete attitude that is tangible through actions. Spirituality is understood as the transcendence of self to enter into union with God through and with others. This is why the Catholic Church, as an institution, but also through many lay or religious organizations, is so much involved in diverse humanitarian and charitable activities.

From childhood, Catholics are educated to love God through the love of their neighbor. In its documents, the church recognizes that children and adolescents have a special role in the ministry to their peers (Vatican II 1966, 12). It is very common for religious education and catechetical programs to include service to others. For instance, in the case of the Holy Childhood Association, children are encouraged to pray, do penance, and do concrete acts of solidarity in order to help other children in missionary countries, through education and food programs but also through evangelization. As John Paul II wrote to these children, members of the association, "showing solidarity to those who are less fortunate helps one to recognize the face of Jesus in poor and needy children" (John Paul II 2003).

There are different and more spiritually profound ways in which children are able to act as ministers. The lives of saintly children reveal how even children can endure and offer suffering for the love of God and the love of neighbor. For instance, little Jacinta declared that she was enduring suffering for the conversion of sinners (John Paul II 2000), while Laura Vicuña, who died at the age of twelve, offered her life for the salvation of her mother's soul (Valentini 1998). This attitude toward suffering is typically Catholic, especially emphasized in the Mediterranean mentality. Many pious Catholic movements exalt the cross of Christ and the cross one has to bear in life. If accepted with, in, and through Christ, suffering is believed to be an efficacious way toward salvation for oneself and also for others. Through suffering, one participates in the mystery of Redemption. Since suffering is one of the constant mysteries humans have to face, it is not surprising that through the family and parish formation, and especially through popular religiosity, children are immersed in the theology of giving of self and the offering of one's sufferings for the redemption of others. For example, the capacity of Nennolina to offer the suffering caused by the amputation of her foot for the church, the pope, missionaries, African children, and for sinners may surprise us, but we begin to comprehend this spirituality when we learn that her father often read meditations to her on the passion of Christ and that her spiritual director taught her to offer sufferings to God (Vanzan 1999).

Participation in the Liturgy

All forms of Catholic spirituality emphasize that the process of sanctification necessitates a community with whom one is nourished by the Word of God, through which one practices the commandment of love, and with whom one celebrates God's presence and saving action in one's life through the liturgy. For Catholics, the liturgy is the summit through which individual members of the community are held together and are directed in holiness (Vatican II 1964, 10).

One of the most visible and most radical changes brought about by the Second Vatican Council was surely in the area of the liturgy. The change from Latin to the vernacular language, the effort to encourage the faithful to participate in the liturgy, and a better understanding of the communitarian dimension of the liturgy are only a few of the changes that have transformed the lives of many Catholics. This shift in mentality brought with it a greater concern to make the spiritual fruits of the Eucharistic celebration accessible to children. The church realized that it was spiritually harmful for children to go to Mass without being able to understand and to participate in the Eucharistic mystery, and thus feel excluded from the community of believers (S. Congregatio de Culto Divino 1974). For the first time in two millennia, the official church suggested practical adaptations of the liturgy for children. This was done in recognition of the specific spiritual needs of children . Being able to celebrate, feeling part of a community, and sharing one's life and the Eucharist with others are basic tenets into which children need to be educated. Indeed, becoming aware that salvation is not a personal business but a communitarian effort is intrinsic in any Catholic spirituality. Thus, an adapted liturgy becomes the perfect place to meet Jesus and to stand by him in the presence of the Father. The Eucharistic sacrifice and meal are the source of strength needed to live the perfect Christian life and to be better witnesses of the kingdom of God in everyday life.

The liturgy is not only a tool in the hands of the parish community. Through the liturgical calendar, families, schools, and associations have powerful means to educate the young to sense the presence of God in the history of one's community and in one's own life. Apart from the particular periods of Advent, Christmas, Lent, and Easter, the veneration of Mary and the saints helps to educate in particular virtues, and in the sense of prayer through concrete models of faith. For instance, the months of May and October are traditionally dedicated to Mary with special attention given to the praying of the rosary. Through the twenty mysteries of the rosary (each category of mystery—joy, light, sorrow, and glory—refers to five New Testament-based events), the child is educated in the school of Mary, who is considered to be the true pointer to the Way, the Truth, and the Life (John 14:6). Contemplating with Mary and asking for her maternal intervention open the door to an abundance of Grace. Through the rosary, the child is educated in silence, perseverance, in becoming aware of the incessant presence of God, and on the central place of Christ, among other things. On the other hand, the feasts of saints are special occasions to educate in particular virtues and spiritualities. For instance, the feast of Saint Francis of Assisi, celebrated on October 4, helps us remember our connection with nature and to pray and act for peace, while the feast of Saint Martin of Tours, observed on November 11, directs us toward the virtue of compassion. The meaning of these feasts is made concrete through simple rites, such as the blessing of pets or the donation of fruits.

Growing in a Catholic Community

Spirituality is concretized in everyday life through real communities. Growing in Malta means growing in a country strongly formed and immersed in Catholic traditions, where 98 percent of the population profess to be Catholic and more than 80 percent claim to participate in the liturgy at least once a week. Children and adolescents are spiritually and religiously formed by the family (both nuclear and extended), the parish, the school (both public and private), and Catholic associations. From the first weeks of their life, children are immersed in the Catholic community. The administration of the sacrament of baptism, normally during the first month, parents' use of holy images, scapulars, and relics to protect the child from evil, and the presentation of the infant, normally after the first birthday, to Mary, introduce the newborn to the Catholic world.

The first years of the child are heavily marked by religious practice. Through morning prayer, grace at meals, and night prayer the child is encouraged to develop a relationship with God. Devout families teach their children to say the rosary and to pray the Angelus (a prayer to Mary) with the ringing of the church bells at 8:00 a.m. and at noon. Before going to school many mothers take their children to mass. The first quarter of an hour of school is dedicated to an assembly that includes a religious thought and a prayer. Catholic religious education is obligatory in both primary and secondary schools. Furthermore, students can avail from the service of a priest who is responsible for pastoral care that includes spiritual direction and the administration of the sacrament of confession (reconciliation).

At the age of six, the child starts attending parish catechesis two times a week in preparation for receiving First Holy Communion. Catechesis is obligatory till the child reaches the age of ten, when children receive the sacrament of confirmation. The Society for Christian Doctrine, an organization of celibate laypersons, is very involved in the catechesis and pastoral care of the young. Apart from catechesis, the society also provides social activities and aims at forming the whole child. After receiving confirmation, many adolescents continue to attend Catholic organizations. Research conducted by the author among thirteen- to fourteen-year-olds found that 38.6 percent attended a Catholic group. These adolescents account for 66 percent of all those attending some form of association (Gellel 2005). It is clear that the church, through its various organizations and through scholastic programs, has much influence on the lives of many children and adolescents.

The social and religious calendar also sustains the spiritual development of the child. Advent, Christmas, Lent, Easter, and the feast of the village patron saint are the major periods of the year through which both children and adolescents are introduced to a number of religious and spiritual activities, such as concrete acts of charity, retreats, processions, and special paraliturgical celebrations. Apart from these festive periods, there are other devotions, for example, the first Friday of the month, dedicated to the Sacred Heart of Jesus, the crowning of Mary, Corpus Christi (the feast of the real presence of Christ in the Eucharist celebrated with devout processions in all parishes), and All Souls' Day (a school holiday on which many visit the cemeteries with their families). These festivities aim at instilling devotion toward saints and at building a special relationship with Jesus, presented as their best friend and ideal companion.

While the church, school, and culture continue to sustain religious activities, there are also clearly emerging signs of change and of erosion of meaning. The picture is not altogether rosy. Many participate in the liturgy and perform devotions without reflecting and without internalizing the spirituality of age-old practices, and thus without benefiting from the spiritual grace these should bestow. The reaction to this situation, especially from conservative quarters, is greater insistence on doctrine, rather than more work toward spiritual maturity. Some seem to fail to understand that God works in wonderful ways and is always present in the lives of his children. It is the job of the faith community to help the young become aware that there is an all-loving Father, a Brother, and a Wise Guide who craves to enter into an intimate relationship with them. This should help them start a journey of love that leads to self-perfection. In this sense, spiritual awareness should precede and accompany religious education and catechesis.

The Christian message is concerned with the here and now just as much it is concerned with the ultimate union with God in paradise. Building an intimate relationship with each person of the Blessed Trinity is also an earthly concern that leads the person to be more authentic with self and in perfect communion with others.

References

Ariès, Philippe. 1962. *Centuries of childhood: A social history of family life.* Translated by Robert Baldick. New York: Vintage Books.

Athanasius. 1882. *On the incarnation of the word.* Translated by P. Schaff and H. H. Wace. Vol. 4 of *Nicene and Post-Nicene Fathers.* Peabody, Mass.: Christian Literature Publishing.

Borriello, Luigi. 2002. Anche i bambini possono essere santi. *Rivista di Vita Spirituale* 56:443–68.

Braido, Pietro. 1991. *Lineamenti di storia della catechesi e dei catechismi: Dal «tempo delle riforme» all'età degli imperialismi.* Turin: Elle Di Ci.

Catechism of the Catholic Church. 1992. Vatican City: Libreria Editrice Vaticana.

Congregation for the Clergy. 1997. *General directory for catechesis.* Vatican City: Libreria Editrice Vaticana.

Denzinger, Heinrich. 1996. *Enchridion Symbolorum. Definitionum et declarationum de rebus fidei et morum,* ed. Peter Hünermann. Bologna: EDB.

Downey, Michael. 1997. *Understanding Christian spirituality.* New York: Paulist Press.

Del Genio, Maria Rosaria. 2000. Nennolina: Una "Santa" di sei anni. *Rivista di Vita Spirituale* 54:317–29.

Gianetto, Ubaldo. 1986. Prima Comunione. In *Dizionario di catechetica,* edited by Joseph Geavaert, 514–16. Turin: Elle Di Ci.

Gellel, Adrian. 2005. Adapting religious education to individual requirements. Ph.D. diss., Università Pontificia Salesiana, Rome.

Guroian, Vigen. 2001. The ecclesial family: John Chrysostom on parenthood and children. In *The child in Christian thought,* edited by Marcia J. Bunge, 29–60. Grand Rapids, Mich.: Eerdmans.

John Paul II. 1979. Apostolic exhortation: Catechesi tradendae. *Acta Apostolicae Sedis* 71:1277–1340.

———. 1998. Apostolic letter: Divini amoris scientia. *Acta Apostolicae Sedis* 90:930–44.

———. 2000. Beatification of Francisco and Jacinta Marto Shepherds of Fatima. http://www.vatican.va/holy_father/john_paul_ii/travels/documents/hf_jp-ii_hom_20000513_beatification-fatima-en.html (accessed October 29, 2004).

———. 2003. Message to the young people of the Pontifical Society of the Holy Childhood. http://www.vatican.va/holy_father/john_paul_ii/speeches/2003/june/documents/hf_jp-ii_spe_20030614_holy-childhood-en.html (accessed October 29, 2004).

Kinerk, Edward. 1981. Toward a method for the study of spirituality. *Review for Religious* 40:3–19.

Pius XII. 1954. Allocutiones. *Acta Apostolicae Sedis* 46:44–49.

S. Congregatio de Culto Divino. 1974. Pueros baptizatos. *Acta Apostolicae Sedis* 66:30–46.

S. Congregatio de Sacramentis. 1910. Quam singulari. *Acta Apostolicae Sedis* 2:577–83.

Teresa di Gesù Bamino. 1997. *Storia di un' anima.* Rome: Postualzione Generali dei Carmelitani Scalzi.

Turner, Paul. 2000. *Ages of initiation: The first two Christian millennia.* Collegeville, Minn.: Liturgical Press.

Valentini, Eugenio.1998. Laura Vicuña. In *Enciclopedia dei Santi. Appendice prima,* 1431. Rome: Città Nuova.

Vanzan, Piersandro. 1999. Antonietta Meo, detta Nennolina: Una mistica di sei anni. *La Civiltà Cattolica* 150:466–76.

Vatican II. 1964. Constitution on the Sacred Liturgy *Sacrosanctum concilium. Acta Apostolicae Sedis* 56:97–138.

———. 1965. Dogmatic Constitution on the Church *Lumen gentium. Acta Apostolicae Sedis* 56:5–71.

———. 1966. Decree on the Apostolate of the Laity *Apostolicam actuositatem. Acta Apostolicae Sedis* 58:837–64.

Weigel, George. 1999. Roman Catholicism in the age of John Paul II. In *The desecularization of the world: Resurgent religion and world politics,* edited by Peter L. Berger, 19–35. Grand Rapids, Mich.: Eerdmans.

CHAPTER 8

After a Child's First Dance with God: Accompanying Children on a Protestant Spiritual Journey

Catherine Stonehouse

Since the sixteenth century, the spiritual nurture of children has engaged the attention and energies of Protestant Christians. Church leaders such as Martin Luther (Reed and Prevost 1993, 194) and John Wesley (Stonehouse 2004) endeavored to impress on parents the importance of their role in the nurture of their children. They also sought to establish schools that would communicate the Christian faith. Since the last decades of the eighteenth century, volunteers have invested their time and energy, teaching children the Bible and moral values in Sunday schools around the world. Organizations have been formed to foster the faith of young people, and churches provide youth groups where adolescents and adults explore issues of faith and life together.

What view of spirituality lies behind these efforts on behalf of children and youth? In this chapter we will explore foundational assumptions supporting a Protestant understanding of spirituality and explore how that spirituality forms and is nurtured during the early years of life.

Foundational Assumptions

The Bible holds a special authority for Protestant Christians. Since the beginning of the Protestant Reformation they have turned to its pages to discover knowledge of God, God's ways, and God's intent. In line with this tradition, therefore, we will begin our discussion of a Protestant understanding of spirituality by exploring foundational biblical assumptions.

CREATION DESIGN

In the biblical account of creation, we find our first clue for understanding spirituality. Human beings, we learn, are created in the image of God: "So God created humankind in his image, in the image of God he created them; male and female he created them" (Genesis 1:27). Since God is Spirit, those created in the image of God are spiritual beings. Dallas Willard (2002) describes the spirit within as "the fundamental aspect of every human being." He goes on to note that the spirit takes its character "from the experiences and the choices that we have lived through or made in the past" (13). Children and youth, as well as adults, are spiritual and are being formed through all the experiences of life.

The brief account of human creation in Genesis 1 provides a second clue for understanding spirituality. In verse 26 God says, "Let *us* make humankind in *our* image, according to *our* likeness." Notice that God uses the pronouns *us* and *our* in this verse. God is "us," a community in relationship. The Christian God is a trinity of persons, God the Father, God the Son (Jesus), and God the Holy Spirit, in a relationship of perfect communion and unity. Those created in the image of God, then, are created for relationship, to desire communion and connection with God, and with other humans. By creation design the youngest child is a spiritual being with potential for relationship with God and others.

JESUS' AFFIRMATION

In the New Testament we also find Jesus affirming the spiritual potential of children. Three of the four Gospel writers, Matthew, Mark, and Luke, tell of parents who wanted to bring their children to Jesus. There was something about Jesus that made them think he would take time for the children and bless them, and they were right. Mark reports that when the disciples tried to turn the children away, Jesus was indignant and commanded, "Let the little children come to me; do not stop them; for it is to such as these that the kingdom of God belongs." And he took them up in his arms, laid his hands on them, and blessed them (Mark 10:14, 16). Jesus, God in human form, welcomed children, took time to hold them, and blessed them.

Notice that "the kingdom of God" belongs to children. Being part of the people of God, knowing God, and participating in what God is doing in the world is not just for adults. Children also have a place in God's kingdom.

In several settings we see Jesus presenting children as examples for adults to follow. For three years Jesus had tried to teach his disciples about the ways of God's kingdom, God's rule in their lives, but they were not getting it. Their highest value seemed to be greatness, and they wanted to know who was the greatest. Jesus shocked his disciples with his response. He set a child before them and said, "Truly I tell you, unless you change and become like children, you will never enter the kingdom of heaven. Whoever becomes humble like this child is the greatest in the kingdom of heaven. Whoever welcomes one such child in my name welcomes me" (Matthew 18:3–5).

Children, in their awareness of their need for care and guidance, and with their readiness to love and trust those who love them, show adults the way toward relationship with God. Jesus points to a child, the least in society, who has no status, power, or wealth, as an example of the greatest, the most important in the upside-down value system of God's kingdom. The child in the midst of the disciples helped Jesus turn their attention from the pursuit of greatness in terms of status, power, and wealth, toward

God's understanding of greatness in humility, welcome, and care for children, and all the vulnerable and least in society.

Notice how Jesus identifies with children. To welcome a child in Jesus' name is to welcome Jesus (Matthew 18:5). When we welcome children in Jesus' name, we welcome them on behalf of Jesus, with the love of Jesus, allowing the child to experience the love of Jesus through us. And through these acts, in some mysterious way, the Christian disciple has the joy of offering the gift of welcome to Jesus.

From this statement on welcome in Matthew's Gospel, Jesus moves into a warning to any who would cause "little ones who believe in me" to stumble (Matthew 18:6). Notice two points in this verse. First, Jesus affirms the faith of children, referring to them as ones who believe in him.[1] And second, not only does Jesus offer the blessing of his presence to those who welcome children (verse 5), he warns of punishment for those who cause them to stumble (verses 6–7). Jesus takes seriously the child's faith and the protection of it.

In the teachings of Jesus, we see a high view of children and their spirituality. Their faith is real, not just a weak forerunner of adult spirituality but an example for adults. The spiritual life of children is to be respected, protected, and nurtured.

ELEMENTS OF SPIRITUALITY

With these biblical concepts in mind, we now turn to consider more specifically an understanding of the term *spirituality* that is in harmony with biblical perspectives. As spiritual beings, all humans, irrespective of age, gender, cultural, or religious influences, share some basic elements of what might be called general spirituality. It is the awareness that there is more to life than the material; an awareness of oneself as a human being, responsiveness to beauty, sensitivity to ethical concerns, as well as experiences of engaging mystery, awe, and wonder (Hay and Nye 1998, 9, 59). It is the inner source of thoughts, feelings, intentions, choices, and actions (Willard 2002, 13–14).

David Hay and Rebecca Nye, through their research with children from different religious backgrounds and no formal religious background, affirm the reality of this general spirituality as a universal human awareness (Hay and Nye 1998, 4). They identify the core of this spirituality as relational consciousness. From the children in their study, they heard evidence that the children were aware of " 'I-Others' . . . 'I-Self', 'I-World' and 'I-God'" relationships. They see in this "relational consciousness" the "rudimentary core of children's spirituality, out of which can arise meaningful aesthetic experiences, religious experience, personal and traditional responses to mystery and being, and mystical and moral insight." This understanding of spirituality points to the potential for the young to move outside of, or transcend, the self and sense relatedness with others, including God (114, 172).

Protestant Christian spirituality embraces general spirituality and moves beyond to name the "Great Other." Christians believe that the transcendent one is the God who created human beings for relationship and desires relationship with them. The spiritual life, for Christians, is life lived in relationship with God, the Father, the Son Jesus, and the Holy Spirit. Spirituality is not one piece of the person, or something laminated onto life; it involves the whole person relating to God (Lee 1985, 7).

In response to a question from a sincere Jewish leader, Jesus captured the goal of the spiritual life in a quote from the Old Testament. " 'You shall love the Lord your God with all your heart, and with all your soul, and with all your mind, and with all your strength.' The second is this, 'You shall love your neighbor as yourself.' There is no other commandment greater than these" (Mark 12:30–31). Christian spirituality focuses on a growing love relationship with God that flows into the love and service of others. The model for that life of love for God and others is Jesus Christ, and spiritual growth is often identified as becoming more Christlike.

Children, as we have said, are born spiritual beings with potential for relationship. Jesus respects and values the spirituality of children, commanding his followers not to hinder the children who desire to come to him to pursue relationship with God through Jesus. Children and adolescents, therefore, are on the spiritual journey and are blessed when adults walk with them, encouraging their responses, guiding them around dangers, and enjoying with them the wonder and awe of knowing God on the journey.

Spiritual Journey: Divine-Human Interaction

UNDERSTANDING SIN

The understanding of another aspect of Christian theology is essential for comprehending a Protestant perspective on spirituality—the concept of sin. Although the first human beings were created for perfect communion with God and each other, their relationship with God was soon broken. Genesis 3 tells the story. Tempted by the offer to become like God, the first woman and man exercised their freedom of choice and disobeyed God; they sinned, breaking their union with God and consequently with each other.

From that point on, every child has been born with great potential for relationship with God, and also with the infection of sin that in time pulls him or her toward selfishness and evil. Children are also born into a world of brokenness and sin, often experiencing wounds to their spirit from those who should protect, nurture, or befriend them. Such wounds can contribute to violent responses from children that are destructive to themselves and others. All this is the result of sin.

Some theologians ignore issues of sin when describing the spirituality of children, whereas others see children primarily as little sinners. Both of these extremes lead to parenting and religious instruction that can be damaging to children. The theologian Marcia Bunge (2004) challenges those who care about children to hold a richly complex theology of the child's spirituality:

> [A] solid and biblically informed model of parenting must . . . incorporate a
> complex view of the child that holds together the inherent tensions of being
> a child: fully human and made in the image of God yet still developing and

in need of instruction and guidance; gifts of God and sources of joy yet also capable of selfish and sinful actions; metaphors for immature faith and childish behavior and yet models of faith and sources of revelation. (51)

The good news of the Christian Master Story found in the Bible is that God has prepared a remedy for the reality of sin. Because of God's love, Jesus came to make possible the forgiveness of sins, and God's Holy Spirit offers insight and power for humans to grow spiritually and live in God's ways of health and wholeness—holiness.

GOD'S INITIATIVE

Not only must we hold a belief in the child's great spiritual potential together with a belief in the reality of sin, but there is a third critical element in the equation, grace, the unmerited love of God that seeks to draw us into relationship with God's self. John Wesley, the eighteenth-century father of the Methodist movement, believed that the early awareness of God and sense of right and wrong seen in children were not simply a natural phenomenon, they were evidence of God's seeking love at work within the child. He called this activity of God preventing or prevenient grace. It was the love of God drawing the child toward relationship with God before that child took any initiative to call out to God. This prevenient grace is active from the beginning of life and continues until the child, adolescent, or adult responds to God's love.[2]

Walter Wangerin Jr. describes God's first encounters with children as a dance with God. God first comes to the child in the experiences of sunshine, a familiar place, the earliest universal experiences of life. "And though, at first, the child has no name for this Someone so Significant, this Other, the Dear, or the Terrible Almighty (*El-Shaddai*), yet the holiness and glory, the power and even the righteousness of the Other are very real to him—and the love." Wangerin believes this experience, this beginning of the faith journey, comes to all children. "We all have danced one round with God. But we danced it in the mists," he claims, in the mists before language (Wangerin 1996, 20–22).[3]

God takes the initiative in the spiritual life of children and continues that initiative throughout childhood, adolescence, and adulthood. God also, however, awaits the response of the person. The spiritual journey is one of divine-human interaction.

THE PROCESS OF SPIRITUAL GROWTH

As we begin to examine this interactive spiritual journey, it is important to note that spirituality is not explainable in terms of human development. However, the spiritual interfaces with and is influenced by all facets of human development.

During the first years of life, children construct their initial image or understanding of God. Drawing from important relationships with parents and other significant adults, the words they have heard about God, and rituals they have experienced, children are putting together their understanding of the great "Other" whose presence they have sensed. This image of God is formed before we know we are forming it, and this primal understanding can influence us throughout life, helping us love and respond to God, or making it difficult to do so. If our first concept is of a loving dependable God, a trusting, loving response to God will probably come easily. But if the child attributes to God the unpredictable, angry responses they have experienced from adults who care for them, or if comments about God's displeasure with the child are used in discipline, God becomes one to be feared. Even into adulthood, after a person has learned that "God is love," the now forgotten first image of the angry God often keeps the person from being able to embrace the love of God for himself or herself. The first thing children need to know is that God loves them unconditionally.

As children learn the stories of Scripture and participate in faith traditions in the home and congregation, they grow in their understanding of God. From the stories of the Old Testament they see God as the powerful One who delivers those who trust in God. In the New Testament they meet God as Jesus, with the people, loving and forgiving them. In my research I found that many children, when asked about God, think Jesus and talk about God as Jesus (Stonehouse unpublished). As James Loder (1998) looked at the development of young children through the lens of theology, he saw "a longing that anticipates but does not know the Face of God until it is revealed in the image of God in Jesus Christ. This is a revelation," Loder claims, "that must be grasped and appropriated Spirit-to-spirit" (170). Children come to know and love God in Jesus. Learning the stories of Jesus is important to children, but there is more. In those stories, as the child is ready, a Spirit-to-spirit encounter awakens the human spirit to relationship with God.

Many children seem to easily love Jesus and readily accept the premises of faith given to them. This faith is not a transplant of their parent's or their Sunday school teacher's faith, however. It is the set of beliefs and values the child puts together from his or her interpretation of what has been taught, their life experiences, and their encounters with God.

With the developmental changes of adolescence comes the need to examine the faith of childhood, to dig more deeply into the meaning of life and understanding of God. Questions arise from within the young adolescents, and culture around them may challenge their faith. In a research interview, ten-year-old Joel (not his real name) amazed us with his insights. At one point he talked about things he could not understand. "Like, how can God not have a beginning. I'll never understand that," he said, "but I believe it." The interviewer asked, "Can you believe things without understanding?" "Yep," Joel replied. "The Bible says it, and I just believe it." In an interview with his parents eighteen months later, when Joel was on the threshold of adolescence, his parents commented, "He has started asking, 'But how do I know it's true?'" The beliefs of the child were being challenged from within (Stonehouse unpublished).

Building on the work of James Marcia (1980) on identity formation, we can extrapolate that adolescents may respond to these faith challenges in a variety of ways, each having a different impact on the young person's faith identity. According to Marcia, adolescents may (1) critically examine their faith and own it (identity achieved); (2) critically examine their faith and disown it, or not have an understood faith to examine (identity diffused); (3) fail to critically examine their faith and never own it for themselves, instead choosing to follow the faith set for them by authority figures, usually parents (foreclosure); or (4) begin to critically examine their faith but not be ready to decide to own or disown it (moratorium). In Marcia's identity formation stages noted with the above responses, we see both the importance of critically examining faith during adolescence and the value of having a faith to examine. The child's faith and relationship with God are a significant beginning for the lifelong journey with God, a journey of "becoming" as we grow in our knowledge of God and God's ways, and as the Spirit of God transforms us to be more and more like Jesus.

CRITICAL RESPONSES

Christian spirituality involves not just knowing about God but being in relationship with God. That relationship calls for critical choices and responses along the spiritual journey. As the child or adolescent becomes conscious of God's great love for him or her, that awareness calls for a response of love. Without a loving response the relationship withers and dies.

As children develop morally they discover how self-centered, sinful attitudes and actions break relationships in the family and between friends. Within the Christian faith community they also learn that sin breaks our relationship with God, but that through Jesus' death and resurrection God offers forgiveness of sins to all who come to Jesus. As these understandings dawn upon children or adolescents they are faced with a choice: to go on in their selfish, sinful ways, or to turn to Jesus, acknowledge their sinful selfishness, by grace receive forgiveness and new life, and enter a new relationship with God through Jesus. While the best choice might seem obvious, adolescents in particular often see a false third option—that of earnestly seeking God while attempting to satisfy their own selfish desires. Only when they realize that living in relationship with God calls for giving themselves heart, soul, and mind to God will they find their true self.

For some, this turning to God for forgiveness and new relationship involves a critical event that over time stands out in their memory. They identify a time when they "became a Christian." Others have simply responded to God's love from early childhood, and when they became aware of selfish sinfulness, sought God's forgiveness. They know they belong to God, even though they cannot identify a beginning point in that relationship.

Living life in relationship with God, like any other relationship, involves critical encounters and responses to God and calls for the ongoing process of coming to know the "Other" more and more fully, continuing to receive and give expressions of love, and the willingness to seek forgiveness as needed. Children and adolescents can and do experience such a relationship with God.

Nurturing the Spiritual Life

We have affirmed that God comes in seeking love to every child; we all dance at least one round with God. But what is needed for that relationship to continue and grow?

RECEIVING THE LANGUAGE OF FAITH

Wangerin (1996) claims that so few children continue their initial dance with God "because when they needed language to name and to save the experience, it was not given unto them. . . . No system came to cradle the truth of their experience," and consequently what had been experienced "fell into discredit" (24–25). Without language to name it and the system of religion to support it, the child's awareness of his or her early relationship with God will die of neglect (48).

How does language work in the nurture of the child's spirituality? First, language gives a name to the child's private experience of God. Naming it brings the experience into the external world where others affirm its reality and goodness (Wangerin 1996, 23). In the Christian family children hear the name of God and of Jesus. In rituals of prayer and blessing, with others they enter into conversation with God and experience God's presence. As children worship with adults at home or in the church, they often sense God's presence, they hear the adults they love sing God's praises and speak the name of Jesus. They have a shared language to keep alive their experience of God. And using that language, they can enter into the experience of God with others.

To preserve and grow in their understanding of God, children need the language of sacred stories telling of God's acts in history, stories that picture God in relationship with men and women, boys and girls. As children grow toward adolescence, they profit from a deeper explanation of their faith, often offered in catechetical or confirmation classes. In these settings children are helped to pull together what they have learned about God and further explore the greatness and mystery of God. Children are not well served by a class or adult that packages God in terse, simple explanations. Rather, they need to be guided to affirm and celebrate what they can comprehend of God while they stand in awe of the mystery that beckons them to continue the exploration. They need to begin to realize that getting to know God takes a lifetime.

Giving children the language of faith serves one other crucial purpose. It gives them language with which to confess their faith and make their vows of love and intention to continue in relationship with God. The language given to children is not the final word on God. As they continue to grow and experience God and life, that experience will likely explode their understanding of the language. They will need to discover, sometimes painfully, new language, or at least richer meanings for their growing experience of God and the demands of life (Wangerin 1996, 23–24).

MEETING GOD IN THE STORIES OF SCRIPTURE

In one of my early attempts to learn from children about their thoughts and experiences of God, I asked a young friend, "John, what have you learned about God that you think other children ought to know?" "Oh, I haven't learned hardly anything about God," he replied. Later in our conversation I asked whether he had ever felt God close to him. "Yeah!" he responded with excitement. "Like when I was thinking about Adam and Eve in the garden and how they sinned and God gave them a second chance." Even though John could not answer my cognitive question with a list of God's attributes, he had learned about God. In a Bible story he met God as the God of second chances, a God of mercy and grace. And that discovery had been so meaningful that he connected it with feeling God close to him (Stonehouse 1998, 161).

Through narrative, children like John intuitively and affectively connect with the reality of God that they most need. In story they can get in touch with concepts they would not grasp if presented to them in propositional statements. They may know intuitively what they do not have words to express. Children learn about God most naturally and profoundly when they enter into the stories of the Bible, meet God there, and wonder about God and God's ways. Let me briefly describe one worship approach that leads children to do just that.

Building on the work of Italian Hebrew scholar Sofia Cavalletti (1983), Jerome Berryman (1991) developed a means of leading children into the story of the Bible that he calls Godly Play. Sonja Stewart and Berryman introduced this approach to churches through their book *Young Children and Worship* (Stewart and Berryman 1989).[4] In this approach to worship, children are welcomed into a quiet place "to be with God, to talk with God, to listen to God, and to hear the stories of God" (57). To the amazement of those who have never seen it before, even the most active children willingly enter the peace of this special place.

They sit in a circle on the floor and after a greeting, a brief time of talking with God through prayer and singing, the children are invited into a Bible story. The story is told simply, often using the words of the biblical text to present the essence of the story. With voice, simple wooden or laminated figures, and hand movements, the storyteller dramatizes the event, with eyes focused on the materials. By not making eye contact with the children, the story, not the storyteller, becomes central and the children enter the story to live in it for a time, to meet God there, and to hear what God has to say to them. At the end of the story, children and adult leaders wonder together about its meaning. By inviting the children to wonder about the story, we infer that God can speak to them, that God's Spirit will guide them to grasp meaning in the story, meaning that the adult leader may not realize is important to the child. After this time of wondering, the children select how they wish to respond to the story. They may choose to work with the materials of a story, telling it themselves and living in it again, or they may express their feelings and thoughts through art. Whatever their choice, they have time and a place without distractions to process their response to God's story and presence.

For Christians the Bible contains the Master Story of their faith, the story that makes sense of life. It is important to the spiritual life of children and youth that they know and value the Master Story. How that story is presented to them is critical. The young need to know the flow of the whole story, not just unconnected bits and pieces of it. The spirituality of children and teens will be enriched when the important adults in their lives acknowledge the mystery of God's ways and lead their young companions to the Bible, not simply to learn a fact or prove a point, but through wonder to discover the new understandings that are there for them each time they come. Sofia Cavalletti (1983) believes that adults should introduce the greatest truths to children in parables and story, not expecting them to fully comprehend the truth now, but to experience the unfolding of that truth across a lifetime (76).

EMBRACED IN COMMUNITY

Christian spirituality is not a solitary way. The spiritual journey of the child and adolescent is greatly enhanced when they are embraced by a family and faith community who love God and in response to God's love live a life of love for others.

Learning through Experience

Children learn first through experience. When they are present in family prayers, in the friendship and worship of a faith community, they experience what is happening long before they can understand, or even do on their own the faith practices. They watch what adults do and model those behaviors, which become part of their behavior patterns.

As children mature, they note the consistency of adult words and actions, or the lack of it. In families and faith communities where adults truly believe in, trust, and put into action the truths they teach, many children and adolescents embrace those values and learn to live into them as they watch the lives of their parents, friends, and mentors. In families and faith communities where adults teach one set of values to their children and live by a different set, many of the young become disillusioned, cynical, and turn their back on the faith of their parents and church. Children and teens are blessed when they have a faith community to show them how to be Christians and live as Christians.

Identity Formed in Community

Identity forms best in community. When the young are welcomed into full participation in the faith community, when they are known and loved by many in the community, they have a sense of belonging and identity. They know themselves as Christians and possibly as a certain kind of Christian. When the pressure is on to go against their Christian values, the young person's identity with that community of Christians and awareness that others share their values can strengthen their resolve to live out their values.

Processing Questions

A spiritually healthy faith community gives children and teens a safe and supportive place to ask and process questions about faith and life. Children think deeply and often wrestle with disquieting questions. In the process of making their faith truly their own, teenagers have many questions to answer. Questions are often an indication of readiness for new growth and significant changes in perspectives. Adults who care about youth will not fear those questions but provide youth with a safe place for asking their questions, assistance in finding answers, and support to continue the quest when answers come slowly, or do not come at all.

Sometimes we do not have good responses for the questions our children ask. In those cases honesty is always best. We can acknowledge the mysteries we do not comprehend along with sharing the pieces of an answer that we have found helpful. By this approach we model for those watching us that the life of faith includes the need for continual growth in understanding and knowing God. In addition, we can acknowledge to the young that we are as much on the journey as they are; though farther along, we have not arrived.

Learning to Serve

Christian spirituality, as we saw earlier, is summed up in loving God and loving others. The family and faith community give children and teens a place to experience love and to learn to love and serve others. Learning to serve may begin with children experiencing simple acts of sharing and not always getting their own way. At Sunday school, through experience, they may learn how to include, serve, and enjoy the friendship of a child with a handicap. A group of children and adults can learn the hard work and joy of serving as they do yard work for an older person, or clean up around the church. Older children and teens can begin taking on regular responsibilities in the faith community, working with adults to usher, teach young children, or sing in the choir. And they can work to provide resources for those in need of the basics of life. Christian spirituality requires service to others, and the young are spiritually enriched when service becomes part of who they are during the early years of life.

Structures for Nurture

Since the early part of the twentieth century Protestant churches have been characterized by the structures, or programs, they have provided for teaching the faith to children and youth. Most Protestant churches around the world provide Sunday school for children and youth and may also offer clubs, choirs, and youth groups. For many these programs have supplied spiritual nurture as they brought together adults and children or teens for regular, planned teaching and learning, in settings where significant relationships take shape. But too often the full potential for spiritual enrichment has not been realized as teaching focused on merely learning facts, not on forming the spirit. And unfortunately many churches depend on these programs to nurture the young, failing to see that it is the responsibility and privilege of the whole church to nurture the spiritual life of its children.

The values, attitudes, faith, and actions of a family and a congregation are like the air our children breathe. As they live in the community they take in that air, whether it is health giving or polluted. One Sunday school teacher, reflecting on her childhood experiences with the adults in her African American church, commented, "I gathered my spirit from theirs" (Haight 1998, 5). The spiritual life of children and adolescents is nurtured as they are embraced in a family of faith and a vital faith community.

Concluding Reflections: Encouraging Signs and Concerns

In recent years interest in the study of spirituality during childhood and adolescence has exploded. Protestant scholars and ministry leaders are actively engaged in research and in conversations that bring together perspectives from the human sciences and theology. In many contexts persons from differing faith traditions and representing many countries meet to think deeply about spirituality in the early years of life. The new research and writing of scholars and these conversations promise to enrich our understanding of spirituality and our ability to come alongside children and youth in ways that enhance their spiritual formation.

Many Protestant churches are taking seriously their responsibility to the young and are hiring staff to work with children, teens, and their parents. I celebrate those who invest their lives for the spiritual nurture of children, youth, and their families. Two trends concern me, however: the age segregation of many churches and the role given to programs and technology for nurturing faith. Too often hired age-level specialists are expected to develop a team and minister with children or teens in isolation from the rest of the congregation. But it takes an intergenerational community to form faith in healthy ways.

In technologically advanced, media-saturated societies, influential voices call for rapid-paced, high-tech mediums to communicate God's good news to children and teens. Although there is a place for technology and media in the church's ministry, such tools cannot provide the faith nurturing needed by the young. As persons created in the image of God, the faith of children and adolescents is nurtured in relationship, in the community of family and congregation where we find ways of knowing one another, celebrating our faith, and journeying together with God.

Notes

Appreciation is expressed to James Hampton, Professor of Youth Ministry at Asbury Seminary, for reviewing this chapter and offering helpful insights on spirituality during adolescence.

1. It is important to note that many commentators believe that in Matthew 18:6 Jesus is referring to believers who are young in their faith rather than to children. However, even if Jesus is expanding his discussion to include adults who are young believers, the fact that the child is in the midst of the disciples and has been the object lesson in the preceding verses leads me to believe Jesus still has children in mind.

2. For a fuller discussion of a Wesleyan perspective on sin and grace, see Stonehouse (2004).

3. It is important to note that not all Protestant theologians agree with Wesley and Wangerin. Some believe that the sovereign God reaches out to and saves only certain persons who have been elected by God for salvation. This, however, is not the perspective of the author.

4. For additional resources on Godly Play, check www.godlyplay.com.

References

Berryman, Jerome W. 1991. *Godly play: A way of religious education.* San Francisco: HarperSanFrancisco.

Bunge, Marcia. 2004. Historical perspectives on children in the church: Resources for spiritual formation and a theology of childhood today. In *Children's spirituality: Christian perspectives, research, and applications*, edited by Donald Ratcliff, 42–53. Eugene, Ore.: Cascade Books.

Cavalletti, Sofia. 1983. *The religious potential of the child: The description of an experience with children from ages three to six*. New York: Paulist Press.

Haight, Wendy L. 1998. "Gathering the spirit" at First Baptist Church: Spirituality as a protective factor in the lives of African American children. *Social Work* 43 (3):213–21.

Hay, David, and Rebecca Nye. 1998. *The spirit of the child*. London: Fount.

Lee, James Michael. 1985. *The spirituality of the religious educator*. Birmingham, Ala.: Religious Education Press.

Loder, James E. 1998. *The logic of the spirit: Human development in theological perspective*. San Francisco: Jossey-Bass.

Marcia, James E. 1980. Identity in adolescence. In *Handbook of adolescent psychology*, edited by Joseph Adelson, 1959–87. New York: Wiley.

Reed, James E., and Ronnie Prevost. 1993. *A history of Christian education*. Nashville, Tenn.: Broadman & Holman.

Stewart, Sonja M., and Jerome W. Berryman. 1989. *Young children and worship*. Louisville, Ky.: Westminster/John Knox Press.

Stonehouse, Catherine. 1998. *Joining children on the spiritual journey: Nurturing the life of faith*. Grand Rapids, Mich.: Baker Book House.

———. 2004. Children in Wesleyan thought. In *Children's spirituality: Christian perspectives, research, and applications*, edited by Donald Ratcliff, 133–48. Eugene, Ore.: Cascade Books.

Wangerin, Walter, Jr. 1996. *The orphean passages: The drama of faith*. New York: HarperCollins, 1986. Reprint, Grand Rapids, Mich.: Zondervan (page references are to reprint edition).

Willard, Dallas. 2002. *Renovation of the heart: Putting on the character of Christ*. Colorado Springs, Colo.: NavPress.

CHAPTER 9

In Right Relationship with God: Childhood Conversion in Evangelical Christian Traditions

Kevin E. Lawson

A Church Baptism Experience

My daughter and I arrived at the Corona del Mar beach on a sunny Sunday afternoon in May and headed over to a grassy area where several families had begun to gather. Within a few minutes our pastor called for our attention and introduced the twenty people who had come to be baptized as a sign of their faith in Jesus Christ as Lord and Savior. The group stood in front of us and our pastor asked each one either to share their personal testimony of coming to faith in Jesus Christ or to answer a few questions that affirmed their faith in him.[1] For several minutes we heard stories from the baptismal candidates of their faith journeys and their affirmations of Jesus Christ as Lord and Savior of their lives. The group ranged from eight years of age through middle-aged adults, with several children and teenagers participating. When their testimonies were finished, we headed up over the rocks and down to a cove for the baptism service. There, surrounded by crowds of people enjoying their day at the beach, two pastors waded out into the water and then invited those to be baptized to come out one at a time. When a child went into the water, a parent went as well to assist with the baptism. With the waves washing around them, the baptismal candidates were immersed in the ocean and raised up to the applause of the congregation. When the last one had been baptized, two members of the congregation brought out guitars and led the gathered crowd in songs of praise to God. Our baptism service was ended, and we rejoiced at God's gracious work in the lives of these new believers.

Although not all evangelical churches practice believers' baptism, this experience, repeated in congregations around the world, is one example of the results of an evangelical view that children and youth are capable of coming to faith in Jesus Christ. But what does this mean in the life of a child or youth? How do children and youth get to this point of faith in Christ, and how does this relate to the concept of Christian "conversion"? Are their spiritual need and salvation experience the same as those of adults? How does the evangelical church understand the spiritual state of children and youth, and how should this understanding influence what it expects of them and how it ministers with them?

The Evangelical Christian Faith Tradition

The evangelical movement within the Christian church is not confined to any one denomination or ecclesial group. It crosses denominational boundaries and has within itself various subgroups, making it difficult to identify one particular understanding of the spiritual life of children and how they relate to God and the church. Nor does the evangelical movement have a single theological tradition at its root but rather is characterized by an adherence to a few theological distinctives that influence personal and ministry priorities. In a previous publication I have described these distinctives as the following:

1. An acceptance of the Christian Scriptures as God's divinely inspired revelation to humankind, with a majority seeing them as inerrant in all they affirm. Scripture then is viewed as God's authoritative Word for faith and life and is central to the Christian education process, including the church's ministry with children.
2. From the Scripture, an affirmation of classic Christian doctrines that focus on Jesus Christ as God incarnate, on His redemptive work for humankind through His death and resurrection, and on the necessity of receiving salvation by God's grace through faith in Jesus Christ alone. Evangelism, the call to personal faith in the atoning work of Jesus Christ, is one critical characteristic of evangelical preaching and teaching, including teaching directed to children.
3. An emphasis on personal and corporate spiritual growth, transformation into the image of Jesus Christ in character, attitudes, and actions as the indwelling Holy Spirit works within people's lives. (Lawson 2004, 438)

Evangelical church ministry then is characterized by a strong emphasis on the study and application of Scripture to life, the active presentation of the gospel of Jesus Christ's atoning death on the cross and encouragement of a personal response of faith to that good news, and a priority on nurturing and pursuing continuing growth both in faith and faithfulness in character and life as God works within us.

Evangelical Christian Spirituality

In light of these theological foundations, there is within the evangelical Christian tradition a tension when considering the concept of spirituality as an intrinsic human capacity for self-transcendence in which the individual participates in the sacred. On the one hand, like all Christian faith traditions, evangelicals understand that people are made in the image of God and made for relationship with God. There is a created capacity for knowing and relating to God, for a rich and vital spiritual life. However, due to the pervasive impact of sin in human nature and its alienating influence, human spirituality is viewed as distorted and incapable of allowing people to participate in the sacred without God's help. God must take the initiative to address the sin problem and its alienating impact on our lives. From an evangelical perspective, genuine spirituality begins with God's gracious work to draw us to faith in Jesus Christ so that we might be regenerated and justified, renewed in our inner person by the saving work of God in Jesus Christ that is received through faith, resulting in our being in right relationship with God. This new relationship with God enables true spiritual growth as God's Holy Spirit indwells and transforms us over time, remaking us into the image of God. The apostle Paul, in 2 Corinthians 1:17, 18, describes it this way: "Now the Lord is the Spirit, and where the Spirit of the Lord is, there is freedom. And we, who with unveiled faces all reflect the Lord's glory, are being transformed into his likeness with ever-increasing glory, which comes from the Lord, who is the Spirit."[2] This new spirituality is manifested in a reconciled relationship with God and new relationships with others around us characterized by love and forgiveness.

On the other hand, if this regeneration does not occur, the individual is seen as "spiritually dead," incapable of genuine participation in the sacred. Any attempts at fostering spirituality apart from this basic foundation of the regenerating work of God are viewed as ultimately fruitless because they do not address the separation from God resulting from the sinfulness of human nature. Again, the apostle Paul describes our condition this way in Ephesians 2:1–4: "As for you, you were dead in your transgressions and sins, in which you used to live when you followed the ways of this world . . . But because of his great love for us, God, who is rich in mercy, made us alive with Christ even when we were dead in transgressions—it is by grace that you have been saved."

Evangelical spirituality views the "conversion" of people, God's regenerating and saving work in us, as paramount for any meaningful spiritual life. God works before this experience occurs to draw people to faith in Jesus Christ so that they might be given new life and relationship with God through the Holy Spirit. God also works following conversion to bring about the transformation of the individual into the image of God. Evangelicals emphasize the importance of the proclamation of the gospel, or "good news" of God's saving work in Jesus Christ. But what exactly is that gospel? What does this have to do with conversion? And are children and youth capable of experiencing it? Should they experience it?

The Christian Gospel

> For God so loved the world that he gave his one and only Son, that whoever believes in him shall not perish but have eternal life. (John 3:16)

The preceding verse from the New Testament is a key passage for evangelicals and is seen as the heart of the "good news" of Jesus Christ. In 1999, *Christianity Today* published an article titled "The Gospel of Jesus Christ: An Evangelical Celebration." This article presented a statement on the gospel developed by the Committee on Evangelical Unity in the Gospel and endorsed by evangelical leaders from a wide variety of Protestant denominations (e.g., Methodist, Presbyterian, Pentecostal, Baptist, Lutheran, Anglican, free churches). It represents an evangelical consensus on the nature of the gospel that is at the heart of the ministry of the church. It is important to understand this "gospel" and how it shapes an evangelical view of the necessity of personal faith in Jesus Christ as part of a "conversion" experience and how this influences our understanding of human spirituality and our ministry with children.

According to the committee's statement, the gospel of Jesus Christ includes the following:

> Through the Gospel we learn that we human beings, who were made for fellowship with God, are by nature—that is "in Adam" (1 Corinthians 15:22)—dead in sin, unresponsive to and separated from our Maker. We are constantly twisting his truth, breaking his law, belittling his goals and standards, and offending his holiness by our unholiness, so that we truly are "without hope and without God in the world" (Romans 1:18–32, 3:9–20; Ephesians 2:1–3, 12). Yet God in grace took the initiative to reconcile us to himself through the sinless life and vicarious death of his beloved Son (Ephesians 2:4–10; Romans 3:21–24) . . .
>
> The heart of the Gospel is that our holy, loving Creator, confronted with human hostility and rebellion, has chosen in his own freedom and faithfulness to become our holy, loving Redeemer and Restorer. The Father has sent the Son to be the Savior of the world (1 John 4:14): it is through his one and only Son that God's one and only plan of salvation is implemented . . .
>
> God's justification of those who trust him, according to the Gospel, is a decisive transition, here and now, from a state of condemnation and wrath because of their sins to one of acceptance and favor by virtue of Jesus' flawless obedience culminating in his voluntary sin-bearing death . . . Sinners receive through faith in Christ alone "the gift of righteousness" . . . and thus become "the righteousness of God" in him who was "made sin" for them (2 Corinthians 5:21) . . .
>
> The Gospel assures us that all who have entrusted their lives to Jesus Christ are born-again children of God (John 1:12), indwelt, empowered, and assured of their status and hope by the Holy Spirit . . . The moment we truly believe in Christ, the Father declares us righteous in him and begins conforming us to his likeness. Genuine faith acknowledges and depends upon Jesus as Lord and shows itself in growing obedience to the divine commands . . .
>
> By his sanctifying grace, Christ works within us through faith, renewing our fallen nature and leading us to real maturity, that measure of development, which is meant by "the fullness of Christ" (Ephesians 4:13) . . .
>
> We learn from the Gospel that, as all have sinned, so all who do not receive Christ will be judged according to their just deserts as measured by God's holy law, and face eternal retributive punishment . . .
>
> We affirm that saving faith includes mental assent to the content of the Gospel, acknowledgement of our own sin and need, and personal trust and reliance upon Christ and his work. (The Committee on Evangelical Unity in the Gospel 1999, 52, 53)

Christian Conversion

> In reply Jesus declared, "I tell you the truth, no one can see the kingdom of God unless he is born again." (John 3:3)

The gospel points to the need for a response of faith to God's gracious work of redemption available through Jesus Christ. Traditional Christian language would say that there is a need for one to be "converted" from one's old sinful life to a life marked by repentance and trust in the atoning work of Jesus Christ on the cross on one's behalf and acceptance of him as Savior and Lord. This is viewed as a gracious work of the Holy Spirit in the heart and life of the person. Gordon Smith's *Beginning Well: Christian Conversion and Authentic Transformation* (2001) describes conversion from a biblical perspective as involving seven different elements:

1. *Belief:* the intellectual component of believing the gospel.
2. *Repentance:* the penitential component, remorse and rejection of the way of sin.
3. *Trust and assurance of forgiveness:* the emotional or affective component.
4. *Commitment, allegiance and devotion:* the volitional component of loyalty to God, resolve to obey Christ in life practice and serve God.
5. *Water baptism:* liturgical/ceremonial component: an external act that complements and confirms what has happened internally.
6. *Reception of the gift of the Holy Spirit:* charismatic component of consciousness of the presence of the Holy Spirit in one's life.
7. *Incorporation into the Christian community:* corporate component of joining with others for growth toward spiritual maturity. (2001, 138–41)

Although not all evangelicals would agree that the full list of seven elements is critical for genuine conversion, there would generally be a consensus that conversion does include the elements of belief in the gospel of Jesus Christ, recognition and repentance of one's sinfulness, and willful trust in Jesus Christ as Lord and Savior of one's life. With this would come the indwelling of the Holy Spirit, admission to the universal church, and a new commitment to obedience to God, not to earn favor with God, but as a demonstration of love and desire to please God.

If that is what is involved in conversion, then to what degree do children need this experience? If they do, then what does conversion look like in the life of a child? Is it even possible?

The Spiritual Status of Children

Evangelical Christians are not united in their understanding of the spiritual state of children and how the church should minister with them. Scripture does not provide a clear statement about the spiritual state and experience of children as compared with adults, so theologians must draw conclusions based on biblical examples and theological affirmations in related areas. The result is that evangelical Christians from different theological traditions have developed four basic views regarding the spiritual state of children, what they are capable of and need, and how God's work of conversion is understood to happen. Gideon Yoder (1959) and Scottie May (1993) provide helpful summaries of these four traditions and how they understand the spiritual life of children.

CHILDREN VIEWED AS SPIRITUALLY LOST

Rooted in the theological work of Augustine (fourth-century church leader and theologian) concerning human nature, this view sees children as similar to adults in their basic human condition—that is, sinful by nature and separated from God, spiritually dead. God's grace must come to them in some fashion if they are to be made spiritually alive and in right relationship with God. This view of the spiritual state of children has resulted in two basic approaches to the church's ministry with them—infant baptism for regeneration, and child evangelism at an early age.

Infant Baptism for Regeneration

Infant baptism in the church is seen as beginning spiritual life for the child, but the parents must nurture that life so that the child will be able to understand its meaning and benefits (Little 1982, 13, as cited in May 1993). This view is affirmed in one form or another by Roman Catholic and Lutheran theologians and traces its roots to early church theology and the resulting practice of baptism of infants as a sacrament that enables God's grace to regenerate the child and bring the child into right standing with God (Issler 2004). The impact of inherited guilt for sin is addressed, and the child is now able to grow in relationship with God as the church and family instruct and nurture the faith that God has begun.

Child Evangelism at an Early Age

Some evangelical groups have understood that the impact of sin alienates children as well as adults from God. The only way to address this separation is to explain the gospel to children and encourage them to respond in faith to God's grace, at as early an age as possible. Donald Joy (1990) reports that with some groups, evangelistic efforts could begin with children as young as three years of age. Leaders in these groups view Scripture as revealing only one way for salvation to be received: through faith in Jesus Christ as a conscious conversion experience (May 1993). Some view evangelistic efforts with children as a great window of opportunity, reaching them while their spirits/hearts have not yet become hardened due to the habits of sin. Child Evangelism Fellowship, begun in 1935 by J. Irvin Overholtzer, is one example of this understanding of the need for evangelism and conversion of children at a young age (Yoder 1959). Conversion for children is shown in a conscious belief that Jesus Christ died for their sins, personal recognition and repentance for sin, and a trusting in Jesus Christ for salvation that should be a memorable experience.

CHILDREN OF BELIEVERS SAFE WITHIN THE COVENANT COMMUNITY

Another understanding of how the problem of the impact of sin in the life of a child is to be addressed is shown in the practices of churches within the Reformed tradition.

Although seen as sinful by nature, children of Christians are viewed as members of the covenant community of God's people and recipients of God's grace (Sisemore 2000). In many of these groups, the solidarity of the family in its covenant relationship with God is stressed. "In Scripture children are always counted with their parents and reckoned in solidarity with them" (Marcel 1953, 205). From this view, baptism in the New Testament is what circumcision was in the Old Testament, a sign and seal of membership in the people of God (Yoder 1959). The child grows up within the church as a member of the covenant community and is taught and nurtured in the faith and encouraged to make a personal profession of that faith at a later "age of discretion." Conversion is seen as gradual growth in the faith rather than a sudden experience. It is not clear in this tradition what the spiritual state of children is for those whose parents are not Christians, and there has been some debate concerning this in the past century. The conclusions reached by various theologians has a lot to do with their views of God's sovereign election of those chosen for membership in the Kingdom of God.

CHILDREN ARE INNOCENT UNTIL AGE OF DISCRETION

Some Anabaptist groups within the evangelical tradition have understood children to be innocent of any guilt for their inherited human sinful nature. In this view, human depravity does not become sin or make someone guilty until a person accepts one's own sin nature by personal choice. All children are provided for in the atonement before they reach an "age of accountability" when they are responsible for their own sin (Yoder 1959). Children, then, are not in need of conversion or salvation until they grow to the point where they decide to identify or refuse to identify with God and the church through faith in Jesus Christ (Yoder 1959, 58). John Inchley has been a proponent of a form of this view in his book *Kids and the Kingdom* (1976), as has Clifford Ingle in *Children and Conversion* (1970).

CHILDREN ARE SINFUL BUT UNDER GOD'S GRACE UNTIL AGE OF DISCRETION

Related to the previous view, many within the evangelical tradition do believe that all people, regardless of age, are sinful by nature and guilty before God, but some, due to developmental limitations, are not held accountable for this until they reach an "age of discretion" or "age of accountability" (Issler 2004). In this view, all people are in need of salvation, and salvation is only through the work of Jesus Christ. "Even though infants cannot exercise faith in him, he can remove their depravity" (Zuck 1996, 223). Young children are not in need of conversion and salvation, but as they grow and reach a point of committing conscious and deliberate sin, and develop an ability to comprehend the basic elements of the gospel, they then become accountable before God and in need of salvation. Groups in this tradition tend to focus their evangelistic efforts on older children and adolescents instead of young children. Due to the individualistic nature of this "age of accountability," the gospel message tends to be broadly communicated to children and youth, with invitations given to respond in faith and counsel provided by adult believers as the Holy Spirit prompts the child or youth to respond. This view has been broadly accepted in many Baptist groups as well as some free church traditions.

VIEWS OF CHILDREN LEAD TO BASIC MINISTRY APPROACHES

In light of evangelicals' differing views of the spiritual status of children and how they come into right relationship with God, three major approaches have been developed in the church's ministry with children. The first is a *spiritual nurture approach* that views the child already in relationship with God through God's gracious work in infancy. The role of parents and church leaders is to nurture that "seedling" faith through instruction, modeling, and encouragement into its fuller potential. The second is a *conversionist approach* that sees the child as separated from God owing to sin and begins by seeking a conscious conversion experience and then nurturing the new believer in the faith. The third is a *combined approach,* which focuses on a coming "age of discretion" or "age of accountability," begins with instruction and nurture in the Christian faith, encouraging children to love and seek to follow God, and then, as the children grow older, encourages them to exercise their own faith commitment as they recognize the need for forgiveness and the claims of Jesus Christ on their lives.

Nurture and Conversion of Children and Youth

Can children and youth exercise faith in Jesus Christ, believing in ways that show a regeneration of the spirit and being in right relationship with God? The answer, based on evidence from both the Scriptures and the experience of the church, would be yes. In the preceding chapter, Catherine Stonehouse presents an excellent overview of Scripture references that indicate how Jesus welcomed and blessed children and said that children can have a place in God's kingdom. In Matthew 18 Jesus warns against causing children who believe in him to sin, and pronounces woe on those who would look down on children. It is clear from the Scripture that children, at least at some age, are capable of belief and faith in Jesus Christ.

AGE OF CONVERSION

This question has been one of interest to researchers in the field of religion for a long time. In fact, the prevailing view has been that the first two decades of life are the *primary* time period for people to be converted or come to faith in Jesus Christ. At the dawning of the twentieth century, Starbuck, in his *Psychology of Religion*, wrote that "one may say that if conversion has not occurred before 20, the chances are small that it will ever be experienced . . . Conversion does not occur with the same frequency at all periods in life. It belongs almost exclusively to the years between ten and twenty-five. The number of instances outside that age range appear few and scattered" (1901,

28, cited in Lamport 1990). Starbuck's own research showed coming to faith in Christ beginning at seven or eight years of age, increasing gradually to age ten or eleven, accelerating to age sixteen, and declining quickly to age twenty and gradually after that.

Other researchers over this past century have found similar patterns, with the average age of conversion among Christians occurring being between twelve and sixteen (Clark 1929; Johnson 1959; Lamport 1990). Lamport's more recent study of adult Christians showed that 60 percent of them reported experiencing conversion before the age of twenty (1990, 22). For another view of the issue, George Barna's (2003, 33) national research project with thirteen-year-olds in the United States indicates that by this age, an estimated 34 percent of these children have a "born again" faith commitment that fits with the gospel as described above. Children, at least older children, are evidencing a capacity to understand and respond to the Christian gospel in ways that fit with an evangelical understanding of spirituality rooted in relationship with God through faith in Jesus Christ.

WHAT KIND OF CONVERSION?

While it is clear from these and other self-report studies that many Christians say they came to faith in Jesus Christ in the first two decades of life, what kind of spiritual experiences did they have? Are these conversion experiences as described earlier in this chapter? If so, how is this conversion experienced? Scottie May (1993) describes three dominant types of conversion experiences in the lives of Christian children and youth as identified by theologians and social science researchers.

Sudden Conversion

A sudden conversion takes place in a short period of time as a conscious event, often accompanied by a strong emotional response. This has been the dominant model for adult conversion in the evangelical Christian church and is seen in the biblical story of the conversion of Saul of Tarsus in the Acts of the Apostles. Evangelicals who take a conversionist approach in ministry with children are more often than not expecting this kind of experience in the life of the child. Coming to faith in Christ should be specific and memorable. Other evangelicals who emphasize childhood as a time of innocence before God, or a time when the child is not yet held accountable before God for his or her sin nature, may still expect this kind of conversion experience in adolescence when the child reaches an "age of discretion." A time comes when the child or youth must respond in faith and repentance to the love of God revealed in Jesus Christ for conversion to occur. Because for many this "age" seems to occur in early to mid-adolescence, it is normally expected to be a conscious event that the child or youth can later recall. Many evangelical Christians describe this kind of conversion experience in their childhood or adolescence.

Gradual Conversion

A gradual conversion is often described as a series of encounters with God, a movement over a period of time toward awareness of God and acceptance of the claims of the gospel. Mulder claims that though this experience of gradual conversion is harder to describe than sudden conversion, it "is perhaps the most common in the history of Christianity" (1990, 162, as cited in May 1993). Evangelical groups who emphasize the covenant nature of the church and the child's belonging within that covenant people, or who view children as innocent, or not yet accountable before God for their sin, may view this as a legitimate conversion experience in the life of the growing child. Conversion then may come in a series of episodes culminating in a genuine personal faith commitment as the child grows. It may be hard for the child to identify when the faith they have experienced and been taught became their own because it came together over time. Many evangelicals who grew up within Christian families describe this kind of faith experience in their childhood and adolescence. They know that they have responded to God many times in the past regarding their sin and Jesus' saving work, and they know they currently have faith in Christ, but they cannot identify a specific time when their conversion occurred. Some churches that emphasize this approach will have classes in early adolescence for students to review the basics of the Christian faith and confirm their faith in Jesus Christ.

Unconscious Conversion

Unconscious conversion describes individuals who cannot remember a time when they did not have faith in Jesus Christ. As Bushnell described it in his major work, *Christian Nurture* ([1861] 1979), the child grows up never knowing a time when he or she was not a Christian. May comments: "In a way, the description of an unconscious conversion is not unlike the manner in which most children grow up in their families of origin. They have no doubt of who they are, but they have no recall of how they became part of that family or exactly when it happened" (1993, 33). The focus here is on the present reality of the experience of the child, not how it came about. From the perspective of the child, he or she has faith in Jesus Christ and does not recall ever being without it. Evangelical groups that practice infant baptism would view this type of conversion experience as a desirable one for their children. Owing either to the regenerating work of God, or to the covenant relationship of the family with God, the child would be in a special relationship with God from the beginning. Like the "gradual conversion" groups, these kinds of groups generally have a time of instruction in early adolescence in which the youth of the church "confirm" their faith as their own.

Concerns and Cautions Regarding Conversion Approaches

As we have seen, how an evangelical church understands the spiritual status of children has a great impact on how it approaches the task of encouraging spiritual growth. Some view it as a work of God already begun in the life of the children of Christian parents. Others view all children as either innocent or not yet accountable for their sin nature, while still others see a need for conscious, sudden conversion at as young an age as possible. All groups in the evangelical tradition recognize the need for God to regenerate the child at some point as he or she grows and becomes more responsible for his or her own relationship with God. These different understandings and approaches have at times fostered abuses and confusion in the church's ministry with children.

CONCERNS WITH SUDDEN CONVERSION APPROACHES

When the "sudden conversion" of children is viewed as the critical ministry of the church, there can tend to be aggressive efforts to achieve this, often putting pressure on children to respond to emotional invitations to "receive Jesus into their heart," without a clear understanding of the true nature of the gospel (Downs 1994). This can also lead to watering down the gospel message in order to get results. In addition, the high value evangelicals place on people coming to faith in Christ sometimes leads to weak efforts in spiritual nurture and instruction leading up to and following a salvation decision. It is as if these churches focus on obstetrics, bringing new spiritual life into the world, without also emphasizing pediatrics, the health and growth of the young. Finally, these groups may push for decisions before children are actually able to discern and respond to God's work within them, getting children to respond to adult leaders because they want to please them, not because of God's promptings in their own spirit. It is no wonder that some children growing up in evangelical churches are confused about their relationship with God, responding to salvation invitations multiple times (Soderholm 1962).

CONCERNS WITH GRADUAL AND UNCONSCIOUS CONVERSION APPROACHES

Evangelicals who view the conversion of children as a work of God generally occurring in either unconscious or gradual ways may assume too much as children participate in the life of the church and in their own families. As John Westerhoff (1980) describes faith development, children and adolescents have an "affiliative" faith experience as they participate in their faith communities. However, if that faith is to take root and grow into one that is personally owned, the child or adolescent must have a "searching" faith opportunity, testing it to see if it can be personally affirmed. If this examination is not encouraged and facilitated in the church, youth may go through the motions of affirming Christian teaching and joining the church as a way of appeasing their parents and church leaders, an act that is not representative of a genuine spiritual reality in their lives. Confirmation classes can become "conformity" classes where youth go along with the program to avoid conflict at home. Care must be taken to discern the condition of the heart before God, not just what youth can remember of what they have been taught.

AFFIRMATIONS AND IMPLICATIONS FOR ENCOURAGING CHILDHOOD CONVERSION

As one who stands within the "age of accountability" tradition, I believe it is important for the gospel to be shared with children and youth in a nonpressured way, and as they grow, where there is responsiveness to this message, provide counsel toward conversion.

I believe that as children grow they eventually reach a time of discernment and respon-sibility before God regarding their sin nature and separation from God. I do not think that all children or youth will have a sudden conversion experience, but many will be able to identify when they placed their trust in Jesus Christ as Lord and Savior. If we are to nurture children toward this faith commitment in caring and responsible ways, parents and church leaders need to consider the following principles:

1. Before sharing the gospel with children, instruct and nurture them to encourage a desire to know and be in right relationship with God. Children have a natural credulity that should be informed and shaped toward faith in Jesus Christ (Downs 1994, 214).
2. Avoid anxiety-producing appeals to children, having confidence in God's work through the Scripture message and the Holy Spirit (Hayes 1986, 407).
3. Avoid public invitations, relying instead on private conversations with those who would like to respond to the gospel and encouraging a response out of pure motives and accountability before God, not people (Hayes 1986).
4. Provide ongoing nurture and instruction for children who profess faith in Christ, to ensure a growing spiritual life and integrated faith.
5. For adolescents, provide multiple opportunities for reexamining the faith they have been taught, for questioning, and for testing out the faith to ensure that it is under-stood and freely and personally owned. Unfortunately, confirmation classes that all students of a certain age go through have potential social pressure concerns that can make it difficult for honest questioning and decision. These opportunities need to be more voluntary in nature and not tied to a particular age. Richard Osmer has some excellent suggestions in this area in his book *Confirmation* (1996).

IMPLICATIONS FOR FUTURE SCHOLARSHIP AND DIALOGUE

With the different understandings among evangelical communities regarding the con-version of children and youth, it is no wonder that we have controversy over what is appropriate in our ministry with them. Future discussions regarding ministry approaches will need to articulate the theological perspectives behind them to aid in understanding and assessment. Research regarding the experiences of children growing up within these differing approaches would help shed light on their impact on chil-dren's spiritual lives. It would also be beneficial to compare this research with that of how other children in other religious traditions come to their religious identity and beliefs to better understand the impact of varying experiences and instruction approaches in family and religious community settings on the spiritual life of children.

Notes

1. All baptismal candidates had earlier shared their faith testimony with church elders or, if in grade school, with the Children's Pastor, to ensure a personally "owned" faith commitment.

2. All Scripture quotations are taken from the Holy Bible, New International Version (1986), published by the International Bible Society.

References

Barna, George. 2003. *Transforming children into spiritual champions.* Ventura, Calif.: Regal Books.

Bushnell, Horace. [1861] 1979. *Christian nurture.* Reprint, Grand Rapids, Mich.: Baker Book House.

Clark, Elmer Talmage. 1929. *The psychology of religious awakening.* New York: Macmillan.

Committee on Evangelical Unity in the Gospel. 1999. The gospel of Jesus Christ: An evangelical celebration. *Christianity Today,* June 14, 51–56.

Downs, Perry G. 1994. *Teaching for spiritual growth: An introduction to Christian education.* Grand Rapids, Mich.: Zondervan.

Hayes, Edward L. 1986. Evangelism of children. In *Childhood education in the church,* edited by Robert E. Clark, Joanne Brubaker, and Roy B. Zuck, 399–415. Chicago: Moody Press.

Inchley, John. 1976. *Kids and the kingdom.* Wheaton, Ill.: Tyndale House.

Ingle, Clifford. 1970. Moving in the right direction. In *Children and conversion,* edited by Clifford Ingle, 142–57. Nashville, Tenn.: Broadman Press.

Issler, Klaus. 2004. Biblical perspectives on developmental grace for nurturing children's spirituality. In *Children's spirituality: Christian perspectives, research, and applications,* edited by Donald Ratcliff, 54–75. Eugene, Ore.: Cascade Books.

Johnson, Paul Emanuel. 1959. *Psychology of religion.* New York: Abingdon.

Joy, Donald. 1990. Child evangelism. In *Harper's encyclopedia of religious education,* edited by Iris V. Cully and Kendig Brubaker Cully, 116. San Francisco: Harper & Row.

Lamport, Mark A. 1990. Adolescent spirituality: Age of conversion and factors of development. *Christian Education Journal* 10(3):17–30.

Lawson, Kevin. 2004. Marginalization and renewal: Evangelical Christian education in the twentieth century. *Religious Education* 94:437–53.

Little, Ann M. 1982. Childhood salvation: A study of current theories. M.A. thesis, Trinity Evangelical Divinity School.

Marcel, Pierre Ch. 1953. *The biblical doctrine of infant baptism.* London: James Clarke.

May, Scottie. 1993. Reflections on childhood religious experiences: Patterns of similarity and variability in perceptions of adults from three evangelical churches. Ed.D. dissertation, Trinity Evangelical Divinity School.

Mulder, John M. 1990. Nurture. In *Harper's encyclopedia of religious education,* edited by Iris V. Cully and Kendig B. Cully, 10–16. San Francisco: Harper & Row.

Osmer, Richard Robert. 1996. *Confirmation: Presbyterian practices in ecumenical perspective.* Louisville, Ky.: Geneva Press.

Sisemore, Timothy A. 2000. *Of such is the Kingdom: Nurturing children in the light of Scripture.* Geanies House, Fearn, Ross-shire, UK: Christian Focus Publications.

Smith, Gordon T. 2001. *Beginning well: Christian conversion and authentic transformation.* Downers Grove, Ill.: InterVarsity Press.

Soderholm, Marjorie. 1962. *Explaining salvation to children.* Minneapolis, Minn.: Free Church Publications.

Starbuck, Edwin Diller. 1901. *The psychology of religion: An empirical study of the growth of religious consciousness.* New York: Scribner.

Westerhoff, John H., III. 1980. *Bringing up children in the Christian faith.* Minneapolis, Minn.: Winston Press.

Yoder, Gideon G. 1959. *The nurture and evangelism of children.* Scottdale, Pa.: Herald Press.

Zuck, Roy B. 1996. *Precious in his sight: Childhood and children in the Bible.* Grand Rapids, Mich.: Baker Book House.

CHAPTER 10

From Naming to Initiation: Childhood and Adolescence in African Christian Spirituality

Nicholas Otieno

Children are the embodiment of the creative power of life in African society. They are a gift that resembles the very presence of God in the community, and they should never be discriminated against. The idea of the flourishing of life is always associated with children. Children are at the heart of the reality of life in Africa today and therefore present an occasion for reflection on the authentic spirituality of a struggling people. They symbolize in the most powerful way the budding of life and the guarantee of fruitfulness, which includes the promise of a new future for the community.

Among indigenous communities in Africa, children are regarded as an investment of hope in the whole society, because the community not only survives but thrives through children. No individuals or parents can claim exclusive "ownership" of a child: ultimately children belong to the human community as well as to the ancestors and to God, the giver of life. With the names they give their children, the proverbs that enrich their discourse, the songs they sing, and the art forms that decorate their environment, Africans answer what is the most profound question of humanity: What is the human person? The African responds by saying, The human person is life (Ehusani 1991).

The cosmos is a sacred place in which relationships between human beings and the world of nature symbolize the manifestation of the kindred spirits. Children mediate this spiritual reality because they come from the very vortex of life. The vitality of life is present in all human beings and is brought to fruition during the birth of a child. A child not only continues the physical line of life (thought in some societies to be a reincarnation of the departed) but also takes on the intensely religious focus of keeping the parents in a state of personal immortality (Masolo 1995). The more people are remembered after death, the more they live in the existential domain of the individual conscious world; but with time depending on generational memory, they gradually recede into the world of collective unconscious. Memory of the "living dead" is inevitably linked to their being named in the world of the living. The ancestral world of kindred spirits is connected to the temporal world through procreation as well as, ultimately, through the embodiment of memory in the naming of a child. The birth of a child ensures that there is no discontinuity in the great chain of being that connects both the temporal world and the ancestral world with the kindred spirit. This spirit is cultivated as a child grows from infancy into adulthood, a journey that is carefully marked and charted in traditional societies, and one that involves an element of endurance and some physical ordeal.

This chapter highlights key markers on this path, first discussing the naming of a child and initiation into adulthood, and then showing how the HIV/AIDS pandemic in sub-Saharan Africa is unraveling the social fabric that sustains this spiritual journey. It is first helpful, however, to understand the rich and deep spiritual context of Africa.

The Spiritual Matrix of Africa

Africa is a religiously and spiritually diverse continent, with high proportions of the population adhering to Christianity and Islam, in addition to traditional beliefs and practices, as well as other world religions (Barrett, Kurian, and Johnson 2001). Despite preconceptions in the West, African Christian spirituality has its deep roots in biblical history. In the Hebrew scriptures, Africans appear as part of the narrative of their love for God (Sheba in 1 Kings 10:1–10; Ebed-Melech in Jeremiah 38:7). In the Christian Testament, Jesus has multiple encounters with Africa, including his sojourn as a child to Egypt (Matthew 2:13–15) and the African, Simon of Cyrene, who carried Jesus' cross on Good Friday (Matthew 27:32). The first non-Jewish Christian was an African—the Ethiopian or Sudanese official converted by Philip the deacon (Acts 8:26–40).

It is in Africa, and especially in Egypt, that we find the greatest number of martyrs, spiritual fathers, and theologians in the first centuries of the movement of Christianity. The central doctrine of Christian faith, the Trinity, was first articulated and formulated by Africans (Ogbonnaya 1994). Western monastic spirituality has its roots in the Egyptian desert.

Yet this history is lost in the geographic expansion of Europe and its hegemonic designs as the protagonist of the Christian faith. Not only did Western civilization seek to submit the world to its memory, it also sanctioned and produced unimaginable evils: the slave trade and its politics since the fifteenth century; colonialism; imperialism at the end of the eighteenth century and throughout the nineteenth; and fascism and Nazism in the twentieth (Mudimbe 1994).

Despite the violent changes that have taken place in Africa since the incursion of Western civilization (and in spite of all we hear about corruption and brutality among African leaders), it could be said that today's African society is still closer to its spiritual matrix than European or American society. The vast majority of Africans are still poor peasants, who survive the harsh realities of life by holding on firmly to faith in the human person, in the human family, and in the human community (Ehusani 1991).

At the heart of African spirituality is the reality of God's omnipresence as intrinsic in every condition and a social landscape that is filled with the abundance of life. The presence of God is not an abstract idea; neither is it a anthropomorphic extrapolation of perfection. Rather, every spiritual experience is an existential prerogative to the very essence of life. God's blessings are often invoked during moments of encounter between two or more human beings. The generosity of God is so great that it is inadmissible for death to overcome life. It is through birth that life is replenished in the universe.

African traditions embrace the innocence of spiritual childhood as a moral paradigm of life. Every aspect of human experience is valued and connected to the whole continuum of things on the basis of ritual and celebration. The distinctiveness in the diversities of everything in the universe are not by themselves contradictions but rather opportunities for growth. The spirit of death breeds intolerance of distinctiveness, whereas the spirit of life enthuses with the celebration of diversity as a gift. Children symbolize the giftedness and sacred nature of the variety of forms that signify abundance of life. The vital force of life in Africa's moral universe becomes the principal means by which all things are connected and recollected together in the unending influx of change toward the new earth and the new heaven.

In African tradition, the deepest foundation of all existence is nothing but God. Ancestors are the guarantors of this moral cosmology, and therefore God is the basis for Africans of moral life. No thought, word, or act can be understood except in terms of good and bad, in the sense that such an attitude or behavior either enhances or diminishes life (Magesa 1993). This approach is never justified on the basis of any rational premise or any system of knowledge. It is signified by a moral vision of the world in which relationships between all things are held as sacred and intrinsic for the ultimate meaning of life and well-being of humankind. A child was always perceived as a gift from the spiritual world of ancestors to the human community. African spirituality consists of oral narrative of rituals and practices with detailed regulations that relate the ontological realm to the challenges of daily living. These practices protect the community and strengthen its collective sense of identity.

This cultural context leads the preeminent African Christian theologian John S. Mbiti to argue that Africans need no conversion to Christianity. They already live the Christian message (Mbiti 1969). They need no teachings on the life to come, because they already participate in that life in the present. African Christian theology is therefore the systematic formulation of African thought to describe their ideas or conceptions of God and their religious experience in general (Masolo, 1995). These ideas of God's omnipresence and the sacredness of life are manifested in how African cultures mark the birth and growth of children, as well as their passage to adulthood.

The Naming of a Child

The generosity of God is signified in the flourishing of life in the universe. The moment of birth is the moment in which the vital forces of life become visible in the countenance of the newborn baby. Life comes anew as a blessing to the community. Such ineffable moments are preserved by the norms and rituals of most communities in sub-Saharan Africa. In African societies, the birth of a child is a process that begins long before the child's arrival in this world and continues long thereafter. It is not just a single event that can be recorded on a particular date. Nature brings the child into the world, but society creates the child into a social being, a corporate person. For it is the community that must protect the child, feed it, bring it up, educate it, and in many other ways incorporate it into the wider society (Mbiti 1969). This whole process is connected to a moral cosmology that guarantees continuity of life with the ontological embellishment of the kindred spirits.

Africans consider the kindred spirit and the multiplicity of named relationships as a manifestation of the divine reality. Even God is called by many names in order to show the many types of relationships that flourish within the community. The naming of a child signifies the continuity of life between the ancestral realm and the human community. Children have always been held as sacred members of the community. It is also customary among most African communities to name children after the ancestors and great men and women whose exemplary lives have left wisdom and a moral legacy.

The African naming of a child also signifies the intrinsic and symbiotic relationships between the cosmic realm and the spiritual world of ancestors. Most names indicate the unique occasion of the child's birth. For example, among the Nilotic communities of the Luo people in East Africa, the naming of a child is more determined by the events and time of birth. When a child is born in the morning, afternoon, or evening, he or she is given a name that describes that particular moment. In addition, cosmic events at the time of birth are considered a phenomenological connection between the reality of coming into being and the naming of new life. Thus, most Bantu ethnic groups emphasize phenomena such as rain, drought, floods, the appearance of locusts, or even social upheavals and times of abundant harvest.

The joy or sadness accompanying such events is integral to the naming system. The Wolof people of West Africa, for example, name their children one week after birth. For this occasion friends and relatives are informed beforehand, and, if it is the first child, a large gathering takes place. On the appointed day just before noon, the ceremony is performed where the birth occurred. The child's mother extinguishes the fire, sweeps the house, and takes a bath; the baby is washed with medicinal water. These are symbolic acts marking the end of one phase of life and the beginning of a new one. Visitors and guests bring presents. Women give their presents to the child's mother; men give theirs to the father (Mbiti 1969).

The basic foundation of naming systems in African traditions is that of the meaning being derived at the moment of birth. The meaning is not just an appropriation of a natural phenomenon in relation to the human person at the time of birth; rather it is a spiritual affirmation of the goodness of creation of which we are the custodians. It is also customary among most African communities to name children after the ancestors and exemplary men and women. The foundation for early childhood development in Africa is therefore based on a pedagogy of the sacredness of children as custodians of the continuity of life.

The sages, mediums, or community leaders merely facilitate on behalf of the community the urgency of the safe passage into life, as well as other passages (such as from childhood to adulthood, marriage, and the life hereafter). No one, not even the tribal chief, had the authority to change or negate the specificity and detail of ritual observance at birth. It would be a bad omen for the whole clan if a child were not named in time according to the rubrics of oral faith. It would haunt and torment the entire community for generations to come unless some kind of cleansing rituals were applied.

God is often revealed in the context of the dynamism of the kindred spirit whose presence is exemplified in the performance of rituals and celebration of life including the events of birth, rebirth, and death. In naming ceremonies, therefore, new life is venerated as a miracle from the ancestral world. The event of human life is marked by the passage from birth through adulthood and death. The moment of birth is marked by a sense of bewilderment and joy of the gift of new life to the human community.

Becoming Part of the Community

In the first years of life a child learns to either trust or mistrust those who are its care-takers. A child needs love, food, security, and a close relationship with its biological mother or someone who fills that role. Trust develops when these needs are met. When only some or none of these needs are provided for, or care is inconsistent, the child will grow up with a sense of distrust in the community. A child is curiously aware of what goes on in the community, even if it cannot verbalize the experience. A child knows whether the environment is secure and hence experiences fear and lack of safety whenever it is threatened.

In the moral traditions of most African communities, the individual exists only in relation to the group. Human beings achieve wholeness of meaning in their encounters with the ultimate reality present within the realm of the ultimate concerns of the community (Kobia 2003). To be alone is not only an affliction but a curse. It is equivalent to death, the ultimate isolation. Life in community also means responsibility for other human beings, especially the poor, the weak, the widow, and the orphan (Ehusani 1991). Therefore, during the early years of life the African child grows within the communal family environment, learning to obey the values and traditions of his or her people. At the same time, African communalism recognizes ontological pluralism and asserts the individuality of those making up the "we" (Coetzee and Roux 1998).

In most African traditions, children and young people are ritually introduced into the art of communal living. As in many societies, children in Africa grow physically, learning to walk, exercise bladder control, and speak between the ages of two and four. This is when they begin to distinguish between their own reality and that of the objective world. They develop a deep sense of autonomy and begin to act more independently. Even in a communal setting, the young child becomes more cognitive in separating self from others and initiates a process of personality development in making independent decisions that affirm its claim of autonomy. The child makes independent judgments whenever possible and asserts himself or herself occasionally by rejecting social indoctrination. The child begins to say no to what it rejects and yes to what is morally acceptable.

Regardless of the tradition or social setting into which a child is born, the process of developing the human conscience and a profound distinction between the boundaries of the self and the objective world are universal. Cultural particularities are negotiated between the dual interaction between specific social norms and the internal configuration of values that the child develops. A sense of the spiritual world, however, requires exposure to the narrative of faith and belief systems, an exposure that in turn requires some degree of assimilation. Most of the spiritual values in African societies are accompanied by ethical considerations for the growth and moral health of the child. If guidance is too harsh or the environment unsafe for the young child, then it learns to doubt even that which is claimed to be good for its well-being in the community. The traditional rites of passage in the coming-of-age ritual for children, especially among the Nilotic communities in Africa, include separation of both boys and girls by their respective male and female adult mentors. In the evening the boys sit by the fireplace next to their grandfather and the girls do the same next to their grandmother. They listen to stories of heroism that are meant to provide moral and spiritual instruction for the well-being of the community. Every story is laden with riddles and paradoxes of life that transmit moral teaching on values and norms that will the shape the consciousness of the new generation. Children are taught how to live in community and build solidarity with the weaker members of their society. They develop leadership skills, teamwork, collective responsibility, and learn how to make morally sound decisions and live in confidence with their beautiful heritage.

The Spiritual Passage to Adulthood

The passage from one life stage to another is of great significance in African spirituality. One must be initiated and exposed to the secrets of the community that are necessary and relevant to one's new social status. Through these rites of passage, the candidate is introduced to adult life and allowed to share in the full privileges and duties of the community.

In anticipation of adulthood, African young people go through a period of withdrawal from society and absence from home, during which time they receive secret instruction. This is a symbolic experience of the process of dying, living in the spirit world, and being reborn (resurrected). The rebirth that is the act of rejoining their families emphasizes and dramatizes that the young people are now new: they have new personalities and have lost their childhood. In some societies, they even receive new names (Mbiti 1969).

The time of initiation is a time of moral idealism, of testing strengths and limitations, of finding meaningful relationships and exploring vocational interests. It is important to young people to be part of a group and to be recognized and valued for who they are and for their own talents. They enter into the state in which they can now be held fully responsible for their actions. Young adolescents inherit new rights and obligations that will determine their future roles as elders in the community. This incorporation into adult life also introduces them to ancestral life as well as the life of the community's heroes. They are initiated in matters of sexuality and responsible living. Their sense of patriotism and commitment to the ethos of the community are tested and rewarded. When the community is threatened by external interests, they are called upon to fight for its values and autonomy. Initiation rites have a great moral and pedagogical value. The occasion of initiation often marks the beginning of a new life in which practical knowledge and social skills that were otherwise preserved for adults become accessible to young men and women.

Initiation is a spiritual occasion in which the heart is awakened to many things not known during childhood. It is the dawn of a new season in which the eyes of the grown-up child are opened to things that were once hidden by the shadows of time. The testing dimension of initiation includes the mandatory endurance of hardships and certain discomforts that are necessary for personal maturity and the well-being of the community. Young adults must learn to live with one another, and through obedience they must also learn how to be custodians of the secrets and mysteries of the community to which they were born. Youth are ritually introduced to the art of communal living. This happens when they withdraw from other people to live alone in the forest or in specifically prepared huts away from the villages.

Among the Maasai of East Africa, for example, circumcision rites take place every four to five years, for young people between twelve and sixteen years of age. There are certain myths surrounding female circumcision and procreation, for example, that the young woman becomes more fertile and is also likely to be more faithful to her spouse. Circumcision for the girl child was also considered the most significant rite of passage to adulthood because it enhanced social cohesion and increased the chances of marriage and hence the status of the girl's family within the community. Repeated denunciations of female genital mutilation by humanitarian and women's organizations have led to fewer female circumcisions among the Maasai and other tribes.

All those who are circumcised together form a lifelong cohort and take on a new special name. As preparation for the ceremony, all the candidates first assemble, covered with white clay and carrying no weapons. Then they spend about two months moving about the countryside. On the day before the ceremony, the boys wash themselves in cold water. When their foreskin is cut off, the blood is collected in an ox hide and put on each boy's head. For four days, the boys are kept in seclusion, after which they emerge dressed like women, their faces painted with white clay and their heads adorned with ostrich feathers. These practices are a ceremonial exhibition of the ancestral accompaniment of the young in their pilgrimage to adulthood.

A few weeks later, when their sex organs have healed, their heads are shaved; the boys now grow new hair and can become warriors (Mbiti 1969). Young people are exposed to the existential fact that we live in a complex world, one that includes evil and suffering. It is therefore imperative that one be prepared to live and flourish in such a world with the blessings of the ancestors and guidance of the wise men and women in the community. Through initiation they are summoned to a spiritual search for ways to grow, to develop themselves, and to transcend the prevailing confusion of the world.

The Spiritual Crisis of the HIV/AIDS Pandemic

These rituals and roles form the foundation of a village-based system for the social upbringing and moral well-being of the African child. However, due to the embracing of Western modernity and the emergence of an urbane and class-conscious society, the social safety net that provided the basis of communal affection toward children in Africa is fast unraveling. To make the situation worse, the HIV/AIDS pandemic across Africa has left innumerable children orphaned, especially in rural areas. Because the African household economy that supported affection toward such children is no longer viable, these children have no one to whom to turn.

Communities, families, and individuals in Africa are helpless as they watch their own sons and daughters bound in hopelessness without medication or preventive facilities to combat the pandemic. Obviously, the misery that comes with death in any culture leaves many unanswered questions in the minds and hearts of the bereft. The cumulative effects of HIV/AIDS demoralize young people, leading to social despondency and nihilism. The young give up on life early when they see their parents helpless and their communities engulfed and ravaged by fear of the unknown.

One must enter into the world of orphaned children to comprehend the degree of psychosocial anguish that HIV/AIDS brings to their lives. The misery that accompanies the death of parents and loved ones leaves so many children helpless and with unanswered questions about life. The tendencies to stigmatize people living with HIV/AIDS are often based on social taboos and mystical attributes of human sexuality, which children often do not understand.

In a sense, the prevailing situation with HIV/AIDS suggests the apocalyptic option in which the drama of the intrusion of the divine into the human condition must overwhelm our understanding. We are admonished, however, to see in these times a new moment of grace in which God is inviting the whole of humanity to embrace anew the spirituality of childhood, learning from children's resilience and being willing to be drawn to the wonderful things God is doing among the orphans and abandoned children of Africa. These children carry the banner of hope and compassion for a new future, revealing with new eyes the compassion of God reaching out and being mediated through the innocence of childhood.

HIV/AIDS cannot be considered an epidemic in the classical sense—that is, a disease that appears, affects people in a community or region, and then disappears. It has become an endemic and pandemic malady that has come to stay in human communities and that acquires global proportions in terms of its reach and consequences (George 2003). Statistics show that in South Africa, between 1,500 and 2,000 people are infected every day; more than 600 people die every day from HIV-related causes; approximately 800 babies are born to infected mothers every month (Pietermaritzburg Agency for Christian Social Awareness 2004). A child born into a poor family also inherits all the ills associated with poverty.

Few can improve their situation, and HIV/AIDS intensifies their suffering. Many are infected by mother-to-child transmission of the virus. In 2003, South Africa had at least 88,500 orphans, and 3 percent of all households were headed by children less than eighteen years old (Pietermaritzburg Agency for Christian Social Awareness 2004). This trend is aggravated by the economic demands of child labor, especially in rural communities. Throughout rural Africa, children become involved in farming and domestic chores at an early age. Boys herd livestock, and girls assist their mothers with preparing food and collecting water and firewood. West African children are estimated to be net contributors to the household by the age of ten (Devereux and Maxwell 2001).

The HIV/AIDS pandemic has had its own social and cultural repercussions in the care and well-being of children in Africa. Children are today without parental care and protection. Uprootedness becomes part and parcel of the HIV/AIDS phenomenon. Children in rural communities are simply struggling for access to basic needs, such as clean water and one meal a day. They are denied the kind of education that would prepare them to become self-reliant and responsible citizens in the future.

Vast numbers of people and communities in Africa are becoming alienated and uprooted from their ancestry and nationhood as a result of HIV/AIDS. Furthermore, the political upheavals that give rise to the uncontrolled movement of people across borders make children vulnerable to rape and other forms of sexual abuse. Reported rapes in Zimbabwe have increased 30 percent; more than half of the cases in 1997 involved children, a large number of them under five years of age (Murphy 1998). These situations are greatly exacerbated by economic modernity, which distorts the values of equanimity that once knitted the web of relationships within communities and gave the promise of a new sustainable future for the people of Africa.

The HIV/AIDS pandemic results from complex individual, social, economic, and political factors, including the alienation of young people from a healthy way of relating with one another and to their environment. For example, in many parts of Africa, the moral fabric for healthy living is threatened by the poverty and economic hardships of the working poor. Rural and urban migration patterns are creating a social setting in which many single mothers and fathers are encouraged to live polygamous lives both in the city and rural areas. Some leave their spouses in the countryside with children whom they cannot support with their meager resources. These forms of estrangement are linked to the phenomenon of uprootedness, which must be faced with new courage and a spirit of hope.

The dilemma posed by the fact that the old are burying the young in African communities has a direct impact on the valued ancestral memory, and it calls to mind the profound effect of the pandemic on African spirituality. No extinction is worse than the extinction of memory. In essence, African moral traditions and even Christianity are spiritual systems that are nourished and ritualized through the act of remembering. In this regard African thinkers must strive toward a process of spiritual discernment enabling them to transcend HIV/AIDS as an apocalyptic event that threatens the future of young Africans.

The loneliness associated with HIV/AIDS, chronic drought, and even war has created a social climate full of anguish and misery. Children in African villages no longer sit around in the fireplace in the evening to listen to stories that promote the values of respect, integrity, peace, and love in the community. They seek to belong once more to a new future of a possible world in the making. Children are yearning for a new ethic of life in which their survival is guaranteed and grounded on the moral foundations of love. Many children in rural Africa, although impoverished and perplexed by the emerging realities of life, are seeking the chance for a new future through the moral traditions of wisdom, modern education, and spiritual discipleship.

References

Barrett, David B., George T. Kurian, and Todd M. Johnson. 2001. *World Christian encyclopedia: A comparative survey of churches and religions in the modern world.* 2nd ed. New York: Oxford University Press.

Coetzee, P. H., and A. P. J. Roux. 1998. *The African philosophy reader.* New York: Routledge.

Devereux, Stephen, and Simon Maxwell, eds. 2001. *Food security in sub-Saharan Africa.* Pietermaritzburg, South Africa: University of Natal Press.

Ehusani, George Omaku. 1991. *An Afro-Christian vision: "Ozovehe" toward a more humanized world.* Lanham, Md.: University Press of America.

George, K. M. 2003. The threat of HIV/AIDS: Some theological considerations. Paper presented at a consultation jointly sponsored by the World Council of Churches, the Board of Theological Senate of Serampore College, and the South Asia Theological Research Institute, September 10–12, Bangalore, India.

Kobia, Samuel. 2003. *The courage to hope: The roots for a new vision and the calling of the church in Africa.* Geneva, Switzerland: World Council of Churches.

Magesa, Laurenti. 1997. *African religion: Moral traditions of abundant life.* Maryknoll, N.Y.: Orbis.

Masolo, D. A. 1995. *African philosophy in search of identity.* Nairobi, Kenya: East African Educational Publishers.

Mbiti, John S. 1969. *African religions and philosophy.* Nairobi, Kenya: East African Educational Publishers.

Mudimbe, V. Y. 1994. *The idea of Africa.* Bloomington: Indiana University Press.

Murphy, Dean E. 1998. Africa's silent shame. *Los Angeles Times,* August 16.

Ogbonnaya, A. Okechukwu. 1994. *On communitarian divinity: An African interpretation of the Trinity.* New York: Paragon House.

Pietermaritzburg Agency for Christian Social Awareness. 2004. *Gender, poverty, and HIV/AIDS.* Pietermaritzburg, South Africa: Author.

CHAPTER 11

The Child on Loan: The Pathway from Infancy through Adolescence in Islamic Studies

Ruqayya Yasmine Khan

Given the vast number and prominence of Muslim children and adolescents in the world, there is surprisingly little research and reflection on their lives and their spirituality. And though there is within the tradition an understanding of an infant as a "pure uninfluenced soul" (Giladi 1992, 51), there is also a stream of thought that contends that "growing up means forgetting childhood, wiping it out, and suppressing it. One becomes an adult in our traditional societies by scorning childhood and by repudiating femininity" (Bouhdiba 1977, 130). These contrasting images speak to the diversity and complexity of Islamic scholarship and to the ways in which Islamic scholars have understood children, childhood, and adolescence.

Within Islamic studies there are at least four trajectories of scholarship: identity issues with Muslim children and youth; Islamic textual studies (legal and historical) regarding children and childhood; children and childhood in specific regions of the world (primarily those that are predominantly Muslim regions); and childhood in Muslim literature. Drawing primarily from the first two of these streams, this chapter introduces several preeminent scholars in Islamic studies as a way of examining Muslim understandings of the nature of childhood and the process of spiritual change through childhood and adolescence. Before doing so, it is important to provide some insight into the nature of Islamic scholarship.

The Diversity of Islamic Studies

This chapter aims to provide insight into ideas and conceptions regarding "spirituality" (a term defined in the editors' introduction) as it is associated with childhood, children, and adolescents in recent scholarship of Islamic studies. Of course, the research on childhood, children, and adolescents in Islamic studies includes the work of anthropologists and ethnographers, specialists in area studies, historians, sociologists, historians of religion, and philologists. The majority of these would not call themselves "scholars of religion."

132

Indeed, were we to circumscribe the consideration of current research on childhood and children in Islamic studies to, for example, those who describe themselves as "scholars of religion," the trajectories of scholarship become far narrower. This begs the question of whether those who describe themselves foremost as "scholars of religion"—irrespective of the disciplinary framework(s) within which they situate themselves—will produce research and scholarship on childhood and children that is qualitatively different, because the research frames its inquiries differently and/or because it taps into debates specific to the study of religion. I think part of the purpose behind this edited volume is to pursue precisely this kind of question.

Furthermore, the interdisciplinary nature of Islamic studies points to how the constructs "Islam" or "Islamic tradition" are, as many scholars have pointed out (Hassan 1991, 39), not monolithic and instead encompass many kinds of Islam, or many "Islams." Apart from chronological and geographical variations, it is possible to talk about textual Islam (containing the major canons such as the Qur'an, Hadith, legal schools, etc.) being not quite the same as "lived Islam" (which itself varies within different contexts such as metropolis, village, suburban). Moreover, there are distinct, often fiercely contesting, orientations within Muslim communities, including but not limited to mainstream Sunni, Ismaili, Wahabi, progressive Islam, Ahmadi, and Twelver Shi'ite. My focus is confined to a consideration of a limited number of Islamic practices and trajectories of recent Western scholarship concerning childhood and children relating to primarily Middle Eastern Muslim regions.

The Idea of Childhood, the Realities for Children

Consistent with the notion of textual Islam and lived Islam is a distinction between the idea of childhood and the realities of children, which is highlighted by several Islamic scholars. Erika Friedl's term "folklore of childhood" (Friedl 1997, xv) is similar to Elizabeth Fernea's phrase "idea of childhood" (Fernea 1995, 3) and Avner Giladi's phrase "concepts and images of childhood" (Giladi 1992, 3–4). Although this distinction between childhood and children is not specific to Islamic thought and writings (it is also found in scholarship on the history of childhood in medieval Europe, and similar distinctions are found in the social and natural sciences), several Islamic studies scholars have remarked on this distinction as an important theme in their work.

Giladi, in *Children of Islam: Concepts of Childhood in Medieval Muslim Society* (1992), distinguishes between studying "concepts and images of childhood" versus "the reality of children's lives" (3–4). Giladi discusses several Islamic pediatric and child-rearing manuals pertaining to "childhood" as a life stage:

> Muslims writing on the subject—be they doctors, religious scholars or others—accepted some of the basic Hellenistic concepts of childhood. They regarded childhood as a unique period, different physically and psychologically from other periods in human life; they recognized a gradual process of child development, and were aware of certain definable phases in it. Since they discerned the long-term influence of infancy and childhood experi-

ences, they attached great importance to methods of childrearing and education; they tended to take into account individual differences in children as
well as special inclinations and needs. Although childrearing manuals do not
necessarily reflect the real treatment given to children, they do mirror concepts of childhood and basic attitudes towards children which were prevalent at least within the upper strata of urban society. (34)

Fernea appears to make a similar distinction between what she terms "the idea of
childhood, the place of the child, the duties of the child," on the one hand, and "the
cultural ideal of the place of the child, as expressed by people who live in the area, by
religious leaders, and by ethnographers and sociologists who are both inside and outside the culture," on the other (Fernea 1995, 3). Likewise, in *Children of Deh Koh:
Young Life in an Iranian Village*, Friedl (1997) observes:

> All individual differences notwithstanding, however, "child" (*bacce*) and
> "children" (*baccyal*), in the abstract, exist in the minds and language of the
> [Iranian] people and prompt adults and children to behave and to relate to
> each other in certain ways, to expect others to behave in certain ways, and to
> be disappointed, if not necessarily surprised, if the expectations are not met.
> This normative aspect we might call the folklore of childhood—the customs
> and their rationalizations surrounding child-stages. I try to mind both: the
> folklore of childhood with its normative categories and assumptions, and
> what children and adults make of it in the course of everyday life. (xv)

It should be mentioned that while the category of childhood is suggestive of a
divide between "norms, concepts" (read: childhood as defined by adults) and "experience" (read: children's subjective and social lives), undoubtedly the construct has
experience embedded within it. In other words, these adult-engendered normative
concepts, categories, and assumptions regarding child stages are, at least in the practice of child rearing, often conditioned by what adults think of and about *children*.
And what adults think of and about children is often strongly influenced by what
they themselves experienced as children, what they themselves felt and perceived the
adults in their child world thought of them. It is in this sense that Freud's famous
remark that "the child is father to the man" can be partly understood. As noted in
Fernea's *Remembering Childhood in the Middle East: Memoirs from a Century of
Change* (2002):

> Rarely do children represent their own lives—how many books like *The
> Diary of Anne Frank* can one recall? Rather adults speak for the children they
> were. Children never do have control over their lives. Each person has her or
> his own imaginary childhood homeland, and therefore to write the autobi-
> ography of one's childhood is to share adult conceptions of a very personal
> and unique past. (1–2)

The preceding quotation draws our attention to how the term *childhood* has yet
another meaning (apart from its significance as normative or social construct), that is,
childhood as "remembered experience." Lesleigh Cushing (2003) referred to this

notion when observing that "Jewish experience is recorded in one of two ways: as sociological memoir or as fiction." What we find written and expressed about childhood in the memoirs and autobiographies (and in various other genres) of adults is important for the study of religion. Both the ubiquity of human beings engaging in the act of recalling their childhood and the content of the childhood memories recovered and recorded are crucial for understanding the intersections between religion and childhood, between religion and life stages. And as Robert Fernea points out, part of "the paradox is the singularity of each childhood against the universality of childhood itself" (Fernea 2002, 2). This paradox is evident throughout discussions of the process of spiritual nurture during childhood and adolescence.

Elizabeth Fernea's *Remembering Childhood in the Middle East* (2002) provides an important window into the "idea of childhood"—through the memories of adults. Indeed, the idea for the book came about when her husband received a childhood narrative with an accompanying letter that stated: "I heard your wife was doing a book about children in the Middle East. Maybe she would be interested in my story" (vii). Spanning the twentieth century, the thirty-six personal narratives by men and women from fourteen different Middle Eastern countries are organized around four pivotal historical phases for most Middle Easterners of the modern era: the end of the Ottoman Empire; colonial rule and the rise of Arab nationalism; the phase of contemporary wars (Israeli-Palestinian) and revolutions (Iranian); and the postcolonial Middle East.

Within this context, it is important to acknowledge that Muslim scholars have, for centuries, examined issues of children and childhood. In his analyses of premodern Islamic treatises and legal texts, Giladi (1992) sheds light on issues such as infancy, child education, and child mortality. He documents that, as early as the tenth century, Muslim authors produced treatises devoted to pediatrics:

> Muslim doctors attached much importance to pediatrics; perhaps more than their Hellenistic predecessors did—and against this background the compilation of special pediatric treatises, apparently not a common practice in the Hellenistic world and unknown in medieval Europe before the thirteenth century, should be examined . . . [W]hatever their sources, Muslim physicians possessed rich and diversified knowledge which implied an understanding of some of the unique characteristics of children from the physical as well as the psychological points of view. (5)

Early scholarship had a particular focus on early childhood, with great emphasis in recent years on middle childhood and adolescence. The work of two premier scholars—Fernea and Giladi—provides a framework for examining how Islam has addressed spirituality across the first two decades of life.

In doing so, we must recognize that the "boundedness" of childhood and adolescence as phases is not "natural" to Islam. Through her ethnographic observations, spanning more than a ten-year period in Egypt, Iraq, and Morocco, Fernea (1995) concluded that "childhood was not seen as a specific bounded time period, and adolescence, as perceived in Western modern thought, scarcely existed. One moved from babyhood through childhood to puberty and adulthood" (10). She also notes that "a child was said to be without 'aql or reason, and the goal of child rearing was to instill and develop reason which is seen to be necessary for successful adult life in the society" (8). That said, clear practices and emphases occur during these developmental years that allow for exploration of the spiritual dimensions of growth through the first two decades of life.

INFANCY: AN ETHIC OF BREASTFEEDING

Giladi, an Israeli scholar, makes significant contributions to Islamic studies of childhood and children through his medieval Arabic textual studies. Giladi is influenced in part by psychoanalytic object relations theorists such as Donald Winnicott (Winnicott 1982), and this factor, along with Giladi's training as an Arabist, makes for fascinating research on premodern Islamic textual canons. In *Infants, Parents and Wet Nurses: Medieval Islamic Views on Breastfeeding and their Social Implications* (1999), Giladi examines breastfeeding in three Islamic textual canons—Qur'anic, medical, and legal—and provides a focus for exploring Islamic approaches to young children. He begins with the following premise:

> Any attempt at reconstructing the nature of infant feeding in the past and the prevalence of the methods involved helps to shed light on vital aspects of family life and in particular of the lives of women and children in premodern societies: women's status with the family and their relationships with their husbands and infants, the physical treatment children received, the psychological relationships that evolved between children and their parents and nurses, and so on. (1)

Giladi introduces the foundations of an Islamic "ethics" of breastfeeding as laid out in the religious canons of the Qur'an, Qur'anic commentaries, and the Hadith (sayings or dictums attributed to the Prophet Muhammad).

A central concept of childhood identified in the historic Islamic childrearing manuals is that the infant is a "blank, clean slate" or a "pure uninfluenced soul" (Giladi 1999, 51). This idea is also captured in a well-known Hadith: "Every infant is born according to the fitra (Allah's kind or way of creating), then his parents make him a Jew or a Christian or a Magian" (Giladi 1992, 139).

Implicit here is the notion that "childhood is especially important . . . owing to the view that in its pristine state the child's soul is pure and open to influences: its qualities are inscribed upon it just as smooth stone may be engraved" (Giladi 1992, 51). Al-Ghazali, a famous medieval Muslim theologian and mystic reformer, declares:

> The child is by way of being on loan in the care of his parents . . . If he is accustomed to good and is so taught, he will grow in goodness, he will win happiness in this world and the next, and his parents and teachers will have a share of his reward. But if he is made accustomed to evil and is neglected like the beasts, he will be woeful and lost. (Cited in Giladi 1992, 50)

"BEARING WITNESS" DURING CHILDHOOD

As the child moves from infancy into childhood, a central emphasis for nurturing spirituality is the concept of "bearing witness." This concept is enshrined in not just the Islamic creed ("I bear witness that there is no god but God and Muhammad is his prophet"), but also in the modes and practices by which spirituality is fostered and shaped in Muslim children (e.g., the creed is uttered in the infant's right ear upon birth).

As would be true of any religious tradition, the familial unit, including parents and/or other kin figures, plays a pivotal role in inspiring, shaping, and inculcating spiritual awareness in children. Fernea (1995) has remarked that in the Islamic Middle East, "socialization of the child took place primarily within the home, and the father and mother were ultimately responsible for their offspring. However, grandparents, aunts, uncles and cousins were also expected to participate in a child's rearing and usually did so" (9). Obviously, the spirituality of children is often formed and shaped primarily through what they witness, hear, and experience within their homes and related contexts.

For instance, *salat*, an Islamic daily worship practice and ritual, plays an exceedingly important role in the formation of Muslim children's spirituality, and the sheer frequency with which Muslim children observe and witness their kin performing this ritual profoundly molds their spirituality. Salat or daily prayer densely interweaves sacred time with ordinary time, sacred space with ordinary space. This very interweaving, as witnessed and experienced several times a day by Muslim children in their homes, is a vital factor in shaping their awareness of the realm of the sacred. Moreover, while this worship practice ideally entails the bracketing of the adult's attention from all distractions, small children, who often experience this bracketing as a form of inattentiveness on the part of the parent, are not to be ignored.

As any Muslim parent knows, whether in the home or the mosque, small children often fidget and fuss, as well as engage in horseplay during salat. Apposite here is the mention of the Hadith concerning how the prophet "prolonged the prostration posture in one of his prayers so as not to disturb his grandson Husayn who, at that moment, was riding on his back" (Giladi 1992, 48). With time and frequency, however, parents hope that the child's reaction will change from discomfort and a sense of deprivation to silent observation and at times, mimicking the adult's physical worship postures. An element related to salat often under the scrutiny of young children in a Muslim household is the ablution performed before prayer, known as *wudu*. One can only surmise the extent to which toddlers and small children—given their own life stage's preoccupations with the body and toilet training—would readily take notice of this adult bodily ritual visibly taking place in the bathroom.

Indeed, the so-called Five Pillars (the *shahadah,* or bearing witness to the truth claims that there is only one God and that Muhammad is his messenger, as well as the four ritualistic acts of daily prayer, salat; charity or *zakat*; fasting during the month of Ramadan or *sawm*; and *hajj*, pilgrimage to sites in and around Mecca during a given time period) are instructive in the light they shed on the matter of fostering and inculcation of Muslim children's spirituality. I will never forget the "magic" I as a young child associated with the bottles of Zamzam water brought back by my father from his hajj pilgrimage to Mecca. The water, from the sacred well of Zamzam, was a ritual object bestowed on me by my father, and one that I as a child could see and touch—all of which powerfully conveyed to me the spiritual and numinous qualities of the pilgrimage even though I obviously was too young at the time to perform it. For months, I hid those little plastic bottles of sacred water under my pillow, only occasionally sprinkling my hands with it. The hajj pilgrimage therefore is a ritual that forms and transforms the spirituality not only of those undertaking it but also of their kin.

Another means by which the spirituality of Muslim children is shaped is through what they hear in the form of sacred narratives and oft-quoted Hadith, which are employed to inculcate ethical precepts, moral principles in children and adolescents. One such sacred narrative that my mother was fond of relating to us was that concerning Hagar (Hajara) and her son Ishmael. According to Islamic tradition, Hagar, the Egyptian concubine-spouse of Abraham (who bore him his first child, Ishmael), was deposited by the patriarch in a valley of Mecca and left there in the sweltering desert.

When my mother related to us children the story of Hagar's experiences in Mecca, I would curl up next to her and listen raptly. My mother—who had a skill for dramatization—would linger over the part about how Hagar, abandoned by Abraham with her infant in the sand, wandered for days in search of water. My mother's voice become excited as she described to us how finally, Hagar, in desperation, set the bawling infant down and frantically ran over the seven hills looking for any sign of water. Eyes round with awe, I would always imagine hearing the sound of the baby's crying.

Then my mother would come to the part that I liked the best—the part in which Hagar, exhausted and utterly dejected, came back to her wailing infant. As she knelt down to cradle him in her arms, she suddenly noticed that where his heels had been kicking the sand, there was moisture! She put the baby down and began clawing the sand with her hands. She dug and dug, and lo and behold, a spring bubbled forth. This is how the miraculous spring of Zamzam acquired a magical significance in my child's mind. My mother would then conclude the story with a sermon about how God always helps those in need and, just as important, she would stress how Hagar was a Muslim heroine, an ideal mother who went to all lengths to help her needy child, and how God had rewarded her.

Finally, a mode by which spirituality and religiosity are inculcated in children and adolescents is through hearing the constant and frequent use of Islamic devotional phrases and invocations in Arabic. For example, the Qur'anic *basmallah* functions as the equivalent of "saying Grace" before meals in Muslim households. "In sha 'Allah" or "God willing" is said by Muslims with reference to any future plan or any event or occurrence desired for the future. The basmallah and numerous other sacred phrases, formulas, and invocations are often on the lips of devout Muslims throughout the day, and each is pronounced or uttered in different contexts—for instance, at mealtimes or after having sneezed or when embarking upon any new plan or project. In addition to the two aforementioned ones, such phrases include "Al-Hamdolillah" (Praise be upon God), "Subhan al-Allah" (Holy is God), "Allah huwa Akbar" (God is great), and "'Astaghfar al-Allah" (God forgive me).

Of course, the contexts within which such expressions are used or expected to be used can vary greatly, and these contexts often are culturally determined as seen from a childhood anecdote from Maysoon Pachachi, an Iraqi filmmaker whose early years were spent in the United States. She recalls the impact upon her as a young girl, hearing one of these formulas uttered and rationalized by a school friend in Baghdad:

> Learning Arabic was easy compared to the many other things I had to try to understand. In the first week of school, during recess I was doing cartwheels and handstands with a newfound friend. She kept saying "*istakhfar Allah*" (God forgive me), and I began to wonder whether there was something inherently sinful about cartwheels. "You must say that whenever you turn the sole of your shoe to God, up there in the sky, so He knows you mean no disrespect." (Fernea 2002, 273)

Muslim children internalize these phrases, and they become part and parcel of their daily discourses and interactions. The frequent utterance and invocation of these phrases "sacralize" time and space for those who use them.

PARTICIPATION IN QUR'ANIC SCHOOL

Despite the centrality of family, spiritual practices and socialization do not occur only in the home. Fernea (1995) notes that mainly boys past puberty were taken to the mosque for the Friday congregational prayers and that children were not required to fast during the month of Ramadan, but "some often choose to do in imitation of their parents" (7–8). Furthermore, "religious socialization took place not only in the home (for boys and girls) and in the mosque (for boys) but also in the Qur'anic school, or *kuttab*" (9).

In terms of insights into the formation of spirituality in childhood and children, probably the most important thread of information in Fernea (2002) is to be found in the references to Qur'an reading and/or Qur'anic schooling in numerous narratives. Those experiences are not always positive. Indeed, narratives of several adults in remembering their childhood often point toward poignant, if painful, memories of "Qur'an classes" during adolescence.

In many modern-life stories and autobiographies by Muslims, especially those from the Middle East, childhood experiences associated with Qur'an classes are marked by a recurrent feature: one or another kind of experience of stress or discomfort associated with the learning of the Qur'an. Such a feature is found, for example, in one of the most famous autobiographies by a modern Muslim, *The Days—Taha Hussein: His Autobiography in Three Parts (al-Ayyam)* by the Egyptian scholar and author Taha Hussein (Hussein 1932). In the autobiography, Hussein "relates in detail his experience of memorizing the Qur'an as a blind child. Despite his great pride in this achievement, through lack of practice he forgot it and to his shame was found out in a very painful moment in front of his father, and a guest. He then memorized it again and again forgot it, and finally on the third try, did he succeed in memorizing and retaining it" (Reynolds 2001, 85–86).

A number of the male narrators also recall the severe physical discipline exercised by the Qur'an teacher. For example, Ali Eftekary (born in Iran) shares:

> The teacher held a stick that was long enough to reach every child. Anyone who made a mistake in reciting the Qur'an or the Persian textbook would find that stick crashing down on shoulder or head. The man was stern, harsh but dedicated, and he really wanted to teach us something. He tried hard to achieve this goal, because he truly believed if we could read the Qur'an, we might some day say a prayer for him so he would be rewarded in the next world. But we were only children and did not think about such matters. (Fernea 2002, 249)

In spite of this, hearing the recitation of the Qur'an in the home or traditional Qur'anic school no doubt played a key role in the ingraining of spiritual values in Muslim children and adolescents. For instance, Nazik Ali Jawdat, of both Syrian and Iraqi background born in 1903, remarks on her aunt Hadije's worship: "Aunt Hadije then devoted herself entirely to praying and fasting . . . I remember her on her rug, praying and telling her beads or reading the Quran on her cushion by the window" (Fernea 2002, 24).

IDENTITY ISSUES AND MUSLIM CHILDREN AND YOUTH

Another key issue that emerges, particularly following puberty, is identity. Especially since the 1960s, there has been an increase in emigration from Muslim-majority countries to different parts of the world, notably the United States (Haddad 1994, xx–xxi).

This has yielded Muslim populations abroad made up of immigrants (including those that have arrived as adults or children) and first and second generations born in their parents' new homelands. This change has sparked a growing body of scholarship that examines identity-related issues that have arisen and continue to arise among immigrant Muslim populations in different parts of the world—especially Europe and the United States (see, for example, Chaudhry 1998; Hasnat 1998; Hermansen 2003; Ostberg 2000; Parker-Jenkins 1995). Among the chief themes addressed by these works are those of acculturation and identity formation. In an article titled "We Are Graceful Swans Who Can Also Be Crows: Hybrid Identities of Pakistani Muslim Women," Lubna Chaudhry employs the concept of "hybrid identity" to explore how four young women "asserted their 'American-ness' in contexts where it was overlooked and stressed their Muslim and Pakistani origins when they were negated" (49) Likewise, Naheed Hasnat implies the hybrid, contextual, and situational aspects of identity in her essay "Being 'Amreekan': Fried Chicken versus Chicken Tikka" when she first lists the components of her identity in order of priority (female gender, Muslim faith, American citizenship, and Pakistan ethnicity) and then declares "I am an amalgamation of these" (Hasnat 1998, 39).

The identity-related works also include research with Muslim children and youth living in Muslim-majority nations and regions, such as the Arab Middle East or Turkey.

Generally speaking, the identity-related research contains studies of children and youth in which either ethnic or religious identity is made prominent and examined (e.g., El-Shamy 1981; Saktanber 1991). In some cases, ethnicity and religion are studied together. Issues pertaining to immigration and education loom large in this trajectory: again, an indication of how many of the identity issues examined address the processes of acculturation, assimilation, and/or alienation that are inherent in the experiences of immigrant/diasporic Muslim communities.

Closing Observations

Despite the rich insight gained from existing scholarship, there is a paucity of research and scholarship on childhood, children and adolescents in Islamic studies—particularly in the North American milieu. This paucity is more alarming when one considers that globally Muslims number approximately one billion, a significant portion of whom are children. Fernea, in *Children in the Muslim Middle East* (1995), has observed that "children under the age of fifteen . . . constitute more than 40 percent of the population in the majority of the countries of the Middle East" (4) Likewise, Friedl (1997) points out that more than half the population of Iran is under the age of fifteen (xiv).

In addition, Muslim children and adolescents—at this historical juncture—are some of the poorest, angriest, most marginalized, and underprivileged in the world. Apart from the academic and intellectual needs for filling in the gaps with regard to this topic, it would not be incorrect to state that, given the contemporary international controversies swirling around and in the Islamic world, it is imperative that far more attention be paid to the categories of childhood, children, and adolescents in the Islamic tradition and Muslim societies.

References

Bouhdiba, A. 1977. The child and the mother in Arab-Muslim society. In *Psychological dimensions of Near Eastern studies*, edited by L. Carl Brown, 126–41. Princeton, N.J.: Darwin Press.

Chaudhry, Lubna. 1998. "We are graceful swans who can also be crows": Hybrid identities of Pakistani Muslim women. In *Patchwork shawl: Chronicles of South Asian women in America*, edited by Shamita Das Dasgupta, 46–61. New Brunswick, N.J.: Rutgers University Press.

Cushing, Lesleigh. 2003. I will also forget thy children: Childhood in Jewish studies. Paper presented at the annual meeting of the American Academy of Religion, Atlanta, Ga.

El-Shamy, Hasan. 1981. The brother-sister syndrome in Arab family life, socio-cultural factors in Arab psychiatry: A critical review. *International Journal of Sociology of the Family* 2:313–23.

Fernea, Elizabeth, ed. 1995. *Children in the Muslim Middle East*. Austin: University of Texas Press.

———. 2002. *Remembering childhood in the Middle East: Memoirs from a century of change*. Austin: University of Texas Press.

Friedl, Erika. 1997. *Children of Deh Koh: Young life in an Iranian village.* Ithaca, N.Y.: Syracuse University Press.

Giladi, Avner. 1992. *Children of Islam: Concepts of childhood in medieval Muslim society.* New York: St. Martin's Press.

———. 1999. *Infants, parents and wet nurses: Medieval Islamic views on breastfeeding and their social implications.* Leiden: Brill.

Haddad, Yvonne. 1994. *Muslim communities in North Africa.* Albany: State University of New York Press.

Hasnat, Naheed. 1998. Being "Amreekan": Fried chicken versus chicken tikka. In *Patchwork shawl: Chronicles of South Asian women in America*, edited by Shamita Das Dasgupta, 33–45. New Brunswick, N.J.: Rutgers University Press.

Hassan, Riffat. 1991. Muslim women and post-patriarchal Islam. In *After patriarchy: Feminist transformations of the world religions*, edited by Paula M. Cooey, 39–64. Maryknoll, N.Y.: Orbis Books.

Hermansen, Marcia. 2003. How to put the genie back in the bottle? "Identity" Islam and Muslim youth cultures in America. In *Progressive Muslims: On justice, gender and pluralism*, edited by Omid Safi, 306–19. Oxford, UK: Oneworld.

Hussein, Taha. 1932. *An Egyptian childhood: The autobiography of Taha Hussein.* Translated by E. H. Paxton. London: Routledge.

Ostberg, Sissel. 2000. Islamic nurture and identity management: The lifeworld of Pakistani children in Norway. *British Journal of Religious Education* 22 (2):91–103.

Parker-Jenkins, Marie. 1995. *Children of Islam: A teacher's guide to meeting the needs of Muslim pupils.* London: Trentham.

Reynolds, Dwight, ed. 2001. *Interpreting the self: Autobiography in the Arabic literary tradition.* Berkeley and Los Angeles: University of California Press.

Saktanber, Ayse. 1991. Muslim identity in children's picture-books. In *Islam in modern Turkey*, edited by Richard Tapper, 171–88. London: Tauris.

Winnicott, Donald. 1982. *Playing and reality.* New York: Tavistock.

CHAPTER 12

Entering the World, Entering Torah: Moving from the Natural to the Sacred in the Jewish Life Cycle

Roberta Louis Goodman

The Jewish life cycle is filled with moments of celebration and sadness, remembering and rejoicing. Jewish publishers are printing numerous books to help Jews prepare for various life cycle phases and marker events. These books come with titles such *The New Jewish Baby Book. Names, Ceremonies, Customs: A Guide for Today's Families* (Diamant 2000), *For Kids. Putting God on the Guest List: How to Claim the Spiritual Meaning of Your Bar or Bat Mitzvah* (Salkin 1998), and *Parenting as a Spiritual Journey: Deepening Ordinary and Extraordinary Events into Sacred Occasions* (Fuchs-Kreimer 1998). All of these books are aimed at helping Jews prepare for life cycle stages.

Life cycle events or ceremonies are powerful, highly symbolic, emotionally charged happenings. Jewish life cycle rituals and customs often include aspects that are biblical, rabbinic, historical, and contemporary, as well as religious or spiritual, cultural, familial, communal, and individual. Life cycle rituals have evolved over time and space.

In today's world, many people are searching for meaning, purpose, and spirituality in their lives combined with a desire to do rituals themselves rather than have someone else do these rituals for them. These factors have precipitated a revival in life cycle ceremonies. Many more Jews are preparing for these life cycle events in creative and thoughtful ways. This interest has led both to recapturing traditional ways and to creating new interpretations of blessings, ceremonies, and customs. The rituals reflect the values and hopes of a community and give direction for the person's development as an individual as well as a member of the Jewish community.

This chapter explores what Jewish life cycle rituals in childhood and adolescence can teach us about spiritual development. What can children named Max, Sam, and Sophie, good names from past generations of immigrants, or Jacob, Rachel, and Leah, good names from the Bible, or even names like Vered and Ariel, good modern Hebrew names, do to illuminate our understanding of spiritual development? What does the emphasis on Jewish schooling for young children and elementary school-age children suggest about the connection between learning and spirituality? Why are bar/bat mitzvah students often involved in *tikkun olam* (literally, "repairing the world") projects as part of this rite of passage at puberty while at the same time learning to read or chant lengthy sections of Torah or haftarah (selections from Prophets)? What is the significance in terms of a teenager's development when his grandfather says that his grandson's bar mitzvah was one of the best days of his life? Why would an educator say that for the family the bar/bat mitzvah is a turning point when parents can be engaged deeply in their own Jewish journey? These are just some of the questions that begin to uncover what Jewish life cycle ceremonies, customs, ritual objects, and prayers have to say about the spiritual development of children and adolescents.

This chapter draws implicitly and explicitly on the work of many developmentalists. Key to the understandings presented are the work of James W. Fowler, Erik Erikson, and Jean Piaget, as well as many who have written about, applied, and even expanded their theories. Fowler's (1981) theory of faith development, a holistic theory of the self, posits meaning making as the primary functioning of human beings. Fowler draws on the work of both Erikson and Piaget. Erikson's (1980) work on psychosocial development is foundational in seeing life as a cycle and the many phases that constitute the life cycle. In addition, his theory is concerned with identity formation that is applicable to the task of learning to live in and preserve a spiritual and cultural tradition. Piaget (1967) introduces the concept of stages, the idea that children and adults are different developmentally, and grounds that discussion in the cognitive aspects of the individual.

The focus of this chapter is on three life cycle events that mark transitions into new stages in childhood and adolescence: entering into the world (brit milah and brit habat, covenantal naming rituals), beginning Jewish schooling, and becoming Jewishly responsible (bar/bat mitzvah). The life cycle events are analyzed first individually and then collectively for what can be learned about the spiritual development of children and adolescents.

Entering into the World: Brit Milah, Brit Habat, and Naming

Birth marks the entry point into Jewish spiritual life. Through procreation or even adoption, parents fulfill the first of the biblical commandments, "p'ru u'revu," to be fruitful and multiply (Genesis 1:28). The actual birth of a baby is a miraculous occasion when one marvels at God's creation. Many parents, when asked to describe a time in their life when they felt close to God, will speak about childbirth. Giving birth to a child is an act of optimism. As David Novak, a Jewish scholar, writes, "Parenthood for Jews at times has to be a conscious act of faith that God will not allow either the earth or the Jewish people to be destroyed. 'There is hope of your future, says the Lord' (Jeremiah 31:16)" (Novak 1993, 13).

More than just the birth of the child, Novak views creation as an example of a long-term partnership among parents and God in raising a child. He interprets the rabbinic passage that states that there are three partners in the creation of a human being: God, father, and mother (Kiddushin 30b), to demonstrate that parenting is an ongoing sacred act (Novak 1993, 12).

The best-known Jewish life cycle ritual at the time of birth is the brit milah, the covenant of circumcision that usually takes place when a male child is eight days old. Circumcision is a sign between God and the Jewish people of their interdependent covenantal relationship. When Abram is circumcised, he enters into a new status in his partnership with God. His name becomes Abraham, the father of monotheism, the father of a new nation. The command to Abraham to circumcise his son, Isaac, when he was eight days old, establishes the Jewish custom of circumcision as a sign of the covenant between God and Abraham's descendants (Genesis 17:12). The male child thus becomes identified with the Jewish people physically and spiritually from his earliest days.

More and more, celebrations for girls are being conducted either at home or at the synagogue similar in stature to a brit milah. There were always naming prayers for girls recited in a public forum. But these public ceremonies in the synagogue stood in sharp contrast to the home-based, highly ritualized brit milah ceremony. Now girls are being welcomed into the covenant. Parents and clergy are devising and adapting rituals creating a brit habat (covenant of the daughter) to signify the female baby's entry into the world and membership in the Jewish people. This ritual change reflects an increase in the stature and responsibilities being accorded to females in religious life, recognizing that they, like their brothers, are spiritual beings created in God's image and integral parts of the covenant.

Part of both the brit milah and the brit habat is the giving of a name. Names are important in Judaism. The crown of a good name is greater than even Torah, the priesthood, or royalty (Mishnah Avot 4:13). Often children receive two names, a provincial or "English" name, and a Hebrew name. In some cases, the names are the same. When the names are different, biblical names are often favorite choices to demonstrate the strong connection to Jewish ancestry. These Hebrew names and their meanings are spiritual links to the family's Jewish heritage.

The giving of a name connects the lineage of Jews throughout the ages and the baby to his or her own personal family history. Ashkenazic families with roots in Eastern or Western Europe generally name only for deceased relatives; Sephardic families with roots in North Africa or the Middle East will name a child after a living relative. As 1 Samuel 25:25 relates, "Like his name, so is he," a person reflects the qualities and attributes of the name given to him or her. Names are suggestive of one's essence. Passing on a name becomes symbolic of passing on one's soul from generation to generation.

After the child officially is given his or her name, the blessing offers a framework for the child's life. The prayer expresses the following expectations and hopes: "As he has been entered into the covenant, so may the child grow into a life of Torah, *huppah* [marriage canopy], and *ma'asim tovim* [good deeds]." This prayer, which is recited not only by the officiant of the ceremony but by the entire community that is present, anticipates the steps that will mark the individual's ongoing covenantal relationship with God and the Jewish people.

Through these birth rituals children are linked to the Jewish people and to God from the beginning of their lives. It is not only the parents but the Jewish community as a whole that accepts responsibility for the ongoing spiritual life of the child. Faith developmental theorist James W. Fowler speaks of a "pre-stage of faith development" that characterizes the infant usually until the emergence of speech. He acknowledges that this development really begins in the womb.

Judaism recognizes children born of Jewish parents as Jewish from birth. Traditionally, children born of a Jewish mother or converted to Judaism are considered Jewish. Some movements will accept as Jewish a child whose father alone is Jewish and who is raised as a Jew.

Covenantal birth rituals underscore the components essential in spiritual development, connection to a community, a sense of belonging to a heritage, and a relationship with God. Often the child has remainders and reminders of this early celebration in the form of ritual objects and mementos. These may include a kiddush cup for wine used at most Jewish life cycle and holiday celebrations, an artistically done naming certificate with Hebrew and/or English, and pictures or videos of much of the ceremony or celebrants. From the start, a child is introduced and surrounded by the tools and language of his covenantal heritage. The birth ritual inaugurates a framework in which the routines of daily life from eating to sleeping are understood in light of the sacred.

The birth of a child is connected not just to creation but also to another major theological theme, redemption. Children are not just wonders of creation, they also present the possibility for redemption of the world. Made in the image of God, with a yet-to-be-tested capacity for good and evil, they represent the hope that their actions will bring about the renewal and repair of the world in partnership with God. Each newborn child could be the Messiah. Most symbolic of the redemptive capacity of children is the presence of an empty chair for Elijah, who is traditionally part of a brit milah. Jewish tradition imagines that Elijah will return to earth announcing the Messiah, ushering in the messianic age. At the birth of a child, this hope is renewed.

All children are created *b'tzelem elohim*, in the image of God, imbued with a spark of God, given a soul, the breath of life. All are God's creatures. But the Jewish child is inducted into the covenant with God and his or her people, shown a path for living from the very beginning of life. Jean Piaget, James Fowler, and more recently the brain development theoreticians and others have acknowledged that significant development begins from the earliest days of one's life before the acquisition of speech. So too does the covenantal ritual welcome the Jewish child into a life of relationship to God. Long before he or she is responsible for performing God's commandments, the Jewish child's connection to the covenant is affirmed. Being welcomed into the covenant signals to the parents and the community their responsibility to raise the child physically as well as spiritually. The ability to relate to God and comprehend the holiness of the universe is a capacity and an expectation that a child has from birth.

Entering Torah Study

The next most significant Jewish life cycle event after birth is the entry of the young child into formal Torah study. The Torah represents the relationship between God and the Jewish people. It provides a worldview, values, and purpose for each and every Jew. It has been said that when one prays, one speaks to God, but when one studies Torah, God speaks to us. The study of Torah, broadly understood as the whole of Jewish learning and not just the five books of Moses, is a sacred task that seeks to provide knowledge, deepen commitment, and ignite the soul. As one Jewish day school motto states, "A child is not a cup to be filled, but a light to be kindled." Torah study by children is held in high esteem. As the rabbinic text states, "The world endures only for the sake of the breath of schoolchildren" (Shabbat 119b). Rabbi Akiva taught that the Torah is life itself for the Jew. To quote a phrase from a Jewish folk song: "The land of Israel without the Torah is like a body without a soul." Without Torah, the Jew cannot survive spiritually. Torah constitutes the very identity of the Jewish people.

Today nearly 80 percent of Jewish children ages six to seventeen have received some sort of formal Jewish schooling, according to the National Jewish Population Study 2000/2001. Jewish learning is a widespread activity for males and females. Although at one time most formal study was for male children only, today girls and boys are participating in all levels and kinds of Jewish study as children and adolescents. In more traditional circles, the curriculum may be different and girls and boys may be separated as they approach puberty, but the importance of providing Torah study to both girls and boys is upheld across Judaism.

There are multiple points of entry into formal Jewish schooling. Some begin with parent-tot classes. Other children go off to a Jewish preschool at age three or four. Some start in kindergarten as part of a congregational "Sunday" school or others at a five-day-a-week parochial Jewish day school. Still others wait until second or third grade to enter afternoon Hebrew school. The length children stay in formal Jewish study and its intensity vary, but for the most part, Jewish schooling is an activity in which children engage from ages two to eighteen.

This emphasis on Jewish learning and schooling has an ancient history in Judaism. The words *Torah, moreh* (teacher), and *horeh* (parent) share a common root related to teaching. A rabbinic text suggests that teaching a child is like giving birth to that child, because learning and existence are inextricably linked. The obligation of parents to teach their children about God's commandments arises in the Torah. As the Israelites are preparing to enter the Promised Land, God provides these instructions:

> Hear, O Israel: The Lord our God, the Lord is One. Love the Lord your God with all your heart, with all your soul, with all your might. And these words which I command you this day you shall take to heart. You shall teach them diligently to your children. You shall recite them at home and away, morning and night. You shall bind them as a sign upon your hand, they shall be a reminder above your eyes, and you shall inscribe them upon the doorposts of your homes and upon your gates. (Deuteronomy 6:4–9)

These words from the Torah form a central part of the daily Jewish liturgy.

The earliest schools in the Jewish community were started more than two thousand years ago by Simon ben Shetah for those children who were orphaned or had no parent able to teach them Torah. While not all Jews in earlier times received a formal Jewish education, the teaching of Torah by tutors, in schools, and in the home was clearly a religious obligation and fairly widespread. The Talmud contains discussions of the importance of building a school, instructions on how to educate children, and even the qualities of a good teacher. Furthermore, the Talmud teaches that one is forbidden to live in a town without a school (Talmud, Sanhedrin, 17b and Rambam, Mishna Torah, Hilkhot Deot 4:23).

Jewish study is viewed as preparation for taking on the responsibilities of the commandments that occurs when one becomes a bar or bat mitzvah, beginning the transition into adulthood. Rabbinic writings clearly show this sequencing as well as differentiating childhood and adolescence from adulthood by outlining different tasks associated with different ages from five through one hundred. Those of childhood, adolescence, and young adulthood are included here:

> At five [one begins the study of] the Bible. At ten the *Mishnah*. At thirteen [one takes on] the [responsibility for] the *mitzvot*. At fifteen [one begins the study of] the Talmud. At eighteen [one is ready for] marriage. At twenty to pursue [a livelihood]. (Mishnah Avot 5:21)

Formal study begins with classical Jewish texts. Study of these texts precedes responsibility for performing the mitzvot. Learning prepares one to lead a moral and sacred life. Young children and elementary-age children learn a great deal from imitating and modeling behaviors expected of adults in a religious sense. They learn not just what these acts are and how to do them, but as they study and grow older they begin to understand their spiritual, historical, and cultural significance for the Jewish people and themselves. Jewish educator Steven M. Brown suggests that children are more likely to be developmentally ready to follow the positive commandments (e.g., observing Shabbat, holidays, and kashrut) before they are ready to follow the negative commandments (e.g., not stealing, not coveting). He explains that the negative commandments "often have much more philosophical, obscure, or even frightening reasoning behind them. Here, time must be taken for a child to understand what is involved and the reasons behind the forbidden action" (Brown 1993, 37). A deeper understanding and sense of self, community, and God come from study of Torah.

Many liberal synagogues have consecration and connect the entry into Jewish schooling with a Jewish holiday, making it a public ceremony. The Reform movement that began in the 1800s initiated the ceremony of consecration for children as they entered congregational "Sunday" or religious schooling. This ceremony is often connected to the holiday of Simchat Torah, the day of rejoicing with the Torah that usually occurs shortly after the beginning of the school year. On this holiday, both the ending and the beginning of the Torah are read. Children recite blessings such as the Shema, are blessed by a rabbi, and receive miniature Torahs or certificates in recognition of this milestone. Dancing, music, flag waving, unrolling the Torah are all for the purpose of celebrating the joy of Torah and study. A special *aliyah* (honor of being called up to the Torah) is reserved for children on this holiday alone. Being called up to the Torah is a reenactment of the Jews receiving the Torah from God on Sinai, at which children as well as adults were present. Even though these young children are not fully responsible for following the Torah until they reach bar or bat mitzvah age, they are to learn and uphold its teachings as a way of partaking of God's love.

A few synagogues hold consecration in connection with Hanukkah. Hanukkah is a festival of "rededication" of the Temple in Jerusalem. The word *Hanukkah* shares the same root as *hinuk,* meaning "education." Consecration becomes a time of dedicating oneself to God through study.

The first day of Jewish schooling in most places is welcoming, but not necessarily one so well framed with great symbolism and ritual. One tradition was to have children lick honey from a slate of Hebrew letters when they began Jewish learning. In this way the community expressed the hope that the words of Torah would be sweet in their mouths. Today there is a need for developing other rituals and ceremonies that would solidify the significance of the moment. The beginning of school often is a missed opportunity for connecting children and their families to the sacred act of Jewish learning.

The entrance into formal Jewish learning acknowledges the ability of even the youngest children to grasp the sounds, stories, symbols, values, wisdom, and worldview of Jewish texts and traditions. This life cycle stage focuses on cultural literacy, learning how to live within a Jewish framework. This is no simple challenge in an open society where so many options and choices are available. In an open postmodern culture, tradition is no longer learned through "osmosis" in the home or community; it must be intentionally taught. Furthermore, just knowing what to do is no longer sufficient, but the "why" behind customs, values, rituals, blessings needs to be answered. In these preschool and elementary school years, the immersion into the what and how of Jewish life is essential before children reach the adolescent years that come filled with questions about their own identity in particular and the world in general.

Entering into Responsibility: Bar and Bat Mitzvah

Bar and bat mitzvah literally mean "son and daughter of the commandment." The origin of bar/bat mitzvah is traced to the rabbinic quotation from Mishnah Avot 5:21 cited earlier: "At thirteen one takes on the responsibility of the mitzvot." Originally the domain of boys, the first recognized bat mitzvah was in 1922, when Judith Kaplan Eisenstein, the eldest of four daughters of Mordecai Kaplan, the founder of Reconstructionism, celebrated her bat mitzvah in a congregation. Today, even in Orthodox circles, most girls become bat mitzvah at age twelve or thirteen with some demonstration of Torah learning.

Even though a baby is brought into the covenant as a Jew at birth, bar/bat mitzvah represents the commitment of the young person to the covenant between God and the Jewish people. At this age, one is counted in the quorum of ten needed for communal worship, puts on tallit and tefillin (prayer shawl and phylacteries), and is called to the reading of the Torah. In affirming one's identity as a Jew and taking responsibility for one's relationship to God, the focus here is a connection to community and God.

A bar or bat mitzvah is a ceremony that embodies the transition from childhood to adulthood on multiple levels. Perhaps no greater reminder of thirteen as a time of transition are the physical changes that the adolescent is undergoing. Bodies begin to turn from looking and sounding like children into looking and sounding like adults. The body is a

visual reminder of the major changes the adolescent is undergoing intellectually, emotionally, socially, and spiritually. Even the word used to refer to the bar/bat mitzvah is
symbolic of the individual's change in status. When called to the Torah, the bar or bat
mitzvah is referred to as a *bachor* or *bachora,* literally, the "one who makes choices," rather
than using a term either for child or for adult. The bar or bat mitzvah is making choices
about his or her spiritual direction and connection to the Jewish people. The ceremony
signifies changes in relationships between the parents and the child and the child and the
Jewish community as a whole. Symbolic of the change from dependence to independence, parents traditionally recite a prayer stating that they are freed from the "punishment" of this child. Such an affirmation acknowledges the beginning of the young
person's independence and his or her ability to make moral choices.

Thirteen is the beginning of a transition into adulthood rather than an indicator
of one's full arrival into this stage. Other ages better represent a full attainment of, an
arrival at adulthood. Twenty is the biblical age to be counted in the census and to go to
war (Numbers 1:3) and in modern Israel, seventeen or eighteen is the age at which one
usually begins military service.

Bar/bat mitzvah preparation focuses on learning to read or chant in Hebrew a
selection from the Torah and/or haftarah reading (from Prophets) and prayers from the
service. Participation in religious schooling helps lay the foundation for this occasion.
Usually, the bar/bat mitzvah delivers a d'var Torah, an explanation and interpretation
of the textual readings. This task supports Piaget's theory of cognitive development.
The bar/bat mitzvah is leaving behind concrete thinking and entering the stage of
abstract thinking. From Fowler's perspective (Goodman, 2002), the bar/bat mitzvah is
challenged to make meaning of life's significant questions addressed in tradition's sacred
texts and to reflect upon the significance of his or her future responsibilities and status
as a Jewish adult. Bar/bat mitzvah is the beginning of the transition when the individual begins to seek a personal relationship to God. This transition is mirrored in the bar
or bat mitzvah making a public commitment to the Jewish community.

Much of the bar/bat mitzvah preparation also focuses on actions. Some b'nai mitzvah are required by their congregations to participate in tikkun olam or to engage in a
"mitzvah" project of a substantial nature. Some b'nai mitzvah choose to donate money
to a worthy cause. Many engage in community service projects. These actions stress the
social responsibility and moral consciousness of becoming a Jewish adult and underscore the Jewish understanding that the spiritual life is nurtured through moral action.

While bar/bat mitzvah generally builds on past knowledge and experiences, it challenges the individual to grow in new ways. For this reason, bar/bat mitzvah is better
understood as an expression of the transition into adulthood, the taking on of a lifetime
of responsibility, of study and mitzvot, rather than as a culmination of study. Still, too
many mistakenly view the bar/bat mitzvah as an ending, a graduation of sorts.

Erik Erikson's theory of psychosocial development highlights how this event is a
transition between two phases, the struggle between industry and inferiority typical of
elementary school-age children and the identity and identity confusion of adolescents.
In many ways, becoming bar/bat mitzvah demonstrates a child's industry in a Jewish
way through the mastery of liturgical skills in a public setting. Even more so, the
emphasis is on the tension between the onset of the new phase of identity and identity

confusion. The bar or bat mitzvah makes public "belief" statements about his or her commitment to God and loyalty to the Jewish people at the same time that the community expresses its desire for the young person in terms of how he or she should grow as a member of the Jewish community. The bar or bat mitzvah makes these testimonials as he or she leaves behind the certainty of parental lessons and enters what is often a confusing time of self-discovery and self-definition in the midst of peer pressure. The wisdom of having the bar/bat mitzvah at age twelve or thirteen rather than the middle or end of the transition into adulthood helps ground the individual's identity formation. The ceremony comes at a time before most adolescents leave the security and comfort of their community for entry into the larger world.

Parents, congregational leaders and members, educators, and clergy struggle with keeping the bar/bat mitzvah celebration appropriate socially, religiously, and economically. To put it in a Fowlerian framework, they struggle with the meanings, the values that emerge out of this life cycle function. Celebrations can be extravagant and inappropriate. Even tasteful celebrations are quite expensive. The social pressure on the bar/bat mitzvah and the parents to match, if not surpass, the ceremony and celebration of others can be strong. At ages twelve and thirteen the peer group is becoming increasingly important in a young person's life. The bar/bat mitzvah wants to fit in and be part of a social group, a dynamic that can add to the pressure on both child and parents. Children with different learning capabilities can struggle with being singled out for not performing on a level comparable to that of their peers. Despite these concerns, many parents and adolescents find this life cycle event to be a meaningful, often transformative experience.

At a time when hormones, emotions, intellectual or cognitive capacity, sense of self, and relationships with others are in a state of flux, this ritual models a "holding place" where emerging young adults can feel safe, competent, and valued while trying to figure out who they are. This life passage presents a rich opportunity to put these Jewish adolescents in contact with people who can be positive role models—teachers, clergy, community members, and even Jewish peers—at an age when they seek guidance beyond their parents. These life cycle events bring together the people who provided and will continue to provide support and guidance for many years to come.

Learning about Development from Jewish Life Cycle Events

This chapter focused on the Jewish celebrations connected to three life cycle events that serve as markers of different ages or stages for children and adolescents. Five important lessons emerge from examining these life cycle functions:

1. Developmental changes need to be acknowledged and celebrated; through acknowledgment and celebration, life cycle events can become spiritual and theologically centered occasions.
2. These life cycle events wisely come at the beginning of a transition rather than at the end, thereby presenting rich educational opportunities.

3. Because development represents change, it involves both gains and losses, resulting in a variety of feelings such as sadness, joy, grief, relief, and anticipation.
4. These life cycle events leave relics, reminders, and memories that influence the individual throughout his or her lifetime.
5. Individual development not only occurs in relationship to others and God in the context of community, but this development is informed and strengthened by this interaction.

ACKNOWLEDGING AND CELEBRATING

Being human involves spiritual, emotional, physical, and social growth. Children, adolescents, and adults move through life passages, from one stage to another, whether or not any type of secular or religious ceremony formally marks these periods in life. Judaism understands that the individual from birth is capable of living in a covenantal relationship with God. In Jewish life, learning is connected to spiritual growth both in terms of understanding God and increasing one's love of God. Judaism takes the ordinary moments of life and connects them with the sacred. Religious rituals that mark life transitions make clear statements about what is of value. In our world today, while growth and development are expected, the framework that helps provide a cosmic order, direction, purpose, and meaning to a person's life is not automatic. Without that framework, life can be void, vacuous, even self-destructive and lacking in hope.

The three life cycle events described in this chapter are markers of developmental change that point to the sacred nature of each developmental stage. Each of these changes—birth, beginning of Jewish study, and bar/bat mitzvah—is an occasion that conveys some of the core ideas and values of the Jewish people and their covenantal relationship to God. Each event acts out this relationship to God in highly symbolic ways. These rituals tell stories about the Jewish people. The brit milah and brit habat reenact the miracle of the world's creation and renew the covenant between God and Abraham. The giving of a name reflects back on the first naming in the Garden of Eden.

Ongoing Torah study continues the process of God's revelation to the Jewish people today. The Torah is the story of the relationship between God and the Jewish people. Learning Torah is a way of understanding and relating to God. It is a process not only of acquiring information but also of interpreting it. For children, reading their lives into Torah is a way of binding the history of the Jewish people with one's own personal story.

Engaging in tikkun olam, mitzvah projects, are ways of helping to bring about redemption. Living out Torah, not just studying Torah, is important. Saying blessings, leading a prayer service, reading Torah or haftarah, delivering a sermon in the context of a communal prayer service are ways of reliving the revelation of the Torah at Mount Sinai. Bar/bat mitzvah is an act of affirmation, a restatement of the words spoken by the people at Sinai upon the receiving of the Ten Commandments, "na'aseh v'neshmah" (we will do and we will hear). As our ancestors freely chose to follow God's ways, so too does the bar/bat mitzvah choose to take responsibility to live by God's commandments.

All three of these life cycle events use symbols and rituals to connect the celebrant to his or her family, the community, the Jewish people past, present, and future, and

God. The drama that the stories, rituals, and symbols create sets the child and adolescent in a spiritual direction that can influence the many years of each stage or phase of development. Spiritual life is understood not only as a life of belief, but also as a life of study, moral choices, and actions. It is expressed not solely as an individual but within a community.

The question should be raised of what is lost when these marker events are not recognized or celebrated: What is missing when a child is born, circumcised in a hospital, and given a name to put on a state birth certificate? Why should anyone need to make an occasion of it when a child begins his or her schooling, secular or religious? Why go to the fuss of celebrating a bar/bat mitzvah? Jewish children who reach the age of thirteen are considered to have become a bar/bat mitzvah regardless of whether they participated in a service.

Fowler's theory of faith development implies that all people are engaged in "faithing," the process of making meaning out of their lives, an active, not static process. Although faith is universalistic, Fowler advocates that individuals follow a particular path, especially one offered by a religious tradition, as way of embodying one's faith. Erikson would say that not having these events as part of one's personal history or story would affect one's identity. These marker events are an opportunity to connect growth and development, something common to all human beings, to the sacred, to the ways and values of a religious tradition. If this is not done, other meaning systems—secularism, narcissism, commercialism—take over or a sense of moral or spiritual emptiness can prevail. Celebrating these marker events concretizes the connection of a child to a tradition, a community, and God. They help young people face life's challenges, affirm their accomplishments, and provide opportunities to engage in life's significant questions.

MARKING THE BEGINNING OF A TRANSITION

All three ceremonies—brit milah or brit habat, starting Jewish schooling, and bar/bat mitzvah—are events that mark transitions. They are finite events for which the preparation and anticipation can be as significant as the event itself. They are launching pads for stages that last for several years. Developmental theories are often very good at explaining or characterizing a stage, but less complete or detailed in their handling of transitions. Transitions can be a time of great emotional, intellectual, social, and spiritual activity, an opportunity to gain new skills and knowledge, deepen relationships, cultivate identity, and take on new roles.

GAINS AND LOSSES, JOY AND SADNESS

Life cycle events draw attention to the fact that growth and change that are a result of development trigger many emotions for which those involved can benefit from guidance and support. Growth and change are both exciting and rewarding, frightening and sad at the same time. Development means finding new ways, reaching new understandings, or obtaining new responsibilities, but it also represents the loss of old ways, sometimes very comfortable and comforting ways of being and knowing. William Perry (1981), who theorizes about cognitive and ethical development, writes about the importance of grieving for the "lost" ways of knowing. Perry uses the metaphor of a bridge that is firmly anchored in the existing way of knowing and extends toward the new way of knowing, advocating that the learner be accompanied across the bridge by a teacher, counselor, clergy, parent, or other adult. Addressing these different feelings presents opportunities and possibilities for providing learning, support, and direction.

RELICS, REMINDERS, AND MEMORIES

The three life cycle marker events reviewed create holding times with highly symbolic actions that dramatize values, core narratives, expectations, and hope. These events leave behind relics, reminders, and memories in the form of names, ritual objects, gifts, family stories, memories, photographs that continue to inform the phase of development. Many of these items stay with the person throughout his or her lifetime. They help the individual remember, reflect, and communicate the experience to others. These items help carry the stories throughout a person's life journey.

THE ROLE OF COMMUNITY

The life cycle is not just about an individual in isolation. Rather, it is about an individual embedded within a family, community, and society. While Erikson lays out the life cycle as if it were a linear progression by an individual, the image that comes from Jewish experience is that of a circle with multiple intersections with other people's lives. Some developmentalists provide an egocentric focus that is often excessively individualistic, making it seem as if the child or adolescent is developing on his or her own. Other theorists give more emphasis to the role and significance of parents, teachers, rabbis, peers, friends, and community members that affect the development of an individual.

These developmental marker events remind us that others affect and are affected by these changes in the life of a child or adolescent. A brit milah or brit habat is as much about the person being celebrated, the baby, as it is about his or her parents' and other relatives' life cycles. Becoming a parent or grandparent is a major transition in one's life. The same is true when a child starts school or becomes a bar/bat mitzvah. Strassfeld (2002) explains this connection not just between child and parent, but in many ways, to all the generations that proceed and follow one:

> For parents, the bar/bat mitzvah is a rite of passage that marks this transition in the life of their child. They can take pride in the accomplishment of their child learning what they needed for the ritual. They can feel bittersweet about reaching this stage in their child's life. And they can realize that their

child is a marker of their own life. Thus the bar/bat mitzvah serves as a
reminder of their own passing years. As on all such family occasions, there is
a connection to the past and to the future. There is often the remembrance
of past bar/bat mitzvahs. There is a collection of family members who have
died, but whose presence is felt on this occasion. There is recognition of the
new generation as the future of the family with the hopes and concerns that
that raises. (348)

What seems to be individual experience turns out to mark us as part of a larger community.

All the life cycle events are essentially about *inclusion*—about welcoming the individual into the Jewish community, about becoming a more fully participating and
active member of Klal Yisrael, all of Israel, about linking us spiritually to both past and
future generations of Jews. Each step of the life cycle, and the meaningfulness it evokes,
not only preserves Jewish tradition but also brings the individual closer into the community, enabling her or him to experience the riches thereof, and so to move forward
spiritually within that community.

Being a witness at or participant in these life cycle events in Judaism is considered
to be fulfilling a commandment—the responsibility to help raise the child, to influence
his or her spiritual development; the child's connection to God falls not just only on the
parents but on the entire community.

Implications for Religious Leaders

Judaism, like other religious traditions, has many life cycle events that are markers of
transition. They are times of developmental change spiritually, emotionally, socially,
intellectually, and physically. These life cycle events affect not just the individual who is
passing through this time but also the individual's family and community. They are
highly charged moments of uncertainty and seeking, powerful times with potential for
learning and change. Religious tradition through ritual and study can serve as a bridge
and a guide to deepen the individual's connection to God and sense of spirituality.

As Fowler tells us, people are constantly making meaning out of their lives. Development concerns the fundamental qualitative changes in how meaning is made. As
spiritual leaders, educators, clergy, counselors, mentors, and role models, we need to
enter into that conversation, to touch people's lives in significant ways. If not, our
silence may send the message that religion has nothing to say about human growth and
development. Life cycle events are times in people's lives when they tend to be open to
spiritual searching and learning as children, adolescents, and adults. Our religious traditions, texts, prayers, and ceremonies offer glimpses into how these life cycle stages can
be fulfilling and meaningful.

We have much to offer children and adolescents at a time when they are open to
hearing, filled with questions, searching for answers, and seeking joy. We need to open
the gates of understanding, exploring the background and significance of different customs, engaging them in taking responsibility in ways that merge tradition and their

personal lives for the celebration of these occasions. If we capture their imaginations at these times of change, we have a better chance of helping them fill out each stage by finding and experiencing the holy, the sacred in the day-to-day, year-to-year flow of life. Parents, educators, and clergy have the opportunity to make a difference. As we connect or reconnect children, adolescents, and adults spiritually, we can guide them on the path of working together as God's partners in filling out each stage, of reaching toward truth and understanding as one humanity.

Note

I am grateful to Sandy Sasso for her insight that birth ceremonies, entrance into Torah study, and participation in tikkun olam reflect the themes of creation, revelation, and redemption, respectively, and for other contributions throughout this chapter.

References

Brown, Steven M. 1993. Parents as partners with God: Parenting young children. In *Celebration and renewal: Rites of passage in Judaism*, edited by Rela M. Geffen, 32–52. Philadelphia: Jewish Publication Society.

Diamant, Anita. 2000. *The new Jewish baby book. Names, ceremonies, customs: A guide for today's families*. Woodstock, Vt.: Jewish Lights.

Erikson, Erik. 1980. *Identity and the life cycle*. New York: Norton.

Fowler, James W. 1981. *Stages of faith: The psychology of human development and the quest for meaning*. San Francisco: Harper and Row.

Fuchs-Kreimer, Nancy. 1998. *Parenting as a spiritual journey: Deepening ordinary and extraordinary events into sacred occasions*. Woodstock, Vt.: Jewish Lights.

Geffen, Rela M. 1993. *Celebration and renewal: Rites of passage in Judaism*. Philadelphia: Jewish Publication Society.

Goodman, Roberta Louis. 2002. Nurturing a relationship to God and spiritual growth: A developmental approach. In *Teaching about God and spirituality*, edited by Roberta Louis Goodman and Sherry Blumberg. Denver, Colo.: ARE.

National Jewish Population Study 2000/2001. 2003. *A summary of findings from the US National Jewish Population Survey*. New York: United Jewish Communities.

Novak, David. 1993. Be fruitful and multiply: Issues relating to birth in Judaism. In *Celebration and renewal: Rites of passage in Judaism*, edited by Rela M. Geffen, 12–31. Philadelphia: Jewish Publication Society.

Piaget, Jean. 1967. *Six psychological studies*. New York: Vintage.

Salkin, Jeffrey K. 1998. *For kids. Putting God on your guest list: How to reclaim the spiritual meaning of your child's bar or bat mitzvah*. Woodstock, Vt.: Jewish Lights.

Strassfeld, Michael. 2002. *A book of life: Embracing Judaism as a spiritual practice*. New York: Schocken.

CHAPTER 13

Educating the Warrior: A Tibetan Buddhist Approach to Spiritual Growth

Richard C. Brown

THE EDUCATION OF THE WARRIOR

That mind of fearfulness
Should be put in the cradle of loving-kindness.
And suckled with the profound and brilliant milk
of eternal doubtlessness.
In the cool shade of fearlessness,
Fan it with the fan of joy and happiness.

When it grows older,
With various displays of phenomena,
Lead it to the self-existing playground.
When it grows older still,
In order to promote the primordial confidence,
Lead it to the archery range of the warriors.
When it grows older still,
To awaken primordial self-nature,
Let it see the society of men
Which possesses beauty and dignity.
Then the fearful mind
Can change into the warrior's mind,
And that eternally youthful confidence
Can expand into space without beginning or end.
At that point it sees the Great Eastern Sun.

—Chogyam Trungpa, Rinpoche[1]

This chapter will explore the rites of passage and stages of spiritual development for children and adolescents in Shambhala Buddhism primarily through an examination of the preceding text (Trungpa 1984, 89). Traditionally, Tibetan Buddhism has not considered notions of child and adolescent development. Only after the emergence of this text in the West did Jeremy Hayward (1981) and David Rome (1991), two senior students of Chogyam Trungpa's, suggest correlations with developmental stages. This examination extends their pioneering work.

Having arrived in England in 1963, Chogyam Trungpa was among the first and most successful lamas to establish Tibetan Buddhism in the West. In the late 1970s in North America, he also revived the ancient Tibetan lineage of Shambhala, teachings he saw as essential for the secular, nonmonastic Western culture. Thereafter, a rich artistic and educational culture flourished within the Shambhala communities of Europe and North America. Starting before his death in 1987, the Shambhala and Buddhist teachings have gradually merged. Now, under the leadership of Trungpa's son, Sakyong Mipham, the synthesis is known as Shambhala Buddhism. This chapter draws from their work as well as the perspectives of Tai Situpa, a prominent lama who is their contemporary.

Essential Shambhala Buddhist Teachings Related to Spiritual Development

BASIC GOODNESS AND EGO DEVELOPMENT

Fundamental to understanding spiritual development in the Shambhala Buddhist tradition is the notion of basic goodness, which is akin to the idea of buddha-nature, or intrinsic enlightenment. "Buddha-nature is not a seed that has to grow; it is already the flower. Beings are already Buddha; in reality there is nothing to be attained" (Thayer-Bacon 2003, 33). The essence of basic goodness is that all beings are fundamentally whole, healthy, and awake. It is a primordial goodness, the very nature of beings before any conditions arise. Even the confusions or disabilities that do arise are ultimately experiential aspects of interconnectedness, completeness. "It is not just an arbitrary idea that the world is good, but it is good because we can *experience* its goodness. We can experience our world as healthy and straightforward, direct and real, because our basic nature is to go along with the goodness of situations" (Trungpa 1988, 31).

However, one danger of exclusively holding the view of basic goodness is that one may dwell in a blissful "all is good" mentality. Adolescents, for instance, may seek euphoric states of mind in an effort to bypass irritating and confusing everyday realities. Adults trapped in this view may strive to preserve children in a condition of primordial oneness, despite the natural development of a personal ego.

Along with the primordial perfection of basic goodness, children and adolescents grow and develop within the imperfect, conditioned realities of the world. This means that within an ultimate perspective of basic goodness, there is a relative reality of stages of development. The relationship between the two is essential in Tibetan Buddhism. "For roughly twenty years, a person's outlook is not only formed but deeply rooted by experiences. Those experiences come out of the environment" (Situpa 1992, 38). To integrate those conditioned realities into one's individual manifestation of basic goodness, a path of spiritual development is necessary. "In . . . each step of life one has to cross a threshold. If there is not healthy growth and development, these stages become disordered, and a person ends up pretending he has grown into the next stage when he has not . . . he will eventually have to face that reality. Usually people are not willing to face it, and because of this all kinds of problems come into their lives. Recognizing and acknowledging where one is and working with whatever situation life presents—accepting it just as it is—is an important step toward mental and spiritual maturity" (61).

Ambitious notions of spiritual development can preoccupy adults who wish only the best for their children. One danger of exclusive preoccupation with the relative path of stage development is that one might ignore basic goodness. The tendency to propel the young into stages of development they aren't ready for can obscure their daily spiritual manifestations. This preoccupation could also inhibit establishing stability within developmental stages.

The challenge becomes to appreciate the goodness of children and adolescents when they are resting within a stage or even regressing. "Everyone has the potential for achieving all the possibilities of the perfect human being. Through the growth process a person develops or liberates that potential, just like a seed that germinates. If a person does not grow that potential becomes distorted or wasted" (Situpa 1992, 60).

Spiritual development from this perspective of the union of relative stages and ultimate goodness is not a linear process. The underlying dynamics and daily realities of this unfolding are in practice rhythmic, cyclical, and relatively unpredictable. Shambhala Buddhists aren't only focused on the goal of spiritual awakening; the journey itself is also the goal. The practice is to recognize and cultivate both basic goodness and the unfolding stages of innate brilliance from birth onward.

INDIVIDUAL IDENTITY AND SOCIAL CONTEXT

As the child matures, he or she adjusts in varying degrees to the relative experiences within the context of the domestic culture. This adjustment results in the formation of individual identity, ego. The emerging experience of a separate self, or ego, is seen from an ultimate perspective in Buddhism as an artifice. Independent identity is also a relative truth, however: the reality of human development. Relative ego and ultimate non-ego coexist in this view.

Each culture highlights and reinforces certain attributes of the child's emerging experience and identity while negatively reinforcing others. As will be explored here, the culture and practices of Shambhala Buddhism tend to soften ego stage development. By relating compassionately, yet directly, ordinary experiences become supple and workable for the young person, as well as somewhat more highlighted. Individual identity experienced in this interplay allows for freedom within limitation—ordinary yet boundless manifestation.

RELATIONSHIP

On the relative level, individual spiritual development of the young happens in relationship, in society, and not in isolation. As shall be seen in Chogyam Trungpa's "The

Education of the Warrior," each stage is described in a social and cultural context—first within the family, then ever more broadly in the world. When spiritual development of the individual is seen as inseparable from the community and the environment, there is less anxiety-producing focus on the individual developing self; there is less of an individual "problem mentality." Traditionally, only after a certain level of maturity is reached (age eight in Tibetan Buddhism) does individual spiritual development become important, but never to the exclusion of the social matrix.

One important dimension of this communal journey of spiritual development is that leadership or guidance by the contemplative elder beneficially influences the young person's journey. The elders have experience and understanding of the spirituality, culture, and society in which the young are being raised. Another related dimension to understanding spiritual development from the point of view of this text is that spiritual unfolding applies to both the child and the adult. Such mutual development amplifies the interdependent nature of spiritual paths in Shambhala Buddhism. Even though there are clear characteristics in each unfolding stage experience of the child and adolescent, the underlying dynamics of spiritual development are continuing and common to all, including adults. When development is seen as interdependent, then social and spiritual bonds between the young and old are strengthened.

The success of this interdependent approach requires that the adults in the society practice basic goodness nonconceptually. The practices of Buddhist mindfulness awareness in meditation and in daily life involve noticing, letting go of conceptual fixations, and opening to the fullness and richness of immediate experience. This entails both humbly embracing and releasing conceptions of right and wrong. This approach does not reject thought and concept per se, but they are to be experienced within the context of nonattachment.

From the ultimate perspective one can be fully awakened and pass through the stages of spiritual journey within the context of any social or environmental conditions. This explains how it has been possible for ordinary beings to have great spiritual achievement, when their upbringings, circumstances, and surroundings have seemed so alien to enlightened development. This perspective can be very liberating, because it means that the young do not need to have perfect developmental conditions, including enlightened elders, to experience awakening or to journey to further awakening.

Rites of Passage through the Lens of "The Education of the Warrior"

Within Shambhala culture are ever-evolving programs and rites for children and adolescents. The "Education of the Warrior" text has served as the foundation and inspiration for them. We will examine the text in sections corresponding to the stages of development and associated rites.

INFANCY AND TODDLERHOOD

That mind of fearfulness
Should be put in the cradle of loving-kindness.

This first section corresponds to the stage of the infant and suggests how adults can nurture spiritual development. "The early part of life is the most important for forming attitudes and responses . . . Confusion and emotional or physical difficulties in the life of a pregnant woman will have an effect on the child she is carrying" (Situpa 1992, 38). For this reason, despite the demands of child rearing, Chogyam Trungpa emphasized that it was of the utmost importance for parents to continue their meditation practice to cultivate a peaceful and synchronized mind and body.

It may seem odd that the state of mind of the infant is called "fearful." "When we talk about beginning with a state of 'fearfulness,' this is not a statement of condemnation. Fear is the sense of challenge . . . When we are working with children—or with others in general—both fear and fearlessness are always present. There will be times when a child is not just opening like little petals in the sun. Fear manifests as resistance, doubt, and confusion. It is important to respect those feelings, and not just label them as bad. Doubt and fear are the mirror image of inquisitiveness and curiosity, and the stepping-stone to growth" (Rome 1991).

In Shambhala Buddhism, fear is related to insecurity and estrangement. Whenever there is any experience of an alien, dangerous "other," anxiety arises. The birth process or the separation of the infant from primary nurturing contexts produces a fearful mind. From this point of view, no matter how carefully prepared, any separation experience will always produce some fear. Since Shambhala Buddhism acknowledges fearfulness as part of the spiritual journey, there is not excessive concern about protecting the infant or anyone from fearful situations.

The cultivation of fearlessness comes not by suppressing fear, but by developing awareness of its underlying energy. Through meditation adults learn not to react impulsively to their own fears. When emotions arise, one notices them, lets them go, and returns one's attention to the breath. The adult who becomes familiar with fear and practices fearlessness will tend not to react by excessively trying to eliminate, distract, manage, or ignore the infant's fear. Adults in the community practice responding fearlessly to the immediate needs of the situation itself, and not to fear. By not complicating their own or children's anxieties, those anxieties are tempered, and an atmosphere of fearlessness and confidence arises. Otherwise, the young may sense additional anxiety from the adult and become even more afraid. In time children may come to associate their experience of fear with an expanded, environmental anxiety.

The adult at this stage practices both fearlessness and loving-kindness. His or her role is to create a loving, womb-like, yet spacious, environment for the infant that is secure, nurturing, and sympathetic. For the child to thrive in "the cradle of loving-kindness," emerging energies, whether fearful or not, should be met fully and lovingly. "We're talking about an atmosphere in which we don't reject. It refers to loving kindness that isn't withheld as a punishment" (Hayward 1981). Unconditional loving-kindness is traditionally represented in Buddhism by the image of the mother: complete devotion and selflessness in the practice of loving-kindness and compassion to all beings. From the perspective of basic goodness the adult is not trapped in the duality of "good and bad" childhood behavior. The adult offers loving-kindness and respect to the infant's fearfulness. This section of Chogyam Trungpa's text highlights the ongoing, delicate interplay in development between the challenge of fearfulness and the nurturing of loving-kindness.

And suckled with the profound and brilliant milk
of eternal doubtlessness.

The offering of "profound and brilliant milk" suggests the nature of spiritual nourishment. "The early environment should be nurturing and feminine, but even at this stage there is a definite reality principle operating—we are not just providing a safe cocoon. The milk is nourishing . . . at the level of development he or she is at—but it is also a profound and brilliant milk. It is *real* milk, milk that nurtures real growth and change. There is a quality of dignity that exists in the parent or teacher, and the whole environment. As with birth itself, one enters a world of stimulus, of challenge" (Rome 1991).

"When we present [milk] to children, we present it with a sense of doubtlessness . . . We take the attitude as teacher or parent that we do have something to teach; we do have a heritage or a tradition . . . We can bring up children within the context of . . . thousands of years of tradition . . . We don't just invent [tradition] on the spot and make up anything that seems like it will work to get out of the tight corner that we happened to have gotten in at the moment" (Hayward 1981).

The doubtless manner in which one presents and manifests sacred world and tradition to the young could be quite ordinary. Adults simply live and present their world and tradition in a very straightforward, everyday manner. One doesn't need to force-feed the "milk" or fortify it with extra vitamins. If children don't take the "milk," the adults are not insulted or defeated. Indeed, from the ultimate perspective the whole environment is nourishing. But the "milk" is still regarded as the basic food, the traditional food, so adults don't abandon it. They keep gently offering and including it in the domestic culture.

Authority for the Shambhala Buddhist adult is based on personal, direct experience of his or her heritage, not on philosophies or credentials. The basis of the adult's engaged leadership is awareness of each momentary encounter of present reality in the context of the tradition and the adult's particular upbringing. This interaction between past experience and present moment provides a lively, connective experience of adult authority, one that distinguishes it from authoritarianism.

In the cool shade of fearlessness,
Fan it with the fan of joy and happiness.

This stage corresponds to the older infant or toddler. "Here we have moved from the cradle to the cool shade. The child is no longer in the nursery, but outdoors, presumably in the garden, still within the family compound" (Rome 1991). The attentive spaciousness and gentle activity implicit in the images of the cool shade and fanning are fundamental to nurturing spiritual development. "The image of fanning is two-sided; on one hand it is comforting, but it also provides a gentle stimulus. Rather than introducing a foreign element, you are taking the air that is already there and moving it. You are making what is already there more vivid, bringing it to the attention of the child. [Chogyam Trungpa] talked about creating an atmosphere of delight, which allows a child to expand and experience more" (Rome 1991).

The "fan of joy and happiness" indicates that adult engagement in the world of the very young child could be a fundamentally joyful experience of the basic goodness of life. "When the adult is aware of the inherent space within herself, the environment, and the child, then the atmosphere of delight can be genuinely cultivated . . . 'The cool shade' refers to that, at some point we begin to not smother the potential warrior with our love. In other words, we give it some space, as we say. They have the opportunity to open up themselves" (Hayward 1981).

Buddhism does not define joyfulness narrowly, however. "The fundamental experience of joy or delight does not necessarily manifest with a smooth experience of path. It could also manifest with the experience of your hatred, jealousy, passion, aggression or pride for that matter" (Ponlop 2002, 41). If joy is valued and suffering rejected, then whenever misery arises, one might conclude that there's a fundamental problem in one's life, family, or spiritual path. The full range of aware emotional experiences represents valued features of spiritual life, and it is all joyful.

The adult appreciates sacredness in whatever arises in youthful experiences but does not indulge it. The same attitude of nonattachment applies to adult reactions to pleasant experiences or culturally valued behaviors. By excessively isolating and praising natural spiritual experiences such as awe, the adult may unintentionally promote self-consciousness and, thereby, feelings of separation and fear in the child.

Within the stable and fearless presence of the aware adult, the child can feel a spacious sense of well-being, a delightful ordinariness about everyday experiences. As the child grows older, spiritual experiences, whether fearful or magnificent, become just ordinary life. The child learns to work directly and skillfully within fearful and joyful situations. In this way, fearfulness begins to transform into fearlessness, and ecstasy into equanimity.

The Children's Welcoming Ceremony in the Shambhala Buddhist tradition introduces the infant or young child to the community. It is also a way of reminding parents about ways of fostering spiritual development. During one part of the ceremony the parent holds the young child, introduces her or him to the community, and describes the child in a word or two—a practice that has the effect of revealing one's ideas about one's child. Parent and child later pass before a vertical mirror over which water is sprinkled. While they gaze together into the blurred image of themselves, the preceptor gives a blessing.

The preceptor may make a brief presentation to the parents such as the following: "This a Shambhala ceremony, which means we are acknowledging the basic goodness of our children and of ourselves as parents. The Shambhala tradition speaks of the natural magic of the world, how there is a way in which the elemental qualities of the world speak to us directly, nonconceptually. Very often in our daily lives, we cannot actually see this quality. We are too busy with things—preparing breakfast, doing the laundry, and taking out the trash. But our children see this magic very naturally and have a sense of wonder and discovery that awakens us. That is why we have the ceremony of looking into the mirror" (Simmer-Brown 2000).

At the end of the ceremony everyone recites the following: "We aspire to raise our children in an environment of compassion, fearlessness, and good humor, in which they can grow into full human beings who walk through this world with dignity and care for others with joy and loving-kindness."

CHILDHOOD AND PREADOLESCENCE

When it grows older,
With various displays of phenomena,
Lead it to the self-existing playground.

This stage begins at the age of the older toddler and continues until about age eight. At this stage the adult metaphorically leads the child out of the garden and shows her the world outside. Having been nurtured but not overfed, having been protected but not smothered, the child begins to manifest and extend naturally. The "various displays of phenomena" that emerge both from the child and the expanding perceived world are an indication of that natural outward movement. Thus, the child should be in active contact with the sacred environment. "Everything that is in the outer physical environment can affect what is going on in the internal physical environment" (Situpa 1992, 22).

"Throughout this journey a progression of different environments is presented to the warrior. This is a central idea of the educational process—the appropriate environment is introduced at the appropriate time. [Chogyam Trungpa] placed great emphasis on creating appropriate, uplifted environments for activities to occur within" (Rome 1991). The environment of the "playground" is not necessarily completely safe. Naturally, there is a strong sense of protection and guidance, but adults allow children to explore in creative interaction with the environment and each other. There might be small things to climb on, natural conditions that might have a small risk, or the ordinary emotional encounters of childhood.

This continuation of the practice of fearlessness in spiritual development suggests that adults should not particularly hide self-existing phenomena from children. Chogyam Trungpa emphasized in his teachings not to conceal the truth from children or they would lose fundamental trust in adults. Obviously, this does not mean that one should go out of one's way to expose young children to the suffering of the "real" world. But occasionally bits of the "real" world naturally appear in the "playground." A cat may be seen killing a bird; two parents may be heard shouting at each other; or a police siren may be heard. The adult responds to such situations straightforwardly and with an open heart.

The environment provided for the spiritual unfolding of children at this age is not artificially "spiritual." Offering a self-existing playground at their earliest age of exploration affirms the sacredness of the ordinary world. At the same time that the playground is self-existing, it is ideally designed for young children with adults enhancing or enriching the playground in a way that reflects the best of their culture. "There is still some sense of a prepared environment. But this is a self-existing playground, not an artificial one full of plastic toys" (Rome 1991). The playground is further transformed when it is revered, uplifted, and cared for by the community, including children. This is how the ordinary becomes more overtly sacred.

Affirming the child's nonconceptual sensory experiences of their world is basic to spiritual development at all stages in Shambhala Buddhism. "We simply show the child this, this, this, and this. We don't show it this is good, this is not so good, this is bad, etc. We let the child explore . . . its senses, its world, the richness, the qualities, the dangerous qualities, the qualities that seem to be enjoyable, the qualities that seem to be the cause of fear. All of the qualities of the phenomenological world we show without judging, without providing all kinds of little bits and pieces of opinion about everything" (Hayward 1981).

A central purpose of the rite of passage for the eight-year-old in this tradition is to introduce the child to the culture and contemplative practices of the adult Shambhala Buddhist society. Whether he or she chooses to continue with any of those arts is completely up to the child. Because of the inherent power and meaningfulness in the rite, many non-Buddhist children regularly participate without any intention of entering the community afterward.

During weekly classes leading up to the ceremony, children sing songs, learn calligraphy, compose poetry, practice kyudo (zen archery), learn ikebana (flower arranging), and practice the fundamentals of marching drill. Children are also taught simple forms of meditation. (Eight years is the traditional age in Tibet when children could enter the monastery.) All the classes are led by accomplished adults and young people in the community.

At one point in the actual rite of passage ceremony, each child, accompanied by her parents, offers to the shrine a symbolic possession from her childhood, such as a treasured stuffed animal. Then, in a poignant moment of symbolic separation within the family, the child and parents bow to each other before the assembly and separately take their seats with their peers.

Toward the end of the ceremony adolescents from the community perform dances of the elements (earth, water, fire, wind, and space), affirming direct sensory experience. First, each element dances alone, celebrating its unique qualities while interacting playfully and meaningfully with the eight-year-old spectators. At the end, the elements dance together, manifesting their spontaneous relational dynamics.

The eight-year-olds take the following vow near the end of the ceremony: "As a warrior I will be kind to myself. As a warrior I will be kind to others. As a warrior I will be kind to the world. The warrior's way is fearless and gentle. Today the seed of warriorship has been planted in me. Ki Ki! So So! [a Tibetan warriors' cry]."

When it grows older still,
In order to promote the primordial confidence,
Lead it to the archery range of the warriors.

This stage spans roughly age eight to preadolescence. "This is a big step, an abrupt change in the environment, which is no longer so safe. It is still not at the level of being fully on one's own in the world—there is still a quality of undergoing training . . . and it involves considerable responsibility" (Rome 1991). The nature of discipline in this approach derives from the root meaning of the word *disciple*, "follower." The adolescent follows the forms of discipline because there is trust, not just in the adults and the older adolescents who are leading, but also in the whole culture. "One develops the correct way of handling oneself in sports, in archery, or horsemanship. A teenager could develop an immense sense of inheritance, realizing that discipline is not being imposed on him but that he is actually beginning to receive and take possession of the inheritance of his ancestors" (Dorje 1979).

Trungpa's phrase "archery range of the warriors" illustrates an important dimension of spiritual education of this stage. At the conclusion of the rite for eight-year-olds, children are presented with a gift from their parents. Sometimes this is a "weapon," such as a pocketknife or a calligraphy brush. The confidence the parents have in the child and a sense of sacredness and power are transmitted. Such a gift denotes the challenge of the next stage of development they are entering, namely, the archery range. The challenge is to work with fear and fearlessness—the ground for the union of relative and ultimate. "Weapon is simply the analogy [of] whatever embodies the power and dignity of being fully human. So in some traditions, it is, indeed, an actual weapon. For example, the samurai sword always right up until World War II, was *the* embodiment of the power and dignity of being fully human . . . In some traditions, it could be the pen or the calligraphy brush, the coat of arms, or the plowshare. It always has some sharp, cutting quality and therefore, in some sense, some weaponlike quality. Not a weapon with which to destroy others at all, but the sense of weapon here is that there is no hesitation in fully living in the world. It represents some sense of mastery" (Hayward 1981).

"It is very important at this point for the mentors to present the students with that challenge and to allow them the space to take real risks. Only in this way can the student discover genuine confidence. The image of the archery range also tells us that learning only takes place through doing, rather than just receiving instructions" (Rome 1991). Because preadolescents have naturally strong affiliations with peers, the "archery ranges" for children at this stage use peer grouping and are staffed largely by older adolescents and young adults. These young leaders are generally well experienced in the disciplines and act in a kind, empathetic, and respectful manner.

The youth may or may not be attracted to any of the particular disciplines that have been presented to them up to at that point. However, there is encouragement and sometimes insistence by the parents for them to experience those practices of the society. Because this "leading" by adults is related to the "doubtlessness" discussed earlier and is not based on adult ego, the young adolescent is likely to follow the lead of the adult—but not always. When our own children were at this stage we suggested, then insisted, that they attend Sun Camp in the Colorado Rockies with the understanding that after the one-week program, they'd never have to go back if they didn't like it. Once there, they instantly loved the camp, because of the camaraderie, spaciousness, and the gentle discipline of the older adolescent and young adult leaders. They have returned every year since with enormous enthusiasm.

ADOLESCENCE

When it grows older still,
To awaken primordial self-nature,
Let it see the society of men
Which possesses beauty and dignity.

"This is the stage of socialization, of finding and entering into a relationship with society . . . The suggestion here is that one's identity isn't fully realized until one is in mature relationship with others, able to express and contribute one's unique warriorship for the benefit of all. There is a movement from dependence to independence to social *inter*-dependence. This is similar to the old-fashioned idea of 'becoming a useful member of society' " (Rome 1991).

"At this point then we introduce them to the entire heritage of the world of men and women, and the best of that world that possesses beauty and dignity . . . In some ways, we expect the teacher and the parent to try and embody that to whatever extent they can . . . Wisdom, from this point of view, comes about through embodying one's culture, one's tradition" (Hayward 1981).

The Shambhala Buddhist notion of enlightened society into which the adolescent is introduced is not some utopian ideal. "We are saying that a society of such caliber, so to speak, is here, right here. You are the enlightened society, every one of you, with no mistakes, of course. If there were a mistake, you wouldn't be here" (Trungpa 1978). This convergent view of relative and ultimate society extends into the past, into one's upbringing. In order to fully embrace enlightened society, Chogyam Trungpa encouraged his students to accept their own social cultural upbringings, no matter how confused or harmful they may have been. By discovering the essential compassionate and uplifted intentions in how one was raised, one can transform and extend one's heritage.

The final rite of passage for the young person in the Shambhala Buddhist community is the Rite of Warriorship for sixteen-year-olds. This secret rite takes place over several days in a natural, often mountainous setting. It involves meditation, group rituals, and a challenging period of time alone: it is a profound, sacred experience of transforming fear into fearlessness.

Following this rite there are often informal opportunities for interconnections between young adults and the adult Shambhala Buddhist society through apprenticeships and community engagement. These may be explicitly within the Shambhala Buddhist community, such as working with a painter, an archer, or a flower arranger, or they could be in the larger world..

FRUITION

Then the fearful mind
Can change into the warrior's mind,
And that eternally youthful confidence

Can expand into space without beginning or end.
At that point it sees the Great Eastern Sun.

The warrior's mind or warriorship in the Shambhala Buddhist tradition refers to the awake, courageous, and gentle dignity of being fully human in the world. Awake mind is both an inherent quality and a developmental process. "That which is most essential about us as human beings is already in us. The challenge, or process, is one of waking up to that, or of recognizing that that in itself is already awake" (Rome 1991). The purpose of awakening is to become fully oneself and also to be of benefit to others. "Warrior is the term that we use to represent someone who lives fully in the world . . . The warrior's mind appreciates and understands where it came from and, therefore, where others come from. There is always the feeling of connection with one's origin in basic goodness and the tendency toward cowardice and to close up . . . The warrior still has the sense of tender heart that can touch others, and help others to see their own tenderness, their own possibility of growing" (Hayward 1981). At this stage the warrior is engaged in enlightened society, in which "no human being is a lost cause. We don't feel we have to put a lid on anyone or anything. We are always willing to give things a chance to flower" (Trungpa 1988, 58).

The warrior fully participates in and serves a world that extends beyond our ordinarily perceived world into ultimate space. Awakened mind, beyond individual mind at this unconditional level of confidence, is known as the Great Eastern Sun, a central symbol in the vision of enlightened society. "The Great Eastern Sun is a rising sun rather than a setting sun, so it represents that dawning or awakening of human dignity" (Trungpa 1988, 54). "The warrior who confronts his existence and fear produces a powerful form of dignity—*wangthang,* a Tibetan term that literally means 'field of power' . . . Such a feeling of power provides profound confidence that radiates and puts us in direct contact with reality. It is life force manifested at its peak" (Midal 2004, 215). "The confidence which is innate, but which in the beginning was characterized as the mind of fearfulness, has woken up, matured, to manifest as full-fledged confidence. It is not the end of the journey. The warrior is now ready to expand, to participate in life as a full human being" (Rome 1991).

Up to this point in the series of rites we have briefly examined, no formal religious commitment to Shambhala Buddhism has been made. Within the religious path of Shambhala Buddhism, however, are numerous formal levels of spiritual practice, such as Shambhala Training and Warrior's Assembly; and vows, such as Refuge, Bodhisattva, and Vajrayana vows. One can also continue nonreligious practices within the community, such as archery or flower arranging.

In Shambhala Buddhism, the ground of young people's spiritual nature is never lost. Since it is innate, one can awaken to it at any time, age, or circumstance to glimpse the sacred wholeness of life. One experiences spirituality differently throughout the stages of one's life and also from moment to moment. Certainly this experience of sacredness can be covered over or forgotten for many reasons. But spirituality is not some *thing* to be grasped or realized once and for all. As one grows and takes on further dimensions of maturity, there are more possible obscurations and at the same time more spiritual connections to be explored. As the context of one's identity becomes more complex, so too do the links to unconditioned goodness. As young persons develop and come to see the extent of their interdependence, they can understand that spiritual development is not solely an individual experience. From the view of the union of relative stages and ultimate goodness, beings are simultaneously fully complete and individually limited— still on the path to further spiritual awakening. When adults are able meet the young where they actually are, then the magic of the present moment dances with the child, and development unfolds naturally and unexpectedly.

Note

1. From *Shambhala: The Sacred Path of the Warrior* by Chogyam Trungpa, copyright 1984. Reprinted by arrangement with Shambhala Publications, Inc., Boston, www.shambhala.com.

References

Dorje, Loppon Lodro. 1979. Education, society, and Shambhala vision. *Vajradhatu* (February/March).

Hayward, Jeremy. 1981. The family in the Shambhala tradition. Talk for the Foundation Class on the Family, January 21, Boulder, Colo.

Midal, Fabrice. 2004. *Chogyam Trungpa: His life and vision*. Boston: Shambhala.

Ponlop, The Dzogchen. 2002. *Penetrating wisdom: The aspiration of samantabhadra*. Vancouver: Siddhi Publications.

Rome, David. 1991. Education of the warrior. *Banner* (April).

Simmer-Brown, Judith. 2000. Children's welcoming ceremony remarks. Talk for the children's welcoming ceremony. Boulder Shambhala Center.

Situpa, Kenchen Tai. 1992. *Relative world, ultimate mind*. Boston: Shambhala.

Thayer-Bacon, Barbara J. 2003. Buddhism as an example of a holistic, relational epistemology. *Encounter* 16 (3):27–38.

Trungpa, Chogyam. 1978. Education for an enlightened society. Talk delivered at Naropa Institute, Boulder, Colo.

———. 1988. *Shambhala: The sacred path of the warrior*. Boston: Shambhala.

PART III

RITUALS AND PRACTICES TO NURTURE THE INNER LIFE

Most scholars and practitioners recognize the inner life as central to spirituality. Through this inner life, adherents shape their sense of meaning, purpose, identity, and connectedness to each other and to the divine and/or the transcendent. They adopt a wide range of individual, family, and communal disciplines, practices, and rituals that have, often for centuries, sustained and guided people on their spiritual journeys. Furthermore, they have created a variety of institutions, settings, and resources—monasteries, schools, congregations, media—that cultivate the inner spiritual life.

The authors in this section explore how their religious traditions understand and nurture the inner life through individual practices and communal rituals. They address questions such as: What individual and communal practices are encouraged, nurtured, or taught to cultivate young people's spiritual lives? How are the narratives or stories of the tradition used to shape young people's spirituality? What rituals, holy days, or celebrations are emblematic of their tradition's approach? Although it is impossible to do justice to the vast diversity and depth of approaches represented here, the chapters introduce important themes that link the spiritual life of children to the rituals and practices of faith traditions.

The Dzogchen Ponlop Rinpoche begins by introducing Tibetan Buddhist perspectives on the vital importance of cultivating in young people an awareness of their highest potential, then offering the tools they need to reach that potential. He notes the wide array of rituals, symbols, art, and practices within Tibetan Buddhism that nurture the spiritual lives of the young, then focuses specifically on the meditative disciplines that imbue the sacred stories, rituals, artwork, and ceremonies with "life, meaning, and transcendent value." The quest for meaning and life in the world involves awakening the "youthful buddha" within, which requires study, meditation, and mindful action, all three of which are forms of meditation that cultivate "mental sharpness, concentration, and mindfulness, as well as intuitive understanding."

A vital part of cultivating the spiritual life of children and adolescents is for them to embed themselves in narrative and story that convey meaning and connection to others and across time. Howard Schwartz shows how stories and storytelling play a central role in Judaism in linking the mythic past to the desire of children to develop their own spirituality. He notes that, within Judaism, the child is viewed as a paradigm of spirituality, with spiritual truth being present, but hidden, in each child's life. This spirituality is drawn forth and shaped through the biblical narrative and the process of storytelling, as "Jewish children over the ages have attempted to emulate the holy ways of the patriarchs." Schwartz focuses on the biblical and Midrashim of Abraham, highlighting how the tradition understands Abraham's spiritual life as a child, and how that story serves as a rich resource for nurturing children's spiritually.

Shoshana Silberman, also writing from a Jewish perspective, asserts that children's spirituality must be actively formed, not just nurtured. Historically, this formation has focused on ethical behavior, although there is growing interest in a more explicit emphasis on spirituality as well that builds on the Hassidic saying that "we reach out in three directions: up to God, out to other people, and into our own hearts." Silberman describes how teaching children and teenagers to pray and actively engaging them in holy days each week and throughout the year are concrete means by which the spiritual life is developed. And, key to Jewish thought, she points out that spiritual life is incomplete if it does not lead to ethical behavior.

However, as Robin Maas suggests, religious communities are not always attentive to the inner life of young people and, in fact, may not even take it seriously. She critiques the U.S. Catholic Church for neglecting to tap its rich spiritual resources in service to young people, leaving them instead in a spiritual famine in which they are only "entertained and out of mischief." She calls for educating the heart of adolescents in "the school of prayer," offering them the wealth of historical resources available in the church's two-thousand-year history that can help them navigate the emotional ups and downs of adolescence. She draws on the teaching of Saint Teresa of Ávila, who learned how to meet her passionate longings and desire for relationships (key issues in adolescence) through disciplined prayer that nurtures a relationship with the divine.

Whereas some rituals and practices are more individually focused, others emphasize community-wide experiences. For example, in Hinduism, writes Melukote K. Sridhar, religious, historic, and seasonal festivals are vital opportunities for cultivating the spiritual life. Indeed, each year is filled with many festivals, each with its own meaning, purpose, and rituals. Through these celebrations, both children and adults are taught the stories and expectations of the tradition, and people are bound together in a sense of community while also being reminded "of the presence of supreme reality, or God." Through both observation and dialogue about the festivals and their meaning, parents introduce children to the festivals from an early age, teaching them the expectations and practices associated with each. Sridhar illustrates the centrality of these festivals by describing key celebrations and how they cultivate young people's spirituality.

Finally, Kathy Dawson and Shin-Kyung Park offer a snapshot of the dynamic interaction of culture and religious tradition in establishing institutions that support children's spiritual journeys. They do so by describing the past and present similarities and differences in Presbyterian preschools in South Korea and the United States. Although guided by similar goals from within the Reformed Christian tradition, the institutions that emerged in these two countries in the twentieth century for nurturing children's spirituality were dramatically different, shaped largely by the culture in which they were formed. Furthermore, each faces new challenges as it seeks to remain relevant and effective in changing cultures across time.

Each religious tradition offers a web of interconnected practices, rituals, expectations, and experiences that seek to cultivate the spiritual life. The snapshots in this section begin to introduce and explore some of that richness—although more remains to be done in both deepening the exploration within these traditions *and* expanding it to other traditions and cultures. Yet, as many of these authors suggest, religious communities face the persistent challenge of ensuring that rituals and practices that are intended to enliven and develop the life of the spirit do not inadvertently become empty routines without meaning and relevance. If the chapters offered here provide any insight into that question, it lies in remembering intent (such as strengthening the life of the spirit) and rediscovering for each generation the practices, rituals, narratives, and celebrations that have, through time, offered people of faith a sense of meaning, purpose, and connection.

CHAPTER 14

Young Minds, Youthful Buddhas: Developmental Rituals and Practices in Tibetan Buddhism

The Dzogchen Ponlop Rinpoche

All philosophical traditions uphold truth as a virtue, akin to qualities such as authenticity, genuineness, and even reality itself. If this is so, then when truth is inaccessible to us—or when we fail to recognize it—our lives become inauthentic, less than genuine, and in some sense unreal. Therefore, from the perspective of the Tibetan Buddhist tradition, it is essential to nurture the spiritual lives of children and youth by cultivating in them an awareness of their highest potential and providing them with the knowledge and skills to realize that potential. This perspective can be applied to our experience as social beings, as members of the interconnected and complex fabric of humanity. It can also be applied to our innermost experience, to the very nature of our journey as spiritual beings. For example, from birth, the fundamental qualities of gentleness, love, and compassionate wisdom are always present within the hearts of all beings. However, these qualities may not be obvious or manifested clearly to oneself or others. When there is no recognition of one's true nature, one falls subject to mistaken views about the self and experiences a state of confusion. Therefore, the process of education and the support of a nurturing environment play important roles in helping one reconnect with this nature—so that its radiance can extend out into the world, where it is most needed.

Ritual and Practice

The Tibetan Buddhist tradition employs many skillful methods to promote spiritual awakening and support the development of genuine wisdom and compassion—the chief aim of spiritual education and practice. This tradition is especially rich in ritual elements, symbolic expressions of spiritual aspiration and transformation conveyed through forms such as liturgies, ceremonies, storytelling, and art. It is also rich in its systems of meditation practice, methods of working directly and simply with the mind. Ritual practices are regarded as an essential aspect of the training of young Buddhists, as well as important vehicles for enhancing the spiritual life of the monastic and lay communities. However, while there are many ritual forms that are vital to sustaining the Tibetan tradition and to nurturing the spiritual lives of children and youth, this chapter focuses on the meditative disciplines, which are the means of gaining direct experience of the reality expressed through symbolic form. The knowledge, or *prajna,* that results from the practice of meditation is what gives life, meaning, and transcendent value to the chanted liturgies, the formal ceremonies, and the depictions in sacred stories, sculpture, and painting of enlightened beings and states. Prajna, which is the natural sharpness of awareness, has two forms: mundane prajna associated with worldly knowledge, and higher prajna, which refers to wisdom itself—the realization of the selflessness of phenomena, or the direct knowledge of things as they are. Meditation, in this context, refers to those disciplines that develop qualities of concentration, mindfulness and awareness, and insight and that support the development of loving-kindness and compassion.

The educational processes described here are primarily based on (1) the traditional philosophical and meditative training provided within the monastic systems and *she-dras,* or monastic colleges, of Tibet and their counterparts in India, and (2) the customs of Tibetan families who have largely maintained their Buddhist traditions as they have moved from Tibet to India and the West. Because the Buddhist tradition as a whole, and the Tibetan tradition in particular, is a composite of many schools encompassing diverse cultural communities, differences will always be observed—in content of training, methods used, and resources available—in addition to changes effected by the shifting needs of students and communities. It is significant to note that the age at which a child might engage in a particular level of study or practice will vary according to his or her abilities and spiritual development; recognized reincarnate lamas, for example, may demonstrate high levels of accomplishment and be prepared for advanced study at a very early age. By the age of nine, His Holiness the Seventeenth Karmapa, supreme head of the Kagyu lineage of Tibetan Buddhism, had memorized perfectly more than two hundred pages of prayers and supplications and knew by heart all the ritual practice texts of the lineage—amounting to hundreds of additional pages (Martin 2003). Furthermore, there is no set age for a child to enter a monastery; thus, children of different ages may be found in the same classroom. Finally, it is interesting to see how Western culture is embracing Buddhism in its many forms; students in Europe, North America, and South America are studying the dharma, practicing meditation, and doing long retreats, while simultaneously developing careers and raising families. The dharma, which refers to the teachings of the Buddha, can be viewed in two ways. There is "scriptural dharma" and the "dharma of realization." Scriptural dharma refers to Buddha's teachings as they appear symbolically in the form of books, letters, speech, and thought; the dharma of realization refers to one's experience of these teachings in meditation and, in particular, to the insight that sees the true nature of phenomena.

Many of the educational processes described here are already available to—and evident in—a new generation of young, Western Buddhists, who will become educators and spiritual guides for their own children and for a whole generation.

Mind and Its World: Understanding Buddhist View

To understand the Tibetan Buddhist approach to cultivating the spiritual lives of children and youth, it is necessary to have some understanding of its view of reality, of the nature of mind and its world. From the perspective of this tradition, the genuine reality of our mind is always in the state of utter purity and is always fully awakened. It is full of compassion and free of any confusion, faults, or stains of self—the ego-centered view. This nature is the primary state of a child's mind as well as the minds of adults and all beings.[1] This genuine mind, always shining like the sun in a cloud-free sky, is who we truly are.

At the same time, our experience in the world is predominantly a continuum of confusion and suffering, with intermittent glimpses of happiness. We do not perceive the radiance or experience the wisdom of our own nature because it is temporarily obscured—blocked from our view, so to speak—by another aspect of our mind. That aspect is a deeply rooted ignorance, from which various delusions arise, including the manifestations of ego and ego-clinging, the destructive emotions, or *kleshas,* and the forceful momentum of karmic actions. *Klesha* can be translated as a "destructive state of mind" that brings more suffering into our lives. The kleshas include states such as passion, aggression, ignorance, pride, and jealousy. When we look at what we normally think of as "our mind," and cling to as a "self," we can see that it is our dualistic consciousness—a momentary stream of sense perceptions, mental constructs, thoughts, and emotions that arise and dissolve ceaselessly, like the waves on an ocean.[2] Entranced by the energy and activity of the waves, we do not see the ocean itself; we do not see the profound and vast wisdom that is the source of the mind's projections.

Our vision is further clouded by the conditioning we receive from our environment in the present and our habitual tendencies from the past. This state of bewilderment is reinforced by our continual mindless actions. When considering a child's educational needs, it is also necessary to pay attention to and work with this more disturbed aspect of mind. It is said to be easier to remove the defilements of mind when one works with them from a young age.

There is an image known as the "youthful buddha in a vase," which illustrates this situation. A youthful buddha is fully shining in the state of complete enlightenment; however, that light is concealed from view as this buddha is inside a thick, lidded vase. When the container is opened or when the vase is broken, the light fully manifests, illuminating everything in its surroundings. The light seems to be new light, but the youthful buddha has always been glowing. A child's mind is like the "youthful buddha," which is concealed within the "vase" of dualistic concepts, ego-clinging, fixation on objects, labeling, kleshas, and karma. *Karma* means "action," and it refers to the principle of "cause and effect," or the relationship between an intentional action and its inevitable consequence. Actions include mental actions, as well as the actions of speech and body, which arise from our fundamental intentions and thoughts.

When we fail to recognize the true nature of our mind, that is the beginning of *samsara,* the repetitive cycle of suffering arising from ignorance, kleshas, and karma. However, it is possible to rediscover and reconnect with mind's empty yet luminous nature because what is obscuring it is not part of that nature and has no inherent existence of its own. It is simply a state of bewilderment or "mindlessness" that clouds our perception and covers our awareness. Our current state of existence is therefore like a dream, and the goal of the spiritual journey is to awaken from that dream.

All the teachings of the Buddha point to this awakening and can be summed up in three topics called view, meditation, and action. Like the pillars that hold up a house, these three support us on our journey of discovery, our quest to find the meaning of life and the world. Having the correct view is like having flawless eyesight—a precise and clear vision of the path. Meditation is like having good feet to walk on that path. Action is what we do, how we conduct ourselves so that our view and meditation become useful and meaningful—a living dharma that will bear fruit in the world.

These three concepts are inseparable aspects of the wisdom that is the foundation for the spiritual training of children. When we are working with view, meditation, and action, we are simultaneously working with what Buddha taught as the "three wheels."[3] As we progress on our path, we study to develop the view of each stage; we meditate to develop the realization of the view; and we engage in the actions, or conduct, appropriate to each stage. The view is developed through working directly with conceptual mind. Formal meditation is developed in stages, through various methods, both conceptual and nonconceptual. Engaging in mindful action is the method of bringing our understanding of the view and our experience of meditation into our everyday life situations. In fact, all three wheels—study, meditation, and mindful action—are regarded as forms of meditation, involving the cultivation of mental sharpness, concentration, and mindfulness, as well as intuitive understanding. Altogether, the trainings in view, meditation, and action inform each stage of a child's education.

Karmic Threads

In the Buddhist view, a child does not come into this world as a blank slate, to be inscribed by present conditions. Each child possesses an individual and unique thread of karmic qualities that influences their way of learning and acting in the world (Gampopa 1959, 74–90). Therefore, although you can apply the same training to each child, you will not get the same result. At the same time, education and environment have a tremendous impact on the young, fresh minds of children and play a central role. All of these factors—past karma, education, and present conditions—determine the outcome of the training and how each individual will manifest his or her spirituality. For example, with the same education and environmental conditions, twins may display very different qualities of gentleness and aggression, different capacities for intellectual or intuitive understanding, and different degrees of artistic or scientific skill. In the same way, their connection to and the development of their spirituality will be very personal and individual.

It is said that those who have a karmic connection from the past with Buddhist teaching will naturally connect with it after they are born and will develop that connection throughout their childhood and adult lives. One example is the renowned eleventh-century Tibetan yogi, Milarepa, who, in his youth, amassed many negative karmic deeds. Through acts of black magic, he avenged the evil treatment of his mother and sister at the hands of greedy relatives; in one incident, he magically produced a hailstorm that rained death and destruction on these relatives and some of their supporters. Later, overcome by remorse, Milarepa turned toward the practice of dharma. His connection to this path was so profound that he overcame his negative karma and discovered the nature of his mind. He became a holder of the Kagyu lineage of Tibetan Buddhism and the most celebrated yogi in Tibet. Others who have a genuine karmic connection to the practice of dharma may come to sudden glimpses of realization that transform their experience of this world. They can spontaneously experience the world as sacred world, as appearance-emptiness—like the moon's reflection on water or a colorful rainbow. At that point, their perception of the world and their interaction with this life become quite different.

When we do not have such a strong karmic connection or developed wisdom, when we are not very habituated to such a path and its practices, then our experience of the world is not so transcendent. Most of us experience the "truth of suffering" on many levels, as well as the "truth of the cause of suffering," the destructive states of mind known as kleshas. In his first cycle of teachings, the Buddha elucidated this aspect of our experience in his teaching on the "four noble truths," which express deep, pervasive truths about the nature of our human suffering, as well as its causes, its cessation, and the paths and methods that bring one to the state of peace, the state in which suffering is overcome.

Therefore, creating a productive educational environment in the present and providing training in loving-kindness, compassion, and mindful action are very important for the development of children. Rarely do we see the manifestation of exceptional qualities in someone without extensive training. The majority of people manifest such qualities only after going through a graduated process of learning. Furthermore, children can be guided and taught to work with their individual karmic tendencies, whether positive or negative. Those negative impulses that an individual mind exhibits can be trained and transformed into more genuine, positive, and mindful expressions. Those individuals who naturally demonstrate many positive tendencies and a strong connection to the spiritual path can receive training that will further cultivate those qualities and help bring them to fruition.

Early Training

Because of the opportunities that human birth enjoys, it is regarded as precious and difficult to attain (Gampopa 1959, 14–29). It is most precious when we possess the causes and conditions that support us in following a genuine spiritual path. In the homes of traditional Tibetan Buddhist practitioners, wisdom and compassion are cultivated right from the beginning of a child's existence. For example, three days after birth, an infant is brought into the presence of a spiritual master who invokes the enlightened qualities of the child's inherent nature through the bestowing of blessings. The minds of young children are particularly receptive, possessing the qualities of openness, inquisitiveness, and innocence, which are considered essential for the cultivation of genuine spirituality. Such fresh and bright minds are full of potential. They possess a capacity for precise and complete learning that can be realized at great depth, often in a much shorter time than is possible for an adult. Thus, to bring about the utmost benefit, it is essential to begin training early.

In lay communities, from birth to approximately the age of ten, a child receives preliminary education and learns basic life skills from parents and elders. Spirituality is first taught by example and through the environment created by parents in their home. Children learn by participating in family meditation sessions and prayers. For example, the father will lead the whole family in a morning meditation session and an evening prayer session. During the day, the father will teach a few basic principles of dharma, and the mother will observe the child's conduct and encourage mindful and compassionate action. For example, a child will be taught not to harm any beings, starting with tiny insects. At the same time, a child receives important lessons by observing the conduct of his or her parents and their practices in everyday life activities. In this way, the child receives instruction and training in the basic principles and methods of the Buddhist path from a very young age. Such early exposure to formal and informal practices has a deep impact on a child's mind. As a result, the child's innate wisdom naturally manifests in expressions of kindness, compassion, and uncontrived devotion. These interactions lead the child forward on the path of spirituality and become the basis for the deepening of his or her experiences.

In the monastic setting, young children begin their training in spiritual practice as early as the age of six. At the time of entering the monastery, a child receives novice ordination (the Tibetan term is *getsul*), which is based on the Refuge Vow, the ceremony that signifies the moment when one formally becomes "a Buddhist"; thereafter, one relies solely on the Three Jewels of Buddha, Dharma, and Sangha for guidance and support on one's individual path to enlightenment. In this ceremony, the child "goes for refuge" to Buddha Shakyamuni as a supreme teacher and as an example of one's own potential; to the Dharma as the methods of the path that free one from mental afflictions; and to the Sangha, the community of noble, realized beings, or bodhisattvas, as companions on the path. At some point, this outer form of refuge transforms into a sense of inner refuge; it becomes simply a confirmation through body, speech, and mind of the discovery of one's own fundamentally awakened nature of mind as being the same as the Buddha's wisdom. At a later stage, in conjunction with the bestowal of tantric initiations, or empowerments,[4] a young Buddhist also undertakes the Bodhisattva Vow, which signifies the engendering of *bodhichitta,* the altruistic attitude that resolves to lead all sentient beings to enlightenment—a state of joy, peace, and permanent happiness.

Monastic training is usually carried out by classroom teachers, resident teachers, and personal tutors. Teachers working in a classroom setting train groups of young monastics in Buddhist philosophy, tantric arts, and other subjects. Resident teachers take full responsibility for the physical well-being of their apprentices. They oversee areas such as housing and meals, and they introduce children to the ethical disciplines of monastic life. Personal tutors provide training in a progressive path of study and meditation, teach the daily ritual practices, and refer each child to other appropriate spiritual friends—scholars and meditation masters—for further training.

For both the lay and monastic communities, another important means of inspiring devotion and conveying essential points of spiritual practice is the retelling of the life stories of great figures of the Buddhist lineage. The life of Shakyamuni Buddha, "the sage of the Shakya clan," and the historical Buddha of our age, is an especially popular and instructive story. In the same way, the Jataka tales, or "birth stories" of the Buddha, which relate remarkable and instructive incidents from his previous lives, provide fundamental life lessons. Other important narratives include the lives of the eighty-four mahasiddhas, Indian Buddhist saints, who came from all walks of life and often displayed unique and unconventional behaviors on their paths to enlightenment. There is also a practice of observing special days that commemorate the lives and spiritual attainment of great teachers. The primary such day in the Tibetan calendar is Saka Dawa Duchen,[5] the celebration of the birth, enlightenment, and parinirvana of Buddha Shakyamuni. In addition, the Losar festival celebrating the Tibetan New Year is a major event in the Buddhist community. At this time of renewal, special offerings are made; the young visit and pay respects to their elders and venerated teachers; and socializing and feasting may continue for several days.

In practice, the course of training varies, reflecting the customs and resources of each community and monastery. For example, not all monks will enter the shedra system that provides advanced philosophical training. Around the age of fourteen, each monk will choose whether to enter the shedra or to focus on training in the ritual practices that are essential to monastic life, such as the construction of sand mandalas; the making of *tormas,* or offering cakes; the chanting of liturgies; the playing of musical instruments used in the performance of *pujas,* or devotional ceremonies; and the meditation practice known as "lama dancing." Monks not entering the shedra may also seek private, advanced instruction in philosophy or meditation by approaching a respected teacher and requesting individual instruction on a specific text or practice. Members of the lay community may also seek private instruction in this way.

Since Buddhism in the West is only beginning to unfold, practitioners here are adapting this training in accordance with their own communities and resources. Parents may bring their children, from infants to preteens, to "children's blessings" offered by eminent teachers. Young children may also be taught how to make offerings of candles or flowers to the shrine, recite supplication prayers to the Buddha, meditate for short periods, and dedicate the merit of these activities. Increasingly, dharma programs, retreats, and sangha-sponsored social events are organized for teenagers. The Refuge and Bodhisattva Vow ceremonies are available in the West outside of the monastic setting—for children and teens, as well as their parents.

Spiritual Friends: Elders, Masters, and Gurus

While parents and elders are the initial guides for most children, especially the very young, at a certain point in their early training, students encounter what is known as a "spiritual friend." Generally speaking, the idea of the spiritual friend is a very down-to-earth concept. A spiritual friend is simply a compassionate teacher who may be a learned scholar or may be an enlightened, realized human being.

In the Buddhist view, the ultimate spiritual friend is one's own fully awakened nature of mind, which is not separate from the enlightenment or realization of Buddha Shakyamuni. While the absolute spiritual friend is fully present within our ordinary state of confused being, for the student to make that discovery personally, it is necessary for him or her to develop a relationship with a living human teacher.

Making a connection with a spiritual friend is similar to making a connection with someone who later becomes one's best friend. For example, when we meet a sympathetic person with whom we feel compatible at school or in a nice coffee shop, we generally go through a process of exchanging questions and answers—with each discussion leading us to a deeper and closer heart connection. This too is how we make our connection with the spiritual friend on the path of Buddhism.

There are three levels of such teachers: the elder, the spiritual master, and the vajra guru (the term *vajra* means "indestructible" or "invincible"; the vajra guru is one who is accomplished in the vajrayana teachings and is capable of transmitting their essence to others through a variety of skillful means). Students need the close guidance of each in order to follow the spiritual journey egolessly. In one sense, the function of a spiritual friend is to find the student's faults and weaknesses and bring them to his or her attention. Traditionally, the spiritual friend will counsel the student and help keep his or her motivation and intentions pure and genuine on the path.

The student's first contact with a spiritual friend may be with a teacher who is regarded as an *elder*. This relationship may develop very early, even before school age. The elder may also be a continuous presence throughout the student's training. This is someone who is older and wiser in understanding and realization, someone with mature experience in spirituality. The elder is a trustworthy friend, in whom the student has confidence. Much like a good friend in the mundane sense, the elder is someone the student can talk to, someone who can provide understanding, encouragement, and reliable guidance. The elder is also is the person who gives students their first instruction in basic dharma—what genuine dharma is, who the Buddha is, and what refuge means. This good friend helps young students on their spiritual path in many ways.

As the student's understanding matures, the *spiritual master* replaces the elder in the role of primary teacher. This master is someone who holds a particular lineage of philosophy and training in dharma and, therefore, holds a certain authority regarding the dharma. At the first stage, the student related to the elder primarily on the level of ideas; at the second stage, the spiritual master can offer guidance that is more concrete and pragmatic. For example, when a student faces obstacles on the spiritual journey, the spiritual master can help him or her deal with those problems. Working with others is not only theory and ideas; the spiritual master has gone through the process personally.

The third kind of spiritual friend is the *guru*, or the vajra master. The vajra master possesses qualities of wisdom and compassion that manifest vividly and powerfully, with a sharp edge. That sharpness cuts inwardly and outwardly at once—cutting through our grasping on to inner and outer phenomena, as well as through any misunderstandings that develop on the path. This extraordinary teacher is the one who gives the student pith instructions, or "pointing out instructions," which awaken and ripen the student's mindstream. The vajra master also gives the student individualized, detailed instructions for personal practice.

The spiritual master and the vajra guru may appear in the life of the student at any time, depending on his or her karmic connection and readiness for particular levels of training. However, it is more typical to formally work with these teachers after the age of eight to ten. In some instances, a student may have only one primary teacher, a highly realized master who has the capacity to manifest the qualities of all three levels—elder, spiritual master, and vajra guru, each at the appropriate time. Through exploring and developing a relationship with these spiritual friends, the student has a greater opportunity for deepening his or her understanding. It is difficult to fully comprehend Buddha's teachings on one's own, or to fully realize the true nature of mind without the guidance of a teacher. Such relationships, based on trust, confidence, openness, and mutual respect, are invaluable for actualizing the path of dharma. In particular, the spiritual master and the vajra guru are regarded as lineage holders, as embodiments of the enlightened wisdom transmitted from realized master to student in a succession stretching back to Buddha Shakyamuni. Therefore, their instructions are regarded as especially significant for helping the student connect with the heart of Buddha's teachings.

The Three Wheels of the Path

Buddha taught in the Vinaya Pitaka,[6] the collection of teachings on discipline, that monastics as well as lay practitioners should engage in three principal areas of training known as the three wheels: (1) the wheel of learning and contemplation; (2) the wheel of *dhyana,* or *samadhi* (meditative concentration); and (3) the wheel of action. Buddha said that these three trainings should be taught from the first day of entering the path of liberation. Therefore, most monastic institutions in Tibet, India, and many other Buddhist countries treasure this instruction and regard it as the basis of training for both monastic and lay sanghas. My own tradition of Tibetan Buddhism especially adheres to the practice of these three wheels—from the very beginning of the spiritual journey—regardless of the age at which one enters. These three constitute the foundation for training the youthful mind in spirituality in Tibetan Buddhism; all levels of education and instruction are built on the basis of these three. Generally, this training has tremendous influence on everyday life in the monasteries as well as in the communities of lay practitioners. Training in the three wheels is connected to the development of transcendental knowledge, or prajna.

THE WHEEL OF STUDY

The wheel of study represents the stage of listening to or studying the dharma. In a sense, the spiritual journey for a child begins simply with a curious mind, a mind that is full of questions. If we start our journey with the mind-set that says, "I know everything," then there is nothing more to find out. However, when our minds are fresh, open, and keen to explore the world and discover how it works and what it means, that is the beginning of our true spiritual journey in Buddhism.

The most important training with which to begin a child's education is training in the art of listening, which means listening with mindfulness and an open, compassionate heart. Generally, this training is a natural part of childhood; for example, one learns from one's parents how to listen to their words, how to listen to others, and how to listen to one's friends and teachers. This interaction develops informally at home or in the monastery whenever a child hears discussions of dharma and stories of the Buddha or great masters, or is instructed by parents or elders on Buddhist principles, such as karma, or acting with loving-kindness and compassion.

Formal study may begin around the age of eight, with advanced studies beginning around the age of fourteen. Study involves the reading of dharma texts, memorizing of passages, and attending classes and teachings given by learned scholars and realized masters. This stage of the path works with developing the student's conceptual mind, communication skills, and language comprehension. Through study, the student develops a clear understanding of the view of the entire spiritual journey—its basis, its paths and stages, and its final fruition.

The second aspect of the wheel of study is the practice of contemplation, which is the process of internalizing knowledge developed through formal studies. The great yogi Milarepa said that, at this point, our knowledge is like a patch sewn over a hole on our clothes. Even though the patch covers the hole temporarily, that does not mean the patch has become one with the original cloth. It is still separate. In a similar way, the knowledge the student has accumulated so far through listening or studying has not become one with his or her mindstream. Whenever doubts arise, one can apply an intellectual patch; but that does not really solve our problems or heal our suffering. True contemplation develops the prajna of experience. Through this practice, the student becomes one with his or her intellectual understanding and is no longer frozen in theory. Instead, this knowledge becomes part of the student's being, rather than remaining a part of his or her notebook or computer. Thus, this instruction becomes the second most essential point to train in, as it is through the practice of contemplation that a student develops his or her own certainty in the view. Generally, the seeds for this type of training can be found in a child's upbringing: for example, when a child is encouraged to examine something and then come to his or her own conclusion based on that analysis.

The actual practice of contemplation is done through analytical meditation, either in formal meditation sessions or in postmeditation, as a kind of experiential investigation. For example, the student might bring a verse of dharma to mind, contemplate it, and penetrate its meaning; or the object of contemplation might be the fixation on a "self." In this case, the student mentally tries to discover what the self is, where it is, and so forth. The student's investigation may be guided by recollecting what he or she has read in books or been taught by a spiritual friend. In this way, the student relates present experience to theoretical descriptions learned earlier.

The actual point of meditation is to develop awareness, insight, or prajna—the precise function of analytical meditation—which is the process of cutting through dualistic confusion. This method of conceptual meditation was practiced in the past at Nalanda University, the most renowned educational institution in ancient India.[7] It is still done frequently in the great institutions in India and in most of the Tibetan monastic institutions.

At this stage, the student is developing genuine experience, but it has not yet developed into complete realization, or the full state of wisdom. Milarepa said that our experiences in meditation are like the thick mist that appears in the early morning. It seems to be so solid and so real, but later in the day, when the sun has risen, the mist simply disappears. Likewise, meditation experiences are temporary. They come and go like the morning mist. This indicates that it is necessary to go on to the next stage, which develops the prajna of meditation.

There is sometimes a misunderstanding of study: Students may think that it is not *real* dharma practice in the same sense that meditation is. However, as far as the spiritual path of Buddhism is concerned, studying or listening to the dharma *is* practice, *is* meditation, and *is* a genuine path. It is through study that the student develops a precise conceptual understanding of the nature, logic, and methods of the path. Studying *becomes* the path. It is not simply listening or talking. It is much more precise, much more sharply concentrated than that.

The Accumulations of Merit and Wisdom

Through study, a student accumulates both merit and wisdom. The term *accumulation* suggests the gathering of many small pieces—in this case, the gathering of pieces of knowledge, wisdom, and acts of compassion. For the student, this translates to the practice of working with or being mindful of every single action in his or her life and making it into positive, meritorious, virtuous action. Actually, action and karma cannot be separated; so in one way, positive action itself *is* what merit is. Thus, the path of accumulating merit is the path of generating positive deeds. It is a practice that, through living in a mindful, wholesome way, makes each life more workable and beneficial to all.

The accumulation of merit is based on working with ego-clinging; thus, it involves the practice of detachment, or training the mind in letting go. In the Buddhist tradition, this notion is introduced to youthful minds with the practice of generosity, in which the student begins to work with his or her clinging to material objects. With this practice, the student learns to let go of clinging to outer objects first, and then increasingly begins to work with letting go of conceptual clinging—of clinging to the whole universe of ego, inside.

Because the student has developed a certain degree of prajna and an understanding of mind through study and contemplation, it is possible to extend this practice to working with the vivid kleshas. The objective is to see every aspect of one's clinging and to let it go. When a student is able to do this, the habitual tendency of grasping and ego-clinging is reversed. Ordinarily, we cling to whatever we perceive or whatever arises in our mind, and each time the mind grasps, an imprint of that clinging is made in our mindstream. With each imprint, we build up ego and solidify our belief in a self. When we practice letting go, over and over, the tendency to *not* grasp is imprinted in our mindstream instead. Thus, the accumulation of merit leads to the higher realization of egolessness, of transcendental knowledge, or wisdom, and a total sense of freedom. And as the student personally goes through the process of surrendering ego, one's self-centered view, the generous heart of loving-kindness and compassion naturally develops.

THE WHEEL OF MEDITATION

This wheel plays a crucial role in children's education and the development of their spirituality. For young children, meditation is often taught with simple and practical methods that involve a great deal of concentration and mindfulness. One method, for example, teaches how to wear the monastic robes properly; another teaches how to clean the shrine hall while contemplating the cleansing of one's own mental defilements. In the latter method, the student reflects on the inherent purity of mind, which is like the clean floor upon which the dust of emotional and cognitive defilements falls again and again, to be swept away by mindfulness and awareness. Additionally, simple forms of formal meditation, such as breathing meditation or meditation with chanting or music, are introduced to groups of students, while personal tutors continue the training of individuals in smaller groups or in one-on-one sessions.

In the Buddhist path, many methods of meditation are taught, but what is the essence of meditation? According to Milarepa, meditation is not meditating *on* anything; rather, it is simply a process of familiarization—familiarizing ourselves with the nature of our mind. Here, meditation refers to the practice of "resting meditation." At this stage, the practice of the student is to go beyond concept and simply rest in the state of nondual experience. The ability to rest in that way comes from contemplation, from analytical meditation, which gradually leads us to the stage of nonconceptual meditation. Thus, the wheel of meditation is the actual cause that produces the genuine prajna of realization. Milarepa said that realization is like the sky or space, which is always the same. Therefore, once you have reached that level of realization, it is unchanging. That realization is always there. It is not like the morning mist that comes and goes.

Through the practice of meditation, the student comes into close contact with his or her mind, seeing it just as it is, beyond the filters of religion, philosophy, or culture. The mindfulness and awareness that are developed illuminate and tame our habitual agitation that is characterized by restlessness and dissatisfaction. Our obsessive concern with past and future is pacified, and we can rest wakefully and at peace in the present. Mind's natural clarity becomes more brilliant, and we discover the actual remedy for our suffering and the suffering of others.

Shamatha and Vipashyana

Although Buddha taught many varieties of meditation, all of these are included in the two most fundamental practices, *shamatha* and *vipashyana*. A student first trains in shamatha, which means "calm abiding." Shamatha meditation is a practice that supports the development of a stable, one-pointed concentration, which brings the mind to a state of peace and tranquillity. Thus, it is also known as resting meditation. The practice of shamatha brings about a remarkably close connection with mind and the discovery of its profoundly rich and powerful qualities. Once the student can rest in a state of nondistraction, he or she begins training in the practice of vipashyana. Vipashyana means "clear seeing" or "superior seeing." Its nature is a lucidity or clarity of mind, which enables one to determine the characteristics and ultimate nature of all things in an unmistaken manner. Fundamentally, it consists of the recognition of the nature of mind, and it is marked by a sense of openness and spaciousness.

With these two forms of meditation, the student develops transcendental knowledge, which has the quality of awareness, or self-aware wisdom. In that awareness, one discovers a basic quality of compassion, a genuine heart of love for all beings. Such compassion is our natural state, and at its fullest point, it becomes egoless compassion that takes us beyond clinging to a self and dualistic phenomena. In the Mahayana tradition of Tibetan Buddhism, this is known as *absolute bodhichitta,* the union of compassion and emptiness, in which compassion manifests spontaneously, unconditionally, and without bias. At this transformative stage, a student's concern for the peace, happiness, joy, and freedom from suffering of other sentient beings surpasses concern for his or her own liberation. Because this experience may come and go on the path, it is the practice of the student to continually generate this noble heart and to bring the aspiration to benefit beings into everyday activities.

THE WHEEL OF ACTION

The third and final wheel, the wheel of action, works in unison with the wheels of study and meditation. Buddha taught that these three wheels should not become separated. All of the teachings of the Buddha are to be put into action, into practice; otherwise, the dharma becomes a useless philosophy. When the student becomes skillful at putting the view and meditation into action, the dharma becomes a living teaching. It becomes personally useful and meaningful and brings a positive result to one's community.

The key point in the Buddhist teaching on the third wheel of ethical conduct, or mindful action, is to see that each of us is responsible for our actions and that from these actions we produce different results. Through studying and contemplating these teachings, the student begins to see directly how he or she has the power to create happiness and bring it to the world, as well as the power to create and bring suffering to the world. This understanding leads to a recognition of the importance of discerning harmful actions from those that are beneficial for oneself and for others. In this regard, Buddha taught the ten nonvirtuous actions and their opposite, the ten virtuous actions (Patrul Rinpoche 1994, 102–18). Three actions are related to body, four to speech, and three to mind. The three nonvirtuous actions of body are killing, taking what is not offered, and sexual misconduct. The four nonvirtuous actions of speech are lying, inciting discord, harsh speech, and idle chatter. And the three nonvirtuous actions of mind are covetousness, malicious intent, and wrong view (or misunderstandings about karma). Refraining from these constitutes the ten virtuous actions.

Buddha also taught that our beliefs and assumptions about what constitutes a positive action and what constitutes a negative action should be thoroughly analyzed. Mindful action is dependent on this analysis, as it is essential to determine which actions are universally positive, providing for the happiness of all regardless of their individual backgrounds, and which actions are positive only in a limited or subjective sense. For example, some actions will be viewed as positive and constructive in one social, cultural, or religious context and as negative and harmful in another. Thus, the student is challenged to bring this discriminating mind to his or her own actions.

The qualities necessary for bringing this practice into everyday life are mindfulness, awareness, and a sense of relaxation, which come from meditation. The most important quality, however, is nondistraction. When the mind becomes distracted, one's actions are governed by heedlessness, and this becomes a cause for generating harmful actions, either directly or indirectly. Therefore, the student is instructed first to be as mindful and aware as possible, and then to simply relax. Relaxation is taught to be the key to maintaining mindfulness and the quality that makes the accomplishment of all our intentions possible.

It is also important, however, for the student to realize that maintaining a state of continuous mindfulness, without any gaps, is not possible. Rather than losing heart and losing interest in engaging with the world, the student is encouraged by the spiritual friend to appreciate that each moment we have awareness is perfect. If it is gone in the next moment, that is all right. Each moment presents a new opportunity; and when we have that opportunity, we should be curious about it and take the best advantage of it.

This is the general idea of action in the Buddhist teachings. However, there are many more aspects of Buddhist ethics and conduct taught in relation to the Hinayana, Mahayana, and Vajrayana, the three vehicles or stages of the Buddhist teachings.

Finding Our Way

Modern society offers us an endless variety of opportunities for distraction: from the Internet to iPods, from cell phones to handhelds, from video games to high-definition TV, and so on. Or our passions may run toward eco-adventure-travel, extreme makeovers, fashion-forward wardrobes, or karaoke bars. Surrounded by this overwhelming display of modernity and materialism, young people may be disinterested in following a spiritual path at all, while older practitioners may lose heart and abandon their initial interest in this wisdom. This is ego's magic—the deepening of the dream until we lose all contact with the reality of our wakefulness.

Those with a genuine connection to this tradition of ancient wisdom inevitably find their way back and return to their practice; however, if the continuity of its transmission is interrupted, if its wisdom is not realized and fully held by each generation, then there is a danger of losing it. Thus, the most critical challenge now faced by the Tibetan Buddhist tradition is simply the question of how to continue this tradition in the face of modernization and the unprecedented material development of the past half century.

Continuing a genuine lineage of Buddhism in our modern world will be possible only by each practitioner going deeper into the heart of dharma, the heart of experience and realization. However, this means breaking free of any fixations we may have on purely cultural forms of Buddhism, to which we so easily become attached because of their "foreignness," their novel and exotic qualities. It is entirely possible for our attachment to such forms to become so strong that it blocks us from achieving any genuine realization. If, for example, we find our Buddhist practice only in the shrine room (where we are more or less alone) and not equally in the shopping mall (where we will find our children and neighbors), then we are missing the point and losing our way. Our fixation on spiritual culture is something we need to transcend. The question is, how *can* we go beyond?

Long ago, Buddha instructed his disciples to "act in accord with the times and the society" in which they found themselves. Likewise, we can look at our own time and place for the *upayas* or skillful means best suited to it. The responsibility for this rests with the mutual efforts of teachers, students, and the lay population. It is a universal responsibility in the sense that this effort has as its goal the liberation of all beings from suffering.

While we essentially possess the same spiritual nature throughout our lives, the spiritual education and training of children and youth merit special attention because they have such an immediate impact on lives that are newly forming. When the spiritual training of children is applied consciously and with care, it nurtures the development of genuine knowledge—a profound understanding of both our inner and outer worlds. Insights generated from such knowledge are inherently liberating and meaningful. They support the aspiration for and accomplishment of positive relative qualities in relation to others—understanding, generosity, loving-kindness, and benevolent, skillful activity—and the recognition of one's own fundamentally pure, wakeful, and transcendent nature.

Notes

1. These statements are representative of the teachings given by Buddha Shakyamuni in his third cycle of teachings known as the Third Turning of the Wheel of Dharma. They are also known as the teachings on buddha nature, or *tathagatagarbha.* Sutras in this cycle include the Tathagatagarbha Sutra, the Srimala Devi Sutra, and the Mahayana Mahaparinirvana Sutra.

2. For the Buddhist view of mind and phenomena, see Khenpo Tsultrim Gyamtso Rinpoche (2002). Also see the works of Dignaga and Dharmakirti, seventh-century Indian philosophers and logicians who composed authoritative texts on valid cognition.

3. Of the three baskets, or *pitakas,* of the Buddha's teachings, it is the Vinaya Pitaka, the collection of teachings on discipline, which contains instructions on the three wheels. The other baskets are the Sutra Pitaka, the collection of teachings on meditation, and the Abhidharma Pitaka, the collection of teachings on discriminating knowledge. Their function is to remedy the three primary kleshas of passion, aggression, and ignorance.

4. Young monastics, as well as the lay population, may attend some Vajrayana empowerments primarily for the purpose of receiving its "blessings" and creating an auspicious connection to its wisdom, rather than as a means for entering the actual practices associated with the empowerment. Both the Refuge and Bodhisattva vows are integral aspects of all empowerments, whether received as "blessings" or as entrance to its actual practices.

5. This holy day is variously called "Vesak," or Buddha Day, and the Tibetan calendar may differ from other calendars with regard to the calculation of the date on which it falls.

6. The collection of teachings on discipline; see note 3.

7. Nalanda University was established in the fifth century B.C.E. and flourished for more

than one thousand years. Located in the state of Bihar, its curriculum encompassed not only spiritual studies but also secular subjects such as grammar, logic, medicine, arts, and crafts. It attracted scholars from China, Korea, Japan, Tibet, Sri Lanka, Indonesia, and all the regions of India. Among the abbots and masters of Nalanda are many of the most important figures in the history of Indian and Tibetan Buddhism. See Lyons (2004).

References

Gampopa. 1959. *The jewel ornament of liberation.* Translated by Herbert V. Guenther. Berkeley, Calif.: Shambhala.

Khenpo Tsultrim Gyamtso Rinpoche. 2002. *Progressive stages of meditation on emptiness.* Auckland, New Zealand: Zhyisil Chokyi Ghatsal.

Lyons, Tim. 2004. Nalanda Mahavihara. *Bodhi* 7(special inaugural edition):94–97.

Martin, Michelle. 2003. Music in the sky: The life, art and teachings of the 17th Karmapa. Ithaca, N.Y.: Snow Lion.

Patrul Rinpoche. 1994. *Words of my perfect teacher.* San Francisco: HarperCollins.

CHAPTER 15

Narrative and Imagination: The Role of Texts and Storytelling in Nurturing Spirituality in Judaism

Howard Schwartz

> I will set aside the life-giving Torah for you, by which you and your
> children will live in health and tranquility.
> *Sephardi Mahzor*

When we speak of children's spirituality in Judaism, we must address two separate issues. One is whether children are intrinsically spiritual. On this point there is no question in Jewish tradition but that the child is a spiritual being. The other issue is how spirituality is instilled in Jewish children. The answer is that it is developed using the techniques of storytelling and the stories found in the Bible to provide examples of spiritual men and women, as well as spiritual children, who can serve as role models. Nor are these stories limited to the Bible, but are found in all of postbiblical Jewish literature. An examination of these texts reveals an attitude of deep concern not only for the welfare but also for the spirituality of children. The best way to discern the traditional Jewish views about the spirituality of children is to examine these texts.

The key concept underlying the spirituality of children in Jewish tradition is the purity of the soul. Unlike Christian teachings, Judaism does not include a belief in original sin, nor is there a Jewish ritual equivalent to baptism. Therefore, a newborn child is regarded as having been born sinless, with a pure soul. Indeed, the purity of the child and the purity of the newborn soul are synonymous. These souls of the unborn are said to be kept in the Treasury of Souls in Paradise, where they await their turn to be born. When the time comes, the angel Lailah directs the soul to enter a seed and sees to it that the seed is planted in an embryo. The angel accompanies the infant in the womb, reading to the unborn child and revealing secrets of great wisdom. Just as the infant is born, Lailah puts her finger to the infant's lips, as if to say, "Shhh," and this causes the child to forget everything he or she had learned and creates an indentation above the upper lip.[1] This fascinating myth suggests that from the time of birth, the spiritual aspect of a newborn child has already been cultivated and that at some unconscious level we are aware of spiritual secrets we have otherwise forgotten. Thus spiritual truth is to be found beneath the surface, if we would only seek it out.

An oral variant of this tale describes God as sitting in a circle with many baby spirits that are about to be born.[2] God knows that the babies won't experience the same joy on earth that they experienced in heaven, and he doesn't want them to be dissatisfied. So God touches his finger just below their noses, leaving an indentation on their upper lips. This makes them forget the joys of heaven, so they can adapt to the world into which they are born. God's concern for the unborn babies is palpable in this tale, as well as his awareness that life on earth involves suffering.

In the Torah there are many examples of direct communication with God. God speaks to Abraham on several occasions, and Moses remains in close contact with God through the entire Exodus. And when Rachel, Jacob's wife, is desperate to bear a child, she goes to Mount Moriah, where Abraham was once about to offer Isaac as a sacrifice, and she inquires of God.[3] For young readers of these texts, God appears as a fatherlike figure to whom they can confide their hopes and fears, and who will personally care for them. The trust in God instilled by these crucial biblical stories goes a long way toward creating the kind of I-Thou relationship that is the underlying basis of spirituality.

Indeed, one of the primary metaphors for God's relationship to Israel is that of a father to his children, as expressed in the identification of the people of Israel as the Children of Israel. This presumes the tenderness of a father for his children, and reflects the father's love, as well as the father's awareness of his children's love for him. The father assumes the innocence and spiritual purity of his children and the perfection of their love. This view of the love between God and Israel is projected onto the belief of the spirituality of children in Jewish tradition. This metaphor works both ways: just as a parent has a tender love for his children, so God has a tender love for his children, the Children of Israel. And just as a child has a natural love for his or her parent, so do the Children of Israel love God, their divine Father.

God's fatherlike concern for his children finds expression in a famous midrash that describes a nurturing God who raises the male children of the Israelites after they were abandoned because of Pharaoh's decree against newborn boys (Exodus 1:22). After they were grown, the boys returned to their families. When they were asked who took care of them, they said, "A handsome young man took care of all our needs." And when the Israelites came to the Red Sea, those children were there, and when they saw God at the sea, they said to their parents, "That is the one who took care of us when we were in Egypt."[4]

God's role in guiding the Children of Israel through the wilderness finds expression in the Torah in the verse "God went before them in a pillar of cloud by day, to guide them along the way, and in a pillar of fire by night, to give them light" (Exodus 13:21). However, in the midrash the verse "God went before them" (Exodus 12:21) is interpreted literally to mean that God himself took a lantern and went before the people, escorting them in the wilderness. This personification is elaborated by describing God "like a father holding a torch for his son," and Rashi, the preeminent biblical commentator, emphasizes that "in this way God showed the nations of the world how dear the children were to him." This midrashic interpretation presents a powerful anthropomorphic image of God carrying a lantern and striding before the people through the wilderness, as well as that of a father guiding his children.

Remarkably, considering that Judaism is monotheistic, the Children of Israel also have a mother figure. This is the Shekhinah, who is also identified in kabbalistic literature, particularly in the *Zohar,* the central text of Jewish mysticism, as the Bride of

God. Earlier, in the talmudic era, around the fifth century, the term *Shekhinah* was identified as the Divine Presence, or God's presence in the world. However, by the thirteenth century, the feminine term had evolved into the notion of a largely independent mythic figure, God's Bride, whose home was the Temple in Jerusalem, and whose children are the Children of Israel, who are said to be sheltered under the wings of the Shekhinah.

The devotion of the Shekhinah to her children, the Children of Israel, is found in a startling myth from the *Zohar* in which God's Bride confronts God over the destruction of the Temple in Jerusalem and the exile of her children. Here God's bride makes the decision to abandon her spouse, God, and to go into exile with her children, the Children of Israel. This exile will last until the Temple is rebuilt and her children all return to the Holy Land. Reading between the lines, it is not hard to see here that a mother's responsibility and devotion to her children are expected to be even greater than her devotion to her husband, their father.

Another perspective to this exile is found in the Talmud, where it is said, "Alas for the children who have been exiled from their father's table."[5] From both points of view, the people of Israel are viewed as children in a family. From the perspective of this talmudic aphorism, the children have been exiled from their father's table, thus from his favor. This is a tragic estrangement of the father-child relationship. But in the *Zohar*, after having been cut off from their father, the children seek refuge with their mother. God's bride places most of the blame on God for this tragic turn of events that caused the Temple in Jerusalem to be destroyed and sent her into exile with her children. This motherly protection provides great consolation to the children. The myth reminds us that children need to be protected, and that they need both a father and a mother to be complete. But no matter what, their mother will be loyal to them, even if it results in estrangement from her husband.

This dual portrayal of father and mother figures, and the identification of the people of Israel as their children, clearly reinforces the key kabbalistic principle of "as above, so below." Just as children normally have a father and mother, so the Children of Israel also have the parental figures of God and the Shekhinah. From this perspective, it can be seen that children represent an archetype of spirituality in Jewish tradition, for in this metaphor their lives are parallel to the divine family, where human parents are implicitly linked with divine figures. This expresses the sacredness of the family unit and is reinforced in the commandment to honor your father and mother (Exodus 20:12). Here we can recognize that not only is the child viewed as a paradigm of spirituality, but the family unit in itself is regarded as sacred.

To a large extent, children's spirituality in Judaism has been shaped by biblical narrative and by the process of storytelling. The biblical accounts of the lives of the patriarchs, Abraham, Isaac, and Jacob, became so well known to the people that they came to think of the patriarchs as a part of their family. Abraham was referred to as "Abraham Aveinu"—our Father Abraham. Moses was known as "Moshe Rabbenu"— our teacher Moses. Just as children naturally attempt to emulate the ways of their parents, so Jewish children over the ages have attempted to emulate the holy ways of the patriarchs. Further, the extensive clusters of legends about the patriarchs found in rabbinic literature, which were also very much a part of the daily study of children, strongly enhanced the sense of incorporating a personal family narrative into their lives. They sought, above all, to emulate these holy lives.

One of the primary models used to create a sense of spirituality in children is that of unusually spiritual children. Naturally, children were encouraged to emulate these spiritual models. The best known is Abraham, who is presented as an exceptionally spiritual child. Abraham was seen by Jews as their first ancestor, yet nothing is said about his childhood in Genesis. When he first appears, he is a grown man. Yet there are, remarkably, as many rabbinic legends about Abraham as a child as there are about Abraham the patriarch, despite the fact that Abraham's childhood is never mentioned in the Bible. This is surely no accident. Abraham represents the symbol of the purest faith in Judaism, and his frequent portrayal as a child clearly indicates that his primary characteristics of purity and faith in God are associated as well with children in Jewish tradition. It is not surprising, then, that in his dying vision,[6] Abraham is suddenly transformed into a happy child, and he sees a great many happy children coming toward him. Abraham plays with them and runs with them to hear the wonderful songs of the angels. They walk among sweet-smelling trees and rest under the Tree of Life.

Above all, the ancient rabbis were very curious to know how Abraham discovered God's existence, and in one famous midrash they imagined a deeply spiritual child who sought to comprehend who ruled the world:

> When Abraham was still a boy, he saw the sun shining upon the earth, and he thought that surely the sun must be God, and therefore he would serve it. So he served the sun all that day, and prayed to it. But when evening came and the sun had set, Abraham said to himself, surely the sun cannot be God. And Abraham wondered who had made the heavens and the earth.
>
> That night, when Abraham lifted his eyes to the sky, he saw the stars and moon before him, and he thought that the moon must have created the world, and the stars were its servants. And Abraham served the moon and prayed to it all night.
>
> But in the morning, when the sun shone upon the earth again, and the moon and stars could not be seen, Abraham understood that they were not gods, but servants of God. From that day on Abraham knew the Lord and went in the ways of the Lord until the day of his death.[7]

This is an important midrash, in that it offers an explanation of how Abraham discovered the existence of God, and therefore it provides the origin of monotheism. Above all, it shows that Abraham's intrinsically spiritual nature found expression in his childhood, and that he felt a need from an early age to discover and worship the true God.

Another midrash about Abraham's childhood reveals God's intense concern about him from the time of his birth:

> Abraham's mother went to a cave to give birth to escape King Nimrod's decree that all newborn boys be put to death. For Nimrod had seen a sign that a child born at that time would overthrow him. After giving birth, Abraham's mother grew afraid for the safety of her family, and at last she abandoned the infant in the cave and returned home. Then the angel Gabriel descended to the cave and fed the infant with his thumb, from

which milk and honey flowed, and because he was fed in that miraculous way, the boy began to grow at the rate of a year every day. And on the third day, while exploring the cave, he found a stone glowing in one of the crevices of the cave. Then the angel, who knew how precious that glowing stone was, put it on a chain, and hung it around Abraham's neck.

Thirteen days later Abraham's mother returned to the cave, for she could not put the fate of the infant out of her mind. She expected to find that the child was no longer living, but instead she found a grown boy, who said that he was her child. She refused to believe it at first, but when he showed her the glowing stone and the sacred light it cast, she came to believe that a miracle had taken place.

Abraham wore that glowing jewel all the days of his life, and it was said that whoever was ill and looked into that stone soon healed, and that he also used the stone as an astrolabe, to study the stars. Some say that after Abraham's death it was hung on the wheel of the sun.[8]

Of course, Abraham had a special destiny, as the intercession of Gabriel indicates. But this midrash also conveys the sense that even as a child Abraham had a naturally spiritual nature, which was enhanced by the divine food provided by the angel Gabriel. So too was his finding of the stone destined, itself the subject of a chain of legends. Here the stone can be identified as a higher soul. When Abraham receives it, he achieves a new depth of spirituality, and grows up to become the patriarch who communicated with God and founded the Jewish religion. Indeed, in kabbalistic tradition there are five levels of the soul, where the two highest levels exist on high. In receiving the sacred stone, Abraham can be seen as receiving a higher soul, which fuses with his earthly soul.

The identification of an enchanted stone with the soul is made explicitly in a tale found in Jewish folklore of a wonder child whose soul is contained in a jewel she clutched in her hand when she was born.[9] This child is described as having been conceived from the prayers of her parents at midnight on Shavuot, the observance of the giving of the Torah at Mount Sinai, at the moment when the sky opened. This is a particularly holy time, when, it is believed, all wishes made will come true. In the story, this child is not only exceptionally talented and beautiful, but also spiritually pure. Much like Sleeping Beauty, when the wonder child is separated from the jewel, she falls into the sleep of death until it is restored to her. It is significant that the soul of this exceptional child is found inside a jewel, an object that is a symbol not only of beauty but also of spiritual perfection.

Usually there is some indication of the unusual nature of a holy child. Noah, described as the most righteous in his generation (Genesis 6:9), was born with an aura radiating from his face.[10] Such a child is considered a manifestation of divine purity and wisdom and is acknowledged as a deeply spiritual being. Yet all children are regarded as pure beings.

In addition to storytelling, a great deal of the teaching of Jewish texts, especially the Torah, the first five books of the Bible, consists of exegesis. Students are not only taught the traditional interpretations of the Torah, they are encouraged to arrive at their own interpretations through a process of discussion and debate. This challenge of attempting to resolve the kinds of problems that crop up in the text has the effect of drawing the students even deeper into the spiritual realm the texts represent, which, out of their deep involvement in studying, the students make their own. Sometimes perplexing passages yield unexpected explanations, which, in themselves, reinforce the spiritual underpinnings of the sacred texts.

One unusual midrashic interpretation seems to indicate a parallelism between the birth of souls and the birth of children. Since souls represent the pure essence of being, the identification of souls and children underscores the intrinsic spirituality of children. This interpretation grows out of the reading of the verse "And the souls they had made in Haran" (Genesis 12:5). The usual interpretation of this verse is that "souls" refers to the converts that Abraham and Sarah made in Haran. In this reading, however, "souls" refers not to converts but to souls, and therefore, although "Sarah was barren; she had no children" (Genesis 16:1), Sarah gave birth to souls. In this interpretation, "the souls they had made in Haran" suggests that Sarah did give birth, but to souls, not to children. Thus, Sarah is portrayed as a goddesslike figure who gives birth not to human children but to souls.[11]

This brings us to that central, inescapable episode of the Binding of Isaac in Genesis 22, what is known as the Akedah. Here Abraham seems to value God's command to sacrifice Isaac more than his love of his long-awaited son. God, too, cannot but be seen as harsh in his demand. After all, this is the son Abraham has awaited all his life, born to him when he was one hundred years old, the son who holds the key to the covenants between Abraham and God. To compound the matter, Abraham does not dispute God's command to sacrifice his son, while in Genesis 18:20–32 Abraham is determined in his efforts to convince God not to destroy the people of Sodom. How can this portrayal of Abraham be reconciled with the tradition that closely associates Abraham with the spiritual purity of children? The answer, I believe, can be found in the ultimate fate of Isaac—the Angel of the Lord intervenes from heaven, demonstrating that for God and the angels, the life of a child is the most important of all, and establishing for all time the principle that there will be no more child sacrifice. At the same time, Abraham, like Job after him, is perceived at having passed a grueling divine test, demonstrating that his faith in God was more important to him than anything else, even his beloved son Isaac. While modern readers may not find this explanation satisfactory, and continue to regard the entire story of the binding of Isaac as perplexing, Abraham's role as God's loyal servant is reinforced, while Isaac is saved, and heaven has clearly acknowledged the precious value of a child's life. Naturally, the first step in developing spirituality is to recognize the precious nature of life, and ultimately the story of Isaac does convey this important lesson.

Yet there is a late midrash, from the thirteenth century, that changes the very basis of the narrative in which Abraham does *not* slay Isaac, insisting instead that Abraham *did* slay Isaac, and Isaac's soul ascended on high to the celestial academy of Shem and Eber. There his soul was taught all the secrets of heaven and shown all of heaven and hell. And after three years, the soul of Isaac descended into his body and he was reborn.[12] It is apparent that having his soul spend three years on high strongly indicates that Isaac was a holy person. Even his later blindness is explained in mythical terms, that the tears shed by the angels witnessing Abraham's upraised knife, fell into Isaac's eyes and made them grow dim. Thus, in his old age Isaac was blind to the world around him but still able to perceive the secrets of heaven.

Although the legends about Isaac's ascent on high seem to encourage the study of mysticism, since Isaac was said to have been taught the secrets of heaven, the opposing view predominates. Here concern about the spirituality of children is reflected as well in some warning tales, such as one about a certain child of exceptional understanding who read the Book of Ezekiel in his teacher's house and lost his life. The warning is clear: children should not be permitted to study mystical texts, which Ezekiel's vision represents.

Yet this stern view of the dangers posed by mystical teachings is turned on its head in a tale found in the story of Rabbi Gadiel the Child.[13] This legend is one of the fullest expressions of the belief in the purity and wisdom of children. Two disciples of the talmudic sage Rabbi Shimon bar Yohai met a child in a city they were visiting. Each time he spoke, mysteries from on high were revealed. The rabbis began to feel they were in the presence of an angel. They asked the child how it was possible that he was acquainted with such mysteries, and he told them that his soul was the soul of Rabbi Gadiel, who had been martyred in an earlier life at the age of seven. Even then he had been recognized as a great scholar and one of great purity. His soul had been received at once in heaven, where he was made head of his own academy. Still, even though the greatest sages in Paradise sat at his feet, he had longed to know what it meant to live a full life. And when God recognized his great longing, Rabbi Gadiel had been reborn into that family, but he had brought all of his knowledge with him.

As we have seen, the central role of stories and storytelling in Judaism creates a powerful link to the mythic past and a desire, on the part of children, to develop their own spirituality, modeled on that of the patriarchs and matriarchs, especially Abraham. In such a universe, ruled over by God, all things and all people have a purpose and destiny. The act of storytelling thus reinforces this spiritual view of existence, both by the act of storytelling and by the stories themselves.

Notes

1. Babylonian Talmud (hereafter B.) Niddah 16b, 30b; B. Sanhedrin 96a; Midrash Tanhuma-Yelammedenu, Pekudei 3; Zohar Hadash 68:3; Sefer ha-Zikhronot 10:19–23; Be'er ha-Hasidut 1:216; Aseret ha-Dibrot 79; Avodat ha-Kodeah, Introduction; Nishmat Hayim 2:18; Anaf Yosef on B. Niddah 30b; Amud ha-Avodash 103b; Avkat Rakel in Beit ha-Midrash 1:153–55; Likutei ha-Pardes 4d—5c.

2. Oral version collected by Howard Schwartz from his uncle, Maury Schwartz. Variants are B. Niddah 16b, 30b; B. Sanhedrin 6a; B. Avot 3:1; Midrash Tanhuma, Pekudei 3; Zohar Hadash 68:3; Sefer ha-Zikhronot; Be'er ha-Hasidut 1:216; Avodat ha-Kodesh, Introduction.

3. Genesis 25:21–26

4. Exodus Rabbah 23:8, 23:15. This might also be read as a myth about the continued existence of the multitude of Hebrew boys that were slaughtered because of Pharaoh's decree that all firstborn boys be put to death. Unable to accept so many deaths, the myth explains that the boys were still alive, being taken care of by God. In this midrash, the boys point out God, clearly per-

sonified, at the Red Sea. God had taken the form of a young man. Who can better testify about the one who had saved them than the boys themselves?

5. B. Berakhot 3a.

6. Yalkut Shim'oni, Hayei Sarah; Testament of Abraham (A) 11:1; Vita Adae et Evae 25:3, 42:4; Zohar 1:212a.

7. Sefer ha-Yashar 9:6, 9:13–19.

8. B. Bava Batra 16.

9. Israel Folktale Archives (IFA) 6405. Collected by Ilana Zohar of Egypt from her mother, Flora Cohen. Aarne-Thompson (*Types of the Folktale*; hereafter AT) 412: The Maiden with a Separable Soul in a Necklace. A variant is IFA 4859, told by Esther Mikhael of Iraqi Kurdistan to her granddaughter, Esther.

10. Sefer ha-Yashar.

11. Rashi on Genesis 12:5; Zohar 1:79a, 3:168a; Zohar Hadash, Balak 53; Megaleh Amukot on Genesis 30:23; Or ha-Hayim on Deuteronomy 21:10–11; Tiferet Shlomo on Genesis 12:5; Sihot Shedim 1 in Sifrei Rabbi Tzadok ha-Kohen.

12. Targum Pseudo-Yonathan on Genesis 22:19; Genesis Rabbah 56; 3 Enoch 45:3; Pirkei de-Rabbi Eliezer 31; Hadar Zekenim 10b in Beit ha-Midrash 5:157; Perush Ramban al Sefer Yetzirah 125. This radical myth grows out of the absence of Isaac at the end of Genesis 22. Abraham descends the mountain and rejoins his young men, who had accompanied him to Mount Moriah. But Isaac is not mentioned. The rabbis wondered why Isaac was missing, and this alternate version of Genesis 22 offers a radical explanation—because Abraham slew Isaac. The parallels to the death and resurrection of Jesus after three days are obvious, making this a rare Jewish myth likely inspired by Christian sources.

13. From Seder Gan Eden in Beit ba-Midrash, edited by A. Jellinek, 3:136–37. Also found in Otsar Midrashim 1:87. A variant is found in Zohar 3:186a.

CHAPTER 16

Sanctifying Time: A Jewish Perspective on Prayer, Holy Days, and Blessings in the Life of Children

Shoshana Silberman

A well-known Hassidic tale depicts the deeply spiritual nature of children:

> There once was a farmer who had a son who could not distinguish one Hebrew letter from another, nor could he recite a single prayer. This father thought it was a waste of time to take his child to the synagogue to pray. One Yom Kippur, however, the father decided to take him along. In his pocket, the child put the little silver flute that he played when he tended his father's sheep. The child was so moved by the sad, soulful melodies, that he longed to play his flute. When he asked his father's permission, the farmer scolded him, for it was forbidden to do such a thing on the holiest day of the year. All day long the child tried to restrain himself, but finally could no longer resist. He reached for his flute and blew one long, powerful note, much to the dismay of his father. The founder of the Hassidic movement, the great Baal Shem Tov, spoke out, telling all present not to be angry or embarrassed, for the child spoke to God in his own way. So strong was the child's desire to pray that his prayer on the flute not only went straight to God, but also carried the prayers of the entire congregation up to the gates of heaven. (Based on Ruthen 1986)

From a Jewish perspective, children have an innate capacity for spirituality. The Talmud even describes children in sacred terms: "Children receive the presence of the Shechinah [the Divine Presence]" (Kallah Rabbati Baraita 8) and "The world itself rests upon the breath of children in the schoolhouse" (Shabbat 119b).

My own research (Silberman 1998) supports this viewpoint. I studied how children from eight to twelve years of age conceptualize God. Nearly nine hundred students (from three Jewish movements: Conservative, Reform, and Reconstructionist) were surveyed. The methodology included a survey form, open-ended questions, and drawings.

On the whole, these children hold a strong belief in God, especially the belief that God is everywhere and that God is someone to whom they can talk and who answers their prayers. They see God as omniscient, although not necessarily omnipotent. Their God creates daily. Although God sometimes punishes, God is also described as an "enabler," giving them strength and power. The children I surveyed reported feeling close to God both in synagogue and when alone, especially at times of great emotion (when they were happy, sad, troubled, lonely, or when someone died or was born). Their "proof" that God is real is that creation itself points to God's existence.

Although the capacity for spirituality resides in children, the predominant Jewish view is that children's sense of the divine must be actively developed as opposed to merely being nurtured. The Torah itself (Deuteronomy 11:18–20) instructs parents to teach spiritual lessons to children:

> You shall love Adonai your God, with all your heart, with all your soul and with all your might. And these words which I command you today shall always be in your heart. Teach them to your children. Speak of them when you are at home and when you are away. Repeat them when you lie down at night and when you rise up in the morning.

The rabbis of the Talmudic period (200 B.C.E. to 500 C.E.) interpreted this text to mean that one should teach a child Torah as soon as the child can speak (Bialik and Ravinsky 1992, 635). A child was also instructed to recite prayers and follow Jewish law as soon as possible. For example, a child who knew to whom a benediction was addressed was invited to participate in reciting the Grace After Meals with the adults (Brachot 48a). The child who could shake a lulav (a palm branch with willow and myrtle) properly, don a prayer shawl, or care for tefillin (phylacteries—small leather cases containing scriptural verses worn on the forehead and arm during morning weekday prayers) was encouraged to do so, even though he was not legally responsible for fulfilling Jewish law until the age of thirteen.

The purpose of early instruction of Jewish observance was to create a "mensch," a kind and decent child, with a strong moral character. Although the rabbis of the Talmudic period spoke of religious instruction, they did not speak of "spirituality" in the ways we do today. For them, spirituality was associated with ethical behavior. Acts of loving-kindness, such as feeding the hungry, visiting the sick, and welcoming guests, were sacred expressions that imitated the divine. For the rabbis, these ethical acts flowed from studying Torah (scriptural and oral teachings of traditional Judaism) and observing the commandments.

This historical emphasis remains a strong component of the development of Jewish spirituality today. Contemporary Judaism, however, is actively seeking additional ways that speak to today's children. Nonetheless, the challenge remains the same. While Genesis teaches that each child has a divine spark within him or her, that spark must grow to sustain both the relationship to God and, simultaneously, the relationship to other humans. There is a Hassidic saying that we reach out in three directions: up to God, out to other people, and into our own hearts. The secret is that all three directions are truly the same. When we reach out to another person, we find ourselves and God. When we find God, we find others and our true selves. When we find ourselves, we reach God and other people. This, in essence, is the spirituality Judaism challenges parents and educators to teach children.

Prayer as a Means for Spiritual Growth

The Jewish prayer book was not composed by one person or a single authoritative synod. The whole prayer book spans about three thousand years (Garfiel 1958, 24). It not only contains the religious ideas and beliefs expressed in the prayers but also alludes to the historical events, the social and theological changes and hopes of the Jewish people. God's mercy, kindness, compassion, and love are frequent themes. Although all Jews use a prayer book with the same essential prayers, there are variations by geographic location as well as ideology. All prayer books, though, have three basic kinds of prayer: praise, thanksgiving, and petition. There are also prayers of meditation and reflection.

Most prayers are in the first-person plural, emphasizing group consciousness, so as to encourage a sense of comradeship and responsibility. Although one may pray individually, there are certain prayers that can only be said in a prayer quorum, for example, the prayer celebrating God's holiness. For Judaism, the spiritual life is nurtured with others in community. Some prayers are sung or chanted, whereas others are said silently. Prayers are meant not just to communicate with God but also to be reflective, inspiring a person to action. As one recites God's attributes, one should be moved to imitate the divine. Although prescribed prayers constitute the framework of Jewish prayer, the rabbis taught, "Do not make your prayers a fixed thing" (Pirkei Avot 2:18). Maimonides, the great codifier of Jewish law, wrote, "Prayer without devotion is not prayer" and "one must pray with feeling" (Garfiel 1958, 28)

In the Jewish tradition, there are no special prayers written solely for children. However, two prayers in particular have often been taught to and said with children, including very young ones. The first is the Sh'ma/V'ahavta, which are said together. The Shema ("Hear O Israel: Adonai our God, Adonai is One") speaks of God's unity and uniqueness; the V'ahavta (previously translated) tells of the need to love and have God at the center of one's life. This prayer is often said with children in the evening before going to bed. The second prayer, the Modeh Ani, is said upon rising: "I give thanks to You, eternal Sovereign, Who with mercy has restored my soul within me. Your faithfulness is great." Perhaps these prayers have been recited with children because they occur at very intimate times that parents and children share together. In a close setting, these prayers are a way of offering both comforting words and a sense of inner security.

That reciting the Shema/V'ahavta prayer with children can be a very spiritual moment has been recognized by both educators and parents. In many religious schools today, pajama parties are held for young children where they learn to recite the Shema. Elementary school children are creating Shema pillows, with the words of the prayer, to take home. Some are singing another prayer that follows the Shema at bedtime: "In the name of Adonai, the God of Israel, may (the angel) Michael be at my right hand and

Gabriel at my left; before me Uriel; behind me Raphael; and above my head the Shechinah, the divine presence."

Besides these special prayers, children are usually introduced to prayer through "blessings." Blessings are formulaic prayers that begin with the introductory verse: "Blessed are You, Adonai our God, Sovereign of the world," followed by the appropriate ending such as, "Who brings forth bread from the earth." There are blessings, for example, before one eats fruit, drinks milk, smells a fragrant spice, or sees a rainbow. There are also blessings upon seeing special people, such as those with great Torah wisdom.

Teaching a child to recite blessings is meant to create a more grateful person, one who is continuously aware of God's presence in his or her life. A blessing ensures that an orange or an ocean, for example, will not be taken for granted. In this way, even the everyday becomes sacred.

One of the challenges of engaging children in Jewish prayer today is that the prayers from the Jewish prayer book are in Hebrew. Although they can be translated and said in the vernacular, the Hebrew words connect Jews not only to the past but to Jewish communities around the world who use the same language in prayer. Consequently, children must first be taught to read the prayers fluently and often sing them using the appropriate melodies. They must also learn the order of prayers and the "choreography" of the service. Some schools require that students be able to translate the prayers; others expect that students know only key words or phrases. When students reach the age of thirteen and celebrate their bar/bat mitzvah (coming of age) ceremony, they are expected to learn to lead some or all of the service, as well as to chant selections from the Torah and Prophets, using the correct ancient musical notation system. This is quite an awesome task.

Although teaching these skills is necessary, teaching for meaning is equally important, if the goal is to help children search for meaning and purpose in their lives. Children must be shown the value and importance of what they have been taught to read or recite by rote. Students need to explore concepts in the prayer book such as God's oneness/uniqueness, God's omnipresence, and God's covenantal relationship with them. Children need to understand how God is viewed metaphorically in the tradition as a Rock and Shield, a Protector and Savior, as well as a Healer and Redeemer.

Prior to the mid-twentieth century, children attended the Sabbath services geared to adults. They could come and go, staying longer as they felt more comfortable. As Jews moved to suburbia, more attention was paid to the needs of children. It was thought that children should have their own Sabbath morning service, usually called a junior congregation, modeled after the synagogue at which it took place. The Torah portion of the week was either read or told in story form, depending on the age of the students. Communal lunches or treats followed the service. These practices continue today. Congregations have also recently begun to offer special "family services" where parents and children can both learn and pray together.

One thing that has recently changed is the liturgy written for children. The prayer books have begun to include commentaries on the prayers, stories, poems, and experiential activities. New also is the idea of using art to entice the young reader to further explore the text. This is done with graphics, micrography (the practice of using minuscule script to create abstract shapes or figurative designs), and illumination. Also included are the thoughts and spontaneous prayers of children themselves, such as the following (Silberman 1993, 8):

> Dear God,
>   You are the one that makes miracles. You help everyone, and worked so hard to make the earth and keep it alive. You made people, rainbows, the sun, moon, and stars. You made the sun to rise and set. You made all living things. Thank you so much, so very much. Love from one of your many creations,
>   Melissa Sands
>   Princeton, N.J., age 8

Through movement and dance, children are now encouraged to express their prayerfulness. Art projects, such as creating a mural with prayers that express the theme of God's love, help children delve deeper into the meaning of prayers and discover how they themselves are connected to them. Signing has also become a way for children to explore prayer. By using either standard American Sign Language or simply creating motions themselves, children experience not only the reinforcement of prayer vocabulary but the meaning as well.

Additional strategies are being tried to help children understand the prayer experience. One approach that challenges children to develop a more mature outlook is to ask them what is "wrong" with certain prayers such as: "Please make sure my friend gets a bad grade on his test." "Please make the baby my mom is going to have a girl." "Please give me an A on my math test, even if I did not have time to study." The ancient rabbis discouraged prayers that asked God to change the course of nature. A strategy used with adolescents to expand their thinking about prayer is to ask provocative questions such as: What difference does it make that God is One? Is mentioning ancestors in a prayer an attempt to bribe God?

As children grow, their conceptual ability expands and their emotions deepen. Preteens and adolescents are often searching for a personal relationship with God and are receptive to prayer and spirituality. At times their spirituality is very private. Some, for example, enjoy expressing their thoughts in journals and poetry. Simultaneously, they also are influenced by their peer culture, often preferring their own prayer services, with their own style of music. With their skills and enthusiasm, they can be wonderful service leaders and great role models for elementary-age students.

Because of the developmental differences between childhood and adolescence, any specific prayer can be approached at varying levels. Consider the prayer Mah Tovu (How Beautiful) that is sung when congregants first enter the sanctuary. It is based on a biblical story found in Numbers 22:2–25:9. Balak, king of Moab, was so against the Israelites passing through his land on their journey that he hired a magician named Balaam to stop Israel by cursing them. Balaam climbed a mountain and looked down on the Israelite encampment. Their peaceful dwellings and beautiful sanctuary touched his heart. Instead of a curse, words of blessing came out of his mouth: "How beautiful are your tents, O people of Jacob, and your dwelling places, O Israelites." Knowing the origin of this prayer makes it come alive for adolescents. The story can illuminate the concept of sanctifying God's name in the world and inspire teens to live in a way that will continually draw praise from others as well as make themselves proud. They can also be asked to recall periods in history when Jews were forbidden to pray together. Then, they can discuss how the synagogue and other sacred spaces are important to them, their family, and the community. They can also do "imagery" work, to reflect on other transitions in their lives, leading them to explore what helps them connect with God.

Children can be drawn to the same prayer by using a graphic with the words forming a tent to pique their interest from the start. Using this same text, they can also be engaged by asking them to count the number of times the word *I*, *me*, or *my* is used in the second paragraph of the Mah Tovu prayer: "Through Your loving-kindness I enter Your house to pray. Here in this special place, I will bow before You. Accept my prayers, Elohim, and answer me with mercy. Teach me Your ways of truth." This activity can lead to a discussion of why this prayer is in the singular (when the rest of the prayers to follow are in the plural) and how one makes the spiritual transition from individual concern to communal caring.

Stories have always been a way to engage children. At the center of the Sabbath service is the reading of the Torah. In Judaism, prayer is not only praise, petition, and thanksgiving but the reading of the sacred text, study, and reflection. Children are introduced to these narratives at home and in the synagogue.

Holy Days as a Means for Spiritual Growth

The Jewish holy days provide a multitude of spiritual moments, though each in a unique way. There are too many to discuss in one chapter, even briefly, but a sample can provide a window into the variety of spiritual opportunities for children to experience in the Jewish calendar year. The holy days include rituals that, through words, gestures, and actions, open the door to deep emotion and feelings of closeness to God (Wolpe 1993).

Because the Sabbath comes once a week, it offers a consistent opportunity for families to share sacred time together. Since work ceases on the Sabbath, there is much to prepare ahead of time. This business adds to the anticipation of a special occasion. When children help polish silver candlesticks or set the table, for example, or teens have the honor of braiding the Sabbath hallah (bread), or baking cookies for dessert, they, too, help usher in the Sabbath Queen on Friday evening.

The meal begins with candle lighting and the blessings over the wine and hallah. Traditionally, a hymn is sung to welcome the Sabbath Queen. Songs are sung by the husband (and more recently the wife, as well) to show praise and devotion for one's spouse. This expression of love is important for children to witness and teaches a lesson about a Jewish view of marriage. At the dinner table, it is customary to bless the children in the family. The parent(s) place both hands on the head of each child. The traditional blessings are, for girls, "May you be like Sarah, Rebecca, Leah, and Rachel" and for boys, "May you be like Ephraim and Manasseh" (the sons of Joseph). It is also appropriate for parents to add their own personal blessings. They conclude with the threefold benediction, recited by the priests of old: "May Adonai bless and protect you. May Adonai shine upon you with graciousness. May Adonai look upon you with favor and grant you peace."

In this intimate moment, a spiritual bond is created. Even children at camp or adolescents who are traveling or away at college can receive this blessing by telephone or e-mail to demonstrate that a parent's love, like God's, is unconditional and unending. A child once described the experience of receiving a blessing as being "zapped, but in a good way" (Grishaver 1980).

On Sabbath morning there are synagogue services, followed by a festive lunch. The afternoon offers families a chance to relax and be in harmony with the rest of creation, such as finding a pleasant route to take a walk; sitting in a garden to observe and smell; spending time talking to close friends; playing board games (without keeping score); reading Bible tales, Talmudic legends, or modern holiday stories; viewing family albums; and having grandparents share stories about when they were young.

The Sabbath ends at sunset, with a beautiful ceremony called Havdalah. In the dark, huddled together, the family recites blessings over wine, a braided candle, and spices. Children are often given the task/honor of holding the ritual objects. For example, they can pass around the spice box so that the fragrance, symbolic of the Sabbath day, will linger during the week. The Sabbath teaches the importance of focusing on the spiritual. Without words of instruction, children experience and internalize this sacred moment in time.

While worship and study in the synagogue are an important part of the Sabbath, it is the home where much of the Sabbath is celebrated. The spiritual is not something reserved for a designated sacred place but created in the everyday—at home, with family.

Although children are not required to follow the commandments regarding a holy day, parents involve them, as much as possible. They may not attend the complete lengthy Rosh Hashana (New Year) service, but parents make sure children come into the sanctuary to hear the blast of the shofar. Children do not fast on Yom Kippur (the Day of Atonement) but are taught the importance of saying how sorry they are to God, family, and friends for the wrongs they did during the year. They, too, can experience God's forgiveness.

The three major festivals in the Jewish year—Sukkot, Passover, and Shavuot—have certain rituals that involve children. On Sukkot (Tabernacles), children participate in decorating the family or synagogue sukkah. They sit out under the stars and offer prayers acknowledging God's bountiful gifts. At the conclusion of this eight-day festival, the holiday of Simhat Torah (Rejoicing with the Torah) takes place. Simhat Torah celebrates the completion of reading the Torah cycle and beginning anew. Children march in joyous parades, waving gaily decorated flags. Although usually one must be thirteen to be called up to recite a blessing when a selection from the Torah is read, children are honored on this holiday and called up to the Torah. Either wrapped in a prayer shawl or placed beneath a prayer shawl spread like a canopy, the children in the congregation proudly recite the special blessing. In this way, children are seen as part of the ongoing life of Torah.

Some congregations now use this occasion to hold a consecration ceremony, usually for first or third graders. It officially marks the beginning of children's Torah study. Gifts such as miniature Torahs and prayer books are distributed. Often the children are given the opportunity to lead some prayers that they have learned. This is a way of acknowledging the children's new status as Torah learners and to demonstrate that the Torah is their inheritance, too. Based on a medieval custom, the children are given something sweet to associate Torah learning with sweetness.

The festival of Passover is referred to in the Torah as the "holiday of matzah," "the holiday of spring," and "the time of our liberation." One might add "the holiday of children." That is because so much of the Passover seder revolves around them. First and foremost are the "Four Questions" that traditionally the youngest, but often all of the younger children present, ask. Children tirelessly practice these verses each year before Passover, in order to recite them competently:

> How different this night is from all other nights!
> On all other nights we eat bread or matzah (unleavened bread). On this night why do we eat only matzah?
> On all other nights we eat all kinds of vegetables. On this night why must we eat maror (a bitter herb)?
> On all other nights we do not have to dip vegetables even once. On this night why do we dip vegetables twice?
> On all other nights we eat our meal sitting any way we like. On this night why do we lean on pillows?

The Four Questions are indeed important because they are recited early in the seder. They focus on the differences the child sees between the seder and a regular meal. The child's role is crucial: the ritual cannot proceed without these questions being asked. The rest of the seder will tell the story of the exodus from Egypt, which, along with the creation of the world and the revelation on Mount Sinai, comprise the central narratives of the Jewish people.

For children, asking the Four Questions is their big moment, not only because they display their Hebrew chanting skills, but also because the recitation marks their centrality. Their questions are an intellectual kind of appetizer to help those present start the spiritual journey ahead. Their questions are a model for the seder experience in which all are invited to inquire and exchange thoughts with each other to fulfill the injunction that "in each generation, everyone must think of himself or herself as having personally left Egypt."

The festival of Shavuot, the time of the revelation at Mount Sinai, is the festival that celebrates the covenantal relationship between God and the Jewish people. If the message of Passover is freedom, Shavuot is a time of choosing to enter God's service. Revelation, however, is also viewed as continuous, unfolding in the study of the Torah and following its commandments.

Sons on the eighth day after their birth have been welcomed into the covenant through the ritual of circumcision and girls by being named during a synagogue service or at a home celebration. A new ritual, a confirmation ceremony, has begun to be associated with Shavuot. It is an occasion for adolescents, usually sixteen or seventeen years of age, to publicly affirm their commitment to accepting the covenant. It is not done as an individual experience, such as the coming of age ceremony, bar/bat mitzvah, but rather as a class event.

This communal experience can be spiritually challenging as students create their own texts and explore what their religion means to them. Although they, at birth or through an early conversion, became Jewish, these teens now formally establish their commitment. I believe that the confirmation experience could be spiritually enhanced by adding the kabbalistic custom of staying up all night on Shavuot, studying Torah and connecting to God. The kabbalists believed that for a brief period, the heavens would open on Shavuot to answer one's deepest prayers. This custom could be a way to introduce adolescents to the more mystical aspects of the tradition.

Central to Jewish theology are the themes of creation, revelation, and redemption. Through the three pilgrimage festivals, children are invited to feel themselves present at Sinai on Shavuot, redeemed from Egypt on Passover, and connected to the natural world of creation on Sukkot. Through the drama of ritual, story, and prayer, they connect their lives with the ongoing experience of the Jewish people.

The minor holiday of Hanukkah has much importance to American Jewish children, not only because of its placement close to Christmas, but also because of its unique appeal. Children are, understandably, taken with the success of the Maccabean revolt, a victory of the small over the mighty. It is the story of the cruse of oil, found when the Temple was restored and about to be rededicated, that burned miraculously for eight days and nights, however, that speaks to children. As they light their own small menorahs to commemorate this miracle, they sense the courage that it took to light the small cruse in the first place and the faith it took to believe in a hopeful future. As they light the Hanukkah candles, they can see themselves as part of a long history and tradition. They can imagine what it must have been like to stand up for religious principles so long ago and be grateful that the courage of the Maccabees enables them now to proudly express their own faith.

The Everyday as a Means for Spiritual Growth

Although Jewish holy days are numerous, something must still be said of the "everyday." As previously mentioned, daily blessings and prayers give ordinary days a spiritual quality. These prayers, as has been noted, are said at specified times. There is also a recent movement that extends the Jewish sanctification of the everyday by creating life cycle rituals to make the secular events of children's lives feel sacred. These rituals run the gamut from learning to tie shoes to obtaining a driver's license, from toilet training to leaving for college.

Sometimes, existing blessings are employed to mark these life cycle events. For example, the traditional prayer of gratitude that one recites upon reaching a special occasion is recited to mark a milestone such as toilet training, a birthday, or learning to read. Or, the priestly benediction (cited previously) can be offered as an adolescent leaves for college. Sometimes, a personal blessing is created for a child. For instance, a child who has learned to tie his or her shoes may be blessed with words: "May you continue to grow and learn to do many things by yourself." Or, words of Torah can be shared when a teenager obtains a driver's license, such as: "Before you I have placed life and death, the blessing and the curse. Choose life, so that you and your descendants may live" (Deuteronomy 30:19). A parent and child may create a "covenant" to spell out the responsibilities each now has. The prayer one traditionally recites upon beginning a journey can be placed on a key ring or visor or even put next to a child's computer as she or he surfs the Internet.

Although children were prayed for when ill, they themselves were not usually a part of the prayers to heal others. This is changing, as children in classrooms and junior congregations or at family services are encouraged to pray for family and friends. Whether reciting the traditional Jewish prayer for healing or using the words that Moses spoke when he prayed to God to heal his sister Miriam, "Please God, heal her" (Numbers 12:13), children are experiencing the power and solace of prayer.

Final Thoughts

Judaism's sacred books define the religious requirements of the Jew. Performing these required acts, however, does not necessarily ensure a spiritual attitude, unless performed from the heart. Noted theologian Rabbi Abraham Joshua Heschel taught that if the inner dimension is not nurtured, then the external commandments cannot be properly fulfilled (Heschel 1976). Yet, for Jews, spiritual awareness without religious expression is incomplete. Judaism teaches that religion is not only about awe and wonder but also about the creation of holiness even in mundane acts. Prayer and ritual may be personally meaningful, but only if they lead to ethical behavior. Judaism sees study, prayer, and ritual as mechanisms for living a good life. Torah is the guide; prayer is the source of inspiration; and rituals are the reminders to help one live such a life. This is obviously why it has always been so important to impart knowledge and skills to a child and to encourage that child to participate in the religious life of the community as early as possible.

References

Bialik, H. N., and Y. H. Ravinsky, eds. 1992. *The book of legend.* Translated by David Stern. New York: Schocken.

Garfiel, Evelyn. 1958. *Service of the heart.* New York: United Synagogue of America.

Grishaver, Joel. 1980. *Shema is for real.* Chicago: Olin-Sang-Ruby Union Institute, UAHC.

Heschel, A. J. 1976. *God in search of man.* New York: Farrar, Straus and Giroux.

Ruthen, Gerald C. 1986. *Daniel and the silver flute: An old Hassidic tale.* New York: United Synagogue Commission on Jewish Education.

Silberman, Shoshana. 1998. How Jewish children conceptualize God. *Reconstructionism Today* 6 (Autumn):1.

Wolpe, David J. 1993. *Teaching your children about God.* New York: HarperPerennial.

CHAPTER 17

Schooling the Heart: Introducing Catholic Youth to the Meaning and Practice of Prayer

Robin Maas

Those passionately enthusiastic and chronically critical creatures we call adolescents give rise to many secret fears in the hearts of adults; and it is a great irony that just at the time in their lives when teenagers are most susceptible to religious conversion, American churches have found so little to offer them besides undisciplined discussion in which opinions are allowed to substitute for knowledge of the facts, pizza for prayer, and hayrides or "lock-ins" for service to their own "poor," namely, those youth among them who suffer because they are somehow different and don't fit in. Just keep them entertained and out of mischief. That's pretty much all modern parents seem to care about; and then they wonder why, as young adults, their offspring wander away from organized religion.

It is not a real lack of resources that has caused this form of spiritual famine for our young. It is mostly ignorance of the past and the real treasures found in Christian tradition—treasures that have the power to light up the world of the young and to transform individual lives. Roman Catholicism, which boasts of a two-thousand-year legacy, has an embarrassment of riches in this regard, and it is a pity so little of it has been made available in service of the younger generation. In particular, Catholicism, with its dual concern for faith and reason, for prayer and virtue, has ample resources for dealing with those souls whose lives are consumed with navigating a range of emotions that ebb and surge like breakers on the beach heralding a hurricane. It is a religious tradition that does not pit the head against the heart but proposes, instead, to send both of them to "school." About schools for the head, youth already know. About schools for the heart, they have much to learn.

The Heart in Scripture

Actually, the modern, Western understanding of "heart" is quite narrow. The tendency is to equate it almost entirely with our emotional life, our capacity to feel, and, especially, our romantic or erotic desires. The word *heart* appears in Scripture frequently. One scholar claims that it occurs about a thousand times in the Old Testament, with twenty-six of these occurrences referring to the heart of God. In the New Testament, a much shorter document, the word occurs about one hundred times.

The ancient Hebrews had a different understanding of the function of the heart. For them it was not just the seat of the emotions; in fact, *very* deep feelings, such as empathy for the suffering of others or personal sorrow, were thought to be found in the bowels. (Hence the term "gut feelings.") It comes as something of a surprise to hear that in the Bible the heart is, above all, the organ of *understanding*, of will, of conscience—along with the affections. This is why King Solomon, according to legend the wisest of men, asked God not for a brilliant mind or great wealth and fame but for an "understanding heart." And because he asked for a wise heart rather than riches, God gave him what he asked for—and more—in abundance. God gave Solomon what Scripture calls "largeness of heart" (1 Kings 3:4–14).

Scripture does not artificially isolate reason from feeling but locates both in the very heart or, we could say, at the *core* of the person. (The word for heart in Latin is *cor*.) So when the biblical writers want to speak about the deepest center of a person, her most essential character or, in a sense, a man's very soul, it speaks of the "heart." (We use the word in the same sense when we speak of "the heart of the matter.")

The condition of the individual's heart is a matter of great importance in both the Old and New Testaments. It can be pure or corrupt, single or double, open or closed, warm or cold, divided or whole, proud and hard, or broken and contrite. Scripture affirms that our status before God will be determined by the condition, not of our intellect and the degree of polish it has attained, but of our heart (in the biblical sense of the word); not just our feelings, but our deepest center: "Man looketh on the outward appearance but the Lord looketh on the heart" (1 Samuel 16:7).

Thus one does not achieve sanctity by being smart—though there is certainly no great virtue in being dumb. Holiness has to do with a capacity for love. This being the case, the truly wise will certainly want to send their hearts to school, and the sooner the better. Why? Because in Christian tradition the natural condition of the human heart is a wounded condition. In consequence of the Fall, it is fatal to trust completely in the human heart. Jeremiah writes, "The heart is deceitful above all things" (17:9), and the person our heart plays the biggest tricks on is ourself.

It is for this reason that it is dangerous to rely on a purely self-taught heart. Scripture warns that we are really fooling ourselves if we think we can read our own heart accurately without the help of some supernatural illumination. It follows that we need to send our hearts to school, and the best school for hearts is the School of Prayer.

The School of Prayer

Ironically, only a broken heart is really ready to be schooled. The heart that does not know its own weakness is unteachable. The contrite heart, the grieving heart, the yearning heart is a heart that has been broken open and can therefore receive what God has to offer it. This is why awareness of our own need, our own sorrow, is the essential prerequisite for enrolling in the School of Prayer.

If a broken heart is the one essential admission requirement to the School of Prayer, it is also the one thing youth want to avoid at all costs; at the same time, however, most of them know exactly what this entails. Perhaps they have experienced a deeply wounding loss in their lives; on the other hand, what looks like a small fissure to an adult may feel like a death blow to a fifteen-year-old. Ironically, although youth may feel brokenhearted about things an adult would find rather trivial, serious, soul-searing suffering in the life of a young person, while increasingly a common occurrence, is often completely hidden from them. When we are young, it is easier to mourn the superficial wound than the potentially deadly one.

Yet any person, especially any young person who has experienced a significant loss and who is suffering as a result of that loss, is ready to enroll in the School of Prayer: "A broken and a contrite heart," says the Psalmist, "thou wilt not despise" (51:17). When all other doors are closed, prayer remains the only secure path to hope. Unfortunately, a common response to the breaking of a fragile young heart is a determination never again to suffer such pain. The sufferer, quite logically, reasons that his heart must in the future be well defended and so a hardening process sets in: "If I don't care so much, I won't hurt so much." When this happens, it's more difficult to gain admission to the School of Prayer. The hardened heart lends its owner a false sense of security.

The School of Prayer, like any school, intends certain outcomes. It has goals for its graduates—a vision of what a well-schooled heart looks like. To identify these goals, let us consult some key passages in Scripture. These will supply a clear picture of what will be included in the curriculum. And as we describe these goals, let us consider whether young people will find them compelling.

1. A New Heart: This is the true goal of the School of Prayer. What a steady life of prayer begins to accomplish in the human heart is not simply a mending of what has been broken or befouled but actually a new creation—a new heart. The work of the Spirit in the human heart is akin to the work accomplished in the creation of the world. The prophet Ezekiel explains it this way: "I will give them a new heart and put a new spirit within them; I will remove the stony heart from their bodies and replace it with a natural heart, so that they will live according to my statutes" (Ezekiel 11:19–20). What we see from this passage is that the new creation is really a restoration. The new heart is a *human* heart, one that can truly feel, a heart capable of love, sorrow, joy, and compassion. What looks like a completely "new" heart is actually what God created in the first place—a fully human heart that was free to love fully because it was not enslaved to sin.

The possibility of a new heart is immensely appealing, especially for youth who are habitually attracted to what is new, yet perpetually discouraged by the inability to live up to their own high ideals. The person who has confessed the same fault over and over again begins to wonder: Will it ever get better? Will I ever change? Am I a hopeless case? Why bother even trying? I believe the impulse we all feel to secure a fresh start so frequently in so many areas of our life is rooted in a supernatural reality—our own new creation in Christ. We want more than to be forgiven. We want to be healed of what ails us.

2. A Forgiving Heart: This new heart is a living, beating human heart, not shriveled with grief or self-pity nor hardened by an unforgiving bitterness. And because it is

a heart of real flesh and blood, it virtually throbs with compassion, tenderness, and forgiveness. Like the living Sacred Heart of Jesus from whence flowed blood and water, a
truly human heart, especially in its capacity to forgive, is a source of "living water" to
all who are touched by it (John 7:38).

Although it is not so difficult to imagine the heart of youth as alive and throbbing,
what it often throbs with, along with unmeasured passions, are harsh, unsoftened judgments. The vibrant idealism of youth lends itself to easy disillusionments. High hopes
are quickly dashed and great bitterness can result. This is true not only in the case of
real or perceived disloyalties among friends or in shame-producing disappointments
with parents. It is especially true in relation to the institutional Church. When the
Church, in its witness, in its clergy, in its rank-and-file laity, fails to live up to youthful
expectations, the young will often turn away in disgust and discouragement, embarking on a self-chosen exile that can last long into adulthood.

What the School of Prayer teaches the young heart is humility and patience. An
increase in prayer always brings with it an increase in self-knowledge, a greater and
more vivid awareness of our own weaknesses and failings. And the beginning of this
awareness, providing it comes in the context of prayer, should be a source of great hope
and encouragement. Just as we read that when our own heart condemns us, "God is
greater than our heart" (I John 3:20), so when our youthful heart condemns the
Church, God is greater than the Church—yet loves it still. As God will never surrender
it to the gates of Hell, so will he not let it be defeated by the untempered judgment of
those who need it to be what it actually is rather than what they think, in light of current cultural values, it should be.

3. An Obedient Heart: Obedience, says Scripture, is the straight and narrow path
to wisdom. "Behold," says the Psalmist, "thou desirest truth in the inward being; therefore teach me wisdom in my secret heart" (51:6). The one thing each and every heart
has to learn to face is the truth; but without obedience this will never happen. Ironically, that which the heart most needs in order to heal it is also most certain to flee.

So how can the truth, God's very own medicine, reach the heart?

The heart that has been schooled in prayer will become increasingly humble, pli-
ant, and soft. In fact, it will become so soft and so receptive that it will be able to receive
the mark of the promised New Covenant on its very flesh. Discouraged by Israel's constant disobedience, the prophet Jeremiah dreamed of the day when the Law of God
would actually be written, or *engraved*, on the hearts of the faithful. When that finally
happened, the people would no longer need teachers to instruct them in Torah or God's
Law, because they would all know that Law "by heart" (Jeremiah 31:33–34). Obedience would come freely, without effort and without resentment. Rather than being the
mark of immaturity, obedience would be the sign and seal of full spiritual adulthood.

Jeremiah's promise of a heart that has the truth engraved upon it is another way of
saying that knowing what is really true and important will someday seem instinctual,
something one knows without having to be taught (what Roman Catholic tradition
calls "infused knowledge"), and doing what is right will no longer be a struggle (what
the Church calls "virtue"). What a promise! If the obedient heart is the heart that
knows—that has the truth engraved upon its very flesh—then who wouldn't be willing
to exchange the old for the new?

You will protest, of course, that obedience is not generally a virtue to which the young aspire. Today especially, many find the notion of obedience positively repellent. To the immature, obedience represents just that: immaturity, minority status, the absence of freedom. When you are struggling to become an autonomous adult, obedience sounds like a return to what you are trying to outgrow. And this legacy of repulsion for what God requires can last well into adulthood, seriously inhibiting the process of spiritual maturation. Some people never learn to relish obedience to the Law of God; and when this happens it is a tragedy, for the Law of God is the Law of Love.

It is not too early to introduce youth to the truth that the obedience God asks of us is quite different from the kind of obedience that is a response to coercion. Obedience learned in the school of prayer is a response of love, of adoration. It is freely given out of a deep desire not only to please the One we love but to unite ourselves with him. And because it is freely given (and not exacted), it requires a certain autonomy and maturity in the first place. Prayer brings with it, first, the desire to be obedient to the Lord and then, increasingly, the capacity to give true obedience (rather than mere compliance) in precisely the same measure that we give love.

4. A Whole Heart: Finally, and perhaps most important, the renewed, re-created heart is a whole heart. Only a whole heart can give undivided love. Only a whole heart can obediently respond to the command to love the Lord with all our heart, mind, soul, and strength and our neighbors as ourselves (Luke 10:27).

There is perhaps no other goal so attractive to the young as the prospect of a total gift of self, both spiritually and physically. (Witness their affection for the word *totally*—it permeates their speech.) The young always aspire to the dramatic gesture—the radical choice to risk all for a single love.

Perhaps this is because they sense that a whole heart signals an end to incompleteness, to the unfinished, unpolished state of being that plagues every person who is not yet grown up or "knit together." Just as a broken heart is the fundamental prerequisite to admission to the School of Prayer, a whole heart is a sign that the lessons have been fully and probably painfully learned.

The Faculty in the School of Prayer: The Teacher Within

Well, you say, this sounds terrific, but how do I send my heart to the School of Prayer? And how do I convince the young that they should, too? The simplest way to answer this question is: First, find a good teacher. Find the *best possible teacher* you can, and then, "move in" with him or her. Like the apprentice of old, be willing to start with the mundane and menial tasks assigned to you by the teacher for the sake of simply being present with and to that authority, day and night. Learn the subject by *learning the teacher*.

Before dealing with particular teachers in the School of Prayer, however, we need to talk about the principal or headmaster—the one who helps the pupil find just the right course to take, who assigns the right teacher at the right time. I am speaking, of course, of the Holy Spirit who, says Saint Paul,

helps us in our weakness; for we do not know how to pray as we ought, but
the Spirit himself intercedes for us with sighs too deep for words. And he
who searches the hearts of men knows what is the mind of the Spirit, because
the Spirit intercedes for the saints according to the will of God. (Romans
8:26–27)

This is an amazing passage, worth many hours of pondering. It promises us that
the Spirit knows better than we ourselves the condition of our heart and can place our
needs before the Heart of the Father in a way that corresponds with God's will for us.
The Spirit truly is our advocate before the Throne of Grace for he prays *in* us, *for* us,
and *in our stead.*

I have seen the Holy Spirit referred to as the "Teacher Within,"[1] and perhaps the
single most important principle learned in the School of Prayer is the necessity of trusting in the intercessions of the Spirit on our behalf rather than in our own personal skill
at praying. So the first, very simple but essential lesson is always to begin prayer with a
heart full of trust, not in our own abilities but in the Spirit, who is the great Reader of
Hearts, who knows what we mean, what we most need, and how to communicate all
that in the most effective way possible to our Father in heaven.

This is a tremendous message of hope to the young who are so often inarticulate,
embarrassed by silence and religious sentiment, and obsessed with their own inadequa-
cies and needs. Let them learn to rejoice that no matter how religiously unskilled they
believe themselves to be, the Holy Spirit, the Teacher Within, will pray with, in, and for
them; and therefore they can rest assured that God will hear their prayer.

I have found in my own experience that the Teacher Within can also be trusted to
assign us to the right tutor at the right time. I have been blessed throughout my journey toward God with many wonderful teachers of prayer, most of whom have
instructed me by means of the printed page; and what I have learned is that newer is
not always better. In fact, the best of the new are those works that rest on the sturdy
foundation laid by the saints—those who know God best. One of the greatest of these,
whose teaching has been given special recognition in Catholicism, is Teresa of Jesus,
better known as Saint Teresa of Ávila.

A bright, attractive, and socially charming woman who, as a youth and young
adult was very dependent for happiness on her interpersonal relationships, Teresa
came from a family that had secrets to keep and worried much about what other people thought. Her many close friendships were both her greatest consolations as well as
the source of much of her suffering because they provided, as human relationships
always do, constant occasions for sin. In prayer, Teresa learned how to redirect all her
passionate longings and considerable skills for friendship to her relationship with
Christ. And in this relationship she found a friendship that never failed to satisfy and
to challenge.

Because she was so oriented toward finding emotional solace in relationships, her
teachings on prayer have a special value to the young; yet because these teachings are
embedded in material that remains largely inaccessible to all but the most dedicated
readers, relatively few young people can benefit from what Teresa has to say. These
insights deserve to be shared nonetheless. With a little help from her friends (i.e., you),

this superb teacher in the School of Prayer will offer youth much encouragement and consolation. Teresa will offer them *Jesus*.

A Teresian Tutorial on Prayer

Teresa of Jesus had great compassion for anyone trying to get serious about learning how to pray and developing a rich inner life. Her life's work, both in the establishment of her monastic reform (the Order of Discalced or "Barefoot" Carmelites) and in her writings, devolved around helping people scale the heights of prayer; and as one who had actually done so, she recognized that this could only occur where a proper foundation had been laid. For Teresa this foundation consists of three essential practices: recollecting the senses, reflecting on the past, and meditating on the life of Christ, especially his passion.

Because she was accustomed to finding inspiration in nature, Teresa famously uses the analogy of bringing water to a garden, beginning with the most laborious method (drawing water from a well) to the most effortless (rainfall) to describe the various stages of prayer and the ways in which each stage differently reflects the relationship between human effort and divine grace. The earliest stage, the one that concerns us here, requires the most effort on our part. Beginners, she says, necessarily

> tire themselves in *trying to recollect their senses*. Since they are accustomed to being distracted, this recollection requires much effort. They need to get accustomed to caring nothing at all about seeing or hearing, . . . and thus to solitude and withdrawal—and to *thinking on their past life*. Although these beginners . . . must often reflect upon their past . . . [i]n the beginning such reflection is even painful, for they do not fully understand whether or not they are repentant of their sins. If they are, they are then determined to serve God earnestly. They must strive to *consider the life of Christ*—and the intellect grows weary in doing this.[2]

RECOLLECTION AND THE PROBLEM OF DISTRACTION

Prayer is most generally satisfying and fruitful when it is offered in a state of "recollection"—a word Teresa uses often to describe what we are more likely to call a centered state. Our roving thoughts and senses need to be re-collected, like so many sheep that have wandered away, distracted by their hunt for tender grass. A recollected soul is a quiet, undistracted, fully attentive soul, ready to receive what the Lord is offering. If you have ever tried to keep your attention focused on a single subject for any length of time, you will know how difficult this is; and if you spend much time around teenagers you may be tempted to despair over this initial requirement.

Yet no teacher is more compassionate and understanding about the problems of distraction than the saint from Ávila. The first thing we learn from her on the subject is that we should not succumb to discouragement about distractions in prayer. Many of us launch bravely into the "I will pray daily and well, *starting now*" syndrome and then flounder the minute we meet with obstacles to our success. Teresa, always a shrewd instructor, warns us in advance of the types of temptation we are likely to encounter when we get started in prayer, and the worst and most persistent of these temptations is the problem of almost constant distractions: I'm hungry: What will we have for dinner? Should I try to sit next to Jimmy in geometry today? Why did I flub that last shot? What I *should* have said was . . . Gee, maybe I better quit praying and start studying for the chemistry exam!

First, what we find most consoling is Teresa's wonderful way of describing her own distracted state of mind in prayer. By doing so she relieves the reader of a sense of guilt about our all-too-human inability to concentrate our attention on a single subject. This tendency, she says, is ever with us as part of the human condition, although there are things we can do to strengthen our abilities to attend to the Lord. Once she has put us at our ease by assuring us that she too suffers from this plague, she ensures that we will be readier to hear what can be done about it.

The same strategy works with the young. When they know that *we* know what they are going through, then they can hear what we have to say on the subject. But nowadays it's even harder to gain ground with youth on the subject of dealing with distractions in prayer. More than previous generations, today's young people come to this task with some serious handicaps.

We are accustomed to expect the young to have a shorter attention span than the adult. Reading is fast becoming a lost art. Now in competition with television and video games, it seems to require way too much mental and imaginative effort—not to mention an emotional payoff that seems far too long in coming whenever the attempt is made to read anything written before the late twentieth century.

Yet the qualities that enhance the art of reading—attentiveness, patience and persistence, imagination, and the ability to savor pleasures slowly—are the same qualities that enhance the art of prayer. The young person who has not had to struggle mentally (or any other way) to achieve something of great value and interest will have a hard time developing a capacity for the kind of interior life in which prayer thrives.

Moreover, the rigid perfectionism of the young is a terrible obstacle to persistence in prayer. If they can't get it right the first time, the temptation is to simply drop it. Teresa won't let us do that. The one thing she says we must never do is to stop praying—no matter how sinful or inadequate we feel, no matter how discouraged we get about our own weaknesses, no matter how many distractions we have to endure. Our prayer has a value to God, whether or not it meets our own exacting standards of what prayer should be. That that value is hidden from us should not deter us from doing what God bids us do.

A correlative problem arises out of a naive overoptimism about what to expect in the beginning stages of serious prayer. When we read about the great spiritual heights reached by the mystics, we normally feel a strong desire to experience something of the same. The younger we are, the thirstier we are for experience, especially exciting or "sensational" experiences. A typical beginner's response is to look for strong emotional reactions (what Teresa calls "consolations") from prayer; or, because Teresa talks about different stages of prayer, to want to push oneself, through sheer force of effort, to a more advanced stage of prayer. This, she says, we can never do. When we are ready for more, and not before—and it is always God who decides this—we are moved *by the Lord* into a different kind of prayer. When we are preoccupied with our own progress, we are not being fully present to the Lord.

The good news is that there are things that parents, teachers, and youth ministers can do (better late than never) that qualify as a kind of remote preparation for serious prayer because these practices tend to develop the capacities that will make it easier for us to be "recollected" or attentive to God.

First: Help youth develop an aptitude and an appetite for silence and solitude. Today's young people are prisoners of noise. Some of them go through withdrawal pangs when they have to unplug from the ever-present noise producers in their life. Much of their need for noise is born of habit; but noise is also a way of not having to be "alone." Some youth have grown up in noisy households, but many have learned to plug in as a way to tune out those parts of reality they find too threatening. And the big threat for all noise addicts, young or old, is the terror of inner chaos and emptiness. Hence the television left on all day to keep them company; MTV so that their fantasies will go on thriving; soap operas and movies to stave off the banal ordinariness of their existence; ear-splitting music to keep the adrenaline flowing—*anything* to avoid looking at what's really going on. Inside.

Because they run in herds, the best way to start with adolescents is to let them be quiet and alone *together*. By inviting them to experience small doses of silence and solitude en masse you are, in effect, giving them permission to do it on their own. And many will require this kind of permission so that they will not feel "too weird."

Second: Encourage any wholesome activity that requires concentration and self-discipline. Scholastic achievement, athletics, especially team sports, music, and the arts all require personal dedication and long hours of practice before significant results are achieved. Teens understand this, and those who want to go for the gold will put themselves through the necessary rigors to achieve their goal. If in some cases, say in art, achievement comes relatively easily because of natural talent, there should be plenty of encouragement for undertaking an additional goal, such as academic achievement or athletics, where more effort will be required.

The acquisition of true excellence in any field is a form of self-transcendence that hints at a far greater glory than worldly fame can offer. But more to the point, the persistent and hard work from which true excellence springs has "transfer value" into other areas of young lives. The boy who practices his trumpet for hours on end, like the girl who works overtime in the school lab, will be less likely to despair when serious prayer and the following of Christ turns out to be harder than they thought.

REFLECTING ON OUR PAST AND THE PROBLEM OF DENIAL

Adolescents are walking furnaces in which feelings constantly churn and roil. We remember, if we are honest, that we too were once walking furnaces, that during adolescence we were at the mercy of turbulent and unpredictable emotions; and that when we are *ablaze*—with anger, jealousy, or lust—it is almost impossible to believe that we are fit to place ourselves in the Presence of God, recollected or not.

Teresa's teaching[3] will help youth begin to understand that it is appropriate to share *all* of who we are with the Lord in prayer—not just our thoughts, not just our high-minded hopes, but also, and especially, our deepest feelings, including our negative feelings—all the sad and bad and hidden corners of our heart, the heart God already knows is deeply wounded. The parable of the prodigal son or the parable of the Pharisee and the tax collector are instructive here. The Lord welcomes the prayer of the desperate and defeated, and especially the prayer of the young, who so often feel this way, with open arms. But first you have to know how desperate you really are, and this is where most of us get defeated—by something the psychologists call "denial," that is, by our mostly unconscious resistance to seeing what's really there.

Adolescents are experts at a particular type of self-examination—the kind that takes place in front of a mirror. Hair, skin, body shape, and size are all the subject of intense and daily scrutiny. There are clearly defined standards of acceptability in their social world, and these standards are rigorously enforced by the group and by individuals. Give the kids credit: there is an almost heroic quality to the effort they make to gain acceptability, to live up to the high standards they and their peers set for themselves. So we know that youth do cherish certain ideals and do, in fact, want to meet "high" standards.

How sad, then, to see how misguided, unwholesome, and even destructive some of these standards actually are. Almost all of them qualify as worldly and are therefore superficial, because they are concerned with appearances and popularity rather than with personal integrity and fidelity to God. The need to look good takes on overwhelming importance to teenagers at a time when a challenge to grow into real goodness is, in fact, their paramount developmental need. Is it possible to harness this desire to meet or even surpass the standard set by peer pressure for better purposes? Can a look into the soul compete with the daily tryst with the mirror?

Teresa is adamant about the importance of accountability in the spiritual life. For her, self-knowledge is the essential foundation to a genuine experience of God. Without that knowledge we cannot pray with the honesty and integrity that the Lord demands. In this sense we could say that we must face our own personal reality before we can face God, who is Ultimate Reality. In another sense, we could also say that it is almost impossible to face our own reality without the sustaining presence of the Lord in our lives.

Young people can be encouraged to end their day with a review that does not take place in front of a mirror but is instead conducted in the sustaining presence of the Lord, the Healer of Hearts:

> What things have I done or said that I am pleased to present as an offering to Christ?
> What things would I rather he not know about?
> Are there things I should have done today and didn't?
> Do I have the courage to lay these failings at the Lord's feet anyway?
> Can I believe that once I do this, he will be able to do something with these failures?

Will he love me in spite of my failures?
Is it possible he will be especially pleased if I have the courage not only to acknowledge my failures but to entrust my imperfect self to his mercy?

Another stratagem is to encourage adolescents to review the important relationships in their lives: with parents, siblings, teachers, friends, and, of course, "enemies":

What have I done to strengthen weak relationships or heal broken ones?
In what ways have I further weakened or wounded those relationships that aren't doing so well?
Can I entrust *all* these relationships to the Lord, or only some of them?
Am I willing to let him take charge of the important relationships in my life, or do I want to maintain the illusion of control?
Would I actually prefer that some of these relationships not be healed or purified? If so, what does that tell me about myself? About the relationships?

And what about all those past mistakes that we can't undo? Once a person begins to practice self-examination on a regular basis, he or she may begin to feel real remorse about callous and sinful behavior that cannot be recalled. Absolution is essential to spiritual well-being, but if we cannot shield the young from experiencing the long-term consequences of their own sinful behavior, we can and must encourage them to bring every sorrow to the Lord in the firm belief that everything about us, including our past, can be redeemed.

God's response to his people's repentance is not a stern "I told you so!" but a joyous outpouring of the Spirit: "Your sons and your daughters shall prophesy, your old men shall dream dreams, and your young men shall see visions" (Joel 2:28). In this remarkable passage we find a clue to the connection that links repentance and—what Joel calls "vision"—the basis of all virtue. Ethical behavior is grounded in seeing what is actually going on, in *reality*. And the main obstacle to plain seeing is the demon whose name is "denial"—the veil that only God's gift of tears can wash away.

Injustice is always easy to spot *somewhere else*. Children and youth are quick to react to anything they think is "unfair," especially when it touches them. And they can easily be led to believe they are actually "doing something" about injustice by protesting loudly. Not so. In fact, the louder they protest, the less likely they are to spot injustices they themselves might be perpetrating. It is honest recognition of our own character flaws—our own "heartsickness"—that turns out to be the only solid foundation for genuine compassion and empathy; and without these moral capacities, no healing charity will be offered and no satisfying justice done.

Most youth ministry programs recognize the immense character-building value of service projects, with work camp usually topping the list of mind- and heart-expanding experiences that reap immediate rewards in terms of heightened awareness for participants of the legitimate needs, rights, and gifts of those who are less socially and financially fortunate than themselves. However, when Christian service is something our privileged youth simply "bestow" on worthy beneficiaries, there may be plenty of self-satisfaction but relatively little "vision" resulting. All too often the service project simply becomes a way of making the self-indulgent suburban teen "feel good about themselves" (i.e., *useful* for a change) when what they should be feeling—or saying—is "Pray for me, brother—or sister! I too need help but of a different kind!"

Personal repentance is where moral vision begins; and lessons learned the hard way are still lessons learned and therefore blessings. Young people need to hear that even the bitterest regret, if offered to the Lord, is returned to us in the form of a blessing, often in the form of an opportunity to help a fellow sufferer. Indeed, how many adult ministries are redemptive precisely because they flow from bone-deep sorrow for the sins of our youth?

That is Teresa's excuse for all the good she did. Contrition for her own "sins"—which many are inclined to discount—fueled her monastic reform. So Teresa never tires of telling us that there is a clear connection between our ability to practice virtue and our faithfulness in prayer. Alas, we cannot be virtuous simply by willing ourselves to be. This is the great discovery and discouragement of the young. They want so much to be good and get so fed up with themselves when they fail to live up to their own, often unrealistic ideals.

What Teresa teaches is that we all have to learn—usually the hard way—that goodness is a work of divine grace in us. Goodness comes with God's "takeover" and "makeover" of our wounded, broken heart. We cannot do this by ourselves. And God will not do it unless we give him leave with tears and prayers of repentance. By the same token, we cannot expect to make progress in prayer if we do not attempt to practice virtue. A sinful life gives the lie to what we ask for in prayer.

So somehow we must at the same time be honest with God and with ourselves. We must place our hearts in God's hands and trust him with them. Then he can really do something—*for* others—*through* us.

CONSIDERING CHRIST AND THE PROBLEM OF SUFFERING

The average American looks at prayer as yet another thing to put on the "to do" list, seen negatively as an irksome duty, or positively as a spiritually fulfilling experience that will yield personal benefits. From Teresa we learn that prayer is not about acquiring a technique or being dutiful (Take your vitamins; recite your prayers . . .) but about friendship and love. Specifically, she teaches that prayer lays the foundation for a deep personal relationship with Christ: "I tried as hard as I could to make Christ present," says Teresa. "That was my way of prayer."

Many Christians pray exclusively to the Father. Teresa believed that the intimacy we all yearn to have requires constant personal contact with the Word *made flesh*. Try as we might, we can never be intimate with an idea—only with a person—and the enfleshed divine Person we call Jesus is the dearest gift the Father has given his children. And so Teresa talks ceaselessly of a tender and growing intimacy between herself and Christ that developed in the same way all close personal relationships develop. As the partners gradually reveal more and more of themselves to each other, the desired closeness begins to materialize; but like any successful human friendship, our relationship with God requires time and effort. In her words, "Mental prayer in my opinion is nothing else than an intimate sharing between friends; it means taking time frequently to be alone with him who we know loves us."[4]

Teenagers, especially teenage girls, are obsessed with relationships. How to make and keep friends—or even how to dump a friend—are subjects that preoccupy them. As they struggle daily with these dilemmas, one of the first things they learn is that there are rules that must be followed for relationships to flourish; and once they learn these rules, they are often meticulously, even rigidly, enforced.

First, and more superficially, they learn that when it comes to making friends, there is a certain way they must be, look, dress, act, and speak if they are to be accepted by the crowd they hope to join. More important, they learn that if they want to keep a friend they must be loyal. Sharing someone else's secret to curry favor with a third party is death to a friendship. Many young people learn the hard way that when trust is gone, the friendship evaporates, leaving bad feelings in its wake. Eventually, they learn that if they want to get really close to a friend, they must be prepared to make personal sacrifices. For example, intimate friendships require spending a considerable amount of time alone with another (generosity and unselfishness); they call for consistency of commitment (fidelity and self-discipline); they stand or fall on telling the truth (honesty and courage); and finally, when there is sufficient trust, they require us to begin sharing our secret joys and sorrows, and intimacy is achieved.

It is not too great a leap for youth to recognize that the requirements of our earthly friendships mirror those of our friendship with Christ. Time alone with the Lord, personal courage, honest self-revelation, self-discipline, and fidelity form the foundation for intimacy with Jesus. If we can meet him halfway through our efforts to cultivate these virtues, he runs to meet us. And a wonderful by-product of a deeper relationship with Christ is the gift of better relationships at home and truer, finer friends at school. These good things happen because deeply personal relationships always leave their mark on us. The people we learn to love in a sense "remake" us; and this is never more true than when it occurs in that perilous transition between childhood and adulthood. When our hearts are molten.

How does this work?

Through intimate, sustained contact. Consider the following: Teresa particularly loved to meditate on Jesus at those moments in his life when he was alone, misunderstood, rejected, betrayed, or suffering from grief and physical pain. She believed that if she offered him her own friendship and consolation in *those* moments—moments when he suffered deeply in his own humanity—he would welcome her company and take solace in it.

Such moments of loneliness and misunderstanding are very familiar to youth. In fact, all those who yearn for more human intimacy can be richly comforted by an experience of intimate communion with Jesus, who came in the flesh precisely so that he could be Immanuel or God *with us*. With the onset of what Jean Piaget terms formal-operational thinking, adolescents can begin to empathize more deeply with Christ's humanity, his suffering, and his sacrifice on their behalf. It is suddenly possible to grasp that in God's own "humanity"—Jesus of Nazareth—there is a real, fully human *Person* who can hear their prayers, who can love them enough to die, not just for the whole world but for each one of those walking furnaces alone—as if he or she were the whole world. Love like this, as the young would say, is a love *to die for*.

In Christ-centered prayer our youth will discover a fountain of grace that captures their hearts and fixes their attention on worthy goals, strengthens their hearts with courage to face reality and do justice, and enlarges their hearts so that all who need compassion and forgiveness will find a haven there. In Christ-centered prayer, the young will find a hero worthy of their highest aspirations, a friend who will bend to their smallest need, a trustworthy guide to each one's unique mission and personal destiny. And as their relationship with their Lord deepens, they will learn that to imitate Christ is not simply to honor but also to *love* him. To follow Jesus is to say to the world, "I belong to *him*"; and every teenager knows that once you realize where you belong, you finally know who you are. And that, for sure, is the answer to every teenager's prayer.

Notes

1. This designation for the Holy Spirit was used by Sofia Cavalletti in *The Religious Potential of the Child*, trans. Patricia M. Coulter and Julie M. Coulter (New York/Ramsey: Paulist Press, 1983).

2. See Teresa of Avila, "The Book of Her Life," in *St. Teresa of Avila: Collected Works*, vol. 1, trans. Kieran Kavanaugh, O.C.D., and Otilio Rodriguez, O.C.D. (Washington, D.C.: Institute of Carmelite Studies, 1976), 11.9, p. 114, my emphasis.

3. Most people who want to read Teresa start with her most famous work, *The Interior Castle*. This is a mistake. The first part of "The Book of Her Life" and *The Way of Perfection* are much more helpful for the neophyte.

4. "Book of Her Life," 8.5.

CHAPTER 18

Sacred Celebrations: The Role of Festivals in Nurturing Hindu Children's Spirituality

Melukote K. Sridhar

India is a land of festivals. Hindus, Buddhists, Jains, Sikhs, and others of different faiths and traditions celebrate various festivals during the year. These festivals bring people together and add a new dimension to the otherwise routine life. Although most Hindu festivals are religious by nature, they have cultural and regional diversities and often have mythological, ethical, social, and spiritual appeal. However, the essence and spirit of Hindu festivals remain the same throughout the country and anywhere Hindus reside. The festivals teach us to be physically and mentally pure, and help people in resolving conflicts and bind them together for harmonious living and welfare. Hindu festivals reflect the mind and philosophy of India in various epochs. Hindu festivals also have a deep spiritual meaning and purpose and remind us of the presence of supreme reality, or God.

Hindu festivals can be broadly classified into three categories: religious, historical, and seasonal. These festivals are celebrated at specific times during the year, based on Hindu solar or lunar calendars. The Hindu calendar has 365 days and fifty-two weeks. The seven days in a week are named after the sun, the moon, Mars, Mercury, Jupiter, Venus, and Saturn. Each day commences with a specific star; altogether there are twenty-seven stars that move cyclically throughout the year. Hindu religious festivals are based on the advent of the specific and auspicious star on a day or an auspicious day, or both.

The solar calendar begins when the sun enters the Aries sign of the zodiac and covers the next eleven signs over the course of a year. Generally this event occurs in the second or third week of April. The lunar calendar begins when the moon enters the Ashvini star during the bright half of the month of Chaitra and covers the next eleven months. This event generally falls on the fourth week of March or first week of April. There will be a difference of two weeks between those two calendars and sometimes even a month. The religious festivals are Deepavali or Diwali (the festival of lights), Shivaratri (the marriage of Lord Shiva), the births of Lord Rama (Ramanavami) and Lord Krishna (Krishna Janmashtami), and the nine nights in autumn dedicated to worshipping the divine in the female form (Navaratri). Historical festivals are associated with the birth of historical personages, saints, and spiritual teachers. They are the birthdays of Mahavira (Mahavira Jayanti), Shankara (Shankara Jayanti), Ramanuja

(Ramanuja Jayanti), Madhva (Madhva Jayanti), Basava (Basava Jayanti), and Guru Nanak (Guru Nanak Jayanti). The seasonal festivals are associated with nature and agriculture. They include Makara Sankranti, Vasant Panchami, Sharad Purnima, and Holi.

Festivals at Home and Children

The observation of festivals and religious activities in homes by parents becomes an integral component in facilitating spirituality in children. Hindu parents teach their children from an early age the significance of each day, as to how one should dress while offering a prayer, combing of hair and tying of the plait while offerings are made, removal of sandals and shoes before entering the sanctum sanctorum, the methods of saluting the deities and elders with folded palms (*namsthe*) or prostrating oneself on the ground, circumambulating the icon (*pradakshina*) in the clockwise direction, proper posture for prayer and meditation, maintenance of silence during worship, receiving of the sacred water and offerings (*prasad*), and such other physical and mental disciplines that prepare them for a spiritual life. Parents also teach a few verses in their mother tongue to children that praise various deities and, by inculcation, instruct the children to recite or chant them both in the morning and evenings and during festivals. This method of memorizing and reciting the divine verses from early childhood until entering school at the age of six imparts to children a spiritual feeling. In the second phase, parents perform several important sacraments for children and initiate them into prayer, worship, and studies.

HINDU SACRAMENTS

Everyone who is born a Hindu is expected to undergo a process of refinement that brings an awareness of the sacredness of life and the divine order of the Lord. The refinement rituals are called sacraments (*samskaras*), and they sanctify a person and prepare him or her for living a religious and spiritual life. They are sixteen in number and cover the life of a Hindu from the very moment of birth till death. This system energizes a Hindu for leading a pragmatic, healthy, happy, and spiritual life. Among the sixteen Hindu sacraments, a dozen of them are meant to assist in the development of children into balanced adults. I will describe here three sacraments that nurture children's spirituality.

Tonsuring of the Hair

The first tonsuring of a Hindu male child (*Chudakarma* in Sanskrit) is done at the end of either the first or the third year. The father (or, these days, a barber) cuts the hair of the child for the first time on an auspicious day, and later the priest performs the act by reciting Vedic hymns. This sacrament is intended to enhance the beauty and longevity of the child, according to the Hindu sages and physicians (Buhler 1892). The Yajurveda (3.33) declares that by this sacrament the longevity, physical strength, and spiritual virtue of a child will be enhanced. It is not performed for females, since cutting their hair is considered inauspicious.

Initiation into Learning

The child is initiated into the learning of the alphabet during the third or fifth year. This sacrament is performed during the first half of the year on an auspicious day. After the worshipping of deities such as Lord Ganesha (the deity for warding off obstacles), Brihaspati, the divine preceptor, Sarasvati (goddess of learning and wisdom), and the family deity, the child is seated facing the East. The father holds the child's index finger and thumb and writes on a plate of raw rice the names of gods, goddesses, and the letters of the alphabet. Thus are boys and girls spiritually initiated into future studies (Shama Shastri 1920).

The Sacred Thread Ceremony

One of the important sacraments performed for boys is the sacred thread ceremony or spiritual initiation (called *Upanayana* in Sanskrit), which denotes a starting point for the individual for formally acquiring knowledge from the teacher. With this ceremony, boys enter the first stage of Hindu life, the student life, also called the life of celibates. The ceremony is elaborate and extends for an entire day, during which the father, with the guidance of a priest, initiates the son into the mystic hymn of Gayatri, after adorning him with a sacred thread (called *Yajnopaveeta*). The son from then on should perform obeisance to the sun three times a day, chant the hymn of Gayatri and know its secret meaning, and vow to lead the life of a bachelor until the completion of Vedic studies. This ceremony is treated as the second life for the Brahmins (Muir [1805] 1967). Among the four classes of Hindu society in earlier days, it was suggested by traditional texts that this ceremony should be performed at the age of eight for Brahmins, at eleven for warriors and public servants, and at twelve for traders; laborers were not eligible for the ceremony (Buhler 1892).

The main purpose of this ceremony is to impart complete spiritual education to a celibate. According to the Vedic sages Apastamba and Bharadwaja, the student, apart from seeking spiritual knowledge, should also practice high ethical values in life, further leading to a spiritual life. The Gayatri hymn goes as follows: "We meditate on the adorable Light of the supreme creator of the universe. May He, or the Light existing in our hearts, guide our intellects in the pursuit of truth." This hymn was also used to initiate Hindu girls until the onset of foreign invasion in India in 800 C.E.

The Significance of Hindu Festivals

Every Hindu festival has a component of sacredness and purity and is intended to serve as a holy occasion for a deep contemplation of God and our association with him. The fasts associated with festivals give Hindus an opportunity to look within and visualize the supreme reality. Some days are sacred to Lord Vishnu, believed as the sustainer;

some to Lord Shiva, the involutor of the universe; and some to goddesses such as Durga and Lakshmi, the presiding deities of prosperity. On these sacred days, men and women fast, read sacred texts, and sometimes stay awake the entire night. Festivals are meant for the purification of the soul and feeding the body and mind with spiritual food. The Bhagavadgita (2.39) declares: "That which is night to all beings, in that the self-controlled man wakes. That in which all beings wake, is night to the Self-seeing sage."

Every festival celebrates the glory of a specific god or goddess and denotes not only the ultimate triumph of good over evil but also the "One Ultimate Reality" behind the plethora of gods and goddesses. The arrival of festival brings a joyous atmosphere to the home and necessitates many activities—buying essential commodities for the festival, cleaning and decorating the house the previous day, arranging worship materials, the taking of baths by family members, the preparation of special clothing for the occasion, displaying the *tilaka* on the forehead, and making special dishes. If the festivals fall on holidays, the daughters help their mothers with arranging materials required for the worship and with cleaning and decorating the worship area, whereas sons help their fathers with decorating the house, tying flower garlands and mango leaves to the doorways, and arranging lighting for the icon and worship area.

Proper worship during the festival is performed by the householder, his wife, and children, being ably guided by the family priest. Hindus who have settled in the West may not have ready access to a family priest. Hence, they usually perform the worship with the help of books meant for those purposes or with the help of audio- or video-cassettes.

The deity specific to the festival is worshipped on that day. The worship consists of sixteen types of practices sanctioned by the treatises of Hindu tradition and later strengthened by Shankaracharya, who founded the school of Advaita (absolute nondualism) philosophy twelve hundred years ago. This worship replicates the sixteen services that are offered to a beloved guest: (1) invoking the presence of the deity (*avahana*); (2) the offering of a seat (*asana*); (3–4) the offering of sanctified water for the washing of the feet and hands (*padya* and *arghya*); (5) the offering of water for drinking (*achamana*); (6) the bathing of the icon (*snana*); (7) the offering of clothes (*vastra*); (8) the offering of the sacred thread (*upaveeta*); (9) the offering of sandalwood paste (*gandha*); (10) the offering of flowers and ornamentation (*pushpa*); (11) the offering of incense sticks (*dhupa*); (12) the offering of dishes of food (*naivedya*); (13) the offering of camphor light (*dipa*); (14) the offering of betel leaves and areca nut (*tambula*); (15) the recitation of Vedic hymns (*mantra pushpa*); and (16) obeisance to the deity (*pradakshina*).

Children ten to fifteen years old are guided by their parents to follow this order of worship and advised to continue later in their married life. Thus the worship serves as a solid foundation for children to shape their spiritual life. It is common that younger children (five to ten years old) watch these rituals out of curiosity and start questioning their parents about them:

> Why do we celebrate the festivals today and what is their significance?
> Will those icons know what you are doing?
> Will those icons receive those flowers, fruits, and sweets you offer?

Why don't the icons speak or walk like we do?
Why shouldn't those fruits and dishes be offered to us first and why should
we wait to eat anything until the worship is over?
Why one should take a special bath on these days?

Parents need to provide answers about the religious and spiritual significance of these festivals and rituals in a language that can be easily understood by their children. They may narrate a symbolic story associated with the festival. Parents, especially mothers, start narrating mythological and spiritual stories to their children at a very young age. The range of stories may vary but generally they include incidents from the two major Indian epics, the Ramayana and the Mahabharata, the life and achievements of Lord Krishna from books of lore, including the *Bhagavata Purana*. Sometimes parents may narrate stories from the lives of Buddha, Mahavira, Guru Nanak, Chaitanya, Ramakrishna Paramahamsa, Swami Vivekananda, Sharadadevi, and other spiritual teachers and saints. These stories have either moral or spiritual messages and are frequently interconnected with the religious festivals observed in homes, thus creating tremendous curiosity among children of all ages. Children are advised to have such role models in their life. Let us examine the form and content of some of the major Hindu festivals and their religious and spiritual significance.

MAKARA SANKRANTI OR PONGAL

The year begins with this seasonal festival, which is connected with agriculture. This festival is celebrated during the second week of January when the sun changes the course of his direction from south to north and from the zodiacal sign of Capricorn to Cancer. People pay their respects to nature, which has nurtured them, and they exchange fruits, freshly grown grain, and vegetables. Farmers offer prayers in the fields along with family members and also decorate their implements and bullocks, ably assisted by their children. These offerings are symbolic of identifying the same soul in all animate and inanimate objects of the world. At this time, the parents explain to children the need to respect Mother Earth, which is treated as a goddess in the Hindu tradition. A hymn in the Sama Veda (616) describes nature thus:

> Rejoice in all the moods of Mother Nature.
> Experience the unseen sacred moods.
> *In its variegated and pompous forms*
> Spring is the season of cool breezes and flowers
> Which fill the hearts and give joy.

SHIVARATRI

This festival is dedicated to Lord Shiva, considered the involutor of the universe. It falls on the fourteenth day of the dark fortnight during the months of February or March. The festival lasts a whole day, including the night. Parents offer worship in the home, particularly to a *Linga*, symbol of Lord Shiva and the macrocosm. The Shiva Linga is bathed in a mixture of water, milk, curds, honey, ghee, and sugar. It is decorated with sandalwood paste, flowers, and colored clothes. Generally we see children pouring the liquids on the Linga while the priest or the father recites the hymns. Sons who have been initiated into the sacred thread ceremony are guided systematically by their parents to chant mystic hymns silently. Parents also fast that day and visit the temple of Lord Shiva, accompanied by their children. Shiva is considered the foremost among the gods who practiced Yoga, and therefore devotees who cherish those attributes sit in silence, meditate on the mystic word *Om,* and pray to the Lord to rid them of ignorance and indolence. Some may sing and dance in praise of Shiva. There will be spiritual discourses on the various feats performed by Shiva and his final victory over evil and evildoers.

HOLI

A month after the Shivaratri festival, on full-moon day, Holi, a seasonal festival of colors, is celebrated with pomp and grandeur. Men and women of all ages offer prayers to the Lord, sing, dance, and sprinkle colored water on each other. The colors captivate the eyes of children and are representative of the outward expression of our deepest emotions. This festival is also a tribute to Mother Earth for having provided us with food and nurturing. People light a bonfire, which is symbolic of burning off the passions. The festival is associated with the mythological story of Holika, a sister of the demon king (Hiranyakashipu). Parents narrate the story to children: "Prahlada, the son of the demon king, was a great devotee of Lord Vishnu, considered the sustainer of the universe. Driven by greed, the demon king motivates his sister Holika to kill her nephew. It appears that Holika had obtained a favor from Lord Brahma the Creator that she should not die, even though she, too, would enter the fire. She entered the fire along with Prahlada and was burned to ashes, as she had only evil desires. Thus was Prahlada saved by Lord Vishnu." They also explain the moral of the story: that true devotees of Lord Vishnu will emerge safe in difficult circumstances, but evil people will be punished for their sins. The celebration of this festival teaches children to be true devotees of God and to harbor spiritual qualities for self-development and emulate the attributes of Prahlada and not the qualities of a demon king. As the life of a Hindu is based on the foundational principles of the fourfold values, meritorious acts (*punya*), unmeritorious acts (*papa*), and atonement (*prayaschitta*), as well as the doctrine of action and theory of rebirth—the elders explain these philosophical concepts to children in simple and illustrative language and create in them an ethical mind-set regarding the performance of meritorious acts and refraining from wrong behavior throughout their life.

YUGADI

Yugadi is a historical festival heralding the New Year according to the traditional Hindu calendar. It also denotes the first day of the spring season. Like New Year's Day in the

West, this festival is celebrated with hope and joy. The emphasis is on taking an oil bath that has medicinal benefits and eating a mixture of neem leaves and jaggery (unrefined sugar) with the recitation of a hymn that signifies the joys and sorrows of life. Parents explain to children that the eating of neem leaves makes their body strong like a diamond for one hundred years, for warding off all evil and obtaining all types of prosperity. Parents also advise their children to be strong physically and mentally, like heroes such as Lord Hanuman and Bhima, one of the mythological epic heroes, and to cultivate their qualities. Children are encouraged to read the related tales from the epics and books of lore.

THE BIRTHDAYS OF RAMA AND KRISHNA

The festival associated with the birth of Rama, believed to be the incarnation of Lord Vishnu, falls on the ninth day of the bright fortnight in the month of April. The celebrations include the offerings of worship to Lord Rama, recitation of the Ramayana in a week, visiting the shrine of Rama, treating guests, and fasting by elders. Philosophically, Rama represents the universal soul, and his consort Sita represents the individual soul; their marriage is a unification of the individual soul with the universal soul. The battle between Rama and his archrival, Ravana, is symbolic of the battle of good over evil thoughts, and hence children are advised by their elders to "emulate the noble qualities of Rama and not the ignoble qualities of Ravana." Every Hindu is generally familiar with the story of Rama, and parents encourage their children to read the stories during the festival and absorb the morals associated with it. The love life of Rama and Sita teaches youth to be chaste and follow a balanced married life.

Generally around the middle or end of August, Hindus celebrate the birthday of Krishna, who also is considered the incarnation of Lord Vishnu. This is a festival of heroism, love, and devotion. On this day, special worship is performed for Lord Krishna at home and in temples wearing a festive outlook. Multitudes of devotees sing, dance, and praise the glory of the Lord and stay awake till midnight, the time of his birth. Children and youths engage in sportive activities such as breaking the pot blindfolded and gymnastics. The major Krishna temples bring out massive decorated chariots in which the icons of Krishna and his consorts are placed and taken out in procession. One can see young children and youth engaged enthusiastically in pulling those chariots, breaking the coconuts, waving lamps, and distributing sweets and savories. Some young children take part in religious competitions meant for that purpose, some being dressed as Krishna and drawing the attention of the crowd, some acting in dramas related to Lord Krishna. These activities obviously enhance the religious and the consequent outlook of children in their formative years.

GANESHA FESTIVAL

Lord Ganesha is the son of Lord Shiva and Parvati. He is believed to be the lord of obstacles, the remover of obstacles, and the lord of knowledge. Hence worship is primarily offered to him in all the religious festivals. The exclusive worship of Ganesha comes in the month of September. Marketplaces are flooded with clay icons of Ganesha in various poses, and children take delight in visiting those stalls and purchasing miniature Ganeshas. After the completion of worship at home, children are asked to visit 108 houses in the locality and offer salutations to Lord Ganesha. The number 108 is symbolic of twelve months multiplied by nine planets. Some children and youth come together and install a Ganesha icon in their neighborhood and arrange cultural and religious programs and after a week process through the neighborhood with the icon before immersing it in a nearby lake or tank. Children and youth are naturally drawn toward Ganesha as he is considered the presiding deity for knowledge.

THE BIRTHDAYS OF SPIRITUAL TEACHERS

Because Hinduism has given great importance to spiritual teachers, one can see in temples all over India the icons of spiritual teachers along with the icons of gods and goddesses. They were the great devotees of the Lord, and through their spiritual courage and divine strength, they conquered the forces of evil and helped their fellow mortals in removing the veil of ignorance and passing through worldly life (*samsara*).

Foremost among these spiritual teachers was Shankaracharya, propounder of nondualism (*Advaita*); Ramanujacharya, founder of the school of qualified nondualism (*Vishishtadvaita*); Madhvacharya, propounder of dualism (*Dvaita*); and Chaitanya and Basavanna, founders of the Vaishnava and Veerashaivism schools (the schools worshipping Lord Vishnu and Shiva, respectively, as supreme reality). The birthdays of these preceptors are celebrated with great enthusiasm by Hindus belonging to subsects of Hinduism. Generally on these days, there will be worshipping of the teacher concerned, the pulling of the decorated chariot carrying the icon or the portrait of that teacher, special lectures and discourses by eminent scholars, literary and religious competitions related to the works of the teacher, and screening of films. Children are encouraged to participate in the pulling of the chariot and literary competitions. In the case of a holiday, the elders accompany the children to religious congregations and also narrate the role of these preceptors in revitalizing the spiritual legacy of India.

It is amazing to find that the birth, enlightenment, and death of Buddha all occurred on the full-moon day of Vaishaka month (April–May). The followers of Buddhism all over the world celebrate this day as Buddha Jayanti. The birthday of Mahavira, the founder of Jainism, is celebrated on the thirteenth day of the bright fortnight of Chaitra month (April). The birthday of Guru Nanak, the founder of Sikhism, is celebrated on the dark fortnight of November. Their followers observe these days with great reverence and engage in charitable acts, such as mass feeding of the poor, medical and health-care camps, and the distribution of clothes to the poor. You can see Indian children from eight to twenty years of age enthusiastically engaging in volunteer services in all these activities. They slowly come to understand that charity, compassion, sharing, loving, and caring are integral components of one's religion and that practicing such virtues will contribute to their spiritual growth.

RAKSHA BANDHAN

Raksha Bandhan is a festival of brothers and sisters that falls in the month of August (Shravana) on a full-moon day. On this day, a sister binds a thread around the wrist of her brother as a symbol of her protection by him. Brahmins wear a new sacred thread around their shoulders denoting their commitment to ritualistic and religious practices.

In ancient times in India, a preceptor used to tie the orange thread around the wrist of his pupils at the time of the initiation ceremony. The color also indicated the renunciation of worldly activities in the fourth stage of one's life. The Hindu traditions treat father, teacher, and guest as one's god and mother as one's goddess (Taitirriyopanishad, Shikshavalli, Anuvaka I). This Vedic concept of treating elders as gods and goddesses was later extended to sisters and women in general. Hence in Hindu tradition, a woman who does not have her own brother sometimes ties this thread around the wrist of a friend whom she considers as a brother. Seeing this practice performed by elders helps children develop a deep respect and familial attitude toward the other gender. This respect becomes a powerful moral and spiritual force in shaping their future married life.

NAVARATRI

This festival is basically meant for the worshipping of female divinities of Hinduism. The festival is celebrated during October and is celebrated over nine nights. The first three days are for the worship of the goddess Durga, the protector; the next three are for the goddess Lakshmi, the benefactor of wealth; and the last three are for the goddess Sarasavati, the bestower of knowledge and wisdom.

The festival is indicative of the immense potentialities of female deities and their power in destroying evil forces. In fact, in the Hindu tradition, male and female children are considered gods and goddesses till they attain puberty, and hence sixteen girls or virgins (*Kanya*) are worshipped by elders of the household. The number sixteen represents the noble attributes to be cherished and cultivated by the people for the overall development of one's personality, especially spiritual growth. Boys who observe these rituals tend to develop a respectful attitude toward girls and women.

The tenth day of Navaratri is called Dussera or Vijayadashami, as it was on this day that Rama killed his archrival, Ravana, and saved his wife, Sita. According to a mythological account, on this day the goddess Durga killed the demon called Mahishasura, which speaks of the victory of good over evil. Children learn through the Navaratri festivals that the final triumph belongs only to truth, righteousness, and good. They are inspired to adopt these values in successive phases of their lives.

DIWALI: THE FESTIVAL OF LIGHTS

Deepavali is a Sanskrit word meaning a series or row (*avali*) of lights (*Deepa*). The people in northern India call it Diwali. The festival is celebrated either for three or five days commencing with the dark fortnight of Ashwayuja month and the first two days of the bright fortnight of Kartika month (October–November), according to the Hindu lunar calendar. During the festival, the women light lamps at dusk and decorate their homes; businesspeople decorate their establishments with lights; and children burn a variety of crackers. The needy are given donations. Special services are held in temples.

The second day, which is the fourteenth day of the dark moon, is celebrated as the victory of Lord Krishna over the tyrant demon Narakasura, who ruled the kingdom called Pragjyotishapura (now the state of Assam). According to the mythological account in the *Bhagavata Purana*, Narakasura, ruling in the Dwapara age, had let loose a reign of terror in the triple world. He stole the earrings of the goddess Aditi, the mother of the gods. Krishna, at the behest of the gods, sought the help of his wife, Satyabhama, as a charioteer. He killed the demon during the night and returned the earrings to Aditi. The demon was the son of Mother Earth (Bhumi) and was called Bhauma. To this day, symbolically the effigy of Narakasura is burned in many places all over India. Mother Earth requested Krishna to announce the day as marking the triumph of good over evil. According to an account in the Ramayana, after the killing of Ravana by Rama, his trusted devotee Hanuman flew from Lanka to Ayodhya and announced the triumphant arrival of Rama's party to the kingdom.

It is mentioned in the *Bhagavata Purana* that Krishna, in order to relieve his battle fatigue, took an oil bath. This tradition is practiced by people at dawn even now and has multiple health benefits according to Charaka, the ancient Indian physician. The first day of the bright fortnight of Kartika month is in great honor of Bali, the demon king. According to the mythological story, Emperor Bali ruled the triple world in the Krita age. He was the grandson of Emperor Prahlada, a devotee of Lord Vishnu. Indra, the lord of the gods, became jealous of Bali and requested Lord Vishnu to dethrone him. Vishnu agreed and came down to Earth in the form of a dwarf and requested Bali to give him a piece of land, where he was performing a sacrifice. Bali offered Vishnu however much land he could cover in three strides. Vishnu covered the earth with one foot and covered the heavens by growing tall (considered the second foot). He then asked the emperor where he should place the third foot. Bali asked the dwarf to place the third step on his head, and thus Lord Vishnu pushed him to the netherworld. Because of this extraordinary feat, Vishnu was popularly called Trivikrama (a god of three giant strides). In accordance with the request of the demon king, Vishnu made him immortal and allowed him to visit the citizens of his kingdom once a year for a few hours. For this reason, people greet Bali the emperor on this day and also worship Lord Shiva in the evening. For certain regions of India it is also the beginning of a new lunar year of Vikram Samvat. Vikramaditya was a great emperor in whose memory the counting of years was begun. But in most places in northern India the fourth day is celebrated as a day of victory of Krishna over Indra by lifting the mythical Govardhana mountain. According to a mythological account, the denizens of Gokula were worshipping Indra, the lord of the rains. Once they offered worship to Mount Govardhana. Indra became furious and arranged for torrential rains, creating havoc among the residents. Krishna came to their rescue and held Mount Govardhana on his index finger, thus sheltering the whole village. Hence in Indian states such as Rajasthan and Maharashtra, people prepare a hillock of food and feed the poor and the needy.

Diwali helps Hindus in pursuing the fourfold values of life. The lamp represents the five primary elements of the universe (earth, water, fire, air, and ether) as the lamp is made out of clay, the oil is the liquid medium, and the wick burns with the help of air and is symbolic of ether. Diwali is indicative of the triumph of light over darkness, good over evil, truth over falsehood, and knowledge over ignorance. The eating of roasted or puffed rice during the festival is indicative of the annihilation of innate desires in us. Taking an oil bath during the Diwali festival is like taking a holy dip in Ganges, the most sacred river of India. According to a mythological story, Rama, who was born and brought up in Ayodhya, returned on Diwali day after an exile of fourteen years. Krishna, who resided in Dwaraka in the West, went to the Northeast and killed Narakasura. These two historic heroes thus united India from North to South and East to West. Children learn and understand the religious and spiritual symbolism of the Diwali festival by way of participation, discussion, and reading related literature.

GITA JAYANTI

The Bhagvadgita, or the Song of the Lord Krishna, is treated as one of the basic Hindu Scriptures. In sum and substance, it deals with the philosophy of knowing oneself and the ways and means of attaining that goal. Generally in December, the festival is celebrated wherein the Gita is recited, discourses are organized, and the war scenes from the Mahabharata are enacted by children and youth. Memorizing the verses of the Gita will have a lasting impact on growing children. It impels them to know the philosophical dimensions of their religion in later years.

We find from the foregoing accounts that festivals play a crucial role in the religious and spiritual development of a Hindu family. These religious festivals are inextricably associated with various kinds of stories such as mythological accounts, folklore, and other wondrous tales. The method of introducing any idea or a concept through stories is the most ancient one in all civilizations, as stories foster curiosity, imagination, and liveliness in the minds of hearers.

In the Indian tradition, this method was employed for thousands of years to narrate the daring exploits of the gods and demons, their titanic struggles, and the valorous deeds of emperors and kings. Traditional literary critics contend that the story should be endowed with many sentiments, be imaginative, and be able to arouse the curiosity of the people (Vamanacharya Jhalakikar 1907). Hence, every religious and philosophical book in the Hindu tradition has one story or another with a moral or spiritual theme. Apart from the national festivals discussed here, people belonging to various castes, sects, and subsects, as well as those residing in villages, celebrate numerous festivals that have regional, folk, and indigenous cultural significance. The localized dimensions of these regional and subaltern festivals are too highly period specific to be covered here.

I have observed over the past three decades that Hindu children from five to fifteen years old imitate the acts of their parents, their elders, and their teachers. In fact, parents and teachers become their role models and testimony for all their actions. As they enter high school, and as the mind and brain blossom and puberty sets in, they slowly start questioning the contemporary relevance and scientific basis of all these religious practices. From the ages of fifteen through twenty, they are confronted by various issues. The college atmosphere, discussions of religious matters with classmates, the widening generation gap, the instruction they receive from various teachers, the physical and emotional changes they undergo, and the sociopolitical environment all combine to change the mind-set of these young people. Unable to face the pressure and challenges, they may question the rationale behind all these festivals, rituals, and practices and sometimes even refuse to participate in them. They try to seek answers by talking with their peers and trusted teachers.

When growing older, the young person tries to find answers from within or outside the tradition through reading books, talking with parents, elders, relatives, friends, teachers, or gurus, or by self-examination. They make a logical and scientific analysis of those issues or gnawing questions and often arrive at a synthesis or a broad opinion. Young people develop their personalities from the physical, mental, moral, cultural, social, religious, and spiritual dimensions based on those experiences. As Hindu festivals are spread throughout the calendar year, active participation in them continually impacts Hindu children and youth, contributing to their leading a spiritual and balanced life. The balanced life is based on the pursuit of the fourfold values of life, called in Sanskrit the *Purusharthas*: righteous value (*Dharma*), economic value (*Artha*), emotional value (*Kama*), and spiritual value (*Moksha*). Children learn through participating in festivals and reading religious and spiritual books that gods appear on earth in the form of incarnations for helping the distressed and for warding off evildoers. Some children even practice Yoga and breathing exercises for finding answers, guided by teachers.

According to Hindu thought, the ultimate aim of existence is to free oneself from the snare of ignorance (*Avidya*) and cycles of birth and death, thus leading to spiritual salvation (*Moksha*). Cherishing and practicing these values pave the way for the individual to reach his or her ultimate goal.

Acknowledgments

I am grateful to Beth Kulkarni and Monica Johnson for reviewing this chapter.

Sources

Benfey, Th. 1848. *Sama Veda*. Leipzig: n.p.
Buhler G., ed. 1892. *Gautama Dharmsutra*. Bombay: Nirnaya Sagara Press.
———. ed. 1892. *Vasista Dharmasutra*. Bombay: Nirnaya Sagara Press.
———. 1937. *Manu Smrti*. Bombay: Nirnaya Sagara Press.
Kane, P. V. 1946. *History of Dharma shastra*. 5 vols. Poona: Bhandarkar Oriental Research Institute.
Muir, John. [1805] 1967. *Rig Veda* with the commentary of *Sayana*, Original Sanskrit texts. 5 vols. Reprint, Amsterdam: n.p.

Shamashatri, R. 1920. *Kautilya Arthashastra*. Mysore: Oriental Research Institute.

Srimad Bhagavad Gita. 1942. Gorakhpur: Gita Press.

Susruta Samhita, Sarirasthanam. 1945. Varanasi: Chowkamba.

Vamanacharya Jhalakikar, ed. 1907. *Amarakosha with the commentary of Maheshwara*. Delhi: K. C. Publishers.

Yajurveda. 1940. Varanasi: Chowkamba.

CHAPTER 19

Reformed Spirits: Christian Practices in Presbyterian Preschools in South Korea and the United States

Kathy Dawson and Shin-Kyung Park

We come to this task as Presbyterians. Even though thousands of miles separate our research, we share a heritage of the Reformed tradition. This branch of Christianity claims the theological work of John Calvin (1509–64) as foundational for its belief system, and John Knox (1505–72) for the structure and governance known as Presbyterian. Neither of these forerunners of our Reformed faith set foot in either country represented in this chapter. So we share gratitude to the nameless missionaries who brought this version of the Christian faith to our respective soils, and look to uncovering the adaptations made to a transplanted faith as it regards the spiritual formation of children.

Since the early catechetical schools of Calvin's Geneva, the Reformed faith has taken the education and social welfare of young children seriously. It may surprise some to know that Calvin actually had a high view of children's spirituality. In his commentary on Psalm 8:2, he writes that the very real infants of this passage "even before they pronounce a single word, speak loudly and distinctly in commendation of God's liberality toward the human race" (Pitkin 2001, 166). Calvin also promoted instruction for young children in the catechism (a simplified summary of the Christian faith usually published in question-and-answer format), as well as a solid background in the humanities and character formation. He wished to pass a regulation within Geneva requiring all parents to provide such education for their children, and could for this reason be seen as the first promoter of public schools. The Presbyterian outgrowth of this Reformation movement continued its interest in the schooling and social welfare of children.

The remaining portions of this chapter will deal with four snapshots of children's spiritual formation from the South Korean and U.S. contexts. We begin with the historical forces that have led to current practice. This will be followed by a look at the present situation in Presbyterian church-related children's programs. The focus will then shift to spiritual formation as we look at current curricular practices and new models emerging for the future. In each section we will begin with a look at the South Korean context followed by practices in the United States. This cross-cultural comparison highlights both the commonality in religious tradition as well as the unique accents that emerge within particular cultural contexts.

South Korea: Past and Present Context

Institutions for early childhood education were first introduced by American missionaries to Korea during the Japanese occupation era (1910–45).[1] The Christian missionaries from the United States regarded kindergarten[2] education as an instrument of their missions, so they founded kindergartens and attached them to churches or schools they had previously established in Korea. Until that time, early childhood education was a task performed exclusively by family members.

Since Ewha Kindergarten was born in 1914 as the first kindergarten in Korea, many kindergartens were established in a short time, not only by American missionaries but also by Korean people (Park 2001, 133f.). Being connected with the resistance movement against Japanese colonialism, this kindergarten movement quickly expanded to the whole nation. Koreans assumed that early childhood education was the only hope for a future independent Korea and that kindergartens would lay the foundation for it.

By the 1930s, more than five hundred kindergartens existed in Korea, 80–90 percent of which were Christian kindergartens. From the beginning, the Christian church played an important role as the largest founder and supporter for Korean early childhood education. Through this mission, it endeavored to deliver Christianity to Korean people, to educate their children, and to nurture their spirituality in the light of the Gospel. This role played by the South Korean church in early childhood education continued into the 1970s until the South Korean government took ownership of public early childhood education and became the main founder of public kindergartens.

Since the 1980s the number of Christian kindergartens in South Korea has dropped, which indicates that the commitment of churches to the spiritual formation of young children through kindergartens has gradually been withdrawn. For example, 822 Protestant church kindergartens were registered in 1988, but only 569 were registered in 1995. In contrast with the decrease of Christian kindergartens, the number of kindergartens in other religions has increased (Buddhist kindergartens increased by 58 percent in the same period from 114 to 181). In 2003, there were 303 Protestant, 192 Catholic, 123 Buddhist, 4,329 public school kindergartens, and 3,125 private kindergartens in South Korea (*Statistical Yearbook of Education 2003*). This implies that while Christian churches still play a major role in educating South Korean children, the influence of the church on social education has become weaker (Park 1998, 367).

Currently in South Korea there are three kinds of educational institutions that are comparable to American Presbyterian preschools: church kindergartens, *Urinichib* (day-care centers), and *Sunkyowon*. Their founders are Christian churches, religious corporations, or private persons.

The church kindergarten is an institution for the education of young children from three to six years of age before public school. Generally it is sponsored by a church or by a person who intends to lead his or her kindergarten in the light of Christian educational principles. The church kindergarten belongs, like other kindergartens, to the public school system as a primary-level institution and stands under the guidance and control of the Ministry of Education and Human Resources. In order to meet the increasing day-care needs of young children whose mothers hold full-time jobs, many kindergartens have all-day groups, in addition to half-day groups.

Urinichib (children's house) is day care for young children from newborn to six years of age. Originally, their focus was on day care, but now they are trying to integrate educational activities into the caring tasks. According to their care time, there are three kinds of groups: a morning group, an all-day group, and a twenty-four-hour group. Administratively, Urinichibs are overseen by the Ministry of Health and Welfare.

These two types of church-related preschools are legal (accredited) institutions that are supported financially and also supervised by the South Korean government. Therefore, there are certain restrictions on their religious educational work. Owing to the diversity of religious beliefs in South Korea, it is difficult for these preschools to put an educational focus on Presbyterian beliefs and to make explicit their intention for spiritual formation in their regular curriculum.

Sunkyowon (missionary kindergarten with children ages four to six) is a nonaccredited institution, although it is sponsored by the Christian church. It is registered merely as a special institution for children's missions in the Ministry of Culture and Tourism. For this reason Sunkyowon is not recognized as a legal educational institution. However, the church, as the founder of Sunkyowon, insists on staying outside government control owing to difficulties in religious spiritual formation at public accredited preschools.

Moreover, many small churches with a weak financial basis that aren't able to found a legal kindergarten prefer to organize a Sunkyowon for the education of young children in their neighborhoods. Unfortunately, because Sunkyowons do not receive subsidies from the government, many have financial problems, a circumstance that influences the quality of their educational work. In spite of all these difficulties, they have been fighting for recognition and identification as qualified preschools for church missions.

The United States: Past and Present Context

In the United States the relationship between churches and the child-care programs they house is a fairly recent one. Although the early-twentieth-century industrialization and the periods of both world wars provided the impetus for the creation of "day nurseries" and day-care centers for the children of working-class mothers, most child care until the 1960s was provided within the family. With the increase of working parents from all social classes, rising birth and divorce rates, the mobility of job situations, and increased cost of living, families demanded child-care for their young children. But why would churches take on this role?

As mentioned earlier in this chapter, Protestant churches saw children as fertile ground for faith instruction. They had already responded to the call in earlier times for children's education in the form of Sunday school (Boylan 1988). In the Presbyterian

Church (U.S.A.), much work with children was attributed to both scriptural texts (such as Jesus' welcoming of little children) and to vows that the parents and congregation take as an infant is baptized—vows that promise a nurturing of the growing child in faith. There were also economic reasons for churches to open their doors to a new mission with children in the 1960s and 1970s. Mainline church membership was declining. Large churches with extensive classroom space were sitting empty during much of the week. Housing a child-care program was good stewardship, in religious vocabulary. Children could be educated, unused space occupied, and potential new member families introduced to the church setting, and perhaps the schools could bring some income to a declining church at the same time.

It is this last point that makes the spiritual formation of young children in church-related preschools in the United States a difficult topic. A 1982 survey conducted by the National Council of Churches identified more than eighteen thousand church-related child-care programs. Of these, half were operated by congregations and half were simply housed on the church property through a contractual arrangement with a private provider (Lindner, Mattis, and Rogers 1983). Regardless of their status, 94 percent of the programs received some subsidy from the church in which they were housed. Over 33 percent also received government funding to subsidize their lower-income students. Only 16 percent indicated that spiritual development was the main goal of their curriculum.

As the financial decline of mainline churches increased in the 1980s less church money was allocated and more outside grant sources were sought to sustain the preschools. These grant sources often stipulated that money could not be used for religious instruction. Some weekday programs interpreted this condition to mean that the spiritual growth of children would need to be accomplished in settings other than the church-related preschool, a point that has implications for the amount of explicit spiritual content found in church-related preschools in the United States at present.

A 1993 survey found that Presbyterian Church (U.S.A.) preschools and day-care settings in the United States were housed in 28 percent of Presbyterian churches, serving 288,523 children annually.[3] These figures, now more than ten years old, are the most recent data available for this denomination on weekday programs for children housed in church settings. This percentage includes preschool, day-care, and after-school programs, which were not differentiated in the data collection. For purposes of this chapter we focus on the first two that offer either morning or full-day education and care for young children (ages three to five). Accrediting agencies such as the National Association for the Education of Young Children and the Ecumenical Child Care Network are not attached to the government as in the South Korean context. Individual states do offer government licensing to church-related child care. Requirements vary among states, and some states offer religious exemptions to those programs housed within religious institutions.

In continuing conversations with a number of Presbyterian Church (U.S.A.)—related early childhood programs, it would seem that very few devote an explicit part of their regular curriculum to spiritual formation. Some attribute this to increased funding from government sources and other agencies that discourage religious training. Others fear a loss of accreditation or licensing would result from a focus on specific spiritual practices. Some preschool programs, although beginning as missions of the local Presbyterian church in which they are housed, have through personnel changes and changes in governance become less connected to the church than they were originally. They will often cite the growing diversity of religious beliefs among their families and parents' fears of indoctrination into a Presbyterian brand of religious belief. Other preschool programs rely on the pastor or educator of the Presbyterian church in question to provide a periodic chapel or religious education time in a separate space that is offered as an option to families. Finally, some define their time of spiritual formation more implicitly, relying on the hiring of staff with Christian values who model the Christian life without actually mentioning the source of their faith.

There are Presbyterian weekday schools that see spiritual formation as a part of the development of the whole child. These will often be explicit in their mission statement, listing spiritual growth along with cognitive, social, physical, and moral development. One such center is St. John's Children's Center in Reno, Nevada. Pam Ramseth, director of Children's Ministries, and Donna Young, director of the Children's Center, have intentionally created a close link between the church and the preschool beginning with the mission statement:

> St. John's Children's Center is a non-profit religious organization which is part of the ministry of St. John's Presbyterian Church to children and families. The purpose of the Children's Center is to provide a well-rounded, developmentally appropriate program for children which is grounded in the values of the Reformed Tradition of the Christian Church and is designed to provide educational, social, and spiritual activities promoting the well-being of each child.[4]

Each parent receives a copy of the mission statement, which also contains three explicit statements concerning how the center will carry out its spiritual formation:

- Each child is a unique and special creation of God, worthy of unconditional love and respect.
- Christian values are a critical part of our daily interactions with others.
- Programs at St. John's Children's Center are inclusive and respectful of all genders, races, cultures, and while promoting the Reformed Tradition of the Christian Church will be respectful of other religions.

Beyond this statement of its philosophy, St. John's Children's Center also requires each employee to sign an agreement that he or she understands the "Christian Values Policy" of the center. Teachers are not required to be Presbyterian or even Christian, but they must uphold the values that undergird the philosophy. This is certainly not the norm for Presbyterian-related preschools, but represents a school that makes its relationship to the church's ministry explicit. Churches, like St. John's, that have a close relationship with their weekday programs and view them as a mission of the church should have fewer ethical dilemmas involved with children's spiritual formation.

Current Practices and Emerging Models

The spirit of this cross-cultural study is that context does make a difference to practice. We turn our attention now to the specific spiritual practices and new models that have grown out of these two contexts. In addition to examining current practices, we highlight some new models of spiritual formation suggested by recent research from our respective cultures.

SOUTH KOREA: CURRENT PRACTICES

The spiritual practices of South Korean church-related schools of each of the three types described earlier do not seem very different from one another. Their dominant place of spiritual formation is a time of worship together once a week. Prayers and gospel music are also important expressions of their religious practices. They are normally integrated into daily work: for example, prayers before (and after) group activities and meals, as well as hymns and stories for group programs. In addition, church-related preschools make use of Christian holy days and celebrations as religious educational opportunities.

Rituals and Practices

Rituals used in Christian preschools, according to my field observations, are generally very similar to church rituals in their essential forms: gospel music, prayers such as the Lord's Prayer, and Bible stories. Most preschools have worship services once a week together or in small groups. New church songs are taught before worship time or during small-group time. Church songs for young children are often accompanied with rhythmical hand gestures or body motions, so that the melodies and lyrics can be better understood and memorized by young children.

In church-related preschools, a pastor or an educator sent by the church tells children Bible stories. His or her educational expertise determines the quality of the whole service. Usually the teachers pray, but sometimes children follow after the teacher's prayer. Before the start of daily work teachers hold a prayer time. Many directors of preschools emphasize the modeling of teachers' religious attitude.

Holy Days and Celebrations

In church-related preschools Christian holy days and celebrations are used as important occasions for spiritual formation. Especially on Christmas, Easter, and Thanksgiving holidays a more elaborate worship service is planned with special activities and events, such as puppet shows, performances, parties, special offerings, and craft displays. Also, in preparing for the celebrations, children can learn about Bible stories and their meanings for our life. Parents, relatives, the congregation, and members of the community are invited to these celebrations. Since the majority of children are from non-Christian families, it is a good opportunity to share the gospel with them.

Narratives or Stories

As mentioned earlier, Bible stories are a core part of periodic chapel services. Biblical themes are mainly about God, Jesus, creation, church, family life, human relationships, and church festivals. Sometimes Bible stories are integrated in small-group activities. Bible stories are often performed with audiovisual materials or books. The storytelling is occasionally followed by related activities such as drawing, painting, and handicrafts. These bring children to conversations about the stories, which leads again to spontaneous worship.

Besides direct spiritual practices related to education, church-related preschools try to maintain contact with parents through letters, which include some religious educational information. Some schools have parent groups who want to know more about Christianity, and they offer Bible-learning opportunities to them.

SOUTH KOREA: NEW MODELS

Recently a reform movement for the traditional practices of nurturing spirituality in young children is emerging in South Korea, especially from churches. Several alternative models have been developed successfully. They are weekday church-school programs, in which young children learn about God with their mothers. It is an attempt to stretch the restrictions of Christian education, which have been limited to Sunday schools inside the churches until now.

Baby School (Choongshin Presbyterian Church, Seoul)

Designed for toddlers two to four years old and their mothers, baby school is a weekday church-school program for early childhood education. At baby school the mother helps the early socialization of her baby, and the baby learns and plays God's words with its mother. Baby school therefore has a dual set of goals that benefit both the children and their families.

Choongshin Presbyterian Church initiated this program in 1986, and it has since found echoes in many churches. The program is generally held for two twelve-week terms a year, during the spring and autumn. It is a half-day program, from 10:00 to 12:00, two days a week.

The educational activities consist of free play, singing and dancing, gym, worship, Bible stories, as well as family play, field trips, doll play, concerts, presentations, Mothers' class, and other special activities.

The daily schedule is as follows:

> 9:30–10:00 Teachers' meeting and praying time
> 10:00–10:30 Free play

10:30–10:55 Singing and dancing, gym
10:55–11:15 Worship service and special activities
11:15–11:30 Snacks, announcements, calling out names in small groups
11:30–11:55 Bible stories and follow-up activities
11:55–12:00 Benediction and good-bye
12:00–2:00 Teachers' lunch, cleaning and rearranging the room, preparation
for next day, prayer time

In this program, children participate with their mothers and perform all activities together. Through these common experiences children and their mothers teach and learn from each other. If needed, parents can get instructions about options for their children's education through printed materials, special lectures, or Internet contacts.

Teachers for baby school are trained in a four-day course ("Seminar for Arranging Baby Schools") about two to three weeks before the beginning of baby school.

A second model would be the Eunice school (Youngnak Presbyterian Church, Seoul). This program focuses on the training of parents as core teachers for nurturing their children's spirituality. The program was named after Timothy's mother, who was a good model of faith for her son (2 Timothy 1:5). It is set up similar to the baby school: two days a week, from 10:00 to 12:00.

The themes of learning are composed mostly of aspects of Christian family life. The program accentuates, above all, the home as a place of God's grace and its delivery to children, and mothers as stewards and models of spiritual formation for their children (Department of Education of the Korean Presbyterian Church, 1998).

THE UNITED STATES: CURRENT PRACTICES

Spiritual Practices and Prayer

The major difference in spiritual practices between the South Korean and the U.S. context is that in the latter, spiritual practices are often not part of the daily life of Presbyterian preschools but occur either in isolated moments or special celebrations apart from the daily routine. Taking prayer as an example, it is not the practice of preschools to begin and end each group activity during the day with a prayer. If prayers are in evidence during a typical preschool day in the United States, they would most likely take the form of grace before meals or snack times. These prayers range from reciting or singing a communal prayer such as "God is great. God is good. Let us thank God for our food. Amen" to a teacher or child leading the group in prayer. Some preschools with diverse student bodies will use a moment of silence as the grace before the meal or snack.

Other occasions on which prayers are sometimes used in U.S. preschools are times of grief, illness, or fear. Acknowledging the intense feelings of children through prayer connects them with the Divine, who is protector and comforter. Young children are also able to bring the names of those in their immediate family who are ill to the gathered community in prayer. They may describe this practice as "talking to God."

Holy Days and Celebrations

Another time when spiritual practices are often present in Presbyterian weekday schools is during the Christmas or Easter season. A nativity display is a part of many classrooms. Some schools will also acknowledge other traditions and their holy days, such as Hanukkah and Kwanzaa in winter or Passover in spring. Many schools blend sacred and secular symbols of these holidays much as the larger American culture does. It would not be unusual to see the baby Jesus side by side with Santa Claus and the reindeer in the celebrations of young children in these schools.

Narratives or Stories

Children's literature is another place in which spiritual issues are made explicit in the classroom. Some of these may be actual Bible stories. Others are less explicit in their focus on Scripture, but may promote Christian spiritual practices and values. Books that invite conversation of a spiritual nature can be windows into the spiritual life of some children, as they bring their questions and observations to the story. Karen Marie Yust has provided a helpful framework for acquiring these types of books that can be used by both families and church-related weekday schools in the United States (Yust 2004).

What seems to be missing from spiritual practices as found in the preschools of the United States is the sense that the spiritual nature of the child is just as likely to be nurtured during times of informal interactions as during prayer and the reading of literature. One recent study from the National Center for Early Development and Learning shows that teachers from preschools with religious affiliations are more likely to endorse "group-centered" activities in which everyone engages in the same activities at the same time rather than the "child-centered" activities advocated by teachers of public school and Head Start programs (Early, Clifford, and Howes 1999). Such attention to children in groups could mean missing the faith expression of an individual child. Children bring their own spiritual questions and stories to school each day. A spiritual practice for the teacher of young children is to listen and be attentive to these unexpected times. Often questions will arise as children contemplate items from God's creation, including class pets. The death or illness of a family member may also be a time of many spiritual questions. The environment and curriculum of the classroom can invite or stifle such critical inquiry.

Rituals

Finally, the spiritual formation that most Presbyterian preschools would point to as explicit religious training and most influenced by the Reformed tradition would be periodic chapel services or educational times with the pastor or educator. In the schools whose teachers I have conversed the most frequently with, chapel times were twice a week for four- and five-year-olds. Some schools had chapel as infrequently as once a month or even just at Christmas and Easter. Again this points to the view that the spiritual life of children is not something that is deemed to be as important or as natural as their cognitive, motor, and language development. Those who lead these services are usually outside of the daily classroom community, thus continuing the idea that spirituality is something separate and alien to a child's education.

The quality of these services or educational times also depends on how adept the pastor or educator is at structuring the services at the preschool child's developmental level and interest. Most of these services include music, storytelling, and perhaps some call and response of Bible verses. Many gifted pastors and educators have also learned the importance of creating rituals of gathering and departing in order to create sacred space in their time with the children.

THE UNITED STATES: NEW MODELS

There are a number of new models being used in Presbyterian weekday schools in the United States to foster children's spiritual formation. Some schools are moving to a more conversational format of spiritual instruction. Using programs that combine spiritual practices with a Montessori style of children's education like Godly Play, Young Children and Worship, or Catechesis of the Good Shepherd, children are being asked to wonder about the Judeo-Christian stories of Scripture (Berryman 2002; Cavalletti 1992; Stewart and Berryman 1989). These modes of teaching have rituals of welcoming and leaving, and a time of storytelling with manipulative objects that invites the child to enter into the story. They also set aside time for responding to the story through art, story retelling, conversation, and a time of feasting and prayer. One of the unique aspects of this style of teaching comes after the story has been told and before the response time. The children are invited into a time of wonder centered on the story. Statements like, "I wonder where you are in this story," and "I wonder where this place really is," prompt children to voice their own interpretations and insights as well as hear what the storyteller is wondering about the story presented.

There is also a resurgence within Protestant circles in the United States in looking at spiritual practices as a way of daily life. Dorothy Bass, Don Richter, and Craig Dykstra, among others, have published books asking Presbyterians and other mainline Christian denominations to reclaim such spiritual practices as honoring the body, keeping Sabbath, hospitality, saying yes and saying no, and singing our lives (Bass 1998). All of these practices and others are accessible on a child's level and could be incorporated into a curriculum or named as spiritual formation if they are already present. The Valparaiso Project, founded with Lilly Endowment money, offers grants to congregations and other ministries in the United States that want to target specific practices or a broad constellation of practices for education and growth.

In 2003 a grant was awarded to the Newbury Center for Childhood Education, a laboratory preschool connected with Union Theological Seminary and Presbyterian School of Christian Education in Richmond, Virginia. Over the course of an academic year a team of seminary students, early childhood educators, parents, a research fellow, and a Christian Education faculty member observed the specific spiritual practice of "shaping community" as it was naturally occurring in the school day. The team was attuned to the behaviors and conversations that occurred during times of gathering, storytelling, and breaking of bread. Partway through the year, a time of explicitly Christian education that also embodied these three forms of community shaping was added to the weekly schedule in the form of Godly Play, and observers looked for any changes in community shaping that occurred.

The data are still being sifted, but some preliminary observations are offered here. First, community was created on at least two levels. Researchers watched as teachers and students began creating rituals, rules of behaving, and relationships within the classroom. But the researchers themselves also created community with monthly lunches at which they, too, gathered, told stories, and broke bread in sacred space. Relationships were formed between parents, seminary students, and teachers that would not have developed if it had not been for the research. This observation is offered here to encourage schools and churches to take their partnership more seriously and view the strengthening of relationships centered on the spiritual lives of children as a practice of faith.

Second, the depth of theological play around the explicitly spiritual stories surprised the researchers. It was not unusual to discuss the role of Mary in relation to Jesus, the reason for God's creation of the world, or the importance of Abraham's building of altars in thankfulness for God's providence. The language was simple, but the theological wrestling of these children between the ages of three and five would be worthy of a seminary classroom or critical adult Bible study.

Finally, it was discovered that conversations of a spiritual nature went on constantly in the classroom, if one were but to listen closely. The frequency of these conversations aids children in more fluently expressing their questions and thoughts regarding matters of faith. It also leads to an acknowledgment on the part of the preschool staff that children's spirituality is an integral part of the whole lives of their students. This speaks to a growing spirituality that cannot be stifled by funding or methodology. It remains for adults to decide whether they want to be part of the conversation.

What We Have Learned

The authors are grateful for the opportunity we have shared in working together by means of e-mail on this project. The Internet can only go so far in cultural comparison, however. We had the advantage of having met while Professor Park was doing sabbatical research in the United States. The comparison would have been aided significantly by a similar cultural exchange by Professor Dawson visiting Korean schools. Only through this type of mutual indwelling can we hope to truly understand what we share and how we differ.

As claimed in the opening paragraphs of this chapter, we share a common heritage in the Reformed tradition. In some ways the emerging trends articulated here move us closer to our Reformed roots. In the Korean context, the movement to empower families to nurture their children spiritually is reminiscent of Calvin's efforts with the parents of Geneva. In the American context the movement to daily spiritual practices that inform our lives is akin to a Reformed pietism that finds its expression in the real world.

The appropriation of both these trends within the life of early childhood programs housed in Presbyterian churches would greatly strengthen the link with the local church and the tradition that formed and reformed us. We hope that others will join the conversation, so that we may learn from each other how best to promote spiritual practices with young children throughout the world.

Notes

1. The early part of this historical context would hold true for all of Korea, but since 1953 early childhood education has taken different directions because of the division between North and South Korea.

2. The Korean context uses the term *kindergarten* to refer to educational institution for ages three to six. The United States context would use the same term to refer to the year that directly precedes first grade, usually ages five to six, and so will use the term *preschool* to designate its early child education for ages three to five. Other cultures may have different designations and ages specified within the realm of early childhood education related to religious settings.

3. The survey was sent to all Presbyterian Church (U.S.A.) congregations with a response rate of 89 percent (10,177 of 11,456 congregations), according to Jack Marcum, Research Services Division of the Presbyterian Church (U.S.A.). E-mail correspondence, October 4, 2004.

4. St. John's Children's Center Philosophy Statement, October 14, 1996, provided by Ramseth and Young at the Association of Presbyterian Church Educators' annual conference, February 4, 2005.

References

Bass, Dorothy, ed. 1998. *Practicing our faith: A way of life for a searching people.* San Francisco: Jossey-Bass.

Bass, Dorothy, and Don Richter. 2002. *Way to live: Christian practices for teens.* Nashville, Tenn.: Upper Room Books.

Berryman, Jerome W. 2002. *The complete guide to Godly Play.* 5 vols. Denver, Colo.: Living the Good News.

Boylan, Anne M. 1988. *Sunday school: The formation of an American institution, 1790–1880.* New Haven, Conn.: Yale University Press.

Cavalletti, Sofia. 1992. *The religious potential of the child.* Chicago: Catechesis of the Good Shepherd Publications.

Department of Education of the Korean Presbyterian Church. 1998. *With mother, baby and God resource book.* Seoul: Korean Presbyterian Publishing.

Dykstra, Craig. 1999. *Growing in the life of faith: Education and Christian practices.* Louisville, Ky.: Geneva Press.

Early, Diane, Richard Clifford, and Carollee Howes. 1999. A survey: Quality practices. *NCEDL Spotlights,* no. 10. (Accessed at www.ncedl.org September 2004.)

Lindner, Eileen, Mary C. Mattis, and June R. Rogers. 1983. *When churches mind the children: A study of day care in local parishes.* Ypsilanti, Mich.: High/Scope Press.

Park, Shin-Kyung. 1998. Role of Christianity in the founding process of kindergarten education in Korea. Youngnam Theological College and Seminary, *Theology and Ministry* 7:343–69.

————. 2001. *Öffentliche Kleinkindererziehung: Vergleichende Untersuchungen zur Entwicklung und zum gegenwärtigen Stand in Deutschland und in Südkorea.* Munich: Biblion Verlag.

Pitkin, Barbara. 2001. "The heritage of the Lord": Children in the theology of John Calvin. In *The child in Christian thought,* edited by Marcia J. Bunge, 160–93. Grand Rapids, Mich.: Eerdmans.

Statistical yearbook of education. 2003. Seoul: Ministry of Education and Human Resources Development/Korean Educational Development Institute.

Stewart, Sonja M., and Jerome Berryman. 1989. *Young children and worship.* Louisville, Ky.: Westminster/John Knox.

Yust, Karen Marie. 2004. *Real kids, real faith: Practices for nurturing children's spiritual lives.* San Francisco: Jossey-Bass.

PART IV

CONNECTING THE INNER LIFE WITH ETHICAL ACTION

In examining the relationship of "inner" to "outer" spirituality, the six authors in this section explore the following questions, among others: What rituals, practices, and obligations of the spiritual life guide young people to meaning, purpose, and ethical action? How does each tradition understand the relationship between spirituality and social/ethical obligations, including service and social action? How does spirituality relate to issues of vocation, or finding one's "right livelihood" in the world?

Michael Warren, a Roman Catholic, explores the relationship between what he calls "two spiritualities." "Lowercase spirituality" refers to the idea that "everyone has a spirituality," since we are all embodied spirits; but this spirituality can be directed to any number of outcomes, negative or positive, depending on what we "stand for" in our lives. "Uppercase spirituality," on the other hand, involves an "active disciplined search for God" in which we take responsibility for our entire way of living, including our ethical actions. Warren argues that Christian communities must make a concerted effort to involve youth in "uppercase spirituality" by helping them to understand the images that affect their life structures and encouraging them to assume ethical responsibility for all outcomes of their lives. This kind of spirituality—symbolized by the Eucharist as the core of Christian living—leads to thankfulness and generosity, countering the contemporary self-centered consumerist mentality.

Evelyn L. Parker offers another view (which could be described as an illustration of "uppercase spirituality") from the Christian Methodist Episcopal Church, a historic African American institution. She suggests that "singing songs of hope," such as "We Shall Overcome" and "Keep Your Eyes on the Prize, Hold On," symbolized the values of this church during its first century from 1870 to 1970 and continue to do so today. Further, Parker says that the spirituality of African American adolescents during this era was uniquely influenced by the "emancipatory hope" embodied in these songs, which are rooted in the resurrected Christ and the power of the Holy Spirit. This hope and the ethical actions based on it lead to the transformation of all human relationships and dehumanizing social structures. Parker offers the example of Ruby Doris Smith, an African American civil rights activist who died in 1967 at the age of twenty-five, to illustrate her view and provide a model for contemporary adolescent spirituality.

Sherry H. Blumberg describes the embedded relationship between the inner life and ethical action in the Jewish faith. In Blumberg's view, Jewish tradition implicitly assumes that outer ethical action comes first and inner understanding later, and she suggests that the developmental concept that "children learn by doing" supports this approach. She demonstrates how the traditional Jewish concepts of *mitzvot* (God's ritual and ethical commandments or "good deeds"), *gemilut hasadim* (acts of loving-kindness), and *tikkun olam* (repair of the world: working for justice or social action) offer a focus for children's and adolescents' ethical development, both in terms of doing good deeds and then reflecting on them. Blumberg traces a developmental trajectory in which ethical actions are transformed from learned behaviors to ethical reminders and finally to fully reflective actions that nurture the inner life.

Lori M. Noguchi offers a perspective from the Bahá'í faith, suggesting that because this religion has faced intense persecution since its establishment, the education of children has always been central to Bahá'í community life and is a significant factor in its survival. Instead of becoming bitter toward those who persecuted them, people of the Bahá'í faith have instead demonstrated a strong commitment to equanimity in the face of suffering and work for social progress and ethical justice. The formation of youth reflects this attitude, with a focus on character education and "the transformation of society through selfless service." Indeed, the development of personal potential is always seen in the context of service to others. The virtues of love of others, trustworthiness, truthfulness, and justice are continually cultivated in the educational process. Youth are trained in group interaction processes and oriented toward community service at the same time as they are educated in developing inner methods of "spiritual perception."

Afeefa Syeed and Nusaybah Ritchie demonstrate that the basic rituals and obligations of Islam, known as the Five Pillars, embody both the ethical guidelines that support children and adolescents in making sound choices in respect to their actions throughout their lives as well as ideals of service to local communities and society. They suggest that Islam is a complete way of life that includes all ethical action as part of the religion itself. These Five Pillars include a declaration of belief in the oneness of Allah and the negation of any other deities; regular communication with Allah through prayer or supplication; sharing one's wealth with those less fortunate; regular fasting to promote the ethical qualities of peace, generosity, and thankfulness; and Hajj or pilgrimage, which promotes multiculturalism and diversity through global awareness. When children are raised with these five practices, the authors suggest that ethical action becomes embedded in the personality.

Monte Joffee suggests that Soka education, a Buddhist-inspired pedagogy, is inherently ethical and can be integrated into both "secular" and religious educational settings. This chapter gives a biographical sketch of Tsunesaburo Makiguchi, the founder of Soka education, as well as an example of its principles as an educational system based on values. Joffee explicates how this method is deeply rooted in the Nichiren Buddhist sect of the Mahayana tradition in which the "Buddha nature" is seen as the sustaining force of each individual. Educational practices support the Buddha nature, so that even though they are somewhat restricted by individual karma, young people can feel interconnected with and ethically responsible for others. Joffee then offers an example of the integration of this method into a public charter school in New York City where he is a principal. In this school, spirituality, meaning making, and ethical values are intertwined in the curriculum. As a result, students exhibit social awareness, racial understanding, ethical commitment, and a strong sense of engagement.

All of these authors suggest that it is vital to develop a spirituality of youth in which the "inner life" is intricately connected with the "outer life." Each proposes that her or his tradition understands the relationship between spirituality and social-ethical obligations to be essentially inseparable. While these authors have demonstrated the potential of the spiritual path in each of these religious traditions to lead to a life of engaged service and strong vocation, many questions remain: Which practices are most effective in forming ethical action? Why do some religious traditions seem to "fall short" in this area, with adults emerging from religious formation as self-centered and intolerant of others? Will the increasing consumerism and materialism and resulting egocentrism of many contemporary youth mean that religions must intensity or modify their efforts to form youth who can resist these forces? What new rituals and practices might be necessary to accomplish this shift? These essays offer a beginning point for the extended conversation needed in the field to explore these remaining questions and others that will emerge over time.

CHAPTER 20

A Way of Mind and Life: The Relationship of Adolescent Catholic Spirituality to Life Structure

Michael Warren

Spirituality has a thousand definitions today. For some it is an individual religious matter, "me seeking my god." For others it is a search for inner peace, a peace of one's "spirit" that has nothing to do with communal religious practice. American television regularly offers gurus of "spiritual" wisdom, most of whom have insights into the human condition and proposals for being happier and more at peace. Some might claim that behind such searching is a kind of "spirituality consumerism" looking for the right spiritual product for Number One. For still others the word is understandable only in the context of the centuries-old quest for communion with God and an equal quest to shun false gods. The literature regarding the spiritual quest is ancient and voluminous. My concern as a Roman Catholic pastoral theologian is defining the meaning of *youth spirituality* for the Christian tradition, and to get at this I must offer some clarifications about what I have in mind. I will do so without going into the history of the term *spirituality*. Instead, I will focus on some popular but problematic approaches to spirituality and their correctives.

Mistaken Approaches to Spirituality: Conjunctive and Disjunctive Errors

There are two approaches to spirituality that lead away from the sort of holistic understanding I wish to propose. Each approach makes an opposite sort of error. The first makes a conjunctive error, equating two realities (prayer and spirituality) that are not quite the same; the second approach falls into a disjunctive error, separating two matters (spirituality and way of life) needing to be conjoined. The "conjunctive" error equates spirituality with prayer. One might think the first error (equating prayer and spirituality) had been ended in many denominations, especially Roman Catholicism, by the worldwide theological renewal ratified by Vatican II, but the error persists. The Sri Lankan theologian Aloysius Pieris finds in Roman Catholic Church documents a tendency to name contemplation as spirituality par excellence, if not also as spirituality per se.[1] Spirituality must not be equated with prayer.

In conjoining prayer and spirituality as identical, the idea seems to be: get praying and one will become more "spiritual." But not all prayer is authentic, and commentators on the prayer of Jesus point to the many times in the New Testament when Jesus warns of the dangers of inauthentic prayer (see Sobrino 1978, 146–78). To find the proper relationship of prayer and spirituality, one must be ready to lay out a definition of Christian spirituality that will not permit it to be equated with prayer. Among Christian denominations over the past quarter century there have been many attempts to heal the inappropriate conjunction and to recover a broader, more holistic understanding of spirituality than the one that puts spirituality and prayer into the same shoe.[2]

The disjunctive error separates two elements of Christian life that need to be related, even conjoined. These elements are prayer/worship and life structure/life patterns. Liberation theologian Gustavo Gutiérrez (1973) claims that "a [Christian] spirituality is *a concrete manner*, inspired by the Spirit, *of living the Gospel*; it is a *definite way of living* 'before the Lord,' in solidarity with all persons" (204; my emphasis). Here Gutiérrez sees spirituality as broader than prayer, because at base it is a concrete way of living. Spirituality is about a concrete way of living the gospel that allows for authentic prayer. In all his writings, but particularly in *We Drink from Our Own Wells* (1984), Gutiérrez specifies what this solidarity with all persons, and especially with the oppressed, might mean for a local church. As the "wells" metaphor in its title implies, his book sees spirituality as a religious culture imbibed in particular ways of living and perceiving; these ways structure one's commitments.[3]

Carolyn Osiek (1976), highlighting the relation between the habits of the heart and the actual concrete way of living one's life, has described spirituality as "the experience, reflection and articulation of the assumptions and consequences of religious faith *as it is lived in a concrete situation*" (231). This matter, the priority of our lived way over our verbal way, is not always front and center in youth ministry—or, for that matter, in the churches themselves. I will return to this issue later.

"Lowercase" and "Uppercase" Spirituality

An assumption grounding my way of looking at spirituality is that everyone has a spirituality. We cannot *not* have a spirituality. Every person is an embodied spirit who has been shaped by commitments, choices, hopes, uses of time, and so forth. The question can never be, "Will we have a spirituality?" Rather, it must be, "What kind of spirituality will we have?" Adolf Hitler had a spirituality, as, sadly, did Harry S. Truman. Their spirits stood for something. In consumerist societies some who call themselves "spiritual" and even "religious" in fact have a consumerist spirituality, with their hearts ever intent on the next things they will buy.[4] Life-directing desires represent a root kind of spirituality, a fact that should give pause to all concerned with Christian spirituality. A life fundamentally directed by consumerist desires is directed by a spirituality of consumerism, just as a life directed by abuse of the world's resources is a spirituality of abuse. Sacralizing the word *spirituality* can be a conceptual error. We can get in touch with this basic kind of spirituality when we stand at a person's coffin and find ourselves reflecting on what this individual stood for in his or her life. Perhaps we could refer to this kind of "everybody" spirituality as "lowercase" spirituality.

We cannot get at the actual spirituality of young people without discerning their commitments and stances, and neither can young people understand their own spiritualities unless they are willing to examine their stances and the actions that flow from those stances. Such stances are specific and discernible, even when overlooked by the very people living those commitments and stances. Not all such stances come from individual choices; some of them develop incrementally through the influence of images, metaphors, cultural assumptions. Cultural pollution can seep into one's spirit just as easily as environmental pollution can permeate one's membranes. Youth ministry has not yet given enough attention to this crucial dimension of spirituality. Without such attention youth ministry is marked by a certain shallowness.

"Uppercase" spirituality involves an active disciplined search for God, the result of a religious transformation seen as a gifting act of God. For a thumbnail description of spirituality in this explicit religious sense, I propose the following: *Spirituality is a systematic way of attending to the presence of God.*[5] Several features of this description are helpful. First, it sees every theistic religious system as having its own spirituality, because each is a spirituality or a way of paying attention to the presence of God. In spite of the impression sometimes given by Christian writings, spirituality is not an exclusively Christian term. While acknowledging spirituality as something they have in common with all other faiths,[6] Christians know their particular spirituality attends to the presence of God in the first-century Galilean Jew, Jesus of Nazareth.

Also valuable in this description is its stress on "way," modified by the sort of purposefulness implied by "systematic." In this sense spirituality can also be examined as a discipline. The key to the word *discipline* used this way is the word *disciple,* on which it is based. A disciple is one who learns the Way of a master. To learn certain crafts might mean, as it did for many centuries, apprenticing oneself to a master who would then pass on skills over time to the apprentice. Apprenticeship meant submitting oneself to being a learner, a "noticer," attending to the teacher's ways. Apprenticeship, that is, the careful way of following worked out by those who wished to be disciples of a master, often lasted several years. The same process of "careful following" is needed for learning to play the violin.

The way we follow provides us access to its consequent form of attention; our way of living determines our consciousness and the matters we choose to attend to. If it is true that we live in a time of fractured attention, then this inattention functions as a kind of antispirituality. I want to name that very inattention as a *spirituality,* because it is a systematic way of *not paying* attention. Finally, if we accept this understanding of spirituality, the whole matter moves from abstraction to the level of concrete acts. Ways are specific and thus discernible.

A WORD ABOUT CHRISTIAN SPIRITUALITY

I do not wish to lay out all the whats, whys, and wherefores of a distinctive Christian spirituality, except to note that it is clearly sketched for Christians in the Eucharist. The Eucharist is all about gift and giftedness: the multiple gifts of the loving God. A marvelous exhibition of this core of Christian spirituality is *The Blackwell Companion to Christian Ethics*. Its thirty-seven scholarly essays all point to the sensibility of the Eucharist as the core of a Christian way of "doing" and living. Jesus is the core gift, and the Eucharist declares in subtle and nonsubtle ways that those who live in the Spirit of Jesus live within an ambience of life's giftedness. "Thanksgiving" is the most natural impulse of one enchanted by the glad tidings brought to humankind by the Rabbi from Galilee. The most natural impulse of a consumerist spirituality is not thanks but pining and griping and dissatisfaction. Ads are crafted to feed that impulse. The character of gift is its givenness; the character of consumerist desire is possession and grasping.

The disjunctive error in spirituality is the one that separates spirituality from the world in which we live and from how we live in that world. As a disjunction, it splits apart things meant to be connected to each other. Although many writers (e.g., Rahner 1970) warn against paying attention to the things of God in such a way that attention is drawn away from pressing human issues the error persists.[7] A youth ministry turned steadfastly inward to the youth group and away from the wider world falls into this disjunctive error and is unfaithful both to the young and to the gospel.

Another side of the disjunctive error emerges when a local church thinks the young should live attuned to the gospel while the adult congregation lives attuned to consumerism and one-upmanship. All too often, however, the youth ministry program remains stuck at the level of the congregation's unspoken assumptions, lived convictions, and income level. These realities become the elephant in the living room, looming large but unacknowledged. Such situations verify French sociologist Pierre Bourdieu's claim that every social situation is fundamentally conditioned and shaped by the things that cannot be said. If the congregation is fond of itself, "full of itself," and deaf to the implications of its worship, its sacred texts, and its own creed, then a local congregation imagines for youth and youth leaders that such is what the church stands for. The young readily see this contradiction, and it easily sours them. On the other hand, it can also happen that when youth leaders succeed, for example, in opening the young to the implications of Jesus' siding with the poor and oppressed, some adults, possibly their own parents, will not be amused.

If the young see in their church the gospel being lived in its naturally inconvenient way, they absorb such efforts as a normal part of Christian living. That implicit understanding is absorbed as deeply as its opposite would be in an entirely different kind of church.

A Response to These Errors

In the United States, efforts have been under way by Christians in the new millennium to examine the spirituality of the youth group and its relationship to that of the wider church. Behind these efforts is the conviction that whole local church must pursue together an authentic spirituality. One especially noteworthy effort was the Youth Ministry and Spirituality Project, devised and led by ministers and educators at San Francisco Theological Seminary. In this project, church leaders began to understand that the church could not influence the young without understanding their pain and without credible efforts to engage young people in the goals and purposes of the church. They discovered that adults needed the religious energies and insights of the young, just as the young needed the religious energies and insights of adults.

The project worked toward common understanding of the situation of young people, bringing young and old together to talk out their dilemmas in the light of their faith. The written material from this project seems to say the *elders* will help the *youngers*, but when I saw the project in action, what seemed to happen was a mutual enlivening. The elders got to know the young people by paying attention to their interests and pain and by physically attending events young people find important. Those who participated in the effort took on a particular young person as an object of their daily prayer. Communities who undertook this effort seemed to be transformed by mutual caring and mutual healing. This project seemed connected to classic Christian spiritual ways, such as discernment of inner movements (here capitalized): Desire and Yearning; Response to God's gifts; Temptation to run from the good; and Patience to allow for the work of Healing. These movements have been described in the classic literature of spirituality in all denominations.

What was most interesting in this effort was that everyone involved pursued spiritual wisdom, not just personally but communally. So the Youth Ministry and Spirituality Project was in effect a work of individual and communal transformation. Those who designed the project did the work of thinking through a process of entering deeper into the Spirit of Jesus. Along with trying out practical initiatives, theoretical frameworks for youth ministry were also being developed. The project worked to hone skills in what is termed "spiritual accompaniment of the young" and in "the age-old practice of discerning spirits." A lovely aspect of this project saw the young and the old as mutual healers through mutual service.

Spirituality and Life Structure

In order to understand why the response of the Youth Ministry and Spirituality Project might be a model for the Christian community as it responds to and resists the erroneous approaches to spirituality common today, we must explore further my previously stated conviction that spirituality always affects lifestyle. To do so, I want to replace the word *lifestyle* with a term more accurate to the situation and requiring more explanation: *life structure*. Furthermore, I want to make the claim that spirituality, in its explicit religious sense, should always—but in fact does not always—affect life structure, whereas life structure *always* affects spirituality, often as the most decisive factor.

What is life structure? I have found helpful the brief treatment of life structure offered by Daniel Levinson (1978) in his attempt to plot shifts in the lives of middle-age males:

> By "life structure," we mean the underlying pattern or design of a person's life at a given time. A person's life has many components: occupation, love relationships, marriage and family, the relation to oneself, one's use of soli-

tude, one's roles in various social contexts—all the relationships with individuals, groups and institutions that have significance. One's personality
influences and is influenced by one's involvement with each of them. . . .

The concept of life structure—the basic pattern or design of a person's life
at a given time—gives us a way of looking at the engagement of the individual in society. It requires us to consider both self and world, and the relationships between them. (41–42)

Even this description, however, is somewhat vague, and Levinson's readers find
themselves asking many questions about the relationships among various aspects of life
structure and how accessible they are to analysis. Levinson himself seems aware of this
problem, to which he offers the following suggestions:

How shall we go about describing and analyzing the life structure? The most
useful starting point, I believe, is to consider the choices a person makes and
how the person deals with their consequences. The important choices in
adult life have to do with work, family, friendships, and love relationships of
various kinds, where to live, leisure, involvement in religious, political and
community life, immediate and long-term goals. (43)

Our choices and our relationships come to "create" or structure the kind of person
we are. To point this out is not to moralize; instead, it is to bring front and center a
characteristic of all lives that usually hides in plain sight. Young people are in the
process of making big choices in tiny incremental ways. Addressing these choices could
easily be given book-length treatment, but I offer a single example: financial choices. In
my undergraduate classes at St. John's University, I start each course on Christian marriage with a request that students take out their wallets and all the change in their pock-
ets and count it. Then I ask them to count the number of credit cards in that wallet:
plastic that can be used in place of cash. I count mine and give the number. I ask what
they might guess would be the average number of such cards carried by class members.
Then I ask what they would guess the *average* credit debt might be of students in this
class. The last time I asked this question, the most common projection was $7,500 of
credit debt. Almost all of these students are under twenty years of age.

This exercise is the beginning of a semester-long unnamed exploration of life structure and what it means for marriage. Issues never named as life structure include cost
of a wedding; choice of friends; choice of career and decisions about what kind of daily
commute to work might enhance or undermine a marital relationship. I ask students
questions such as: Do any of you know persons who have ended up with (in your view)
the wrong friends? Do you know persons who have been physically or emotionally hurt
by being with the wrong friends? How many hours of work a week do you think would
be appropriate for a young person? For a young married couple? How many hours
would diminish a person's quality of life? How many hours of commuting a week
would harm a martial relationship?[8]

As the teacher, I have no required answers to these questions, but neither are they
asked just for effect. To each question are attached potentially important answers. They
are all about choices that together make up a life structure. All these questions need to

be pondered if young people are to become aware of how choices can cement them into situations unhelpful or harmful to them. These sorts of questions should find some place, some time, some "when" to be asked in the context of youth ministry and of asking what living a gospel life involves. They are questions about spirituality as a way of living, not about spirituality as a set of thoughts or feelings.

Life structure is bound up with what we pay attention to. One could do an in-depth analysis of life structure by examining a young person's checkbook; phone bills (especially if the bills included the numbers actually phoned); a list of the books purchased over a year or of the magazines subscribed to; stubs of tickets that gave a young person admission to various kinds of events; and a time chart gauging the amount of television watched as well as the names of the programs. Out of an intuitive grasp of life structure's significance, a student from Ireland once suggested he could analyze the social situation of Catholic bishops in his country if he knew where the various bishops ate when they took meals outside their homes, with whom they ate, and who paid the bills. He was suggesting that some Irish bishops are out of touch with the unemployed young people of his country and their difficult financial circumstances. The people the bishops share meals with are at the other end of the economic scale.

Christian Spirituality as a Way of Mind and Life

Concern for the connection between spirituality and life structure is not new and is not a side issue. If uppercase spirituality is the systematic approach to the presence of God, then it is a system, a way, and not just a mental construct. A spirituality is a way of walking, a particular way of being in the world. It is entirely possible to have two conflicting spiritualities, a verbal or notional one, which we might claim guides our lives, and a lived one, which is the actual one. The first is an illusory spirituality, which is named and not lived, but which belies the actual spirituality, which is lived but not always named. Persons can claim in verbal declaration that they have a Christian spirituality, whereas the actual way they structure their lives, right down to their simplest decisions, might not be based on the Christian gospel at all. Quite simply, a spirituality that does not affect life structure is not an actual spirituality; it is a ghost of one. Youth and youth ministers often fail in their attempts at "spiritual renewal" when the new programs they create and participate in do not affect their life structures. Similar to dieting, if a program fails to change not just the way people think but the way they act, then it has no effect.

The earliest Christians' lives were jeopardized because of the way they lived, not just the way they prayed. Seekers for admission to their fellowship endured a lengthy period called the catechumenate, which could well be termed "life structure therapy." Origen, the early church father, wrote, "The profound and sacred mysteries must not be given, at first, to disciples, but they must be first instructed in the correction of their life style." Elsewhere, Origen is more explicit: "When it becomes evident that the disciples are purified and *have begun, as far as possible, to live better* [my emphasis], only then are they invited to know our mysteries."[9] A candidate seeking membership had to have succeeded, beyond any merely stated desire, in transforming his or her way of life before being admitted to the community of worshippers. According to Regis Duffy (1984):

> One major characteristic of the catechumenal process . . . [was]: God's Word leads to commitments long before it leads to initiation. . . . Three years "hearing the word" in the catechumenate of Hippolytus at Rome might seem long until we reflect on the quality of commitment that was expected of any Christian at the time. Hippolytus tells us that when the first-time inquirers came "in order to hear the word," the teachers questioned them on their motivation, their life situation, and their willingness to change work that might hinder the practice of God's word. (44)

Without any reference to religion, the nineteenth-century American pragmatist philosopher C. S. Peirce wrote something similar:

> Belief consists mainly in being deliberately prepared to adopt the formula believed in as the guide to action; the essence of belief is the establishment of a habit; and different beliefs are distinguished by the different modes of action to which they give rise.[10]

On this understanding, where the behavior consonant with a belief is lacking, one has grounds for doubting whether there is in fact a belief.

Implications for Christian Youth Ministries

There are implications for ministry with youth in these ideas. Youth ministry can ask questions about the relationship between spirituality and life structure without imposing judgments on the possible answers. Such questions may evoke reflection and possibly decisions that change the way young people embody their spirituality. Furthermore, such questions may help youth see that prayer becomes authentic in the context of the wider way of life called for by a particular religion.[11] Life structure authenticates prayer (Warren 1999, 55–75).

It is impossible to influence a renewal of a young person's Christian spirituality without a shift of that person's life structure, and it is not possible to renew life structure without a change in life-orienting imagery. *If life structure is the vehicle in which spirituality moves, life-orienting images are the tracks or road along which it runs, giving it direction.* One of the tasks of a Christian catechesis of spirituality is to help young people become conscious of the images that in fact underlie their consciousness, direct their attention, and offer plausibility to their life structure; and to encourage them to change those not suitable for disciples of Jesus. Conversely, to seek to renew spirituality by focusing only on prayer is doomed, if only because prayer is all too easily subverted by ways of imagining the world that are at total variance with Jesus' way. I once heard Atlanta-based theologian James Fowler incisively name this subversion: "The churches are the cheering squads leading the cheers for the dominant culture." May this never be true of Christian youth ministry groups.

Notes

1. See Pieris (1988), 3. A study of some of the books on spirituality produced in the 1940s and 1950s shows how they set out the traditional three stages of the spiritual life: the purgative, illuminative, and contemplative. These stages corresponded to the various steps of the ancient catechumenate, which even after its demise in the West were retained by monastic life in its initiation process. In some twentieth-century books, however, these spiritual stages were presented as stages of prayer, or at least, as having their true meaning not so much in a way of living one's life as in a way of praying. Pieris (144) seems to agree with my analysis here.

2. A helpful account of this effort, but in the context of a survey of the denotation of "spirituality" through the ages, is Schneiders (1986).

3. Gutiérrez never actually uses the term *religious culture,* but I find the idea as an important assumption throughout *We Drink from Our Own Wells.* The explicit manner in which he describes spirituality is as a "way," one that he equates with discipleship: "Discipleship is rooted in the experience of an encounter with Jesus Christ . . . in which the Lord takes the initiative, and it is the point of departure for a journey . . . A spirituality is the terrain on which 'the children of God' exercise their freedom" (35–36). See also Sobrino (1989, 1993).

4. As John Kavanagh (1986) has written: "The great paradox of finding one's identity in wealth is ultimately the paradox of all idolatries: entrusting ourselves to our products, our silver and golden gods, *we become fashioned—re-created—in their image and likeness.* Bereft of personhood and human sensibility, we lose our vision. We become voiceless, unable to utter words of life and love . . . To make wealth one's god, is to become brittle and cold, to become like unto a thing, to become invulnerable, impenetrable, unloving" (23).

5. The description is not original and can probably be found in various versions in many works on spirituality. I first came across it when leading a series of sessions for adults on prayer in which we were using as background reading James Carroll's little book, *Prayer from Where We Are* (1970). Chapter 3, "Tending the Presence of God," started me on a long road of reflecting on the question of spirituality behind the question of prayer and on the key matter of attention. Some sense of the book can be gleaned from the titles of chapters 5–7: "The Tending Silence"; "The Tending Solitude, the Tending Group"; and "The Tending Imagination."

6. Schneiders (1986) deals with this matter well.

7. There are many ways of effecting this split. Several years ago in a review of a book on spirituality, Vincent Rush (1983) took issue with its unacknowledged assumption that there is some stable world beyond change accessible through spirituality. In "Spirituality in a Liberation Perspective," Pieris (1988, 8 n. 2) cites a study of Pope John Paul II's exhortations to priests and religious that claims he makes this same disjunction.

8. For some troubling indications of current youth life structure indications, see Denizet-Lewis (2004); Gogek (2004); Powers (2002); Talbot (2002).

9. Both quotes are found in Capelle (1933) 151, notes 38 and 39. Capelle gives the original references as (1) Hom. V, 6 in Iud. and (2) C. Cels. 3, 59. Regis Duffy first called my attention to this source.

10. Cited in McCarthy (1978), chapter 2, n. 23.

11. Pieris notes how the integral dialogical contact of Christianity with Greek culture found in the first five centuries of Western Christianity diminished when Christianity moved into Europe, not through the power of dialogue and incarnational praxis but through the power of law and governmental authority. Authoritarianism had replaced the dialogue with people's actual lives needed to lead them to discipleship as a way of life. The practice of the people was not considered as important as the theory of the theologians. It took another eleven hundred years for

Europe's religious leaders to recognize that the living practice of the old folk religions had per-dured in the religious ways of the common people. Thus the Protestant Reformation and Catholic Counter-Reformation were basically programs of *conversion*, i.e., of entire life orienta-tion. This point is found, of course, many places in the literature dealing with the period lead-ing to the Reformation, for example, Albert Mirgeler's *Mutations of Western Christianity* and John P. Dolan's *History of the Reformation*. Pieris traces Christianity's mistake of being more interested in religious thought than in religious practice and way of life back to the early Chris-tian apologetics of Iraeneus and many others. Pieris's argument is worth close study; see Pieris (1989), 17–42, esp. 18–23.

References

Capelle, Bernard. 1933. L'Introduction du catéchumenat à Rome. *Recherches de théologie anci-enne et médiévale* 5:151.

Carroll, James. 1970. *Prayer from where we are.* Dayton, Ohio: Pflaum.

Denizet-Lewis, Benoit. 2004. Friends, friends with benefits, and the benefits of the local mall. *New York Times Magazine,* May 30.

Dolan, John P. 1965. *History of the Reformation.* New York: Desclee.

Duffy, Regis. 1984. *On becoming a Catholic: The challenge of Christian initiation.* San Francisco: Harper and Row.

Gogek, Jim. 2004. Putting caps on teenage drinking. *New York Times,* August 25.

Gutiérrez, Gustavo. 1973. *A theology of liberation.* Maryknoll, N.Y.: Orbis.

———. 1984. *We drink from our own wells: The spiritual journey of a people.* Maryknoll, N.Y.: Orbis.

Hauerwas, Stanley, and Samuel Wells, eds. 2004. *The Blackwell companion to Christian ethics.* Oxford, UK: Blackwell.

Kavanagh, John. 1986. The world of wealth and the gods of wealth. In *Option for the poor, chal-lenge to the rich countries,* edited by Leonardo Boff and Virgil Elizondo, 17–23. Edinburgh: Clark.

Levinson, Daniel. 1978. *The seasons of a man's life.* New York: Knopf.

McCarthy, Thomas. 1978. *The critical theory of Jürgen Habermas.* Cambridge, Mass.: MIT Press.

Mirgeler, Albert. 1968. *Mutations of Western Christianity.* Notre Dame, Ind.: University of Notre Dame Press.

Osiek, Carolyn. 1976. Reflections on American spirituality. *Spiritual Life* 22:230–40.

Pieris, Aloysius. 1988. Spirituality in a liberative perspective. In *An Asian theology of liberation,* 3–14. Maryknoll, N.Y.: Orbis.

———. 1989. Western Christianity and Asian Buddhism: A theological reading of historical encounters. In *Love meets wisdom: A Christian experience of Buddhism,* 17–42. Maryknoll, N.Y.: Orbis.

Powers, Ron. 2002. The apocalypse of adolescence. *Atlantic Monthly,* March, 58–74.

Rahner, Karl. 1970. The church's commission to bring salvation and the humanization of the world. In *Theological investigations,* vol. 14, 295–313. New York: Herder & Herder.

Rush, Vincent. 1983. Steps along the way: Review of Benedict J. Groeschel, *Spiritual passages: The psychology of spiritual development. Cross Currents* 33:377–79.

Schneiders, Sandra. 1986. Theology and spirituality: Strangers, rivals, or partners. *Horizons* 13:253–74.

Sobrino, Jon. 1978. *Christology at the crossroads.* Maryknoll, N.Y.: Orbis.

―――. 1989. *Spirituality of liberation: Toward political holiness*. Maryknoll, N.Y.: Orbis.

―――. 1993. Spirituality and the following of Jesus. In *Mysterium liberationis: Fundamental concepts of liberation theology,* edited by Ignacio Ellacuría and Jon Sobrino, 677–701. Maryknoll, N.Y.: Orbis.

Talbot, Margaret. 2002. Girls just want to be mean. *New York Times Magazine,* February 24.

Warren, Michael. 1999. *At this time, in this place: The Spirit embodied in the local assembly.* Harrisburg, Pa.: Trinity Press International.

CHAPTER 21

Singing Hope and Practicing Justice: Emancipatory Hope Embodied in the Life of Ruby Doris Smith

Evelyn L. Parker

> When the load bears down so heavy, the weight is shown upon my brow.
> There's a sweet relief in knowing, O', the Lord will make a way somehow.
>
> —Thomas A. Dorsey

Singing songs of hope during the first one hundred years of its life, from 1870 to 1970, was a familiar practice that formed the spirituality of children, teenagers, and adults within faith communities of the Christian Methodist Episcopal Church (CME) in the United States. Although other practices included reading hope-filled Scripture passages and offering hope-filled prayers, singing was a mainstay, a constant practice for spiritual formation. Thomas A. Dorsey's gospel song "The Lord Will Make a Way Somehow," written in 1943, was one of those songs of hope. Its lyrics touted confidence in a God-given solution to struggle and sorrow experienced by Black people as a result of sociopolitical, socioeconomic, and sociocultural injustice. Its rich metaphors, including a ship tossed about in the storms of life, capture the troubles of African American people. Values of courage, patience, and a worry-free heart follow episodes of strife, misfortune, and being misunderstood. The refrain offers a constructive response to the problems of the Black American by emphasizing the cultural proverb "The Lord will make a way out of no way." The Lord will make a way somehow when burdens become unbearable and are revealed in visible signs on the faces of Black people. The mere act of giving problems to the Lord Jesus Christ brings assurance that the Lord will somehow solve them. There is "sweet relief" when one knows the Lord will make a way somehow.

The spirituality of adolescents coming of age during the 1950s, '60s, and '70s in the CME Church was uniquely influenced by songs of hope expressed in their sociohistorical milieu. During the civil rights era they sang "The Lord Will Make a Way Somehow," "We Shall Overcome," "Keep Your Eyes on the Prize, Hold On," "We've Come This Far by Faith," and other freedom songs with their congregations and in their youth choirs. These songs provided meaning during their search for identity amid tumultuous times of social, political, and economic injustice. Singing songs of hope is an important practice among several others that shaped the spirituality of young people in the CME Church, as will be discussed later.

Situated in the southern states of Tennessee, Kentucky, Mississippi, Georgia, and Alabama, the young CME Church sought to offer hope to African Americans in the post-emancipation era. Through Reconstruction, World War I, the Great Depression, World War II, and up to the civil rights revolution, the CME Church sought to be a beacon of God's liberating hope for African Americans in a lethally segregated society. Jim Crow laws imposed strict social codes that maintained the separation of Black and White people. These included segregated public facilities such as bathrooms, waiting rooms, and water fountains, as well as schools. Violation of the social codes of Jim Crow could lead to public humiliation and even death for African Americans.

The CME Church sought to refashion its own identity, changing its name from Colored to Christian in 1954. The previous name was intended to reflect the designation Black people used during the mid-nineteenth century, as well as to signal the self-determination of an emancipated people. The name change came about under the shadow of the U.S. Supreme Court's 1954 *Brown v. Board of Education* decision declaring racial segregation in public schools unconstitutional. It also occurred as ordained and lay leadership of the CME Church were becoming involved in the civil rights movement.[1]

This chapter is about hope-filled practices that fashioned the spirituality of adolescents within the CME Church for the first one hundred years of its existence, including singing songs of hope. Spiritual formation among African American teenagers is captured in the concept of *emancipatory hope*. This idea is best illustrated through the life of Ruby Doris Smith, a member of the CME Church who, as a teenager, came of age during the turbulent times of the civil rights movement and was one of its most prominent leaders during her young adult years. Ruby Doris Smith embodied emancipatory hope as she lived an integrated life of Christian hope, holiness, and social activism (Parker 2003, viii). What follows is a fuller discussion of the idea of African American adolescent spirituality as emancipatory hope, demonstrated in the life of Ruby Doris Smith. I illustrate emancipatory hope by connecting her story with hope-filled practices of the CME Church during her time in history. I conclude with an assessment of current practices of spiritual formation among youth in the CME Church and a challenge for new ways of fostering emancipatory hope among teenagers.

Emancipatory Hope

"To possess emancipatory hope is to expect transformation of hegemonic relations and to act as God's agent ushering in God's vision of equality for humankind . . . Emancipatory hope is to expect that hegemonic relations will be transformed and to acknowledge personal agency in God's vision for human equality" (Parker 2003, 15). Emancipatory hope expresses anticipation of liberation/freedom from all forms of supremacy within human relationships while exercising personal agency in God's liberating process. Anticipation of freedom from oppression is far more than optimism; it connotes the absence of a transcendent source or a divine power. Optimism is based on human strength or ingenuity and not God's divine power. Anticipation of freedom/liberation from human dominance requires an act of faith in God who promises freedom and flourishing for all humankind regardless of assessments of worth connected to race, socioeconomic status, gender, or other differences. "Christian hope moves within the morass of life, confronting the state of what is because of the expectation of what will be. The reign of God is in the midst of the morass of life, and at the same time is a transforming and liberating divine force" (Parker 2003, 17).

In addition to vividly defining the verb *to hope,* Gayraud Wilmore (1982) connects the epistemological benefit of this action to the verb *to know*: "To hope is to know" assures that your worth is not a result of your economic circumstance or your point of origin. "To hope is to know" expresses the belief that your humanity is far greater than any burden imposed on you because of your race, class, gender, sexual orientation, or physical abilities. These human actions are attributes of emancipatory hope.

Emancipatory hope is rooted in the promises of God, the resurrected Jesus Christ, the power of the Holy Spirit, and the possibilities that can be realized through the work of the Holy Spirit. We see emancipatory hope when an African American adolescent expects transformation from all forms of dehumanization and exploitation in human relationships and acts as God's agent of justice and love. Or emancipatory hope can be evinced in a black teen's confrontation of oppression with self-confidence, emulating Jesus Christ the liberator and his vision of justice. Emancipatory hope is seen in a Black teen's anticipation of a better world free from domination and her or his action in the power of the Holy Spirit to bring this hope to reality.

African American adolescent spirituality as emancipatory hope is related to a broader understanding of spirituality as the capacity for self-transcendence through the power of the Holy Spirit in the face of seemingly hopeless situations. Jesus the liberator is the example of self-transcendence above pain and despair. This spirituality feeds the hunger for spiritual depth and lends meaning to meaningless situations. It satisfies the yearning that popular culture, materialism, and unbridled sexual activity could never satisfy. It moves teens toward awareness of the work of the Holy Spirit within and among us to bring about wholesome relationships between God, ourselves, and all of creation (Talvacchia 2003; Thompson 1995). It propels ethical action that transforms domination and oppressive systems that prohibit human potential. Spirituality of this nature yields centuries-old Christian practices that include prayer, hospitality, discernment, seeking justice, and singing (Bass 1997; Bass and Richter 2001) integrated with social witness. Emancipatory hope is Christian spirituality ordained by God, who creates, liberates, and transforms.

Ruby Doris Smith

Emancipatory hope, a seamlessly woven Christian spirituality of piety and social activism, was embodied in the life of Ruby Doris Smith.[2] She was born April 25, 1942, in Atlanta, Georgia, to John and Alice Smith. Of her seven siblings, Ruby Doris was the second child and second daughter. Her father was a strict disciplinarian regarding appropriate behavior for the children, both at home and socially. Because of his strong religious beliefs, he would not allow them to attend parties or dances, or be out late on dates. Her mother, also religious, engaged in forms of social activism in addition to being a beautician and encouraging her children to focus on high academic achievement and to become socially well rounded.

In 1945, when Ruby Doris was just three years old, she insisted that she should attend the church-sponsored kindergarten with her older sister, Mary Ann. Her parents complied with her protest, and at age four Ruby Doris entered the first grade. Her self-reliance and strong will continued throughout her childhood and teenaged years. As she grew older, she resonated more with her mother's values but experienced friction with those of her father. In an interview about the influence of her parents, Ruby Doris had this to say about her mother:

> When I was little—our house was on the escape route for Negro men on the prison chain gangs. You know, Negroes used to be really brutalized on the chain gangs not so long ago, and they escaped when they could. It's still pretty bad for Negro men in prison . . . Once or twice I remember a lotta commotion in the house and whisperin' and a strange man in the kitchen in the middle of the night.
>
> She took a big risk. Didn't matter what he did or who he was—he was a Negro man off the chain gang and if they caught him, they'd beat him to death. So she helped him escape. My daddy was very angry about it. He was afraid we'd all be killed if they caught us.[3]

Ruby Doris emulated her mother's social activism as a young teen. At age thirteen she was strongly influenced by the 1955 Montgomery, Alabama, bus boycott. Each day she would rush home from school to watch the events of the boycott unfold on national television. She longed to play an active part in this historical event and recalled "being impressed by seeing elderly people walking and walking" (Ross 2003, 198). Although an armchair activist, she supported the bus boycott and sought ways to resist that form of Jim Crow in Atlanta as her consciousness about racism developed.

Another foreshadowing of her leadership occurred when Ruby Doris was about fourteen years of age. The fledgling movement had deeply captured her conscience. Her youngest sister, Catherine, recalls some of Ruby Doris's reflections during that time:

> One particular conversation we had and she told me, she said, "I know what my life and mission is." And I said, "What is it?" She was a teenager, and she said, "It's to set the black people free," and she said, "I will never rest until it happens." And she said, "I will die for that cause." (Fleming 1998, 36)

Following the wishes of her mother, Ruby Doris and her siblings were active participants at school, in the community, and at church (Fleming 1998, 36). Her high school activities included being on the yearbook staff, the student council, serving as a majorette, and being on the track, basketball, and tennis teams. These activities ranked second to her excellent academic performance. Ruby Doris's high school leadership was a blueprint for her future accomplishments. Her leadership skills were also molded at the West Mitchell Street CME Church, where her family actively participated in worship and the church's ministries. As a teen at West Mitchell, Ruby Doris sang in the youth choir and participated in the Christian Youth Fellowship (CYF). The latter is the official connectional youth group of the CME Church operating under the General Department of Christian Education and focusing on Christian discipleship and leadership development among teenagers.[4] The CYF involves youth in activities on local, district, annual conference, and connectional levels.

In 1956, when Ruby Doris was fourteen, she was an alternate delegate to the National Youth Conference of the CME Church held in Memphis, Tennessee. This was a significant honor for Ruby Doris, for it demonstrated the confidence her faith community placed in her ability to represent the congregation well. Another delegate to that conference was a friend who grew up in the church with Ruby Doris and attended college with her, Dr. Carol Stemley. During an interview (September 15, 2004), Carol described other local and regional youth conferences in which she and Ruby Doris had been active participants. As Carol pointed to a picture of Ruby Doris, herself, and other girls attending the 1956 Youth Conference, she recalled their participation in the Conference Choir. She recalled the powerful preaching of Bishop William Yancy Bell, who earned his Ph.D. from Yale University and served as dean of the School of Religion at Howard University. Carol also remembered the charismatic leadership of Bishop Nathaniel Linsey, who in 1956 was a young preacher and civil rights activist in the Alabama Christian Movement for Human Rights in Birmingham and the Southern Christian Leadership Conference (SCLC) with his schoolmate Martin Luther King Jr. (Linsey, e-mail to the author, August 23, 2004).

The 1956 National Youth Conference was situated in a sociohistorical context of increasing racial and social awareness in the United States and in the CME Church. Also, this conference convened at a time when Bishop B. Julian Smith, general secretary for Christian education from 1934 until 1954, developed comprehensive programs for children and youth. These programs included leadership training schools in each Episcopal district and the development of the popular "Youth Jubilees" into the National Youth Conference. The spirituality of Ruby Doris and other CME youth of her time was shaped in local, state, and national conferences, where teenagers learned to lead worship, pray, sing, and read Scripture equally as much as they learned to conduct meetings, pass motions following Robert's Rules of Order, and strategize for youth events.

No doubt her participation in local, state, and national youth activities was an incubator for this budding young leader. Ruby Doris participated in several areas of her faith community, including the youth choir.

Youth choirs in the CME Church have always provided a setting for African American adolescent spiritual formation. Traditionally, the second Sunday of each month has been designated Youth Sunday, when the youth choir sings. Additionally, youth provide leadership with the liturgy, as ushers, announcing clerks, and in other capacities, depending on the local church. But the youth choir, through rehearsals, is where teenagers learn theological principles, learn to pray, express their emotions freely, and move their bodies freely while singing. Carol Stemley recalled favorite songs she and Ruby Doris sang in the youth choir. These songs included "Have You Got Good Religion?" and "Swing Low, Sweet Chariot," two Negro spirituals, and the hymn "Is Your

All on the Altar?" Carol and Ruby Doris also enjoyed singing their favorites, "Kum Ba Ya" and "Spirit of the Living God," at the Georgia Leadership Training School.

Biographer Cynthia Fleming and ethicist Rosetta Rose have written about the shaping of Ruby Doris as a young leader through her self-confident, independent spirit, take-care-of-business personality, combined with a pastoral nature with her peers and outsiders. She and a teenage friend and neighbor, Brenda Jefferson Smith, had very different personalities even though they identified each other as best friends. "Ruby Doris was bold, brash, and blunt, while Brenda was painfully shy and very insecure" (Fleming 1998, 28). Brenda also dealt with a learning disability that contributed to her insecurity. Ruby Doris's sense of fairness and caring for those on the underside of life motivated her to support her friend on several occasions. One of those times occurred when Brenda attended a school play rehearsal, left her lunch in a classroom, and returned to find that someone had eaten it. This pattern continued for several days. Frustrated, Brenda shared her experience with Ruby Doris, who promptly implemented a plan. She sprinkled large amounts of hot sauce on Brenda's sandwich, and they left it in the usual place. After that, Brenda's sandwich was no longer stolen while she attended play rehearsal (Fleming 1998, 29; Ross 2003, 198).

When Ruby Doris and Brenda became first-year students at Luther Judson Price High School, Ruby Doris convinced Brenda to enter the race for campus queen and served as Brenda's self-appointed campaign manager. She accompanied the shy and introverted Brenda to various classes and made speeches to their peers on Brenda's behalf:

> Every time Ruby Doris and Brenda prepared to enter another classroom, Ruby Doris paused to speak a few reassuring words to her candidate before striding purposefully into the room. She was greeted by new rows of desks where polite students were seated with their notebooks open and their pens poised to take notes. Standing next to a nervous Brenda who was trying very hard to appear calm, Ruby Doris went to work on her audience. Her pitch was short, and her quick mind provided her with just the right words she needed to persuade her fellow students. After she finished, she politely thanked the teacher and ushered her nervous candidate out of the room. All the hard work paid off when Brenda was elected first runner-up to Miss Price High School. (Fleming 1998, 30–31)

The school and church were both training grounds for the leader Ruby Doris would become.

As a young adult woman Ruby Doris demonstrated qualities of emancipatory hope as a free-spirited woman similar to some women in the New Testament who participated in the Jesus movement. According to Elisabeth Schüssler Fiorenza (1999), the Jesus movement was emancipatory. It sought to resist the powers of domination and exploitation and usher in an egalitarian model of life among humankind (123–41). Among the many accounts of Jesus' liberating power are those about women who experienced freedom through him. Jesus and the Samaritan woman in John 4:7–30 is a story of Jesus' ignoring tradition and crossing the border of difference. Jews avoided contact with Samaritans because they were considered outsiders. Yet, Jesus' conversation with the Samaritan woman freed her to confess her infidelity with men and give testimony about Jesus' power that brought others to see him. Likewise, Jesus liberated Mary Magdalene from debilitating "spirits" after which she became one of his faithful disciples. Eventually, in John 20:1–18, she bore witness to the other disciples of the resurrected Lord.[5] These stories demonstrate the transformative power of the Jesus movement in the lives of women. Jesus' interaction with these women freed them from heavy burdens and pain and allowed them to come forth in the capacity of their human potential.

Ruby Doris's independent spirit, however, created tension with her father throughout her high school years (Ross 1998, 195). When she was a senior she left home to live with Ruby O'Neal, her maternal aunt for whom she was named (Ross 1998, 195). We can only speculate how this setting influenced her spiritual and social development given her newfound freedom. Biographical data suggest that Ruby Doris's last year of high school provided a smooth transition into college. Her independence and personhood influenced her selection of the Atlanta-based, all-female Spelman College, a choice that met the approval of all her family members (Fleming 1998, 37).

Ruby Doris entered Spelman College in 1959 with her CYF friend Carol Stemley. The college atmosphere welcomed the seventeen-year-old and her budding activism. Many of the faculty and students participated in boycotts and sit-ins. In February 1960, after seeing the reports of the Greensboro, North Carolina, sit-in, Ruby Doris began imagining the same kind of thing happening in Atlanta, but she wasn't ready to act on her own (Fleming 1998). Soon after, students and seminarians from the Atlanta University Center organized themselves as the Atlanta Committee on Appeal for Human Rights and published a statement in the *Atlanta Constitution*. Ruby Doris's sister, Mary Ann, secretary of the Morris Brown College Students' Government, signed the document. The group organized its first sit-in for March 16. Ruby Doris admonished her sister to "put me on the list." Ruby Doris was among the first two hundred students selected for the demonstration (Fleming 1998, 199).

Ruby Doris also participated in the Atlanta kneel-ins, when student and adult civil rights activists attempted to desegregate White churches. She held a lot of hope in Christian churches to turn away from their separatist way of life. Prior to the kneel-ins, Ruby Doris protested against clothing and grocery stores that practiced Jim Crow and did not have African American clerks. Segregated White churches offered a different challenge. Her eighteen-year-old's idealism blinded her to the reality of hard-hearted segregationist Christians. She was disconcerted and stunned when refused admission by White ushers. The White members of the congregation disappointed her as they turned to see what the commotion was about. When they saw her, some quickly turned around as if she was invisible. Other White congregants gave her evil and hateful looks. Although she wanted to retreat, simultaneously she wanted to shout, "But this is the Lord's house!" (Fleming 1998, 56). She only stood there and refused to leave. She said, "I pulled up a chair in the lobby and joined in the singing and worship services which I enjoyed immensely" (Fleming 1998, 56). Ruby Doris's faith and idealism were indestructible even in a situation as upsetting as that one:

> I feel that segregation is basically a moral problem, and for this reason, I feel that Church is the one institution where the problem can be "thrashed out."

> I think the kneel-in movement is an appeal to the consciences of Christians, who are primarily "good" people. Even if we were not admitted to worship, as was true in my case, I think that the attempt in itself was a success, because the minds and hearts of the people who turned us away were undoubtedly stirred. (Fleming 1998, 56)

Ruby Doris believed in the innate goodness of people that results from their identity as Christians. Her actions were based not simply on a critical assessment of racial prejudice but also on the belief that a Christian conscience can overcome prejudice.

During the spring of 1961 Ruby Doris left Spelman College for full-time activism in the Atlanta movement. In 1962 she joined the Student Nonviolent Coordinating Committee's (SNCC) summer voter-registration project. The next year she accepted the position of administrative assistant to SNCC's executive secretary, James Forman. She also married Clifford Robinson, who participated marginally in SNCC. In the summer of 1964, when her son was born, Ruby Doris provided essential leadership in the Freedom Summer Project sponsored by a coalition of SNCC and other civil rights organizations. In 1965, she received a B.A. in English after being readmitted to Spelman College in the fall semester of 1961 (she convinced the admissions committee that she would work equally as hard academically as she had as a social activist; Fleming 1998, 91). Ruby Doris's leadership skills and compassionate manner with SNCC field workers was rewarded when on May 16, 1966, she was elected to succeed James Forman as executive secretary. This achievement made her the first woman to hold the highest-ranking office of any of the civil rights organizations. Her tenure as executive secretary was short lived, however. In January 1967, while on a fund-raising trip in New York, Ruby Doris became ill. She was diagnosed with a rare form of cancer, lymphosarcoma, and died on October 7, 1967 (Fleming 1998, 189; Ross 2003, 217).

The life and contributions of Ruby Doris Smith provided a model of emancipatory hope for teenagers growing up in the CME Church and the Atlanta community during the 1960s and '70s. Her spiritual formation yielded a seamless life of Christian hope, holiness, and social activism (Parker 2003, viii). Also, Ruby Doris embodied central values of the CME Church that were rooted in its heritage, among them a Christlike character, racial uplift, strong leadership, and educational achievement. During her time CME Church values were apparent in the preaching, teaching, liturgical expressions, service-oriented ministries, and the social and political stance of the church as it responded to North American society and West African society.

As the CME Church moves into the twenty-first century the values that sustained it over its first one hundred years are still fundamental among its Episcopal leaders and faith communities. These values inform the current spiritual formation of African American adolescents in a more subtle way, unlike that of the 1950s, '60s, and '70s. The sociohistorical events of the twenty-first century have not pushed the church to fashion adolescent spirituality as emancipatory hope. However, the CYF and Second Sunday youth worship in local congregations, along with leadership training on regional levels and the quadrennial National Youth Conference, remain the primary "connectional" or national contexts for spiritual formation among the church's youth.

The General Department of Christian Education encourages local CYF groups to emphasize adolescent spiritual formation through education about Christian doctrine, heritage and CME Church traditions, Christian discipleship and evangelism, and Christian fellowship and stewardship. The glaring absence of Bible study from the list raises questions about the role of the Bible, not only within the CYF, but also within the enterprise of youth's Christian spiritual formation in the church at large. However, Bible study does take place among youth in the CME Church, although with particular biblical and theological emphases in each local congregation. The youth worship service held each second Sunday throughout the connectional church remains the most vibrant site of adolescent spiritual formation in the CME Church. As mentioned earlier, the youth choir is at the heart of that worship service.

The twenty-first century is bringing new challenges to spiritual formation among adolescents in the CME Church. One significant challenge is the shifting racial and ethnic makeup of the denomination. Although the church remains predominately African American, its members and mission field are increasingly multicultural and multiethnic. The youth of the church represent this trend. Latino and Latina youth are joining CYF groups and youth choirs of those churches intentional about evangelization among this population, which oftentimes lives in the neighborhood of the church.

How will the CME Church speak to the yearning for spiritual depth that is synchronized with youth's realities? How will the church quench the spiritual thirst that popular culture cannot satisfy? How will the church help youth who struggle with poverty and benefit from middle-class advantages amid a materialistic and capitalistic society? How will youth cope with the social relic of racial injustice? How will teenage girls come to know that they are created in God's image, free from objectification and exploitation? How will adolescents' spirituality take shape in a holistic manner where prayer, economic power, and political power are interwoven? How will they shape an adolescent spirituality of emancipatory hope?

The search for answers to these questions involves a focused and committed effort among both teenage and adult CME leaders as well as the entire communion. Since we are not situated in a sociohistorical moment that can galvanize sustained acts of justice like the civil rights movement in which Ruby Doris Smith was involved, the CME Church needs to rethink its strategy for spiritual formation among teenagers that shapes both their piety and their political power as a "whole" spirituality. Although this daunting task is not unique to the CME Church, we must educate members of our communion to understand that practices of prayer, meditation, and discernment are intertwined with political, economic, and social activism. We have Ruby Doris's life as a witness to this form of spirituality. Currently, our relationship to the National Council of Churches of Christ USA, through the leadership of Bishop Thomas Hoyt, Ph.D., the current president of the NCCC, provides the structure for CME congregations to become involved in political, social, and economic events that seek to eliminate injustice in society.

Also, perhaps the answers to the preceding questions are immediately connected to spiritual formation of African American adolescents in local congregations. The youth choir is one avenue toward adolescent spirituality as emancipatory hope. Hope-filled music with theological and biblical integrity has the power to transform apathy, cynicism, and despair. Singing songs that defy racism, classism, sexism, materialism, and capitalism fosters emancipatory hope. The youth choir is the focal point of youth-led worship services. In youth choir rehearsals teenagers (and within small congregations usually their younger siblings as well) learn to pray, read, and interpret Scripture, and teenagers provide leadership for their peers. The challenge is for youth choirs to create songs and liturgy that articulate their realities while maintaining solid biblical and theological principles. This demands music and liturgy for black teenagers that is more than just praise music, but music that will sustain our children in times of crisis. The teens' new music will have different words but will reach back to age-old CME Church beliefs and values of justice that have upheld us throughout the church's history. With new words African American teens will sway and clap their hands as they sing, "There's a sweet relief in knowing, O', the Lord will make a way somehow" (Dorsey 1943).

Notes

1. For a detailed account of events influencing the name change and other aspects of the sociohistorical context of the CME Church, see Lakey (1985). Also see accounts of conversion among ex-slaves and the origin of the CME Church in Whelchel (2002), 84–119.

2. Biographical information about Ruby Doris Smith is summarized from Ross (2003) and Fleming (1998).

3. Quoted from Ross (2003), 196–97, who quotes Carson (1968), 253–54; Carson refers to Ruby Doris as Sarah.

4. For details on the history, nature, purpose, and structure of the Christian Youth Fellowship, see Johnson (1977) and Crutchfield (2003).

5. The New Interpreter's Study Bible offers commentary on both stories; see 1912–15 and 1948–49.

References

Bass, Dorothy, ed. 1997. *Practicing our faith: A way of life for a searching people.* San Francisco: Jossey-Bass.

Bass, Dorothy C., and Don C. Richter, eds. 2002. *Way to live: Christian practices for teens.* Nashville, Tenn.: Upper Room Books.

Carson, Josephine. 1968. *Silent voices: The southern Negro woman today.* New York: Delacorte.

Crutchfield, Carmichael D. 2003. *Organizational guide for Christian education in the Christian Methodist Episcopal Church.* Memphis, Tenn.: CME Publishing.

Dorsey, Thomas A. 1943. The Lord will make a way somehow. In *National Baptist hymnal 1977–80.* Nashville, Tenn.: National Baptist Publishing.

Fiorenza, Elisabeth Schüssler. 1999. To follow the vision: The Jesus movement as Basileia movement. In *Liberating eschatology: Essays in honor of Letty M. Russell,* edited by Margaret A. Farley and Serene Jones, 123–41. Louisville, Ky.: Westminster/John Knox Press.

Fleming, Cynthia Griggs. 1998. *Soon we will not cry: The liberation of Ruby Doris Smith Robinson.* Lanham, Md.: Rowman & Littlefield.

Johnson, William R. 1977. *Developing the educational ministry of the local church: A manual for Christian educators.* Memphis, Tenn.: CME Publishing.

Lakey, Othal Hawthorne. 1985. From "colored" to "Christian": Change and conflict 1946–1970. In *The History of the CME Church*. Memphis, Tenn.: CME Publishing House.

Parker, Evelyn L. 2003. *Trouble don't last always: Emancipatory hope among African American adolescents*. Cleveland, Ohio: Pilgrim Press.

Ross, Rosetta E. 2003. *Witnessing and testifying: Black women, religion, and civil rights*. Minneapolis, Minn.: Fortress.

Talvacchia, Kathleen T. 2003. *Critical minds and discerning hearts: A spirituality of multicultural teaching*. St. Louis, Mo.: Chalice Press.

Thompson, Marjorie. 1995. *Soul feast: An invitation to the Christian spiritual life*. Louisville, Ky.: Westminster/John Knox Press.

Whelchel, Love Henry. 2002. *Hell without fire*. Nashville, Tenn.: Abingdon Press.

Wilmore, Gayraud S. 1982. *Last things first*. Philadelphia, Pa.: Westminster Press.

CHAPTER 22

Repairing the World: The Place of Mitzvot in Children's Spiritual Lives

Sherry H. Blumberg

Children learn by doing. Educational theorists such as John Dewey (1938) and Jean Piaget confirm that active "doing" plays a major role in how children learn to think and reflect. Young children, especially, explore the world they live in through their senses— touch, smell, sight, hearing, and taste. Many—perhaps most—young children are primarily kinesthetic learners. They seem to act first and then later to understand what they are doing and (later still) the consequences of their actions. Although children use all their senses to learn and many will later learn best by visual and aural/oral means, a multisensory approach that stresses "learning by doing" seems to be best for most young children.

While we know that this progression is true for children's intellectual growth and even for emotional and social growth, there is less certainty about how a child's inner spiritual world grows. Although the recent interest in this topic may generate new research and findings, this chapter's use of the term *spiritual growth* will refer to the combination of the child's extrinsic actions and his or her intrinsic thoughts, meditations, and reasons for acting. Jewish tradition has implicitly assumed that a child's inner life reflects learning by doing. Jews, by their actions, implicitly believe that the doing of mitzvot (the commandments), focusing for the young on ritual and *ma'asim tovim* (acts of loving-kindness) will eventually lead to a healthy moral and spiritual life.

In the Book of Exodus, Moses tells the Israelite people all the laws and rules that God has commanded. The people respond: "All that God has commanded we will do" (Exodus 19:8 and 24:3) Then, Moses writes down the commandments and reads them to the people, and the people respond, "All that God has commanded, we will do and we will hear [*na'aseh v'nishmah*]" (Exodus 24:7). *Na'aseh* means "we will do." *V'nishmah* can be translated either "and we will hear" or "and we will understand."[1] For most of Jewish life and Jewish history, this two-verb phrase has been interpreted to mean that first a person should do the mitzvot and that understanding of them would follow later. In recent history—particularly with the rise of rationalism—there have been challenges to this established approach to Jewish life. For some modern Jews, the nishmah (understanding) must come before the na'aseh (doing).

The debate about which should come first is important not only in theological discourse but also in educational circles. For the development of children's spirituality, the debate and its resolution are critical because of the role that "doing" may play in the inner life of the Jewish child. While children, in the past, learned to do the commandments because their families observed the commandments, we do not know if the parents helped explain the connection between the doing of the commandments and the spiritual life of the doer. Still, for many individual Jewish doers, the links were formed. Whether or not the parents understood the link between the commandment and the spiritual life of the individual, there was family and community pressure to do the commandments. Thus, na'aseh v'nishmah continued as the primary method of connecting children to their inner lives and to God. It was generally understood that doing the commandments was what God wanted, and that understanding was a secondary and less important consequence.

In our modern world, Jewish community life has changed. Families are more scattered, and the Jewish community (except in a very limited number of demographically concentrated areas) is not always available to support a child's religious or spiritual growth. Many Jewish adults neither do the mitzvot nor have any conscious or unconscious connection between Jewish action and their own spiritual lives. If any understanding or connection is to be attained for these Jews, and thus for their children, the nishmah (hearing and understanding) often must come before the na'aseh (doing). These modern Jews want—perhaps need—a reason for doing a commandment, a reason that is meaningful for their own lives. They often need such a reason before they will even consider doing anything Jewish, especially Jewish rituals. Some modern Jews are secularists, believing in the Jewish people but unsure of the nature or role of God, and particularly the role of God as "Commander."

The liberal movements of Judaism helped resolve this problem by transforming the meaning of *mitzvah* from "commandment" to "good deed." One common modern approach posited that the ethical and moral commandments were imperatives, but that the ritual commandments needed to be updated and were, therefore, not binding. Other Jews countered that it was the ritual that reinforced the ethical. Under that view, the theological debates became critical. Liberal Jews, seeking an a priori rationale for doing, stressed prophetic ideals of social justice and social action, while more traditional Jews, retaining the "do first, then understand" approach, stressed all the ritual commandments as well as the ethical and moral ones, trusting that only through doing *all* the commandments would complete understanding come. In these debates, some of what became lost was what Saul Berman has called the "permanent and temporal functions of mitzvot," that is, the way in which the mitzvot relate to a human being's basic nature by transforming a person into a more perfect and spiritually connected human being (Berman 1973, 342).

These theological debates—na'aseh v'nishmah versus nishmah v'na'aseh and whether to define mitzvah as "commandment" or as "good deed"—and their resultant differences in actions have had profound effects on the education and spiritual development of children. Because even international law has recognized, at least since 1924, children should be allowed to develop normally, in material and spiritual respects (Schweitzer 2004 and UN archives),[2] it is important to examine how "doing" the actions of the mitzvot affects the spiritual development of the child.

In this chapter, we will examine the role that *mitzvot, gemilut hasadim,* and *tikkun olam* play in the lives of our young. And, although we will not necessarily be able to answer the question of which approach is correct (whether the action is to be done first and understood later, or vice versa), we can begin to clarify the role that "doing" plays in the development of the spiritual life of the young Jew. A better understanding of the role mitzvot, gemilut hasadim, and tikkun olam can play in shaping a Jewish child's spirituality may enable parents and educators to make better decisions about how to include these actions and concepts in the child's maturing life.

Definitions

For the purposes of this chapter, mitzvot will be defined as those actions that are traditionally believed to be commanded by God. Thus, this definition includes both the commandments that are ritual and those that are ethical (whether one approaches mitzvot as "commandments" or as "good deeds"). In applying this definition to the different philosophical movements within Judaism, readers will understand that some groups of Jews will attempt to perform all the mitzvot possible and others will not—depending on whether the group's belief is that the commandment is the "word of God" or the "word of people trying to interpret God's will or in search of God."

Gemilut hasadim (deeds of mercy) and its nearly synonymous term, *ma'asim tovim* (good deeds), both refer to those ethical commandments that are considered to be "acts of loving-kindness" or deeds that are ethical in nature and that lead toward tikkun olam. Tikkun olam (literally, "repair of the world") originated as a mystical concept concerning the human responsibility to reunite "sparks" of the divine that had been scattered over all the earth. As used here, tikkun olam will be defined as "repair of the world" and will include all those actions that constitute working for justice and social action. Again, some Jews will believe that all the mitzvot are needed to accomplish tikkun olam, and other Jews will not.

One further definition is required to help the reader understand how these three concepts (mitzvot, gemilut hasadim, and tikkun olam) can promote the inner spiritual life of a child or an adolescent. The growth of a Jewish child's spirituality can be more accurately examined as "Jewish religious experience." Jewish religious experience consists of both the inner feelings of connectedness to God and the call to action that results (Blumberg 1991). As such, one can educate for Jewish religious experience and provide opportunities for the growth of the person's moral, intellectual, social, and spiritual connection to God, Judaism, and Jewish life. It is of major importance to examine the role played in a person's education by the actions of (1) performing mitzvot, (2) doing deeds of loving-kindness, and (3) helping to repair the world.

In addition, the studies by Edward Robinson of English children's religious experiences suggest that long-buried experiences can grow into full religious experience when they are reflected upon (Robinson 1983). Thus, while mitzvot, gemilut hasadim, and tikkun olam should be understood as only one part of how a Jew's religious experience and spirituality grow if they are reflected upon later in life, they can be critical in helping the adult feel that, even as a child, there was something more to life.

Mitzvot as Teacher

In Jewish law, children do not become "responsible" for carrying out the commandments until the age of bar (thirteen for boys) or bat (twelve and a half for girls) mitzvah. Before that age, the responsibility is upon parents and teachers to teach the mitzvot and how they are performed, and thus to teach children how to live their lives as adult Jews.

Young children learn by doing the mitzvot, by seeing their family members doing the mitzvot, or by observing their teachers' actions. The job of parents and teachers is to reinforce good behavior and extinguish or discourage less desirable behavior. This job is often accomplished by praising the child for correct actions. As children develop a moral and ethical sense, their inner desire to do the right thing will grow from their original fear of punishment.[3] At the age of *chinuch* (education), age six, children are taught to recite the blessings before eating and before doing mitzvot. One may teach a younger child the blessing, and certainly a child is taught to say "Amen" to a blessing recited by others (Cohen 1993, 21–22).

If children are praised appropriately for their early learning, their feelings of self-worth and self-esteem grow. Feelings of self-worth enable the young child to reflect upon the doing of mitzvot as a way in which he or she gains praise and lives happily and appropriately within the Jewish community. Doing the mitzvot, such as saying a blessing before eating or helping to light Shabbat candles, also adds structure and predictability to the life of a child. This structure can lead to a sense of inner satisfaction and security (Kelemen 2001, 38).

The mitzvot themselves are also teachers, especially for the child. Inherent in some of the mitzvot are the values that, while not yet fully understood, satisfy other inner needs of the child. Some of the mitzvot enhance the sensual needs of the child, such as decorating the Sukkah (harvest hut), lighting candles (on Shabbat and holidays such as Hanukkah), tasting the special food with the appropriate blessings, hearing the shofar (the ram's horn), or the reading of the Scroll of Esther. Other mitzvot enhance the sense of belonging to a community (such as making up a minyan, the quorum of ten people required for communal prayer). Some mitzvot nurture feelings of safety and security such as the regularity of prayer and of Shabbat. Still others promote basic fairness, since all Jews, rich or poor, are seen as responsible for doing the mitzvot and giving something to help others. This required "giving" is called *tzedakah* in the Jewish tradition—an act not of "charity" but of "righteousness." Many families give tzedakah right before the beginning of Sabbath as their way of regularly acknowledging this obligation, and their children usually remember the small tzedakah box in their home in which they would put their coins just before Sabbath. It is comforting to contemplate this obligation to give, not only because giving can cause pleasure by itself, but also because there is security in knowing that if *I* am truly in need, *my* needs will be provided for.

In more traditional Jewish communities, the mitzvot act as teachers to mark the distinction between men and women—something that may be problematic in more liberal Jewish communities whose members tend not to make such definite distinctions with regard to the mitzvot. By simply observing, the child learns what mitzvot she or he must perform and which ones are not going to be required. Because they tradition-ally care for children and the home, women are exempt from the time-bound mitzvot (for example, the obligation to attend public prayer at three set times each day). They are not prohibited from, for example, wrapping tefillin (phylacteries), but rather they are allowed to put the needs of their children and family first. They pray but are exempt from the obligation of communal prayer. Girls are taught, early on, to take a small piece of dough from the challah loaf that is burned before the bread is baked, as a remem-brance of the temple sacrifice. This act can be done by men or women, but it is a woman's mitzvah. Young girls learn this early in their education. There are other obli-gations incumbent upon women, such as the ceremonial lighting of candles and keep-ing the laws of family purity. Today, within the liberal movements, the stated theology is that there is no distinction between women and men in regard to the mitzvot.

Finally, many of the mitzvot teach values that can be directly transferred into a child's spiritual life, including patience or delayed gratification, the importance of learning, and honoring other human beings. For example, delayed gratification comes from knowing that one does not eat without first saying a blessing. The importance of learning and growing is found in the daily learning that is expected. A child learns to honor others because the sacred texts that are part of their education require that every human being be treated with dignity, especially parents and teachers. For children to have time to explore their own spiritual selves, they must be able to delay their own gratification and wait for what they want. Learning as a daily activity allows children to make mistakes and to reflect on how to do better, as well as how to be excited by the world and the opportunities around them. The mitzvot that prohibit gossip or harm-ful words (Leviticus 19:14–16) teach the sanctity of speech, require that we refrain from doing unto our friends what we would not want done to us (Hillel, in Babylon-ian Talmud, Shabbat 31a), and teach that each human life deserves respect and dignity.

Mitzvot as Connection to God

A child's God image is formed at an early developmental age. According to some of the research, the image of God a child forms can be understood by using a child's ability to represent his or her ideas about God in art. Often these early images are of a God that is geographically and emotionally distant (Heller 1986). According to Michael Samuel (1996), "Children have a natural affinity for God" (30). Samuel explores how that nat-ural affinity is eroded as the child grows, unless a relationship to God is encouraged.

Living and teaching children in their Jewish tradition provide just such encour-agement. The Jew asks, "What does God require of us?" The mitzvot are seen as ways of fulfilling what God requires of us—children included. Performing the mitzvot can help the child develop a more lasting connection to God.

A child's first emotional human need, according to developmental psychologist Erik Erikson (1962), is a sense of trust in others and the world, developed by experiencing trusting relationships with the first caregivers. Thus, when children first learn to do a mitzvah, they are trying to please their parents. Lawrence Keleman (2001) characterizes this process of meeting early emotional needs as a way that the child can develop strong and committed relationships with God "kindling a child's soul," relating to the child's developing spirituality (198). Later, if properly guided, feelings of self-worth children have when they experience success, or feelings of sadness when they experience failure, can enable them to consider their actions as those that please God.

According to the Talmud (Sotah 14a), children can learn to model themselves after God by doing what God wants and imitating God's actions. Thus, they learn that they are performing acts of loving-kindness (ma'asim tovim) when they visit the sick (as God did after Abraham circumcised himself), feed the hungry (as God did, feeding the children of Israel in the desert), honor the elderly, refrain from cruelty to animals, practice the sanctity of speech, engage in the study of Torah, and do other acts that emulate those of God.[4] In this way Jews act in the knowledge that they were created in the image of God. Such acts help shape a child's inner world so that the partnership between God and child grows. And, while the Talmud (Sotah 49a) adds that "a child cannot be pious," it is certainly possible for a child to develop a friendship or a positive, ongoing relationship with God.

In prayer services, children read that "God loves Israel and the world," and they also read, "And you shall love the Lord your God . . ." (Deuteronomy 6:8–9). Children may conclude from these that that they have to love God because God loves them (a simple covenant). Fulfilling the mitzvah of loving God helps the child discover the mutual love between God and Israel, of which the child is an important part. Recognizing and attempting to give effect to this covenant can be both emotionally satisfying and conducive to developing a trust in God. That trust can satisfy the child spiritually and lead to a richer, more complex trust as the child matures and grows into adulthood. The development of *emunah* (faith) grows from such mutuality.

A connection to God is also the foundation from which one can elevate one's soul and ultimately become able to transcend one's self. Self-transcendence may be a natural function of the human brain as it develops, or it may need to be encouraged. In a study of brain science and belief, researchers construct a theory of how the self emerges and how the mind gives meaning and substance to a person's perceptions and thoughts. They call this process "reification" and define it as the ability to convert a concept into a concrete thing. A child's mind grows in its ability to connect with something larger than himself or herself by first finding concrete reality in certain actions, ideas, and feelings (Newberg, D'Aquili, and Rause 2001). Performing actions that are conceptually connected with developing a relationship with God (such as acts of loving-kindness) may encourage this kind of growth, which, in turn, encourages self-transcendence.

Mitzvot as Connection to People

Children need trust (Erikson 1962) and love (Kelemen 2001) to develop strong and committed relationships with people. A major mitzvah that not only allows but encourages this kind of love and trust is the observance of Shabbat. Shabbat can be a day of prayer, study, contemplation, and ritual. Shabbat is also a day for families and friends to spend together, connecting with each other without the interference of work and other everyday distractions. Traditional Jewish families may not answer phones, watch television, use their computers, go shopping, cook meals, or even drive or ride in a car. Taking the time to be with those whom a child loves and needs is one way for the child to develop a healthy relationship with others. Taking time on Shabbat for reflection allows a child's inner world to develop, because it encourages self-reflection, imaginative play, and an ability to be quiet.

An additional benefit for a child's spiritual life comes from the traditional form of study that occurs on Shabbat. This study, often done in *hevruta*—the form of two friends arguing over a text—can allow a child to understand that divergent opinions counted in the past and that they are still cherished today. The child realizes that the Talmud and other ancient sources honored a variety of opinions. Moreover, by observing study in hevruta, the child learns both friendship and respect for such diversity. The rabbis kept interpreting verses in different ways, and while one of the ways was finally chosen—either by consensus or by majority vote—to be the way a mitzvah was performed, all of the materials and the argument were retained in the text. These preserved opinions often provided a basis for later generations to adopt formerly minority views as more appropriate for their later changed situations. The understanding that one can disagree with and yet respect opposing viewpoints enriches the child's ability and willingness to develop and to think his or her own thoughts. This recognition can lead to compassion, empathy, and respect for other points of view.

Developing compassion and empathy are the outcomes of several of the mitzvot. A child needs to know that there are others who need him or her and that he or she needs others. In Ecclesiastes (11:9) we read, "Young children should walk in the ways of their hearts." Learning by acts of love between themselves and others will nurture a heart that is filled with compassion and empathy.

Tikkun Olam for the Adolescent

Developmentally, teenagers are often rebellious (Erikson 1962; Kohlberg 1981).[5] They may believe that they can do things better than their parents. A young teenager may be idealistic and enthusiastic. It is at the outset of this developmental period (at bar/bat mitzvah) that young people begin to learn responsibility by actually accepting the responsibility for carrying out the commandments and entering into adult learning. This is the time when ideas about tikkun olam may help shape an inner spiritual life that can make a difference in this world.[6]

Dewey (1938) posited that young people had to be trained from childhood to follow certain societal rules and norms of behavior, but that they also had to be taught to criticize those very traditions and values. Such criticism can be learned through the hevruta techniques of Jewish study, and the kind of logic and reasoning found in Talmud and later writings. Teenagers can also learn this critical thinking skill by performing actions to improve on their own world and by being guided to see their actions as helping to shape the kind of world that God would want. This critical attention to actions can thus be channeled into a concentration on tikkun olam.

In addition, the teenage years and adolescence as a whole are a time of social development for young people. A young adult's spiritual life may also grow and mature as that young person reflects on his or her place in a social group and on the potential power of that social group itself. Most projects that can help repair the world are group projects in which people have to work together to accomplish a worthy goal. A prominent example of such group projects would be Habitat for Humanity. If the organizers take time during such projects to help their group members reflect on the transformative aspects of the work they are performing, they will improve the odds that the project will foster growth in the participants' spiritual lives.

In biblical and Talmudic times, it was often the young person who brought the family's or community's sacrifices to the Temple in Jerusalem (Talmud, Chagigah 6b). Being entrusted with that responsibility and making the pilgrimage not only brought youth to the center of the cult of worship, it also brought them into contact with other young people who had likewise undertaken this family and communal responsibility. They could see that their actions led to the well-being of their community. In today's world, a young person's understanding that his or her actions are important in tikkun olam can allow the inner life of that youth to grow with a sense of purpose. Feeling needed and reaching beyond the immediate problems of adolescence are strong motivators for finding an enriched spiritual life in the community.

From the research on youth programs in Jewish education (Alexander and Russ 1992), we know that successful programs pack lots of activity into the available time, call upon the adolescent participants to express (by words and action) an amount of idealism, have a high emotional impact, and provide critical role models through support staff. Programs that focus on tikkun olam have, inherent within them, all of these characteristics and, thus, are encouraged in Jewish tradition.

Nurturing the Connections between Mitzvot, Gemilut Hasadim, and Tikkun Olam

The inner workings of the heart and mind of learners include the imagination, the emotions, and the spiritual world that children and adolescents encounter as they grow. Mitzvot, gemilut hasadim, and tikkun olam are concepts and actions that can help focus and develop a child's or young person's inner life. But at least as important as the deeds themselves is how the young person reflects upon those deeds. Whether that reflection is done before (nishmah v'na'aseh), during, or after (na'aseh v'nishmah), it probably is both the doing and the reflection (the action and the understanding), the drawing close to God and to others that allow the individual child's inner life to be enriched.

Reflection for the young child may take the form of play. In educational settings today students are encouraged to "play" at doing the mitzvot, to play-act doing deeds that are kind and loving, and then to talk about the experience. This encouragement is intended to help children begin an inner dialogue of imagining as well as of verbal exchange. Other kinds of activities that can help develop skill in self-reflection include (1) pattern making and recognition, (2) artistic creation as responses to an emotion or event, and (3) conscious discussions that encourage the appreciation and gratitude of the child. All of these activities can be guided by adults, teachers, and parents. These adult guides can help balance inner reflection with group participation (Blumberg 2002, 167–69). Questions designed to prompt critical reflection, such as, "What does doing this mitzvah teach you?" or "Do you feel closer to God when you . . . ?" are designed to prompt critical reflection.

As young people grow, other kinds of reflection, especially reflection that involves writing, metaphorical ideas, and even meditation, can be added. Here again, it is important that the action of the mitzvah be linked with the inner life of the child by helping the child reflect, verbally or in writing, on how the performance of the mitzvah affected her or him emotionally. As adolescence approaches, the use of paradoxical issues and ethical dilemmas can be added with regard to the performance of the mitzvot. Group processes and group reflection upon the mitzvot and an examination of the purpose for which they are performed can enhance young adults' inner life. Examples of questions that can be added at this stage might include, "How did you decide which action was more just, or more merciful?"; "Can performing a mitzvah create a tension in your family or the community?"; and "How can we repair a world when so many are bent on destroying it?"

By connecting the doing of both ritual and ethical mitzvot to gemilut hasadim and then to tikkun olam, a young person's spiritual development will continue to grow. The role that these actions play will change from rote behaviors to ethical reminders and finally to actions that nurture the adult's inner life. And, while some young people may still continue to do the mitzvot because they believe God has commanded them and that our purpose is to do what God wants, the concurrent growth in the individual will help create a meaning that goes beyond the doing of the deed. Closeness to God, closeness to humanity (in general) and the Jewish people (in particular), and a sense of hopefulness and *shalom* (wholeness) can only benefit the individual and the community as a whole. For the Torah tells us: "Surely, this instruction which I enjoin upon you this day is not too baffling for you, nor is it beyond reach . . . No, the thing is very close to you, in your mouth and in your heart, to observe it" (Deuteronomy 30:11–14).

Notes

1. A couple of more modern translations curiously render the two verbs in this passage as, "we will faithfully do."

2. The Geneva Declaration of the Rights of the Child of 1924, adopted by the League of Nations, stated, "The child must be given the means requisite for its normal development, both materially and spiritually." This statement was transformed by the United Nations in 1959 into Principle Two of its Declaration of the Rights of the Child: "The child shall enjoy special protection, and shall be given opportunities and facilities, by law and by other means, to enable him to develop physically, mentally, morally, spiritually and socially in a healthy and normal manner and in conditions of freedom and dignity."

3. See the works of Lawrence Kohlberg or of Gabriel Moran for more information on the growth of this ethical consciousness.

4. Many of these mitzvot are more commonly referred to by their Hebrew equivalents. For example, *kedushat halashon* (sanctity of speech), *talmud torah* (study of torah), and *tzar ba'alei chayyim* (noncruelty to animals).

5. Adolescence, according to developmental psychologists Erikson, Kohlberg, and others, is often characterized by rebelliousness, as young people attempt to disengage from their caregivers and to establish their own unique identities.

6. Although beyond the scope of this chapter, the concept of tikkun olam could, for older adolescents, be used to help develop a sense of connection to self—*tikkun ha-nefesh* (repair of one's own soul or spirit).

References

Alexander, Hanan A., and Ian Russ. 1992. What we know about youth programming. Chap. 10 in *What we know about Jewish education: A handbook of today's research for tomorrow's Jewish education*, edited by Stuart Kelman. Los Angeles: Torah Aura.

Berman, Saul J. 1973. The extended notion of the Sabbath. *Judaism* 22:342.

Blumberg, Sherry H. 1991. *Educating for religious experience*. Ann Arbor, Mich.: University Microfilms.

———. 2002. Educating for self transcendence. In *Teaching about God and spirituality: A resource for Jewish settings*, edited by Roberta Louis Goodman and Sherry H. Blumberg, 164–73. Denver, Colo.: Alternatives in Religious Education.

Cohen, Rabbi Simcha Bunim. 1993. *Children in Halachah*. Brooklyn, N.Y.: Mesorah.

Dewey, John. 1938. *Experience and education*. New York: Collier.

Erikson, Erik. 1962. *Childhood and society*. New York: Norton.

Heller, David. 1986. *The children's God*. Chicago: University of Chicago Press.

Kelemen, Lawrence. 2001. *To kindle a soul: Ancient wisdom for modern parents and teachers*. Southfield, Mich.: Targum Press.

Kelman, Stuart, ed. 1992. *What we know about Jewish education: A handbook of today's research for tomorrow's Jewish education*. Los Angeles: Torah Aura.

Kohlberg, Lawrence. 1981. *Essays on moral development*. San Francisco: Harper and Row.

Moran, Gabriel 1987. *No ladder to the sky: Education and morality*. San Francisco: Harper and Row.

———. 1996. *A grammar of responsibility*. New York: Crossroad.

Newberg, Andrew, Eugene D'Aquili, and Vince Rause. 2001. *Why God won't go away: Brain science and the biology of belief*. New York: Ballantine Books.

Robinson, Edward. 1983. *The original vision: A study of the religious experience of childhood*. New York: Seabury Press.

Samuel, Michael. 1996. *The Lord is my shepherd: The theology of a caring God*. Lanham, Md.: Jason Aaronson.

Schweitzer, Friedrich. 2004. *Children's right to religion and spirituality: Legal, educational and practical perspectives*. Collegial paper presented at the International Seminar on Religious Education and Values, Villanova University, Philadelphia.

CHAPTER 23

Nurturing Young People's Spirituality as a Force for Social Change: A Bahá'í Perspective

Lori M. Noguchi

The Bahá'í Faith traces its roots back to the middle of the nineteenth century, when Bahá'u'lláh proclaimed that the various religions of the world are successive stages in one Divine Plan and that the peoples of the world belong to a single family. Human beings have been created noble, and all share the same purpose: to know and worship God. Bahá'u'lláh's writings, together with those of the Faith's other central figures, His son 'Abdu'l-Bahá and His forerunner, the Báb, cover the range of human experience, and while the Faith has profound mystical teachings that aim to nurture the spiritual life of the individual, its vision extends beyond the individual to cultivate the collective life of humanity. The writings explain that humanity stands on the threshold of its coming of age, and our challenge today is to lay the groundwork for a global civilization that reflects the oneness of humankind. And just as with individual development, civilization building must address both the material and spiritual aspects of human existence, for neither can be neglected indefinitely without detriment to the other.

The Bahá'í writings place strong emphasis on the pivotal periods of childhood and youth in the individual. Numerous passages guide parents in the education of children and call on youth to contribute to the advancement of society. These writings recognize young people's spirituality as a powerful force that can effect social change.

A Historical Perspective

To gain a perspective on how an influential segment of the Bahá'í community has understood and applied the guidance in its sacred writings, it is helpful to look briefly at the early days of the Bahá'í community of Iran. This community, the first with large numbers of believers working together to apply the teachings of the new religion, was directly guided by its central figures.

Since the Faith's establishment, the Bahá'ís in Iran have faced intense persecution. In its early years, thousands of believers were killed in horrific circumstances. Countless others suffered imprisonment, lost their homes, or were rejected by friends and family. Children were no less likely to be ostracized for their beliefs than parents; not only did they suffer when their parents were victimized, they were also open to ridicule, humiliation, and abuse by their peers. Such persecution has continued in Iran in varying degrees until the present day, influencing the nature and identity of the Bahá'í community there.

It is not difficult to see how, under such conditions, the education of children was central to Bahá'í community life; indeed, emphasis on the spiritual education of children was one factor in the remarkable survival of the community despite severe persecution. Children's spirituality was nurtured at home and through participation in community life. Formal classes for the spiritual education of children and youth ages six to eighteen were established throughout the country.

At home, family practices such as dawn prayers and the memorization of Holy writings instilled basic habits of Bahá'í life and shaped individual spiritual identity. Stories of the heroes and heroines of the Faith contributed greatly to this process. Of particular influence were the lives of youth such as Badí', who, though troubled during adolescence, was transformed by meeting Bahá'u'lláh. At the age of seventeen, Badí' suffered torture and ultimately gave his life to deliver a message from Bahá'u'lláh to the Shah. Another such hero is Rúhu'lláh, who, at age twelve, was imprisoned with his father for his beliefs. When a government official, having already killed Rúhu'lláh's father, offered Rúhu'lláh high positions and riches if he would say he was not a Bahá'í, he refused and was hanged.

The family as a whole approached Bahá'í community life with a sense of anticipation. Attendance at holy day celebrations and the nineteen-day feast (a gathering that takes place every nineteen days combining worship, consultation on community affairs, and fellowship) was presented to children as a privilege; many adults tell of times when, as children, they were reminded to behave, lest they not be allowed to attend the feast. Children were accepted as full-fledged community members. They were seen as a trust of God: to educate another's child was considered the same as educating one of Bahá'u'lláh's own children. Thus, the entire community was responsible for the welfare of children. To be a teacher of children became one of the highest honors.

Some salient features of the educational process that gradually took shape were its emphasis on the application of spiritual principles to daily life; its encouragement to strive for high moral and intellectual achievement; the use of Bahá'í history to shape identity; the stress laid on service; and the weight given to study of the Faith's writings. While an evaluation of the effectiveness of spiritual education in the Iranian Bahá'í community, which would involve an analysis of its strengths and weaknesses and their causes, goes beyond the scope of this chapter, a survey of some of its accomplishments is relevant to the theme under review.

Individuals raised in this process were taught to recognize the Hand of God, even in persecution. Bahá'í writings call on believers to "see the end in the beginning" (Bahá'u'lláh 1991, 15). Confident that whatever difficulties the community faced would result in its ultimate advancement, Bahá'ís were able to maintain high levels of hopefulness and to meet opposition with a renewed desire to serve.

Another characteristic of the individuals that emerged was their strong sense of purpose and a keen awareness of their spiritual nature. They were concerned with achieving excellence in material, intellectual, and spiritual aspects of life and considered service an imperative. Bahá'ís everywhere today see in the accomplishments of some five generations of Iranian believers as evidence of the triumph of the human spirit when illumined by the spirit of faith and kept free from fanaticism and bigotry. Its significance, they would argue, lies not so much in the personal and family achievements of the community's members, nor even in its solidarity, but in the absence of hatred or bitterness toward those who persecuted them and their extraordinary commitment to work for social progress.

A 2003 message from the Universal House of Justice, the governing body of the Bahá'í world community, to the Iranian Bahá'ís analyzes the historical development of the Faith in that country and underscores a point pertinent to the theme being explored here. Reminding Bahá'ís in Iran that they are not alone in enduring injustice in this world, the message asks them to bear in mind how they have escaped the spiritual effects oppression has on its victims such as loss of confidence, bitterness, and the deadening of the spirit of initiative. Iranian Bahá'ís, it explains, were able to keep their hearts free from resentment and act with magnanimity toward their oppressors, even after more than a century of oppression, because they successfully applied Bahá'í teachings in their lives.

A few examples of Bahá'í writings that have shaped the lives of the believers in Iran and enabled them to maintain both confident mastery of their moral purpose and an abiding love for their homeland are as follows: "O well-beloved ones! The tabernacle of unity hath been raised; regard ye not one another as strangers. Ye are the fruits of one tree and the leaves of one branch." "Love is light, no matter in what abode it dwelleth; and hate is darkness, no matter where it may make its nest." "In this day, all must cling to whatever is the cause of the betterment of the world and the promotion of knowledge amongst its peoples." "Women and men have been and will always be equal in the sight of God" (Universal House of Justice 2003, 6).

Conceptual Framework

Soon after its appearance in Iran, the Faith began to spread, and it now represents an organized worldwide community of several million with a closely connected network of institutions that administer its affairs and propagate its ideals. Child education is one of the most pressing concerns of all national Bahá'í communities, and the conceptual framework for spiritual education that guides their actions continues to evolve on the basis of the Faith's writings. Questions of identity and purpose are fundamental to the framework, and in addressing them, Bahá'ís everywhere draw inspiration from the experience of the Iranian community.

According to the Bahá'í writings, human nature has two aspects: one material and the other spiritual. If the material aspect is allowed to dominate human consciousness, the consequences are injustice, cruelty, and selfishness. The higher nature expresses love, generosity, kindness, and all the virtues and qualities of the human spirit. The implications for education are expressed by 'Abdu'l-Bahá (1978, 130): "Every child is potentially the light of the world—and at the same time its darkness; wherefore must the question of education be accounted as of primary importance."

Developing the spiritual nature so that it dominates the lower nature is a fundamental aspect of human purpose, and therefore of spiritual education. Bahá'í writings
related to human purpose take a variety of forms, but within them one can identify two
major themes: the transformation of one's character through the development of spiritual potentialities and the transformation of society through selfless service and the
application of spiritual principles.

These two aspects of human purpose are inseparable. One does not develop spiritual qualities and talents in isolation but through efforts to serve others. Outside the
field of service, it is difficult to judge the development of one's qualities as there is no
concrete result by which to measure progress. Lacking attention to the social dimension
of moral purpose, individuals are prone to subtle forms of ego—combinations of guilt,
self-righteousness, and self-satisfaction. Yet social transformation is equally dependent
on personal transformation. Without recognition of the need for personal growth,
efforts at social transformation are likely to be misdirected. When change in social
structures is seen as the answer to all problems, ignoring individual responsibility, it is
easy to lose respect and compassion and become inclined toward acts of cruelty and
oppression.

Bahá'í efforts in spiritual education, therefore, seek to cultivate recognition of one's
identity as a spiritual being with a twofold moral purpose: striving for one's own spiritual growth and contributing to social advancement. The process must begin, according to the Bahá'í writings, in early childhood, when emphasis is placed on character
development.

The period of childhood is especially important for the shaping of character
because, as 'Abdu'l-Bahá explains, "Children are like unto tender branches, they grow
just as they are educated . . . if they are given a divine education they become divine,
and obtain heavenly character from the Sun of Reality" (Research Department of the
Universal House of Justice 2004, 2). Spiritual qualities, concepts, and attitudes
acquired during childhood influence the individual throughout life. Among the fundamental principles that are to be instilled is the recognition of the oneness of God and
of humanity.

Another essential quality to be developed is love. According to Bahá'í teachings,
God's love for humanity is boundless. As human beings grow spiritually and the limit-
less love of God permeates their thoughts and actions, they gain insight into the true
meaning of spiritual teachings and moral values. Love is also intimately linked to thirst
for knowledge of the laws of the universe. As knowledge and insight grow, so does a
feeling of infinite love. One's love for family, friends, community, nation, and humanity becomes less dependent on transitory emotions and more rooted in the reality of
human existence. Further, the interaction between love and knowledge engenders faith,
which the Bahá'í writings refer to as conscious knowledge in action. Through the application of one's growing knowledge, faith is strengthened. Faith in one's potential to
change, faith in the possibility of creating a new society, faith that life has meaning—
all are necessary to develop one's potentialities and contribute to civilization building.

Another set of qualities that the Bahá'í writings view as essential to a spiritual
human being are those associated with rectitude of conduct such as truthfulness, trustworthiness, and justice. Bahá'í writings call truthfulness the "foundation of all human

virtues" (Universal House of Justice 1991b, 338). Without it, "progress and success, in all the worlds of God, are impossible for any soul" (338). Trustworthiness is fundamental to the progress of society: "Trustworthiness is the greatest portal leading unto the tranquility and security of the people. In truth the stability of every affair hath depended and doth depend upon it" (Bahá'u'lláh 1978, 37). Clearly, truthfulness and trustworthiness entail more than keeping one's word and refraining from telling lies. Both are essential to perceiving truth and maintaining an attitude of learning, without which personal and social transformation are impossible. They are also closely related to questions of justice, at personal and societal levels.

Like truthfulness, justice is a spiritual quality that enables us to investigate reality and to acquire knowledge:

> The best beloved of all things in my sight is Justice; turn not away therefrom
> if thou desirest Me and neglect it not that I may confide in thee. By its aid
> thou shalt see with thine own eyes and not through the eyes of others, and
> shalt know of thine own knowledge and not through the knowledge of thy
> neighbor. (Bahá'u'lláh 1985, 3)

Justice also has a profound social dimension; it is a necessary precondition for unity and harmony in society. Without it, peace and tranquillity are, at best, fragile.

Love, knowledge, and faith, and virtues associated with rectitude of conduct such as trustworthiness, truthfulness, and justice, are primary themes in Bahá'í educational programs that nurture spirituality in children and youth. These, along with other qualities like generosity, purity of heart, and courage, are considered essential characteristics of the human soul and building blocks of human character. Although each quality is indispensable in itself, they all stand in need of modification by others. Thus love, for example, is to be complemented by justice and justice by compassion.

The conceptual framework within which Bahá'í communities strive to nurture spirituality does not limit itself to issues related to the acquisition of virtues and praiseworthy habits. Spirituality also implies a well-developed spiritual perception, which involves the ability to recognize spiritual forces, identify relevant principles, and apply them. Spiritual perception is used here as an aspect of spirituality as distinct from religion or religious belief. Spirituality is rooted in that "mystic feeling that unites man with God" (Bahá'u'lláh et al. 1994, 543). It is a state in which one reflects the attributes and qualities of God and is conscious of sacredness in one's actions. True spirituality is linked with action: "That which is truly spiritual must light the path to God, and must result in deeds" ('Abdu'l-Bahá 1984, 107).

Spiritual perception is developed in childhood and further sharpened in adolescence. Educators are encouraged to let children "open wide their eyes and uncover the inner realities of all things, become proficient in every art and skill, and learn to comprehend the secrets of all things even as they are" (Universal House of Justice 1991a, 277).

Bahá'í communities everywhere are becoming increasingly aware of the importance of early adolescence in spiritual and moral development. Recent messages from the Universal House of Justice underscore the significance of junior youth, those aged twelve to fifteen. No longer children, but not yet in full possession of their powers, junior youth begin to explore social reality and determine their place in it, shaping their own identities and worldviews and standing in need of spiritual perception. They are able to analyze and apply spiritual concepts of greater complexity than those dealt with in childhood and to undertake acts of service to their communities. Programs of spiritual education for junior youth are expected to introduce themes related to the social implications of spiritual principles, and emphasize areas of service that contribute to social transformation—this, without neglecting the development of spiritual qualities, knowledge of the sacred writings, and the consolidation of the habits of daily prayer and meditation.

The ages between fifteen and thirty are considered the period of youth when individuals "must assume serious spiritual obligations and duties" and realize that they "are themselves alone ultimately responsible to God for the progress of their own souls" (Universal House of Justice 1992, 1). During this stage of development, "the mind is most questing" and "the spiritual values that will guide the person's future behaviour are adopted" (Universal House of Justice 1966, 1). Bahá'í youth strive to understand and apply the teachings; share them with their contemporaries; overcome the pressures of the world; and demonstrate leadership for their peers and succeeding generations. Bahá'í writings say of youth that it is they "who can contribute so decisively to the virility, the purity, and the driving force of the life of the Bahá'í community, and upon whom must depend the future orientation of its destiny, and the complete unfoldment of the potentialities with which God has endowed it" (Bahá'u'lláh et al. 1994, 214).

Messages to individuals and groups of youth remind them of their high destiny and of the services they can render. They are urged to distinguish themselves "by [their] sanctity and detachment, loftiness of purpose, magnanimity, determination, noble-mindedness, tenacity, the elevation of [their] aims and . . . spiritual qualities" (Research Department of the Universal House of Justice 2004, 2). They are encouraged to investigate and analyze the principles of the Faith and to correlate them with academic and current issues (Research Department of the Universal House of Justice 1995).

For this age group, then, programs of spiritual education try to address fully the dual purpose of striving consciously to grow spiritually and of contributing to social transformation. Much current learning among Bahá'í educators is related to developing moral capacity, spiritual perception, and the ability to study the Bahá'í writings in depth and apply the teachings to social action. If this is done, and balance between the personal and social aspects of moral purpose reached, youth will not only arise to shoulder the responsibilities of their Faith but will also challenge the community to "explore ever more audaciously the revolutionary social implications of Bahá'u'lláh's teachings" (Universal House of Justice 2001, 101).

It is important to note that, in the framework being discussed here, contributing to social transformation is not defined in terms of isolated individual acts of service. Statements in the Bahá'í writings point to a profound connection between personal growth and changes in social structure:

> We cannot segregate the human heart from the environment outside us and
> say that once one of these is reformed everything will be improved. Man is

organic with the world. His inner life molds the environment and is in itself deeply affected by it. The one acts upon the other and every abiding change in the life of man is the result of these mutual reactions. (Research Department of the Universal House of Justice 1989)

The need for organic change in society's structure is one implication of the principle of the oneness of humankind, the establishment of which is the very aim of Bahá'u'lláh's teachings:

> The principle of the Oneness of Mankind—the pivot round which all the teachings of Bahá'u'lláh revolve—is no mere outburst of ignorant emotionalism or an expression of vague and pious hope. Its appeal is not to be merely identified with a reawakening of the spirit of brotherhood and good-will among men, nor does it aim solely at the fostering of harmonious cooperation among individual peoples and nations. Its implications are deeper, its claims greater than any which the Prophets of old were allowed to advance. Its message is applicable not only to the individual, but concerns itself primarily with the nature of those essential relationships that must bind all the states and nations as members of one human family. It does not constitute merely the enunciation of an ideal, but stands inseparably associated with an institution adequate to embody its truth, demonstrate its validity, and perpetuate its influence. It implies an organic change in the structure of present-day society, a change such as the world has not yet experienced. (Shoghi Effendi 1974, 42)

Such organic change implies achieving balance between the spiritual and the material in the fundamental processes and relationships that shape society: the relationship between human beings and nature, among individuals and groups, within the family, and between individuals and institutions. Just as the individual's life has material and spiritual aspects, so must civilization be understood as advancing in material and spiritual dimensions: "No matter how far the material world advances, it cannot establish the happiness of mankind. Only when material and spiritual civilization are linked and coordinated will happiness be assured" ('Abdu'l-Bahá 1982, 109).

To educate youth to contribute to the advancement of civilization in both dimensions, Bahá'í communities are learning to give attention to moral capabilities, the development of which requires the understanding of concepts and the acquisition of sets of qualities, attitudes, and skills. Youth developing such capabilities will seek, for example, to be builders of unity; to establish a united and harmonious family; to transcend and rectify relationships of dominance; to interact harmoniously with nature; and to defend victims of oppression.

To advance in these capabilities, youth require certain spiritual habits in the realm of group interaction. They must learn to practice the art of consultation, that is, cordial and dispassionate investigation of a situation with the intent of coming to a common understanding of reality. They are to be taught that consultation, undertaken according to provisions set out in the writings, is the process by which they will reach decisions throughout their lives. They should see how progress can be achieved through a continuous process of consultation, action, and reflection. One investigates reality and enhances one's understanding of spiritual principles through study, prayer, and consultation; strives to apply that understanding in action; and then reflects on the results of one's action. Not infrequently, renewed study in light of experience brings fresh insights. One discovers the shortcomings of one's previous notions and recognizes the spiritual principles that must now be taken into account.

Recent Developments

Bahá'í programs of spiritual education around the world represent an evolving understanding of how to apply the framework described here in practice. Recent years, in particular, have witnessed a systematization of efforts worldwide. Although conditions vary from place to place, this systematization tends to address both patterns of community life and formal classes of spiritual education. In most countries, programs to increase human resources among adults include courses about the spiritual education of children. As a result, a great deal of attention is being given to the child's spiritual well-being from his or her earliest days—indeed, from the time that prayers are said for the expectant mother. Groups at which parents support one another in the spiritual education of their children and consult about challenges they are facing also flourish. Some communities have established counseling programs to assist families. Communities increasingly celebrate the achievements of children and youth, and their participation in community activities ranks high in priorities.

Formal educational programs are also being further systematized. Spiritual education classes existed historically, but such classes were generally regarded as exclusively for Bahá'ís, were usually composed of mixed age groups, and often used materials created by teachers on an ad hoc basis. Recent years have witnessed a steady influx of participants from the wider community into Bahá'í activities. Bahá'í children's classes and junior youth programs, in particular, have seen an increase of young people from other faiths. In some communities, participants from diverse religious backgrounds far exceed those from Bahá'í families.

Content is being formalized so that classes use age-appropriate materials that build systematically from level to level. Although no overall evaluation of such classes has been made, stories abound of their impact on children. For example, nine-year-old Anisa Kintz from the United States approached her school principal about involving young people in meetings to prevent racism; her efforts led to a series of race unity conferences in schools reaching more than two hundred children (Coastal Carolina University 2004).

At the junior youth level, a set of materials is being developed to address junior youths' relationship with society. Apart from Bahá'í programs, these materials are being incorporated into the educational programs of nongovernmental organizations. A study by a Harvard University graduate examined the effects of one such program on secondary students in rural Honduras. In addition to academic subjects, the program tackles such issues as developing spiritual qualities, resisting propaganda, and the meaning of service. Participants in the program demonstrated significantly greater orientation to helping others, indicated more willingness to remain in rural areas to support their communities, and valued spiritual qualities more than did students in comparable rural Honduran schools (Honeyman 2004).

Although varying considerably, most programs for youth combine intensive study of the Bahá'í writings, analysis of how to apply the Faith's teachings, and use of the arts to demonstrate their efficacy to others. Through dance, music, and traditional arts and crafts, youth convey social messages about the importance of spirituality in young people's lives, addressing such issues as racism, violence, and the dangers of drugs and alcohol. A program developed in Russia, for instance, employs drama to examine social concerns. At the point of climax, a scene is frozen and the audience asked to explore the relevant spiritual principles and possible solutions. So successful has the approach been that it was made into a national television show.

Programs in which youth offer dedicated periods of time to community service, in their own countries or abroad, are also becoming more systematic. Considered preparation for a life of service, such programs provide youth with a unique opportunity to put into practice newfound skills and abilities. Serving with other youth, they see spiritual development in a new light, acquire skills of cooperation, and learn to integrate service into daily life. Participation in such service programs raises awareness of community needs, inspiring many participants to choose vocations that will help meet those needs.

Finally, spiritual education programs in many national Bahá'í communities are complemented by Bahá'í-inspired academic schools that strive to integrate spiritual and academic concerns. Where formal schools do not exist, short courses and seminars on academic and social issues stimulate youth to consider the implications of Bahá'í teachings for social change. These courses often influence career paths chosen by youth.

Emerging Challenges and Research Implications

Several challenges have emerged as Bahá'í communities have striven to cultivate spirituality in youth. Foremost among them is the need to develop appropriate human resources. Establishing a system based on the framework in the Bahá'í writings requires communities to conceptualize an educational system, elaborate curriculum, and train teachers in its use. All of these tasks demand human resources. Whereas appropriate educational materials are gradually becoming available, systematic training of teachers remains a challenge.

Another set of challenges relates to the process of change itself. As insights emerge about the spiritual education of children and youth, communities need to adjust their patterns of behavior. Behavioral change is far from easy and, not infrequently, brings fresh tests that require individuals and institutions to develop new capacities. For example, as youthful creativity and sometimes impetuosity is brought to bear on community service, Bahá'í institutions must learn how to nurture and guide such efforts. Institutions must undergo their own maturation process to develop the capabilities that will enable them to effectively guide young people, allowing them to take their rightful place in a vibrant community life.

New insights can also raise new questions. Questions confronting Bahá'í communities today include: What constitutes the meaningful participation of children in community life? What principles and concepts should junior youth learn? How will traditional views about childhood and adolescence, as well as child-rearing practices, be modified in light of the ongoing application of the Bahá'í writings?

Related to these questions is the challenge of differentiating between the universal and the particular in educational practices and patterns of community life. What is the role of culture in a system of spiritual education based on a common framework? To what extent does culture define the part young people can play in the process of social transformation? How can one respect variations in applying spiritual teachings without falling into the trap of cultural relativism?

These questions and many others are now the object of investigation and experimentation in Bahá'í communities worldwide. Shared by religious communities everywhere, such questions can represent fruitful areas of collaborative research by academics and religious practitioners who seek to release the spiritual power of young people to bring about social change.

References

'Abdu'l-Bahá. 1978. *Selections of the writings of 'Abdu'l-Bahá*. Haifa, Israel: Bahá'í World Center.
———. 1982. *The promulgation of universal peace*. 2nd ed. Wilmette, Ill: Bahá'í Publishing Trust.
———. 1984. *'Abdu'l-Bahá in London*. London: Bahá'í Publishing Trust.
Bahá'u'lláh. 1978. *Tablets of Bahá'u'lláh revealed after the Kitab-i-aqdas*. Haifa, Israel: Bahá'í World Center.
———. 1985. *The hidden words*. Wilmette, Ill.: Bahá'í Publishing Trust..
———. 1991. *The seven valleys and the four valleys*. Wilmette, Ill.: Bahá'í Publishing Trust.
Bahá'u'lláh, the Báb, 'Abdu'l-Bahá, Shoghi Effendi, and the Universal House of Justice. 1994. *Lights of guidance: A Bahá'í reference file*. 3rd revised ed. New Delhi: Bahá'í Publishing Trust.
Coastal Carolina University. 2004. Calling all colors: Ten years after. *Coastal Carolina University Magazine*, September 10. http://www.coastal.edu/magazine/fall2002/feature03.html.
Honeyman, Catherine. 2004. An orientation toward human progress: Developing social responsibility in rural Honduran youth through the Sistema de Aprendizaje. Undergraduate honors thesis, Harvard University.
Research Department of the Universal House of Justice. 1989. *Conservation of the earth's resources*. Haifa, Israel: Bahá'í World Center.
———. 1995. *Extracts from the writings of Bahá'u'lláh and 'Abdu'l-Bahá and from the letters of Shoghi Effendi and the Universal House of Justice on scholarship*. Haifa, Israel: Bahá'í World Center.
———. 2004. *Spiritual, moral, and intellectual education of children and youth*. Unpublished extracts from the Bahá'í writings and from letters written by and on behalf of Shoghi Effendi. Haifa, Israel: Bahá'í World Center.
Shoghi Effendi. 1974. *World order of Bahá'u'lláh*. Wilmette, Ill.: Bahá'í Publishing Trust.
Universal House of Justice. 1966. Letter addressed to Bahá'í youth in every land, dated June 10. Haifa, Israel: Bahá'í World Center.

————. 1991a. *The compilation of compilations prepared by the Universal House of Justice: 1963–1990.* Vol. 1. Maryborough, Victoria, Australia: Bahá'í Publications Australia.

————. 1991b. *The compilation of compilations prepared by the Universal House of Justice: 1963–1990.* Vol. 2. Maryborough, Victoria, Australia: Bahá'í Publications Australia.

————. 1992. *Manner of appealing to youth.* Letter addressed to individuals, dated October 28. Haifa, Israel: Bahá'í World Center.

————. 2001. *Century of light.* Haifa, Israel: Bahá'í World Center.

————. 2003. *To the Bahá'ís in the cradle of the faith.* Letter dated November 26. Haifa, Israel: Bahá'í World Center.

CHAPTER 24

Children and the Five Pillars of Islam: Practicing Spirituality in Daily Life

Afeefa Syeed and Nusaybah Ritchie

As a "way of life" or *deen* (see Haneef 1982; Voll 1991, 206), Islam not only encourages but expects Muslim children to be contributing members of civil society and to be engaged in efforts for social justice, as an integral part of their spiritual development and religious practice. The basic rituals of Islam, known as the "five pillars of Islam" (*Arkan al-Islam*), are foundational supports for the spiritual growth of Muslim children. They concretize the ethical guidelines against which children can make sound choices throughout their lives, and provide models and methods for how children may serve their local communities and society as a whole.

This chapter begins with a brief overview of how the concepts of spirituality and childhood are understood in Islam. Next, we will introduce each of the five pillars of Islam and discuss them in the context of Muslim children's experiences of Islam as a way of life. Finally, we will explore ways in which the practice of the pillars of Islam is playing an increasingly significant role in shaping how children view themselves as contributing members of the global community.

Throughout we will use the Qur'an and the Sunnah (traditions of Prophet Muhammad)[1]—Islam's two authentic sources of sacred knowledge—to support our view that the activities of observing, learning, contemplating, practicing, and sharing each pillar's rituals and their underlying meanings promote a child's sense of ethics, vocation, and social responsibility that is balanced with the child's development of a rich inner spiritual life marked by *taqwa* (God-consciousness), *iman* (faith), and *ihsan* (virtue).

Although we are Muslims writing about Islam, we speak neither for the entire Islamic faith nor for all Muslims worldwide. The core identity we bring to this discussion is that of *Muslim*, meaning that we identify as humans who are engaged, by belief and action, in the willing submission to the One God, called Allah[2] in Arabic. We assert this core identity as part of our religion's mandate to avoid creating schisms or adhering to sects. While there are three major sects of Islam—Sunni, Shi'a, and Sufi— we choose not to identify ourselves with these or any other sects, which have arisen over the centuries mainly owing to political disputes. Rather, our approach is to avoid sectarianism by relying on the foundational sources of the Qur'an and Sunnah, which provide the normative and prescriptive framework subscribed to by adherents of Islam throughout the world.

As we will describe, our conviction is that the beliefs and practices of the Islamic deen connect a child's private or inner dimension of spirituality with the child's behavior in the public realm, especially in terms of ethical choices, vocation, and community service. We describe the five pillars of Islam as rituals that support children in both the private and public realms, serving as threshold spaces connecting the two.

Spirituality in Islam

Since this chapter is concerned with spirituality, and yet our focus is ostensibly on ritual, we would like to recognize a trend in intellectual thought that pits spirituality against both religion and ritual, as if religious rituals rob the individual of his or her spirituality. Muslims are aware that Islam is frequently criticized for overemphasizing ritual, and the religious laws that govern ritual, to the detriment of spirituality:

> [T]o Western eyes this faith appears to be a "lawyers' religion," whose theologians in addition, if not as a matter of priority, have to be legal experts, because Islam tries indeed to shape and regulate the entire course of a believer's day. (Hofmann 1997, 41)

The spiritual and ritual aspects of Islam are often portrayed as existing at opposite poles, represented by conflicting branches of Islam. We argue that, instead of empty rituals performed mindlessly by rote, the five pillars of Islam are meant to enhance the inner spirituality of Muslims, including children, while connecting them with an outer community of believers as well as with Allah. Islam necessitates both ritual and spiritual awareness performed in balance with one another and practiced in accordance with the Qur'an and Sunnah. Spirituality is not the sole domain of any single sect of Islam. Concern for the spiritual dimension of Islam is inseparable from concern for ritual observance:

> An 'Ibabah [worship] devoid of spirit, though correct in procedure, is like a man handsome in appearance but lacking in character and an 'Ibadah full of spirit but defective in execution is like a man noble in character but deformed in appearance. (Mawdudi 1980, 97)

Furthermore, ritual observances in themselves constitute a form of spiritual experience. Since many rituals in Islam are performed in community, a certain consistency and conformity in practice enhances cooperation and spiritual feelings of brotherhood and sisterhood. Making sure one is properly observing ritual is also a method of developing spiritual awareness, concentration, and discipline in the service of obeying Allah. Attention to the rules of ritual is not intended to promote a concern for outward appearances. It should manifest a desire to please Allah and avoid what displeases Him, not according to one's own human whims and guesses but according to the divine specifications He has revealed through His Prophet.

The quality of desiring to do what pleases Allah and avoid what displeases Him is rooted in a spiritual state of simultaneously fearing Allah, loving Him, and holding Him in awe—this state is called taqwa (God-consciousness). Being one of the *muttaqeen*, or those who have taqwa, is a level of spirituality all Muslims must constantly strive for in their worship. Muslims who are strong in their level of iman (faith) are called the *mu'mineen*. The pillars of iman (*Arkan al-Iman*) are to believe in Allah, His angels, His revealed scriptures, all of His messengers, the Day of Resurrection and Reckoning, and to believe in Allah's determination of all affairs. Another spiritual quality for which all Muslims should strive is ihsan (virtue). Ihsan is defined as worshipping Allah as if we could see Him; and knowing that although we cannot see Him, He definitely sees us. Those who worship Allah at this level of spirituality are called the *muhsineen*, or those who have ihsan.

These concepts are familiar to Muslims regardless of sect and are firmly established in the Qur'an and Sunnah. As Muslim children throughout the world learn the beliefs and practice the rituals of Islam they are guided in how to promote their own experiences of such inner spiritual qualities as taqwa, iman, and ihsan, among others.

Childhood in Islam

The Qur'an establishes the integrity of every child and his or her sacred connection to the Creator (*Al Khaliq*) well before the child's birth. Allah asserts His total dominion over the creation of life and His intimate knowledge of everyone (Qur'an 42:49–50). Allah's descriptions in the Qur'an of how He fashions the embryo and fetus serve to emphasize the power and intentionality of Allah's Will as well as to underscore the utter dependency on Allah of every human being (Qur'an 23:12–14).

The Qur'an and Sunnah inform us that each child is born free from any sin or blemish. The newborn child is born in a natural state (*fitrah*), which is inclined toward the good. The idea of "original sin" is antithetical to the Muslim concept of fitrah:

> The notion of Original Sin is one which Islam emphatically denies, affirming that every human being comes into the world innocent and sinless. Accordingly, he will be held accountable only for what he himself inscribes upon the unblemished *tabula rasa* of his nature, not for what his ancestor Adam (or anyone else whomsoever) did or did not do. (Haneef 1995, 182)

One of the most important roles a parent has "is to help children maintain the original nature (fitrah) in their hearts," and training children in performing the pillars of Islam is an important method of helping them maintain their fitrah (Mohamed 2003, 21).

As the child grows, he or she enters three stages of development according to one model of childhood proposed in Islamic tradition (Magid 2003). The first seven years are the years of play and exploration. During this time, parents and other adults are to see that the child is protected while also being encouraged to discover the wonders around him or her. It is important to note that children who have not reached puberty are not required to observe the rituals prescribed through the pillars.

The second seven years of the child's life are the years of discipline and learning. At around the age of seven, children reach what is called the "age of discretion" roughly equivalent to what others have called the "age of reason," when children can discern between right and wrong and begin to make ethical decisions. From age seven to fourteen, or the "age of sponsorship," the child learns Islamic manners, the consequences of behavior, and how each of us is connected to the other. Parents and community leaders coach children in how to perform the pillars of Islam. During this time, children start to be disciplined for not performing the Islamic prayer, *salat*. Children become adults in Islam in that they become responsible before Allah and the community for their beliefs and actions; however, they remain under the sponsorship of their parents and other community elders. The father's role as *wilayah* (custodian or sponsor) to the children is increasingly recognized, whereas the mother's connection to the children continues to remain strong throughout their lives.

During the last seven years, from fourteen to twenty-one, children are befriended by their parents and other adults. Adults welcome them into society as equals in brotherhood and sisterhood, although there is no formal induction ceremony to mark adulthood. Now that children have been properly introduced to the tenets and practices of the faith, the Qur'an states that they are to be held fully accountable for their actions. Friendship and understanding between elders and these young adults will further increase their sense of belonging, duty, and spirituality.

Prophet Muhammad's caring and respect for children and their love for him is well established in Islam, as exemplified by traditions related to the warmth with which they greeted each other. Anas Ibn Maalik, the Prophet's servant and Companion, "reported that when he used to walk with the Prophet and when they would pass by a group of children, the Prophet would extend greetings of peace to them" (Ash-Shulhoob 2003, 65). When Prophet Muhammad immigrated to Medina from Makkah (Mecca), crowds of young girls from Medina greeted him with a song of welcome still sung by Muslim youth around the world to this day. Prophet Muhammad's wife Aisha reported that "when the noble Prophet would see her [his daughter Fatima] coming towards him, he greeted her and stood up in respect and kissed her. He then escorted and seated her. In the same way she would greet and stood up in respect and kissed when the noble Prophet would visit her" (Sunan of Abu Dawood, in Talukdar 2004, 77).

The Five Pillars

Having defined the concepts of spirituality and childhood in Islam, the discussion will now turn to how the core practices of the religion, the five pillars of Islam (Arkan al-Islam), support children in the individual, spiritual dimensions of their faith—the experiences of taqwa, iman, and ihsan, for example—and the practical expressions of their faith in terms of ethical choices, vocation, and community involvement. The five pillars of Islam provide concrete training in the kinds of service-oriented activities and life choices they are expected to make as Muslims. As Lang (1994) has indicated, "The five pillars of the Islamic faith, which are the ritual embodiment of Islam's ideology, conspicuously unite humanity's duty to God and individual's obligations to humanity" (124).

Across Muslim communities and within Muslim families, the intergenerational initiation into religious practices such as prayer, fasting, and charity can be readily observed. Whether it is sending the child out with a bowl of food to the beggar who comes to the door in a village in Kashmir, or having a four-year-old put coins into the charity box in a mosque in New York, children are taught to take responsibility and carry out "important" tasks. Through the performance of these tasks, children develop awareness of the spiritual dimension of their daily lives, build relationships with the people around them, and integrate themselves as valued members of their religious community.

SHAHADA: THE DECLARATION OF BELIEF IN ISLAM

Practicing Muslims hear and say the *shahada* (declaration of belief in Islam) many times throughout their day. It is heard at every significant event from birth to death, it is repeated in the call to prayer and within the prayer itself, and it is the single statement that one needs to make to become a Muslim. For children as well as adults, the repeated hearing and saying of the shahada reinforces their identity as Muslims.

The meaning of the shahada is the core belief of Islam, and its utterance is Islam's central practice. The first part of the shahada—"There is no deity except Allah"—is at once an affirmation of belief in Allah and a negation of any other deities or partners in Allah's divinity. The second part of the shahada is "Muhammad is the Messenger of Allah."

Whenever a Muslim says the shahada, he or she declares belief in the Oneness of Allah (*tawheed*) and the oneness of his or her religious community (*ummah*) united under Allah's final Message to humanity, revealed to Prophet Muhammad. With this belief comes a sense of wholeness, of order within a seemingly chaotic universe, and a center to which all matters can be oriented. Children learn the shahada as a simple statement of Allah's divine attribute of Absolute Oneness (*Al Ahad, Al Wahid*). Understanding the Oneness of Allah gives proper meaning to the rest of the pillars of Islam, which must be performed for the purpose of worshipping Allah alone.

Children begin their lifelong quest to connect with Allah by studying Allah's sacred revelation to humanity, the Qur'an, and contemplating the meanings and implications of Allah's various attributes. By learning and reciting suras (chapters) from the Qur'an in Arabic, children are preparing for the requirements of prayer while also acquiring tools to boost self-confidence. For example, children recite the last three suras of the Qur'an to feel empowered in times of fear or anxiety. These suras refer in simple language to the Oneness of Allah and seeking refuge in Allah from all sorts of dangers.

Striving to emulate Allah's attributes is a spiritual practice that impacts children's choice of vocation as they seek to live lives that reflect the divine qualities. For example, careers in medicine and social work reflect Allah's attributes of the Most Merciful and Compassionate (*Ar Rahman, Ar Rahim*) and the Protector (*Al Muhaimin*). The pursuit of scientific knowledge is in keeping with Allah's command to ponder Him as the Creator (Qur'an 2:164). Striving to emulate Allah's attributes of the Wise (*Al Hakeem*), the Just (*Al 'Adl*), and the Source of Peace (*Al Salaam*) might inspire children to become teachers, judges, and peacemakers.

When children learn about Prophet Muhammad, they discover the best model of a human being who practiced Islam throughout his daily life in a way that pleased

Allah. Muslim children's sense of vocation is influenced by learning about the life of Prophet Muhammad, his wives, and his Companions. Lives devoted to trade, scholarship, nursing, politics, family, teaching, social services, and the like can be traced back directly to the Prophet and his community.

In addition to its impact on children's vocation, the belief in Allah and the prophecy of Muhammad provide the basis for the ethical system in Islam that children will use to make choices throughout their lives. Since the Qur'an is Allah's unaltered, divine message to humanity and Prophet Muhammad was the living example and divinely sanctioned interpreter of the Qur'an, both must be referred to when making ethical decisions. Therefore, knowledge of the Qur'an and Sunnah, as well as knowledge of Arabic, the language of these sacred revelations, become critical in terms of teaching children how to make informed ethical choices within the framework of Islam.

SALAT: COMMUNICATING WITH ALLAH

Having accepted the Oneness of the Creator, we are asked by that Creator to regularly communicate with Him. This communication is not something He needs, but it is a requirement. Praying to Allah helps us to attain spiritual peace. By "talking" to Allah, we can be more reflective of our actions, our intentions, and our aspirations. Without this daily ritual, we can easily lose our spiritual grounding and forget the importance of serving our Creator with humility.

Salat is the Arabic term most often translated as "prayer," but this English word does not fully convey the dimensions embodied in the Arabic. The Arabic word *du'a* more accurately corresponds to what most people understand by the words prayer or supplication. Most du'a can be made at any time, anywhere, as a means of contacting the Divine, usually in the form of acknowledging one's need of Allah and requesting Allah's help. Making du'a is more spontaneous and informal than salat.

The salat is formal, requires preparation, and is precise in its timing, movements, and design. For children especially, learning these positions and movements is part natural imitation of adults, and part learning about concentration, self-control, and discipline. Because the salat is required at definite times of the day—between dawn and sunrise, early afternoon, midafternoon, sunset, and night—it is directly related to the natural world and its movements, to space and time. Furthermore, the direction of the prayer—toward the Ka'bah in Makkah—is a fixed geographic point and shared focus (*qiblah*) for all Muslims in prayer, providing the sense of a unified global community. The salat creates a natural rhythm in one's lifestyle (Hamid 1990) that is easily translatable to children, who desire routine and order in their lives. Children learn to be aware of their position in the world and changing conditions in the natural environment precisely because they must rely on it to carry out their acts of worship. At a young age, Muslim children discover how to ascertain the time of day by the sun's position in the sky and find the direction of the qiblah wherever they are.

Children appreciate that movement is a form of worship, not something to be condemned as overactive or disrespectful of sacred space. In fact, there is a high tolerance for children during prayer times in mosques. Children can be seen prancing about, playing, and mimicking the postures of adults in prayer. Children's involvement in the sacred space of the *masalla* (prayer area) has always been an important part of Islam. Prophet Muhammad recommended that the *imam* (prayer leader) should shorten his recitation of the Qur'an when he hears a child crying in the congregation, but tellingly did not recommend that the child be removed from the masalla. Even though the salat requires maximum concentration and is composed of an orderly and precise series of actions that must be performed correctly or else the prayer might be invalidated, men and women are permitted to carry children during the performance of salat (Mohamed 2003). Prophet Muhammad himself was the model for including young children within the sphere of adult prayer:

> The Prophet also loved his little granddaughter Umamah, who nearly always accompanied her mother Zaynab. Once or twice he brought her with him to the Mosque perched on his shoulder and kept her there while he recited the verses of the Koran, putting her down before the inclination and prostrations and restoring her to his shoulder when he resumed his upright position. (Lings 1983, 211)

To prepare for the performance of salat, believers must purify themselves with water by making *wudhu* (ritual cleansing). Wudhu teaches children that they are responsible for their hygiene and about the importance of cleanliness in our faith. The child must cleanse in a certain order and manner, making sure that water touches his or her hands, mouth, nose, face, arms, head, ears, and feet. This act of cleansing provides the child with the opportunity to reflect and to reconnect with his or her body and realize that prayer is based on a readiness to talk with the Creator. During wudhu, children reflect on what their hands have done, what their mouths have said, and where their feet have taken them. Have they been engaged in actions that please Allah?

In addition to its function as a preparation for salat, wudhu is also used to teach children self-control. Prophet Muhammad instructed his followers who become angry to stop and make wudhu so that their physical sense of calmness is restored. Washing with water can relax and cool down hot tempers; children are taught that they can use wudhu as a tool for anger management. Prophet Muhammad also instructed his followers to conserve water when making wudhu as a way to protect the natural resources Allah provides for our use.

Children frequently serve as the *muedhin* (caller) for daily prayers. The *adhan*, or call to prayer, is a simple one recited in Arabic, and parents and community leaders give children the responsibility of making the adhan to give them a sense of participation and acknowledgment. Calling believers to prayer is an honor for children at any age and any level of Qur'anic study. To lead the prayer, one must have reached the age of puberty and be well versed in the Qur'an. Leading prayer teaches children the importance of leadership in Islam. A child leading the prayers as the imam realizes that his or her actions are being followed closely and that others are counting on him or her to perform the prayer well. This experience prepares Muslim children for the responsibility of being role models and leading others.

ZAKAT AND SADAQA: SHARING THE WEALTH, SHARING OF OURSELVES

Islam emphasizes the importance of balancing the spiritual and material aspects of existence. Muslims strive to ensure that others are taken care of in this world. *Zakat,* the duty of Muslims to give a certain percentage of their wealth, means to "purify" or "cleanse" in Arabic. Our wealth is cleansed through giving it as we remember that it was not our actions alone that created our wealth, that our wealth is a provision from Allah, and that Allah is the Provider (*Ar Razzaq*). Children learn that adults are successful because they trust in Allah and fulfill their duties as believers. At the same time, material success is a test from Allah: Will Muslims remember their duty to share their wealth with others? Will they hoard money? Will they spend extravagantly while others are suffering around them?

Every human being carries the trust (*amaanah*) from Allah to be active in ensuring that social welfare is maintained for all. Islam teaches that the poor and the deprived have a "title" or a "right" to the wealth of the rich (Qur'an 70:24–25, 9:60). Those endowed with material wealth are called upon to meet this obligation, and if they do not respond to the call of the poor, Allah will call them to account for it. The funds that zakat is paid on will receive blessings from Allah and multiply because they have been properly cleansed. Those who do not pay zakat on their wealth will see it turn into non-beneficial wealth in this world, and it will testify against them in the next.

Children are taught to make concern for social welfare a natural part of their lives. Zakat is an obligation they see their elders meeting with confidence that this process of sharing is necessary for the good of the larger community. This is a tremendous lesson for children: that we are asked to give, not because it is a nice thing to do or makes us feel good, but because it is an action in which social justice is rooted. Sharing wealth is not a luxury or a choice; it is a fundamental part of what makes societies fair and equitable. The underprivileged in society have a right over those who have been privileged with wealth: "The one who needs to ask and the outcast have a title or share in your wealth" (Qur'an 51:19). In order to remove arrogance on the part of the giver and humiliation on the part of the receiver, giving charity should be done willingly, with a smile, and without reminders of one's generosity.

The other aspect of social welfare is *sadaqa* (voluntary charity). This act of sharing whatever is possible at any time, even sharing of ourselves, is encouraged and its scope extended so that even the poor can offer sadaqa (Hamid 1990). Children, who do not have access to wealth themselves, are encouraged to give sadaqa in many ways. Prophet Muhammad taught that removing a branch from the walkway, smiling at another person, helping someone with his luggage are all forms of sadaqa that can be practiced by children.

SAWM: KEEPING THE FAST

Fasting is a powerful means to achieve spiritual connection with Allah. Children learn that fasting is the fulfillment of an obligation (Qur'an 2:183–87) that Allah has required of other faith communities. In Islam, refraining from eating and drinking from dawn until sunset is the ritual requirement for fasting, but its spiritual implications run much deeper. While fasting, particularly during the blessed month of Ramadan, when fasting is obligatory, Muslims have the opportunity to better practice the tenets of their faith. Allah ordained fasting on humans primarily for them to gain taqwa, and Allah describes fasting as a shield against sins. Fasting also promotes peace (salaam), generosity through voluntary charity (sadaqa), patience (*sabr*), thankfulness (*shukur*), and spirituality through prayer (salat). Prophet Muhammad practiced these aspects of Islam with particular intensity during the month of Ramadan.

Experiencing firsthand how others suffer because they lack the basic needs of food and drink instills in children a sense of solidarity with the poor and oppressed. In addition, the discipline of fasting teaches Muslims to become aware of their health and how what they consume affects physical and emotional well-being. Children are taught that Prophet Muhammad encouraged us to manage our eating habits by not taking more than is necessary and leaving aside space in our stomachs for digestion. The Prophet's saying "A Muslim is not a believer if he goes to bed and his neighbor is hungry" is reiterated. It is important for a fasting person not to get angry when fasting; if a fasting person is annoyed or provoked to anger, he or she is advised to repeat, "I am fasting."

Again, children who have not reached puberty will not be required to fast, but many do practice fasting between meals or for half-days. They associate special Ramadan foods and treats with fasting. In some regions, work and school are interrupted during the fasting month and certain expectations are made about how much will get done during this time. Children in non-Muslim-majority communities understand that not everyone participates in Ramadan; they can still share the principles of Ramadan with those of other faiths in their schools, neighborhoods, and other community forums. Eid al Fitr is the festival marking the end of Ramadan and is a joyous time for all Muslims, especially children. Communities across the globe celebrate Eid by praying in large gatherings, visiting friends and relatives, eating special sweets and pastries, and wearing new clothes.

In the same way that prayer sanctifies the day with spiritual fortification, Ramadan helps to punctuate the year with a time for remembrance and reconnection. Since Muslims follow the lunar calendar, the timing of Ramadan changes every year, arriving around ten days earlier each time around. When it comes during the winter season, the fasting day is shorter and the physical sacrifice is less. Ramadan in summer means more sacrifice with hope for more spiritual reward. Witnessing the eventual, slow movement of Ramadan through the years as they grow older, children relate to their natural environment and the rhythms of creation of which they themselves are an integral part.

THE HAJJ: PILGRIMAGE TO AN UMMATIC PERSONALITY

To make the Hajj is to heed the call of the Creator and disrobe one's self of material concerns. It is to understand that the collective called "humanity" is indeed a reality and that our duties to Allah and our relationships with each other should not be taken for granted. During the Hajj, individuals learn to understand and forgive others who come from all walks of life, from every corner of the globe, and who are at various levels of commitment to the Creator. Hajj is a time to practice the Islamic ideal of brotherhood and sisterhood and to learn that experiences of injustice, conflict, and hardship must inspire us to pursue peace, social justice, and mutual respect according to our religious values and teachings. Allah states, "O Mankind! We created you from a single pair of a male and female and made you into nations and tribes that you may know each other not that you may despise each other" (Qur'an 49:13).

Many of the rites of Hajj go back to the Prophet Ibrahim, his wife Hajar, and their son Prophet Ishmael. Children are reminded that as Muslims we follow the same religion as Prophet Ibrahim. Remembering and reenacting events that took place in another time bonds those who perform the rituals to ancient traditions and to all the Muslims in history who ever performed the same rituals. The Hajj reflects the "ummatic"—global Muslim community or *ummah*—aspect of being Muslim. Pilgrims performing the Hajj rituals in Makkah present the ultimate scene of multiculturalism and diversity. Returning pilgrims (Hajjis) relate their unique Hajj experiences to eager children back in their hometowns, cities, and villages. In schools and around dinner tables across the globe, Muslim children pore over photographs showing the millions of Hajjis congregated in a relatively small area during a short time frame to fulfill their obligations to their Lord (*Ar Rabb*). Almost invariably, it is the visual impact of the simple Hajj attire—two white pieces of seamless white cloth—and the sea of people of all nationalities and ethnicities performing the prayers in unison that impresses young people most. The stories of Ibrahim, his wife, and their child are recounted to children who relate to them on a basic level: a mother and child left in the desert with no water; only prayer and perseverance reward them with water from the well of Zamzam.

For those who do not make the Hajj, the end of the rituals brings the celebration of Eid ul Adha which commemorates Ibrahim's willingness to obey Allah when asked to sacrifice his son and Allah's Mercy in replacing the sacrifice with a ram. Children are taught this story with the lesson of trust in the Most Merciful (*Ar Rahman*) as a cornerstone of Islam. At this time, children may witness the ritual slaughtering of a sheep in commemoration. They learn that animals are not to be mistreated and that humans are placed as custodians on earth to take care of creation. Children are taught a special du'a that is said before the sacrifice and learn that the sacrificial animal is made calm by stroking and being given water to drink. Meat of the animal is then distributed to the needy and is considered a gift from Allah to sustain humanity. Children are involved in this pillar by making replicas of the Ka'bah, drinking Zamzam water, and welcoming back pilgrims from Makkah. On Eid ul Adha, as with Eid ul Fitr, special congregational prayers and community celebrations are organized in which children's participation is a special part.

The Five Pillars Supporting Muslim Communities across the Globe

Muslim children, like their parents, come from every country in the world. Islam has long been an international religion. As it spread after the seventh century, it took on the flavor and nuances of the cultures it encountered. For the most part, integration into existing cultures was in keeping with the faith. Allah states in the Qur'an (30:22): "Among His signs is the creation of the heavens and the earth, and the variations in your languages and your colors: Verily in this are signs for those who know." Prophet Muhammad and the leaders who succeeded him encouraged multicultural relations and cultural sensitivity. For example, Prophet Muhammad noted to his wife Aisha the cultural preferences of the natives of Medina (*Ansar*) with regard to entertainment at wedding celebrations (Abu Ghudddah 2002, 58–59).

As Islam spread, cultural variations influenced certain practices. The five pillars of Islam are shared by all Muslims, however, regardless of their geographic or cultural identity. One Muslim may pray with his hands on his chest, another may pray with his hands to his side, but both strive to pray according to legitimate scholarly interpretations and both teach his or her children that prayer is basic to Islam. All Muslims try to follow Prophet Muhammad's example by breaking their fasts with dates or water, yet Muslims in Jordan, Pakistan, Indonesia, China, Senegal, and the United States will enjoy vastly different cuisines for their main meals.

Ideally, in Muslim-majority communities, the social systems and family life are organized so that children see the tenets of Islam practiced around them as a normal part of life. They are taught by example, not just by their parents, but also by their teachers, peers, extended family, and society at large. It is only natural to fast when others are doing so, and it only makes sense to pray when the call to prayer is heard from a neighborhood mosque. In these places, the support networks make it easier to teach children about spirituality, and children's practice of Islam follows seamlessly.

In contrast, Muslims living as minorities face constant reminders that they are minorities living in a non-Muslim-majority land. Their children are not exposed to the same practices outside the home as they are inside. There is often no uncle, teacher, grandparent, or coach to reinforce the teachings through example. In Muslim-majority countries, the salat is an integral part of daily life. The adhan is called five times a day from numerous minarets. Businesses and schools break for salat, and prayer times are a convenient way to organize one's activities: "Meet me between the noon and midafternoon prayer." On the other hand, in communities where Muslims are in the minority, there are virtually no auditory or visual indicators of salat in the public sphere. Nevertheless, children are taught to tell time by the sun's position. To reduce isolation and build a sense of Muslim community, it becomes crucial to establish and make the extra effort to attend congregational prayers in the home as well as the mosque. In general, Muslim minorities must be far more conscientious in teaching their children the sacred sources and rituals, and the underlying spirituality of their religion.

Until recently, even sizable or Muslim-majority communities oftentimes did not have access to authentic religious sources without the intervention of forces like governments or politically polarized organizations. Consequently, regard for the spiritual aspects of the faith and interest in Islamic scholarship waned. Unfortunately, in such constrictive sociopolitical environments, ritual practice devolved into a series of motions and mystifying rituals. In the former Soviet republics, for example, where religious expression was suppressed, even though large communities had been culturally Muslim for centuries, an entire generation came up without full comprehension of the spiritual side of the Islamic faith. Children, alongside adults, are reacquainting themselves with the five pillars of Islam and their integral spirituality.

At present, vibrant discussions are taking place within Muslim communities on issues of governance, theocracy, and scriptural interpretation. Still, Muslims throughout the world continue to teach their children the same five pillars of Islam, with increasing emphasis on the spiritual, ethical, and social implications of these rituals. Parents, teachers, and community leaders are reawakening to the notion that it is not enough for their young ones to imitate them; they must become more aware of *why* they do what they do. Children, in this age of the Internet and satellite communications, are being taught that to practice Islam well they must care for people in their own neighborhoods as well as for the range of human faces they see on their computer and television screens. They are learning suras at deeper levels of comprehension with more emphasis on linguistic meanings and exploring Qur'anic links to the Sunnah. The Qur'an and Sunnah are calling on youth to worship Allah, reflect within themselves, and take peaceful action for social justice in their families, local communities, and the world at large.

How will this sort of discussion impact Muslim children? We believe that, at the very least, it will bring to light the need for Muslim children everywhere to have access to authentic religious sources, learn Arabic as an indispensable tool of religious scholarship, define their own approaches to modernity within the context of their religion, and empower their peers, as well as their elders, with authentic knowledge of what the faith stands for and how the five pillars can support them in the spiritual choices they will make throughout their lives.

Notes

1. Muslims invoke Allah Almighty's Peace and Blessings on Prophet Muhammad, and all prophets, whenever their names are mentioned.
2. Muslims proclaim Allah's Glory, Greatness, and other attributes whenever He is mentioned.

References

Abu Ghuddah, Shakh 'Abd al-Fattah. 2002. *Islamic manners*. N.p.: Awakening.
Ash-Shulhoob, Fuad ibn 'Abdul-'Azeez. 2003. *The book of manners*. Riyadh: Darussalam.
Hamid, Abdul Wahid. 1990. *Islam, the natural way*. London: Muslim Education and Literary Services.
Haneef, Suzanne. 1982. *What everyone should know about Islam and Muslims*. Chicago: Kazi Publications.
Hoffman, Murad. 1997. *Islam: The alternative*. Beltsville, Md.: Amana.
Lang, Jeffrey. 1995. *Struggling to surrender*. 2nd ed. Beltsville, Md.: Amana.
Lings, Martin [Abu Bakar Siraj al-Din]. 1983. *Muhammad: His life based on the earliest sources*. Kuala Lumpur, Malaysia: Foundation for Traditional Studies.

Magid, Mohammad. 2003. Rights and Responsibilities of Parents and Children in Islam. Lecture presented at the ADAMS Center, Sterling, Virginia.

Mawdudi, Abul A'La. 1980. *Towards understanding Islam*. London: Islamic Foundation.

Mohamed, Mamdouh N. 2003. *Salaat: The Islamic prayer from A to Z*. Dr. Mamdouh N. Mohamed. N.p.: Author.

Talukdar, Mohammad H. R. 2004. *Ten women of paradise*. Kuala Lumpur, Malaysia: Noordeen.

Voll, John O. 1991. Islamic issues for Muslims in the United States. In *The Muslims of America*, edited by Yvonne Yazbeck Haddad, 205–16. New York: Oxford University Press.

CHAPTER 25

Value-Creating Education: A Nichiren Buddhist Perspective

Monte Joffee

The Renaissance Charter School (TRCS), a New York City school of 500 students in grades K–12, opened in 1993 and converted to charter status in 2000. TRCS founders hoped to create a school in which spirituality, meaning making, and ethical action were core values. As a cofounder and the school's principal, I brought to my work perspectives I gained from my practice of Nichiren Buddhism.

The school's founders envisioned nurturing students of character and capability who as adults would rise to levels of leadership and help reinvigorate their communities, hence the school's motto, "Developing Leaders for the Renaissance of New York." In addition to a strong academic program, we would emphasize projects and small-group work to strengthen the net of social and ethical obligations and "community involvement" to build both norms of service and social action.

If rituals have a powerful effect on developing a spiritual life, schools, as institutions imbued in rituals (Erickson 1982; Herrera 1988; Jackson 1990; McLaren 1993), have great impact in guiding or impeding this quest. Ratcliff (2001) notes, for example, how the seemingly simple school ritual of students walking through the hallway can have an effect on their spirituality. The premise of TRCS's founders was that a guiding school ethos would permeate the very life and walls of the school—affecting both routines and instruction—to develop character, ethical awareness, and spirituality.

As I observed our middle school's dismissal recently I saw strong evidence that our routines were promoting such latent spirituality. In most urban middle schools students are quickly (and hopefully orderly) evacuated from the building at the end of the day. Rather than being pushed out of the building by staff, the approximate hundred students who were dismissed from class gathered in the school's common area where they spontaneously sat on tables in loose self-selected groups for about a half an hour. Faces were relaxed, conversation was animated, friendships were highly evident, and factors such as race, class, age, gender, and academic ability were not apparent in the groupings. This simple ritual promoted several characteristics of innate spirituality described by Hay and Nye (1998). Students were immersed in a "relational consciousness" as they intensely interacted with peers, their environment, and themselves. There was a sense of oneness, peace, and an acute sensing of the here-and-now.

At the same time, in another room, a group of staff members was scrutinizing, over and over again, a videotape of a very unfortunate fight that had broken out after a recent basketball game. The leaders of the school had come into school over the weekend to begin discussions about the facts, causes, and impact of the regrettable incident. One student had confessed to starting the fight. Four staff members, however, spent the majority of the week procuring witness statements, interviewing players, speaking to parents, and, most important, engaging in reflection. Reminiscent of the jury proceedings in the film *Twelve Angry Men,* the result of these deliberations was the forging of a consensus about the incident that was radically different from the boy's statement. The staff members had modeled ethical action and it prevented great damage to the life of one student; this devotion of time and care might very well have not happened at another school. The slow, nuanced, and communal response resulted in a stronger and more just and ethical community as well.

As the school's cofounder and principal, while rigorously maintaining the separation of church and state and honoring the belief systems of others, I believe my values from Nichiren Buddhism have contributed to the culture of the school. Buddhism recognizes the concept of "dependent origination" (Japanese, *Engi;* Sanskrit, *pratitya samutpada*) that posits a fluid web interconnecting all things, people, and events. Whereas most of the literature on the acquisition of spirituality among youth focuses on the individual dimension (an excellent review of the literature is contained in Mojzisek 2001), as a Nichiren Buddhist I tend to look at inputs that may encourage the growth of spirituality: building a caring culture, providing time and space for relationship building, shielding students and staff as much as possible from some of the destructive aspects of the current accountability movement, and strengthening the community of caregivers who actually have the responsibility of inculcating values.

We were all horrified to learn of the fight after the basketball game. But Nichiren Buddhism views the problems and ambiguities of life as the entry point into spirituality and broad religious sentiment. "When we dig into the inner reaches of our own being, the common foundation of life that all people share comes into view. This foundation is none other than the eternal life of the universe" (Ikeda 1997). From the standpoint of Nichiren Buddhism, spirituality is thus seen as an individual's deep inner reflection to respond to the strict realities of life. The spiritual revolution emanates upward and outward from the core of life to manifest as ethical awareness and, finally, as ethical action.

The Buddhist Concept of Spirituality as Viewed through Nichiren's Teachings

This process is also called the theory of the Nine Consciousnesses (Sanskrit, *vijnana*) in Mahayana Buddhism. To simplify, the Ninth Consciousness (Skt, *amala*) is the spiritual state in which an individual is in communion with universal life force. This alters the equation of all the invisible webs of causes and effects that comprise the Eighth Consciousness (Skt, *ayala*). Ethical stance, embedded deep in spiritual awareness, lies within the Seventh Consciousness (Skt, *mano*), which affects ethical decision making, a part of the "conscious consciousness" of the Sixth level. This, in turn, is the basis of our ethical actions that are based on our sensory consciousnesses, which constitute the first five levels of consciousness (English Buddhist Dictionary Committee 2002).

Thus Mahayana Buddhism considers spirituality to be a condition interconnected and embedded in daily actions within the mundane world. According to the scholar T'ien-t'ai (538–97), who clarified Mahayana teachings as they expanded into China, the state of Buddhahood is seen as a life condition of absolute happiness that exists within all the other conditions human beings experience; likewise the other life states all are contained within Buddhahood. The Buddha nature—brilliant and unique for each individual—is seen as the sustaining force that generates the wisdom and energy necessary to navigate fully and well through life. The possibility of attaining Buddhahood thus exists equally within all people.

Nichiren Buddhism, as one example of a wide variety of Buddhist approaches to ethics, presents an interesting case study of how Buddhism views the fostering of spirituality in childhood and adolescence. It is based on the life of the Japanese Buddhist priest Nichiren (1222–83), who, against the backdrop of the military shogunate and an array of entrenched clerics, called for grounding Buddhist practice on the fundamental and humanistic principles of Shakyamuni's Lotus Sutra. He identified what he deemed to be its essential teachings, which if invoked, he asserted, would liberate the human spirit and make it directly accessible to all people without the intervention of esotericism or clergy. He was adamant that as people embraced the essential teachings of the Lotus Sutra, "the threefold world will become the Buddha land, and how could a Buddha land ever decline?" (Gosho Translation Committee, 25). This was his call for universal world peace.

Nichiren Buddhism does not have a formal theory about the development of spirituality in children and adolescents. The Buddhist view of the dignity of human life, however, makes it clear that this is a quality of potentiality that is inherent in all stages of life, from earliest childhood to the final stages of the dying process. Further, the future-oriented outlook of Buddhism creates a natural emphasis on youth. Within the Soka Gakkai International (SGI), a lay organization of some twelve million Nichiren Buddhist members in 190 countries and territories, youth have always been accorded a visible and responsible role. This reflects strong faith both in their capacities now as well as in their future promise. Daisaku Ikeda, president of the SGI, has written numerous books for children and young people, including *The Way of Youth* (2000), a collection of responses to questions posed by young adults on complicated issues surrounding friendship, families, tolerance, peer pressure, emotions, education, work, and building character. Writing from a Buddhist perspective, Ikeda nurtures spirituality but not sectarianism.

Spirituality is thus seen as an individual's capacity to challenge and surmount his or her personal limitations and the shackles of circumstances through courageous and compassionate action. This outlook is clearly evident in the following interchange between Nichiren and one of his followers, an anguished mother who had written to him about the illness of her daughter. In his response, although at the time suffering himself from the privations of exile, Nichiren demonstrated the state of his spirituality—his compassion and confidence that prayers can awaken the universal forces necessary to surmount difficulties. He exhorted his follower to summon forth similar faith and courage in order to activate these forces and prolong the life of her child:

> Since I heard from you about Kyo'o, I have been praying to the gods of the sun and moon for her every moment of the day. . . . Wherever your daughter may frolic or play, no harm will come to her; she will move about without fear like the lion king. . . . But your faith alone will determine all these things. A sword is useless in the hands of a coward. The mighty sword of the Lotus Sutra must be wielded by one courageous in faith. (Gosho Translation Committee, 412)

Over the course of subsequent centuries Nichiren Buddhism lost much of the founder's revolutionary fervor and humanistic impulse. This historical trend was sharply reversed in 1930 with the formation by Tsunesaburo Makiguchi (1871–1944) and Josei Toda (1900–1958) of the Soka Kyoiku Gakkai ("Educational Value Creation Society"), the forerunner of today's SGI.

Makiguchi's life provides a vivid example within a single individual's lifespan of the development of spirituality, its representation in the form of ethical stance, and finally its transformation into ethical action. Abandoned by his parents in his infancy, Makiguchi was raised by relatives in a remote and impoverished fishing and agricultural village off the Sea of Japan. At the age of fourteen, Makiguchi traveled alone to the island of Hokkaido, then Japan's frontier outpost. Largely self-educated, having attended only four years of primary school and studying briefly at the Sapporo Normal School, Makiguchi began working in the Japanese equivalent of the one-room schoolhouse, where he struggled with the challenges of teaching socially and economically marginalized children with limited resources. His incipient ethical stance was based on an egalitarian appreciation of the dignity and worth of all students:

> They are all equally students. From the viewpoint of education, what difference could there be between them and other students? Even though they may be covered with dust or dirt, the brilliant fight of life shines from their soiled clothes. Why does no one try to see this? The teacher is all that stands between them and the cruel discrimination of society. (Ikeda 1996)

Pagan (2001) theorizes that Makiguchi's relative escape from Japan's regimented form of education actually enabled him to think powerfully and independently about life and education and led him to resist the encroaching radical conservatism and jingoism of Japan's educational establishment and government. His own rugged, adventurous, and close-to-nature youth led to a fascination with the interdependence of the human being, society, and the physical world. In his first published work, *A Geography of Human Life* (Bethel 2002), Makiguchi describes the interconnectedness of people and their natural world. "The earth, for Makiguchi, was a miracle. Life was a miracle, and he saw life vibrating and pulsating through all phenomena" (Bethel 2002, xiv). In his major work, *The System of Value-Creating Pedagogy* (Makiguchi 1930), he describes how education could nurture character. For Makiguchi character is synonymous with spirituality: the recognition of the unique inborn potential of each individual and his or her ability to create value. At the basis of all of Makiguchi's works is his theory of value creation. He concluded that "the highest and ultimate objective of life is happiness . . . A happy life signifies nothing but the state of existence in which one can gain and create value in full" (Bethel 1973, 50). Makiguchi's notion of happiness entailed meaning, purpose, and social and ethical obligations, and leads to social engagement and action.

Makiguchi's career as a principal was brilliant; especially notable was how he implemented many of his humanistic ideas despite his clashes with the rising conservatism and nationalism of his times. Makiguchi placed great importance on the development of the teacher's spirituality as the environment that would nurture the student's character. "The teacher needs the sensitivity of a midwife to aid the self-actualization process without trying to control it, to be ready and standing by but not standing in the way" (Bethel 1989, 104). Humbly, the teacher must find value within the living environment, discover the physical and psychological principles that pervade life, and apply these principles to create new value (168). He strongly contended that the home and community had abdicated important educational responsibilities to the school with the effect of "[turning] young people's entire childhood and adolescence into a study hall at the expense of all else" (151). As a result, students become apathetic and lose considerable amounts of physical and emotional well-being. Although he was unable to implement this aspect of his pedagogy, Makiguchi recommended a program of half-day schooling in which students would spend their time outside school in family, community, or vocational pursuits. This would result in "the instilling of joy and appreciation for work" (156) and would revitalize the purpose of study.

Makiguchi embraced Nichiren Buddhism in 1928 at the age of fifty-seven. He was delighted by the similarities between the theory of value he authored and the philosophy of Nichiren; both were invitations for individuals to actively participate in and contribute to life's symphony of interdependence. Thus, his encounter with Nichiren Buddhism was through the eyes of a person who had already seriously contemplated the spiritual nature of life and the possibilities of education in awakening this capacity.

He formed a lay society of Nichiren Buddhists, the Soka Kyoiku Gakkai, which grew to some three thousand families by the outbreak of World War II. Displaying his ethical development, up until his arrest in 1943 at the age of seventy-two, Makiguchi maintained his public speaking appearances, attending more than 240 meetings during the height of the war and defending rights such as the freedoms of thought, expression, and worship; he also railed against governmental authorities and clergy who imposed thought and religious controls.

Gebert and George (2000) reviewed wartime government indictment and interrogation documents about Makiguchi, as well as the letters he wrote home from jail. Makiguchi was charged for expressing opinions such as "the emperor is a common mortal." Although the government portrayed the war as a "holy war" (*seisen*), he labeled it a "national disaster" stemming from Japan's adherence to mistaken religions and philosophies. According to Gebert and George, the documents reveal a person who was "extraordinarily composed" and exhibiting a "philosophical transcendence of his present difficulties combined with an unshaken commitment to pragmatic action." Makiguchi was imprisoned for some five hundred days until his death in 1944.

The link between spirituality, ethical stance, and ethical action can also be seen in Makiguchi's closest disciple, Josei Toda. Imprisoned with his mentor, Toda was determined to unlock the mysteries of the Lotus Sutra for the sake of the common people during his ordeal. "Through thoroughly pursuing the question 'What is the Buddha?' he came to realize that the Buddha is none other than the self, and the great life of the universe; that these two—the self and the universe—are in fact one" (Ikeda et al. 2001, 266). Toda came to the conclusion that the powerful "Bodhisattvas of the Earth" referred to in the Lotus Sutra were none other than common people who manifested their potential, a process he later coined as "human revolution." He believed that the majestic "Ceremony in the Air" portrayed in the Lotus Sutra was the assemblage of myriads of strong and creative common people determined to create a victorious world on the basis of their personal human revolutions. From his release in 1945 to his death in 1958, Toda dedicated himself to building the Soka Gakkai into an organization capable of nurturing numbers of such people sufficient to affect every stratum of society.

The Development of Soka Education

Toda's mission was inherited by his closest disciple, Daisaku Ikeda, who assumed the organization's presidency in 1960. Under his leadership, the SGI became an international organization that supported peace, culture, and education.

"Soka education" is a term created by Ikeda to describe an educational program that nurtures capable, spiritually centered, and socially active youth. Starting in the 1970s, Ikeda founded Soka University of Japan, a group of K–12 private "Soka schools" in Japan, and "Soka kindergartens" in Hong Kong, Singapore, and Malaysia. More recently he founded Soka University of America in California and a Soka kindergarten in Brazil. On a broader scale Soka education is a set of guiding principles that thousands of educators are seeking to implement in public and private pre-K–university settings throughout the world. Members from constituent organizations in various parts of the world have initiated local Soka education projects. Members of SGI-Brazil have organized adult literacy and school outreaches called "The Makiguchi Project in Brazil" (de Melo Silva 2000). Several private schools have been founded on Soka education principles, such as the New School of Collaborative Learning in Beijing and the Centro de Orientación Infantil in Panama; several additional schools in the United States have been founded at least partially on principles of Soka education. Finally, numerous teachers are applying concepts of Soka education in their classrooms. For example, Pagan's dissertation (2001) documents her efforts to apply the principles of Soka education in a middle school science classroom.

Research on contemporary applications of Soka education is in its earliest stages. G. D. Miller (2002), synthesizing many of Ikeda's writings, traces the two roots of Ikeda's educational philosophy to Makiguchi and Nichiren Buddhism. Miller equates the socially responsible, egalitarian, and inclusive concept of enlightenment in Nichiren Buddhism with Ikeda's educational belief that "no being on this planet is incapable of being educated; all have the light within" (13). Miller proceeds to describe

Ikeda's educational philosophy as a "spiritual or cosmic humanism" (48) in which "internal or spiritual revolution is the overarching concept" (51). This involves the "integration of reason and compassion" and the "recognition of the interrelatedness of the self with the universe" (52). Miller pays particular attention to Ikeda's insistence on hope as a moral virtue. "The hope of which Ikeda speaks is the heuristic hope that is like a messenger from the future who tells us that what we do now will matter in the future" (74–75)

Much of the research on Soka education is anecdotal in nature. T. Miller (personal correspondence), a former faculty member at Soka University, reports that Ikeda did not endorse specific methodologies at the Soka schools, stressing mainly matters of the heart; he counted on teaching professionals to use their creativity to employ the most effective methods. Miller argues that unlike many educational philosophers, Ikeda does not espouse a particular learning theory, something he claims is problematic for positivists who look for the observable and measurable. Miller states that Ikeda's contribution is "unique precisely because his focus is on not the tangible but the intangible—things like compassion, affection, courage, creativity, or the spark of enthusiasm for learning and dialogue . . . [and] the heart of the teacher." Thus these spiritual qualities in teachers can awaken the same qualities in students.

T. Miller's comments are substantiated in a collection of Ikeda's essays and speeches about education (Ikeda 2001, 153). Using stories from history, ideas from great thinkers, and sheer exegeses, he attempts to resuscitate the spirits of both educators and students so that they can earnestly engage in the practice of education, and, through their spiritual centeredness, contribute to the restoration of society.

Whereas so much of the contemporary debate on education centers on curriculum, philosophy, accountability, and preferred types of schools, Ikeda tends to raise issues that cut across the divide between traditional and progressive camps. He cautions that spiritual change is more significant than structural or political reforms. Although he clearly recognizes the substantial problems facing education as well as abuses in the educational system, he categorically states that "it would be irresponsible to lay all the blame at the system's door because exchanges between human beings are the soil in which creativity grows" (Ikeda 2001, 131). The essence of education occurs through "contacts between [a student's] personality and the personality of the instructor" (132). Educators must possess the virtues of endurance, courage, affection, effort, and a glowing, appealing personality (133). This student-teacher relationship is the "imperishable 'golden rule' of human education and moral upbringing" (148). Ikeda points to the importance of the "Socratic approach," which is driven by the exemplary compassion of the teacher:

> Socrates was more acutely aware of his era than anyone else. He scrutinized it more keenly and deeply; and more than anyone else, he lived through his time with full vigor, ready to sacrifice his own life. The attractiveness of his lifestyle, the magnetism that emanated from his very humanity, could not but reach the impressionable hearts of the young. Regardless of the times, there lies unchanging in the depths of the young human soul an earnestness that responds to earnestness, a seriousness that reacts to seriousness; this is the true character and prerogative of youth. (147–48)

In the same manner, he enlarges the scope of the educational debate. Claiming that children are the mirror of society, he traces such problems as student absenteeism, bullying and problematic behaviors, and a pervasive "flight from learning" that is occurring in schools to the "overall decline of the educational functions that should be inherent not only in schools but in our communities, families and society as a whole" (Ikeda 2001, 65). What is needed is the "cultivation of spirituality" and "broad religious sentiment" (46–47). Ikeda points to "the heart and guiding ethic of Soka education," which aims to nurture the whole individual (47). Soka education is nonsectarian, but it has the aim of "developing students' abilities to ponder meaning and purpose," to "foster a rich humanism and spirituality" (49). Reviving education through fostering spirituality and broad religious sentiment will require "every individual, every family, every organization and every sector of society [to] pool their energies and resources" (49).

He asserts that overcoming the problems in education will require the courage to resist evil and a confrontation with defeatism, detachment, self-doubt, cynicism, and indifference. These attitudes reveal "a decisive lack of passionate engagement with life, an isolation and withdrawal from reality" (Ikeda 2001, 41), which in fact permit evil to proliferate (42). Overcoming this requires individuals capable of an "inner dialogue" between their self and an empathetic "other" that "has struggled through phases of suffering, conflict, ambivalence, mature deliberation and, finally, resolution" (43).

Ikeda calls for "a paradigm shift from looking at education for society's sake to building a society that serves the essential needs of education" (2001, 70). Humans should not be used as means to an end, whether political or economic; rather, "learning is the very purpose of human life" (70). Referring back to Makiguchi, he emphasizes the importance of reestablishing bonds and interactions between people, human links with nature, and the importance of integrating schooling with work in the community to achieve "spiritually and physically balanced growth" (81). In contrast to the prevailing cynicism and despair in educational circles, Ikeda assures us that as long as efforts toward humanistic education are made, it will be possible for students to transcend the faults and abuses of the system (130).

In 1984 Ikeda published "Thoughts on the Aims of Education," his first major essay outlining integrating perspectives through which education can reconstitute itself. He stresses three points—totality, creativity, and internationalization—as the essential elements of reforming the educational system. The "totality of wisdom" refers to the connection of academic studies to the fate of individuals and humanity (Ikeda 2001, 128–29); highlighting the dangers inherent in the trend toward unregulated fragmentation of learning, Ikeda urges that studies must be related to "the values of human happiness and a better way of life" (128). He invokes the theme of creativity, calling it "the badge, or proof of our humanity" (130). Creativity permits the "flowering of the personality" (131) and must be activated from within. Finally, an international outlook is fostered through culture. Culture must be lived, however, which requires the appreciation and cultivation of one's own culture as well as that of others (134–37).

Ikeda expanded his plan of action in a lecture he delivered at Teachers College, Columbia University, in 1996 (2001, 97–109). In this address he argues that spirituality is, in effect, the ethic of global citizenship, the elements of which are:

- The wisdom to perceive the interconnectedness of all life and living.
- The courage not to fear or deny difference; but to respect and strive to understand people of different cultures and to grow from encounters with them.
- The compassion to maintain an imaginative empathy that reaches beyond one's immediate surroundings and extends to those suffering in distant places. (101–2)

Ikeda points to the Buddhist description of a bodhisattva as a "person who embodies these qualities of wisdom, courage and compassion, who strives without cease for the happiness of others" as an ancient precedent of the "global citizen" (2001, 102). He argues that human transformation, human revolution, should become the focus and goal of human endeavors. In turn, the myriad and interlocking problems facing the world can be counteracted by "fostering new generations of people imbued with a profound respect for the sanctity of life" (98). "Education should be a vehicle to develop in one's character the noble spirit to embrace and augment the lives of others" (104). Furthermore, education at all levels needs to incorporate four curricular themes:

- "Developmental education," which focuses attention on global issues of poverty and justice;
- "Peace education";
- "Environmental education"; and
- "Human rights education." (108)

Partially through Ikeda's advocacy, the United Nations has declared 2005–15 the "United Nations Decade of Education for Sustainable Development," and the United Nations General Assembly announced the start of a World Program for Human Rights Education in 2005.

The Development of Spirituality at the Renaissance Charter School

The principles of Soka education, as described here by Ikeda, are inspired by Nichiren Buddhism but are by no means exclusive to it; in fact, they are ideals that are shared by many religious and philosophical belief systems. Rather than searching for distinctiveness, the appeal of Soka education is its broadness. It is a platform upon which educators interested in developing spirituality and an ethical stance among youth can unite.

I believe that my use of these principals has affected the rituals, practices, and obligations of both TRCS students and staff. I further believe this has enhanced their spiritual life and guided them to meaning, purpose, and ethical action. Although as school principal I was only one of many dedicated staff members, the school culture at TRCS became centered on the responsibilities—and not entitlements—of staff members. Starting with the leadership team, staff members worked hard to live up to the cry, "I will change myself first!" We came to an understanding that in our building all people would be listened to and all would be treated with respect; there would be no yelling, no allegiance to the slogan "The teacher is always right." We did the very difficult retrospective work of recognizing and understanding the pervasive effects of racism and other "isms." We learned how to work together as staff: how to conduct meetings, engage in deep levels of discourse, and develop new levels of leadership. We designed a vibrant school building that physically conveys the concepts of village and community.

Academically our students have been doing quite well, far above their peers in New York City. Most significant is that results from the High School Survey of Student Engagement designed and administered by Indiana University (2004) in which our school participated provide some empirical evidence that we have been successful in transmitting spiritual values to our students. In comparison to a national sample, TRCS students report being more satisfied with their school experience than their peers. They identify themselves as being more engaged in classwork and in relationships with peers and with teachers. They are better able to recognize and appreciate the support they receive from the staff and school. Quite critically, they feel more socially aware; in comparison to the national sample, TRCS students report that they are cognizant of the school's impact on values, self-awareness, and racial understanding. Adding to this evidence, recently five of our fifty graduating seniors received full college scholarships to prominent liberal arts colleges through the Posse Foundation. These scholarships are unique because in addition to academics they are awarded on the basis of students' affect, ability to engage with others, ruggedness, and resiliency.

Thus, there are strong indications that spiritual values have taken root and that TRCS students are developing ethical stances. Our students are young and have not fully walked on the stage of life with all of its inherent contradictions and challenges. However, students who have had to confront major crises such as sickness, severe family problems, and death have done so with courage and dignity and with the great support of their friends. I believe TRCS has contributed to these victories. According to the Buddhist outlook the transmission of values is often silent and embedded into rituals, practices, and human relationships. It is my contention that the leadership of teachers imbued with these qualities has led young people to develop meaning, a sense of purpose, and ethical stance. The Buddhist theory of the Nine Consciousnesses posits that ethical stance is a precursor to ethical action. It seems likely that the educational practices underlying TRCS will nurture ethical action among youth in the future.

References

Bethel, Dayle M. 1973. *Makiguchi the value creator.* Tokyo and New York: Weatherhill.

———. 1989. *Education for creative living.* Translated by A. Birnbaum, edited by D. M. Bethel. Ames: Iowa State University.

———, ed. 2002. *A geography of human life by Tsunesaburo Makiguchi.* San Francisco: Caddo Gap Press.

de Melo Silva, Dilma. 2000. Makiguchi project in action: Enhancing education for peace. *Journal of Oriental Studies* 10 (special issue):62–93.

English Buddhist Dictionary Committee. 2002. *The Soka Gakkai dictionary of Buddhism.* Tokyo: Soka Gakkai.

Erickson, Frederick. 1982. Classroom discourse as improvisation. In *Communicating in the class-room*, edited by Louise Wilkinson, 153–81. New York: Academic Press.

Gebert, Andrew, and Anthony George. 2000. Tsunesaburo Makiguchi: Founder of Soka Value-Creating Education. Soka Gakkai International. http://www.sgi.org/english/SGI/makipaper2.htm (accessed March 25, 2005).

Gosho Translation Committee, ed. and trans. 1999. *The writings of Nichiren Daishonin*. Tokyo: Soka Gakkai.

Hay, David C., and Rebecca Nye. 1998. *The spirit of the child*. Grand Rapids, Mich.: Zondervan.

Herrera, Ebaristo A. 1988. *An ethnography: School life out of classrooms*. Ann Arbor, Mich.: University Microfilms.

Ikeda, Daisaku. 1996. Makiguchi's lifelong pursuit of justice and humane values. Speech delivered at Simon Wiesenthal Center, Los Angeles, California, June 4, 1996. http://www.sgi.org/english/President/speeches/justice.htm#3 (accessed December 25, 2004).

———. 1997. Wisdom of the Lotus Sutra 25. http://etherbods.com/sutra/wisdom/wisdom25.shtml (accessed January 21, 2005).

———. 2000. *The way of youth: Buddhist common sense for handling life's questions*. Santa Monica, Calif.: Middleway Press.

———. 2001. *Soka education: A Buddhist vision for teachers, students and parents*. Santa Monica, Calif.: Middleway Press.

Ikeda, Daisaku, Katsuji Saito, Takanori Endo, and Haruo Suda. 2001. *The wisdom of the Lotus Sutra: A discussion*. Vol. 3. Santa Monica, Calif.: World Tribune Press.

Indiana University School of Education. 2004. High school survey of student engagement. www.iub.edu/~nsse/hssse (accessed January 2, 2005).

Jackson, Philip W. 1990. *Life in classrooms*. New York: Teachers College Press.

Makiguchi, Tsunesaburo. 1930. *Soka Kyoikugaku Taikei* (The system of value-creating pedagogy). Tokyo: Fuzanbo.

McLaren, Peter. 1993. *Schooling as a ritual performance*. London: Routledge and Kegan Paul.

Miller, George David. 2002. *Peace, value, and wisdom: The educational philosophy of Daisaku Ikeda*. Amsterdam: Rodopi.

Mojzisek, John David. 2001. Egocentrism and spirituality in adolescence. Ph.D. diss., Loyola College, Baltimore, Maryland.

Pagan, Iris Teresa. 2001. Makiguchian pedagogy in the middle school science classroom. Ph.D. diss., Teachers College, Columbia University, New York.

Ratcliff, Donald. 2001. *Rituals in a school hallway: Evidence of a latent spirituality of children*. East Lansing, Mich.: National Center for Research on Teacher Learning (abstract retrieved August 31, 2004, from ERIC database, ED 457460).

PART V

WHO IS RESPONSIBLE FOR NURTURING SPIRITUALITY?

All the religious traditions represented in this volume recognize spirituality as being actively cultivated during childhood and adolescence. Although they vary in their understanding of the spiritual nature of children, they affirm that it must be actively cultivated in order to flourish. An important question, then, is who plays this spirit-nurturing role in various traditions? What do faith traditions expect from the community of faith, parents, peers, other adults, and other institutions in nurturing spirituality? The authors in this section explore these kinds of questions, examining the roles of parents, communities, congregations, schools, and other persons and institutions in shaping the spiritual lives of children. Some also assert the central role of young people themselves in taking responsibility for their own spiritual path.

Elizabeth F. Caldwell, writing from within the Presbyterian Church (U.S.A.) tradition, observes that the North American church can no longer assume that the general culture, school, and community will sustain Christian values. She argues that one intention of spiritual nurturing must be to counter cultural priorities of individualism. This responsibility requires a partnership between church and family. Today's family is spiritually impoverished and ill equipped, however, so the task has fallen almost exclusively to the church. Caldwell calls for increased educational opportunities to enable parents to become more comfortable with religious language and talking about God, to live out their faith and engage children in everyday spiritual practices. She notes that, more than doctrinal instruction, children require living examples of faith from the adults they encounter. The church is a necessary but insufficient means of transmitting faith.

Examining Malaysian, Korean, and Western Buddhist communities, Sumi Loundon, Ilmee Hwansoo Kim, and Benny Liow discuss the impact of Westernization and Christian missions on the traditional ways of the monastics and temples in the transmission of Buddhist practice. In response to these influences, Malaysian and Korean Buddhist communities have adapted the Western Sunday school model as a primary way of revitalizing Buddhism. While monastics, parents, and youth themselves play a role, formal Sunday programs of instruction are ensuring the continuation of Buddhist traditions. However, these authors are concerned that, among Westerners who have adopted Buddhism, no one takes responsibility for educating young people.

Remembering their own negative religious experiences, parents have opted to allow their children to explore religion for themselves. Often it is university professors who teach Eastern traditions and increasingly popular mediation classes—not family or temple—that draw young people to Buddhism in the West.

Islam, according to Pamela Taylor, teaches that the responsibility for spiritual nurturing falls primarily on the individual. Still, a partnership of parents, extended family, and community serves to awaken the spirituality inherent in the child's soul. In certain extreme cases, even the government accepts responsibility for the spiritual life of its citizens. Despite the importance of family, especially in the years before puberty, Taylor points to a lack of specific guidance for Muslim parents regarding how and what to teach children. Often education involves adherence to and knowledge of Islamic law with memorization and rote learning the most common methods of instruction. The author laments an excessive legalism, which neglects spiritual life to the detriment of children and youth, and calls for change within the educational process to take into account the spirit of the child.

Hinduism understands each human being to have a spiritual spark, and the role of the parent, educator, and community is to help that spark glow. Venkatakrishna B. V. Sastry explains how that process begins from the time of marriage, even before the child is conceived. Rituals from conception to birth, from naming to toddler routines, are infused with spiritual values. From lullabies containing the names of gods and goddesses to practices handed down from elder women to younger mothers, children are nurtured spiritually in the early years. As children grow, educators become the primary role models. Like the other authors, Sastry is concerned that the modern state is challenging many of these traditions.

Through a discussion of the Jewish ritual of becoming bar/bat mitzvah, Jeffrey K. Salkin describes the changes that have taken place from rabbinic to modern times. Societal pressure, loss of community, and an emphasis on individualism undermine traditional Jewish values that understand study leading to action rather than "belief" as essential for spiritual growth. Salkin offers suggestions for how the Jewish community might transform this widely practiced puberty ritual and help parents resume their primary role as models and teachers. He believes that the guidance and mentorship of community elders, the tutelage of older adolescents, and viewing the synagogue as a community of meaning will help make bar/bat mitzvah part of an educational process that counters the prevailing culture of individualism and consumerism.

David C. Dollahite and Loren D. Marks highlight the primacy of family among Latter-day Saints. While spiritual development is the responsibility of the individual, it is incumbent upon others in the community, particularly the family, to nurture children's spirituality. Parents are primarily responsible for helping children to maintain personal communion with God and to practice charity, thus facilitating the sacred covenant that binds families together. Along with the home, presided over by the father, the church community provides supplemental program and support. Strict codes of family fidelity, belief, and morality often come in conflict with the surrounding culture and present challenges to the community, which is frequently at odds with the sexual mores of the society.

The authors of these chapters all recognize the primary importance of home and the family in the spiritual development of young people and the transmission of the heritage and values of faith traditions. While some communities, such as the Latter-day Saints, retain strong parental influence, others like the Presbyterian Church (U.S.A.), lament the declining ability of parents to transmit traditional values. All the authors agree that cultural influences—particularly society's emphasis on individualism and consumerism—further erode the power of religious traditions to mentor youth. There is a consensus that empowering parents as religious educators and understanding religious education as the transmission of a faith lived out, not only recitation and adherence to doctrine, will better serve the spiritual life of children and adolescents, and ensure the continuation of the priorities of religious communities.

CHAPTER 26

At Home with Faith and Family: A Protestant Christian Perspective

Elizabeth F. Caldwell

In talking with parents about the spiritual practices they observe in their homes, I usually begin with the question, "What practices were a part of your family's life when you were a child?" The answers range from "nothing" to a limited number of intentional practices of faith: blessing at meals, having a Bible story book available for children, nighttime prayers, reading the story of Jesus' birth on Christmas Eve. If I wait long enough, stories will emerge of parents who involved their children in actions of justice and kindness with others and rituals of faith in the home, such as setting up the treasured family nativity. Moving to the next question requires more space for silence, reflection, and response: How would you describe the home you make for faith today? Which of the spiritual practices that were a part of your life as a child have you continued? What new things have you added that have become essential for your continued growth in the life of the Christian faith, ones that are important for nurturing your child's growth in faith?

As a Christian living in the United States, my experiences with teaching about the connection between faith and the home are both particular and varied. I speak and write from the background of being a lifelong Presbyterian. I live and teach in a seminary that reflects the ethnic and religious diversity of the city in which it is located, Chicago, Illinois. My particular religious tradition, the Presbyterian Church (U.S.A.), is shaped in its belief about the connections between faith and life and faith and home in the celebration of two sacraments: baptism and Eucharist. The reformed tradition recognizes and practices infant baptism, which takes place in worship and involves three things: profession of faith in Jesus Christ as Lord and savior by a parent or parents; the baptism with water of the child; and the affirmation of promise by the parents and the congregation to be responsible for nurturing the child in the life of faith in which she has been baptized. Baptized children are welcomed with their families to come to the table and share the meal, the Eucharist or the Lord's Supper. At the heart of this faith tradition is the commitment to welcoming with water the newest one who has been born to or adopted into a family. Equally important but less understood and taught is the role of the family in nurturing this child so that he may grow into the potential of his baptism.

In writing about the connections between faith and the home it is important to make clear some distinctions in terminology. In the United States, people are able to identify themselves as religious or nonreligious. When pressed further with a question such as, "In what ways do you consider yourself to be religious?" people may respond with identifying a faith tradition in which they are active or spiritual practices that are important to them. Spiritual practices such as the ones that will be discussed here emerge from and are evidenced in the lives of people of faith. So faith then becomes the loving response of people to God's activity, God's presence in their lives. This chapter begins with the assumption that spiritual practices are essential for the formation of persons committed to growing in the life of the Christian faith.

The particular perspective on spirituality at the core of a faithful ecology connecting congregation and the home begins for me with two passages from the Bible. The Shema or the Great Commandment from Deuteronomy 6:4–9 represents the simplest yet most complex statement about the relationship between humankind and God, something beyond themselves: "Hear, O Israel: God is our God, God alone. You shall love the Lord your God with all your heart, and with all your soul, and with all your might." The writer then goes on to say that these words should be kept very close, "in your heart," taught to the children and recited both at home and away from home. This affirmation of faith in God should be visible in actions in the world: "write them on the doorposts of your house and on your gates." And in the New Testament, Matthew records the words of Jesus, God's Son, who when asked about which commandments were most important, responded with the words of Deuteronomy and added that there was a second commandment, "You shall love your neighbor as yourself" (Matthew 22:39). So the response of thankful people is loving God and loving others, as you love yourself.

This chapter focuses on families who are formed in faith and choose to live within the culture rather than removing themselves from the culture. Being Christian and growing in a life of faith requires being a part of a congregation. Participation in the life and work of a church sustains Christians for their presence in the world. Yet this alone is not adequate. It is my thesis that parents are partners with the congregation, faith educators, people who claim a Christian identity that supports their living faithfully in the world. Nurturing children in the life of the Christian faith requires the commitment of family members to immerse themselves in spiritual practices that grow with them. The commitment of parents to the spiritual formation of their children is strengthened when they experience practices such as prayer, attentive listening for God, reflection on life and faith, seeing actions through the lens of faith, meditation, reading of Scripture, and caring for others. Such experiences connect children, youth, and adults to the holy and strengthen their Christian identity.

Realities and Challenges

Three realities serve as background for understanding the nature and practice of spiritual formation in the home. They can be stated as tensions: (1) Are Christians a majority or minority presence in the culture? (2) Who is responsible for spiritual nurture, the church or the home or both? (3) In what ways do cultural understandings of time as *chronos* or *kairos* contribute to adult commitments to faith formation in the family?

Living faithfully within the diversity of culture and faith traditions in the United States is a challenge for Christian families who have always assumed their place as majority. As recently as thirty years ago, the culture protected Sunday as Sabbath, a day of rest, a day for families to be in church together, a day when there was little else available to do. Community-organized sports for children now claim Sunday as a prime time for practice and games as do professional sports.

Parents who assume that the culture will support and impart Christian values are becoming cognizant of the reality of the variety of religious traditions present in the schools of their children. Consider the fall season. Christians around the world celebrate World Communion Sunday, and faithful Jews observe Sukkot. For Muslims, Ramadan can begin as early as October or as late as December. The traditional Christmas party for elementary school has been renamed a holiday party where diverse faith traditions can be honored and celebrated—Kwanzaa, Hanukkah, and Christmas.

It has been reported that about 83 percent of Americans define themselves as Christians, and nearly all believe in a deity. Yet according to an ABC News poll in 2002, only 38 percent attend weekly religious services. The National Opinion Research Center has reported that Protestants may lose majority status as soon as 2005. The Protestant share of the population has been steadily decreasing since 1992, reaching 54.2 percent in 2002. Another statistic reveals that fewer children are being raised in Protestant homes in the past forty years. Those who report they have no religious identity increased from 5 percent in 1972 to nearly 14 percent in 2002 (Dart 2004).

Christians have assumed that because of their majority presence in U.S. culture, they can rely on a convergence of institutions such as schools and the community to sustain Christian values. This assumption is no longer valid and must be challenged. Jews in the United States have always known that if they are to survive in a culture where they are a minority, they must be intentional about faith formation, raising their children so that they grow up knowing they are Jewish and what they believe. Christians in the United States must begin to grapple with this same issue—not how to survive within the culture, but how to thrive in the midst of "a new religious America," as Diana Eck has described it (Eck 2001, 1).

A second challenge is the consideration of roles and responsibilities with regard to faith nurturing—of professionals, church leaders, or parents and extended family. Protestant congregations in the United States share a similar model of religious education. Sunday is the day for Christian education (separated by age groups) and worship. Church school is considered to be the primary context for children, youth, and adults to learn the content of the faith tradition and to make connections between content and living the life of a Christian in the world. Some congregations offer midweek contexts for learning and community, and varieties of other settings are offered during the year—church family retreats, vacation church school in the summer, mission trips, and summer church camps. Many congregations have strong mission commitments within their communities and offer opportunities for families to participate together in ministry with homeless, with tutoring and child care, and older adults. In such activities, children grow up learning that being Christian requires living the faith in actions in the world.

Increasingly in the culture, the assignment for raising children in faith, for nurturing their spirituality, has by default been left to the church—to church school teachers and leaders and to the professional staff of pastors and church educators. The obvious question emerges, what happens in the days between Sundays? Martin Marty has said: "Most American Christians are woefully unprepared to be responsible agents of their faith. They know too little of its story, its teaching, and its moral framework to exemplify and testify to their faith in a pluralist culture. So they blend into the culture or are overwhelmed by it or desert the faith for one or another of the options in it" (Marty 1993, 22).

It has been noted by those who observe religious tradition in North American culture that for most Christians, family devotions haven't been practiced for more than 100 years. "Children grow up biblically illiterate in homes where Bibles abound but are rarely opened. We [Christians in the United States] have become a generation incapable of passing on the stories of our faith. The face of our faith has become extremely impoverished. Instead of being rich banquets, feasts of faith and community, our tables of faith become barren with barely enough bread and water to satisfy, and we try to sustain ourselves on this meager diet" (Caldwell 2000, 7).

Many families today find it a challenge even to find the time to share a meal together, which leads to a third challenge for people of faith: the issue of time, *kairos*, Sabbath time, in a culture that places great value on *chronos*, speed, change, and over-scheduled lives, lived by the clock. In American culture, for families with children, time has become the most prized possession. Some say, "At our church we have to have church school for children the same time as worship because parents want it all done in one hour. That's all the time they have." For many Korean, Hispanic, or African American congregations, Sabbath is lived by God's time, *kairos*. Gathering for worship is a time for being in community with each other and with God. This gathering of community is a supportive alternative to a culture in which they are a minority. Yet we all live by watches and *chronos* time, and we are called to live into *kairos* time. If lives are lived by the clock, what happens to attunement to *kairos* time, being with God? It's a matter of priority for use of time.

Spirituality is being attuned to the mystery and wonder of God's presence in our lives. Jean Grasso Fitzpatrick has observed that "a spiritual life is not something we begin to lead—or to cultivate in our children—after analyzing every book in the Bible, or resolving to be do-gooders, or even deciding we believe in God. Spirit is our life's breath . . . Spirituality is not something we need to pump into our children, as though it were nitrous oxide at the dentists. Like oxygen, it is freely available to each of us at every moment of life. Spirit is in every breath we draw and so is spiritual nurture" (Fitzpatrick 1991, 44).

These three tensions of the Christian presence in the culture, the responsibility for Christian nurture, and commitment of time serve as a framework for addressing the importance of intentional faith education in the home. Parents can prepare themselves to be "responsible agents of faith," as Marty describes it (1993, 20). With a commitment to their own growth as a spiritual person, parents become more comfortable with the reality of the presence of God's spirit, which as Fitzpatrick has said is "in every breath we draw."

Making a Home for Faith

The importance of the role of the family in nurturing the Christian faith of children at home is not a new concept. In 1888, Horace Bushnell wrote that the ideal understanding of Christian education from the perspective of those involved in nurturing a child in faith was that "the child is to grow up a Christian, and never know [her- or him] self as being otherwise" (Bushnell 1861, 10).

In 1928, Hulda Niebuhr identified three kinds of parents of children in the church school. First are the parents who believe that they have enough to do and that the religious education of their child is best left to others. They fail to recognize "their own inevitable part in that education." A second group are parents whose time and energy are focused on providing the basics of food, shelter, and clothing for their children. They want to be good parents, but they have no time left over to "learn to be intelligent educators." Third are the parents who are glad to be involved in the Christian life of their children and supportive of Christian education in their church (Niebuhr 1929, 13). Sophia Fahs, a religious educator and contemporary of Hulda Niebuhr's, believed that the natural experiences of children, such as wondering about the death of an animal and the ensuing questions about death and life, mark the beginnings of their religious search (Hunter 1976).

Writing in the 1970s, John Westerhoff asked, "Will our children have faith?" He answered the question with a *yes* and *if*. Children will have faith if families are actively engaged in the life of a Christian community in worship, in education, in mission (Westerhoff 1976). In a later work he identified five guidelines for sharing faith with children, activities that he believed would nurture children in faith through their adolescence: tell and retell the biblical story together as a family; celebrate faith and life as a family; pray together; listen and talk to each other; and be engaged in faithful acts of service and witness as a family (Westerhoff 1980, 37).

Marjorie Thompson speaks of the family as the "forming center," a primary place of spiritual formation through both the everyday and natural opportunities of life within a family and through "intentional practices" that support growth in the life of the Christian faith (Thompson 1996, 21). Growing out of her family therapy practice, Mary Pipher has written about the things that "shelter families." She has identified six qualities that give a family "definition, identity and power: protecting family time; valuing places that have meaning for the family; shared interests; honoring family celebrations; engaging in rituals that connect family members to each other and to friends and extended family; recalling family stories" (Pipher 1996, 245). Missing from this list are two things essential for forming families: faith shelters families, and participating in the life and work of a congregation shelters a family.

The recent work of the Lilly Endowment in faith formation in children is reflected in the work of Karen Marie Yust, who speaks of three themes present in understanding the activity of spiritual formation. First, we accept that faith is a gift of God. This gracious act of a loving God means that when faith is received and acted upon, it has the power to transform life and work. Our being and our doing, our spiritual practices, are an essential part of a faithful response. And third, Yust believes that the best response of the creation to the Creator is "faith-full-ness" through understanding the meaning of and acting in response to the concepts of belonging, thanksgiving, giftedness, hospitality, understanding, and hope (Yust 2004, 13–14).

Christian churches are proud of the varieties of educational ministries they provide for the Christian education of children and youth. A wealth of curricular resources, both in print and on Web sites, is available for the support of creative and effective models of Christian education in the congregation. Congregations know that one of the greatest tools of evangelism is to provide inviting settings and varieties of ministries for children and youth.

This commitment to educating children and youth in the life of the Christian faith has not always been equally extended to preparing and supporting parents and extended family for their vocation as faith educators. Pastors and church leaders seem to think that parents know what to do in raising their child in the Christian faith. Opportunities to learn about simple Christian practices or rituals for the home, whether in a formal class or in informal conversation, do not seem to be a priority in many congregations.

This chapter began with an examination of some of the realities of life for Christians living in the United States in the twenty-first century. This cultural and religious shift is timely in two ways. It means that congregations and their pastoral and educational leaders can examine their role with adult family members in reconceptualizing the home as a place for nurturing children in the life of the Christian faith. Essential questions must be explored: What are we doing to support parents in their role as faith educators with their children? What are we failing to do in this area? It is also time for parents to reclaim their role as faith educators with their children, living into the reality and practices of Christian life.

Martin Marty has observed that "many participants in Christian education are refugees, exiles or rebels" (Marty 1993, 22). This is descriptive of many parents of young children today. These parents left the church after their confirmation as teenagers, and in many cases their return to church is predicated by their wanting their child to be baptized. Many parents today are in exile, searching for meaning in their life and not quite sure how to begin to ask the questions or even ask for help. Some are refugees from a previous Christian faith tradition and have no faith tradition or have not found their spiritual home. Some believe that they want faith and belief for their children but rebel at the thought of needing it for themselves.

In sharp contrast to a culture that places a high value on rugged individualism and looking out for the self, the Christian faith professes a belief in the formative power of the Christian community. The sacrament of baptism, whether of an infant or as a choice by a believer of any age, takes place within worship, the people of faith gathered around the individual and/or the family. Bonnie Miller-McLemore suggests that it is time for congregations "to discuss the radical understanding of parenting as a religious discipline and community practice," because she believes that "the practice of raising children belongs to all Christians, and not solely to parents or to mothers" (Miller-McLemore 2003, 164–65). Baptism is a radical act of faith and community, and as such it has the power to transform lives of everyone present at this sacrament.

What support structures are needed for parents and extended family members that will enable them to become at home with their own faith so that they are able to nurture their children and teenagers in the life of the Christian faith? What areas of spiritual formation need the most attention by parents? It is possible that congregations might consider a new model of religious education, one that supports the spiritual formation of parents and supports them in their role as faith educators. With the implementation of such a model, it is possible that parents who are "refugees, exiles and rebels" can become partners, connectors and translators.

PARTNERS

The text from Deuteronomy that reminds the hearer of the great commandment to love God requires more than intellectual assent. It must be integrated into a believer's very being. If Christian families are to thrive in the multifaith culture in which they live, it is imperative that parents come to accept their call, their vocation, as the primary faith educators with their children.

This affirmation requires both a cognitive and a practical shift in understanding on the part of parents and pastors and educators within the congregation. It means that the commitment to enabling growth in faith, to nurturing spirituality, is a partnership of church and home. It means reexamining goals and objectives for Christian nurture and beginning to focus on how congregations can live out their partnership with parents, grandparents, aunts and uncles, all friends of children—to foster and support the spiritual growth of children and teenagers.

Being a partner means that congregations seek practical ways through education, worship, and mission opportunities in the church to enable adults of all ages to understand that the care of children is the best response to loving God. Being a partner means that congregations enable adults of all ages to live into a community practice of care and love for children. Being a partner means that adults of all ages understand that caring for the lives of children is a religious discipline.

Christian adults who live out a commitment to being a community of faith that practices partnership with families are ones who take seriously their vocation to live their faith with children. In the sacrament of infant baptism, after faith questions are asked of the parents and after the child has been baptized, questions are asked of the congregation: "Do you, as members of the church of Jesus Christ, promise to guide and nurture this child by word and deed with love and prayer, encouraging them to know and follow Christ and to be faithful members of his church?" (*Book of Common Worship* 1993). If a congregation is intentional about its commitment to hold parents accountable for being the primary faith educators with their child, then following through on baptismal promises is imperative.

CONNECTORS

The words of the great commandment in Deuteronomy continue with the instruction to "teach them [Love the Lord your God with all your heart, soul, might] to your children" (Deuteronomy 6:7). As a primary faith educator with a child, a parent becomes one who connects the biblical story with the living of faith in the world. A parent helps a child or a teenager make connections between the faith in which they are immersed and the world in which they live. The great commandment to love God and the second commandment given by Jesus, to love our neighbors as we love ourselves, are so easily affirmed and yet require intention of reflection upon action.

A primary way of helping adults connect with their role as a partner with children is to provide opportunities and experiences with practices of faith. Congregations who seek to help families grow spiritually need to plan for intentional education and support of parents who want to grow in their vocation as faith educators. For example, a congregation could offer periodic workshops or conversations based on a model of spiritual formation for families. Using the seasons of the Christian year—Advent/Christmas/Epiphany, Lent/Easter, Pentecost, and Ordinary time—would provide four natural time frames for providing families with resources. If spiritual formation has as its goal to help people be attuned both to the mystery and wonder of God's presence in their lives and faithful living in response to this relationship, then it seems essential to emphasize three practices that work to answer the question of the Old Testament prophet, Micah. What does the Lord require of you? To do justice, love kindness, and walk humbly with God. Thus three practices can sustain our spiritual lives—acts of piety, mercy, and justice (Micah 6:8).

In writing about Christian practices that nurture spirituality, Craig Dykstra has identified thirteen that he believes to be consistent within the Reformed tradition and important for Christians today: worship, telling the Christian story, interpreting Scripture, prayer, confession of sin and reconciliation, encouraging others, being in service and witness, suffering with neighbors, providing hospitality and care, listening, struggling to understand the context of life, criticizing and resisting the powers of evil, working together to create social structures that sustain life in accord with God's will (Dykstra 1999, 42–43).

Reflecting on this list, it is possible to see how these practices become examples of the three kinds of spiritual practices that can become part of a family's commitment for engaging in rituals of faith at home, rituals that support church participation. A family can make commitments to growing in the grace of piety, of listening for God through participation in worship, reading and interpreting the biblical story, and praying. Ancient Christian practices such as *lectio divina* (hearing or reading Scripture three times, each time listening for something different), the *examen* (reflecting on the activities of the day in terms of experiences of receiving God's love and sharing God's love), praying the Psalms, and walking labyrinths are now being taught and practiced by all ages. Children are learning how to engage in meditative prayer.

Other spiritual practices that can be easily engaged in with children and youth are singing hymns or musical responses Taizé style (simple repetitive singing, as practiced at the Christian community of Taizé in France); sharing stories of faith from the Bible; teaching children about different kinds of prayer—breath prayers, prayers of thanksgiving, intercession, adoration, and confession, or as Gellman and Hartman say, prayers of "thanks, gimme, wow and oops" (Gellman and Hartman 1995, 145–46)]; teaching children how to stop and be still, to meditate; making use of the examen, a ancient spiritual practice for the end of the day, to say thank you to God and to ask God's forgiveness for acts that were not kind or helpful to others; and honoring Sabbath. To this list of simple spiritual practices that help nurture a sense of connection with the mystery of God, Carol Wehrheim adds fasting. She suggests that fasting can take several forms, such as a Lenten practice of simple meals and no desserts and saving the money to give to those who don't have enough food. Fasting can also take the form of giving up something material, such as turning off televisions, computers, or cell phones and replacing them with family activities (Wehrheim 2004).

Families practice acts of love and mercy when they encourage others, are in service and witness, suffer with neighbors, provide hospitality and care, and listen. In writing about the moral teaching of adults, Robert Coles has said that what is most important with children is "the witness of our lives, our ways of being with others and speaking to them and getting on with them—all of that taken in slowly, cumulatively, by our sons and daughters, our students . . . in the long run of a child's life, the unself-conscious moments that are what we think of simply as the unfolding events of the day and the week turn out to be the really powerful and persuasive times, morally" (Coles 1997, 31).

Pastoral leaders can support parents in their ability to help children make the connections between the teachings of Jesus and how their family seeks to live together as a Christian family. The simplicity of the six spiritual practices that define acts of mercy is astounding. These activities are ones in which we engage every day, no matter what our age; naming them and helping children connect are important. When parents are transparent, letting children see the faithful acts they do, children grow up with an identity of faith.

The call to be formed spiritually stands in sharp contrast to the call of the world to accumulate possessions, to keep up with the latest in technology. Christians live with the tension between the call of the culture and the call of Jesus to feed those who are hungry and thirsty, to welcome the stranger, to take care of the sick and those who are imprisoned (Matthew 25:31–46). Spiritual practices of piety lead to and connect with practices of mercy.

Finally, Christians are also called to practice acts of justice: struggling to understand the context of life, criticizing and resisting the powers of evil, and working together to create social structures that sustain life in accord with God's will. Christians are called to live in the world, modeling the faith that sustains them rather than the values the culture offers. The tension between these two callings is astounding.

Families who engage in table conversations about current events and the places where God's presence is needed as each family member faces the reality of evil and the potential for good in the world are raising children who are capable of discerning, criticizing, and forming judgments about faithful actions required of them. Families who join their congregations in acts of justice such as mission projects, serving meals to older adults or homeless shelter guests, building houses with Habitat for Humanity, working together to fight hunger by participating in CROP walks (interfaith community hunger education programs) are witnessing to the challenge of Jesus to his disciples, "Just as you did not do it to one of the least of these, you did not do it to me" (Matthew 25:45).

In writing about the efficacy of spiritual practices, Dykstra has said that they "place people in touch with God's redemptive activity . . . put us where life in Christ may be made known, recognized, experienced, and participated in. They are means of grace, the human places in which and through which God's people come to faith and grow to maturity in the life of faith" (Dykstra 1999, 43). Works of piety, mercy, and justice, when woven together in the faithful acts of a family, help provide a tapestry of support for living in the world.

TRANSLATORS

In recalling the words from Deuteronomy, we need to remember the command to love God with our whole being, our hearts, our soul, and with our strength. And the commandment is given to teach these words to our children and to remember them "when you are at home and when you are away, when you lie down and when you rise" (Deuteronomy 6:7). To support his research about what it means to "grow up religious," Robert Wuthnow conducted interviews over a three-year period with two hundred people. After listening to them tell stories about their childhood experiences, he came to believe that "embedded practices are influential in religious development because they spin out webs of significance that richly connect people with the world around them." Contrary to those educators who believe that children are "mental machines" whose religious formation requires hours of catechetical instruction at church, Wuthnow's evidence revealed that children "assimilated religion more by osmosis than by instruction." For families who intentionally raised their children in a faithful home, faith came to be experienced as natural, as a way of life (Wuthnow 1999, xxxvi).

Many Christian congregations give children's story Bibles or Bibles at important points in the life of a child or youth. Baptism, second or third grade (marking the time when children become able to read on their own), and confirmation or graduation from high school are typical moments in Christian worship when this takes place. If congregations are going to be partners with families in supporting their role as faith educators and growing in their abilities to ones who can connect with faith and translate conceptual beliefs into faithful concrete actions in the world, it is essential to educate parents about reading, meditating on, and being at home with the Bible.

Being at home with faith by engaging in practices of faith must first begin with adults. Parents and extended family members who feel comfortable in their own religious skin, so to speak, are not paralyzed by religious issues raised by children, such as questions of information, analytical questions, questions related to their experience in the world, and questions that concern the mysteries of God.

Parents who are able to use theological vocabulary, such as *sin, grace, judgment, forgiveness*; parents who are able to talk about God's work as creator and God's self-revelation in Jesus; parents who can translate difficult theological concepts such as providence or redemption in terms such as "God plans for a good world" or "God loves you even when you do something wrong" are giving their children a language of faith that helps immerse them in the experience of faith even before the theological language is in place. Such immersion surrounds children like the waters of their baptism, preparing them for the movement through the questions of faith that naturally arise as they move into adolescence.

A Faithful Ecology: Implications for Further Dialogue

Does the Christian faith see the church community or the individual family as primarily responsible for the spiritual education of children? One seems to predominate, but there is a growing desire on the part of parents, primarily women, who want support for spiritual practices for themselves and their families, ideas for rituals of faith for the home.

There is in the Christian churches, and in the United States as a whole, a profound spiritual hunger for something. It is a hunger that I think may be met, at least in part, by a truly theological education in Christian practice. Dykstra has said that Christians in American society are no longer scripturally literate. Their [spiritual] hunger "is not simply the result of a shift in taste; it is the consequence of a radical starvation" (Dykstra 1999, 3–6).

For many Christians in this culture, observing Sabbath is an essential faith-forming family activity, the primary choice for their Sunday life together. For many Christians in this culture, Sabbath participation in worship and Christian education is one among many choices they have in their life, and it may be secondary to sports and other recreational pursuits. If the Christian family is to continue as a formative presence in the culture, its very existence depends upon a faithful ecology that moves between church, home, and living faithfully within the culture.

"Faith education is the shared responsibility of parents and other family members at home and lay leaders, teachers, ministers and educators in the church. A faithful ecology is formed in both contexts where faith, hope and love are practiced. We learn to speak by being spoken to, and later we learn rules of grammar. We learn about love by being loved. We learn about God by singing our faith, practicing our faith, praying in faith, and being faithful" (Caldwell 2000, 73).

Christians in the United States would agree that beliefs and practices that grow out of the biblical story shape families in faith and in the perspective they bring to the world. There is less consensus with regards to two issues that continue to be a major part of Christian dialogue. First, it can be affirmed that there is a diversity of Christian interpretations of biblical text and theological priorities for faithful Christian living. We are not of one mind about faith.

Within a neighborhood it is possible to find parents who teach their children a literal translation of the Bible based on the understanding that everything in the Bible is true and written by God, parents who read the Qur'an with their children, families whose Bible gathers dust on the shelf. Next door is the family in which the parents help their children hear the stories of God's people struggling to live in the ways that God has instructed, learning that the Bible is a collection of different kinds of writing inspired by God. And down the street is the Jewish family who bakes challah and lights the candles on Shabbat. Scattered in the community are families who claim the identity of being Christian but who have no intentional practices of faith. And probably you would find at least one family who claims no religious identity.

The challenge of being at home among the variety of expressions of the Christian faith and the faith traditions of the world represented in our neighbors and in the classmates of our children has clear implications for the role of the congregation in supporting and nurturing adult family members in their role as faith educators with their children. In writing about the task of Christian education in a pluralistic culture, Martin Marty says that the "purpose of education is to take people where they are and help them come to a new point. The purpose of Christian education that is sensitive to pluralism is to provide the widest scope and fairest representation of the surrounding world" (Marty 1993, 22).

A second topic for continued dialogue is family, what constitutes family, and which families are welcome in Christian congregations. One of the realities of the postmodern world in which Americans live is the changing nature and understanding of what constitutes family. Children may be blessed by being raised and nurtured in the Christian faith by a mother and a father or by a loving grandparent. Children may be raised by two parents of the same sex or by a single mother or dad. Children in a family may be biological and/or adopted, and families can be blended because of divorce or other family circumstances.

Christians of all denominations in the United States represent a diversity of theological perspectives. Those for whom a traditional family consists of two parents with children, in which the father is understood to be the head of the family, are oftentimes embedded within a community of faith that supports these roles with biblical teaching. In such a family, it is often the mother who is assigned the role to teach Christian values at home and at church as a teacher of children in the church school. Equally real are the experiences of congregations that welcome families of all kinds and support parents and other adult family members in growing into their roles as ones capable of nurturing a child in the life of the Christian faith. In both settings, families are usually very intentional about Christian practices of Bible reading and prayer, forming their children in the life of faith that will equip them to live in the world as Christian.

In discussing the goal of faithful living at home, Lisa Sowle Cahill has written: "The Christian family is not the perfect family but one in which fidelity, compassion, forgiveness, and concern for others, even strangers, are known. In striving to embody these virtues, however imperfect its success, a family lives in the presence of God and begins to transform its surroundings. A Christian family is such a family" (Cahill 2000, 137).

Congregations foster the spiritual lives of children and youth by taking care of adult family members, teaching them and supporting them in their role as faith educators. Families who are committed to taking time for Christian practices discover how each family member is spiritually nurtured in his or her own unique way. And families who take risks to grow faithfully together in acts of justice, mercy, and kindness are strong families, committed to their faith, to each other, and to their Christian presence in the world in which they live. Such is a faithful ecology for being at home with faith and family.

Author's note: With thanks to my family, who help me keep God's words in my heart.

References

Book of common worship. 1993. Louisville, Ky.: Westminster/John Knox Press.
Bushnell, Horace. 1861. *Christian nurture.* New York: Scribner's Sons.

Cahill, Lisa Sowle. 2000. *Family: A Christian social perspective.* Minneapolis, Minn.: Fortress Press.

Caldwell, Elizabeth F. 2000. *Making a home for faith: Nurturing the spiritual life of your children.* Cleveland, Ohio: United Church Press.

Coles, Robert. 1997. *The moral intelligence of children.* New York: Random House.

Dart, John. 2004. Protestants may lose majority status. *Christian Century* 121:11.

Dykstra, Craig. 1999. *Growing in the life of faith: Education and Christian practices.* Louisville, Ky.: Geneva Press.

Eck, Diana L. 2001. *A new religious America.* San Francisco: HarperSanFrancisco.

Fitzpatrick, Jean Grasso. 1991. *Nurturing your child's spiritual growth.* New York: Viking.

Gellman, Marc, and Thomas Hartman. 1998. *How do you spell God? Answers to the big questions from around the world.* New York: Morrow Junior Books.

Hunter, Edith. 1976. *Sophia Lyon Fahs.* Boston: Beacon Press.

Marty, Martin. 1993. Christian education in a pluralistic culture. In *Rethinking Christian education,* edited by David S. Schuller, 17–30. St. Louis, Mo.: Chalice Press.

Miller-McLemore, Bonnie. 2003. *Let the children come: Reimagining childhood from a Christian perspective.* San Francisco: Jossey-Bass.

Niebuhr, Hulda. 1929. Parental education in the church. *International Journal of Religious Education* 6:13–14.

Pipher, Mary. 1996. *The shelter of each other: Rebuilding our families.* New York: Grosset/Putnam.

Thompson, Marjorie. 1996. *Family as the forming center: A vision of the role of family in spiritual formation.* Nashville, Tenn.: Upper Room Books.

Wehrheim, Carol. 2004. Spirituality and children. *Hungry Hearts* 13:4–7.

Westerhoff, John. 1976. *Will our children have faith?* New York: Seabury.

———. 1980. *Bringing up children in the Christian faith.* San Francisco: Harper and Row.

Wuthnow, Robert. 1999. *Growing up religious: Christians and Jews and their journeys of faith.* Boston: Beacon Press.

Yust, Karen Marie. 2004. *Real kids, real faith: Practices for nurturing children's spiritual lives.* San Francisco: Jossey-Bass.

CHAPTER 27

Sunday School for Buddhists? Nurturing Spirituality in Children

Sumi Loundon, Ilmee Hwansoo Kim, and Benny Liow

The premodern Buddhist tradition has little formal instruction regarding the place and development of children. Early Buddhist scriptures mention a minimum age (twenty) at which boys can become monks, acknowledging that maturity must be brought to this life-changing decision. Informally, children absorbed Buddhist teachings by learning from their parents' modeling, by developing relationships with village temple monastics, and through the moral lessons in scriptures and stories. A formal education for children, a full catechism in the theological and ritual aspects of a Buddhist lineage, however, would have taken place in the context of monastic training. Many monasteries and temples received children from poor or especially devoted families and also took in orphans.

As Asian countries modernized, village life yielded to urban life. Western colonialism recast Buddhism as a religion and introduced the idea of a formal religious education. The success of Christian missionaries displaced traditional Asian religions. Today, globalization is a force in describing cultural norms. Modernity, colonialism, Christianity, and globalization have challenged the role of the temple and of monastics, the bearers of the Buddhist tradition. In response, beginning in the early twentieth century, temples began developing Sunday schools, similar to the Christian Sunday schools. These schools, now found in Sri Lanka, Indonesia, Singapore, Malaysia, Thailand, Taiwan, Korea, among Asian Buddhist communities in the United States, and elsewhere, are highly successful and have become the primary center of education for Buddhist children. Here, dedicated laypeople play an integral role in organizing the children and in teaching. Lay teachers lead educational games, use textbooks and coloring books, teach a choir to sing Buddhist "hymns" with Western melodies, arrange camps, and mobilize community service projects. Increasingly, in some schools there is a brief meditation period. Modern educational techniques from both the secular and the Christian communities are now applied to Buddhist education. Monastics are still highly respected by the youth. In many ways, the idea of a Buddhist monk or nun has become iconic, thanks in part to the West's own fascination with Buddhist monastics. Monastics themselves are making efforts to modernize while remaining faithful to tradition. Younger monastics can be seen hosting an online discussion for youth members on current topics such as intoxicants, sexuality, media, and stress.

There are very few monastics among the Westerners (in the United States, Canada, United Kingdom, Europe, Australia) who took up Buddhism in the mid-twentieth century, so the tradition—yet to be established—will be held and transmitted primarily by laypeople. Many chose, as they began families, to take a decidedly hands-off approach to religion, not wishing to force their children into a religion, as they had perceived their own Catholic, Jewish, or Protestant parents doing. In the past ten years, however, as baby boomer Buddhists age and their children become adults, a small but growing awareness of recruiting and educating a new generation has led to the beginnings of youth-related programs, literature, retreats, and scholarships. Generally, these initiatives center on meditation practices, ranging from explicitly Buddhist to a more secular, psychological focus.

Because so little has been written on the modern education of young Buddhists, this chapter will take a broad social approach. Benny Liow, a lay leader in Malaysia, details the success of Sunday schools among the English-speaking Chinese Buddhists. Ilmee Hwansoo Kim, a young Korean monk, examines how Korean Buddhism is adapting to meet the needs of Korean children in both South Korea and in the United States. Sumi Loundon, a young lay Buddhist who works among the Western Dharma[1] centers, discusses the unique situation of a first generation of convert Buddhists only recently thinking about the needs of their young people. By spanning Buddhist youth in Asia, Asian youth in the United States, and Western youth in America, we provide a global perspective and will conclude with suggestions for future development.

Malaysia's Buddhist Sunday Schools: Origin, Development, and Transformation

Of Malaysia's nearly twenty-four million people, about 25 percent are ethnically Chinese. Buddhism, practiced mainly by the Chinese, is a minority religion set within the larger Muslim, ethnically Malay, majority. Among Chinese Buddhists, most practice the Mahayana form and speak primarily Chinese, while a minority practice the Theravada (Southeast Asian) form and speak primarily English. Underpinning the Theravada communities is a system of Sunday schools that educate the laity on Buddhist teachings in English. These Sunday schools play a central role in transmitting Buddhist traditions. To appreciate the development of Buddhist Sunday schools in Malaysia, it is important to consider the background.

Chinese immigrants came to Malaysia in the nineteenth century, bringing with them their practices of Chinese Buddhism. A number of Buddhist monks also came along to minister to the religious needs of these immigrants. But as most of the newly arrived were not well educated, they could only appreciate the popular practices of Chinese Buddhism, which included an amalgam of Mahayana beliefs and Confucianism, Taoism, and indigenous Chinese folk religion.

Some of the Chinese immigrants decided to send their children to Christian missionary schools in the hope that an English education would provide better career prospects at a time when Malaysia was colonized and ruled by the British. The Christian teachers were quick to seize the opportunity to influence these young students to convert to Christianity by portraying it as a superior religion. Compared to the many rites and rituals practiced by their parents in the name of Buddhism, the Christianity taught by the Catholics and Protestants appeared modern, logical, and scientific.

The Chinese monks who came to Malaysia from China were unable to present Buddhism in a modern manner, nor could they refute the allegations leveled by the Christians against the many rites and rituals practiced in the name of Buddhism by the Chinese. The Mandarin-speaking monks from China were also unable to communicate with the increasing number of young Chinese educated in English schools. The students, on the other hand, were not taught Mandarin in missionary schools and could not understand the technical Chinese terms that the monks used to explain Buddhism. This was the scenario from 1945, the end of World War II, to the 1960s. Naturally, these young students found solace in the Christian priests and pastors who could communicate in English. As a result, many of them rejected Buddhism and became Christians. It was a period of upheaval within families as children newly converted to Christianity refused to pray at the family altar or perform the traditional rituals, including ancestor worship.

The situation among those educated in Chinese schools was quite different, however. The Chinese schools did not emphasize religion, though they did teach moral values. As Chinese literature has many references to Buddhism, students were able to appreciate the importance of Buddhism in Chinese culture and society. There were also many books available on Buddhism written in Chinese. As a result, students were able to differentiate the "popular" or folk Buddhism practiced by their less-educated parents from the "purer" kind of Mahayana Buddhism presented in these books as rational, scientific, and compatible with modernity. Thus, far fewer Chinese-educated students became Christians compared to those in English schools.

By the 1950s, few English-educated Chinese in Malaysia were Buddhist. Buddhism among these Chinese was actually revived from an unexpected source: the arrival in Malaysia of monks from Sri Lanka and also a few Western monks who had been ordained in Sri Lanka. As a result of these missionaries, there are now more than fifty English-speaking, ethnically Chinese Buddhist communities that practice in the Theravada (Southeast Asian) tradition.[2] They are not unlike the Theravada communities in the United States, which are also English-speaking and not ethnically the same as those that traditionally practice Theravada. Other parallels include the emphasis on lay leadership, building small, local communities, and meditation. However, unlike the Theravada communities in the United States, Malaysia's Chinese Theravada have a well-developed system of Sunday schools, which provide a foundation of education and literacy in the tradition. These Sunday schools have been essential to the revitalization of Buddhism among the English-speaking Chinese of Malaysia.

The Sinhalese (Sri Lankan) monks established Malaysia's two earliest Sunday schools: Buddhist Institute Sunday Dhamma School in Kuala Lumpur in 1929 and Mahindarama Sunday Pali School in Penang in 1959 (Pali is the liturgical and scholarly language of Theravada Buddhism). Familiar with Christian missionary activities in Sri Lanka, the monks believed that the Sunday school was a good way to introduce Buddhism to the young. The initial objective of both was to preserve the culture and language of the Sinhala community as well as reinforce the position of Buddhism as an integral part of the community. However, Venerable Dr. K. Sri Dhammananda, the current chief abbot of the Buddhist Maha Vihara, led the way in reaching out to non-Sinhala Buddhists. From 1953 onward, children of all nationalities began attending Sunday school regularly, and English was used as the common language. Many of the former students have since become active lay Buddhist leaders in the temple as well as other Buddhist centers outside Penang. Owing to the efforts of these Sinhalese monks, many English-educated Chinese in Malaysia were able to learn about Buddhism.

The recent interest and mushrooming of Sunday schools in Kuala Lumpur and surrounding areas are due to a number of factors. First, with greater economic prosperity, Chinese parents are now exploring their own religious needs and turning to religion for solutions to their workplace problems and stress. Although many of them are nominal Buddhists, they have a closer affinity to Buddhism than to Christianity or Islam. They also realize the importance of their children receiving some basic religious and moral values while young, and they turn to Sunday schools to meet this need for their children. Second, increased Christian evangelism has pushed some parents to send their children to Buddhist Sunday schools because of their fear that without knowing the basics of Buddhism, considered their heritage and ancestral religion, their children could easily be converted by Christians while at school or in college. Third, Buddhism is now perceived as a modern and scientific religion because of the positive publicity in the Western media and local Buddhist groups' invitations to well-known Western monastics to visit Malaysia to give talks on Buddhism. The image of Buddhism being an old-fashioned Eastern religion has been diminished in the recent past. There are now many more books on Buddhism, in English, easily available in bookstores or printed for free distribution. These developments have resulted in an increased membership in Buddhist societies. When these Buddhists have children of their own, they send them to the nearest Sunday school.

As stated in their workbooks, the primary goal of Sunday schools is to educate children to be better and happier human beings by developing, in an integrated way, their perceptual, cognitive, emotional, and intuitive capacities so that they may reach their ultimate human potential. To achieve this goal, Sunday schools provide a balanced program of learning activities on two fronts. First, there are mental training activities that develop the students' mindfulness, perception, concentration, and memory. For example, children might play a game in which they must race through a series of webbed strings without touching them. Second, schools promote the ethical values of kindness, honesty, and nonviolence by various means, including reference to relevant cultural contexts, histories, and mythologies.

Children are taught to be kind and ethical in part because Buddhism understands that cultivating these qualities leads to greater happiness. The idea of karma is that good deeds and intentions lead to positive results. Children are expected, in some way, to be attentive to karmatic workings in their lives. At a salvific level, however, ethics are considered foundational to meditation practice and to the cultivation of wisdom. In the Theravada tradition, there is no special theological view of the nature of children.

The typical objectives of a Sunday school are to study the basic teachings of Buddhism, encourage Buddhist youth activities, develop the qualities of wisdom and compassion in the practice of the Buddhadharma, train young Buddhists to be leaders of the Buddhist community later in life, and develop friendship among young Buddhists in the community. The Dharma classes in the Sunday school are ideally divided by age, from age four up to age twenty.

The curriculum encompasses a wide array of programming. The program starts with a short devotional ceremony, conducted in English and Pali, in which The Three Refuges and The Five Precepts for Laypeople are chanted.[3] Dharma classes form the core of the day. The syllabus follows the one devised by the Young Men's Buddhist Association (YMBA—patterned after the YMCA) of Sri Lanka and is customized by local examples. Common topics are the life of the Buddha, basic doctrines, daily Buddhist practices, and apologetics. Through choir, Sunday school children learn Buddhist hymns and verses that praise the virtues of the Buddha, his teachings, and disciples. Many of these hymns, originally adapted from the Japanese Buddhist Churches of America during the 1960s, have a Christian syntax and hymnal quality and are well received by the younger children. Noticeably absent from the curriculum is meditation instruction, which Westerners tend to consider the defining element of Buddhism. In recent years, however, meditation, once considered the province of monastics (and only a handful of them, at that) has become popular among laypeople. As a result, children sometimes are asked to do a brief, five-minute meditation. Teachers use meditation partly to help the children calm down and focus, but it is also taught as a way of reconnecting to one's inner self and spirituality. A very few young adults go on to participate in full meditation retreats, and these are gaining in popularity.

In addition to meeting on Sundays, the Sunday schools arrange other activities. New Year caroling, similar to Christmas caroling, is done during the Chinese New Year. A holiday camp is held each December during school vacation that combines Dharma study, games, and fellowship for young people. This is considered more popular than the more serious novitiate program, in which the boys are required to be ordained as monks, shaving their heads and taking just one meal a day.

On Wesak Day (the Buddha's birthday) in May, children make presentations, such as performing a concert and holding an elocution contest. In the evening, the children participate in the annual candlelit Wesak procession, which is held in all major towns and cities in Malaysia. In order to inculcate the teachings of compassion, most Sunday schools organize compassionate activities, such as visits to homes of the less fortunate or collecting clothing for distribution to those in cold countries during winter or to victims of natural disasters such as earthquakes and floods. Compassion is considered an expression of the interconnectedness of all beings: just as our own hand immediately embraces a throbbing stubbed toe, so too does relieving the suffering of others show an understanding of our shared existence.

Monastics, though few in number within Buddhist communities, provide the overall vision and authority for such programming, and also act as exemplars of the ideal Buddhist. Monastics from all the lineages continue to be very much respected. Parents and lay members teach children how to behave properly in the presence of a monk or nun, bowing three times upon greeting, serving food, offering robes, and so on. The primary teaching here is on the virtue of generosity, especially as a way of creating wholesome karma. Monastics are also indirectly essential in nurturing children's spirituality: they are the ones who nurture the tradition in the older lay members and parents, who then become the Sunday school teachers.

While monastics and parents continue to play a traditional key role in nurturing Buddhism in children, the advent of Sunday schools has given dedicated lay members new prominence. While these lay members are themselves parents of the same children in the classroom, there are many others whose children have grown up, who are grand-parents, or who have no children. These laypeople provide the bulk of the energy, funding, and administration for children's programming. They become "aunts" and "uncles," invaluable resources of advice and support for the youth.

Although the concept of Sunday schools in Malaysia has been in existence for more than fifty years, it was only during the past two decades that it has matured into formal organizations with proper administration, qualified teachers, and comprehensive activities and programs for students of all ages. Buddhists have learned much from the way Christians organize their schools, and in the process, Buddhist Sunday schools have developed into effective organizations to train young Buddhists to become responsible citizens of the world.

Korean and Korean American Buddhists

As in Malaysia, South Korea's traditions have been challenged by colonialism, Westernization, and Christianity. From the Korean War onward, South Korea went through a period of rapid modernization. Many Koreans believed that Western culture—especially American culture—was more advanced and modern than traditional Korean society. Because Christianity was identified with the West, it was also seen as a more modern and enlightened religion. Christian missions, particularly the Presbyterian, Methodist, and Catholic denominations, enjoyed great success in converting Koreans by providing much needed relief in the form of food, education, and medical care.

Relative to the socially active missions, Buddhism and Buddhist monastics appeared passive and unconcerned with the immediate suffering of a society recovering from Japanese occupation, war, and social upheaval. Buddhism, which had become integral to Korean culture over its sixteen-hundred-year history, looked increasingly old-fashioned, antisocial, and superstitious in the face of modernity. For many young people, Buddhism became what Grandmother did. Moreover, monastics became preoccupied with a costly power struggle between the married and celibate traditions, a legacy of Japanese colonialism (1910–45). As a result of this infighting and reluctance to change, Buddhism's influence waned as Christianity became the dominant religion in social and political influence.

Starting in the late 1980s, Korean Buddhism began reforming itself. Acknowledging the successes of Christianity, it became more socially engaged. New temples were built in cities and towns, rather than in the remote mountains, as had traditionally been done. Abbots directed the construction of schools and clinics. Monastics began changing their sermons to show how Buddhism could address the everyday concerns of laypeople and of family life. Meditation was revived as a practice to relieve stress and bring calm. Interestingly, it is partly because Americans and other Westerners showed an interest in meditation that Koreans reconsidered the merit of meditation for modern laypeople.

In the 1990s, as Korean society became affluent and settled, Koreans rethought the superiority of Western culture. They began reappreciating their native culture, from local artifacts to shamanism to traditional dance. Buddhism too was newly regarded as an indelible part of Korean cultural identity, and many people began rekindling their interests not only in the rich cultural elements of Buddhism but also in seeking a deeper spirituality from this profound tradition.

In recent years, temples have seen a slow but steady increase in attendance from all generations, including children accompanying their parents. In an effort to modernize, many temples provide youth programming so that young people are drawn in through their friendships. As in Malaysia, the Sunday schools educate the children and provide fun activities while parents attend the service in the main hall. There is also a large governing body, the Korean Youth Leader Association, composed of more than five hundred lay and monastic Buddhist leaders who arrange for and create youth programming across Korea. In addition, these leaders meet twice a year for training and an exchange of ideas.

Upon initiating programs, these leaders base their teachings on Buddhism's traditional beliefs. In Mahayana Buddhism in general, and Korean Buddhism in particular, young people, as are all people, are considered bodhisattvas, those who possess the seeds to become a buddha, a fully awakened one. The Avatamsaka Sutra (the Flower Garland Sutra), one of the most influential scriptures in the Korean Buddhist tradition, epitomizes Korean Buddhism's perception of young Buddhists. At the end of this sutra, Sonjae (Sudhana, in Sanskrit), a young novice, undertakes the path of enlightenment by studying with fifty-seven spiritual leaders, each of whom who sparks his innate Buddhahood, eventually leading the novice to the full realization of his mind. The story of this young novice as a future buddha has impacted lay Buddhists' attitude toward their children.

With Sonjae as a representative figure of a young Buddhist, youth programs communicate three basic teachings. First and foremost, Buddhist leaders teach young Buddhists to believe that they inherently possess the buddha mind (*pulsim*), which is the key doctrinal concept of Mahayana Buddhism. Second, on the basis of their belief in innate buddhahood, young Buddhists are encouraged to illuminate this quality of their minds with their own will. Third, the overarching doctrine, in close relation to the innate possession of the buddha mind, is that nothing can exist alone and we all are interdependent. From this realization of interconnectedness arise love and compassion toward others.

Today, many young people are particularly drawn to the Temple Stay programs in which young lay Buddhists can experience the rigorous monastic lifestyle during a retreat. They join the monks and nuns in waking up at three in the morning for chanting and bowing, eating simple meals, and spending the day working in the temple complex or studying. In fact, some temples have, as a much more effective way than the Korean monastic training system (which requires a lifelong renunciation), adopted the Southeast Asian Buddhist custom of allowing young people to be temporarily ordained for short periods (one week to a month) so that they can try out the monastic life by learning how to rediscover their buddha mind. This program has become quite popular.

Korea also has a division of Club 25, which is a leadership-oriented youth group for those who are twenty-five and younger. This pan-Asian youth club, formed and financially supported under the auspices of the older International Federation of Buddhist Youth, gathers once a year in a different country to learn about the Buddhism of that nation (Thailand, India, Malaysia, etc.) and to plan activities. These club members, many of whom are leaders within the youth groups of their own countries, stay in touch through the Internet. It will be interesting to see what kind of role they create as they grow older in nurturing the spirituality of even younger Buddhists and how, as an international group, they will address globalization as a force in Buddhism.

In Korean Buddhism, the responsibility for nurturing spirituality rests with the monastics, parents, and lay temple leaders, as well as with the youth themselves. Parents model the behaviors of good lay Buddhists, especially with regards to supporting the temples and with proper conduct toward monastics. Lay temple members, working with monastics, are expected to provide programs such as Sunday and winter schools, trips to mountain temples, retreats for youth, and pastoral counseling.

These expectations are the same for Korean Buddhists living in the United States, but the context of being Buddhist in a country that is primarily Judeo-Christian and English-speaking makes the relationships among monastics, parents, lay members, and children more complicated. In the United States, most Korean immigrants are strongly Christian, in part because of the influence of Christianity in Korea and in part because even non-Christian Koreans feel they will adapt better to American culture if they follow a mainstream religion. Furthermore, Korean churches in the United States are active in providing support to Korean immigrants.

In contrast, owing to the shorter history and the weak establishment of Korean Buddhism in the United States, most Korean temples[4] are based in small residential houses and have significantly less funding than Korean churches. The few Buddhist Koreans living in the United States are therefore a minority within the minority Korean population. Korean Christians apply tremendous pressure on the Korean Buddhists to convert. Sometimes the pressure comes even from within families. Thus, the secondary religious status of Buddhism in Korea is lowered even further.

These pressures paradoxically bond the small number of Buddhists together, deepening their emotional attachment to temples in a way that is much stronger than among their counterparts in Korea. To strengthen the identity with Buddhism, many temples offer themselves as a place for immigrants to connect with other Koreans through shared language, food, and cultural values. As a result of these pressures and the importance of the temple as a cultural locus, those few Koreans who are Buddhist are often strongly identified, assertive, and active. In short, Korean Buddhists in America tend to be more consciously Buddhist, in general, than Buddhists in Korea.

Korean American youth whose parents are Buddhists are pulled in two directions: on the one hand, they desperately want to fit in and become as American as possible. Many of their school friends go to church, and friends are more of a pull than the abstract values of religion. On the other hand, devout parents want their children to spend a lot of time at the temple, not only to learn Buddhism, but also to learn the

Korean language and culture. As in Korea, these parents expect lay members and monastics to offer activities for children ranging in age from grade school through university—although most temples have not been able to create a sufficient number of these programs because of a lack of human and financial resources.

At the temples that are able to provide programs, the relationships are complicated by the American context. The monastics and lay members may be Korean and not have complete fluency in English, whereas some of the Korean American children may not have complete fluency in Korean. Then there are newly arrived Korean children who are trying to connect with Korean American youth who might never have even been to Korea. The monks and leading lay members may not have a full familiarity with the American culture that the children encounter in school every day. Further, some of the monastics who are drawn to live in the United States may have been on the edge of the monastic social sphere. They may or may not have good social skills.

The ideal monk is fluent in both Korean and English (and knows the latest youth slang); is young enough to connect with the temple's youth but old enough to guide them; has good social and pastoral skills to counsel not only the youth but also their parents; can transmit not only the tradition of Buddhism but also support cultural events; and has the organizational skills to put together fun and meaningful activities for children of all ages. This is a tall order, and many temples cannot always fill it.

In a model Korean American temple, there is a range of activities for children. Sunday school, in which there are lessons, coloring books, and games, is the foundation. Children learn Buddhist fables, hymns, chants, and rituals. They might also work on a play about the Buddha's life, with a special emphasis on the youth life of the Buddha as a future enlightened one, and perform it in May during the Buddha's birthday celebration. Children and young adults are organized to perform temple functions such as printing a newsletter, making gifts for others, and doing community service. As in Malaysia, meditation does not play a central role in Sunday school, although there are sometimes five-minute meditations. For those in their late teens and early twenties, however, longer meditations are incorporated into retreats, which are primarily constructed around extended periods of bowing, chanting, discussion, study, and social time. Students stay overnight at the temple, usually sleeping on the floor of the worship hall. Youth groups will also plan trips to the mall, movies, bowling, and to visit other temples or Buddhists sites. Finally, many youth groups stay connected online, such as through a chat room or discussion board.

Throughout, dedicated lay temple members, a monk, parents, and the youth group itself are all enjoined to keep the youth active and cultivate buddha mind (*pulsim*) and to stay connected to each other, the temple, and Korean language and culture.

Western American Buddhists

With regards to understanding to whom the Western American Buddhists[5] assign responsibility for nurturing spirituality in children, we run into two issues. First, given that Buddhism has been practiced by the Western Americans for only fifty years at the most,[6] a pattern of transmission from one generation to the next—a tradition—has not been established. In fact, the first generation has only begun thinking about transmission and legacy in the past five to ten years. The short answer to the question is that *no one* in the Western American Buddhist community is assigned responsibility. There are few expectations from community members to nurture spirituality in children. We will have to examine not so much what the tradition has been but what system the first generation is just now beginning to envision. Second, compared to an active synagogue or parish, most Buddhist centers have a striking absence of children, teens, and even university students.[7] The first generation is beginning to consider how youth programming can be created to address the needs of the few committed youth as well as draw in new members.

One unusual feature of the first generation of parents is that they are hands-off in teaching their own children about religion. Many of these parents say they remember, as children, being forced to attend church or the synagogue against their will. They came to dislike catechism, Sunday school, rituals, holidays, the authority of the clergy and the institution. As a result, many Buddhist parents decided they would not force their children to learn Buddhism for either of two reasons. One, they did not want their children to experience what they had from their own parents or, two, they secretly wanted their children to become Buddhist but knew that forcing them would make them rebel against it. Further, in most families usually just one of the two parents is Buddhist. Many couples, having different religious perspectives, decide to let their children explore religion for themselves. Finally, because there are so few Buddhists in the United States—perhaps under a million Western American Buddhists—most parents are isolated, with no local temple or community to be a part of as a family.

As a result, most grown children of Buddhist parents will not describe themselves as Buddhist, though they admit to being influenced. Some children of Buddhist parents go so far as to rebel against that "hippie stuff" and seek more conventional lifestyles. In short, one thing is quite clear about whom the Western American Buddhists designate as being responsible for transmitting the tradition: it is *not* the parents.

If not parents, then who is drawing young adults to Buddhism? Most of those in the second generation that I have informally surveyed cite the following origins for their interest in Buddhism (ranked in order of frequency):

1. A high school or college course on philosophy, world religions, Eastern religions, or Buddhism
2. A book on Buddhism from the library
3. Travel to Asia
4. Seeking the counsel of an older friend, friend of parents, or teacher who seems wise and calm because of a Buddhist or meditative practices
5. Through meditation as a component of yoga or martial arts

It is striking that the most influential group here is university professors, who themselves may or may not be practicing Buddhists. Neither the universities nor the Buddhists expect professors to nurture spirituality among students, and yet these professors are probably the single biggest influence on the second generation. It may be that the classroom format offers a neutral, safe place for young adults to explore something as culturally unfamiliar as Buddhism, in the same way that Sunday schools provide a familiar secular format for highly Westernized Asians. Professors may be able to articulate the Buddhist tradition in terms that Western students are able to understand. It is not unusual that someone outside a religion can be more articulate and comprehensive than one practicing it. Today's professors of Buddhism often present the tradition in a lively and engaged way, with skill, charisma, and even a touch of reverence. Some students in these introductory Buddhism courses continue to study and practice Buddhism on their own, traveling to Asia, and attaching themselves to a nearby Buddhist center, much like those students in their parents' generation in the 1960s and 1970s. These independent studies and travels often lead to a lifelong commitment to Buddhism.

With each of these five sources, we see that there is no directed, active engagement on the part of the first generation to recruit the second generation. Rather, most first-generation Buddhists have a passive stance, preferring to be available should they be approached by a younger person. Because of this reluctance on any Buddhist's part to be directive in others' religious maturation, first-generation Western American Buddhists think more in terms of "creating a space," "creating opportunity," and "making retreats and scholarships available" for those in the second generation who actively seek it out.

It is clear that the second generation will not be primarily composed of adult children of Buddhist parents. Rather, the second generation will be, like the first, formed almost entirely from converts to Buddhism. As converts making conscious choices about their religion, most become Buddhist in their late teens and early twenties. Programming and mentoring are therefore geared toward young adults rather than toward children. Several meditation centers now offer retreats for teenagers, and other youth age ranges (college, postcollege, etc.), which have shorter sittings (thirty minutes, rather than forty-five), permit talking between sits, and offer time for music, art, and hanging out. Beliefnet.com has a lively teen Buddhist discussion board. Roshi Norman Fischer has worked with teenagers to develop initiation rituals and to explore what it means to mature.[8] In the past ten years, university Buddhist groups have grown and become more active, often counseled by a sympathetic professor or liberal-leaning chaplain.[9]

Buddhist communities are developing new programs for young adults in response to several factors. First, as the leading Dharma teachers of the baby boom generation age, they are beginning to recognize that they need to cultivate, at a minimum, well-trained young adults to replace them. Second, these same teachers, as well as mature dedicated Buddhist students, in connecting with the younger generation recognize that young adult beginners have different spiritual questions (how do I survive stress at college?) and needs than do middle-aged beginners (how can I parent my teenage daughter?) and that they also have different generational values. Programming specific to age and generation addresses those unique needs. Third, young adults themselves, often being the minority among the larger community of middle-aged Buddhists, feel a need to bond with peers and to form spiritual friendships. Young Buddhists are increasingly taking a lead in creating programs[10] and literature[11] for themselves.

Although the emphasis of care is placed on youth in their late teens and early twenties, to some extent younger children are receiving exposure to Buddhism. In the past few years, the power of meditation as a technique, decoupled from the Buddhist and

Hindu traditions that developed it, has been entering the mainstream. The Associated Press published an online article titled "Meditation lowers teens' blood pressure."[12] Public schools have brought in TM (Transcendental Meditation)-trained youth to teach that type of meditation (Hindu-based) to reduce stress and behavioral problems. The August 4, 2003, issue of *Time* magazine included a cover article on meditation, with photographs of public school students taking time out to meditate.

It is hard to say whether this is a transmission of the Buddhist tradition per se because meditation is presented as a nonreligious psychological technique that can relieve stress, cultivate emotional intelligence, and provide tranquillity and ease of well-being. In these cases, Buddhist teachers, experienced young Buddhists, and seasoned older Buddhists will visit the schools to teach meditation,[13] but they tend not to display their religious affiliation in these settings. Will this secular form of meditation be an avenue by which young people are further drawn to Buddhism as a tradition? Or might it draw them to bring meditative rituals to their religious traditions of birth? These issues will take another ten years to answer.

Because Buddhism is so new to Western American Buddhists, and because the community at large has begun thinking about its successor population only in the past ten years, Western American Buddhists have not developed theological views about the nature of childhood nor have they articulated what theology would be taught to children and adolescents. Indeed, Western American Buddhists tend to be anti- or, at best, atheological in their approach to Buddhism, emphasizing practice over doctrine. The growing discourse about children is cast primarily in psychological, not theological, terms, and the motivation to reach out to young adults stems from a feeling that meditation practice can relieve the psychological suffering of young people.

Further Reflections

Among Asian and Asian American Buddhist communities, is the development of Sunday schools a good thing? In the view of these three writers, on the whole, they are of tremendous benefit to children. First, Sunday schools provide peer communities in ways that traditional temples have not. These friendships help retain young Buddhists in the face of pluralism. Second, Sunday schools have raised literacy regarding Buddhism among laypeople overall to higher levels than in the premodern tradition. Third, given that Asian youth are already Westernized, the Sunday school format is more familiar and therefore comfortable to them. Fourth, Sunday schools encourage parents and lay members to be actively involved in developing the spirituality of children. And fifth, Sunday schools have not marginalized the role of the monastic: rather, monks and nuns are given new prominence and a clear role in assisting laypeople with nurturing Buddhist children. If we were to mourn any loss of the premodern traditional expressions of Buddhism, we would have to mourn the effects of centuries of colonialism, in the past, and globalization, in the present, on Asian societies as a whole. In a way, Sunday schools are a promising adaptation to the needs of today's Buddhists.

In many respects, Western American Buddhists are behind both Asian American and Asian Buddhists in cultivating a successor generation and nurturing youths' spirituality.

Within the Western American Buddhist lineages of Zen, vipassana and Vajrayana, for example, many of the youth programs tend to focus on meditation but ignore literacy about the tradition in other areas. Western American Buddhists would benefit from studying how Vietnamese Zen master Thich Nhat Hanh's international, Western-based organization has written songs, plays, and encourages artwork for young people. The Buddhist Churches of America, a primarily Japanese American organization that has supported the Jodoshinshu lineage since the early 1900s, has developed excellent programs for young people in a specifically American culture. Likewise, the Soka Gakkai International-USA, also based in a Japanese lineage, has a well-developed youth division that even prints youth-specific pamphlets and books.

Western American Buddhists may want to reexamine their assumption that Asian Buddhism is "ethnic": that Buddhism serves an Asian cultural need rather than a spiritual need. Asian Buddhism is changing rapidly and it has been highly responsive to the modernization—and ironically Westernization—that demands it address the contemporary needs of laypeople and their families. We might reflect on why Korea has been able to adopt the Southeast Asian Theravada custom of having children temporarily ordained as monastics—which is highly popular with Buddhist youth—while Theravada Western American Buddhists have yet to consider such a program. Western American Buddhists can think about why most Asian temples have a youth homepage within their Web site while most Western centers rarely have that feature. Western American Buddhists might learn something from the Asian Sunday schools and other youth programs, while also continuing to develop a system that addresses the particular characteristics of generations of converts. It is unlikely that Western American Buddhists will form programs called "Sunday schools," given that these Buddhists are pushing away from the Christian mainstream from which they came. Yet, educational programming under another name would be of benefit.

At the same time, it is clear that Western American Buddhists are somewhat ahead in developing meditation as an essential part of spirituality. While most meditation teachings are geared toward adults, the new literature on meditation for children, teens, and college students is of high quality. At a time when some Asian countries are becoming more secular, meditation as a semi-Buddhist technique for countering stress, creating well-being, and providing an avenue toward spiritual connection may be a timely reintroduction from the West.

In conclusion, the three authors are encouraged by contemporary developments in both the West and in Asia for clarifying the roles of Buddhists in nurturing spirituality among its children and adolescents.

Notes

1. The word *dharma* can refer to the Buddhist tradition, to the teachings of the Buddha, or to the meaning of Dharma as "the way life is."

2. The majority of Chinese Buddhists practice in the Mahayana tradition, with more than three hundred temples. In recent years, small communities of Tibetan-Vajrayana and Japanese Soka Gakkai have also been established.

3. The Three Refuges are the Buddha, the Dharma (teaching), and the Sangha (community). The Five Precepts for Laypeople are to refrain from harming, stealing, wrong speech, sexual misconduct, and taking intoxicants. There are other chants for gratitude, extending well-being to others, and so on.

4. In 2004, there were ninety-two temples located in the United States and seven in Canada.

5. "American Buddhist" is not a useful label in distinguishing between Asian Buddhists and non-Asian Buddhists because *American* designates a nationality rather than an ethnicity. For the purposes of this chapter, *Western American* refers to non-Asian Americans who were born and raised in the United States. Most Western American Buddhists are converts, and a majority are of European descent.

6. Western Americans began practicing Buddhism as early as the late 1800s, but it was not until the 1960s that a substantial number of Westerners adopted Buddhism as their primary religion. It is reasonable to consider the baby boom Buddhists, those born from 1945 to the early 1960s, as the first generation.

7. However, the Soka Gakkai International-USA is an exception: although the first generation is the largest, there is a strong and active youth division. Unlike other denominations, a high proportion of the youth within the organization are from SGI families and are not converts.

8. See Fischer (2004).

9. Wesleyan College has a dormitory called Buddha House.

10. For example, a weekend workshop in September 2004 at Wesleyan College titled "Buddhism for Our Generation."

11. See, for example, Metcalf (2002), Winston (2003), Levine (2004), Richmond (2003), and Gordhamer (2001). The last four authors are all second-generation writers, and Metcalf is not much older.

12. http://msnbc.msn.com/id/4647377/.

13. The Mindfulness Based Stress Reduction Clinic at the University of Massachusetts Medical Center in Worcester provides training and teacher certification in meditation techniques without tying such training to the Buddhist tradition. Another example in which Buddhist practice has been adapted in a nonreligious way is through Marsha Linehan's Dialectical Behavior Therapy (University of Washington), based on Zen practices, for mental illnesses such as borderline personality disorder.

References

Fischer, Norman. 2004. *Taking our places: The Buddhist path to truly growing up.* San Francisco: HarperSanFrancisco.

Gordhamer, Soren. 2001. *Just say Om: Your life's journey.* Avon, Mass.: Adams Media.

Levine, Noah. 2004. *Dharma punx.* San Francisco: HarperSanFrancisco.

Metcalf, Franz. 2002. *Buddha in your backpack: Everyday Buddhism for teens.* Berkeley, Calif.: Seastone.

Richmond, Ivan. 2003. *Silence and noise: Growing up Zen in America.* New York: Atria.

Winston, Diana. 2003. *Wide awake: A Buddhist guide for teens.* New York: Perigree.

CHAPTER 28

Personal Responsibility with Communal Support: The Spiritual Education of Muslim Children

Pamela K. Taylor

Allahu Akbar	God is Greater
Allahu Akbar	God is Greater
Allahu Akbar	God is Greater
Allahu Akbar	God is Greater
Ash-Shadu a la ilaha ill Allah	I bear witness there is no god but God
Ash-Shadu a la ilaha ill Allah	I bear witness there is no god but God
Ash-Shadu anna Muhammad ur-Rasul Allah	I bear witness that Muhammad is the Messenger of God
Ash-Shadu anna Muhammad ur-Rasul Allah	I bear witness that Muhammad is the Messenger of God
Haya 'ala Salat	Come to Prayer
Haya 'ala Salat	Come to Prayer
Haya 'ala Falah	Come to Success
Haya 'ala Falah	Come to Success
Allahu Akbar	God is Greater
Allahu Akbar	God is Greater
La ilaha ill Allah	There is no god but God

These words—the *adhan,* or call to prayer—are the first words a Muslim child hears, chanted in his or her ear by a loving father, grandfather, uncle, or other relative immediately after birth. They are words that set the child securely upon the path toward the Divine, words that are the first steps in a lifelong spiritual journey and that represent the family's commitment to helping this child fulfill her or his spiritual potential.

This simple ritual may seem small, or even insignificant, in the context of the larger and more complex tasks of giving the child a comprehensive spiritual education; however, it embodies, in a microcosm, foundational Islamic concepts and attitudes that not only inform Islam's understanding of what it means to be human, the relationship between the human and the Divine, and how to teach spirituality, but also that are germane to Islam's view of what spirituality is and the spiritual goals it sets forth for humankind. The ritual is also a manifestation of Islam's normative views on social order and the importance of the family in developing, socializing, and educating children, spiritually and otherwise.

Before one can begin a discussion of whom Islam holds responsible for the spiritual education of children, it is important to understand how Islam envisions this task, in particular how it understands human nature and what it means to be spiritual. The ritual of calling the adhan in a newborn's ear reflects three central concepts of Islam: *tauheed, fitrah,* and *taqwa.* Tauheed is the central thesis of Islam: that the Divine is singular. Fitrah refers to the inherent, natural order of God's Creation, including human nature. Taqwa is an all-encompassing term that refers to piety, fear and love of God, as well as obedience and righteousness.

Foundational Concepts: Tauheed, Fitrah, Taqwa

Tauheed—the belief that God is single, unique—is the central doctrine of Islam.[1] The implications of God's unity are far-reaching; because God is a unity it follows that His Creation is a unity, the universe is a unity, the world is a unity, humankind is a unity, the individual is a unified being (Al-Faruqi 1983). Spirituality, then, is about recognizing the Divine unity in all things and acknowledging it in appropriate ways. A Muslim's relations with the rest of the world, the environment, animals, people, his or her surroundings are envisioned as part and parcel of the spiritual task of acknowledging the Divine unity. Faith and good works are inseparable, as the Islamic understanding of human nature does not allow for a separation between the divine and the mundane, the spiritual and the material.

The concept of fitrah refers to the essential nature of God's creation. Fitrah in the widest sense refers to God's pattern, the natural order in which He created the universe, and it can be compared to natural law, Dao, or Dharma (Glasse 1989, 128). In a narrower sense, fitrah is used to describe the essential and innate parts of human nature, particularly those parts that reflect and respond to the natural order established by God. This fitrah, which is intrinsic to humankind, is composed of several elements:

- An innate recognition of, yearning for, and striving toward the Divine;
- A sense of right and wrong, and the ability to tell the one from the other emotionally, through conscience, and intellectually, through reason;
- The capacity to do good or evil; and
- The desire to do good (Yassien 1996, 3).

The aim of a spiritual education is, then, not so much to teach a child to be spiritual but to enhance, develop, and strengthen the connection to God that she or he was born with, to encourage devotion and the practice of good deeds as a manifestation of that connection.

Muslims believe that acting in accordance with one's fitrah brings harmony and peace, whereas acting against this fitrah creates turmoil, confusion, and unhappiness, both within the individual and to society at large (Al-Attas 1985, 57–58). Furthermore, because it views itself as the final and perfected religion, Islam teaches that the beliefs, principles, and requirements of Islam are perfectly in accord with this fitrah—that is, if one were to practice Islam perfectly, one would be living in complete harmony with one's fitrah. Again, the notion that there can be divisions between the religious and the mundane is rejected: every thought, feeling, and act of humankind is either in accordance with the fitrah on which Allah fashioned Creation and humanity or it is in conflict with God's essential order.

Living according to one's fitrah is synonymous, in the Islamic worldview, with living a life of taqwa. Taqwa is a broad concept that includes spirituality along with piety, devotion, awe, fear, love, righteousness, obedience, and submission to God's will (Ali 1987; see also Siddiqui 2003). The ultimate goal of the Muslim is to embody taqwa in all his or her actions and thoughts. Faith or spirituality, according to Islam, cannot remain at the level of feelings or attitudes; it must be translated into action (Nasr 1966, 121). The Qur'an repeatedly refers to believers as those who *aminu wa amilu salihat*—"believe and do good works."[2] Once again we see that faith, or spirituality, cannot be separated out from good works (Al-Faruqi 1983, 87).

The path to living in a state of taqwa, of awakened spirituality, of good deeds and perfect obedience, as we have seen, begins with the simple ritual of calling the adhan in the newborn's ear. It is, for the Muslim, literally a call to the child's soul, awakening it to its inherent consciousness of and responsiveness to God. The path upon which the child is set is understood to be a lifelong journey. Prophet Muhammad said, "A believer is never satiated with his knowledge. He goes on acquiring it till his death and entry into Paradise."[3] Other oft-quoted sayings include "Seek knowledge from the cradle to the grave" and "Seek knowledge even unto China."[4]

Because the spiritual education of a human being is never finished, the task falls upon various parties at different points in a person's life. Ultimately, the responsibility to obtain a spiritual education/awakening falls on the individual. Islam insists on individual responsibility in all walks of life, whether it be in obedience to law, fulfilling religious obligations, or enhancing spiritual awareness (Al-Anani 1990, 189). At the same time, the parents, the extended family, the local community, and the greater community, in that order, are expected to educate, encourage, and support the individual's spiritual development, particularly before she or he attains majority. Islamic scholars agree, for the most part, that a child attains the age of majority upon entering puberty (Al-Anani 1990, 54). Thus, for the age group covered by this book, Islam places the responsibility for the spiritual education and development of the child upon the family and greater society while the child is young, but that responsibility shifts to the individual in the early teen years.

Individual Responsibility: The Age of Maturity

As stated earlier, in Islam the fundamental human-Divine relationship is between the individual and God, without intermediary. Further, God holds individuals solely responsible for their own beliefs, thoughts, and actions. On the Day of Judgment, the Qur'an tells us, no one will be held accountable for anyone else's deeds, nor will anyone receive rewards for anyone else's deeds: "Each soul is rewarded only for what it earns for itself, nor shall it bear another's burden" (6:164). And, "Guard yourselves against a day when no soul will in any way avail another, nor will intercession be accepted from it, nor will compensation be received from it, nor will they be helped" (2:148).

This responsibility begins at the age of maturity, which is defined as puberty. Various hadith of the Prophet reference this age, some directly and some indirectly. Aisha, the Prophet's wife, related that the Prophet said: There are three people whose actions are not recorded: a sleeper till he awakes, a child till he reaches puberty, and a lunatic till he comes to reason (Abu Daud, book 38, no. 4384). Thus, around the age of twelve or thirteen, Muslims are considered liable for their good and bad deeds, for their spirituality, or lack thereof.

The implementation of this standard, however, as observed by this author, varies widely across the Muslim world. In many countries, young teens are treated as adults, and marriage is common among older teens, especially young women. In others, and especially in Western Muslim communities, modern ideas about maturity have been accepted, and parents remain involved in the education of their children for a longer period of time, often well into the twenties. Perhaps the most interesting phenomenon is a religious-secular divide, where on the one hand, teenagers are viewed as responsible for their religious behavior—they are expected to pray, fast, do good works, and to work to develop their faith and spirituality—while on the other, they are not treated as full adults—parents still consider themselves in charge of their children's education, direct their activities, and monitor their performance of religious obligations, offering encouragement, support, education, and, often, demanding adherence so long as the "child" lives under their roof.

Furthermore, Qur'anic injunctions to "command the good and forbid the evil" (e.g., 3:104, 7:157, 9:67, 24:21, 31:17)[5] are understood, by both scholars and the Muslim community at large, to mean that although individuals are ultimately responsible for their own actions, family and society also have a responsibility to call their relatives, friends, and neighbors toward the good and to prevent them from engaging in wrong.

A third factor is the Qur'anic recognition that communal support is vital to the individual's success in living a truly spiritual life. Most Islamic rituals are congregational: it is highly recommended to observe the five daily prayers in congregation; the Pilgrimage to Mecca is a mass event; the collection of *zakat*, or alms for the poor, has traditionally been a public function handled by the government rather than a private obligation; even fasting is a communal event with shared fast-breaking and extra congregational prayers in the evening. The Qur'an says, "Hold onto the rope of Allah all together" (3:103). Thus, we see on the one hand an insistence on individual responsibility, while at the same time there is acknowledgment of the importance of community in support of the individual and in encouraging each other toward greater adherence and spirituality.

Again, the implementation of these precepts varies widely. Some communities take a very hands-off approach, leaving spirituality completely up to the individual. A common phenomenon in this type of community is the *halaqa* or *dars* (study or meditation circles) where individuals and families join with others for prayer, reading the Qur'an, and learning about the faith. Often the focus of these study groups is deepening the members' knowledge of Islam, or adherence to Islamic norms and performance of the rituals, while any spiritual benefits are considered a pleasant by-product.

On the other hand, many Muslim cultures interpret the injunction to enjoin good and forbid evil in a more inclusive manner, with extended families becoming very involved in maintaining family morality and honor. The more extreme interpretations hold even the national government responsible for the morality and spirituality of its subjects, such as Saudi Arabia with its morality police, the *mutawwa*.

The Qur'an, however, is adamant that responsibility lies with neither family nor government. In several suras, various prophets are told that it is not their fault if family members will not heed their call to worship, and Prophet Muhammad, who was both spiritual guide and political ruler, is told time and time again that he is responsible only to deliver the message, that belief and compliance are between the individual and Allah (e.g., 2:119, 4:79–80). Thus the Qur'an, while encouraging family, neighbors, and society at large to call to good and to speak out against evil, lays the responsibility for heeding that call squarely upon the individual.

Individual Responsibility: The Tasks of Developing Spirituality

Once the individual reaches the age of maturity, Islam expects him or her to pursue religious knowledge and develop his or her spirituality. The ultimate goal, as eloquently stated by Prophet Muhammad, is total accord with the Divine order and complete submission and unity with Allah. "My (God's) devotee keeps drawing closer to Me by performing acts of devotion till I love him; I become his sense of hearing with which he hears, and his sense of sight with which he sees, and his hand with which he grips, and his leg with which he walks" (Bukhari, vol. 9, book 76, no. 509). Islam recommends various disciplines that help the individual cultivate and manifest this depth of spirituality and faith. Paramount among these are:

- Seeking knowledge and reflecting upon it;
- Remembering God (*dhikr*); and
- Performing Islamic rituals and maintaining Islamic manners.

Seeking knowledge, as was mentioned earlier, is considered one of the central tasks of the Muslim adult. Prophet Muhammad said, "It is incumbent upon every Muslim, male and female, to seek knowledge" (Ibn Majah, book 1, no. 224). Knowledge refers not only to religious knowledge, as one might derive from reading the Qur'an or hadith, but also to knowledge of God's Creation and of human history.

Attaining knowledge in and of itself is not the goal; rather, the Muslim is expected to contemplate what he or she has learned and use it to draw closer to Allah. The Prophet used to pray, "O Allah, I seek refuge in You from the knowledge which does not benefit, from the heart that does not entertain taqwa, from the soul that does not feel contented" (Muslim, book 35, no. 6569). The Qur'an reinforces this concept in dozens of verses, asking humankind to study nature, human history, and the Qur'an itself, and then to reflect upon what they have learned as a means to understand Allah and to enhance one's connection to Him. For instance, 16:14 is the last in a series of verses exhorting the believer to reflect: "It is He who has subdued the seas that you may eat from them, and take from them ornaments to wear. You see on them ships that plough the waves that you may seek the bounty of God, and that you may be grateful."[6]

While nature enhances the believer's wonder and love for Allah, awareness of human history increases his or her awe and fear of God, another essential element of taqwa. For example, Allah remonstrates: "How many cities given to wrong-doing have We destroyed and left in ruin; how many deserted wells; how many lofty castles? Do they not travel through the land? Have they no minds to reflect? Nor ears to hear? It is not their eyes which are blind, but their hearts which do not see!" (22:45–46).

Finally, in seeking to know and understand God, the believer must turn to the Qur'an; the verses that describe Allah and His names—ninety-nine Divine attributes— are considered the only direct source of knowledge about Allah. People may experience Allah and feel unified with Him, but they can never truly know God except through His words. As such, reflection on the Qur'an is encouraged to soften one's heart and awaken one's piety. Prophet Muhammad described the verses of the Qur'an as "a blessing, a means of approach to Allah, and a supplication" (Tirmidhi). The Qur'an describes itself in these terms: "God has sent down the most beautiful of all teachings, a Scripture consistent with itself, yet repeating its lessons. The skins of those who in awe of their Lord do tremble when they hear it. And their hearts soften to the celebration of God's praises. Such is the Guidance of God" (39:23). Reading the Qur'an and reflecting on its contents, then, is propounded as one of the easiest and surest ways to strengthen one's awe, fear, and love of Allah.

The second spiritual discipline recommended in the Qur'an and by Prophet Muhammad is that of dhikr, or remembrance of Allah. The Qur'an refers to remembering Allah in more than a hundred verses and advocates remembrance of God as a means to keep one's heart pure, to align one's deeds in accordance with the will of God, and to attain true serenity and felicity. For example, one verse reads, "Those who believe and find peace in their hearts in the remembrance of Allah—surely there is peace of heart in the remembrance of Allah—and those who believe and do good, for them is inner joy and an excellent resting place" (13:28–29). Prophet Muhammad was a man who constantly had God upon his heart and his lips, and who recommended that his followers offer *dua*—short supplications—or prayers at every turn. The clear implication is that conscious and persistent practice of remembrance will lead one to a life infused with continual mindfulness of and responsiveness to God.

In many communities, however, dhikr has taken on formalized, ritualistic structures. Entire books have been written encouraging people to recite verbatim phrases that Prophet Muhammad was known to have said, even in the most mundane of affairs such as using the bathroom or cleaning one's teeth (e.g., Al-Essa 1993; Badawi 1979). Devotees recite "Alhamdulillah," "Subhana Allah," and "Allahu Akbar"—Praise be to God, God be Glorified, God is Greater—one hundred times after each formal prayer, or *salat*. Sufi groups gather to recite the names of Allah, or expressions in praise of Allah, over and over. While the drive behind these practices is to enhance one's spirituality, all too often they devolve into mindless repetition or perfectionist emulations of the Prophet that neglect the more reflective, nurturing aspects that the practices were designed to enhance.

The third discipline that Islam recommends to enhance the believer's spirituality is the practice of five basic rituals: the profession of faith (*shahadah*), ritual worship (salat) performed five times daily, the giving of alms for the poor (zakat), the fast of Ramadan (*saum*), and the Pilgrimage to Mecca (Hajj). While adherence to these rituals is a religious duty, each also serves to enhance the believer's relationship with God and to increase awareness of God's presence in his or her life.

The shahadah is at once a simple statement of belief—I bear witness that there is no god except God, and I bear witness that Muhammad is a prophet of God—and a profound alignment of the soul with the natural order, the fitrah, upon which the universe has been created. The shahadah is the individual's response to his or her innate yearning for connection with the Divine, the recognition and acceptance of the relationship of created to Creator, of dependence upon Benefactor, and acknowledgment that the Creator is not aloof, but interacts with humankind through His intermediaries, the prophets, and answers prayers addressed to Him. The shahadah is not simply a statement or creed, but a significant part of daily life for the devout Muslim. It is repeated in every cycle of every prayer and informs the Muslim's worldview. Acknowledgment that there are no gods apart from God serves as a reminder—that all good comes from Allah, that all evil can be remedied by Allah, that the mundane affairs of the world are not significant when considered in light of Divine Truth (Nasr 1994, 61–62).

Salat serves much the same purpose as the shahadah: it is a time to realign the soul with the Divine order, to remember that the *dunya* (the mundane world) is ephemeral and to focus on the truly important, that is, one's relationship with God. Salat, with its prescribed timings, is a regular, enforced breather from worldly concerns, and places the worshipper in direct communication with the Divine. The physical movements of salat—standing, bowing, kneeling, prostrating—remind the devotee that in everything she or he does throughout the day, sitting or standing, God is paramount. The words of the prayer, which include the first chapter of the Qur'an, as well as repeated praise of Allah and supplication for guidance and mercy, place the devotee squarely in a position of reliance upon the Compassionate Divine.[7] Again, the performance of salat is considered a duty that cannot be neglected, but its role in establishing mindfulness of God is emphasized in the Qur'an: "Surely prayer restrains one from shameful and unjust deeds, but the remembrance of God is far greater" (29:45). Prophet Muhammad told his followers that excellence in salat is to "worship Allah as if you are seeing Him, for though you don't see Him, He, verily, sees you" (Muslim, book 1, no. 1). The importance of salat in the spiritual development of the individual cannot be overemphasized as it presents a repeated opportunity to concentrate on one's relationship to the Divine.

Zakat, which is similar to tithing, is seen not only as an important civic duty that serves the needy and the disadvantaged, but also as a form of purification from worldly temptations, particularly pride, stinginess, greed, jealousy, and the tendency to cling to worldly goods and one's own possessions. Thus, the ultimate goal of zakat is the renunciation of the worldly in order to facilitate reunion with the Divine. This concept is reiterated by Prophet Muhammad, who said the believer is a traveler in the world; he observes everything with wonder, but never thinks to attach himself to the things he passes by (Bukhari, vol. 8, book 76, no. 425).

Fasting during the month of Ramadan is seen as a purification from and protection against physical desires, especially bodily appetites such as lust and gluttony, as well as sins of pride, greed, and arrogance. While zakat is a renunciation of worldly goods, fasting is a renunciation of worldly passions. The spiritual and physical discipline of fasting is recognized as one of the most powerful tools for elevating one's spirituality. The Qur'an says, "A course of fasting is prescribed for you, as it was prescribed for those before you, that you might attain taqwa" (2:183). Ramadan is a time not only for fasting but also for extra prayers (*tarawih*), extra devotion to reading the Qur'an, and '*itikaf*—seclusion for the purpose of meditating on Allah and His Creation. These additional disciplines heighten the spiritual benefits of Ramadan.

Hajj, the pilgrimage to Mecca, the fifth ritual requirement of Islam, is obligatory upon adult Muslims who are financially, emotionally, and physically capable of making the journey. This ritual requires the believer to set aside the worldly—home, family, clothing, work—and dedicate himself or herself fully to the Divine. Abraham's complete trust in Allah, and his willingness to sacrifice everything—even his son—for God's pleasure is commemorated during the Hajj, as is Hajar's perseverance, which was rewarded by Divine Mercy. Like Hajar and Abraham, the Hajjis (those who are performing Hajj) demonstrate their determination in seeking the face of the Divine and their willingness to sacrifice the life of this world to attain true harmony and unity with God. In return, they are assured of the response of the Divine, who turns aside grief from the devotee as He substituted the ram for Ismail and blessed Hajar with a clear-flowing spring. In the Islamic worldview, Hajj is the ultimate ritual of dedication, devotion, and sacrifice: the pilgrim spends ten days as unencumbered by worldly concerns as possible, engaged in reflection, prayer, and worship.

The rituals of salat, zakat, Ramadan, and Hajj integrate to create a comprehensive discipline for spiritual development. They each require, in varying degrees and levels of commitment, remembrance of God and renunciation of the worldly. Islam's ritual program for cultivating spiritual development is quite comprehensive; salat is a small, daily devotion that requires little worldly renunciation, whereas zakat, Ramadan, and Hajj, although less frequent, are more intense and demanding of the devotee. The combined effect is to ratchet the believer up the scale of taqwa. The heightened spirituality developed by giving zakat, fasting during Ramadan, and performing Hajj is maintained by the daily practice of salat, especially when combined with dhikr and reflection.

Of course, all too many Muslims miss out on the spiritual program offered by the rituals of Islam. Indeed, the community is currently plagued by an excessive legalism that focuses on the physical details—Are your hands crossed in the right spot? Are your feet the right width apart?—to the detriment of the intent and feelings expressed and fostered by the rituals. Islam attempts to protect the community from legalism and ritualism; there are numerous hadith that talk about the importance of intention and the dangers of excessive focus on details. Unfortunately, these are largely ignored in the quest for perfect emulation of the Prophet, or, worse, turned into yet another litmus test of acceptability in which a deed is not acceptable if a statement of intent has not been recited before it.

While the performance of Islamic rituals is vital, it is not sufficient. A Muslim is expected to strive to exhibit taqwa in every detail or his or her life. Every action, whether it be eating, getting dressed, going to school, or fighting poverty, bigotry, or injustice, holds the potential to burnish the believer's spirituality, to cement his or her connection to God. Prophet Muhammad once said much to his companion's amazement that even sexual relations with one's spouse could be an act of worship; after all, the husband and wife were fulfilling their needs in a lawful manner, refraining from illicit relations (Muslim, book 5, no. 2198). Adherence to Islam's virtues—honesty, humility, moderation, and so on—and avoidance of the things it forbids, combined with the intention to serve God, are seen as both a manifestation of spirituality and a means to enhancing that spirituality. The more one practices taqwa, the more one achieves it.

This is the path that the teenager is responsible for traveling down. Clearly, some of these disciplines are more applicable to a teenager than others. Reflection and remembrance, salat, and fasting are considered appropriate for and are practiced by many young people. On the other hand, teenagers who do not work will not be obligated to pay zakat, as it is a form of tithe on wealth, but many families encourage their children to set aside a portion of gifts or allowances for charity. Similarly, a teenager probably can't afford to make the Pilgrimage on his or her own, but may go with family members. As discussed previously, the responsibility to adhere to the tenets of Islam and nurture one's spirituality falls squarely on the individual's shoulders, but fortunately, he or she is not alone in this task. Islam regards family and community as vital supporters and encouragers for adults of all ages, and it provides structural support for the individual through congregational rituals and clear disciplines that foster individual development.

The Education of the Child

At this point, I would like to turn to children who have not yet attained puberty. Islam lays the responsibility for the education of children (spiritual or otherwise) solidly on the shoulders of parents. The first task Prophet Muhammad was charged with was to preach to his family. Only after that had been accomplished was he asked to preach to his community. So, too, the believers are told to focus on their families. The Qur'an says, "Believers, save yourselves and your families from a fire fueled with humans and stones" (66:6). Prophet Muhammad was even more explicit in placing this responsibility on parents. Abu Hurairah reported that he said, "No baby is born but upon the Fitrah. It is his parents who make him a Jew or a Christian or a Polytheist" (Muslim, book 33, no. 6426). It is worthwhile to remember that Islam sees itself as the most perfect expression of the fitrah: the values and rules of Islam are seen as being precisely the values and rules that a human being needs in order to live according to his or her innate inclinations, and thus there is no mention of parents making the child a Muslim; every child is born Muslim in the broader sense of one who lives in harmony with God's will. Furthermore, scholars have argued that without parental or societal influences getting in the way, people would, through reason and conscience, adopt a way of life that is in accord with Islamic teachings regarding God, compassion, justice, and truth. Various hadith promise rewards for parents who educate their children properly, especially daughters (Daud; Muslim). One mentions that only three things bring ongoing rewards, one of which is a righteous child. This responsibility, as we have seen, begins at the moment of birth and continues until the child reaches puberty.

Having laid the responsibility at the feet of parents, Islam does not give a whole lot of guidance as to how a mother or father is to accomplish this task. There is a single narration, which says children should be encouraged to pray at the age of seven, and that if they do not pray by the time they are ten, they should be punished (Abu Daud, book 2, nos. 0494 and 0495). The Muslim community has generally assumed that this time frame applies to the other rituals of Islam.

There are also references to treating children with kindness and affection, but very little is said on how one ought to go about educating one's children—recommended teaching methods, whether it is more important to focus on spirituality or legal matters, what verses of the Qur'an to begin with, which parts of Islamic law are most important. Parents are left to extrapolate from the methods and priorities encouraged for adults as outlined earlier here, and these are not laid out clearly in one place but must be culled from the pages of the Qur'an and hadith. Similarly, priorities in teaching the theology of Islam can be derived by looking at the chronology of the Qur'an, but in no place is there guidance on what to teach children when. Moreover, parents are left to their own devices when it comes to awakening their children to the spiritual aspects of the rituals and of the other disciplines.

At first glance, it may seem surprising that Islam, with its insistence upon constant mindfulness of God, does not provide more guidance on how to teach and encourage this mindfulness. This laissez-faire approach is a reflection of the fact that Islam holds that all children are born pure with an innate recognition and yearning toward God. Thus, parents do not have to teach spirituality, or even to awaken it, but only to encourage and protect it. The same methods that the Qur'an recommends for adults— reflection, remembrance, and rituals—are seen as appropriate and sufficient for children, with reflection and remembrance beginning at birth, and rituals being introduced gradually as the child grows up.

As a result, we see a wide range of practice: from families who assume that being born into a Muslim family will ensure their children grow up Muslim, to families who are extremely strict and who require daily reading from the Qur'an and performance of rituals from a very young age. It is quite common for families to encourage young children to participate in Islamic rituals at a reduced level: praying one or two of the salat each day, fasting from a favorite food, or from breakfast until lunch, giving small amounts to charity from gifts they receive or allowances. All too often, however, the education of Muslim children focuses not on enhancing their spirituality, since it is taken for granted that they will be spiritual, but on ensuring that they know all the details of Islamic law. Correspondingly, the methodology used does not reflect the strategies outlined here but relies on rote memorization. As mentioned earlier, sheets of phrases to be said when sneezing, when beginning a meal, when getting in a car, when waking up, and going to sleep are taught by rote. Children are expected to memorize passages from the Qur'an, sometimes with little idea as to the meaning of what they are learning. Often the emphasis is on adherence, with little tolerance for those who have a different understanding, either of Islam or of the world. Ironically, this emphasis on perfect obedience arises from a deeply spiritual idea, that is, the contention that the truer and stronger one's love for God is, the more one seeks to please God, or, in other words, to subsume one's own will to the will of God. Perfect obedience or perfect submission, which has come to be an end in and of itself, was originally seen as the manifestation of absolute love, the loss of the self into the Divine. Sadly, this deep spirit of love is not often spoken of, at least not in the North American context.

Many books have been published in recent years offering advice to Muslim parents in the West on how to educate their children. The vast majority of these perpetuate the aforementioned methods and focus on a legal education to the near exclusion of spiritual development. A notable exception is *Muslim Teens* by Ekram Beshir and Mohamed Beshir (2001), which addresses foundational concepts and recommends an approach that reflects the methods outlined earlier in this chapter for teenagers. The result is predictable: on the one hand, a community that is struggling to keep its youth within the fold of Islam and that is filled with disillusioned young adults who are spiritually dissatisfied and, on the other, a surge in rigid and narrow interpretations and practices. Jeffrey Lang's *Losing My Religion: A Cry for Help* (2004) details this situation and offers substantive discussion for changing course.

Extrapolating from the Qur'an and the practice of Prophet Muhammad, one can, in addition to the three disciplines mentioned here, extract various approaches one might use to enhance the spirituality of young children: direct teaching, storytelling, relating parables, and showing by example. The Qur'an employs each of these methods to convey its message, and Prophet Muhammad also used each of these techniques.[8] The Muslim community has largely wielded these tools to inculcate the practice of Islam, but they can be effectively used to encourage a more spiritual outlook on life and a deeper commitment to living a life of taqwa.

Perhaps more important than the specific tools he used, was the atmosphere the Prophet created in the *masjid*. Children were considered part and parcel of spiritual life; they were (and are) welcome in the mosque as children—at times noisy, at times rambunctious—and Prophet Muhammad took pains to make them comfortable. This feeling that children are naturally participants in, not excluded from, the spiritual life of the community goes a long way to developing their sense of belonging to the Muslim community and, by extension, to Allah.

Islam's assumption that parents will want to educate their children is so strong that provisions for alternatives are made only with reference to the parents' unavailability, not their unwillingness or inability to perform their job. I have found no references on how the extended family or the community should handle the situation in which the parents are negligent or otherwise unable to carry out their duties. If they have died, however, the Qur'an and the Prophet both place a great emphasis on caring for orphans. For instance, Sura Duha says, "Do not wrong the orphan or chide away the beggar, but proclaim the goodness of your Lord!" Or in Sura Ma'un: "Have you seen the one who belies his religion? He repulses the orphan, and does not urge the feeding of the poor." The responsibility for the orphan, as evidenced by Prophet Muhammad's own life, falls to the near relatives (grandparents) and then progressively more distant relatives (uncles and aunts, then granduncles and grandaunts).

In the event that there is no extended family, the community as a whole is responsible for the care of the child, including her or his education. The Qur'an makes repeated reference to the believers being brothers and sisters to one another—and that they treat one another as family: "The believers are indeed brothers to one another" (49:10) and "Hold onto the rope of Allah all together and let nothing divide you. Remember the favor God has bestowed upon you, how after your enmity, He united your hearts so that you are now brothers" (3:103). As mentioned earlier, the Muslim community is described as one that commands the good and forbids the wrong, thereby encouraging and supporting the Muslim in his or her quest to live in harmony with God's will. This familial, nurturing bond extends particularly to orphans.

In practice, the extended family is often very involved in the education of children—again spiritual or otherwise—especially in Muslim countries. Many Muslim communities are communal in nature, with family compounds housing much of the extended family in one location. In the West, the nuclear family has become the norm as families are separated by immigration, school, or work. Even when relatives live in the same town, there is no parallel to the family compound. However, families remain close-knit, and it is not uncommon for members of the older generation to spend months at a time visiting their children and grandchildren.

Similarly, the community is an active participant in encouraging the religious development of children. As mentioned earlier, the current focus is more on adherence to Islamic law, but the system that has been put in place—of weekend and full-time schools, of youth groups and summer camps for Muslim children—could well serve to foster a greater spiritual development among Muslim youth. It is interesting to note that Islamic institutions serving youth in North America have generally been established by the parents themselves. Many full-time Islamic schools started as a group of homeschooling mothers who wanted to help and support one another. As masjids and Islamic institutions have matured, many of these schools have taken on a life of their own, hiring professional teachers and administrators, with the parents' involvement limited to paying tuition and helping in the classrooms much as parents help in public schools. Similarly, weekend schools, youth groups, and summer camps were developed because parents felt a need for support in trying to instill an Islamic identity in their children. Many are still run by the parents rather than by professional youth "ministers" or camp counselors.

Although a comparison to Catholic, Protestant, or Jewish private schools and institutions might be appropriate in some areas, it is important to note that these schools, youth groups, and camps are independent: there is no religious authority, no priesthood, to oversee them, or to encourage the implementation of set standards and/or curriculum. Different scholars and educational organizations have made efforts to offer comprehensive curriculums and to standardize Islamic education in the United States and Canada, but there is no means of enforcement, and as such, the quality and methodology vary greatly from school to school. Some communities have no full-time school at all; others have thriving schools that attract both Muslim and non-Muslim students.

Concluding Comments

Islam, like all religions, puts a strong emphasis on spirituality, and on believers striving to enhance their spirituality and strengthening their connection to the Divine. It perceives piety to be innate, and considers it not only a matter of faith but also a matter of praxis, offering a wide range of tools to the believer who seeks to enrich his or her spirituality, from meditative dhikr, to active engagement in ritual, from the struggle against poverty, inequality, and injustice to the mundane details of life performed in accordance with God's will and with the intention to serve Him. At the same time, Islam is relatively quiet on the matter of raising children, and how to educate them and enhance their spirituality. This is an area the Muslim community would do well to explore further, both by looking closely at its own texts, traditions, and rich history of mysticism, and by studying the experience of other faith groups.

Notes

1. This author uses God and Allah interchangeably as they are equivalent words in English and Arabic, respectively. Allah can be translated literally as God, and in the Arab world, Jews and Christians as well as Muslims refer to their God as Allah.

2. For instance, Sura Asr, verses 2–3: "Surely mankind is at a loss, except those who believe and do good works"; or Sura Al-Kahf, verse 88: "As for those who believe and do good works, We shall bestow upon them a goodly rewards"; or Sura Nisa, verse 173: "As for those who believe and do good works, God will bestow upon them their rewards and enrich them from His own abundance."

3. Narrated by Abu Said Al-Khudri, recorded in Tirmidhi. Narrations of things Prophet Muhammad said and did are known as hadith. The hadith are analogous to the Gospels and serve as a second source of Islamic knowledge and law, the Qur'an being the first.

4. These two hadith are widely quoted in popular Muslim literature and are quoted as a part of Muslim culture. An exhaustive search of the hadith literature has not located them.

5. Although this author prefers to cite verses by chapter name and verse number, for the purposes of this chapter citations will be by chapter number and verse number, i.e., 2:129 will refer to Sura Baqara, which is chapter 2, verse 129.

6. Akhter (1998, 217–35) has an extensive listing of Qur'anic verses and hadith pertaining to different aspects of knowledge.

7. It is beyond the scope of this chapter to discuss in detail the spiritual dimension of each aspect of salat. An excellent discussion can be found in Shimmel (1975, 148–55).

8. There is not enough space in this brief chapter to list examples of each of these methods. Those so inclined may find examples of direct teaching in Suras Kafirun, Falaq, and Nas; storytelling in Suras Yusuf and Mariam; Sura Baqara abounds with parables; and Sura Fatiah is a prime example of the Qur'an teaching by example.

References

Akhter, Syed Hashim Ali. 1998. *The essence of Islam according to the Qur'an and the traditions.* Chicago: IQRA International Educational Foundation.

Al-Anani, Hasan. 1990. *Freedom and responsibility in Qur'anic perspective.* Translated by M. S. Kayani. Indianapolis: American Trust Publications.

Al-Attas, S. M. N. 1985. *Islam, secularism and the philosophy of the future.* London and New York: Mansell.

Al-Essa, Waleed K. S. 1993. *Authentic supplications of the Prophet*. Miami: The Dar of Islamic Heritage.

Al-Faruqi, Ismail Raji. 1983. *Tawhid: Its relevance for thought and life*. Malaysia: International Islamic Federation of Student Organizations.

Ali, Abdallah Yusuf. 1987. *The Holy Qur'an*. New York: Tahrike Tarsile Qur'an.

Ali, Ahmed. 1984. *Al-Qur'an: A contemporary translation*. Princeton, NJ: Princeton University Press.

Badawi, Jamal. 1979. *Selected prayers: A collection of Du'a from the Qur'an and Sunnah*. Indianapolis: Islamic Teaching Center.

Beshir, Ekram, and Mohamed R. Beshir 2001. *Muslim teens: Today's worry, tomorrow's hope*. Beltsville, Md.: Amana.

Dawood, N. J. 1956. *The Koran*. London: Penguin.

Glasse, Cyril. 1989. *The concise encyclopedia of Islam*. London: Stacey.

Lang, Jeffrey. 2004. *Losing my religion: A call for help*. Beltsville, Md.: Amana.

Nasr, Seyyed Hossein. 1966. *Ideals and realities of Islam*. London: George Allen and Unwin.

Pickthall, Muhammad Marmaduke. 1970. *The meaning of the Glorious Qur'an*. Beirut: Dar al-Kitab Al-Lubnani.

Schimmel, Annemarie. 1975. *The mystical dimensions of Islam*. Chapel Hill: University of North Carolina Press.

Siddiqui, Muzammil. Khutabh, February 7, 2003. http://www.isna.net/Library/khutbahs/Hajj_ASeasonOfLovePeaceUnityPiety.asp (accessed September 20, 2004).

Yasein, Mohamed. 1996. *Fitrah: The Islamic conception of human nature*. London: Ta-ha.

CHAPTER 29

Understanding Dharma, Performing Karma: Shared Responsibilities for Spiritual Grooming in Hindu Traditions

Venkatakrishna B. V. Sastry

The traditional Hindu view regarding the responsibility for nurturing spiritual values in children is structured around three key values: *dharma, karma,* and *rina,* all technical terms that come from Vedic Sanskrit. Dharma represents inviolable cosmic law; karma, taking responsibility for the consequences of one's actions; and rina, one's cosmic debt and obligations. Sins and bondage (*papa bandha*) have their origins in violating dharma, trying to avoid karma, and not clearing rina. Sins and bondage impede salvation (*moksha*) and have ill consequences for one's health, prosperity, and offspring.

One way of lessening the burden of karma and rina is to properly discharge one's responsibility for nurturing spiritual values in children. The spiritual grooming of every child in society from infancy through adolescence is progressively assigned to parents, educators, the community, and, finally, the state. This assignment is twofold: (1) to train the child for the compliant performance of dharma and karma and (2) to see the child through the age- and stage-appropriate rites of passage according to dharma-karma. These duties have both intellectual and practical components that answer the *why* and the *how* of dharma-karma. Successfully fulfilling these duties also entails that each member of the team understands his or her dharma and performs his or her karma. These responsibilities are interlinked and interdependent. The summation of diversity in understanding these concepts set in historical traditions is termed *achara sampradaya.* This guides the understanding and practices of spiritual nurturing in Hinduism. The first section of this chapter addresses issues of diversity in understanding key concepts and perspectives; the second section looks at how this understanding guides the team in ensuring that the child is provided with the appropriate rites for spiritual nurturing.

The following schema indicates how the team responsibility is marked by the recommended rites of passage at various stages of growth through adolescence. The approach is to highlight the significance of the rite (*karma samskara*) as a practice of dharma for the clearance of rina to the spiritual benefit of self and the child. The rite of marriage brings together the team of parents, educators, community, and state and endorses the team's commitment to the spiritual nurturing of children that issue from the marriage. Parental responsibilities are marked in three segments: (1) the marriage vows, rites for the spiritualization of a union for the purpose of begetting progeny, rites for confirming conception, and the rite at the moment of birth; (2) after birth till preschooling; and (3) initiation into spiritual exploration and family traditions of spirituality. Educators' responsibilities initially overlap with those of parents and continue till the conclusion of adolescence. The community and state have an ongoing responsibility in all stages, taking on a more dominant role toward the end of formal education. The child's own responsibility for spiritual progress needs to be initiated through a specific rite by the parent–spiritual educator–community team at the right stage and age. Failure to initiate this rite, to explain its significance, and to take the child through the discipline of the spiritual vows in the formative years and integrate it into the child's lifestyle would be seen as a lapse on the part of the team in discharging its responsibilities. What the child does with this discipline at a later phase affects the child's own dharma.

Key Concepts and Perspectives

The child's social and spiritual persona that emerges during the final transition through adolescence is a consequence of cultural and traditional nurturing. The child passes through these processes, as provided and valued by the team of parents, educators, community, and state at various stages of growth. The understanding and commitment of this team to the key values of dharma, karma, and rina determine the progressive rites of passage at home and in school, the community, and society. The rites of passage (karma samskara) performed by the team depends on its members' appreciation of the significance of the key values for self-benefit and the future of the child.

The current wisdom of Hindu teams comes from the following sources:

- Vedic traditions described in the streams of six theistic faith interpretations (which includes Vaishnavism and Saivism), six philosophical interpretations (which includes Vedanta), two humanist (Buddhism, Jainism), and one materialistic way (Charvaka).
- Allied disciplines and auxiliary literature in *vedanga* and *upaveda* discourse literature (which includes Ayurveda and fine arts), religious law codes (*smriti shastras, purushartha shastras*), faith-specific elaborations (*puranas*, which include Bhagavata), mystical mythological narratives *Ramayana* and *Mahabharata* (which includes Bhagavad-Gita)*;* and several literary and popular versions and customized narratives in regional languages.
- Three mystical traditions: Yoga, Tantra, Sufism.
- Parentage-related community order of social identities by tags of religious faith, social recognition of marital status, lifestyle, and vocation (*varna-jati*).
- Individual-related order of social identities by tags related to personal faith affiliation to a lineage, marital status, lifestyle, and vocations (*ashrama*).
- Temples and other religious institutions.
- Independent masters' traditions
- Historical instances in mainstream and subaltern community practices.

- Adaptations made in practices by communities migrating beyond native lands and language environment. This is a complexly connected, continuous stream of tradition, built over five thousand years, in the vast land of Bharath.
- Undocumented oral traditions transmitted in three main scriptural languages—Sanskrit, Prakrit, and Tamil—and more than three hundred regional dialects. This diversity is the springboard of multiple explanations and practices regarding the responsibility for nurturing spirituality of various kinds within families and in a progressive way at school and in society.

DHARMA

Dharma is a concept that has many shades of meaning, defying efforts to provide a single or simple translation. The popular translation of the dharma as "religion" does not convey the true spirit of the word and is often misleading. Note that these meanings accommodate multiple faiths and do not presuppose a faith in terms of a specific god. These are also not limited by any geographic or time boundaries, a fact that makes them truly human and universal. The ancient Hindu source works known as Veda use the word *dharma* to refer to truth and the power that sustains the cosmic law and order. Manusmriti, an ancient Hindu spiritual code, identifies ten meanings for the word dharma: (1) fearlessness; (2) forgiveness; (3) self-control; (4) noninterference with the possessions of others and respect for others' privacy; (5) purity, cleanliness, sacredness; (6) control and regulation of senses in work and pleasure; (7) intellectual freedom; (8) education and vocational skills; (9) truth (*satya*); and (10) control of emotions such as anger.

KARMA

Some major understandings about karma are listed here. These understandings guide, motivate, and decide the practical format of rites of passage conducted by the team in nurturing the child. The word *karma* indicates these concepts in Hindu traditions: (1) samskara (rites of passage); (2) sampradaya (tradition, family practices, model conventions, etiquette); (3) achara (code of conduct and performance); (4) *vrata* (commitment in the form vow); and (5) *niyama* (self-imposed restraint). The core value of dharma permeates all these linked offshoots of karma. The spiritual values recognized in social conduct, ethical behavior, civil and moral codes of law and order (*neeti* and *nyaya*), and religion or spirituality are actions conforming to specific achara and sampradaya.

RINA

Hindu traditions understand this concept of cosmic debt and obligations in relation to the dharma and karma of the team in the following dimensions.

Pitru rina is the obligation to express gratitude to the past and to be responsible for the present. This is the gratitude of the individual to the parents, for having received the gift of a human body, a powerful instrument for spiritual pursuits. It is an acknowl-edgment of being part of a worthy ancestral lineage (*vamsha gotra parampara*). Marriage vows marking the shifting role of the individual in the direction of becoming a parent provide relevant guidance on this point. The parents' role in ensuring that the child is conceived, born, and groomed for a spiritually healthy status is the objective. For the other members of the team, pitru rina is fulfilling the social obligations of spiritual con-tract to the past masters, traditions, and cultures.

Deva rina is the debt of expressing gratitude to cosmic nature. It is the obligation of each member of the team to nature and the environment that sustains and supports life. It is the repayment of a debt to the divine. The rites of passage performed by the parents include guidance for discharging this responsibility. Other team members are to help the child develop values related to ecological awareness, respect for nature, and honoring the sacredness of the cosmos.

Rishi rina is the obligation of each member of the team to express gratitude to the intelligence that maintains the cosmos and the dynamics of existence. This responsibil-ity is discharged through the inculcation of religious values, spiritual discipline, and codes of moral and civil conduct in which the child is trained and instructed at various stages of growth by the parents and other members of the team.

Practices of Spiritual Nurturing

For purposes of analysis, the practices for the spiritual nurturing of a child by the team can be seen as falling into the following life periods: (a) from the wedding till the birth of the child: in this period, the parents bear the primary responsibility; (b) the first six years of the child's life: in this phase, the parents are in the lead and receive supplemen-tal support from day care workers, preschool teachers, and others in informal settings, as well as the family's priest (the spiritual educator), relatives, and elders; (c) formal school-ing: teachers, community, and state take the primary responsibility for nurturing the universal dimension of spirituality; parents and the spiritual educator take responsibility for nurturing spiritual values in the framework of family traditions, religious faith, and lineage, while the child takes responsibility for the practical assimilation of these two streams of spiritual nurturing by submitting to a life of discipline under the guidance of the team; and (d) the passage through adolescence, the phase that marks the shift in the responsibility of the team—from the role of performers and regulators to that of advis-ers. We start this deliberation by looking at the marriage vows, which contain the seeds of the team's commitment to the spiritual nurturing of children.

MARRIAGE VOWS

Hindu traditions recognize the institution of marriage and family life as the reference point for deciding all issues related to children. The parents are the first members of the team charged with the responsibility for their child's spiritual nurturing. Individual and consenting males and females of age become life partners through the religious rite of marriage (*vivaha samskara*). The irrevocable commitments set forth in the marriage vows mark the first commitment of would-be parents. The institution of marriage, through its dharma dimension, firms up the responsibility of those who desire to be parents for the nurturing of spiritual values in the child. The social dimension of the institution of marriage solidifies the responsibility of the other team members for supporting this nurturing. The societal seal of marriage provides the focal point for the following references to the child for future spiritual pursuits: (a) lineage identity (*vamsha gotra paramapara*), (b) caste community guild membership identity (*varna-jati*) tags, and (c) practices and standards for debt clearance (pitru rina).

SPIRITUALIZATION OF THE FIRST UNION

This is a special rite that reiterates the vow-based commitment of the married couple for discharging their responsibility to spiritually nurture a child. The first union (*nisheka*) is performed on an auspicious day that has favorable spiritual cosmic energies for the partners. The day is selected in accordance with guidelines in the astrology and dharma rulebook, which stipulates that union with the intention of begetting a worthy offspring (*garbhadana*) calls for a special rite. Traditional practices link this to the first union of the couple after marriage. The union for pleasure does not call for any special rite and is regulated by a different consideration. The separation of these two types of union with reference to the time of marriage is at the couple's discretion. The Vedic words and passages in this rite reiterate the commitment of the partners to accept their responsibility to spiritually groom their child.

ON THE CONFIRMATION OF CONCEPTION

The fruition of the union, resulting in confirmed signs of conception, is the next critical stage at which the parents-to-be observe two rites of passage (*pumsavana* and *seemanta*). The reference point of these rites for the mother and child is positioned at any convenient time from the third to the seventh month of pregnancy. The parents use Vedic prayers to request that noble spiritual qualities are bestowed on the child in the womb. Tradition provides elaborate instructions relating to dos and don'ts of food, entertainment, travel, and sexual engagements, which may influence the child in the womb. Compliance with the rules is believed to help the child inculcate spiritual values from the earliest stages. Tradition holds that learning commences from the early part of the fifth month of progress in the womb.

AT THE MOMENT OF BIRTH

It is a great moment in creation to recognize when a life is born out of another life. The actual cosmic and relative time of birth (*janma lagna*) is considered to be of great spiritual significance. In Vedic astrology this technical birth time is called *lagna*, and it is used in Vedic astrology to make predictive calculations; Ayurveda uses birth time for suggesting remedies for ailments; Tantra and Yoga use the time of birth for spiritual initiation into the mystical traditions. It is considered the responsibility of the parents to record this auspicious moment on a chart of cosmic stellar and planetary configurations and to take guidance from this record for the child's spiritual care.

There is a special rite of passage (*jatakarma*) that is recommended for observation at the moment of birth. Tradition expects the father to be present at the place of delivery so that he can perform this rite before the umbilical card is cut. There are technical details of the ritual that suggest the administering of certain medicines and chanting of Vedic passages to bring in the mystical dimension of Ayurveda. This rite is intended to help invigorate the child's higher intelligence (*medha*), bring spiritual protection from evil influences (*raksha*), promote longevity (*aayushya*), provide unswerving love and affection for the parents (*preeti*), and bond the child to the family lineage (*rishi vamsha gotra*). The rite is currently not performed at the prescribed time owing to limiting circumstances and issues related to heath, emotions, and various other practicalities. The rite is generally carried out in a modified way after the eleventh day or at some later time after delivery.

GIVING A NAME IDENTITY TO THE CHILD

Namakarana is an important rite of passage for the child and is performed by the parent. The objective is to infuse spiritual value into the primary name identity. The rules suggest that the name identity be chosen as a constant reminder of spiritual, religious, and family identities. The naming of a female child is subject to more guidelines than the naming of a male child. The use of names indicative of evil forces and personalities is prohibited. A festive event with spiritual significance is combined with this rite. Because the place where the child sleeps has an influence on his or her thoughts, sleep, and dreams, a family function is carried out to determine where the cradle is to be positioned and where the child is allowed to sleep. The rite is observed in accordance with family customs as preserved by female elders and incorporates certain principles from the disciplines of *Vastu* (the guidelines for tapping into directional cosmic energies for the benefit of the child), Ayurveda, and Tantra.

FAMILY NURTURE: UP TO THREE YEARS OF AGE

After birth, the first three years of a child's life are marked with special rites of passage, at significant stages, to be done by the parent. This is separate from the daily routines in which the child becomes a nonperforming participant in the parents' spiritual and religious activities. The daily routines of child care are infused with aspects that nurture spiritual value as a part of tradition. The lullabies sung by the mother to soothe the child generally contain names of deities—Rama, Krishna, Shiva, Ganesha, Sita, Gauri, Durga, Lalitha, Lakshmi, Amba—and passages from sacred texts. The themes of songs come from the playful acts of the gods described in the sacred texts of Ramayana,

Mahabharata, Bhagavata, and the Puranas. There is a deep-rooted belief in Hindu traditions that merely hearing the sacred names of divinities has the power to cleanse sins. The child is made to be actively present in an environment where he or she is habituated to hearing the names of the divine.

Mothers also follow many practices, often undocumented, handed down from elder women to young mothers only. These are intended to protect children from minor evils (*balagraha*) that attack the child through magic, causing health problems. Many of these practices are culture, family, and region specific. The rational for performing them is to conform to the diverse aspects of practicing dharma to clear segments of rina. Among the popular expressions of understanding one would receive for such compliances would be the following: "It is an act of merit (*punya*) and therefore to be done; it is an act of sin (*papa*) and therefore not to be done; it is an act that appeases God and therefore to be done; it is an act which clears me of the promise I had made to God seeking a favor. If I don't do it, God will be angry and the child will suffer. I will be punished; my family will be punished." In this way, the basic human instincts of awe and fear toward the mystery called God are effectively used for nurturing spiritual values in children.

First Exposure to the External World

The child's movements on its own are limited to places within the house. A specific rite of passage called *nishkramana* is performed by the parents to mark the occasion of the child's movement beyond the home. The child is carried to a local temple, a sacred place, a religious institution, or into the presence of a blessed soul (Guru), and blessings are sought. This rite is intended to connect the child's inner spiritual energies to a more powerful source. Traditionally, the ritual is accompanied by the chanting of sacred texts. The child is exposed to the rays of the sun and moon, to fire, deity, and Guru to be joined with the sources of cosmic energy.

Switching from Mother's Food to Solid Food

The goal of *anna prashana* is to help the child assimilate spiritual energy from food. This ritual marks the shift from breast milk to solid food, with the objective of integrating physical and spiritual growth. Normally this rite is conducted when the child is around six months old.

The rite of anna prashana is conducted by the parent. The child is always fed warm and freshly prepared food. Stale foods, cold foods, and foods with a strong taste or odor are not given. Meat-based food is not suggested. The nature of food useful for nurturing spiritual values and lifestyle is determined according to the guidelines for pious foods (*satvic aahaara*) for spiritual aspirants, meditators, and saints. The goal is to build spiritual strength and sensitivity through food, together with other requirements of healthy growth.

Piercing the Ears

Karna vedha is a rite of passage (samskara) for the child conducted by the parent. This rite is common to both male and female children, and it is intended to open the inner "ears" of the child for receiving sacred sounds. This rite has deep mystical and symbolic significance. It is believed that merely hearing sacred sounds has merit in that it cleanses sin and nurtures the spirit.

The ear is decorated with golden earrings or similar ornaments. Parents are cautioned regarding the type of sounds, voices, and content to which the child may be exposed. The sounds heard by the child have the potential to leave a deep impression on the mind, for the child listens with full attention without any internal filtering. This is one of the reasons why children are not permitted to be exposed to obscene sounds, adult entertainment, and harsh noises. In current society, the indiscriminate exposure of children to the sounds and sights of popular entertainment ignores this guidance.

Beautifying the Hair

The hair with which the child was born should be removed as a hygienic measure. The first removal of the birth hair is marked by a rite of passage called *chuda karma*. The ritual has specific prayers seeking blessings for spiritual values. This ritual is being relegated to the sidelines in current lifestyles. There is a traditional belief that the hair, because it is black, sometimes represents evil. The removal of the birth hair is viewed as removal of the child's past sins. Many families prefer to take the child to a place of pilgrimage and offer the birth hair to God. This represents an act of purification or cleansing. The offering of hair that results in a clean-shaven head is an external symbol associated with initiation into a saintly order of life. When individuals take to the order of renunciation (*sanyasa*), they have their heads shaved. The offering of hair is also a symbol of surrender to God.

FAMILY NURTURE: THREE TO SIX YEARS OF AGE

In this next dimension, secular and spiritual educators begin to supplement the efforts of the parents. The spiritual nurturing process is aided by the parent and by educational activities through experiential role models and training provided in the home and preschool environment. Toys, storytelling, and songs convey religious and spiritual values through entertainment in a nonsuggestive way. Having children enact stories with religious themes, in which children dress to imitate the gods, is another way of introducing spiritual traditions through religious symbols. The company of children from diverse religious backgrounds in the preschool can be used to build the values of acceptance, tolerance, and coexistence.

In each of these aspects, the parent-educator team grooms the child according to localized versions of dharma understanding. The key values to which the child is guided in this phase are as follows:

• Physical acts of demonstrating respect for God and elders;
• Sharing;
• Not hurting others;

- Identifying something unique as God in the form-symbol-place to be treated with love;
- Respecting and submitting to a disciplined prayer routine; and
- Identifying primary relations of father, mother, master (i.e., the first teacher, whether mother, father, elder brother or sister, grandmother or grandfather, or professional educator), other family members, and others.

The kinds of toys, stories, music, and games provided for the child should strengthen this understanding; these are culture specific, carrying the hidden symbolism of spiritual values. This is the phase when the child is first exposed to religious and faith identities by jati (caste label). The answers provided by the parent or educator to the child for the query "why is it so?" have an important role in shaping the child's understanding of social caste. The child need not be burdened at this stage about the value of this label, by a flawed understanding of the concept, distortions in regional practices, and historical explanations. It is not the time to build a negative connotation for the child about a certain type of religious identity associated with caste because of parentage. A negative explanation would disturb the delicate bond of the child's perception of and relationship with the parent who provides the negative explanation. This hurts the child's position outside the home—at school, in the community, and among his or her friends—and disrupts spiritual progress.

It is considered sufficient to explain the utility of the jati as a unique identification of traditions of faith, religion, culture, and spiritual practices, all of which can be changed. The rigidity of medieval and classical society in the matter of caste practices is undergoing a transformation in modern society. Instead of looking at the negative connotation of the label from a historical perspective, the positive use for spiritual nurturing is being cultivated.

Initiation into the Formal Learning of Language

Aksharabhyasa is a rite of passage that signifies the readiness of the child to begin the formal learning of language; it is recommended that the ritual be conducted by the parents. The formal commencement of learning symbolized by this rite marks the entry of the child educator and spiritual educator in the single person of a religious priest. In the formal rite the parent helps the child write the letters for the sacred mystical sound *Om*. The learning of the sacred sound is a form of initiation into spiritual tradition. This is the formal introduction of the child to the language of the sacred scriptures. This rite marks the initiation of learning the language of spiritual exploration and learning to write to gain proficiency in secular languages. In current practices, this rite has been overshadowed by the stress on preschooling practices. In mystical traditions, initiation into the secrets of sacred texts is done through a similar ritual.

The Learning of Family Prayers

In this age group, traditional families begin teaching the child the oral recitation of prayers using a listen-repeat, correction-repeat approach. The language of the prayers is generally a combination of the spiritual scriptural languages Sanskrit, Prakrit, and Tamil, as well as the regional languages. The belief is that the accurate pronunciation of the name of the divinity or the words of the scriptural texts has the power of cleansing away sin. It is not critical that the child understand the text. The child says whatever it says with a pure heart, and this will accrue merit. The role modeling and involvement of family members of all ages play an important role in shaping and instilling prayer learning as a spiritual practice in the mind of the child. The child is encouraged to learn the prayers, to repeat them with the proper intonation, physical postures, and gestures, and at the correct times and intervals. The child is generally taught to say the prayers at the time of rising after sleep, during and after a bath, before taking food, before going out of the home, before commencing any auspicious activity, when afraid or confused, at the commencement of studies, at the commencement of taking an exam, and before going to bed. The child is told stories of the deities and the demons, magical and moral stories that highlight the ethical dimension of spirituality. The victory of good over evil, the dangers of pursuing wealth and power, the horrors of telling lies are some of the values that are transmitted through bedtime stories. Children are taught to handle fear with prayer, which calls on the presence and strength of God. Connectedness to God is forged as a key to success. This is the stepping-stone for a later strengthening of spiritual values.

The Role of Festivities in the Home

Festivities and religious activities provide an important visual-experiential learning model for facilitating spiritual growth. Such observances fulfill some of the parents' marriage vows, meet cultural religious requirements to accrue religious merit, and rejuvenate family-community harmony. The ambience of good food, festive atmosphere, and participation of family members in a faith bond creates an environment for the fostering of spiritual values in child.

The details of festivities performed over a cycle of one year and on up to adolescence are many and diverse in practical nature, but they share an objective: every activity—the wearing of a new dress, eating, going out of the house, reading a book—is elevated in its significance to the level of the sacred. The taking of food becomes *prasad*; the book becomes a symbol of the goddess of learning (Sarasvati). Dolls become deities in the Navaratri Dasara festival. The forms of nature and animals are seen in the forms of gods like Ganesha. Through congregational and temple worship practices, the convention is learned and observed of offering respectful submission to the deity through the folding of one's hands, receiving the sacred offering (*prasada; teertha*), bowing and prostrating oneself, lighting the lamp (*aaratii*), dressing appropriately, wearing facial marks.

The child observes and absorbs codes of conduct (*acharas*) in this phase, for example, washing the feet before entering the sacred space, wearing freshly laundered clothes, tying the hair, not going to the temple without fruit or flowers, offering money when receiving the blessed light, not wearing shoes during prayer, the correct posture for prayer and meditation, the direction to face, the direction of the deity, the lighting of the lamp and the incense, the need to avoid the distractions of television and the like for the duration of prayer and meditation, the observance of silence, the wearing of auspicious marks on the forehead, and covering the head in certain traditions. These acharas have taken on deep spiritual and symbolic meanings. The acquisition of practical discipline is believed to lead to the next level of curiosity to explore hidden spiritual values, which is the objective of traditional nurturing.

INSTITUTIONAL NURTURE: SIX TO TEN YEARS OF AGE

The overlap between the parent and teachers in the preschool phase is now reduced, with the teacher taking a major role and the parent playing more of a supporting role. At this point, the child becomes subject to state guidelines and policies on education and institution-specific disciplines for nurturing spiritual values in the framework of religious education as passed on by teachers. The younger child learns more from the living role model of the teacher than from books. This is the time when the system considers the kind of education that will deliver universal spiritual values that can be networked with the diversity of personal religious formats and enrich related practices. This is an issue to be decided by state policies with due deliberation. If state administrators are biased with regard to religion or faith, their biases will color the implementation. This in turn leads to the danger of dividing society according to religious identity, doctrine, and inequalities.

Traditional Hindu guidance for the state in this matter is clear: the religion and faith of an administrator or head of state is personal and should be independent of state policy, which needs to cater to a religiously diverse society. The spiritual values honored by the state are the universal human values. How these are delivered to the child is determined by teacher training policies and practices.

There are no traditional rites of passage for this phase. The parent is directed to take the child through a rite of passage called *upanayana* (discussed in the following section) for the purpose of initiating the child into the scriptural spiritual disciplines. The fact that teachers in the modern educational system are not doing what the masters in traditional schooling did to nurture spiritual values in children needs serious discussion in the new social order. Traditional thinking has anticipated this gap and recommends that the parent shall have the primary responsibility for initiating the child into the spiritual traditions. The training and discipline of traditional systems are guided by spiritual values, a timetable best suited for learning religious practices imbued with spiritual values along with other learning. The training is customized by taking into account the child's abilities and family background. The personal attention of the master to the child characterizes the learning in this phase.

The teaching of religion does not involve any proselytization. It is important to note that Hindu traditions do not advocate concepts such as "absolute sin," "eternal sin," "eternal sinner," "eternal damnation," and "condemnation." The individual is considered the spark of the Supreme Divine. Hindus believe that this spiritual spark is always inherent in every being. Circumstances and effort help that inherent spark to glow bright. This is an important concept in understanding the responsibility of Hindus toward the discharging of responsibility for spiritual grooming through the performance of rites of passage. Every human being is welcome to the arms of God and the Supreme to fulfill their desires. The starting point is not the criterion. The desire to move toward the final goal is the criterion.

Initiation into the Study of Sacred Lore

The learning of the child is divided into two categories: disciplines related to worldly needs and those related to spiritual needs. The approach of traditional Hindu thought is to run these two streams together in an integrated, balanced way. Initiation into the spiritual disciplines carries the tags of *varna, rishi vamsha gotra jati*, and information, the tag of *janma lagna* for customizing the rite. *Upanayana* is the rite intended to address the integration of spiritual and worldly learning. Between the ages of eight and sixteen years is considered appropriate for this rite, as determined by the capability of the child's body and mind to sustain the rigors of spiritual training and the ability to grasp the instructions of the master and put them into practice. This rite of passage is a prerequisite for the next phase, namely, married life.

The initiate makes the commitment to observe spiritual vows (*bramhachari vrata*). The goal is a balanced, integrated development of the disciplines needed for worldly use as well as spiritual progress; body and mind together are disciplined through the observance of discipline under the care of the master and community living. The responsibility for taking the child through this rite is primarily that of the parent and spiritual educators. If for some reason the parents fail in this duty, the spiritual educators must take over. The modern schooling system does not provide for the concept of spiritual educator.

INSTITUTIONAL NURTURE: TEN TO THIRTEEN YEARS OF AGE

This phase builds on the preceding phase to mold each individual child in a more rigorous way. There are no additional rites. The child is set on the path of self-discipline under the watchful observation of parents and teachers.

INSTITUTIONAL NURTURE: THIRTEEN TO SIXTEEN YEARS OF AGE

This stage of development marks a significant period in the styles of body-mind functioning that may have an influence on the emotional development of the child. The semiformed logical and emotional personality of the child needs to be carefully nurtured to handle numerous emotional challenges, such as fear, the desire for thrills and entertainment, physical sensations of pain and pleasure, suppressed desires for dress, food, entertainment, tendencies to show off or imitate elders and heroes, feelings of shame and pride, jealousy, depression, falling into the trap of drugs, or falling into the vices of gambling and the like, which may lead to a sense of false prestige and power and an unwarranted sense of achievement. Mass media, music, and sports have a powerful impact on this age group. Greater vigilance is required from the family and social institutions to ensure the child's safe passage through this phase of growth. The state, community, and teachers are squarely responsible for the values that are placed before the growing child. Various toys and games, and state policies in making entertainment available through the media, are important infringements into this area, which previously was tightly controlled by families and teachers.

INSTITUTIONAL NURTURE: SIXTEEN TO EIGHTEEN YEARS OF AGE

In this final phase the successful discharge of responsibility in the previous phases will be vindicated. The child has now entered the domain of "youth." The child has generally seen the soft phase of love and nurture in the team. Now comes the time for the hand of power, authority, and punishment to discipline through the element of fear. Noncompliance with the achara sampradaya is to be strictly atoned for with the appropriate expiation rites (*prayaschitta*). Judgment continues to be made on the dual considerations of pain-pleasure and right-wrong. Parents and educators assume an advisory status. The child has come to a stage of accepting responsibility for himself or herself.

COMMUNITY AND STATE NURTURE

Hindu communities have institutions of many types: temples, Yoga institutions, single-master institutions, monasteries, and chartered institutions dedicated to the propagation of spiritual care and support. Each of these takes the thread of dharma, karma, and rina principles and builds a cover program over it to appeal to individuals for spiritual progress. Community festivities and events involving spiritual leaders are other dimensions of this support. In practice, many of these issues get subsumed under the outer cover of religious appeal and format. Promotion can take place through the visual arts, music, dance, social services, the public dissemination of knowledge, programs using the power of the media for dissemination of traditions, pilgrimages and other religious tours and the like. The state is a reflection of the individual's aspirations in the society. The state has to discharge its responsibility through its various arms of policy making, administration, and implementation. According to Hindu traditional wisdom, the child loses the benefit of spiritual traditions and wisdom for lack of action on the part of the state in certain areas: (a) lifestyles and state policies that separate spiritual values from worldly skill sets; (b) the substitution of preferred or distorted forms of religious education for spiritual education; (c) the creation of imbalanced priorities of licentious entertainment over enlightening education for economic reasons; (d) turning food, education, and religion into commodities; (e) a thwarted judicial system that fails to redress family disputes and address lifestyle needs; (f) the growth of religious institutions as alternate power centers vying with the state. Taken together, these factors result in the slow poisoning of future society by a distortion of traditions. This is an issue that is deliberated in great detail in the discipline called *artha shastra*. The grooming responsibility of a prince as a future head of state is where we find these traditional directives.

Every child is the prince of his parents and the family lineage. The team of parents, educators, and communities must exercise vigilance regarding state actions impacting the child's future.

In Summary

Hindu traditions have identified a team of four for discharging the responsibility of nurturing spiritual values in children through the end of adolescence. Three key values—dharma, karma, and rina—guide and bind the actions of the team. The understanding of these values provides the rationale for the rites of passage (samskara). The practicality of rites of passage brings in the factors of traditional religious diversity (achara sampradaya). Performance of these rites to deliver their true spirit is the way to accomplish the goal. The child carries a unique spiritual personality, which he or she brings from previous life cycles. The rites conducted for the child facilitate progress in building this inheritance.

The last of these rites is initiation into the exploration of spiritual studies. This rite positions the child from the age of eight till the sixteenth year. Passage through this rite marks the beginning of the child's own responsibility for spiritual nurturing through compliance with the disciplines of spiritual life. Team members provide the environment and support for the child to assimilate the benefit of this discipline. The team also helps the child acquire the skills needed for a successful worldly life at the final transition through the phases of adolescence.

Providing this support benefits the spiritual progress of the team. The action formats of team members, rites, and intermediary goals differ in providing this ambience. Practical guidelines are projected on the framework of popular spiritual values terminology ("merit-sin," *punya papa*) and religious identity by varna ashrama jati. The key directives to observe dharma, perform karma, and clear rina, in their supercharged meanings, have created the profound structure of Hindu achara sampradaya. The success of spiritual grooming is marked by the abundance of the qualities of connectedness, meaning, purpose, and ethical responsibility in the youth. Grooming a high number of spiritually elite members is the goal of this guidance.

Note

The description of Hindu traditions and views presented here are drawn from the original source texts in scriptural languages and used in traditional rituals. The understanding presented is the traditional viewpoint. The material is drawn from the author's observations of current social practices in Hindu families.

CHAPTER 30

Transforming Bar/Bat Mitzvah: The Role of Family and Community

Jeffrey K. Salkin

> When I became bar mitzvah, my grandfather, Eleazar of Amsterdam, of blessed memory, came to me one night in a vision and gave me another soul in exchange for mine. Ever since then, I have been a different person.
> —Shalom of Belz, twentieth-century Hassidic master

If we were to search for an accurate illustration of the challenges inherent in American Judaism, we might choose to look no further than the way in which American Jews speak about bar and bat mitzvah.

Ask American Jews, especially twelve- and thirteen-year-olds, to use the term *bar mitzvah* or *bat mitzvah* in a sentence, and this is what you are likely to hear: "My cousin's bar mitzvah was last month." "I'm having my bat mitzvah in a few weeks." "We are still waiting to get our bar mitzvah date from the synagogue." "His bar mitzvah is going to be at the country club." "The rabbi is going to bat mitzvah my daughter next week." "I was bar mitzvahed at this synagogue two years ago."

What emerges from this examination of popular American Jewish syntax? We see bar/bat mitzvah as an object, something to have, a consumer commodity, an event, a party, something that is conferred upon an individual, something that is passive. Even the spell-check in Microsoft Word rebels against this last usage; the program invariably redlines the term *mitzvahed*.

Occasionally, however, a parent or a child gets it "right." Sometimes, and triumphantly, we hear: "My son is becoming bar mitzvah next month." Here, the syntax is correct, for the speaker understands that bar/bat mitzvah is a status that a child *becomes*. We might say that the use of the term *becoming* represents a moral and spiritual shift from Martin Buber's world of "I-it"—a world of using, having, naming, and reducing—to his counterworld of "I-Thou"—a world of being and that which is markedly superior in the Jewish narrative, *becoming*. The models are clear: Abram becomes Abraham through his devotion to the one God; Jacob becomes Israel when he struggles with a nameless being; Joseph becomes mature through suffering; Moses becomes a leader by recognizing his place among his people.

This chapter will seek to understand the contemporary reality of the Jewish adolescent passage of bar/bat mitzvah; to reflect critically on its history; and to wonder aloud how it might be transformed so that the community might take a larger role in educating and therefore transforming the adolescent.

The History of Bar/Bat Mitzvah

The term *bar mitzvah* is a technical term in rabbinic literature for a young man who has reached the age of thirteen years and one day, thus denoting the attainment of religious and legal maturity. Biblical Judaism had placed the age of majority as twenty years. Postbiblical Jewish law lowered the age of maturity to thirteen, at which time a Jewish boy would be obliged to fulfill all the *mitzvot* (commandments of Jewish life).

As a postbiblical, rabbinic concept, bar mitzvah seems to be entirely rooted in midrash (rabbinic interpretations of scripture) and aggadah (rabbinic lore). If anyone could be called the "inventor" of bar mitzvah, it would be the second-century C.E. sage Judah ben Tema. He envisioned the way that a life of Jewish study and responsibility should unfold: "At five, one should study Scripture; at ten, one should study Mishnah; at thirteen, one is ready to do mitzvot; at fifteen, one is ready to study Talmud; at eighteen, one is ready for the wedding canopy; at twenty, one is responsible for providing for a family" (Mishnah, Avot 5:24).

Thirteen became the age of moral maturity. Classical Jewish anthropology endows the mature human being with two impulses: the *yetzer ha-tov*, the good inclination, and the *yetzer ha-ra*, the evil inclination. Some sources state that children below the age of thirteen possess only the yetzer ha-ra, the evil inclination, and that the child acquires the yetzer ha-tov, the good inclination, at the age of thirteen (Avot de-Rabbi Natan, 16). Therefore, thirteen was the age when young people were considered able to control their desires. In addition, until the age of thirteen a son received the merit of his father and was also liable to suffer of his parent's sin; after that each one bore his own sin.

Consider the midrashic retelling of the youth of Jacob and Esau. It is from Bereshit Rabbah, the classic fifth-century midrash on Genesis:

> "And the boys grew." (Genesis 25:27). Rabbi Pinchas said in Rabbi Levi's name: They were like a myrtle and wild-rose bush growing side by side; when they attained to maturity, one yields its fragrance and the other its thorns. So for thirteen years both went to school and came home from school. After this age, one went to the house of study and the other to idolatrous shrines. Rabbi Eleazar the son of Rabbi Simeon said: A man is responsible for his son until the age of thirteen [to have him educated in Torah]; thereafter he must say: "Blessed is He Who has now freed me from the responsibility for this one" [*Baruch shepeterani me-onsho shel zeh*]. (63:10)

Thus we see that Jacob and Esau went their separate ways at thirteen—Jacob to the worship of God, Esau to the service of idolatry. In a broader sense, the midrash is about the limitations of parenting. The *baruch shepeterani* statement could mean: "Whatever this young person does now, he is legally and morally culpable. Thank God it's not my fault."

Some aggadic texts mention the spiritual significance of the age of thirteen. At the age of thirteen Abraham rejected the idols of his father, Terach (Midrash, Pirkei D'Rebbe Eliezer 16). The Talmud states that the architect Bezalel was thirteen years old when he fashioned the ancient wilderness sanctuary (Sanhedrin 69b).

There were also specific religious passages that happened at the age of thirteen. Consider the issue of fasting on Yom Kippur. Two years before he attained his majority, a child would fast until noon. A year before his majority he would fast the whole day. On the occasion of this first fast, he would appear before the elders of the community. They would bless him and pray that he acquire the merit of learning Torah and doing good deeds (Sofrim 18:7).

At thirteen, the boy could help constitute a minyan (the quorum for communal prayer). He was expected to wear tefillin (phylacteries). In the first usage of the technical term *bar mitzvah*, the eighth-century midrash Tanhuma (Ha-nidpas, Bo para. 14, 84a) states:

> Can even minors don tefillin? We are taught: "You shall observe" (Exodus 13:10), for everyone who learns to observe can learn to do. This eliminates minors because they are not obliged to observe. But if a minor is bar mitzvah [old enough to do mitzvot and obliged to observe them] and *bar deah* [knowledgeable], he is obligated to don tefillin.

Finally, the age of thirteen entailed certain legal implications. Mishnah, Niddah 5:6 states that the vows of a boy aged thirteen years and a day old are considered valid. The aggadah spells this out with its commentary on the actions of Simeon and Levi during the sack of Shechem in retaliation for the rape of their sister Dinah (Genesis 34): they were thirteen years old and thus legally culpable for their actions. At the age of thirteen, a youth could serve as a member of a *bet din* (a Jewish court), and could buy and sell property. The notable exception was that the testimony of a thirteen-year-old is not considered valid regarding real estate "because he is not knowledgeable about buying and selling."

Therefore, the age of thirteen becomes a benchmark of moral, religious, and legal maturity. How would the community mark this passage? Classically, this was accomplished through the public reading of Torah. The origins of Torah reading as symbolizing maturity are obscure. There are some narrative traditions in which a youth reads Scripture before a congregation. For example, Josephus had said that he was examined by the elders and found "commendable" at the age of fourteen, but the reference is perhaps only designed so that the self-serving Josephus might prove his own sagacity (Wasserstein 1974, 31). Thirteen-year-old boys may have read the *haftarah* (the prophetic portion for the week's lectionary) in the early centuries of the Common Era; indeed, Luke 2:42–49 records that the twelve-year-old Jesus publicly read from the scroll of Isaiah. But there is still nothing in rabbinic literature about any ritual connected with becoming bar mitzvah.

It might be that the origin of bar mitzvah is both simpler and more profound than we had earlier thought. It may have found its roots in the *brit milah* ceremony that occurs when a boy is eight days old. At that covenantal ceremony, the father says, "As this child has been brought into the covenant of Abraham, so, too, will he be brought into the study of Torah, the marriage canopy, and the performance of good deeds." The marking of bar mitzvah was the way in which the assembled community confirmed that the father had fulfilled the first part of his promise. It thus constituted a passage for the father as well as for the child. To be part of the community, you must bring your child to the study of Torah.

The distinction between a minor and one who had obtained his majority was primarily theoretical and theological. The latter did as a religious duty what a minor did optionally. In other words, it was not that what was done was different, but rather why it was done. On a theological level, the child was now considered to be old enough to be commanded by God to perform mitzvot. In a very real sense, then, the mandate to perform mitzvot is the essence of the Jewish spiritual passage—this, more than belief, defines the competent Jew. The reason is clear: Judaism is a faith that is rooted in action more than in belief—or, to put it more precisely, in actions that inform belief, and vice versa. The purpose of bar mitzvah, then, was quite simple: it bridges the gap between the responsibilities of childhood and of adulthood (Marcus 1996, 120–24).

The age of thirteen had a particularly poignant significance for the conversos, the Spanish Jews who converted to Christianity under duress during the fifteenth century, but secretly maintained certain Jewish practices and beliefs. It was common for parents not to reveal a child's Jewish identity until the age of thirteen (for a girl, it was often twelve years old, or when she first menstruated). If the secret had been revealed earlier, the child's immaturity might have made it impossible to keep this fact the well-guarded secret that it had to be. Yet, if the child had learned later than this, his or her Christian identity would have "taken," making any kind of link to Judaism much more difficult.

If any ritual celebrates the diversity of Jewish expression, it is bar and bat mitzvah. The reason for this is clear: these are customs with no force of law. The more or less "standard" procedure is for the young person to offer the blessings for the reading of the Torah; to read or chant the Torah portion from the lectionary, and to read or chant the haftarah. In the late Middle Ages, it became customary for the bar mitzvah to offer a *drashah* (a learned mini lecture on a Jewish subject) in the home. That drashah has been transformed into the bar mitzvah speech, which usually serves as a *devar Torah* (a sermonette on the Torah portion) or as a personal prayer for the occasion. In many synagogues, the young person also leads the congregation in the Hebrew prayers in the service. In most synagogues, parents, grandparents, and other close relatives are given *aliyot* (the privilege of saying the blessing over the Torah) and other honors.

What about bat mitzvah, the parallel rite for young women? Starting in the second or third century of the Common Era, Jewish girls at the age of twelve had a legal responsibility to observe the mitzvot that pertained to Jewish women: lighting candles; the separation of *challah* (a memory to the ancient grain offering in the Temple) from bread; and the laws of family purity.

It was not until centuries later, however, that families would begin celebrating the girl's new status with some festivity. By the 1800s, some families held a *seudat mitzvah* (a festive meal for a ritual occasion) on a girl's twelfth birthday. Sometimes the girl would deliver a talk and her father would recite the traditional *baruch shepetarani* prayer. A nineteenth-century rabbinic authority, Rabbi Joseph Hayyim ben Elijah of Iraq, mentioned coming-of-age celebrations for girls in his legal writings. There were also such celebrations for twelve-year-old girls in Italy (where it was called "entering minyan") as well as such celebrations in Poland, Germany, and Egypt in the early twentieth century.

The first bat mitzvah ceremony in North America was that of the late Judith Kaplan Eisenstein (1909–96), the eldest daughter of Rabbi Mordecai Kaplan, the founder of Reconstructionism. It happened in March 1922, when, as Judith later recalled, she was "midway between my twelfth and thirteenth birthdays." Her grandmothers wrung their hands over the planned ceremony, each one prevailing on the other to persuade her father to abandon the idea.

Years later, Judith would remember that the night before the service, her father still had not decided on the exact form of the ceremony. The next day, as usual at a Shabbat service, Rabbi Kaplan read the *maftir* (the concluding portion of the Torah reading) and the haftarah. Then his daughter, "at a very respectable distance" from the Torah scroll (because girls traditionally did not read from the scroll), recited the first blessing and read the Torah selection from the *chumash* (a book containing the text of the Torah).

In mainstream Orthodoxy, the bat mitzvah ceremony is basically a devar Torah, followed by a festive meal. Sometimes the girl delivers the devar Torah in the sanctuary, sometimes in the synagogue social hall. Girls are seldom allowed to read directly from the Torah scroll. In some Orthodox synagogues, girls lead the service and read from either the Prophets or Writings sections of the Bible. In Orthodoxy, bat mitzvah services may be held on Friday evening, Saturday evening, or Sunday morning, or even after the regular weekday morning service. Some modern Orthodox women have become b'not mitzvah by chanting from the Torah as part of a women's service—no men allowed! In England, young Orthodox women sometimes become b'not mitzvah as a group ceremony, in which the girls present essays and speeches but do not read from the Torah. So, there is great diversity in the way Jewish communities have adopted this custom.

Neither Reform Judaism nor Reconstructionist Judaism liturgically distinguishes between bar mitzvah and bat mitzvah. In Conservative Judaism, practices range from the girl leading the service and reading from the Torah scroll to simply reading the haftarah. The time of the service might also vary. Some Conservative synagogues let a girl publicly celebrate becoming bat mitzvah on Shabbat morning. Others limit it to Friday evenings, or Monday, Thursday, and *rosh chodesh* (the first day of the Hebrew month) mornings when the Torah is also read.

Confirmation

Early in its history, Reform Judaism was suspicious about bar mitzvah. There were theological objections to the use of the term *mitzvah*. There were aesthetic objections, as well: nineteenth-century German Jews could be quite uncomfortable with a vocally untrained pubescent chanting Torah (Meyer 1988, 36). There were sociological objections; some observers were uncomfortable with a rite that centered upon a single child, believing that this would foster a sense of narcissism in the child.

But the most strident objections were on intellectual grounds. The late-nineteenth-century American Reform theologian Kaufman Kohler wrote:

> Disregarding altogether the false claim of mental maturity of the thirteen
> year-old boy for a true realization of life's sacred obligations, I maintain that
> the bar mitzvah rite ought not to be encouraged by any Reform rabbi, as it
> is a survival of Orientalism . . . whereas the Confirmation . . . is a source for
> the regeneration of Judaism each year . . . the whole bar mitzvah rite [has]
> lost all meaning, and the calling up of the same [to the Torah] is nothing less
> than a sham. (Quoted in Plaut 1965)

Bar mitzvah was replaced by classical Reform Judaism's major contribution to Jewish ritual life: confirmation. Confirmation is first mentioned officially in Westphalia in 1809. This ritual was adopted from Christianity where it represented the culmination of a course of study intended to prepare the young person for adult status in the church. The Jewish ceremony of that name goes back as far as 1803, when it was instituted in Dessau and then spread to Wolfenbüttel, where the founder of modern Jewish scholarship, Leopold Zunz, was confirmed in 1807.

The ceremony originally was held in either the home or the school, and it was an individual ceremony for boys only, at the age of thirteen. The style was catechistic—well-rehearsed answers to questions about belief in God and its sources in names and in Scripture. Such was Zunz's confirmation ceremony, with the confirmand then reciting Maimonides' Thirteen Articles of Faith in response to a question on personal belief. Finally, the teacher gave him a paternal admonition and the young Zunz recited an original Hebrew prayer of thanksgiving.

Confirmation, then, originally was noticeably similar to bar mitzvah, substituting an adherence to a philosophical truth system rather than the traditional mitzvah system. Confirmation itself was subject to a considerable amount of controversy during the early years of Reform Judaism. Many, especially the local consistories that governed Jewish ritual behavior, were uncomfortable with its blatant Christian roots. Not only were the theological assumptions more Christian than Jewish (the idea of faith as opposed to the performance of mitzvot) but at least one confirmation service (at Seesen in 1810) was coauthored by an Evangelical pastor. According to Michael Meyer (1988):

> One writer noted that while the recitation of articles of faith was essential to
> Christian confirmation, Jews did not become Jews by learning religious doc-
> trines . . . Still it was widely felt that the bar mitzvah ceremony had in many
> instances become an empty shell, that it was deficient in that it did not extend
> to girls, and that in an era when powerful centrifugal forces were eroding Jew-
> ish identity there was an urgent need for some ceremony in which the Jewish
> child would solemnly declare his or her commitments. (40)

Within a short period of time, confirmation would expand to include girls as well as boys. It would become firmly rooted as a group (as opposed to individual) ceremony. When Reform Judaism was imported to America, so was confirmation, starting at New York's Congregation Emanuel in 1845. Over the years the ceremony would cease to be connected with chronological age; rather, it would be connected to a particular grade level in secular school—usually tenth grade (though there is some fluctuation in this practice). Therefore, the ceremony was entirely disconnected from any relationship to bar/bat mitzvah; its association with grade level rather than chronological age served to emphasize its academic and intellectual component.

Confirmation emphasized the group experience of Judaism (as opposed to the individual experience of bar mitzvah); equality between the sexes (which had not yet been affirmed through the invention of bat mitzvah), and the raised age of maturity to sixteen. In the (often) absence of bar/bat mitzvah in American classical Reform congregations, it became a major rite of passage, often serving a key social component as well.[1]

But we also note that post–bar/bat mitzvah retention through confirmation has become very problematic. Statistics in this area are sketchy; some would put the dropout rate at higher than 50 percent. There are certain reasons for this: the growing academic, social, and athletic pressures on teenagers; the loss of a sense of community for which the confirmation class might be a model; increased individualism, demonstrated through parents' desires for the "spotlight" to be on their child; and the simple fact that, for all its advantages, confirmation has never taken root within the American Jewish cultural consciousness in any way resembling bar/bat mitzvah.

What Has Happened to Bar/Bat Mitzvah?

In its classical sense, bar mitzvah evoked a certain worldview. It celebrated the value of Jewish learning, which began with the parents—classically, and most notably, the father:

> Our masters taught: With regard to his son, a father is obligated to circumcise him, to redeem him [if he is the firstborn], to teach him Torah, to teach him a craft, and to get him married. Some say: Also to teach him how to swim. Rav Judah said: When a man does not teach his son a craft, it is as though he taught him robbery. (Talmud, Kiddushin 29a)

The father was also required to teach the son ritual competence:

> Our masters taught: A child who knows how to shake the lulav cluster is required to use the lulav cluster [on Sukkot]. If the child knows how to wrap himself in a prayer shawl, he is required to wrap himself in a prayer shawl. If a child knows how to care for tefillin, his father must acquire tefillin for him. If he knows how to speak, his father must teach him the Sh'ma, Torah, and the holy tongue. If the father does not, it is as though the child had not come into the world. What is meant here by Torah? Rav Hamnuna said: The verse "Moses commanded us Torah, the inheritance of the congregation of Jacob" (Deuteronomy 33:4). And what is meant here by Sh'ma? Its first verse ["Hear, O Israel: The Lord our God, the Lord is one" (Deut. 6:4)]. (Tosafot, Hagigah 1:2; Talmud, Sukkah 42a)

Grandparents might also be involved in the transmission of Torah:

> Rabbi Joshua ben Levi said: When a man teaches Torah to his grandson,
> Scripture regards him as though he had received it from God at Mount
> Sinai, for the verse "Make them known to your children and children's chil-
> dren" (Deut. 4:9) is followed at once by "The day you stood before the Lord
> your God at Horeb" (Deut. 4:10). (Talmud, Kiddushin 30a)

Finally, the entire community might be involved:

> Rabbi Samuel bar Nahmani said in the name of Rabbi Jonathan: When a
> man teaches Torah to his neighbor's son, Scripture speaks of him as though
> he had begotten him. Thus it says, "These are the generations of Aaron and
> Moses" (Numbers 3:1), and right after that, "These are the names of the
> sons of Aaron" (Num. 3:3). This tells you that although Aaron begot them,
> nevertheless, because Moses taught them, they are also called after the name
> of Moses. (Talmud, Sanhedrin 19b)
>   Once Rav came to a certain place where, though he had decreed a fast, no
> rain fell. Presently a reader in the synagogue stepped down in front of Rav
> before the Ark and recited, "He causes the wind to blow," and the wind
> blew; then, "He causes the rain to fall," and rain fell. Rav asked him: What
> is your occupation? He replied: I am a teacher of young children, teaching
> Scripture to children of the poor as well as to children of the rich. From him
> who cannot afford it, I take no payment. Besides, I have a fishpond, and I
> bribe with fish any boy who refuses to study until he comes in to study
> Scripture. (Talmud, Taanit 24a)

We now lack the presumption that parents will be involved in the transmission of
Torah to their children. American Judaism, like much of American middle-class life,
has become a referral culture. While the Hebrew term for "teacher," *moreh/morah*,
shares a linguistic root with the term for "parent," it is unclear to what extent Jewish
parents are really involved in the Jewish education of their children.

We also lack the presumption of community. The Jewish world, so sweetly envisioned by Zborowski in *Life Is with People*, has vanished. We can name many smoking
pistols: mobility, the suburbs, affluence, the culture of individualism.

In Europe, bar mitzvah was a *comma* in a Jewish paragraph. It was the celebration
of a child's Jewish maturity, which meant a certain amount of Jewish learning. Ideally
(or in our mythical imagination), it was assumed that the young Jew would continue
learning. In the United States, however, bar/bat mitzvah has become a *period*. Ivan
Marcus, the preeminent scholar of the Jewish life cycle, has noted that many elements
of the Jewish wedding celebration have "trickled down" to the bar/bat mitzvah and that
the rite has become a "graduation" from Judaism (Marcus 2004, 122). The religious
school dropout rates after bar/bat mitzvah are scandalously high—a matter of great
communal concern.

In Europe, bar mitzvah was one of a list of ritual moments that were tied together
through the assumption of Torah and covenant. The parents had brought the child into
the covenant with words of expectation: "As we have brought this child into the

covenant, so, too, we will bring this child to Torah, to the wedding canopy, and to acts of goodness." There was the real sense that the community that had been present at the brit milah ceremony to hear those words of commitment would be there at the bar mitzvah ceremony to be able to mentally check off that first item on the list: "Thirteen years ago, you promised that you would bring your child to the study of Torah. Here we are thirteen years later, and you have kept your promise." Because of the paucity of Jewish ritual moments, and because most Jews do not understand the poetry of Jewish ritual (and indeed, have not been helped to understand that poetry by their religious leaders), we cannot assume that most Jews will make the connection between brit/baby naming and bar/bat mitzvah.

The "Old World" bar mitzvah meant a real change in status, the attainment of religious maturity, the assumption of additional religious responsibilities. In most quarters of American Jewish life, such references would be incoherent. Where, outside of tightly knit Orthodox communities, would a young person experience such transformation?[2]

The "Old World" bar mitzvah was joyous, but it was always a relatively humble celebration. By contrast, American Jewish folklore enshrines numerous stories about the vulgarization and opulence of bar/bat mitzvah celebrations.

The irony is that bar/bat mitzvah is the only Jewish observance that has actually grown in importance in modernity. It is now the center of a multimillion-dollar industry of entertainment, gifts, and catering. There is even the contemporary phenomenon of gentile children asking their parents for bar/bat mitzvah ceremonies (Bernstein 2004). But in some ways, bar/bat mitzvah has shrunk in significance. A comprehensively ordered, fully integrated system of beliefs and behaviors had come undone, its constituent parts disaggregated and reassembled. In the alchemy of America, a new form of Jewish identity emerged—Jewishness—whose expression had as much, and perhaps more, to do with feeling "Jewish at heart" than with formal ritual.

CAN WE REPAIR BAR AND BAT MITZVAH?

The purpose of a religious ritual is to dramatize a myth—to give flesh to an ancient, transcendent tale. In the case of bar/bat mitzvah, the ritual serves two purposes: it marks the passage from childhood to maturity, and it does so by demonstrating that the child has the skills to be a Jewish adult.

Let us imagine, then, two narratives regarding bar/bat mitzvah.

The modern American Jewish narrative (what the majority of Jewish parents might say): Bar/bat mitzvah is an expected part of American Jewish life. It's what you do. This means something to us. It's really not about impressing our friends and family. It's about our child's Jewish identity. We want our child to know that he or she is Jewish and to be proud of it. Bar/bat mitzvah is the way we show that. It is the way that we have shown it in every generation of our family. Therefore, because we want our child to have a bar/bat mitzvah, we recognize that this means Jewish education. This is a good value. Our child should know his or her Jewish identity. So, we will join a synagogue. We will enroll our child in religious school—perhaps in a Jewish preschool, perhaps starting in kindergarten, perhaps in fourth grade which is the "cutoff" requirement for bar/bat mitzvah eligibility. Perhaps in the course of those years, we will come to services and enjoy them.[3] Perhaps, in the course of those years, we will find other aspects of the synagogue program attractive and we will make some friends. In any case, our child will have a bar/bat mitzvah ceremony. If he or she wants to continue with Jewish education and involvement, we will certainly not discourage that.

In order for bar/bat mitzvah to be transformed in American Jewish culture, we would need a new narrative—a new narrative that paradoxically would recapture a piece of the older, premodern narrative of Jewish life.

A new, postmodern narrative about bar/bat mitzvah: As a family, we find meaning in Judaism.[4] We believe that Judaism is worth teaching to our children. While we acknowledge our primary responsibilities as parents to be Jewish role models and teachers for our children, we understand that only a community can truly transmit Judaism. This is because the Jewish community represents the linkages that bind all Jews together, across time and space. For this reason, we will join a synagogue that embodies our sense of Judaism.[5] In the context of this community, our child will learn Judaism and, as part of that process, become bar/bat mitzvah. We expect that our children will continue learning in the midst of this community, because that is a Jewish responsibility.

Note the cultural, almost "Copernican," shift here. Instead of the bar/bat mitzvah being the desired commodity that drives the engine, it is the notion of seeking a community of meaning that provides education, with the ritual of bar/bat mitzvah as part of that process. Here, process replaces product.

Granted, there are many synagogues in the United States in which this second paradigm is already present. Those are synagogues in which a communitarian philosophy is regnant, rather than individualism and consumerism. Ironically, it is the kind of community that most Jews *say* they want. There is a hunger for real community in America today. In the words of the theme song of the old television series *Cheers*: "Sometimes you want to go where everybody knows your name." No matter how large the synagogue might be, that is what people want—to be known.

Moreover, there is a sense that our children need this as well. Hillary Rodham Clinton borrowed from an African proverb when she famously wrote that it takes a village to raise a child. American Jews sense that it takes a synagogue to build a mensch. But despite our highest values, there is an inherent reluctance here, because this is a countercultural wish. There is nowhere in American life today where this happens for our young people. We are locked into an approach-avoidance relationship with community for our children.

More than this: if American Jews say that they want a sense of community regarding bar/bat mitzvah, it would require an overhaul of worship patterns that, frankly, are deeply ingrained into the American Jewish psyche. In Reform congregations, for example, the notion of a Shabbat morning worshipping community may not really exist. In many synagogues, the bar/bat mitzvah ceremony dominates the service. This has led to the phenomenon of many congregations starting alternative worship experiences for the "regulars"—or those who *might* be the regulars but want more intensive prayer than the usual bar/bat mitzvah service provides. Most synagogues welcome a different "congregation" every week, many of whom are unable to participate in the service with any conviction because they are unfamiliar with Jewish worship. With the preponderance of interfaith marriage and other demographic challenges, there is the possibility that Jews might actually be a *minority* at some bar/bat mitzvah services.[6]

We must be attentive to the kinds of liturgical messages that the service sends. If the bar/bat mitzvah ceremony happens within the context of the Torah service—"superimposed," as it were, on the rest of the service—it sends one kind of message: this is a normal part of our community. If the service, however, only exists, or seems to exist, for the sake of the ceremony, it sends another kind of message—one of individualism, in which one family is privileged over the rest of the community.

We need to be attentive to the way we speak about what happens in the sanctuary. Do we catch ourselves praising the child for his or her "performance"? Do we slip and find ourselves describing the congregation as an "audience"? Do we think the child is engaged in a recital, or is the child leading the congregation in a service that would have happened whether or not he or she was there, and which happened before he or she was born and will endure long after he or she dies? Is this the demonstration of a skill for a singular "event," or of a skill that will be needed in the future to be part of a community (Ellman 2003)?

If, in fact, we really want a community—not a faux community of the people that we happen to know and like, but a community in the sense of a group that shares and celebrates certain values—and if we really want the community involved in the religious and spiritual nurturance of our young people, then the process and resultant ceremony will have to look and feel different.

Let me dream aloud. If we care about creating community, then we will have worked all along to create that sense of community in religious school classes.

We would have to require attendance at religious services as a prerequisite for bar/bat mitzvah—but not as a way of "understanding" the service or even "knowing what you will have to do on your special day." Those goals are not unworthy, but a far better goal would be to attend religious services "so that you and your family feel a sense of community here."

A community educator named Stan Crow (quoted in Michael Gurian's book *A Fine Young Man*) has been creating and directing adolescent rites of passage in Seattle for many years. His philosophy is that newly emerging adolescents need mentors, ordeals and tests, rituals, and community celebration.

What would the elements of such a passage be? How can we integrate these elements with the process of bar/bat mitzvah and make them Jewish?

The adolescent should discard his or her old life in some way, in order to symbolize rebirth.

Newly emerging adolescent boys of the Maasai people in East Africa give away their childhood possessions. Jewish adolescents could give away or sell their old toys in a garage sale, donating the proceeds to a charitable cause.

One of the greatest complaints about bar/bat mitzvah is that the teenager does not perceive any change in his or her status. They want an adult version of Judaism, and not one that simply imitates and needlessly repeats the old patterns and content of previous religious training. Recalling the legend about the youthful Abraham breaking his father's idols, the educator might use the bar/bat mitzvah as a time to break some of the idols that our young people have been worshipping. It might be a time for teenagers to reunderstand Judaism, to know that some of what they have learned in the past was appropriate for them as children, but that they are ready for some bigger truths: Hanukkah is not about a jar of oil that lasted for eight nights. There are racy and violent passages in the Bible. God will not always bail us out.

We could use the moment of bar/bat mitzvah for kids to give some of their old and useable religious school textbooks to younger children. It could be done in a ritualized form, even at a public worship service. It could be a way for those young people to say to themselves and to the community: "I have grown. The 'old me' has died. I am passing on my sources of earlier wisdom to another 'generation.'"

Honor teachers.

It never fails to astound me how rarely children's religious school teachers are present at bar/bat mitzvah ceremonies. To be fair, such a "command performance" would become strenuous for most teachers. But here again, we ask for too little. The teachers should be there. And they should be honored during the service. This child did not get to where he or she is today on his or her own.

Establish connections with the community's elders.

The contemporary scholar of religion Mircea Eliade teaches that the puberty initiation represents the revelation of the sacred. In a primitive society, this means not only what we conventionally call "religion" but also an entire body of culture, tradition, and lore.[7]

That's how it used to be. In "the old days," Jewish boys became Jewish men under the tutelage and guidance of the older men in the community. In those days, the elders of the community lived in our homes and right in our midst, not in Sun Belt retirement communities a thousand miles away. We turned to the elders for wisdom, knowledge, and informal tutoring in the skills of life. They could teach you how to *davven* (pray in the synagogue) and how to put on tefillin. Jewish women had business acumen, folk wisdom, knowledge about cooking and marriage and family. Jewish education—life education—was less of a classroom affair and more of an active apprenticeship.

We lack the wisdom of old men and women in the Jewish community. The question is haunting: Has the American Jewish community become too rational and too professionalized? Is it possible to restore a sense of tribal wisdom to Jewish life?

It is time for us to reacquaint the generations with each other. Older laypeople (and not just rabbis, cantors, and educators) could teach Hebrew, Torah, and synagogue skills. Our young people should be able to ask them the questions of life and the questions of Jewish living and belief. The community could honor the elder tutor at the bar/bat mitzvah ceremony. Imagine how powerful this could be. Imagine how this could help redeem and revive our fading concept of "community."

Concretize relationships with older adolescents.

The synagogue needs to foster a sense of bonding between the bar/bat mitzvah child and older adolescents. When possible, teenagers could tutor younger students and work with them on their sermonettes and/or service projects. In a previous synagogue, I experimented with older students bringing the bar/bat mitzvah candidate onto the *bima* (the raised platform in the sanctuary) and presenting the child to the congregation. It created a sense of "tribal solidarity."

Experience community.

Years ago, a close relative of my great-uncle Harry died. One evening during the shiva (seven-day mourning) period, the door to the house opened up and a group of people entered. Their holy task was to comprise the shiva minyan, the ten-person quorum that would make worship possible. With them was a boy in his early teens. He went over to my great-uncle Harry and said to him: "May God console you on your loss." He then distributed prayer books to the mourners in the living room and began to lead the evening service.

After the service was over, the boy went into the dining room, wrapped some pastries in a napkin, shoved the little bundle into his pocket, returned to my great-uncle's side, shook the old man's hand, and left. I turned to my great-uncle and asked, "Who was that boy?" Uncle Harry shrugged his shoulders and answered, "A kid from the *shul.*"

Such a beautiful gesture! The gesture said, "Who knows, and who cares?" Such beautiful words! "A kid from the *shul.*" That was how Harry identified the boy—as part of his religious community. The boy had become bar mitzvah—old enough to do mitzvot. Someone in the synagogue—the rabbi, the cantor, the director of education, or a knowledgeable layperson—must have taken him aside and said, "Now that you are bar mitzvah, and old enough to do mitzvot, we're going to teach you the most delicate mitzvah imaginable. We're going to teach you how to go into a house of mourning and lead a service and walk mourners through the valley of the shadow of death."

In just such ways, our young people can feel the larger Jewish community's investment in their Jewish and spiritual growth. The task is daunting, because it would necessitate the total rethinking of much of contemporary Jewish life—which would necessitate a rethinking of Judaism's entire post-Emancipation project.

A large, even cosmic task. But it may well be worth the effort.

Notes

1. Conversations with women who were confirmed in classical Reform congregations in the 1920s through the 1950s indicate that confirmation may have also been a faux "coming out" ritual as well. There are still some congregations that link cotillion to confirmation.

2. I note the utter incoherency of such statements in liberal Jewish circles, and how often I have been guilty of uttering them. When I tell a thirteen-year-old child that he or she is now eligible to complete the minyan, I sometimes wonder what kind of Jewish world I am imagining

for this child. In a large, classical Reform congregation, the possibility of a teenager being required to help constitute a minyan—even in a house of mourning, where the shiva minyan is rarely observed—is rather small. We have yet to develop a coherent liberal Jewish language about the meaning of bar/bat mitzvah in the Jewish life of a child.

3. Note the ubiquitous use of the term *enjoy* in connection with religious services.

4. The use of the phrase "find meaning in" is deliberate. I have consciously rejected other formulations, such as "believe in," which may be too theological and too catechistic. Here I am guided by Professor Lawrence Hoffman, who has taught that the role of religion/Judaism is to help people make meaning out of life.

5. This is not the usual motivating factor in families choosing a synagogue. Typical reasons are proximity, friendship patterns, liking the rabbi, and the religious school.

6. I have dealt with this entire problem in depth in my doctoral dissertation "Appropriating a Liturgical Context for Bar/Bat Mitzva," Princeton Theological Seminary, 1991.

7. Eliade (1965) virtually ignores bar mitzvah as an initiatory rite: "The puberty initiation represents above all the revelation of the sacred. In short, through initiation, the candidate passes beyond the natural more—the mode of the child—and gains access to the cultural mode; that is, he is introduced to spiritual values" (3).

References

Bernstein, Elizabeth. 2004. You don't have to be Jewish to want a bar mitzvah: More gentile kids get faux post-rite parties. *Wall Street Journal*, January 14.

Eliade, Mircea. 1965. *Rites and symbols of initiation: The mysteries of birth and rebirth.* New York: Harper Torchbooks.

Ellman, Barat. 2003. Defining community: Bar/bat mitzvah ritual. *Conservative Judaism* 56 (2): 32–47.

Gurian, Michael. 1999. *A fine young man: What parents, mentors, and educators can do to shape adolescent boys into exceptional men.* New York: Jeremy P. Tarcher.

Marcus, Ivan G. 1996. *Rituals of childhood: Jewish acculturation in medieval Europe.* New Haven, Conn.: Yale University Press.

———. 2004. *The Jewish life cycle: Rites of passage from biblical to modern times.* Seattle: University of Washington Press.

Meyer, Michael A. 1988. *Response to modernity: A history of the reform movement in Judaism.* New York: Oxford University Press.

Plaut, W. Gunther. 1965. *The growth of reform Judaism.* New York: World Union of Progressive Judaism.

Wasserstein, Abraham, ed. 1974. *Flavius Josephus: Selections from his works.* New York: Viking.

Zborowski, Mark. 1962. *Life is with people: The culture of the shtetl.* New York: Schocken.

CHAPTER 31

Teaching Correct Principles: Promoting Spiritual Strength in LDS Young People

David C. Dollahite and Loren D. Marks

The Church of Jesus Christ of Latter-day Saints (LDS, Mormon) began in upstate New York in 1830 with six members and has grown steadily to a membership of more than 12 million members in 165 nations (as of 2004).[1] With about 5.5 million American members, the LDS Church is now the fifth-largest denomination in the United States and the fastest growing among the fifteen largest churches (Lindner 2004). Twenty years ago, sociologist of religion Rodney Stark (1984) posited that Mormonism was "a new world faith" and used sophisticated demographic analyses to project a worldwide membership of more than 50 million by the year 2040 and as many as 265 million members by 2080. Although historically considered a "Utah Church" or an "American Church," more than half of the LDS Church's members live outside the United States, and Spanish recently surpassed English as the most prevalent language among the Church's members. Given the relative lack of research on Latter-day Saints outside the United States, this chapter focuses on LDS children and youth in the United States.

Key Sources of Information for Chapter

As family scholars, we have interviewed nearly sixty LDS families with children and youth in seven states about the ways their religious beliefs, practices, and communities influence them as individuals and families. Also, in preparing this chapter we conducted focus group discussions on spirituality with about a dozen LDS youth (ages fourteen to eighteen) in Louisiana and Utah, and we obtained feedback on drafts of the chapter from two LDS bishops (lay congregational leaders).

The Authors in Relation to the LDS Church and Their Fellow Latter-day Saints

The authors are both active and committed Latter-day Saints. As "insiders" we will attempt to convey the ideals and strengths of the LDS faith relative to spiritual development in children and adolescents while also addressing some associated challenges, as requested by the editors of this volume.

The Importance of Spiritual Development in LDS Children and Youth

Promoting spirituality among its children and youth is a central goal of the LDS Church, and vast resources and energies are expended to this end. Ultimately, however, spiritual development is considered the responsibility and opportunity of the individual. A fundamental orientation to teaching youth comes from a statement made by LDS Church founder, Joseph Smith, who, when asked how he governed a large group of diverse people on the western frontier (at Nauvoo, Illinois) said, "I teach them correct principles and they govern themselves." Although agency is respected, LDS families, leaders, and teachers consider it their sacred and solemn duty to encourage and instruct children along the way to correct decisions and mature spirituality.

LDS spirituality is highly relational and consciously active in nature. One LDS doctrine states that "men should be anxiously engaged in a good cause, and do many things of their own free will" (Doctrine and Covenants 58:27–28), while The Book of Mormon teaches that "when you are in the service of your fellow beings you are only in the service of your God" (Mosiah 2:17). Observers of LDS life will likely notice less emphasis on contemplative spirituality than on what can be termed an *engaged spirituality*. Although LDS teachings are replete with commandments to worship God, study Scripture, ponder spiritual questions, and pray often, a central emphasis of these efforts is that the individual establish and maintain a close relationship with God so as to more actively serve Him and His children. In fact, the LDS term describing a member in good standing is "active" rather than devout or orthodox.

ASPECTS OF LATTER-DAY SAINT SPIRITUALITY

Spirituality is complex, dynamic, and personal. For the purposes of this chapter, we discuss three broad aspects of LDS spirituality: (1) communing with God, (2) charity toward others, and (3) remembering and keeping covenants.

Communing with God

Jesus stated, "And this is life eternal, that they might know thee, the only true God, and Jesus Christ, whom thou has sent" (John 17:3). For Latter-day Saints, establishing and maintaining a personal relationship with God the Father through his son Jesus Christ is the first and foremost aspect of spirituality. This relationship is developed by means of regular and meaningful prayer, the study of sacred texts, repentance and forgiveness of sin, and learning to receive and respond to inspiration from the Holy Spirit. Helping children develop a strong and deep relationship with their Heavenly Father through the power and grace of Jesus Christ is viewed as a paramount parental religious duty and blessing. A frequently quoted verse from The Book of Mormon states, "And we talk of Christ, we rejoice in Christ, we preach of Christ, we prophesy of Christ, and we write according to our prophecies, that our children may know to what source they may look for a remission of their sins" (2 Nephi 25:26).

Charity toward Others

The apostle Paul taught, "[T]hough I have all faith, so that I could remove mountains and have not charity, I am nothing. . . . And now abideth faith, hope, and charity, these three; but the greatest of these is charity" (1 Corinthians 13:1–2, 13). Charity is further defined in The Book of Mormon as "the pure love of Christ" (Moroni 7:47). Expressions of this pure love include (a) the pure love Christ has for the individual, (b) the love the individual has for Christ, and (c) the Christlike love the individual develops for others when he or she begins to relate to others as Christ would relate to them. In LDS doctrine, spiritual attributes are not equal—charity is the greatest. This rests in the view that charity is the combination of the first two great commandments taught by Jesus, to "love the Lord thy God" and "love thy neighbor as thyself" (Mark 12:29–31). Latter-day Saints are expected to develop an abiding and active love for all of the Heavenly Father's children on earth and to practice lifelong service to members of the family, faith community, neighborhood, and people of the world.

Remembering and Keeping Covenants

Jesus told Peter that he would give him "the keys to the kingdom of heaven: and whatsoever thou shalt bind on earth shall be bound in heaven" (Matthew 16:19). Latter-day Saints believe the Lord restored these same keys to LDS Church founder Joseph Smith (Doctrine and Covenants 27:13; 81:2; 132:19). By the power of these keys, Latter-day Saints make sacred covenants with God at baptism (after age eight),[2] when male members receive the priesthood (at age twelve), and in temples dedicated to providing covenants and ordinances that facilitate the spiritual progression of individuals and the eternal uniting of couples and families. Covenant keeping involves the sacred effort to honor all promises an individual has made to God, family, and the faith community.

In summary, our definition of spirituality includes a relational aspect (communing with God), an affective component (a pure love or charity toward others), and an observable pattern of behavior and commitment in remembering and keeping covenants. From an LDS perspective, all three are needed for spirituality to optimally develop in children, youth, or adults.

An Approach to Research on Religion

In our scholarship on faith and families (e.g., Dollahite, Marks, and Goodman 2004), we emphasize the importance of considering three dimensions of religious experience—spiritual beliefs, religious practices, and faith community—to understand the influence of religion in connection with families and children. Consistent with this view, we will discuss the Latter-day Saint approach to each of these dimensions in connection with the focal topic of spiritual development in childhood and youth.[3] In doing so, we use the following official LDS Church sources: (a) The Articles of Faith, thirteen statements on LDS doctrine written by the founder and first president of the LDS Church, Joseph Smith; (b) a formal statement issued by First Presidency and the Council of the Twelve Apostles (the governing councils of the LDS Church) in 1995 titled "The Family: A Proclamation to the World" (cf. www.lds.org; hereafter referred to as "The Family"); and (c) the canonical LDS Scriptures called the Standard Works.[4]

SPIRITUAL BELIEFS

For Latter-day Saints, spiritual beliefs are doctrines, framings, meanings, or perspectives that relate to God and His Plan of Happiness for His children. We address two central foci of LDS belief: (a) doctrine on God, Jesus, and the Holy Spirit and (b) doctrine on family and children.

Doctrine on God, Jesus, and the Holy Spirit

Latter-day Saints believe that their first prophet, Joseph Smith, communed with God. Smith reported that following a prayer he offered in the woods near his upstate New York home in 1820:

> I saw a pillar of light exactly over my head above the brightness of the sun, which descended gradually until it fell upon me. . . . When the light rested upon me I saw two Personages, whose brightness and glory defy all description, standing above me in the air. One of them spake unto me, calling me by name and said, pointing to the other—*This is My Beloved Son. Hear Him!* (Joseph Smith History 1:16–17, emphasis in original)

Based on this experience by one who came to be held as a prophet by the LDS people, LDS doctrine begins with the belief that the Father and the Son are physically separate beings, who have glorified "bod[ies] of flesh and bones as tangible as man's" (Doctrine and Covenants 130:22), and that God can and does speak to prophets in our day (Article of Faith 9).

In LDS belief, God the Father and His Son Jesus are the first two members of the Godhead. The third and final member of the Godhead is the Holy Ghost (or Holy Spirit) who teaches and testifies of God and Christ, purges sin from the soul, brings important spiritual knowledge to a person's remembrance, and guides people in spiritual paths. For LDS youth, learning how to seek, recognize, and follow the "promptings of the Holy Ghost" (and helping others do so) is one of the most important aspects of their spiritual development. LDS sermons, lessons, and testimonies are replete with accounts of church members and leaders seeking and following "personal revelation," "spiritual guidance," or "inspiration." LDS parents desire that their children will "gain a testimony" or a "witness from the Spirit" that God lives and loves them, and parents teach their children and youth to seek guidance, comfort, and forgiveness from their Heavenly Father through direct spiritual inspiration in their daily challenges and decisions.

Doctrine on Family and Children

A key LDS doctrine regarding family reads:

> The divine plan of happiness enables family relationships to be perpetuated
> beyond the grave. Sacred ordinances and covenants available in holy temples
> make it possible for individuals to return to the presence of God and for
> families to be united eternally. ("The Family")

What Latter-day Saints call "our Heavenly Father's plan" or "the divine plan of happiness" is ultimately familial in nature. This emphasis on family strongly influences a Latter-day Saint's expectations and commitments. Sociologist John Jarvis (2000) has
emphasized, "It is [a] family focus, a veritable 'theology of the family,' that must be
understood before one can understand . . . Mormonism" (245). Further, the LDS "theology of the family" cannot be understood without noting the centrality of holy temples in LDS worship, theology, and culture.

According to LDS belief, a qualifying man and woman may be married to one
another "for eternity" (through priesthood authority) in an LDS temple (Packer 1995).
Indeed, the core aim of the Church is to build eternal families that will return to the
presence of God, the Father of all. This belief has several implications for the importance of children and youth in LDS families. First, the LDS directive is for a couple to
be married by God's authority in God's house (the holy temple) and then to have children, per the teaching that "God's commandment for His children to multiply and
replenish the earth remains in force" ("The Family"). Second, after children are born,
one has a "solemn responsibility" to love them, teach them, and care and provide for
them, because "children are an heritage of the Lord"[5] (Psalm 127:3; "The Family").
Third, Latter-day Saints believe that parent-child responsibilities are so sacred that
"husbands and wives—mothers and fathers—will be held accountable before God for
the discharge of these obligations" ("The Family"). Latter-day Saints teach these doctrines to their children and youth and emphasize the importance of putting marriage
and family above all earthly cares. The fervent desire of most LDS parents is for their
children to grow up and marry a worthy (i.e., covenant keeping) Latter-day Saint in a
temple and faithfully rear their children in the LDS religion.

An important factor in this effort is siblings. LDS fertility is well above the U.S.
average, and most LDS families have multiple children (Mosher, Williams, and Johnson 1992). Subsequently, LDS children are more likely to experience sibling influence
than their non-LDS peers. In many LDS families there is emphasis on all boys serving
a two-year mission and all children marrying in the temple. Although these are high
ideals, there are many LDS families where all or nearly all children achieve these ideals.
Conversely, if an older sibling fails to live the standards of the Church, this is often a
profound concern for parents who may worry not only about the struggling youth but
about the less-than-ideal example being placed before their younger children.

The central doctrines discussed in this section on spiritual beliefs involve potential
blessings and challenges for LDS youth. The doctrine of God as a literal Heavenly
Father seems to provide a secure sense of spiritual identity as a child of God for many
Latter-day Saint youth. On the other hand, the LDS doctrine of God the Father and

Jesus Christ as physically separate beings contradicts the Nicene Creed. As a result of this and other unique doctrines, many clergy and laypersons of other Christian faiths have viewed the Church of Jesus Christ of Latter-day Saints as "non-Christian," and for youth in some environments this has social consequences.

The LDS doctrine of the central importance of family and children can also be a two-edged sword. On one hand, promoting, strengthening, and supporting marital and parental bonds as eternal is a reported boon for many who fit the ideal (Dollahite 2003). Further, given the low LDS divorce rate and the great emphasis on family life, many LDS children and youth benefit from a secure home life and the stability that derives from family ritual (Family Home Evening, family prayer, and Scripture study) and family activities. However, children and youth from families whose structures do not meet the ideal are aware of this from a young age because of the Church's focus on the ideal of a father and mother who have been married for eternity in an LDS temple. Intrafaith LDS marriages are among the most stable in America (Lehrer and Chiswick 1993), and divorce is still rare enough to cause some stigma in the faith community, intended or otherwise.

A final challenge is that the LDS Church forcefully contradicts many elements of surrounding culture (Stark and Finke [2000] refer to it as a "high tension" faith). As a result, joining and/or remaining fully committed to the faith may be difficult from a social vantage. Being a child or youth in a church that has an uncompromising doctrinal framework can bring a sense of spiritual comfort and direction, but if a youth comes to doubt the truth claims of the faith, the perceived costs of time, energy, money, and personal freedom may be too high.

RELIGIOUS PRACTICES

Religious practices are outward, observable expressions of faith including prayer, Scripture study, rituals, and traditions that are religiously grounded (Dollahite, Marks, and Goodman 2004; Marks 2004). We focus on two levels of religious practice: personal (including morality and sexuality) and familial.

Personal Religious Practices

The personal practices of Scripture study and sincere prayer are viewed as keys in promoting spiritual development and personal connection with God, and this message is directed at LDS youth from an early age. A key objective of these religious practices is to increase spirituality and personal morality by strengthening one's relationship with God.

The thirteenth LDS Article of Faith addresses personal morality as follows: "We believe in being honest, true, chaste, benevolent, virtuous, and in doing good to all men. . . . If there is anything virtuous, lovely, or of good report or praiseworthy, we seek after these things."

This statement resonates with beliefs of other world faiths, and the Ten Commandments are salient to the LDS Church just as they are in other Christian faiths, as well as Judaism and Islam. However, two additional aspects of LDS morality deserve attention, particularly in connection with adolescence. These are the Law of Chastity and the Word of Wisdom.

The family proclamation summarizes the Law of Chastity by emphasizing that "God has commanded that the sacred powers of procreation are to be employed only between man and woman, lawfully wedded as man and wife." LDS youth are explicitly taught that engaging in sexual relations of any kind outside of traditional marriage is offensive to God and harmful to spiritual growth. Sexual activity outside of marriage is viewed with profound gravity by the LDS Church, partly because it may involve the spiritually unlawful creation of life (i.e., outside the bonds of marriage) (Holland 1998). The doctrinal and practical stance of the LDS Church regarding sexual morality is unusually strong, and one who violates the Law of Chastity by committing adultery may be excommunicated from the Church (although urged to repent and return to membership). Although an unmarried youth who engages in sexual activity will rarely be excommunicated, a period of limitations on church fellowship nearly always results.

Another aspect of LDS morality is a code of health referred to as the Word of Wisdom, which includes abstaining from alcohol, illegal drugs, tobacco, coffee, and tea (Doctrine and Covenants 89:1–21). Although breaking the Word of Wisdom is not grounds for excommunication, adherence *is* required for full participation in the Church and its ordinances, including temple ordinances.

At the outset of this chapter, we presented an LDS definition of spirituality that included the component of remembering and keeping covenants. Part of the ordinance of baptism involves a Latter-day Saint's making several covenants, including obedience to the Law of Chastity and the Word of Wisdom. Church doctrine, practices, and programs are designed to defend youth against temptations, particularly of sex and drugs. LDS youth are taught not to begin dating until at least age sixteen (and then only in groups) and to avoid R-rated movies and pornography in any form. LDS youth are, of course, not immune to sexual activity and drug abuse, but data indicate involvement levels significantly below U.S. norms (Top 1998). Predictably, LDS youth frequently find themselves in a social double bind because the behavior that qualifies them for full acceptance in one group restricts involvement in the other. Indeed, an "active" practice of the faith typically involves several choices between the LDS religion and popular culture.

An additional challenge for LDS youth who break their baptismal covenants—particularly the Law of Chastity—is that a period of depression and discouragement can result. For some of these youth, choosing peer acceptance over their faith marks the beginning of estrangement from the Church (family relationships often suffer as well, particularly in "active" families). Church leaders and parents are counseled to reach out in love and support for someone who is struggling with spiritual belief and practice, and efforts are often made to help the youth resolve their issues. However, even if repentance and "the road back" are chosen, this journey is often challenging, not only because of guilt or self-doubt but also because one must again face the decision of whether to reject (and at some level be rejected by) core elements of popular youth culture.

Family Religious Practices

Church leaders extol the virtue of prayer and Scripture study in family as well as personal settings, but perhaps the most family-oriented LDS practice is Family Home Evening and some research has addressed the importance of this practice in strengthening and maintaining family relationships (Marks 2004). Although the practice varies somewhat, Family Home Evening is ideally held each Monday night and involves sacred music, prayer, religious instruction and discussion, food, and wholesome recreational activities.

An organizational feature that impacts family religious practice is that all worthy male members of the LDS faith may hold the priesthood. Part of the father's priesthood responsibility is to see that family prayers and Family Home Evenings are being held. It is the priesthood holder's additional right, responsibility, and sacred privilege to administer ordinances, and this is especially true in the case of a father performing ordinances for his children. Specifically, an "active" LDS father may perform ordinances including, but not limited to, giving his newborn child a name and a blessing; blessing his children (or wife) in times of sickness, sadness, or challenge; baptizing his children after age eight; and ordaining his sons to the priesthood. These can be pinnacle moments of connection between family members (Dollahite 2003).

Owing to the familial nature of the priesthood in the LDS faith, nearly all priesthood ordinances are a reminder of the sacred role of fathers. These ordinances and father's blessings ideally facilitate the child's or youth's connection with God, with their father, and with the Holy Spirit (through whose inspiration blessings come). Conversely, for a child from a mother-only family, having ordinances performed by someone other than the father is a departure from the ideal. A concluding point we made in a recent review piece on religions and families may be particularly relevant to LDS congregations; namely, that a key challenge "will be to find a balance between supporting the standard of marriage-based families that are idealized in most American churches, while addressing the pluralistic family realities that confront them" (Dollahite, Marks, and Goodman 2004, 414).

In sum, sacred family practices, including family prayers, family Scripture study, Family Home Evening, and priesthood blessings given by a father to his wife and children, are ideally at the center of LDS religious experience because the home, not the Church, is to be the primary source of modeling and encouragement of spiritual development for children and youth. Research has supported the value of this emphasis on home. Top (1998) found that the most important factors predicting youth belief in and adherence to LDS values and standards were family-oriented variables rather than peer or Church influences. The Church is aware, however, that the ideals of personal and family practice are frequently unmet, and a variety of supplemental church-based efforts and programs are offered, as addressed next.

FAITH COMMUNITY

Having addressed spiritual beliefs and religious practices, we turn now to a third dimension of religious experience, faith community. Specifically, we will focus on the issues of (a) church-produced media, (b) programs for children and youth, and (c) church service callings.

Church-Produced Media

In many parts of the world, a majority of Latter-day Saints are converts (Stark and Finke 2000). As a global religion with a lay, unpaid ministry and a steady flow of converts, a key challenge for the LDS Church is the standardization of doctrine and practice. Media are a key tool in this standardizing effort, not only with adults, but also with children and youth. Global satellite broadcasts and training meetings take place several times a year. Additionally, an array of high-quality videos, books, magazines, pamphlets, and other materials are available at no (or minimal) cost from LDS Distribution Services, and the Church covers postage to encourage ordering and use. Key youth-directed media are given to youth and leaders of youth to serve as the foundation for Church youth programs. These programs are explained next.

Programs for Children and Youth

Children's Primary (similar to Sunday school in other faiths) is the first education-focused LDS program for children and serves children from ages three to eleven. The Primary program integrates the singing of hymns and the learning of doctrine with the objective of preparing children to make and keep baptismal covenants (i.e., obey the Ten Commandments, the Law of Chastity, and the Word of Wisdom).

Upon graduation from Primary, a twelve year-old girl or boy advances to the Young Women or Young Men organization. Following congregational worship on Sundays, the Young Women and Young Men combine for approximately forty minutes of adult-led Scripture study (Sunday School). Following this study, the youth separate into same-gendered classes (Young Women) or priesthood quorums (Young Men) with members in two-year age groups (e.g., ages twelve to thirteen, fourteen to fifteen, and sixteen to eighteen). The Young Women and Young Men also meet one night during each week for an alternating program of education, training, service, and recreation as outlined by the Young Woman of Excellence and Duty to God programs, respectively.[6] The mission of both programs, like that of the Primary, is to prepare the youth to make and keep sacred covenants. The distinction is that Primary prepares children to make and keep baptismal covenants, whereas the Young Women's and Young Men's programs prepare the youth to make and keep sacred priesthood and temple covenants that require additional commitment and spiritual maturity.

Twice a year each youth will have a private interview with his or her Bishop or one of his counselors in which the youth's personal and spiritual development will be discussed. Bishops serve as both "spiritual cheerleaders" who encourage increased faithfulness to gospel principles and as "spiritual physicians" to those who are struggling.

To assist the Young Women's and Young Men's programs in their efforts to prepare youth for the temple, a parallel program called the Church Educational System (CES) provides additional doctrinal and scriptural training. CES has two arms, the Seminary program (which serves high school-age youth) and the Institute program (which serves college-age young adults). Seminary classes for high school-age youth are typically held in the early mornings (before school) for fifty minutes, Monday through Friday during the school year. Consequently, a four-year Seminary graduate will have spent more than five hundred hours in focused study of the Old Testament (one year), the New Testament (one year), The Book of Mormon (one year), and LDS Church History and related texts including the Doctrine and Covenants (one year). As the youth are studying these sacred texts and preparing to make priesthood and temple covenants, they are simultaneously being trained to serve as scriptural and doctrinal teachers themselves. This is vital given that most active adult Latter-day Saints will teach church doctrine and Scripture because of the lay-operated nature of the Church, discussed later.

An additional purpose of Seminary relates to the LDS directive that every worthy (i.e., covenant keeping) and able young man ought to serve a two-year mission for the Church at age nineteen. Seminary provides a scriptural foundation and training for these prospective missionaries. Currently there are 50,000–60,000 full-time LDS missionaries serving in 165 countries, and approximately 90 percent of these are young adults ages nineteen to twenty-five. Not only are full-time missionaries volunteers, it is expected that a young man will provide (if not all) at least a portion of the approximately $10,000 needed to sustain him during his two-year service. Women who choose to serve as missionaries may do so at age twenty-one and are also expected to pay expenses during their eighteen-month missions. The degree of spiritual and emotional maturation that typically occurs during the eighteen to twenty-four months of missionary service is considerable, and, ideally, returned missionaries continue to serve the faith community in positions of responsibility following their missionary service.

In sum, a vital purpose of LDS programs for children and youth is to motivate members to make and keep sacred covenants with God. This is a shared mission of the Primary, Sunday School, Young Women, Young Men, Seminary, and Institute programs. By extension, the aim of the LDS Missionary Program is to invite those who are not LDS to make these covenants as well (and a by-product is substantial spiritual development and preparation of the youth who serve missions). A logical question that extends from this delineation of child- and youth-centered programs is, "How are these programs funded and staffed?"

Church Service Callings

Service "callings" are given to all actively involved LDS women and men and—like most responsibilities in the LDS Church—are assigned (not chosen) for a limited but not predetermined duration. Typically, however, one will serve in a particular calling between six months and five years. Callings are "extended" in personal face-to-face interviews with a priesthood leader. For women and men, personal worthiness (covenant keeping) is necessary for service in most capacities. The sociologist James T. Duke (1997) has estimated that the average LDS ward (congregation) receives between four hundred and six hundred hours of volunteer service per week from those serving in callings—a remarkable pool of human resources at no direct cost to the church. A significant portion of those hours is spent on children and youth programs, along with a significant portion of the congregation's annual financial budget.

Although adults (especially parents) play a critical role through callings to work with the youth, both female and male youth begin receiving formal assignments and callings of their own at age twelve. Callings for youth include serving as president or assisting the president of one's class (girls) or priesthood quorum (boys). Typical assignments also include monthly home visits to specific church members, participating in service projects for individuals or organizations in the community, cleaning church buildings with their families, working at church welfare facilities, and assisting with Primary children's (ages three to eleven) activities.

If they are keeping their baptismal covenants, LDS boys receive the Aaronic (or Lesser) Priesthood at age twelve and immediately begin to assist in priesthood duties, including bringing the Sacrament (Lord's Supper) to members of the congregation during Sabbath Sacrament meeting. As they advance in maturity and responsibility, their involvement in this ordinance subsequently involves preparing and blessing the Sacrament as well. Thus, young men are at the center of weekly worship and church service from a young age.

LDS young women (ages twelve to eighteen) are heavily involved in the Personal Progress program, which involves regular service projects (to local people and institutions), humanitarian aid projects (often making clothing and preparing aid kits for developing nations and disaster relief), preparing for future marriage and parenting by learning basic skills (cooking, sewing, budgeting, child tending, planning, etc.), developing personal talents (e.g., music, academics, art, sports), and serving in their families.

Like other youth actively involved in a faith community, LDS youth often develop close friendships with their church family of various ages and have both a built-in peer support group and a collection of caring adults who show interest in and supervise them, which helps them form their spiritual identity as Latter-day Saint youth. However, one pervasive challenge LDS youth face involves the time and energy demands of church programs. To review, in addition to three hours of Sabbath meetings, youth with church service callings often have additional Sabbath meetings to attend. The youth meet additionally for one or two hours one night a week and for those ages fourteen to eighteen there is also Seminary (typically Monday through Friday mornings from about six to seven o'clock). Furthermore, an explicit LDS doctrine is that one's talents and abilities are sacred gifts from God that should be actively developed. This doctrine can foster disproportionate involvement in music, athletics, and other extracurricular activities. LDS teachings that "the glory of God is intelligence" (Doctrine and Covenants 93:36) and that one should "obtain as much education as possible" also lead to a focus in academics (i.e., high grades, college-track courses). In short, the three (and often temporally conflicting) foci on (a) active involvement in the faith community, (b) development of talents (i.e., extracurricular activities and training), and (c) academic emphasis, create a dizzying schedule for many LDS youth.

A second pervasive challenge LDS youth face in connection with faith community is less direct but can carry significant influence. Because of the lay-operated nature of the Church and its reliance on service through church service callings, those parents who are most committed to the ideals of the faith are most likely to shoulder the heaviest part of the faith community's workload. For the many LDS parents whose church callings do not involve working directly with their own children, these callings can physically separate a parent from children for a number of additional hours a week (cf. Marks 2004). This is the dilemma that many LDS parents face: a family-centered faith that requires at least some separation from family in order to serve in the Church and "build the kingdom." In those families with heavy parental commitments to church service, youth may be forced to take a backseat to their parents' service, and resentment can occur. In recent years, world leaders of the Church have explicitly and repeatedly urged cutbacks in church demands that remove parents from the home. Improvements have been made, but many LDS youth are still overscheduled and so are their parents.

Notwithstanding these challenges, Latter-day Saints ranked highest in reported satisfaction of their faith in a study by Stark and Finke (2000). Apparently, the high temporal costs are offset by even higher perceived spiritual benefits.

Do the Ideals and Efforts to Promote Spiritual Development Make a Difference?

Recent studies indicate that while LDS "emerging adults" (those ages eighteen to twenty-five) share many values and behaviors with highly religious young adults of other faiths, they also have some unique attitudes and behaviors regarding marriage and family life. Nelson (2003) found that LDS emerging adults were significantly less likely than their non-LDS peers to engage in a variety of risky behaviors (e.g., drinking, smoking, drug use) and more likely to focus on and feel confident about marrying, having children, parenting, adequately providing, and running a household.

Another study found that like highly religious young adults of other faiths, LDS young adults report distinctive attitudes and behaviors from nonreligious young adults and that

> highly religious Latter-day Saints are less likely to engage in pre-marital sex, are more likely to support a traditional division of labor in marriage, are more likely to desire a large family, and perceive themselves as being more ready for marriage. (Carroll et al. 2000, 202)

LDS emerging adults also put this perception to the test and tend to marry and have their first child significantly earlier than the national average (Nelson 2003). Although young marriage and childbirth (i.e., early twenties) are generally red flags for divorce, this does not hold true in LDS-to-LDS marriages. However, interfaith marriages involving one Latter-day Saint are nearly three times more likely to end in divorce than LDS-to-LDS marriages (Lehrer and Chiswick 1993). It appears that the challenges and high demands of the LDS Church may be best met by married couples who share a commitment to the faith.

Data from a recent national landmark study of 3,370 teenagers from numerous faith communities showed that on a range of beliefs and activities, LDS youth were more likely to be committed to and involved in their faith than youth from other faiths. In that study, Smith (2005) reports numerous findings, including the following:

- Mormon teens are the most likely among all U.S. teens to hold religious beliefs similar to those of their parents (35).
- Conservative Protestant and Mormon parents are doing the best job retaining their youth with each group retaining 86 percent of their teens (36).
- Seventy-one percent of Mormon teens attend church at least weekly (38).
- Mormon teens are highest in the importance of their faith shaping daily life and major life decisions (40).

- Mormon and Black Conservative Protestants teens are the most likely to hold traditional, biblical religious beliefs (44).
- Mormon teens were highest in having a very moving or powerful spiritual experience and highest in reporting they had "ever experienced a definite answer to prayer or specific guidance from God" (45).
- Mormon teens were the most likely to report that they denied themselves something as a "spiritual discipline" (46).
- Mormon teens appear to pray the most often (47).
- Mormon teens reported being the most involved in religious youth groups and were the most likely to claim to be leaders in their youth groups (53). (This is likely due to the issue of youth leadership "callings" we discussed earlier.)
- Families of Mormon teens appear to talk about religious and spiritual matters the most (55).
- Mormon, Black Protestant, and Conservative Protestant teens are most likely to pray with their parents (55).
- Mormon teens (23 percent) are most likely to frequently express their faith at school (59).
- Mormon and Jewish youth reported noticeably higher levels of pressure and teasing from peers than did Christian teens (59).
- The number of nonparent adults who played a meaningful role in a teenager's life was noticeably higher for Mormons (61).
- In Mormon churches, ministry to youth is quite an important priority (65).
- A significantly higher proportion (65 percent) of Mormon teens rated their religious congregation as "a very good place" for "talking about serious issues, problems, and troubles" compared to more "lukewarm" ratings from teens of other faiths (66).
- Mormon youth were the highest percentage (83 percent) reporting that they anticipated attending the same type of faith community when they were twenty-five years old and the lowest percentage (2 percent) to say they anticipated attending "a different kind of congregation" (66).

These data arguably comprise the most comprehensive view of the religious lives of American teenagers to date. In an effort to make sense of these data, Dean (2005), a Methodist scholar of religion, proposed that Mormonism provides teens with "a consequential faith" characterized by (a) a substantive doctrine of God or "a creed to believe"; (b) a community of consequence or "a place to belong," which for Mormons is "family"; (c) a morally significant universe or "a call to live out"; and (d) being asked to contribute to God's ultimate transformation of the world or "a hope to hold on to."

Dean's (2005) insights are similar to our own, although our concepts were formed independently and although her model was constructed using Smith's large data set, which employed quantitative measures while our conclusions were based on qualitative focus groups, qualitative interviews with LDS families, and personal experience with and in-depth consideration of LDS doctrines, practices, and programs. In review, the central features of the LDS faith we identified were (a) stable, central doctrines on the nature of God and of the importance of family and children, (b) emphasis on both personal and familial religious practices, and (c) church programs for children and youth that involve church service callings. Like Smith (2005) and Dean (2005), our research suggests that LDS doctrines as applied in LDS homes and faith communities do in fact strongly influence the spiritual development of children and youth.

Concluding Remarks

In this chapter, we have discussed three dimensions of religious experience and how each relates to the Church of Jesus Christ of Latter-day Saints' efforts to nurture spirituality in its children and youth. Key related LDS spiritual beliefs include the beliefs that all persons are children of God; that marital and parent-child relationships can be eternal; that marriage and parenting are ordained by God; and that individuals will account to God for their treatment of spouse and children. Key sacred religious practices include prayer and Scripture study, Family Home Evening, and living a sexually chaste life and obeying the Word of Wisdom health code. Additionally, LDS fathers are to bless and serve their wives and children through their priesthood responsibilities and organize their families so that home is the center of religious worship while the faith community acts in a supportive role in children's spiritual development. Faith community efforts to train children and youth include global broadcasts, youth-centered publications, and other media that address doctrine and outline programs. Church-based programs seek to teach, implement, and apply LDS doctrines, while voluntary church service callings provide necessary leaders for the child- and youth-centered programs.

These spiritual beliefs, religious practices, and faith community resources share the common goal of nurturing communion with God and promoting charity (the pure love of Christ) in LDS children and youth. Ideally, a sense of communion with God and charity for others will promote a personal desire in children and youth to make and keep sacred covenants with their Heavenly Father—covenants that will bind them to their parents, their future spouse and children, and ultimately to God.

Notes

We appreciate helpful comments from Edward Kimball, Gloria Nye, Rachel Dollahite, Jen Yorgason, Bishop Paul N. Hyde, Ph.D., and Bishop James L. Marks on a previous draft. We also greatly appreciate the LDS youth who participated in the focus groups.

1. Data reported in *Ensign* 34 (9):76 (official church magazine).

2. Eight years is referred to as "the age of accountability" in LDS doctrine. This means that children have sufficient understanding and awareness to begin making sacred covenants. By implication, children are not fully accountable for their actions previous to this age.

3. For authoritative explanations of all LDS doctrine, practice, and programs we refer the reader to *The Encyclopedia of Mormonism* (Daniel Ludlow, editor), found at most major libraries or the LDS Church Web site: www.lds.org.

4. The LDS Standard Works include the Old and New Testaments of the Holy Bible (King James Version), The Book of Mormon: Another Testament of Jesus Christ, the Doctrine and Covenants, and The Pearl of Great Price.

5. Theological rationale for the importance of children is grounded in the LDS doctrine that

God's "work and glory is to bring to pass the immortality and eternal life of man" (Moses 1:39). Humankind may share in this work by having children and raising them in righteousness—so that if they are faithful they may receive eternal life.

6. In the United States, the LDS Church also offers scouting (Boy Scouts of America) as part of its standardized program for the Young Men.

References

Carroll, Jason S., Steven T. Linford, Thomas B. Holman, and Dean M. Busby. 2000. Marital and family orientations among highly religious young adults: Comparing Latter-day Saints with traditional Christians. *Review of Religious Research* 42:193–205.

Dean, Kenda C. 2005. Numb and Numb-er: Youth and the church of "benign whatever-ism." Paper presented at the International Association for the Study of Youth Ministry, London, England. January 3–7.

Dollahite, David C. 2003. Fathering for eternity: Generative spirituality in Latter-day Saint fathers of children with special needs. *Review of Religious Research* 44:237–51.

Dollahite, David C., Loren D. Marks, and Michael A. Goodman. 2004. Religiosity and families: Relational and spiritual linkages in a diverse and dynamic cultural context. In *The handbook of contemporary families: Considering the past, contemplating the future,* edited by Marilyn J. Coleman and Lawrence H. Ganong, 411–31. Thousand Oaks, Calif.: Sage.

Duke, James T. 1997. Church callings as an organizational device in the LDS Church. Paper read at the annual meeting of the Association for the Sociology of Religion, Toronto, Canada, August.

Jarvis, John. 2000. Mormonism in France. In *Family, religion, and social change in diverse societies,* edited by Sharon K. Houseknecht and Jerry G. Pankhurst, 237–66. New York: Oxford University Press.

Holland, Jeffrey R. 1998. Personal purity. *Ensign* (Nov.):75–78.

Lehrer, Evelyn L., and Carmel U. Chiswick. 1993. Religion as a determinant of marital stability. *Demography* 30:385–403.

Lindner, Eileen W., ed. 2004. *Yearbook of American and Canadian churches.* Nashville, Tenn.: Abingdon.

Marks, Loren D. 2004. Sacred practices in highly religious families: Christian, Jewish, Mormon, and Muslim perspectives. *Family Process* 43:217–31.

Mosher, William, Linda Williams, and David Johnson. 1992. Religion and fertility in the United States. *Demography* 29:199–214.

Nelson, Larry J. 2003. Rites of passage in emerging adulthood: Perspectives of young Mormons. In *New Directions for Child and Adolescent Development* 100:33–49.

Packer, Boyd K. 1995. The holy temple. *Ensign* (Feb.):32–36.

Smith, Christian, with Melinda L. Denton. 2005. *Soul searching: The religious and spiritual lives of American teenagers.* Oxford, UK: Oxford University Press.

Stark, Rodney. 1984. The rise of a new world faith. *Review of Religious Research* 26:18–27.

Stark, Rodney, and Roger Finke. 2000. *Acts of faith.* Berkeley and Los Angeles: University of California Press.

Top, Brent. 1998. *Rearing righteous youth in Zion.* Salt Lake City, Utah: Bookcraft.

PART VI

SOCIAL AND CULTURAL FORCES THAT SHAPE SPIRITUALITY

The relationships among spirituality, religion, and the broader context of society and the world are complex and interlocking. Indeed, one cannot fully understand the spirituality of children and adolescents unless one understands the religious traditions they embrace *as well as* the social, political, cultural, and natural forces that impinge upon and shape spirituality.

In this final section, authors offer perspectives on how religious traditions understand and critique social and cultural forces as they affect the spiritual lives of children and adolescents. The first three chapters look at identity formation within specific (and changing) cultural contexts. Each highlights the challenges of nurturing one's spiritual identity in cultures and contexts that do not reinforce—and sometimes undermine—that process. The last three chapters emphasize the issues and challenges of spiritual formation in the face of difficult economic and political forces that can threaten well-being and even life itself.

Rita M. Gross begins the section with an exploration of Buddhist perspectives on gender, sexuality, and spirituality. Gross anchors her discussion in the core Buddhist belief in karma, noting that one's inheritance, legacy, and identity are shaped not just by biology but also by deeds and relationships in past lives—one's inherited karma. She then describes multiple approaches to sexuality within Buddhism that reflect both monastic and lay experiences and expectations as well as Eastern and Western realities.

Marcia Hermansen and Shabana Mir focus their attention on the identity development issues of Muslim adolescents living in the United States. They identify the challenge of being a religious minority that is currently stigmatized and viewed with suspicion. The authors highlight the range of ways in which high school and college students have sought to develop a Muslim identity through "identity Islam," traditionalism, and Islamic liberalism. They point toward a growing openness to multiple expressions of Muslim identity within American culture in ways that allow young people to flourish at both social and spiritual levels.

Whereas Hermansen and Mir explore how Muslims are seeking to integrate into U.S. culture, Ellen T. Charry suggests that contemporary society—grounded in postmodern philosophy and a business/technology culture—is "malforming" for Protestant Christian adolescents because it undermines "features of a more traditional culture that contribute to forming spiritually healthy persons." She highlights Christian doctrines (creation and redemption) and practices (baptism and foot washing) that she believes may be particularly valuable antidotes for shaping young people's worldviews and theological identity.

Débora Barbosa Agra Junker shifts the focus toward geopolitical forces that affect young people's spiritual lives. She applies her Protestant Christian theological heritage and its concern for justice for the most vulnerable to the economic and social inequities present in Brazil. She calls for religious leaders to become more sophisticated in understanding macro-economic systems of injustice and to support children and adolescents in developing a "spirituality of resistance," which recognizes young people's spirituality as providing support and inner resilience in times of despair.

Building on the theme of economic justice, Joyce Ann Mercer critiques global economic forces and materialism and their impact on young people's spiritual lives. Also writing from a Protestant Christian perspective, she uses three case studies from the Philippines and the United States to show how young people from dramatically different social positions all participate in an economic system of global capitalism that shapes their spiritual lives. She critiques current economic realities, in particular challenging "systemic political and economic practices that allow so many children to live on the edge of survival."

Finally, Arik Ascherman writes from the front lines of the Palestinian-Israeli conflict about the impact of a culture of violence, hatred, and distrust on the spiritual lives and worldviews of children. He draws on the biblical story of the near-sacrifice of Isaac and related midrashic narratives, which, among other things, articulate the ways in which children pay the price for the actions of others. He describes the spiritual crisis that is born of years of conflict that leads to despair, suggesting that a restoration of hope—a spiritual concept—lies at the core of nurturing new generations who will break through stereotypes and work for peace.

These chapters only begin to illustrate a much broader range of topics and perspectives that could be examined regarding the intersections of spirituality, social and cultural forces, and childhood and adolescence. One could add, for example, chapters on the environment and ecology, political and economic philosophy, racial and ethnic identity and relations, media, interfaith relations, educational systems, and health and health care (which is addressed, in part, in Nicholas Otieno's discussion of HIV/AIDS in Africa in Chapter 10), to name a few. However, the selection offered here begins the conversation and underscores the complexity of addressing these issues.

At some level, it would be easier—safer—to avoid these kinds of difficult and controversial subjects, focusing only on the individual practices of young people, their families, and the immediate community where they live. Doing so, however, would impoverish our understanding, squandering the wisdom that faith traditions can bring to the pressing concerns, trends, and realities of our time that either thwart or enrich young people's spiritual journeys.

CHAPTER 32

Scarce Discourse: Exploring Gender, Sexuality, and Spirituality in Buddhism

Rita M. Gross

To speak of Buddhist perspectives on gender, sexuality, and spirituality as they pertain to children and adolescents is rather difficult. For the most part, Buddhist teachings do not say much specifically about children and adolescents, though, of course, Buddhist cultures have developed many practices for introducing their children to issues of gender, sexuality, and spirituality. This lack of doctrinal focus on children and adolescents probably has something to do with the fact that most forms of Buddhism value monastic life very highly. As a result, Buddhism has never focused on family life or reproduction as central concerns, at least doctrinally. Buddhism is perhaps the only religion in which there is no religious duty to reproduce. Nor does it idealize children as model religious believers, though some oral traditions of Tibetan Vajrayana Buddhism do emphasize that very young children do not yet have the dualistic perceptions that advanced practices try to undo. Nevertheless, Buddhist teachings never suggest that all would be well if we could only avoid the complexities of adult consciousness; growing up is the prerequisite for becoming enlightened.

In India, where Buddhism originated, these unusual features were not so noteworthy. Buddhism shared these values with other Indian religions of the Buddha's day, and religious systems that value some form of monasticism over family life have always had a place in Indian culture. But in other cultures in which Buddhism has been practiced, these values were not so familiar. In East Asia, where the indigenous cultures uniformly regarded reproduction as a central religious duty, these Buddhist values were very controversial. The willingness of Buddhists to forgo family life and reproduction in favor of monasticism was labeled "unfilial," the most unflattering term to be found in that cultural context. It meant disloyalty to everything decent and valuable; it was the same as not repaying one's debts or condemning one's family to the extreme distress involved in not being remembered and not receiving the respect paid to ancestors.

As Buddhism has traveled again, this time to Western Europe and North America, a similar unfamiliarity with the classic Buddhist renunciation of family and reproduction has led to different frustrations. Most Western Buddhists are laypeople with jobs and families, rather than monastics, and yet they try to approximate the rigorous schedule of study and practice characteristic of monastics. Such a lifestyle can lead to great frustration about time constraints. Such laypeople have often complained that they receive little guidance and support for family life from Buddhist institutions and teachings.

The scarcity of Buddhist discourse on children and adolescents available to us is in part due to the biases of the elite Buddhisms better known to Western scholars and preferred by Western converts to Buddhism. Buddhist cultures include more than the monastic lifestyles, of course. But these practices and beliefs are usually not recorded in the canonical literature or even in historical sources, and they are not part of the repertoire of teachings and practices brought by Asian meditation masters to the West. Buddhist teachings and practices are especially oriented to mature adults concerned with preparing for death and rebirth. As a result, lay Buddhists in many cultures rely more on other religious traditions to deal with fertility, birth, marriage, and family life. This is clearly demonstrated by widespread Japanese practices that have led observers to suggest that the question for Japanese people is not "Shinto" or "Buddhism." Rather, Japanese practice is to be "born Shinto and die Buddhist" (Reader 1991).

I will address how gender, sexuality, and spirituality pertain to children and adolescents as a scholar-practitioner. By this I mean that I rely equally on my training and values as a scholar of religious studies and on my training and values as a Buddhist practitioner. Both as a scholar and as a practitioner, I have focused on South Asian and Indo-Tibetan traditions. My practice is within the Shambhala and Mindrolling lineages of Tibetan Vajrayana Buddhism and I also teach within both lineages. Tibetan Vajrayana Buddhism is among the most complex forms of Buddhism, and also among the most secretive, which is why it is hard to study accurately as an outsider only. It is also important to note that although I value scholarship highly, my many years of experience as a practitioner and an insider to the world of Vajrayana Buddhism, as taught by Tibetans and practiced by Westerners, have led me to question many of the impressions about Buddhism common among Western scholars who do not practice Buddhism. While I strive to be ecumenical and nonsectarian in my discussions of Buddhism, it is important to acknowledge these various standpoints.

The Parent-Child Relationship in Doctrinal and Popular Buddhisms

Because belief in karma (cause and effect based on moral intentions and behaviors and extending over many lifetimes) is so basic to most forms of Buddhism, a child is assumed to enter the world with a long history and many predispositions that may be unrelated to its family and culture of birth. Buddhists believe strongly in inheritance, but a child inherits more than its parents' biological genes. These karmic "genes," inherited from its past intentions and actions, are thought to be just as real as biological genes. Thus, conflicts can arise between a child's karma and its parents' and culture's plan for its life. Children are not their parents' possessions in Buddhist thought, though, of course, Buddhist parents have and do try to mold their children's lives and preferences.

Throughout countless lifetimes, a being accrues karma in accord with its actions—positive deeds leading to positive rebirths eventually, and negative deeds leading to negative rebirths. Rebirth is not limited to the human realm, nor even to this planet. The Buddhist cosmos is vast and includes many world systems not visible to telescopes. Furthermore, according to traditional beliefs, rebirth will recur unceasingly until a being understands and realizes its true nature and the nature of reality. Even though many Western Buddhists who have received a great deal of Buddhist training often are not convinced that rebirth occurs (McLeod 2002), it is almost impossible to understand traditional and contemporary Asian Buddhism without some accurate understanding of karma and rebirth.

Asian and Western Buddhist parents agree, however, that their (or any) child is especially fortunate because it has attained a human rebirth. Human rebirth brings opportunities that are almost nonexistent in other kinds of rebirth, and human rebirth is extremely rare. Just think of the billions of insects, for example! Because of this preciousness, parents and societies have responsibilities to provide well for their children, materially, socially, and spiritually.

But, unlike parents in many other Asian religions, Buddhist parents do not fundamentally depend on their children for their future spiritual well-being. In doctrinal terms, parents' future rebirths depend much more on their own karma, and much less on the continued ancestral practices of their descendants. Part of that karma, of course, would include how well they rear their children. One of the reasons why Buddhism has never considered reproduction to be a religious duty probably has to do with the importance of inherited karma, both for parents and for children. In terms of their own karma, parents would do better to raise a few children well rather than to have many impoverished, malnourished, and undereducated children. But, since their own spiritual futures don't depend on having offspring who will remember them, it isn't necessary to have any children at all. In fact, a common prejudice of monastic Buddhism claims that the only way one can really benefit the world is to practice intensely and become enlightened, so that one will actually know how to help others. Thus, if one cannot fit both reproduction and spiritual practice into a single lifetime (and, except for Western converts, most Buddhists have assumed that one cannot), it is far more beneficial to humanity to become spiritually wise than to have children, if one has the good fortune, karmically, to devote one's life to spiritual discipline.

However, if people do choose to have children, Buddhist folklore usually assumes that parents and children have been related to each other in previous lives, which is why they are again attracted to each other. (However, both parents and children also inherit karma from previous relationships, which helps explain why they may disagree on so many things, and sometimes not even like each other.) In Tibetan Buddhism, it is often said that all beings have been our mothers in previous lives, which is one reason why we should be kind to all beings and try not to harm them. This popular teaching also demonstrates how complicated and interconnected our relationships are. A current parent-child bond exists for this lifetime, but not forever. This view contrasts strongly with East Asian perspectives widespread in China and Japan, which state that, literally, one no longer exists if there are no descendants who remember you. If this were the case, the parent-child bond would last forever and it would be necessary to reproduce physically. Buddhisms have made some concessions to these popular beliefs, and there are Buddhist practices in which Buddhist children do try to look after their parents spiritually after they are dead. Almost all forms of Buddhism also teach that a good practitioner will share his or her karmically positive merit with all beings, including her or his parents. (These beliefs are not necessarily completely logically consistent; beliefs about the relationships between the living and dead seldom are in any religion, especially at a more popular level.)

The World a Child Inherits

The human rebirth a child inherits because of previous karma is fortunate because a human body and mind are thought to be much more conducive to spiritual practice and eventual enlightenment than any other rebirth, including that of divine beings in pleasure-filled realms. One of the most important Tibetan Buddhist contemplative meditations, called the Four Reminders, or the Four Thoughts that turn the mind to dharma (spiritual practice), begins by contemplating the good fortune of having a human body. One version of the first reminder from the oral tradition states: "Precious human body, free and well-favored, difficult to obtain and easy to lose." To understand the preciousness of this opportunity is considered an important spiritual attainment, as well as encouragement to practice spiritual discipline. It should also result in gratitude to one's parents for providing that human body, though, as already indicated, the best way to repay one's debts is to become a good and wise person who helps others, rather than to give one's parents grandchildren. (Because of their belief that the proper karmic endowments are necessary for this life of spiritual discipline, Buddhists have never worried that everyone would stop reproducing and there would be no more human bodies coming into the world.)

The human condition is thought to be fortunate for two reasons. First, humans experience a mixture of pleasure and pain that is conducive to spiritual discipline. If beings experience too much pleasure, they have no motivation to practice spiritual disciplines; if they experience unremitting pain, they cannot image anything else. The human condition is also fortunate because humans, unlike beings in other realms, have discriminating awareness, which means that they are not completely driven by habitual patterns, but can differentiate between things and make choices.

Gendered Paths for Girls and Boys in Institutional Buddhism

Buddhist teachings state that gender is fundamentally irrelevant to spiritual attainment, but Buddhist cultures and Buddhist institutions, especially the all-important monastic institutions, have seldom honored these gender-free and gender-neutral teachings (Gross 1993). For a human rebirth to be "free and well favored," certain conditions must be met; otherwise, a human rebirth leads to little benefit. Included among these conditions are things such as being reborn in a time and place in which the Buddhadharma is available and having the material and intellectual circumstances to be able to practice dharma. Ominously, however, all traditional forms of Buddhism declare that a "free and well-favored birth" is a male rebirth (Kongtrul 1977, 41), despite the fact that such distinctions contradict more basic Buddhist teachings. As has been the case for most human cultures, gender roles are rigid and inflexible in Buddhist cultures.

Why have Buddhists traditionally sought a male rebirth? Usually, Buddhists think that the problems with female rebirth are social and cultural, not metaphysical. That is to say, women are not flawed in nature; there is no essential female nature that differs from the male nature. But Buddhists looked at the male dominance prevalent in their cultures and quickly realized that boys and men have many more advantages and freedoms than women and girls. The usual solution to this problem, difficult as it may be for most contemporary Western Buddhists to appreciate, is to somehow make it possible for women to be reborn as men, rather than to change the cultural norms that make life so difficult for girls and women. Western Buddhists usually do not recognize that Buddhist practices that assure a male rebirth to girls and women are probably the result of compassion, not prejudice (Gross 2003).

Buddhist cultures value celibate monasticism highly, usually more highly than reproduction and family life. But, giving in to patriarchal cultural practices, Buddhists usually revere monks much more than nuns, and support them much better, even today in many parts of the Buddhist world. Because the world of deep spiritual practice was almost completely limited to monastics, girls are not expected or encouraged to be interested in spiritual practice. Nor, in the past, were they educated. Instead, early marriage and motherhood, often in their teens, were their destinies. Becoming a nun was often thought of as a failure and brought little prestige to the girl's family. A girl's limited access to the spiritual practices so highly valued by Buddhists is the greatest liability of female rebirth, according to traditional Buddhist cultures, although subservience to male authority throughout her entire life and physical aspects of being female, such as menstruation and childbirth, are also frequently mentioned as liabilities of female rebirth (Gross 1993).

By contrast, boys are often placed in monasteries, especially in Tibetan and Southeast Asian forms of Buddhism, both to receive an education and to learn spiritual disciplines. Families are eager for their sons to become monks, at least for a period of time. A son's ordination as a monk, whether temporary or permanent, brings both temporal prestige and spiritual benefit to his parents. Although, as already discussed, an individual's sum total of meritorious and unmeritorious actions is the primary determinant of future rebirths, most forms of Buddhism also allow for a transfer of merit, in which the person doing a positive deed dedicates the merit accruing from that deed to all sentient beings, or to specific individuals. Particularly in East Asia, where descendants owe their ancestors help in the afterlife, Buddhist monks often claimed to be benefiting their parents, especially their mothers, by their practice. In Thailand, to the present day, almost all boys spend at least some time in a monastery. Their monastic ordination serves as their transition out of boyhood. For girls, the parallel ceremony involves having their ears pierced. For boys, the period of forced celibacy is said to make them ripe for marriage when they leave the monastery. In addition, their stay in the monastery earns merit for deceased relatives, often grandparents.

In the world of Tibetan Buddhism, some boys are recognized very early in their lives as having a special rebirth and heavy duties along with that rebirth. These are the *tulkus*, of whom the Dalai Lama is the best known, though there are literally thousands of such tulkus in traditional Tibetan understandings. These boys receive extraordinary educations from childhood, and also have extraordinary privilege and power. It is very difficult for someone not recognized as a tulku in childhood ever to achieve such levels of prestige, power, and spiritual authority. Because there are very few lineages of female tulkus among the thousands of male tulkus, institutional male dominance is reinforced in still another way in Tibetan Buddhism, as is the view that male rebirth is necessary for high spiritual attainments.

Nevertheless, a popular Tibetan literary genre, the spiritual biographies of great teachers, records other stories that express dissatisfaction with the presumed male dominance and presents examples of women who have achieved high levels of attainment and respect. One of these stories poignantly discusses the plight of a girl who wants to study dharma rather than follow the female gender role and marry. Her mother taunts her, saying, "My dear, girls cannot practice the Dharma. It would be far better for you to marry now that you have many suitors." Her reply captures the frustration of generations of girls in cultures with fixed and limited gender roles: "I will prove to her that girls can practice the Dharma." Fortunately for this particular girl, her father, who is a Dharma teacher himself, recognizes her spiritual potential, supports her vision, and teaches her. Eventually, she becomes a lineage holder herself (Allione 1984, 224–26).

Another well-known story presents one of the liabilities for girls who give in to their parents' pressure to marry early, despite their wish to lead a life of practice and study. Nangsa Obum did marry and became a seemingly ideal housewife and mother, despite the cruelty of her sister-in-law. But she still secretly longed to renounce the world to practice dharma. As she nursed her son, thinking of her longings, she began to weep and broke into a spontaneous song:

"My son, children are like a rope that pulls a woman into samsara.
Lhau Darpo, you make it impossible to leave,
And I cannot take you with me as that would create obstacles in my practice.
I wanted to practice the Dharma, but I got married instead." (Allione 1984, 76–77)

A modern feminist would, of course, criticize a system that makes it impossible for girls or women, but not men, to combine family life with serious dharma practice, but such criticisms did not seem reasonable to most traditional societies, including that of Tibet.

Tibet's most famous female practitioner, Yeshe Tsogyel, is often regarded as cofounder of Tibetan Buddhism, along with her teacher and consort, Padmasambhava. She lived an extraordinary life, but when she was a girl, her desire to practice dharma was also resisted to an extreme degree, despite the fact that her parents had received various signs indicating that she was not an ordinary child while her mother was pregnant and when she was an infant. As a teenager, many men competed to marry her, and, fearing that rival kings would wage war over her, her parents put her out of the house, decreeing that whoever caught her first could take her as his wife. Tsogyel resisted her captor and would not go with him. She was beaten until her back was a "bloody pulp," whereupon she finally acquiesced. Later that night, after her captor and his companions had passed out from drinking, she escaped and managed to live in hiding for some time. But eventually the rival who had lost the race to capture her found out where she was living and went to get her. Again war was threatened, and her father pleaded with the emperor to take her as his wife to settle the dispute. By that means, she arrived at the court, where Padmasambhava was teaching. Recognizing her potential, he demanded that the emperor include her as part of the offerings he made in exchange for teachings. Thus, by being traded by men, Tsogyel at last found her teacher and was released from the bonds of ordinary marriage and the conventional female gender role (Dowman 1984, 15–24). One of the implications of this story is that conventional marriage and the prescribed female gender role, not relationships with men, are the problem for serious women practitioners. Yeshe Tsogyel is always portrayed as having a long and successful relationship with Padmasambhava, but they never had a conventional husband-and-wife relationship. That is also the implication of the story of another famous female practitioner and teacher, Machig Lapdron (Allione 1984, 150–87).

Becoming Buddhist in Lay Buddhist Practice

For more ordinary children, introduction to Buddhist spirituality is more an immersion process, at least in traditional Buddhist societies. Some children are immersed in a monastic environment. Novices can be ordained by the age of eight, and monasteries often function as orphanages in Buddhist societies. Abandoned children or poor children often wound up in them, where they were cared for, fed, housed, and educated. This practice is less common for girls, especially in Buddhist cultures that have lost the nuns' ordination lineage or in which nuns have very low prestige. But the Tibetan nunnery in Indian exile with which I am most familiar has its cadre of "little nuns," as they are called, and the infant girl once left at their gate was taken in and cared for. These girls' shaved heads and robes are identical with those of the adults who have made the decision to spend their lives as Buddhist nuns. Right now, while they are girls, their primary concern is to become educated.

Other children are immersed in a Buddhist environment in the same way that children are immersed into their cultures in most traditional settings. Pious Buddhist parents engage in simple daily practices in their homes or in local shrines and monasteries. In traditional settings, children would learn basic Buddhist perspectives from their parents long before they received any formal education. Furthermore, whether they want to go or not, they are taken by their parents to the various gatherings that punctuate daily life in Buddhist communities. Because the monastics and the laity live in a deeply symbiotic relationship with each other and have frequent contact, despite their very different lifestyles, children have ample opportunity to absorb the ethos and values of traditional Buddhist cultures. For these children, there would be less differentiation between boys and girls than in a monastic environment and more acceptance of societal gender roles than exceptional girls exhibit.

Western Buddhist parents and children, living as a distinct minority in a largely Christian culture, face entirely different problems. How does one raise a Buddhist child in an environment in which Buddhism is not "normal," an environment in which children often want to assimilate to the dominant culture? Contemporary Asian Buddhist parents face some of the same dilemmas from the competition of modern, materialistic values, but at least there is much less of a competing spiritual pull. And for Buddhist parents and children in Western societies, immigrant and convert Buddhist communities face different problems. So-called immigrant Buddhist communities may have lived in North America for four or five generations already, but there is little contact between Asian American Buddhists and Euro-American convert communities (Seager 1999).

The Asian American communities frequently have more traditional Buddhist institutions and ongoing connections with Buddhists from their homelands, which means that children are familiar with Buddhist traditions. Often, youth are retained more through sports, music, and cultural activities at community centers than through specifically Buddhist practices, but these youth are developing a Buddhist identity in the process and interacting with other Buddhist children (Seager 1999).

By contrast, Euro-American converts were usually childless adults when they became Buddhists and had little familiarity with more traditional Buddhist cultural practices, including wisdom on how to bring up Buddhist children. These converts struggled to develop practice centers that were more child friendly and more readily included parents of young children. They had no experience and few ideas about how to educate children as Buddhists. In larger communities, some parents began Buddhist or Buddhist-oriented day schools to cope with their situation, but this option was not possible for most parents and children. In spite of this haphazard introduction to Buddhism, many second-generation Euro-American Buddhists are now old enough to make their own choices about Buddhism. Some of them have no interest in following their parents' ways, but many teenagers take on the intensive programs in Buddhist meditation that have been developed at most Euro-American Buddhist centers. It is also obvious that most American Buddhist children and teenagers are far less bound by conventional gender roles than their Asian counterparts, past or present.

Buddhist Perspectives on Sexuality

As with most other aspects of Buddhist life, attitudes toward sexuality differ markedly for monastics and for laypeople. For monastics, sexual activity is absolutely forbidden, whereas for laypeople, there are few specific rules beyond the basic precept to avoid sexual misconduct, which is defined differently in different cultural contexts.

Buddhist requirements for monastic celibacy are often misunderstood by outsiders, especially in Western societies that have been strongly affected by the discomfort with sexuality displayed by some forms of Christianity. Although many Buddhist texts seem to express a great deal of disgust for the body and an aversion to sexuality, especially women's sexuality, it is the *results* of sexuality, not sexuality itself, that are thought to be so dangerous for monastics. If Buddhists thought sex itself was a problem, their attitudes toward laypeople's sexuality would not be so casual and accepting.

Sexual activity usually results in two things that are anathema for the monastic lifestyle: attachment and offspring. Buddhist analyses always see attachment or clinging as one of the pervasive causes of human suffering, to be replaced by detachment and equanimity in the well-trained meditator who is at peace with herself and the world. But it was thought in the ancient Indian culture that produced Buddhism that if one were sexually active, it was virtually impossible to be detached from the pleasure brought by sex and a longing for more such pleasure. Furthermore, sexual activity usually results in children, which are not compatible with a monastic lifestyle on many counts. Children usually also engender attachment, but probably even more problematic are the responsibility and distraction brought about by the need to provide economically for one's spouse and children. Many Buddhist texts praise the freedom of the monastic lifestyle and contrast it with the confinement and narrowness of the householder lifestyle. Most of the Buddhist world concurred with this analysis until recently. The usual norm among Western Buddhists, that one can or should combine the householder and monastic lifestyles by having a job and a family, but also a serious and time-consuming Buddhist practice, is a recent innovation, and it is unclear how well this lifestyle will work in the long run.

Preteen and teenage monastics live in a markedly single sex world and would only rarely see members of the other sex. One wonders how such an experience shapes emerging sexual feelings during these years, when sexual urges and curiosity are at their height. This is not the kind of information easily shared with outsiders, and the canonical texts do not discuss such matters. They only discuss what constitutes sexual contact, and the definition is very strict. For young monastics, any sexual experimentation would have to be homoerotic or homosexual in nature, and both are forbidden in the monastic codes of discipline. Homosexual contact is further forbidden in some Buddhist conventions about sexuality, not directly, but because intercourse in the "wrong" orifice is forbidden, whatever the sexual orientation may be (Gampopa 1971, 76). Nevertheless, according to the noted scholar Faure, male homosexuality was quite common in Japanese monasteries (Faure 1998), as were younger partners. In any case, for monastics, homosexuality or heterosexuality is not the relevant issue; any sexual contact or experience should be off limits.

This strict sexual discipline imposed on young monks may help explain many of the very negative texts about women found in Buddhist scriptures. Although women usually experience these texts as very hurtful when they first read them, I do not think the intended audience is female Buddhists at all. They are written by monks for monks, written to reinforce a code of sexual restraint that must be very difficult for many young monks who may not even have chosen the monastic lifestyle but were placed in monasteries by their parents at an early age. Nevertheless, the fallout from these negative comments about women, intending to discourage men's sexual desire, is considerable. Imagine how this education would affect the attitudes toward women of men who later left the monasteries. Given that monks who were educated in this fashion are the cultural elite, imagine the impact of such youthful indoctrination on cultural attitudes toward women in general.

For laypeople, sexual regulations are much more relaxed and follow the general norms of the culture and the time. For laypeople, a precept to avoid sexual misconduct is their only guiding principle, in contrast to monks and nuns, who are bound by scores of rules concerning sexual behavior. Buddhist attitudes toward sexuality itself are not especially negative or distrustful; in fact, sexual metaphors are commonplace, especially in Vajrayana Buddhism. Sexual pleasure is a legitimate pursuit for laypeople, so long as sexual misconduct is avoided. Sexual misconduct is most often defined as conduct that is perceived as harmful to oneself or another. Definitions of sexual harm can differ widely from culture to culture and these cultural definitions were far more important to most Buddhist laypeople than any specifically Buddhist rules. This helps explain why North American gay and lesbian Buddhists are usually well accepted despite traditional Buddhist disapproval of homosexuality. This acceptance probably has something to do with the fact that the segment of North American culture from which most Buddhists come is liberal in its attitudes toward sexuality.

Because of the flexibility of Buddhist sexual norms for laypeople, Buddhists have lived with all forms of marriage—monogamy, serial monogamy, polygyny, and even polyandry (multiple husbands), which is practiced in Tibet to retain family property in the male line. Multiple wives among the upper classes are quite commonly recorded in Buddhist historical narratives. Remarriage of divorced or widowed women is generally not a problem for Buddhists. Also following cultural norms, for most Buddhist cultures throughout history, men were allowed to visit courtesans or prostitutes without being guilty of sexual misconduct (Robinson, Johnson, and Thanissaro 2004, 57). In fact, prostitutes are important characters in many classic Buddhist narratives. Then, as now, many of them must have been teenage girls, but in classic Buddhist texts, they are usually not represented as living in degraded circumstances or as being social outcasts (Young 2004, 105–32). This contrasts with the current situation, in which socially aware Buddhists are embarrassed and troubled by the fact that a large portion of the world's sexually trafficked girls are Nepali or Thai, nominally Buddhist girls.

Most of the cultures in which Buddhism has been practiced are male dominant and regulate women's sexuality much more closely than men's. Most of them also practiced early marriage, so most girls were probably married during their teenage years and had little or no opportunity for sexual experimentation before marriage. As already narrated, many girls would become mothers in their teenage years. In male-dominant cultures, boys are usually given much more sexual latitude than girls, and there is no reason to suppose that Buddhist boys were discouraged from sexual experimentation. In fact, in many Buddhist biographical narratives, elite boys who are not in monasteries are represented as having great sexual license, with the historical Buddha himself being a paramount example. Many boys would also be married by their late teens, although marriage did not restrict them in the same way that it restricted girls.

An interesting, little known, and controversial variant of teenage sexuality is the tantric consort. Vajrayana Buddhism, as is well known but not well understand, values sexual imagery and metaphors as expressions of its deepest spiritual insights. In these artistic representations, sexuality is not hidden or obscured, though it is of a completely different character from most explicit Western portrayals of sex, which are often pornographic. In some cases, Vajrayana Buddhism also allows physical sexuality as a religious discipline, though there is almost no accurate information about these practices in Western language literature. Both men and women could take or be tantric consorts, though there is much more discussion of the male practitioner having a female tantric consort. Whether the sexuality is metaphorical or physical, it is never to be understood conventionally; it is not about titillation, personal sexual satisfaction, attachment, set-tling down, or raising a family. Interestingly, the ideal age for a tantric consort, whether male or female, whether imagined or actual, is sixteen. Their physical beauty and robust sexuality are often described enthusiastically.

As is the general Buddhist practice, there are no especially Buddhist norms for Western Buddhist teenagers. Because they usually grow up in liberal households, they are taught what liberal parents usually teach their children about sexuality. They are taught to respect themselves rather than harming themselves with indiscriminate sexu-ality, and they are taught that if they are sexually active, they should use birth control. In keeping with liberal Western practice, there is usually no double standard between boys and girls, and gay or lesbian teenagers would usually be supported by their fami-lies and communities. Regarding abortion, however, Buddhist teenagers might not experience the usual liberal norm and be encouraged to have an abortion. Buddhism in general regards abortion as a grave offense because every specific rebirth begins at con-ception. This has always been the Buddhist understanding; it is not the result of mod-ern scientific understandings of the process of conception. However, even more traditional Buddhist teachers who are also familiar with Western cultures sometimes say that the more important precept is to avoid harming, and sometimes abortion may be the least harmful alternative (Traleg 2001, 21–22).

Buddhism has never been a child-centered or a child-oriented religion. It does not have teachings specifically for or about children. It is perhaps the only religion not to require or recommend reproduction as a religious duty or to make reproduction almost inevitable for sexually active people. Although celibacy has been a cherished, valued norm for large segments of the population, Buddhists have never had any trouble sep-arating sexuality from reproduction for people for whom sexuality is appropriate. Chil-dren are almost never represented as ideal religious believers. The discernment and mental discipline so valued by Buddhists are not really available to children, though teenagers begin to receive training in philosophy and meditation. For all these reasons, it is difficult to isolate Buddhist beliefs and practices specifically related to children and adolescents, beyond narrating cultural practices in which Buddhists may participate. But it is not difficult to delineate Buddhist attitudes toward gender, sexuality, and spir-ituality in general, and these same attitudes pertain to children and adolescents, insofar as they are relevant.

References

Allione, Tsultrim. 1984. *Women of wisdom*. London: Routledge and Kegan Paul.
Dowman, Keith, trans. 1984. *Sky dancer: The secret life and songs of the lady Yeshe Tsogyel*. Lon-don: Routledge and Kegan Paul.
Faure, Bernard. 1988. *The red thread: Buddhist approaches to sexuality*. Princeton, N.J.: Princeton University Press.
Gampopa. 1971. *The jewel ornament of liberation*. Translated by Herbert V. Guenther. Berkeley, Calif.: Shambhala.
Gross, Rita M. 1993. *Buddhism after patriarchy: A feminist history, analysis, and reconstruction of Buddhism*. Albany: State University of New York Press.

————. 2003. Buddhism. In *Her voice, her faith: Women speak on world religions*, ed. Arvind Sharma and Katherine K. Young, 59–98. Boulder, Colo.: Westview.

Kyabgon, Traleg. 2001. *The essence of Buddhism: An introduction to its philosophy and practice.* Boston: Shambhala.

Kongtrul, Jamgon. 1977. *The torch of certainty.* Translated by Judith Hanson. Boulder: Shambhala.

McLeod, Ken. 2001. *Wake up to your life: Discovering the Buddhist path of attention.* San Francisco: Harper and Row.

Reader, Ian. 1991. *Religion in contemporary Japan.* Honolulu: University of Hawaii Press.

Robinson, Richard H., Willard Johnson, and Thanissaro Bhikkhu. 2004. *Buddhist religions.* 5th ed. Belmont, Calif.: Wadsworth.

Seager, Richard Hughes. 1999. *Buddhism in America.* New York: Columbia University Press.

Young, Serinity. 2004. *Courtesans and tantric consorts: Sexualities in Buddhist narrative, iconography, and ritual.* New York: Routledge.

CHAPTER 33

Identity Jihads: The Multiple Strivings of American Muslim Youth

Marcia Hermansen and Shabana Mir

This chapter considers some of the spiritual and identity choices faced by American Muslim youth. In the Islamic tradition, the tension between inner development and outward assertiveness is encapsulated in the Prophet's sayings (hadith) about "the greater jihad." According to this narration about an event in the life of the Prophet Muhammad, on one occasion he was returning from a victorious battle attended by his close companions. He addressed them, stating, "Now we are returning from the lesser jihad (struggle) to the greater jihad." He countered their surprise at this pronouncement by explaining, "The greater jihad is the struggle against the *nafs*" (the negative elements of the self or ego).

We have used the term *identity jihads* in our title because for Muslim youth in the contemporary West, identity issues are defining elements in personal and spiritual development. The struggle, as the hadith cited earlier suggests, concerns how to develop a personal and religious identity that enables maturation and self-rectification as opposed to an identity that becomes a brittle shell, defensive and offensive rather than transformative.

Considering Muslim youth in all cultures, classes, and situations is clearly beyond the scope of a single chapter.[1] Therefore, we can only briefly indicate that Muslim youth all over the world are experiencing the challenges of integrating traditional religious beliefs and practices within the rapid social changes accompanying modernization and globalization. In that sense, identity issues are highlighted in many contexts. For Muslim youth in the United States, however, identity struggles occur not only in the encounter of tradition and modernity but are further experienced through the lens of being a minority, and in the current political climate, an increasingly stigmatized minority.

Life Stage Rituals in Muslim Spirituality before College Age

The principal religious rituals of Muslim life from birth to adulthood are *aqiqa* (hair trimming after birth), circumcision, *bismillah*[2] (start of studying the Qur'an), the child's first fast in Ramadan, *khatm* or *ameen*[3] (completion of a first reading of the entire Qur'an). These markers are more or less standard from one Muslim society to another. Within the U.S. Muslim community, as elsewhere, such rituals are gradually evolving in their form and meaning.

Each Muslim society does have its own specific traditions and expectations surrounding youth. In Turkey and Morocco, for example, male circumcision is performed fairly late and is a rite of passage celebrating masculinity, whereas in many other Muslim societies and among Muslims in the United States, it has become a medical procedure performed in infancy. South Asian Muslims perform the bismillah or induction into the reading of the Qur'an during the preschool years. In this Muslim culture and among South Asian immigrants to North America, children are attired for this ritual in traditional dress strongly evocative of the wedding finery of brides and grooms, perhaps anticipating their maturation and inculcating adult gender roles.

In the case of other childhood religious milestones for Muslim children, such as the induction into prayer and fasting, the sense of assimilating to mature practice and community membership is a consistent theme, even when such events are not highly ritualized. Young boys, in particular, are encouraged in their regular religious practice by being given leadership roles in sounding the call to prayer or, on occasion, leading family congregation prayers.

Muslims living in the diaspora have become aware of the need to explain for youth the substance, in addition to the form, of religious ritual. Thus, in the United States, rather than the standard illustrated prayer guides that provide basic details of the ritual prayers (salat) and quotations from the Qur'an and hadith exhorting to it, books on Ramadan and prayer are produced as a genre of juvenile literature (e.g., Ghazi 1996). Since they incorporate more personal perspectives while reflecting on the meaning of the rituals, such books are suitable both for the edification of Muslim youth and for making the ritual familiar and accessible in a non-Muslim educational setting, such as for diversity instruction in a public school.

Despite the diversity of cultural expressions surrounding Islam, in Muslim societies the family plays an important role during childhood, adolescence, and, in fact, throughout a person's life. Some cultural psychologists have spoken of the concept of a "familial" self in such cultures whereby the individual understands himself or herself as part of a larger unit and usually makes major decisions in close consultation with parents, siblings, and other family members. In general, this intense interaction with the family through celebrations, commemorations, and shared mourning constitutes a major location of Muslim spirituality. The extended family is a sphere of influence for youth, and the religious and spiritual practices of grandparents, uncles, aunts, and cousins are important reference points and/or sources of comparison (Mir 2002–3). However, for Muslim youth growing up in the United States, a culture where separation from the family is usually seen as a necessary part of development, some social, identity, and even spiritual tensions may emerge regarding issues of family ties and autonomy.

PRIMARY AND SECONDARY ISLAMIC EDUCATION IN AMERICA

Along with physical and intellectual maturation, a number of the aforementioned rituals signal the importance of acquiring religious knowledge, for example, by developing familiarity with Arabic and reading the Qur'an. In America, the Muslim community is placing increased emphasis on youth gaining further religious knowledge beyond the Qur'an. Conscious attention began to be directed to the education of Muslim youth in the 1970s, and today there are burgeoning numbers of Muslim weekend schools, full-time schools,[4] madrasas, and Qur'an memorization academies. The need for Islamic youth education has inspired a wealth of curricular literature. These curricular guides are designed to impart religious knowledge in the light of modern pedagogical principles in a way that is accessible to children who have grown up in an environment where novelty and entertainment value are prevalent and where rote memorization is not valued as an instructional method.

In addition to academic goals, a significant purpose of Muslim educational institutions is to establish religious identity firmly during the primary and secondary stages of learning. The metaphor of "inoculating" children against the moral dangers of the larger society sometimes appears in community discourse. For example, the title of a tape by the popular American Muslim motivational speaker Hamza Yusuf Hanson is *Lambs to the Slaughter: Our Children and Modern Education* (ca. 1995). This trope of protectionism from Western and/or modern customs and ideas is evident in Muslim literature directed at children that stresses disassociation from widely celebrated American holidays such as Halloween and Christmas, not only because of their alien nature but also because of their pagan roots.[5] Further symbolic life stage events of American culture that may signal a danger to Islamic identity and moral norms and therefore engender a discourse of avoidance and buttressing religious and societal boundaries include "prom night."[6]

The maintenance of a distinctive and visible identity is often encouraged by conservative Muslims on the basis of certain elements of Islamic tradition, in particular hadiths of the Prophet that appear to discourage the emulation of non-Muslim styles of dress or other customs. However, Muslims who feel that isolationist positions are inappropriate may draw on other elements of Muslim tradition and history that exhort to cordial relations with non-Muslim neighbors.

Adherence to Islamic law (shari'a) is considered essential by many Muslims, and this has generally been interpreted as necessitating distinctive dress for females such as the hijab (head cover and modest dress). As yet a minority of Muslims view the interpretation of such laws as flexible and the religious sources as historically contextualized. A somewhat middle ground between conservatives and liberals would be Muslims who favor the development of a jurisprudence for minorities (*fiqh al-aqalliyyat*) based on elements existing with classical Islamic legal interpretations that allow the incorporation of cultural and legal customs already existing in societies into which Islam expands. This sort of contextually sensitive legal reasoning might permit Muslims living in the West to adjust more easily to certain prevailing customs and situations, for example, female dress codes, economic considerations and marriage, as well as divorce and custody proceedings in secular courts.

Among primary and high school level Muslim educators, there is a range of positions as to what is most important within a Muslim educational system. The ideas of three prominent Muslim academics in America during the late twentieth century epitomize discrete approaches to the problem of Islamic epistemology and education that typify more general attitudes. In fact, we will be able to use these categories as a basis for classifying the major religious and spiritual orientations available to Muslim youth.

"Identity" Islam

While very broad in scope, this orientation may be represented by the late Ismail Faruqi (d. 1986), an American scholar-activist of Palestinian origin who espoused an Islamist current in his thought (Esposito 1991). Taking a position with both educational and political implications, Faruqi asserted that the problem of knowledge was that Western colonialism and hegemony had resulted in the dominant paradigms of authoritative knowledge—in the social and hard sciences as well as in the interpretive disciplines—becoming established solely on Western foundations.

The solution, according to this line of thought, is an Islamization of knowledge, a Muslim intellectual nativism that could incorporate a critique of non-Islamic paradigms while attempting to recover frameworks of inquiry more consistent with Muslim ethos and identity (Stenberg 1996).

The identity affirmation approach, since it adopts and adapts the thought of Muslim religio-political organizations, is most emphatic about issues of identity, rather than addressing spirituality directly. Spiritual activities and spiritual growth may be incorporated, but the thrust of most American Muslim organizations had been toward developing an identity for American Muslim youth that is distinct from the dominant (White, Judeo-Christian) majority. Recognizing that only a small percentage, perhaps 5 percent according to Bagby, of Muslim youth will attend full-time Islamic schools,[7] these organizations focus on developing a presence, voice, and some power for Muslims on mainstream campuses and schools.

Among the Muslim community in the West and its youth, identity affirmation seems to be the most prevalent institutional and educational strategy. This trend is encouraged by the dominant voices of Muslim organizations such as the Islamic Society of North America and the Muslim American Society, whose leadership tends to be drawn from the ranks of Islamist activists. Many schools and mosques project this attitude, and the Muslim student associations on college campuses generally are more conservative, nativist, and politicized in their approach to Islamic identity (Hermansen 2003). First-generation immigrants rather unquestioningly have accepted "identity" Islam both personally and for their children, since it answers many questions about preserving religious identity in the face of overwhelming pressure toward assimilation and promotes "Muslim pride" as a response to potential political and cultural marginalization.

Traditionalism

The traditionalist position may be represented by the American scholar of Iranian origin, Seyyed Hossein Nasr, and other Muslim intellectuals and educators who are influenced by classical Islamic philosophy and Sufism. According to this vision of knowledge and critique of the present situation, the main problems faced by Muslims today are secularism and modernity, which fragment and desacralize approaches to life and knowledge. The solution would be to somehow recover a holistic approach to knowledge that would emphasize traditional religious wisdom and spirituality (Hossein Nasr 1994).

Another type of traditionalism increasingly popular among young Muslims is an emphasis on technical jurisprudence (*fiqh*). This interest represents both a body and a culture of scholarship and an attitude of pietistic sacralizing of everyday activities through relating them to divine commands.

It should be noted that consciously espoused "traditionalism" is not the same as being "traditional" according to this framework, although traditionalists would perceive themselves as being the most authentic representatives of the faith. This religious orientation is well received by Muslims from societies in which local forms of the religion allowed more scope for a spirituality that included belief in the mediating powers of saints and prophets. Spiritual practices of traditionalists encourage personal development through individual or group practices such as *dhikr* (repetition of the divine names or other pious litanies). The cult of the Sufi saints traditionally included shrine visitation and acceptance of the authority of spiritual guides. For this reason, this expression of Islamic spirituality must be adaptive in an American context where youth no longer experience the presence of shrines and may be skeptical and wary of the miraculous and of claims to charismatic religious authority. Thirty or more years ago universalist Sufi movements such as the Sufi Order founded by Inayat Khan (d. 1927) appealed to a generation of seekers who were primarily Euro-Americans due to their engaging spirituality as personal transformation by offering techniques such as meditation, chanting, and methods for personal development. In contrast, the most popular Sufi movements among today's Muslim youth, whether converts or children of immigrants, are those that emphasize, along with inner development, the need to follow Islamic law (shari'a) and the punctilious observation of ritual.[8]

Liberalism

The approach of Muslim modernists and liberals may be represented by the late scholar of Pakistani origin Fazlur Rahman (d. 1988), who was a professor of Islamic studies at the University of Chicago (Rahman 1982). To Muslim liberals, the crisis of knowledge in the Islamic tradition today results from intellectual stagnation and a closing of the Muslim mind due to the emphasis on rote memorization and blind following of past rulings. Thus the solution would be a renewed *ijtihad*, the project of returning to the sources and interpreting the Qur'an and Islamic legal pronouncements in the light of reason, critical thinking, and historical contextualization.

More recently a distinct "Progressive Islamic" movement has emerged in contexts such as South Africa and the United States, emphasizing a concern with justice issues in addition to espousing liberal values in interpretation. Some of the most hotly debated progressive issues include "gender justice" or more inclusion of the female voice in matters of interpretation and leadership (Safi 2003). Female Muslim academics in America such as Leila Ahmed, Amina Wadud, Riffat Hassan, and Asma Barlas have produced works that challenge patriarchal readings of the revealed texts and use the liberal strategy of historically contextually laws that are not equitable with regard to women's rights (see, e.g., Wadud's *Qur'an and Woman: Rereading the Sacred Text from a Woman's Perspective* [1999]). Such interpretations have been given prominence in liberal Muslim circles and among non-Muslim intellectuals and activists. Whether they will have a significant impact on Islamic education and Muslim youth cultures remains to be seen. An example of "liberal" or progressive trends espoused by some young American Muslims is the Web site Muslimwakeup.com, which features both political and social critique of conservative Muslim and Western institutions. A regular column on that Web site, "Sex and the Umma,"[9] explores previously taboo subjects regarding sexuality, especially from female perspectives. Other progressive women activists have drawn up an "Islamic Bill of Rights for Women in the Mosque"[10] that challenges the way females are being segregated and allotted inferior physical space in many Muslim institutional settings.

In fact, Muslims may combine these three approaches in various ways. For example, the views of Seyyed Hossein Nasr and Faruqi may be reflected in recent attempts by teachers in some American Muslim schools to develop a "*tarbiyya* model" that aspires to relate all subjects to Islamic religious sources. The goal of this approach is to present Islam as an integrated worldview infusing and sacralizing all other fields of knowledge.[11]

The College Experience for Muslim Youth: A General Description

Going to college represents a significant moment in the lives of Muslim adolescents, as it does for American youth in general. Many Muslim youth will live away from home for the first time and experience a greater degree of freedom and responsibility, as well as the ability to make independent lifestyle choices. Even commuters will experience some freedom from the monitoring and protective gaze of family and community.

This newfound college freedom may be creatively used in Muslim and ethnic enclaves such as the Muslim Student Association (MSA) and cultural student organizations (e.g., Pakistani or South Asian Student Associations). The use of freedom in these contexts—while it stretches conservative parental and/or community tolerance of youth practices—may yet be justified by religious and cultural norms. All in all, while Muslim youth may stretch and even breach community or parental norms, this will not necessarily mean that they will distance themselves from religious or spiritual concerns. For example, youth who are members of Muslim Student Associations are "working for Islam," and in such a context "brother-sister" interaction is tolerated, or even encouraged, by conservative parents more than if the context had been purely social. When they go to college, many Muslim youth—probably the majority of them—will also leave their mostly white and non-Muslim school friends behind, and will for the first time encounter larger numbers of Muslims and coethnics.

Some Muslim youth may also choose to associate less with other campus Muslims because they wish to avoid a religious or cultural clique or enclave, or the appearance of one. To many youth, college means a search for "new" experiences, and associating with fellow Muslims (or Pakistanis, Arabs, etc.) may lead to a limiting of potential horizons of experience. This may happen because it can be relatively easy to associate with similar peers, and youth are afraid that they will then not make the time and effort to reach out, make new friends, and experience new things. Some youth report that they dislike the appearance of constituting a cultural or religious clique: they feel that a group of "hijabis"[12] or a large group of South Asians that always "stick together" is "intimidating" to outsiders, or appears socially unapproachable. Some Muslim youth seem to feel that the American "melting pot" demands that they not restrict themselves to fellow Muslims. This is particularly so in the case of upwardly mobile upper-middle-class youth at wealthy colleges for whom college is an important phase prior to professional life where they must make important connections and be "groomed" for interaction with diverse (or mostly white) elites (Mir 2002–3).

College is also a context in which the prevalent rhetoric of diversity provides the space for students to more freely showcase their religious, cultural, and racial backgrounds. This is where identity affirmation approaches become active; we will discuss some of these options in the next sections.

ISLAMIC IDENTITY AND THE BURDEN OF REPRESENTATION

In terms of the basic identity markers among Muslim youth, practicing or not practicing the religious rituals such as prayer is the fundamental divide. However, not practicing does not necessarily mean being nonidentified as a Muslim. The "cultural Muslim" may find himself or herself stigmatized by broader American culture due to name or ethnicity, and therefore Muslim identity is an inevitable fact of life for most Muslim students, regardless of level of commitment.

Some experts argue that Islam emphasizes "orthopraxy" rather than orthodoxy (Smith 1957). It is the level of observance of ritual proscriptions and taboos rather than doctrine that is the standard of community affiliation, however. But agreement on this point is not unanimous, and orthodoxy is a term often used in popular sources and one deemed appropriate by at least some scholars of Islam (Calder 2000).

While Islamic identities of college students range from conservative to progressive, virtually all Muslim students must deal with the "burden of representation" of their identity. Garbi Schmidt, a Danish sociologist of religion, writes about Muslim student events she attended in Chicago during the 1990s. After describing the context of MSA lectures and especially the events of the annual Islamic Awareness Week, Schmidt theorizes that a posture of "correction" pervades many MSA events, particularly those conceived of as self-presentation to "the Other," that is, the non-Muslim institution and its members:

> But the Other—fellow students, teachers—were more than an audience. They were a means to Islamic interpretation. Interpretations of the role of women, political issues, scientific investigations, and media presentations all pointed to an adoption of powerful topics and opinion formers within the United States. Though this at times included an "apologetic pitfall" it also included a means for collective empowerment. By attacking, formulating against, and arguing to formulate more correct views than majority authorities (scientists, politicians, journalists) Muslims appealed for social recogni-

tion. By "correcting" the errors of the Other they were convinced (and tried to convince) that although they socially were in minority, the knowledge they represented was intellectually superior. (Schmidt 1998, 167)

This mode of "correcting" arises from a combination of the Islamization of knowledge movement of the 1980s with more recent youthful quests for identity among the first substantial cohort of Muslim students born or raised in the United States. In addition to correcting perceived misrepresentations of Islam, the style and tone of certain MSA activities arise partly from the need to assert some sort of control over an imagined Muslim space while also staking a claim to authority as interpreters of Islam. On the part of U.S. Muslim youth this sometimes reflects the oppressive nature of being a minority and feeling the necessity to assert one's claim to a position. At the same time, such claims can become oppressive for those Muslims whose claims to authority may be rejected or marginalized, such as non-Sunnis, and women who choose not to wear hijab, since many conservative and Islamist expressions of authority are at the same time totalizing and exclusionary in nature (Abou el Fadl 2001).

Ethnic or cultural practice of the religion also represents for Muslim youth the world of their parents that may be subverted by appeals to the Qur'an itself, to shari'a, and to the ideal of a "pure," culture-free Islam.

IDENTITY ISLAM, TRADITIONALISM, AND ISLAMIC LIBERALISM AMONG MUSLIM YOUTH

The range of Islamic identities, from traditional Muslim to identity Islam to liberal or progressive Muslim, as described earlier, offers a way of understanding orientations espoused by young Muslims in the United States.

Identity Expressions

For Muslim youth, arrival on campus may be the first—often exhilarating—chance to encounter large numbers of co-religionists who gather on the basis of Muslim identity, and often the first encounter is through the Muslim Student Organizations. MSAs are one of the most obvious sites to look for Muslim student spirituality on college campuses. The major national organization for Muslims, the Islamic Society of North America, grew out of a student movement in the late 1950s. Its early supporters were foreign students, often influenced by the growing Islamist movements, such as the Muslim Brotherhood, that combined religious commitment with the desire for social and political change in their countries of origin. The conservative and politically oriented characteristics of this organization continued as it grew into a nationwide organization based in Plainfield, Indiana. While the Muslim Student Association today is largely an autonomous body, it meets in conjunction with the national body, Islamic Society of North America (ISNA), and is answerable to adult pressure. Most MSAs are dominated by expressions of identity Islam, whereas traditionalist and liberal perspectives are usually found among more reflective students who avoid the conformity instilled within the norms of MSAs. Both Sufism (mystical or cultural expressions of Islam) and liberal trends are often stigmatized in mainstream Muslim organizations and mosques, so their absence from MSA subcultures is not surprising.

Some Muslim youth will avoid Muslim social groups on campus because they think such groups are "too religious," will have an impact on their freedoms, and/or will "judge" their religious practice or the lack thereof. This avoidance may be due to sectarian religious differences; for example, Shi'a1[13] or Ahmadi[14] students may avoid Sunni MSAs because of differences in religious interpretations or because of a fear of— or actual—ostracism.

Among the activities of MSA spirituality are Islamic Awareness Week, classes such as *Tafsir* (interpretation, correct pronunciation and/or memorization of the Qur'an), and events featuring outside speakers, whose talks are generally motivational in nature. Religious practices highlighted by the campus MSAs include the following.

Qiyam al-lail: This involves staying up all or most of the night performing religious devotions. Muslim youth may organize prayer vigils on particular holy days, or they may perform these extra devotions individually or together.

Fasting: Devout Muslims fast during the daylight hours during the entire month of Ramadan, breaking the fast at sunset as a communal celebration. Some may observe additional fasting on certain other days. During Ramadan, Muslim students may gather in private homes, apartments, mosques, or dorm rooms to partake of the predawn meal and pray the *fajr* (predawn) prayer together (discussed in more detail later). They may also congregate to break the fast together at sunset and to pray the dusk prayer. The taraweeh prayer[15] may also be a high priority for many Muslim youth; after a full day of fasting, standing in prayer and listening to long passages of the Qur'an is regarded as uplifting and purifying by many Muslim students.

Juma': Attendance at Friday prayers is obligatory for males, but such services are also heavily attended by female students at college. Sermons are often given by male students since there is no religious requirement for formal clergy to perform this function.

Fajr is the name for the predawn prayer. Occasionally Muslim students may organize this prayer to be performed in a group. Although in Muslim societies it would be highly unusual for females to leave home before dawn in order to join the congregation, it may be practiced in campus settings where dorms are nearby and female students can arrive in groups, especially since they are mobile and may have cars. The experience of uniting as a small group in this religious practice while the rest of the campus community is sleeping evokes a sense of solidarity and uniqueness among Muslim students. It is also a way of demonstrating religious commitment to fellow Muslims.

Halaqas are study circles emphasizing religious knowledge. The fact that Muslim spirituality emphasizes knowledge, often the knowledge of how to properly perform rituals or moral exhortations, makes such study circles a natural mode of expression for Muslim students. At the same time, Muslim-run study circles may form a line of defense against negative representations of Islam in the broader society. Even the academic study of Islam as part of campus religious studies programs may be seen as subversive and threatening by more conservative students, in the same way that critical historical study of the Bible may be avoided by fundamentalist Christian students. The difference is that conservatism among Muslim students tends to be respected by most insiders and is also expected to be the norm by non-Muslim society, unlike fundamentalist Christianity, say, which is considered fringe or marginal on most campuses.

Less prevalent on campus and less easily classified are the more intensively conservative and politicized views associated with Salafism. Within the global Muslim community a certain type of religious conservatism is labeled "Salafi." *Salaf* in Arabic refers to "the path of the pious ancestors," the idea being that the purest and most pristine form of the religion can be recovered from the revealed sources and early practice of Muslims in the time of Prophet Muhammad and shortly after. Among Salafis, cultural expressions of Islamic civilization, including art, music, philosophy, and Sufism, as well as sectarian forms, are rejected. While few youth are explicitly affiliated with such groups, their influence can percolate into specific mosques or groups through Web sites, literature, or speakers invited to campus.

Salafi influence among campus Muslim youth seems to wax and wane depending on the charisma of specific student leaders. Certain Islamic primary and secondary schools that have administrators and teachers with this orientation incorporate Salafi and Islamist writings such as those of Ibn Kathir (d. 1372), Ibn Taimiyya (d. 1328), and Sayyid Qutb (d. 1966) into the curriculum.

Sufi Traditionalism and American Muslim Youth

Sufism is the mystical interpretation of Islam, an inclination rather than a sectarian movement, although specific Sufi practices and institutions have evolved throughout history. American Sufi movements are often global and hybridized. Hermansen (1997) has used the metaphor of a garden in which there are hybrids, perennials, and transplants to describe the variety of attitudes to Islamic identity, spirituality, and practice within these groups.

There has also been a gradual shift among the mainstream Muslim movements in the United States such as ISNA, which has become more accommodating of some aspects of sober, "shari'a oriented" Sufism. Nowadays speakers at ISNA such as Hamza Yusuf Hanson promote an "authentic" Sufism that is simply an extension of regular Islamic concepts such as purification of the soul (*tazkiyya al-nafs*). The Tablighi Jamaat movement, in areas where it is active, also promotes quasi-Sufi attitudes of devotional piety and asceticism among adults and youth.

On the other hand, groups such as the Naqshbandi Haqqani Sufi Order, who are followers of Shaikh Nazim and his American representative, Shaykh Hisham Kabbani, seem to have been influential among particular communities of youth on specific campuses, for example, at the University of Chicago during the early 1990s (Schmidt 1998, 124–25, 183). The stress on affiliation to a particular Sufi order (*tariqa*), its leader (*shaykh*), and its rituals may become a source of tension on campus and in the broader Muslim community. Conflicting interpretations between Shaykh Hisham's group and the "Salafi" youth who reject Sufi interpretations erupted into a long-running battle on the Internet (see Schmidt 2004).

Currently the most popular form of Sufism on urban campuses seems to be that of Shaykh Nuh Ha Mim Keller (born ca. 1952), a Euro-American teacher (shaykh) of the Hashimi-Darqawi branch of the Shadhili Order. Keller visits the United States twice a year, where he has a number of American disciples,[16] mainly young Muslims born of immigrant parents and raised in the West who are seeking a return to Islamic authenticity. Keller's approach to Sufism epitomizes the emphasis on jurisprudence (fiqh) as a vehicle of Islamic authenticity and spirituality simultaneously, and would therefore represent a strand of "traditionalism." More and more Sufi-inclined Muslim youth undertake study trips to either Syria or Yemen in order to combine learning Arabic, studying fiqh, and sitting at the feet of traditional shaykhs.

Liberals

The emergence of the category "progressive Muslim," especially in the United States after 9/11, allows a new self-definition for certain Muslim youth.[17] The mainstream media and academics seek to define the orientation of progressives or "moderates," sometimes confusing being progressive with religious nonobservance. Some elements of an agenda for "progressives" include gender equality, mosque-state separation, nonliteral Qur'an interpretation, interfaith dialogue, embracing modernity, and an emphasis on the arts (Caldwell 2004). On college campuses these trends are more likely to be represented by the secular academic curriculum in religious studies, Middle Eastern studies, or women's studies, thereby exposing Muslim students to ideas that many will find stimulating and others will find threatening. An example of "liberal" Muslim student activities would be sponsoring dialogues with other student groups, for example, Jewish students from the Hillel organization, in order to establish common ground and overcome negative stereotypes and potential animosity.

A bridge between religious American Muslim youth from all three orientations are the Deen Intensives. These are weeklong religious camps and seminars where a roster of Muslim motivational speakers, shaykhs (religious experts), and academics present lectures to assembled student audiences eager to enhance their background in classical Islamic studies and to share fellowship with other like-minded youth.[18]

Concluding Comments

How does contemporary Islam in the United States view and address the social, policy, and cultural forces that are currently influencing child and adolescent spiritual growth within this tradition?

Many American Muslims appreciate elements of the U.S. system that promote pluralism, since they serve to protect Muslim autonomy and freedom of religious practice (Jackson 2004). A more diffuse impression of American culture among immigrant Muslims is that it is a potential threat to a Muslim's moral and spiritual fiber. Reactions among the Muslim community to this challenge are largely directed toward the education of youth, since childhood is constructed both within the tradition and in academic studies as the period that will have the most impact on a person's later value system and sense of identity.

Most of the social, policy, and cultural forces in the United States are beyond the direct influence of the Muslim community. Among Muslim Americans, university education is seen both as the road to social mobility and as the time when youth must be surrendered to the shaping forces of broader systems of knowledge and authority. The community's response thus far has been to offer Muslim students what ideally should constitute a supportive campus networking of Muslims though Muslim Student Associations. Resources such as Muslim chaplains and mosques on campuses are as yet rare, in contrast, for example, to the role of campus Hillel centers for Jewish students (see, e.g., Rossi 2002).

Most Muslim youth in America ultimately find a way of engaging in the inner "jihad" of managing social and spiritual challenges to self-image and eventually engage in successful careers contributing to the broader society. This is done, in the case of liberals and most traditionalists, through achieving extensive integration in mainstream U.S. culture while maintaining a confidence in and affiliation with Islamic religious practice. In the case of more conservative Muslims it is accomplished through negotiating what are essentially separate spheres of work life, where one performs job duties ably but remains aloof from most social interactions, and a more engaged family and religious life largely spent among co-religionists from a similar ethnic background.

The Muslim community in North America is relatively new, and in the current political climate is under extreme pressure and scrutiny. While one may criticize early institutional efforts for focusing too much on maintaining identity at the expense of encouraging spiritual dimensions of religious experience, this reaction on the part of a largely immigrant population is quite understandable. Trends among contemporary Muslim youth suggest a growing openness to embracing multiple dimensions of Muslim identity and accepting the many positive elements in American culture as compatible with Islamic values. It is this increasing openness that will ultimately allow the flourishing of the Muslim community in the United States at both the social and the spiritual levels.

Notes

1. For example, important and unique dimensions of the experience of African-American Muslim youth could not be incorporated in the following discussion.

2. *Bismillah* means "in the name of God" in Arabic and is used as a formula for commencing meritorious actions. Bismillah begins all but one of the 114 chapters of the Qur'an.

3. *Khatm* means "completion or seal." *Ameen* is the Arabic equivalent of "amen."

4. Ihsan Bagby (2001), "The Mosque Report." At http://www.cair-net.org/mosquereport (accessed May 20, 2004).

5. Sakr (1999); Quick (1997). See also "Dealing with Halloween: 13 tips for parents." At http://www.soundvision.com/info/halloween/13tips.asp (accessed May 20, 2004).

6. Samana Siddiqui, "The prom: 8 prom tips for parents." At http://www.soundvision .com/Info/parenting/parent.promtips.asp (accessed May 20, 2004) and The prom: Not just one night of Haram. At http://www.themodernreligion.com/teens/teen_promonenight.htm (accessed May 20, 2004).

7. Bagby, "Mosque report."

8. A phenomenological description of some aspects of this movement and Keller's teachings may be found in Sahin (2003).

9. See http://muslimwakeup.com/sex/.

10. See http://www.muslimwakeup.com/main/archives/2004/09/time_for_muslim.php

11. Information on the *tarbiyya* project is at http://www.4islamicschools.org/parent_curr.htm (accessed June 1, 2004).

12. Hijabi is the term for a Muslim woman who observes modest dress including the covering of the hair with a scarf. *Hijab* literally means barrier or curtain, but in "Muslim English" it has come to refer specifically to the head scarf.

13. Shi'a Muslims are about 20 percent of both the total Muslim population and the community in diaspora. While many Twelver Shi'a are from Iran, a Shi'a majority society, other Shi'a may be Iraqi, Indo-Pakistani, or belong to further Shi'a subgroups such as the Isma'ili sect.

14. The Ahmadiyya is a movement found mainly among Muslims of South Asian origin. While similar to Sunnis in most aspects of their practice, Ahmadis are stigmatized by many other Muslims since some of them believe that a late-nineteenth-century scholar, Mirza Ghulam Ahmad, played a prophetic role, and this violates the doctrine of the finality of Muhammad's message. Lahori Ahmadis believe that Mirza Ghulam Ahmad played a revivalist rather than a prophetic role.

15. Taraweeh prayers are performed every night during Ramadan. During these lengthy optional prayers about one-thirtieth of the Qur'an is recited aloud each night, thereby completing a full reading in the month. The fact that prayer leaders who have memorized the entire book are available even to smaller campus communities is an indication of the increased role of traditional Islamic knowledge within the American context.

16. We have heard this number estimated as in the hundreds or more.

17. Manifestos of the movement are Safi (2002) and Esack (1999).

18. See http://www.sunnipath.com.

References

Abou el Fadl, Khaled. 2001. *Speaking in God's name: Islamic law, authority and women.* Oxford: Oneworld.

Calder, Norman. 2000. The limits of Islamic orthodoxy. In *Intellectual traditions in Islam,* edited by Farhad Daftary, 66–86. London: Tauris.

Caldwell, Deborah. 2004. Something major is happening: Are we witnessing the beginnings of an Islamic Reformation? At http://www.beliefnet.com/story/92/story_9286_1.html (accessed September 20, 2004).

Esack, Fareed. 1999. *Being a Muslim in the modern world.* Oxford: Oneworld.

Esposito, John L. 1991. Ismail R. al-Faruqi: Muslim scholar-activist. In The *Muslims of America,* edited by Yvonne Y. Haddad, 65–79. New York: Oxford University Press.

Ghazi, Suhaib Hamid. 1996. *Ramadan.* New York: Holiday House.

Hanson, Hamza Yusuf. ca. 1995. *Lambs to the slaughter: Our children and modern education.* Videotape. Hayward, Calif.: Alhambra Productions.

Hermansen, Marcia. 1997. In the garden of American Sufi movements: Hybrids and perennials. In *New trends and developments in the world of Islam,* edited by P. Clarke, 155–78. London: Luzac Oriental Press.

———. 2003. How to put the genie back in the bottle: "Identity Islam" and Muslim youth movements in the United States. In *Progressive Muslims: On justice, gender, and pluralism,* edited by Omid Safi, 303–19. Oxford: Oneworld.

Hossein Nasr, Seyyed. 1994. *Young Muslim's guide to the modern world.* Chicago: Kazi Books.

Jackson, Sherman. 2004. Islam and affirmative action. Paper presented at Islam in America Conference, April 8, Wayne State University, Detroit, Michigan.

Mir, Shabana. 2002–3. American Muslim women college students: Identity strategies and campus climate. Unpublished doctoral research. Indiana University, Department of Education Policy Studies.

Quick, Abdullah Hakim 1997. *Holiday myths*. Videotape. Bridgeview, Ill.: Sound Vision.

Rahman, Fazlur. 1982. *Islam and modernity: Transformation of an intellectual tradition*. Chicago: University of Chicago Press.

Rossi, Holly Lebowitz. 2002. Muslim chaplains a new priority for colleges. Religion News Service, May 16. At http://pewforum.org/news/display.php?NewsID=1203 (accessed September 20, 2004).

Safi, Omid, ed. 2002. *Progressive Muslims: On justice, gender, and pluralism*. Oxford: Oneworld.

Sahin, Inayet. 2003. The experience of turning to a spiritual path and healing the emptiness. Master's thesis, University of Maryland, College Park, Department of Education.

Sakr, Ahmad. 1999. *The adolescent life*. Lombard, Ill.: Foundation for Islamic Knowledge.

Schmidt, Garbi. 1998. *American Medina: A study of the Sunni Muslim immigrant communities in Chicago*. Lund, Sweden: University of Lund, Department of History of Religions.

———. 2004. Sufi charisma on the Internet. In *Sufism in Europe and North America*, edited by David Westerlund, 109–26. London: Routledge/Curzon.

Smith, Wilfred C. 1957. *Modern Islam in India*. Princeton, N.J.: Princeton University Press.

Stenberg, Leif. 1996. The Islamization of science: Four Muslim positions developing an Islamic modernity. Lund Studies in History of Religions, no. 6. Lund: Lunds Universitet.

Wadud, Amina. 1999. *Qur'an and woman: Rereading the sacred text from a woman's perspective*. New York: Oxford University Press.

CHAPTER 34

Countering a Malforming Culture: Christian Theological Formation of Adolescents in North America

Ellen T. Charry

Neither psychologists nor theologians have paid much attention to the theological identity of adolescents.[1] Developmental psychologists have shown little interest in religion generally. Further, since the promulgation of "stages" of development and particularly of the "identity crisis" by Erik Erikson, psychologists, as well as religious educators influenced by them, have tended to assume that adolescence is a time of crisis during which youngsters become isolated from the adult world, where reflection on the formative power of one's beliefs about God, human life, and the created order would take place.

Beginning with Freud, and particularly since Erikson, the notion of development has dominated thinking about children's intellectual and psychological growth, and since Kohlberg, there has been attention to their moral development (Erikson 1963; Freud [1905] 1962; Kohlberg 1958). Development as a theoretical orientation eventually spilled over into religious education as well with James Fowler's work on stages of spiritual or faith development (Fowler 1981). Theological formation is a somewhat different focus than development, however.

For their part, theologians rarely think about the psychological reception of the ideas and practices they analyze, like the nature of God, the meaning of salvation, or the content of revelation, and especially not with specific age groups in mind.[2] They are absorbed in getting at "the truth," working through various controversies and details of doctrine and practice often presented in highly abstract terms that can be difficult to penetrate.

Attending to the logical force, intelligibility, and coherence of Christian claims is not sufficient, however, for any theological claim worth taking seriously will affect how we view ourselves as well as others and suggest how we should live in light of its implications. If theological doctrines do not occupy this space in the young, other things will. Despite inattention to what theological beliefs do to us, they will have their way with us. They shape who we are. We must therefore take care in articulating them, especially to the young, for their values, self-concept, and ability to relate to the world hang in the balance. Either neglecting religion or understanding religious instruction as simply assent to notions that do not do anything with, for, to, and in the minds and bodies of adolescents simply will not do.

Theologians and perhaps psychologists as well would leave the question of the shaping power of theological notions and religious practices on the young to religious educators or parents. This hope is, however, naive. Most youth ministers have little or no professional preparation, and those who do (some fresh seminary graduates) are often on their way to somewhere else. Parents are frequently unable to articulate their own religious beliefs and less able to help their children apply religious beliefs to their lives. Interestingly, there has been little attention to the theological identity of adolescents by religious educators either, although attention has been paid to the religious training of younger children. In short, adolescents have been neglected when it comes to their theological identity.

Let us begin by defining formation with particular reference to theology. We may define formation as the nurturing of the soul that includes beliefs, values, attitudes, ideals, virtues, practices, and behavior through both formal and informal means. The intent is that thinking about how beliefs, values, and virtues shape youngsters be from the perspective of the child or adolescent, that is, with the recipients' well-being uppermost in mind.

Now, I will qualify this definition theologically by adding that theological formation is formation within the parameters of a theological heritage. A theological heritage is broader than a specific religious tradition (say, Lutheranism) because it treats doctrines and beliefs that are shared by many religions and spiritual traditions, but narrower than spirituality in general, which does not connote a heritage with articulated beliefs and practices refined over a long period of time.

Within this framework of theological formation, this essay will now argue that as helpful as the developmental orientation has been for psychology, formation is a better rubric for thinking about theological identity. This is because the cultural context within which development—construed as a natural unfolding of the subject's bent and abilities—was most useful has now changed. The model of formation will be more helpful in addressing the needs of adolescents, for it takes account of the shaping power of external forces, especially cultural forces. Further, while religious educators (especially Roman Catholics) have tended to the religious formation of children, theological formation has not been distinguished from the former and so has received less attention. In the first part of the essay I will define and argue for the concept of formation rather than development when speaking of theological identity. In the second part I will define theological formation and illustrate it with two Christian theological doctrines (creation and redemption) and two Christian practices (baptism and foot washing) that might be appropriate for and helpful to adolescents. The question of how these might be delivered to adolescents will have to await the expertise of religious educators and those interested in helping parents tend to the souls of their offspring.

The Case for Formation

In this section I will argue for a model of formation rather than development when it comes to theological identity. The developmental model in adolescent psychology derives from its use for children's physical and neurological growth that readily lent itself to thinking in terms of sequential stages. Development assumes an unself-consciousness process of gradually strengthening abilities and understandings in the normal individual. Babies naturally hold their heads up, turn over, sit up, crawl, stand, and finally walk in roughly that order without instruction, under normal circumstances. The word *naturally* is key to understanding this outlook. It is not something we must think too much about, because the ability to perform the actions described is the outcome of normal neurological development. What adults must tend to is anything that might interfere with normal processes.

The argument here is that the developmental model is inappropriately transferred to the field of religion. Some of the reasons for this are fairly obvious, but others are less so. One reason that development is not as useful a concept here is because theological notions are learned. They are not automatic, although they may be absorbed unself-consciously and informally. Adopting beliefs and practices as one's own is intentional.

Despite the fact that theology itself has often posited natural knowledge of God or at least of conscience, it is likely that what may have appeared as a universal insight to someone like John Calvin in the sixteenth century—who subscribed to this idea—was actually an unself-conscious by-product of Christendom, the accepted assumptions of Christianity throughout Europe at that time.[3] What appeared as natural and universal was actually the result of socialization, but so unself-consciously that it went unnoticed. Informal education formed the young to the extent that theological assumptions filled the cultural "air."

This being the case, those concerned with the theological identity of children and adolescents must attend to the social context for the formation it actually yields. The argument here is that the dominant culture is no longer able to support many moral and religious values, and so can no longer be relied upon for unself-conscious formation of tender souls. For this reason, formation, often through informal socialization, is a more helpful conceptual framework for helping children and adolescents mature. As the Christendom example suggests, culture shapes the soul. I will now turn to how current culture does so.

DYSPAIDEUSIA

Culture is not neutral. It is not possible not to be culturally formed, despite the strong role genetics and family dynamics may play in personal and social development. Culture is always powerful, if for no other reason than that it blankets the self. Its symbols, language, and expectations relentlessly shape personality. The ancient Greeks were concerned with the transmission of their intellectual-philosophical heritage to their young (Jaeger 1944). Their civilization depended upon cultivating *paideia*, the Greek philosophical ideal of the teaching and learning necessary to sustain the cultural ethos of a civilization. Modern Germans called it *Bildung*. It is socialization into the values, styles, and mentality of the highest values of a refined culture. Formation is the art of civilizing the young.

Formation is often suspected by liberal theologians, religious educators, and psychologists, as is the term Greek *catechesis*, meaning teaching or instruction. Christians absorbed the Greek interest in paideia during Christianity's early centuries for adults seeking the Christian way of life. But it faded from view as the Church gained control of society. Religious instruction of children became important with the Protestant Reformation, one of whose central goals was the creation of an educated and informed laity that would be able to hold their clergy morally and financially accountable.

Anxiety about formation is modern and has philosophical roots in Jean-Jacques Rousseau's *Discourse on the Origin and Foundations of Inequality* (1754) and *Émile* (1762) in which he argued against civilization and its transmission as corrupting the natural interests and abilities of the young (Rousseau 1984, 1974). Resistance to theological formation reflects the conviction that religious beliefs should be voluntarily assented to and that teaching or instruction may threaten the child's freedom. Rousseau's work challenges the earlier pedagogical treatise of John Locke, *Some Thoughts concerning Education* ([1697] 1989), that argued for the moral, intellectual, and social education of children to cultivate the ability to become productive members of British society. It is a treatise on English paideia.

At its sharpest, Rousseau's objection is to instruction altogether on the more Platonic view, as expressed in the *Meno,* that we have within us all that we need to flourish and that education is a process of eliciting what is within rather than putting into us that which we need to know and habits we need to form to function well. Rousseau began romanticism with the idea that the young need only the right growing conditions to flourish, not discipline and instruction from adults. Rousseau's romanticism was in turn, and much later, countered by William Golding's novel *Lord of the Flies,* which argued that civilization keeps vicious impulses and desires in check (Golding 1955).

The argument here is about what Christians call original sin. It is the idea that human beings are basically self-absorbed and seek their own advantage and that this fault is corrected by channeling desire outward (toward God, the common good, the poor, the Church). The desire for citizens to internalize the rule of law, on which civilization is predicated, embodies this assumption. At issue are differing assessments of human nature. Basic orientations are unavoidably theological.

Not surprisingly, there are merits to both sides of the argument. The apparent contradiction between the two positions is precisely that—apparent, once we take into account the quality of the society and civilization that forms its citizens. It has been said that the doctrine of original sin is the only Christian teaching that rests on solid empirical evidence. And indeed, the dastardly things done by human beings to one another bespeak a deep flaw in human nature. We can be tragically vicious toward one another. Yet society and its various subcultures cannot be discounted when examining such behavior, as they set the tone and expectations and form the character its citizens will exhibit, to the extent that these are malleable. The point is that the moral and intellectual strengths and weaknesses of the young are shaped by societal exposure, be it for weal or woe.

Rousseau's polemic against "civilization" in the "Discourse on Inequality" should not be read as a totalizing statement but as an objection to the viciousness of the culture of his day as he read it. He need not have gone so far as to posit the "state of nature" in the image of the noble savage who needs to be liberated from the vices of society to make his point. While Rousseau may be correct that bad societal values corrupt the young, that would be the case whether the young are naturally good or are inclined toward the self-absorption that Christians have identified. After all, a vicious society may reflect the viciousness of its members and then reproduce them rather than simply corrupt innocents. The ancient Greek philosophical moralists judged their culture to be an instrument of paideia, whereas Rousseau judged his to be an instrument of *dyspaideusia*: malformation. The issue is not whether civilization per se ennobles or corrupts but whether and to what extent any particular one does so.

The position taken here is that contemporary American culture, now globally exported, is infused with cultural pathogens that render it dyspaideusic, so that healthy formation must now be supplemented with antidotes. As business and technology have reshaped culture they transmit their own values, language, and sensibilities that shape the soul. Further, postmodern philosophy has undermined trust in reason that in its time had replaced trust in tradition. It thus sustained a sense of cohesion regarding the nature of knowledge and of reality. The combined effect of the business and technology culture and the postmodern philosophical sensibility is to eliminate important features of a more traditional culture that contribute to forming spiritually healthy persons. Four of these lost features are the past, skills of care, moral clarity, and the sense of the stability of reality.

The Loss of the Past

Consuming and competing emphasize novelty and change. Change is now so rapid that the present is "shorter" than it once was and the past comes "sooner" than it did and is less pertinent for the present. Things quickly become obsolete and used up and must be got rid of to make room for new merchandise, new features, better, faster performance. The production of trash through the invention of disposability and obsolescence as instruments of economic growth disvalues the past and its accumulated wisdom and accomplishments. Consequently, the value of the past and of learning from it for the present have faded.

Without the past—both its noble heritage and its mistakes—market culture fills the "screen." Without other resources adolescents are located only where market forces place them. They have no historical ballast to counter cultural toxins. Noble ideas and ideals along with saints who embodied them are models for imitation, and past mistakes are especially fit to learn from. To put a sharp point on it, loss of the past is a form of cultural dementia that abandons the young to sloganeering and advertising that even the most resourceful parents cannot counteract.

The Loss of Skills of Care and Loyalty

Disposability and obsolescence of goods deprive the young of developing the skills needed to cherish possessions and repair them in order to enjoy them for a long time. Consuming and replacing rather than restoring and repairing material goods fail to teach the attitudes and skills needed for recognizing and protecting what is old, fragile, and valuable. The loss of training in caring for material goods may well carry over to interpersonal relationships and the environment. This is one reason why parents train children to take care of pets. Stable marriages and a stable work life both require care-taking skills that are best formed early in life. If the virtues of commitment and loyalty fade, youngsters will be greatly disadvantaged in these spheres.

Furthermore, constant change and novelty undermine satisfaction, enjoyment, and that strength of character traditionally known as fortitude. Disposability as a way of life manufactures cynicism, because no product, person, or occupation is adequate for long. Things can be expected to fall apart eventually or be superseded. Little is worth committing oneself to if something or perhaps someone will soon wear out or be used up. Coping with the instability of constant change is exhausting.

The Loss of Moral Clarity

Under Christian influence, the West has long believed that good and evil are independent of personal preference and knowledge of right and wrong. The ability to distinguish virtuous from shameful behavior can and must be transmitted to the young for the sake of healthy societies. In addition to identifying psychosocial stages of development, Freud (1927) recognized the importance of formation for becoming a mature person. He reified this as the "superego": the internalization of culturally normed moral judgments that create the self-discipline needed for morally coherent societies. He wrote when his culture was able to socialize the young into standards of moral knowledge and the skills and discipline to enact it. The superego is the result of good cultural formation.

Although here we are primarily examining side effects of business and technology, it is important to note the filter-down effects of contemporary philosophy. Postmodernism generally supports moral and cultural relativism. Michel Foucault, for example, interprets "morality" as the expression of class interests (Foucault 1976, 1977a, 1977b). A radicalized ideology of emancipation objects to internalized social controls in the name of freedom or perhaps authenticity. Inherited moral authority and reliance on reason and duty have given way to personal preference with deployment of power being the only way to adjudicate among competing claims. Advertising exploits the theme of freedom in order to promote consumer spending, as if having to select one from fifteen types of mustard advances human freedom. Adolescents are, in a sense, victims of these cultural shifts, for they do not carry with them the more stable moral sensibilities that predate consumer capitalism. Not to trivialize the point, but advertising has reshaped freedom so that it precludes self-discipline, because producers of goods prefer to stimulate spending rather than saving.

The Loss of Reality

Confusing our cultural situation yet further is the loss of a reliable reality in which actions have consequences. The world created by television, film, and the virtual reality of the Internet blurs the distinction between actions that have consequences, and fantasy that does not. Moreover, the invisibility of recipients of products and services renders faceless those whom our decisions affect. Danger and folly become more difficult to detect and responsibility more difficult to discern.

Adolescents, especially wealthy, protected ones, gain the cognitive ability to understand the finality of death, for example, and to recognize physical vulnerability only gradually. The confusion of reality with fantasy by the entertainment culture may delay or confuse formation of the ability to make discerning judgments, to recognize danger to self or others, or to anticipate consequences of foolish behavior. Toggle switches, remote control devices, and other devices of instant change trivialize decision making. It is difficult to grasp the consequences of one's actions in a push-button world. Discernment is difficult to learn. All of this militates against learning to think things through carefully and reflecting quietly on them from various perspectives so that the best possibilities and courses of action are considered before a decision is made.

In the foregoing I have identified several virtues and values that the dominant culture no longer supports: discernment, loyalty, commitment, fortitude, caretaking, responsibility, respect for property, and the wisdom of the past. Others that have passed from the scene under other influences are modesty, humility, and self-control. Formation of the young is now in a dyspaideusic context. Our children deserve antidotes.

Theological Formation

Earlier I defined theological formation as the nurturing of the soul within the parameters of a theological heritage. Yet it should not go unnoted that ancient philosophical paths of life functioned similarly. Platonism, Aristotelianism, and stoicism, for example, along with the great world religions, qualify as philosophical traditions within which one may be formed. The reason for preferring theological to philosophical formation is because a philosophical or spiritual sensibility detached from a theological heritage may not provide a strong enough antidote to the cultural pathogens discussed in the previous section, especially a powerful past populated by devoted followers. Thus, theological formation marks a mean between two poles—formation by secular or pagan philosophies that may once have been substantive, but are no longer vibrant, and secular market forces that are powerful but are morally and spiritually vacuous or dangerous.

A further distinction should be made between theological formation as I am developing it here and religious formation. While it may not be evident to the nonspecialist, religious formation suggests more strongly than does the broader term *theological formation* the transmission of a particular religious heritage so that the term *theological formation* helps focus more directly on the needs and abilities of the youngster. This is not to deny that theological formation transmits a heritage but cautions that such transmission be done in ways that are salutary and nurturing for the recipient.

For those remaining skeptical, formation must finally be distinguished from indoctrination. Given the foregoing assessment of cultural forces, we may suggest that indoctrination prioritizes institutional maintenance while formation thinks from the perspective of the needs of the child, as mentioned earlier. Now we are ready to distinguish the influence of market forces from that of religious educators and parents, for whom the well-being of the child is paramount. Parents and educators will attend to the needs of their charges while market forces pursue other interests. Even though parents and educators will have their own ideology in view that others may disagree with, we may assume that they have thought through their commitment and judged it best for themselves and their charges. The same cannot be said of the producers and advertisers, who indoctrinate the young into the business and technology culture for its own maintenance and expansion. The point is that the general culture indoctrinates with less concern for the well-being of the youngster than do those who seek to shape the soul through the accumulated wisdom of a religious or theological tradition. The narrow space circumscribed here for theological formation may be too abstract for some readers to envision, but perhaps it will become clearer in what follows.

CHRISTIAN DOCTRINES AND PRACTICES

Having argued for and defined theological formation, it is time to turn to specific Christian doctrines and how they might be helpful to adolescents, given their needs and stage of life. Adolescence can be a time when youngsters turn inward. They become both self-aware and self-conscious—spontaneity fades. Some will concentrate their energy and interest in specific pursuits like sports or a group of friends if they are outgoing, or their studies, a hobby, the Internet, or playing a musical instrument if they are more introverted. This is the time when a persona is forming. Successes and failures loom large, for they point toward future possibilities and limitations. Appearance becomes an especially important factor in the creation of that persona and in those possibilities. Although it is a time of testing out one's abilities as well as the reliability and loyalty of others, adolescence can be a period of great fragility, sometimes covered over with a swagger or vented through tears. In any case, it is a time of high anxiety for youngsters and those who care about them, because the future is being mapped and missteps become costly.

There are many Christian doctrines and practices. Here we will attend to two central doctrines, creation and redemption, and two practices, baptism and foot washing, as these directly address these adolescent needs. The argument is that they are antidotes to the cultural pathogens identified earlier. No one-to-one correlation between the pathogens and the theological doctrines and practices will be attempted as that would be artificially rigid. Connections can be made in multiple directions and will be pointed out.

Creation

Judaism, Christianity, and Islam share the doctrine of creation. All believe that God created the world and that our identity as creatures of God is essential for proper self-understanding. Jews and Christians share the Book of Genesis, which further designates human beings as made in the image of God. The doctrine of creation is elaborated by many psalms that praise God for the beauty of the world and its orderliness.

This teaching is rich in guidance and help for the young. The doctrine of creation locates one in the cosmic framework that links one's enjoyment and use of the world to gratitude and responsibility for it. All creatures share this common foundation and are linked together by this common identity and mutual responsibility for this treasure. As a participant in God's act of love, the world is to be cared for and cherished. Scripture depicts human beings as stewards and caretakers of God's vineyard and fields for cultivation. By teaching skills of care and loyalty the doctrine of creation is an antidote to the disposable society.

The scriptural teaching that human beings are created in the divine image is itself a powerful antidote to the instrumental view of other persons taught by a society organized around getting one's own needs met. Respect for others is embedded in the idea that all of us, whether we know it or not or understand it or not, belong to God and image him. Precisely what that image is has stimulated theological reflection for centuries, and it is not a bad question for adolescents to ponder as their souls take shape. However the mystery is articulated, the teaching creates a climate of respect for the dignity of every human being.

That our dignity resides in being created in the divine image also provides a powerful bulwark against insult and injury to which adolescents may be quite sensitive. One's beauty is of God, and being harmed by others injures their dignity, not one's own, for they are betraying their nobility as creatures who image God.

Redemption

Judaism and Christianity both teach redemption, but mean different things by it. Judaism's doctrine is political and derives from the liberation of Israel from Egyptian bondage, whereas Christianity's doctrine is personal and refers to salvation from the consequences of sin. In this brief compass I will offer a few words on the Christian doctrine.

Adolescence is an emotionally fragile time. Youngsters experience rejection and see their peers suffer it in various forms. Feelings of inadequacy, ugliness, clumsiness, and unlovableness are not uncommon and may be exaggerated as increased self-consciousness makes embarrassment a new feeling to cope with. The Christian doctrine of salvation is designed to address just such feelings.

The Christian way of putting it is to acknowledge that these feelings are real because inadequacy and failure are real. We are not able to be all that we wish we were. We disappoint others and even hurt those we love. The Christian point is that God's love for us is bigger than our failings. It is displayed in his taking on all our weaknesses by becoming one of us as Jesus Christ and even undergoing death on a cross to show that he is willing to suffer and sacrifice himself for our sake. God enters our suffering and understands it completely, even taking it upon himself. God is our most trustworthy companion, who loves us and gives himself for us no matter how clumsy a failure we are or experience ourselves to be. Those who experience God's love and companionship as comforting and healing have a buffer against the changes and chances of this life that we come to know as fragile and unpredictable, and ourselves as prone to desolation when we cannot make right what is wrong.

The Christian doctrine of salvation assumes a strong superego and sense of guilt and remorse, qualities that I have suggested are fading as a morally coherent world fades. The doctrine of salvation may thus appear to be obsolete—an answer in search of a problem. If there is no sin there is no need for salvation. Ironically, perhaps the answer to a problem that our culture no longer experiences can be a gateway to recovering the salutariness of the doctrine of sin: humility.

Baptism

Baptism is the central Christian rite of initiation. In and through it one formally and publicly comes to belong fundamentally and irrevocably to God and no other master. It is the orienting identity of one's life, trumping nationality, gender, and race. Other traditions have analogous defining rituals. Baptism directly counters the pathogen of anomie caused by the loss of the past and of community. While the doctrine of creation locates one in relation to God and the world, baptism further specifies those relations with regard to the doctrine of the triune God that is Christianity's distinctive reading of theism.[4]

There are many theologies of baptism. Here is a trinitarian one. Traditional Christian teaching is that the Holy Spirit is the agent in baptism. God gives his own holiness to the baptisand, granting her himself. Further, in the New Testament, Paul teaches that baptism is into the death of Christ, so that it joins one to that act of nobility and self-giving on the part of God the Son. For one already created in the divine image, being united to Christ through the Spirit is to be united with the fullness of the triune God.

Understood in this way, being a Christian is not becoming a member of a club of those whom God especially loves, but one who participates in God's plan for the redemption of the world. Adolescents belong to various groups that provide guidance and orientation through the vicissitudes of high school and college. Clubs, teams, friendship cliques, and so on provide islands of security in the midst of continual change. Yet at the end of these school years, all these relationships will abruptly end and the youngster will have to start all over, to make it happen again. Even if high schoolers are relieved to be graduated from a bad experience, beginning a new school or being thrown on the job market will be daunting. Whether high school was a good or a bad experience is irrelevant. They will still have to "reinvent" themselves, as the current rhetoric has it. Yet this phrase itself gives hope, for we take ourselves with us wherever we go. The idea that God goes forth with us wherever the next chapter of life may lead may be a far greater source of hope than having only ourselves to rely upon.

The identity imparted in baptism, by contrast, is not subject to such disruption and never has to be reconstituted. Belonging to the team falls apart after graduation, but belonging to God is indelibly who one is. It can never be undone, taken away, or fail to be present. No sin or suffering can harm that noble identity and purpose to which one is called by simple baptism. Participating in the life of God for the redemption of the world is the highest status in life that can be achieved. Worldly honors and rewards, as well as failures and humiliations, fade in comparison.

Baptism is thus an antidote to the collapse of reality implied by postmodern fragmentation with its concomitant loss of self. Baptismal identity is ballast in the face of the need to reinvent oneself when a family change, such as death, divorce, remarriage, or family relocation (which is far more common than even a few years ago), dislodges childhood security.

Foot Washing

The Gospel of John reports that on the night before he died, Jesus washed the feet of his friends and followers. In the dry, dusty climate of Palestine, the washing of feet was a form of hospitality. Servants brought water for guests to clean their feet. When Jesus washed his disciples' feet he dramatically reversed standard cultural protocol. The leader served the led. The notion of servant leadership that Jesus created with this dramatic act has become a focus of interest of late, although the practice of foot washing has been badly neglected in most Christian traditions.

Washing other people's feet and even kissing them, as the woman in Luke 7 does after washing and anointing Jesus' feet, is a practice that is a direct antidote to the loss of moral clarity discussed earlier. The moral imperative implied by this practice is to serve others. For adolescents caught up in their private struggles, washing dirty feet and having one's dirty feet washed is a mighty lesson in humility, and a reminder of our dependence on others. The culture gives very different messages about the nature and responsibilities of leadership. Where else will adolescents learn that to lead is to serve those with smelly feet, rather than exert themselves for their own glory? Foot washing conveys an identity that authenticates the claims others make on one's time and energy. No words need be spoken; actions speak louder. Still, it may be helpful for adolescents to process the experience and think through the implications of being a person who makes himself the servant of others, and makes himself vulnerable as he exposes his smelly and perhaps misshapen feet to the gaze of others.

I have argued that formation or *paideia* is a better way to think about the theological identity of children and adolescents than is development. Formation now takes place in a dyspaideusic culture whose cultural pathogens easily malform the soul unless other more spiritually healthful factors counter them. The suggestion is that theological traditions with ancient heritages are best suited to this task.

Consequently, I have argued for theological formation through the Christian doctrines of creation and redemption, as well as the practices of baptism and foot washing, as morally and psychologically healthy antidotes to the cultural pathogens of loss of the past, loss of skills of care and loyalty, loss of moral clarity, and loss of a sense of reality. It will not do simply to try to shield the young from pathogenic influences. Positive alternatives must be readily present and articulated in order to captivate the passions of the young so that their considerable energies may be employed for their own well-being and that of others.

Notes

1. The use of the word *theological* in place of *spiritual* is meant to convey the conviction that that aspect of life of which we speak here does not take place in institutional vacuums but rather within discrete religious heritages most of which articulate a vision of divinity, *theos,* in relation to which the spiritual life of individuals is oriented.
2. Feminism has sensitized theologians to this question to some degree.

3. Although Europe was never universally Christian—Jews were always present—Christianity dominated the culture until the seventeenth century.

4. The Christian doctrine is that the one God is distinguished as Father, Son, and Holy Spirit.

References

Erikson, Erik H. 1963. *Childhood and society.* New York: Norton.

Foucault, Michel. 1976. *The history of sexuality: An introduction.* New York: Vintage.

———. 1977a. *Discipline and punish.* New York: Random House.

———. 1977b. *Power/Knowledge: Selected interviews and other writings, 1972–1977.* New York: Pantheon.

Fowler, James W. 1981. *Stages of faith: The psychology of human development and the quest for meaning.* San Francisco: Harper & Row.

Freud, Sigmund. 1927. *The ego and the id.* London: Hogarth Press and the Institute of Psychoanalysis.

———. [1905] 1962. *Three essays on the theory of sexuality.* New York: Avon.

Golding, William. 1955. *Lord of the flies.* New York: Coward-McCann.

Jaeger, Werner. 1944. *Paideia: The ideals of Greek culture.* Oxford: Blackwell.

Kohlberg, Lawrence. 1958. *The development of modes of moral thinking and choice in the years 10 to 16.* Chicago: n.p.

Locke, John. 1989. *Some thoughts concerning education.* The Clarendon edition of the works of John Locke, edited by John W. Yolton and Jean S. Yolton. Oxford: Oxford University Press.

Rousseau, Jean-Jacques. 1974. *Émile.* London: J. M. Dent; Rutland, Vt.: Charles E. Tuttle.

———.1992. *Discourse on the origin and foundations of inequality among men.* In *The collected writings of Rousseau,* edited by Roger D. Masters and Christopher Kelly, vol. 3, 1–95. Hanover, N.H.: University Press of New England.

CHAPTER 35

Resistance and Resilience: Cultivating Christian Spiritual Practices among Brazilian Children and Youth

Débora Barbosa Agra Junker

When we are confronted by inequality and injustice, it is possible to perceive that it is children who suffer the most significant impact of the social and economic systems that generate poverty, marginalization, and exclusion. In a starving world of material and spiritual goods, poverty dominates lives and assumes many faces and expressions. The poor, who can be found anywhere from Paris to New York, from Dhaka to São Paulo, have the same hungry bellies, have the same wounded bodies, suffer from the same diseases and disabilities, and are victims of social prejudice.

As human beings in this disturbed world, we are overwhelmed by social, economic, political, and cultural problems that surround us as a result of discrimination and prejudice, that detract from and diminish our dignity as humans beings and distort in each of us God's image. As Christians who seek to be truthful to God's call, we cannot escape from this dramatic reality.

As a response to this painful situation, we are called to reflect critically on our responsibility as human beings and as Christians. God's identification with the poor calls us to work for justice in solidarity with all who are the most vulnerable in our society. When we encounter the poor, the oppressed, and the defenseless, we are in touch with God and our own vulnerability. The encounter with the needy provides a confrontation with our own limitations. However, more than sympathy is required in reflecting on this matter. To bring about real transformation necessitates constancy and concrete action based on social analysis and commitment. Old Testament professor Walter Brueggemann affirms that justice requires a clear critique and alternative way to reorder society and active intervention designed to transform social power:

> [A]n important educational task, with both adults and children, is to provide some of the awareness and tools for social criticism so that we may begin to think systemically both about the distortions that do us in, and the alternatives that are resonant with our faith. Unless we are equipped for such social analysis, we end up with occasional and isolated acts of social

indignation but without the power or imagination for the long haul, which is necessary if there is to be serious social transformation. (Brueggemann, Parks, and Groome 1986, 9)

The concept of justice played a fundamental role for the prophets in ancient Israel, as well as in Jewish and Christian traditions. According to Abraham Joshua Heschel (1962, 201), the biblical word *mishpat* means "justice" (norm, legal right, laws), and it indicates a type of action. The word *tsedakah* means righteousness, a quality beyond justice, implying benevolence, kindness, and generosity. Different from *justice,* which has a strict meaning, *righteousness* indicates a quality of a person, and it is associated with a "burning compassion for the oppressed." Although he recognizes such a difference, Heschel does not intend to separate the concepts. For him, divine justice involves God's mercy and compassion. "Justice, then, is an interpersonal relationship, implying both claim and responsibility. . . . The sense of justice is outgoing, transitive, inclusive" (204).

In the biblical sense, compassion for the oppressed requires a critical understanding of reality. God is a compassionate God who cares for the vulnerable, for those who hunger for justice. Children and youth therefore are a source of God's care. Justice without love may demonstrate human virtue, but it does not imply opening the way for reconciliation and redemption.

As God's people, we are called to actively bring justice and peace to humankind. There are abundant needs around us to be satisfied, and in order to serve them, each of us must be involved, working to prevent injustice. Furthermore, if we want to change society, we must start with children and youth, helping them in their difficulties and providing equal opportunities to participate in the construction of a new kind of society. We have not, however, treated children and youth with justice, and in not doing so, we have been unfaithful to a loving God.

The Situation for Children and Adolescents in Brazil

The current economic crisis that has hit countries around the world has had a great impact in Latin America, where the gap between rich and poor has intensified poverty and misery. According to United Nations Children's Fund (UNICEF) statistics,

> 30 percent of children born in 2000 will suffer from malnutrition in their first five years of life; 26 percent will not be immunized against the basic childhood diseases; 19 percent and 40 percent, respectively, will lack access to safe drinking water and adequate sanitation; and 17 percent will never attend school. In developing countries, one of every four children lives in abject poverty in a family with an income of less than one dollar a day.

Maria Conde, regional adviser with UNICEF, said that in Latin America and the Caribbean, 114 million children live in poverty and suffer from malnutrition, illiteracy, violence, and sexual and labor exploitation.

Although Brazil has great natural resources, social differences and economic instability generate endless problems such as violence in its different forms. With an estimated 170 million inhabitants, the country has great challenges for continued advocacy on behalf of children and youth, the most defenseless citizens. Even though the mortality rate in Brazil has fallen, 54 million people live below the poverty line and 1.1 million children and adolescents ages twelve to seventeen are still unable to read and write. Today's reality of unplanned growth in urban areas seems unsustainable, and the lower classes are the ones who are most affected by this situation. The ones who remain excluded and crowded into the slums, the so-called *favelas,* often lack basic amenities such as access to clean water, electricity, and sanitation services. In this environment, children are readily vulnerable to child prostitution rings, diseases, exploitative labor practices, drug trafficking, and other dangers. Most of those children and youth experience violence in their own family. Volunteers who work with street children report that sometimes children who live in such conditions take to the streets because they feel safer there than with their own families. These workers know children whose mothers send their daughters to the street to sell their bodies to bring the family income as well as children who are sexually abused by their stepfathers. This reminds us that it is not enough to take children off the streets and send them back to their homes; we must encourage them to develop a spirit of resistance to fight for their rights as human beings and at the same time take responsibility for their future. For this reason, it is necessary to build a web of mutual support through which families will be instructed to take care of their children in a way that leaves no room for despair as they face life's troubles. In such situations, the work of conscientization, as conceived by the Brazilian educator and social theorist Paulo Freire (1921–97), an ongoing process of empowerment through which a person reaches new levels of awareness in order to transform oppressive and unjust reality, is necessary for both parents and children. They need to understand that things go wrong, but that their attitude can change the flow of their lives for the better. When children have other reference points, they gain the confidence to make better decisions.

Along with today's context and circumstances, it is important to recall the year of 1989, when the Brazilian National Congress saw the force of children and teenagers victimized by social exclusion and claimed their rights before the eyes of politicians and Brazilian society. At that time, disadvantaged children and youth were part of an emerging nationwide social movement for the rights of children, joined by community members, church people, minority groups, nongovernmental organizations, politicians, and some government agencies. The teamwork done by those sectors raised children's issues as national priorities on the political agenda, bringing hope in the midst of despair.

Brazilian children's rights legislation, Estatuto da Criança e Adolescente, or ECA (Statute on Children and Adolescents), was signed into law in July 13, 1990. As a national policy and legislation on young people's rights, the ECA ratifies the principles set forth in the 1989 United Nations Convention on the Rights of the Child, giving Brazilian society a new perspective by which to understand children and adolescents as citizens with rights who deserve our affection and care.

Efforts like these have the power to inspire and sustain our work as we continue to construct and shape a more peaceful and enjoyable world for our children. Certainly, the ECA has helped Brazilian society in this process, as well as the church in seeing its mission as extending beyond the security and comfort of its interior walls. Undoubtedly, the faith community faces a challenge, but it also has a contribution to make as its members engage with disadvantaged children, learning about them, their families, and their life situation. The child who accepts being treated as a sexual object can change this perception by seeing and loving herself as a child of God, reconstructing God's image in herself. After learning about disadvantaged children and adolescents, the community is better equipped to offer alternatives as they think about their rights and spirituality without putting the two in different compartments. In this framework, a faith community can provide a safe space where children can share their stories and have the opportunity to enjoy life while they learn new skills. As part of this new big family, they develop a sense of belonging through relationships of trust and love.

We know, however, that there is much more to be done. Transforming laws into concrete actions requires deliberate effort and the participation of as many people as possible to achieve consistency and force change in social structures. In this context, the church appears as a fundamental partner to organize and support actions and programs that work to sponsor initiatives affecting children and adolescents.

The Methodist Church's Perspective Regarding Children and Youth

Methodism and the Wesleyan heritage are infused with a preoccupation with education. The Methodist movement, born in England at Lincoln College, Oxford, is known by its vocation to teach. After the Industrial Revolution of the late eighteenth and nineteenth centuries, England was experiencing the consequences of rapid urban development. Disease, malnutrition, crime, inadequate sanitation, uncontrolled gambling and drinking, and terrible housing conditions were rampant.

Since schools were restricted to the few families who could afford them, many, many children were left to spend their days in city streets and sweatshops. John Wesley's concerns were to reach out to those victims of socioeconomic hardship and to be proactive in trying to provide for children's health, welfare, and education. He wanted schools with high-quality education and steeped in Christian values. Wesley tried to address the situation concretely in order to rescue people's dignity before God.

According to Richard Heitzenrater (2003, 297), Wesley was concerned about children, especially the children of poor families. He often visited orphanages, prisons, schools, and poor homes to check on children's conditions. He collected money, food, and clothing to distribute to families. He also established medical clinics, lending programs, and subsidized housing. From its beginning, Methodism was concerned with both theology and praxis and had as its pillars personal religion and social responsibility.

Following in the steps of its founder, the Brazilian Methodist Church is committed to living out the Christian vocation of justice for all persons. The church has in many ways joined the effort to fight against social injustice, playing an active role in national and local projects that advocate on behalf of children and youth. Brazilian Methodists affirm their Christian responsibility to the integral well-being of people, understanding the social mission of the church as the human response to God's faithfulness.

The Methodist Church of Brazil, through its General Conference, has officially stressed the importance of seeing children and youth as priorities for all its programs and as citizens of God's reign. To improve its prophetic action, the church has more than five hundred programs designed to assist low-income children. Through its mission, the church has invited laypeople, pastors, and educators to enable and empower children and youth to become active on their own behalf as they seek to live fully in faith and God's call to mission.

Several documents and projects attest to the Methodist commitment to children, especially the poor. In a *Carta Pastoral* (Pastoral letter) for 2004–5 (bishop document for 2004–2005, 36), the bishops made the following statement:

> Let children be a priority in the action of the Church: that in local activities children are welcomed as agents of the mission; that a deep ardor in missionary action is raised to favor Church children and all children who suffer any kind of discrimination and injustice. Let infant baptism be celebrated with great pleasure. Let children be always welcomed at the Lord's table. Let them be nurtured in the faith and educated to affirm the baptismal covenant. Let the Church be one with those who are organized in the society to protect children and adolescents. Let pastors dedicate more time to children. Let the Church study the Child's Pastoral.

Pastoral da Criança (Child Pastoral) is another relevant document addressing children's concerns (Colégio Episcopal de Igreja Metodista 2002). The bishops of the Brazilian Methodist Church wrote this pastoral to orient the action of Methodist people regarding children and youth from a biblical and theological viewpoint. The heart of this pastoral is the understanding of children as paradigmatic of the realm of God. Therefore, the community has the responsibility to provide spaces where children and youth can develop their intellectual and spiritual capacities and gifts to become agents of transformation. Their contributions, as active participants, are a vital element in the dynamism of the community's life.

Engaged Nurturing Practices: Envisioning a Spirituality of Resistance

Taking into account the situation revealed by the previously discussed statistics, one could infer that to be a child or adolescent in Latin America, one needs to learn how to confront social contradictions and challenge injustice and oppression. Children and youth living in an inhospitable world must develop coping skills to strengthen and foster their inner ability to live under stressful conditions. To acquire those skills, two elements are imperative. First, to fully and creatively support children and adolescents in resisting all kinds of oppression, Christian leaders must become much more sophisticated in their understanding of the macroeconomic systems of injustice that pervade our society.

Second, through its programs and projects, the church must work on the public dimension of faith, reaching out to the children and youth who are primary victims of street trade, prostitution, drug trafficking, hunger, homelessness, and disease, to mention a few. These children and adolescents need an educational process through which they can gain new insights into dealing with these threats. They need to build strong character without giving up their dreams, getting depressed, or being seduced into inappropriate ways of surviving in their environment.

The church has an important role to play in facilitating the learning experience of these youth by considering the educational process not as an individual enterprise but as a communal endeavor embedded in and profoundly affected by cultural context.

In this regard, the church must see itself as a place of support for these young people, and not a hiding place—a sanctuary—where participants find security while they forget about the world outside. When community members become aware of the horrible events that strip away human dignity, solidarity will find much more fertile soil and will generate more effective and tangible support systems. As a result, Christian life is validated by praxis, by loving God, our neighbors, and ourselves as we denounce injustices and proclaim the good news. To achieve those goals we need to facilitate an educational process that takes into account each human being in his or her wholeness. Heschel (1966) affirms:

> To educate means to cultivate the soul, not only the mind. You cultivate the soul by cultivating empathy and reverence for others, by calling attention to the grandeur, the mystery of all being, to the holy dimension of human existence by teaching how to relate the common to the spiritual. The soul is discovered in response, in acts of transcending the self, in the awareness of ends that surpass one's interest and needs. (54)

As a practical approach to accomplishing this teaching-learning process of nurturing inner spirituality, I propose a "spirituality of resistance" that affirms the belief that the spiritual dimension in the lives of children and youth can provide support and instill resilience in times of despair.

James Poling (1996) analyzes the evil present in societal structures and shows how victims develop an inner ability to overcome those situations by cultivating, in different ways, a spirituality of resistance. According to him, the struggles of resistance help one avoid falling into hopelessness. In the midst of suffering, those who have resisted evil and survived have found that God's love is stronger than the power of evil. Poling defines resistance to evil as "a form of liberated and critical consciousness that enables persons or groups to stand against evil in silence, language, and action" (103). According to him, "a spirituality of resistance requires conversion of the inner imagination so that identity is located in the history of resistance to evil rather than in oppressive structures" (175).

This is a fundamental statement if we think about building in children and youth a strong identity. In a society pummeled by advertisements that sell "perfect bodies" and dictate what we should buy and how we should look, certainly children and adolescents need to find their identity in their ability to resist everything that alienates them.

Poling (1996) identifies Jesus as a "religious resister," who confronts the oppressive power structures of his time:

> Jesus as religious resister reveals authentic humanity in the face of massive dehumanizing evils such as slavery, racism, and patriarchy. We recognize the holiness of the communities of resistance because they are contemporary forms of Jesus' ongoing resistance to evil. (159)

Poling does not relate Jesus' point of view regarding children, but we certainly can affirm that Jesus also resisted the prevailing view of children in his time. Jesus surprises his disciples and the crowd when he places the child in their midst and tells them that to be like a child is the requirement for entering God's realm: "Whoever receives one of these children in my name," he said, "receives me" (Mark 9:37). Later, in Mark 10:14, he says: "Let the children come to me, do not hinder them; for to such belongs the kingdom of God." In this same episode, Jesus confronts and resists the disciples' attitude when he says, "whoever does not accept the kingdom of God like a child will never enter it" (Mark 10:15).

Jesus' special concern for children is also shown when he resists against the death of the young daughter of Jairus (Mark 5:22–41) or when he resists against the affliction that has touched a boy (Mark 9:25–27). Thus, among many assumptions one can make from Jesus' ministry with children is that Jesus perceives the child as capable of feeling God's presence and having meaningful spiritual experiences. From Jesus' example of confidence in children's ability to resist evil in their lives, we are invited to emulate him.

Taking the preceding statements into consideration, I propose that if we give children and adolescents space to grow as spiritual resisters, as they confront ruthless reality, we may come to see them as stronger individuals who have the skills to overcome evil in our world. By nurturing their inner spirituality, we will model a compassionate experience of life instead of a spirit of competition and fear. To fashion a spirituality of resistance from the perspective of children and youth, some principles need to be taken into account. Each of us must strive to:

1. Help children and youth name the evil in their experience through sharing their life stories. Those who have been abused, rejected, exposed to drugs, and subjected to prejudice need safe spaces in which to tell their stories and those of their families. Having others understand the context of where they come from will help children and adolescents think about actions they can take to change the way things are;
2. Help children and adolescents develop a critical consciousness so that they will become proactive on their own behalf;
3. Be aware of the uniqueness and gifts of all human beings and their potential to grow, such as when children discover the joy of learning new skills, thereby developing inner strength and a sense of belonging that will propel them forward;
4. Offer space for sharing joys and concerns (informal meetings, informal conversations, worship times);
5. Build unity through dialogue in order to awaken children's and adolescents' self-esteem, as well as their awareness of their rights and responsibilities as citizens;
6. Respect individual and collective needs (children and adolescents must understand and accept their time and pace for doing things and appreciate other people's needs);
7. Help children and adolescents experience the healing power of art through self-expression (music, dance, song, play, creative writing); and

8. Recognize that children's and adolescents' emergent self-confidence will inspire them to new discoveries of different areas of competence.

From the perspective of community, it is necessary to provide moments of significant experiences through which all children, regardless of age, will achieve a spirituality of resistance. As families and community of faith, we are invited to create with children and adolescents rituals to express and celebrate our hopes, surprises, and gratitude. When we congregate as brothers and sisters to share in the life of Christ, we celebrate the joy of being with each other, but we also need to set aside times when we can be together to lament, to mourn, to doubt, to question, and to name the atrocities perpetrated in the world. Such moments can be a communal effort in which the adults and caregivers will facilitate and organize sharing moments that might be full of silence, tears, or shouts. Surely, we need family and community rituals that can bring forth the agonies, sometimes hidden, sometimes unhealed. We all need rituals to help us recognize the painful experiences of loss, grief, sickness, guilt, and frustration. When we acknowledge, in our worship, times of joy and times of sorrow, we prepare ourselves to be transformed.

To further this process, educators can lead children and youth to write liturgies, litanies, songs, poems, and prayers that express their feelings. One of these experiences has happened with children of a nearby poor community through a music program developed with them. They participate in workshops and later they are invited to create their own songs, liturgies, and dances under the guidance of educators. When they sing during worship, we can sense the joy and energy coming from each of them as they recognize that they have found a source of power to resist the evil in their lives.

I would like to mention another visible example of a spirituality of resistance. It refers to a social project launched by the Brazilian Methodist Church in 2000, *Projeto Sombra e Água Fresca* (Shade and Fresh Water Project) (Moraes 2000). The project seeks to assist children and youth at risk, to offer them opportunities to become responsible members of a family and society. The goal of the project is to contribute to the integral development of children and adolescents, targeting specific areas such as after-school activities; citizenship; sports and recreational activities; culture and art; health; and basic Christian values. This project helps increase self-esteem by fostering a process of healing as participants develop many abilities in different areas. The children and adolescents involved in the project have increased their cognitive skills as they demonstrate increased ability to solve problems, communicate, and relate to others. Some of them have chosen to become part of the faith community, understanding that their integral growth has a spiritual aspect and is not limited to their intellectual and physical development. Some who participated as students have gone on to become teachers helping newcomers.

The experiences related previously have the power to raise children's self-esteem while allowing them to create a new history of their lives from a new context. When they find new areas of competency in their lives, they begin to see themselves with fresh identities and to understand themselves as citizens who can think critically about their lives.

Inspired in the teaching of Jesus, we are called to enlarge the borders of our congregations, resignifying and not just reaffirming our commitment with every child and youth, those who belong to the community and those who do not. I believe that by working in these areas of their lives, children and adolescents will be able to envision a better future for themselves. By resisting the evil in their present time, they come to know that wounds can be healed. This process doesn't happen without external support. It is clear from the forgoing examples that success is a result of family participation. Families in all shapes are important because they bring to the meetings different needs, stories, and expectations. By working together on each problem, they can find a better way to solve them. Thus, it is imperative that everybody be involved in the search for common benefits. If children and youth develop the necessary skills, while at the same time receiving love and Christian guidance, they will be able to develop a sense of self-worthiness.

As Christian educators, our commitment is to perceive every child as our child, meaning that we perceive each child as God's creation. Experiencing such a dimension of God's love, we are able to cross boundaries, to move toward others, and together to reach out for the needs of the society from a broader perspective. Those experiences, tensions, and conflicts create a place for dialogue, to care for others, to nurture, and to exercise the ethic of love, making creative connections, and thus articulating solutions inspired by the Spirit of God with wisdom and discernment.

After all, any process of transformation takes more than words to materialize. It implies tangible projects that act justly by doing, love tenderly by committing, and walk humbly by embracing others who want to participate in this journey.

References

Brueggemann, Walter, Sharon Parks, and Thomas Groome. 1986. *To act justly, love tenderly, walk humbly: An agenda for ministers.* Mahwah, N.J.: Paulist Press.

Colégio Episcopal da Igreja Metodista. 2002. Pastoral da Criança. *Biblioteca Vida e Missão, Pastorais no. 11.* São Paulo: Editora Cedro.

Heitzenrater, Richard. 2003. Santidade e ignorância esplêndida: Wesley e a educação. *Revista de Educação do COGEIME* 22:9–32.

Heschel, Abraham Joshua. 1962. *The prophets.* New York: Harper and Row.

———. 1966. *The insecurity of freedom.* Philadelphia: Jewish Publication Society of America.

Moraes, Stanley de Silva. 2000. *A criança brasileira em números* (Brazilian Child in Numbers). 16 Recriar Projeto Sombra e Aacutegua Fresca. São Paulo: Coordenação Nacional de Ação Docente.

Poling, James. 1996. *Deliver us from evil: Resisting racial and gender oppression.* Minneapolis, Minn.: Fortress Press.

www.unicef.org/media/media_9475.html (accessed 08/10/2004).

CHAPTER 36

Spiritual Economies of Childhood: Christian Perspectives on Global Market Forces and Young People's Spirituality

Joyce Ann Mercer

Jesus' words that a person cannot serve both God and money (cf. Matthew 6:24) often are incorrectly understood by Christians to mean that matters of the spiritual life and economics should exist in two separate realms. Similarly, many eschew all associations between children and economics, influenced by the dominance of a privileged (and Northern Hemisphere) notion of childhood and youth as a protected, innocent space that is best kept separate from the polluting influences of market culture and money matters. In this chapter I step directly into the connections between economics, spirituality, and young people to address the question of how economic forces in the current context of globalized capitalism impact the spiritualities of children and youth, as viewed through the lens of a Christian faith perspective. Here I use the term *spiritual* to refer to young people's ways of meaning making (the larger framework, or the narrative and symbolic means by which they make sense of their worlds and experiences); their relationships with others and with the sacred; how young people experience the limits and possibilities for their own purposive, agentic action in their worlds; and their capacities for self-transcendence. Economic forces operate as "spiritual economics" upon young people's lives, shaping their identities, while they also determine the concrete-material and ideological conditions under which particular young people form relationships, engage in labor and attribute meaning to their labor, and have opportunities to seek and cultivate connections with the divine.

No single voice exists within Christianity concerning economic issues and the forces of materialism upon the lives and spiritualities of young people. For example, some persons assert a "doctrine of Christian materialism," holding that capitalism's dominance and individual material wealth both comprise evidence of divine favor. Highly popular in North America, Bruce Wilkerson's *The Prayer of Jabez: Breaking through to the Blessed Life* (2000) advocates for such a "prosperity gospel" equating affluence with the kind of abundant living God promises to believers in Scripture. Michael Novak (1982, 1996), writing from a scholarly Roman Catholic perspective, presents a neoconservative and heroic view of capitalism's relationship to Christian faith as he argues that Christians should embrace the benefits of capitalism, the accomplishments of which are compatible with the social goals of Christian faith. Schneider (2002), in a revision of an earlier work titled *Godly Materialism: Rethinking Money and Possessions* (1994), parallels contemporary North American affluence with the Garden of Eden and the promised land, as he argues that wealth is a spiritual blessing.

Other Christians, as I have mentioned, consider faith and economics to exist in separate spheres, as is suggested in the title of a volume by Mennonite writer John Haltemann (1995), *The Clashing Worlds of Economics and Faith* (see also Daniel 2003). The notion that money, if not evil itself, at least constitutes "the root of all evil," and therefore should be kept separate from matters of religious life, is one attitude within Christian traditions in relation to economics (cf. McMillan 1987; Sheils and Wood 1987).

In explicit contrast to such views, my approach stands rooted in a feminist Christian theology of liberation that understands economic matters as matters of justice and therefore necessarily as matters of faith and the spiritual life (cf. Andolsen 1998; Bounds, Brubaker, and Hobgood 1999; Couture 1991, 2003). My interest in these matters and the social location informing my writing comes from being a scholar and practitioner of the Christian faith, a woman and mother, and one who has lived and worked in contexts where children and others are afflicted by the oppressive elements of economic systems (principally the Philippines and urban poor neighborhoods in the United States)—all experiences that lead me to hold deep commitments to work on behalf of the flourishing of children and youth.

Tales of Three Children

In Payatas, an area on the edge of metropolitan Manila (Philippines) where the city dumps some ten thousand tons of garbage each day, thousands of the city's poorest people make their homes on a literal mountain of garbage that reaches seven stories high. Whole families make their living picking through the newest of the garbage for items that can be resold or scraps that can be recycled for money. Five-year-old Eva joins her family in this scavenger work. Eva's older sister and mother were among hundreds of people in Payatas who lost their lives or spent hours buried alive under the garbage when the mountain collapsed after heavy rains in July 2000. Still, in spite of such danger Eva and the other children of Payatas have little day-to-day recourse for changing their situations, and the mountainous dump remains their only source of survival.

Garage scavengers are not the only child workers in Payatas, however. Down at the base of the garbage mountain a small group of children and youth sit in sweltering heat, hand-stitching baseball gloves in a single-room shelter made of concrete blocks. The gloves' leather bears the imprint of a well-known U.S. sports equipment company, and a young man named Ruben, who looks about twelve years old, tells me that he will be paid eight pesos per glove for his labor. If he works all day, he can complete five or six gloves, earning the equivalent of around one U.S. dollar for his day's labor. The work is boring, and he would prefer to go to school more regularly, but his work is critical for the support of his family. He laughs when I ask him if he owns a baseball glove. "Maybe someday, like on TV," he says. "Anyway, there is no time or space to play baseball here."

Halfway around the world, in Petersburg, Virginia, a nine-year-old boy named Austin goes with his dad to the nearby Wal-Mart store to buy his first "real" baseball glove. Austin has been saving his money for several weeks, carefully setting a portion aside from his weekly allowance of ten dollars, to accumulate the fifteen needed for his purchase. Austin already owns his own baseball bat and a bucket of balls with which he enjoys holding "batting practice" with his dad. He also possesses hats and jerseys bearing the logos of several of his favorite professional baseball teams, two different baseball video games and the equipment on which to play them, and a collection of baseball-related videos. His interest in baseball is relatively new, starting about six months ago when he attended a game with a friend. Last year at this time, Austin was passionate about his electric train and model railroad set, which now sits relegated to a back corner of his room and receives little attention. Austin's mother plans to surprise him at Christmas with new bedroom decorations—a bedspread, beanbag chair, and rug—all having a baseball theme, replacing the train theme that is now four years old and allegedly too young for Austin.

Austin and his dad arrive at the store after the end of his school day. They both exclaim about how expensive baseball gloves are these days, but even though they find one on sale for less than twenty dollars, they opt to purchase a more expensive glove (Austin's dad chips in the difference) in order to have a desirable sports company logo on the glove. Nothing about the glove Austin purchases, including its price, contains any hint of Ruben laboring in a hot concrete room at the edge of a garbage mountain in the Philippines. And yet, Austin's ability to purchase his baseball glove at a discounted price is tied to the work done by Ruben, which is the result of transnational corporate decision making to "outsource" labor on its products to countries beyond the borders of the United States that do not have the kinds of child labor laws and protections concerning working conditions that allow the company to keep costs down and profits up.

THE RESHAPING OF CHILDHOOD SPIRITUALITY WITHIN A GLOBAL MARKET ECONOMY

The children and youth in these examples all participate, albeit from vastly different positions, in an economic system of late globalized capitalism that shapes their spiritual lives. Austin, living in a middle-class Euro-American household in the United States, participates in a highly consumer-oriented society that has actively formed him from birth, through cultural forces of advertising and various other social practices organized around the consumption of goods, into a thoroughly consumerist identity. Each narrow interval of his childhood years invites the purchase of different commodities, as market forces effectively school children and their parents in a pedagogy of consumption, dividing childhood into age-segmented marketing niches, with new products marking the transition across the years. Consumptive practices dominate his experiences, desires, and consciousness. A living example of what analyst David Harvey refers to as "structured coherences" between economic transitions in the current globalized capitalist economy and the cultural forms of postmodernity, Austin's constant quest for novelty and his use of commodity acquisition and display as a primary mode of form-ing social relationships with others (e.g., he and his father relate around the purchase of the glove; he forms instant connections with peers on the playground based upon their wearing a common product logo on their sports shoes) come to seem like natural and necessary features of childhood rather than constructions of market forces that pro-mote market interests.

Ruben interacts with the same economic system, but from a vastly different posi-tion as an impoverished laborer in the "Two-Thirds World" whose role in the system of globalized market forces is that of the production of goods for other (primarily "First World") children to consume. The global marketing of consumer goods operates to create similar desires in Ruben as those expressed by Austin, but upon which Ruben may never be able to act with purchasing power, given the material limits of his con-text. Businesses willing to exploit the fact that there are no laws regulating Ruben's wages, hours, or working conditions, along with the reality of poverty that drives him to perform such work for low wages under dehumanizing conditions, will profit con-siderably from the connection between Ruben's labor and Austin's materialism. At the same time, Ruben's work has both material and social significance in his context, as he understands his importance to his family's economy.

And Eva, the most invisible of these three children, is situated by this system of gross inequalities as one who is just as disposable as the mountain of garbage where she ekes out an existence from the waste generated by Manila's fancy hotels and businesses. Eva's lack of recourse to any other mode of survival becomes the strange justification for an elaborately organized system of patronage, corruption, and exchange of capital that places the easy, environmentally hazardous, disposal of garbage over the human dignity, survival, and well-being of Manila's poorest children and youth. Living on the edge of existence, the economic forces that produce her identity and her living context set severe limits upon her relationships, forms of agency, and opportunities for conscious-ness of the sacred in life.

With these examples, I am not suggesting that all children in the Philippines expe-rience the same kind of poverty known by Ruben and Eva. Nor do I intend a totalizing understanding of children in North America as equally materially privileged across all distinctions of race, social class, and gender. In telling the stories of Ruben, Eva, and Austin, I mean to problematize the notions of childhood and the impact of global eco-nomic systems on spirituality posed by *each* of them, in relation to Christian theologi-cal perspectives on economic forces and young people. In different ways, each of these children's identities, social relations, sense of purpose/agency, and awareness of the sacred has been defined by economic forces that order their lives.

At the same time, through the stories of these three children I also intend to prob-lematize an unfortunate stereotypical assumption in one strand of Christian economic thought. That strand of thought interprets Jesus' words, "Blessed are the poor" (Matthew 5; Luke 6) to mean that persons in poverty are "more spiritual" or are hap-pier because they have fewer possessions. Rather, in claiming that economics impacts the spirituality of children, I refer to the ways in which the material conditions and eco-nomic class positioning of children have determinative effects on multiple features of their life experiences relevant to their spiritualities. For example, Eva's extreme poverty requires most of her energy to be put toward just surviving. On the one hand, she does so within a close network of familial and nonfamilial relationships that constitute a spiritual resource in her life that many isolated middle-class North Americans might envy. Yet her ability to activate that resource becomes significantly limited in the face of malnutrition, the absence of educational opportunities, and lack of experiences with other life possibilities beyond the Payatas dump. These features shape how she makes sense of her situation (meaning making), her capacities to envision alternatives (transcendence), and the practices by which she expresses/embodies encounters with the sacred when concrete needs for physical survival so dominate her daily life.

Christian Theology, Economics, and Childhood: Four Theological Points

How does Christianity view and address materialism, consumerism, and the economic forces of contemporary globalized capitalism that influence child and adolescent spirituality? Exploring these ideas could be the subject of several books, so for reasons of space I will briefly summarize them in four main points. The first two concern how Christianity views children and youth.

THE SPECIAL ROLE OF YOUNG PEOPLE IN GOD'S REORDERING OF POWER

First, Christianity affirms young people as having a special role in their societies and faith communities, paradoxically accorded them by virtue of their relative lack of status and power. In various sacred texts in the Christian Scriptures of the Old and New Testaments of the Bible, a theme resounds that the "last shall be first" and the powerless lifted up. This theme extends to children in the Synoptic Gospels (Matthew, Mark, and Luke in the New Testament), which narrate Jesus giving importance to children, as he lifted up children and youth as among those who show the rest of the faith community the way to God (see especially Mark 9:33–37; Matthew 18:1–5; Luke 9:46–48), as when he drew a child close to him and said to his disciples, "Whoever welcomes one such child in my name welcomes me, and whoever welcomes me welcomes not only me, but the one who sent me [i.e., God]" (Mark 9:37).

In fact, in these Christian texts, children offer other disciples a key to the divine reordering of power set in motion by Jesus. The way to welcome or receive God and God's new community is through the welcoming of such children as Jesus gathered around him—children and youth who were sick, destitute, poor, the victims of colonial occupation, and without any claim to status or importance in the eyes of the world. In both a metaphorical and a concrete material sense, children and youth thus become keys to the transformation of reality that is central to the Christian message. That transformation is most often named with the symbolic language of the "kingdom of God," a term that simultaneously proclaims that all forms of human rule and power stand relativized in relation to God, and also that God's ways of "sovereignty" involve the over-turning of unjust power relations and a radically egalitarian inclusivity among all persons. Children in every society occupy the bottom rungs of power and influence, and therefore their repositioning by Jesus to such a place of significance is a powerful expression of this eschatological vision of transformation. By virtue of such a perspective on young people, Christianity would therefore be highly critical of economic systems in which children and youth were devalued or oppressed on the basis of their economic lack, vulnerability to exploitation, or diminished social status.

THE FULL HUMANITY OF CHILDREN AND YOUTH

Second, alongside this assertion that children are key among the ones through whom persons can welcome the divine, Christianity also contends that a person's worth and significance come not from his or her status in the world, as marked by rank or occupation, income level, economic productivity, or even the honor that comes from advanced age, but consist primarily in each person's being created in and bearing the *imago Dei* or image of God. That means that even young people cannot be treated as less than fully human by virtue of their low social standing, less developed physical and cognitive capacities, or other features that might mark them as "unfinished" human beings. The Christian understanding that full humanity comes from being created in God's image, rather than being an acquired characteristic that comes with attaining a certain age or stature in life, means that even the youngest persons possess this identity and status as bearers of the image of God from which their personhood derives its significance. Such a view constitutes a fundamental critique of contemporary consumerist notions of identity and status as secured through the consumption and display of commodities.

AN ETHIC OF CARE FOR THE MOST VULNERABLE

The third and fourth theological perspectives I will name focus more specifically upon economic forces per se, and yet it is interesting and significant that both of them do so within the sacred texts of the Christian tradition in a way that locates young people at the center of their ethical critiques. The third theological perspective is an ethical mandate: within Christianity, youth and children stand among those particularly entitled to receive the care and protection of the faith community, as persons among the most vulnerable of the human community by virtue of their relative dependence upon adults and their lesser access to power—including economic power. The tradition speaks of this ethic of care as the command to provide for "widows and orphans" or for the "stranger and the fatherless," that is, those who are without the support and protection of kin (see especially James 1:27; Exodus 22:22–24; Jeremiah 7:6; Zechariah 7:10).

In essence, such an ethical mandate amounts to a reformulation of the nature of kinship, away from an exclusive reliance upon biological ties to define its boundaries, toward a radically inclusive vision of the community of faith as the kinship network responsible for those who are most vulnerable and in need of care. Contemporary

Christians extend this redefinition of the boundaries of responsibility as crossing not simply biological kinship lines but also national boundaries, taking Jesus' redefinition of a neighbor as one in need (see Luke 10:29–37) to be the real criterion for the faith community's responsibility of care. Accordingly, all children and youth, but particularly poor children and youth who have no other recourse for aid, both locally and globally, are included in this ethical claim of community responsibility. By inference, children and youth whose material affluence or social location puts them in the position to extend care and protection in some form have a responsibility to do so (e.g., through the sharing of their resources or through various forms of socially responsible living), recognizing that their agency for enacting such a responsibility is more limited than that of similarly situated adults.

A CRITIQUE OF UNJUST ECONOMIC SYSTEMS

Fourth, unlike religious traditions that separate matters of material existence from the spiritual realm, Christianity asserts an understanding of human material existence, including economic life as a central issue of justice, and therefore as a matter of faith, not merely at the level of individual well-being but at the level of economic systems. This assertion that the justice (or injustice) of economic *systems* is in fact a spiritual concern can be found with Christianity's biblical-prophetic tradition, found in both Old and New Testaments of the Bible, of protest against tributary systems and economically and militarily oppressive imperial regimes. Under these regimes state agrarian policies of taxation and practices of exacting tribute from agrarian peasants to fund imperial building projects or military campaigns resulted in perpetual debt and marginal subsistence living among peasant populations. Across various historical periods represented by texts in the Hebrew Bible there appear depictions of legal codes and prophetic pronouncements calling for debt easement and the overturning of practices of families being forced into selling their land and particularly, having to sell their children as slaves in order to pay off their debt to the state (see, for example, Exodus 21–23 and Nehemiah 5, for two different types of text that focus on the issue of children's sale into slavery for debt easement). The New Testament narrates the stories of Jesus' protest against the tributary system exercised by a Jerusalem-based temple elite in the service of Roman interests.

Contemporary analogies are omnipresent in the current context of global economic relations in which First World, Northern Hemisphere nations control capital, make loans that come with heavy requirements, and enforce debt repayment that requires Two-Thirds World, Southern Hemisphere nations to give up their land to foreign landholders and sell their children into both metaphorical and literal slavery, or leave their children to go in search of work elsewhere, in order to pay off their debts and secure a living. This system keeps them in a perpetual state of economic struggle. In some nations such as the Philippines, children stay at home but their parents must leave them to enter the system of "overseas contract work" whereby parents cannot make an adequate living in their own nation and must leave their families and children for work outside the country.

According to the Christian tradition's prophetic critique of economic systems that force children into unjust labor or deprive them of parents—a systemic critique with analogies from its various biblical contexts to current global economic systems—children figure centrally among those named as the victims of injustice who have a righteous claim to make, as the ones who have the least power within the system but who are also most likely to be exploited or harmed by its excesses.

Problems Practicing What We Preach: Critiquing Christianity with Christian Theology

The preceding four theological perspectives on young people and economic forces present a strong theology of advocacy for children and an equally uncompromising critique of the effects of unjust economic forces on children as central to the faith of Christians. At the same time, however, Christians have an inconsistent record in terms of their ability to live out these four theological tenets in everyday practice. For example, although the Christian faith clearly possesses the seeds for holding children and youth in particular esteem as the ones who show all Christians the way to the new reign or community of God, many congregations in fact ignore or even exclude children from participating in their worship life and do not expect children to participate fully in the faith community beyond its educational programs. Similarly, while Christian theology's emphasis that human worth comes from God who creates all persons in the divine image contains the seeds for a view of children having inherent worth, congregations sometimes treat children as if their primary value rests in their ability to bring their adult parents into the church, or in the "social capital" they bring to the community by virtue of their presence, which makes the congregation appear more vital. Often the children of "others"—those who are economically, religiously, racially, or geographically "other"—are in effect deemed of lesser worth than "our" children, when romanticized, sentimentalized focusing upon children by North American Christians (e.g., wanting to "give them all the best in life") leads to an inward-turning form of the faith that virtually ignores how First World actions on behalf of our children negatively impact children elsewhere.

And although the ethical mandate of care for widows and orphans, the stranger and the fatherless/ones without protection, resounds strongly throughout Christian tradition with the critique of harmful economic systems similarly clear, affluent Christians often remain slow to recognize the connections between their parts in a consumerist way of life encouraged by market forces, and suffering and harm among children and youth brought about by an economic system that constructs children's primary identities as consumers. Nevertheless, in spite of the unevenness with which these theological perspectives become embodied in practice, their presence makes possible a critique of wider social practices of materialism and economic forces affecting young people throughout the world, creating a context for Christians to struggle for a more child- and youth-affirming, more economically just reality. Keeping in mind the hope embedded in these four Christian theological perspectives on economics and young people, let us now consider the current situations of young people under the economic conditions of globalized capitalism and its structuring of societies and individual young people's lives around practices of materialism and consumption.

Changes in the Economic and Cultural Forces Shaping the Lives of Children and Youth

Most economic and social analysts today agree that worldwide economies, and capitalism in particular, have undergone vast shifts from about the 1970s into their present, globalized forms, which are often termed "late capitalism" to distinguish this contemporary market phenomenon from earlier incarnations of free market capitalism and Fordist-Keynesian capitalism. Several features mark the current economic scene.

FLEXIBLE ACCUMULATION

First, markets moved from earlier patterns of fixed accumulation of capital, labor, and manufacturing to new patterns of "flexible accumulation." That is, rather than being tied to a particular product, location, or even group of workers, in the current economy companies attempt to respond to the ever-changing desires and interests of consumers with small-batch and "just in time" production processes made possible by computers and other technologies.

These innovations also become possible because the companies move their production facilities out of the United States in search of cheaper labor markets through "outsourcing" and lower production costs by choosing locations from which the company can quickly move should conditions become more favorable elsewhere. At the same time, fewer U.S. workers enjoy any long-term job security within a company, as increasing numbers work as contract employees who can be quickly laid off as production needs change, without regard for the effects on the workers or their dependents. As businesses move away from manufacturing and production to service, the number of low-paying, unskilled "McJobs" increases. The number of persons with work-related benefits such as health insurance decreases.

ACCELERATED CONSUMPTION

A second shift in the current economy concerns the market's need to keep consumption levels commensurate with its continual increases in production. In a late-globalized capitalist society oversaturated with "stuff," companies have sought new ways to stimulate and accelerate consumption, including making products less durable, which necessitates sooner and more frequent replacement; creating demands for rapidly shifting fashions through advertising in everything from clothing styles to furnishings and children's toys; focusing on the marketing of nondurable items such as experiences and services (e.g., travel, adventure sports) rather than on durable commodities; and the creation of increasingly narrowly segmented marketing niches, among which youth and children constitute one of the most economically significant, such that new products are "required" by each move into a new age group. The role of advertising in creating and stimulating consumer desires, often masked as "needs," can scarcely be overstated.

THE RELATIVE SIGNIFICANCE OF FINANCE OVER PRODUCTION

Third, instead of being oriented primarily around the production, marketing, and consumption of goods, financial markets have assumed an unprecedented place of importance and power in the world economy as it is now possible for individual investors, governments, and corporations to shift vast amounts of money to the other side of the globe in an instant using computer technology. Problematically, the players in these financial games are heavily concentrated in certain parts of the globe—particularly the United States—and all do not come to the games on an equal footing. Currency exchanges may impact the lives of thousands of people, but they take place in virtually unfettered, faceless digital exchanges that obscure their origins and often the interests and commitments guiding them. A related phenomenon concerns the global reach of marketing that renders geopolitical boundaries largely meaningless: Sony advertised its televisions in New York City and the barrios of Manila in a single commercial sweep, promoting a way of life to which these two populations by and large have very different access.

POSTMODERN CULTURAL FORMS IN COLLUSION
WITH THE MARKET

Finally, various cultural forms attributable to postmodernity appear to be in collaboration with market forces. For instance, the postmodern elision of boundaries between art, entertainment, education, and advertising allows market forces to insert themselves in spaces where they formerly would not have appeared, such as children's schools (with product advertising painted on corridor walls under the rubric of an educational celebration of popular culture art forms) or news broadcasts (with some stations notorious for crossing the boundary between entertainment and information services). An amplified trend toward constant novelty and instantaneity colludes with market interests in accelerating consumption of commodities and services, even as these contribute to notions of the temporary nature and disposability of things, relationships, and commitments.

Taken together, these shifts in economic patterns and cultural forms vastly reconfigure not only the material circumstances of young people's everyday lives across the globe but also the meanings and values embedded in these shifts, to which I will now turn in conclusion.

Shaping Young People's Spiritualities through Consumerism

MATERIALISM

The shifting economic forces of late capitalism hold multiple implications for the lives of young people across the globe that, considered from the perspective of the Christian theological perspectives outlined earlier, merit critical attention in terms of the meanings they shape for human life. Primary among these is the lifestyle of materialism that consumer capitalism fosters among all persons, but presently is targeting for children and youth in particular. Materialism refers to an amplification of the value of "things" in human experience—material goods and commodities—over and beyond the value accorded to other, nonmaterial aspects of life, such as close bonds of affinity between people, sharing resources with those in need, the cultivation of an awareness of the holy, or work for some notion of the common good. Among Christians, materialism holds a generally pejorative meaning, as it refers to an *over*valuing of material things, a displacement of desire or inappropriate assignation between a person's deepest desires and something not worthy of such allegiance. In Christian religious terms, then, materialism may be thought of as a form of idolatry, a form of tacit worship of material elements that in effect substitute for God that which has less than ultimate value and power in human life. Given the Christian tradition's opposition to various forms of idolatry, obviously practices of child nurture that fail to discourage inappropriate materialism are problematic and subject to strong critique.

THE UTILITARIAN VALUE OF CHILDREN IN MARKET CULTURE

Current marketing practices directed at children and intended to stimulate in them desires for commodities (e.g., toys, breakfast cereals), as well their influence on family purchases, encourage materialism in children. Advertising plays a key role in stimulating their materialistic consumer desires, a feature that undoubtedly will continue, since children represent big profits in the North American consumer marketplace. In short, children possess significant utilitarian value for the market. As James McNeal (1999, 58–65), a marketing researcher and promoter of advertising to children, puts it, children represent not just one but three market groups: they comprise a "primary market" as consumers now, spending an estimated $35.6 billion of their own money each year in the United States. They also are an "influence market," influencing the spending of another $487 billion by parents and family members each year. And they constitute a "future market" among whom the cultivation of brand loyalty during childhood promises to translate into future profits.

There now exist separate marketing strategies targeting consumers between the ages of eleven and fourteen, a group tagged as the "great tween buying machine." In the early 1990s adolescents spent $82 billion annually and influenced another $45 billion in purchases each year, figures that can only be assumed to have grown over the past decade. From a Christian perspective, market forces that encourage unfettered materialism among children of financial means, perpetuating the gaps and inequities between these children and others who live in situations of lack or poverty, fail not only the prohibitions against idolatry but also ethical claims against unjust economic regimes that enslave children—both in terms of literal enslavement as child laborers, child soldiers, and prostituted children, and in terms of the metaphorical enslavement to material commodities brought about by First World consumption-oriented lifestyles of children.

FROM THE WAR ON POVERTY TO A WAR AGAINST THE POOR

Few changes in the economy have had a greater impact on the lives of children in the United States than the destabilizing of adult labor markets, with the concomitant decline of employment-related health insurance and other concrete supports. Tremendous stress exists in families where the adults must constantly "retool," reinventing their identities to suit the changing labor market, with increasing amounts of time and space formerly devoted to family and children now being given over to work. As adults move around on this shifting sand, the number of children living below the poverty line with little or no health care and diminished educational opportunities continues to increase, while services to poor children simultaneously are decreasing. In only a few decades, in the United States what began as the government-sponsored "war on poverty" essentially has become a "war against the poor," in which children are among the most deeply affected by the losses of safeguards and social supports for economically vulnerable persons. While certainly the welfare system is in need of changes, the past decade's systematic dismantling of state-sponsored social supports, especially for poor women and their children, targets the poor as "the problem," instead of seeing the condition of poverty as the problem and seeking ways to alleviate it. The National Center for Children in Poverty stresses that "after a decade of decline, the rate of children living in low-income families is rising again, a trend that began in 2000." According to the Children's Defense Fund the United States has some 11,746,858 poor children, or one in every six children. Christian theology affirms that those who are most vulnerable—children, the poor, those without networks and resources to protect them—are entitled to the support of the faith community. And yet the conditions I am describing here place those who are most vulnerable at the greatest risk of harm. Such a situation ought to be intolerable to Christians asserting the incomparable worth of young people as bearers of the divine image, alongside the Christian tradition's particular advocacy for children in the face of the abuses of economic systems.

COMMODIFIED RELATIONSHIPS

A further impact of contemporary globalized economic forces on the spirituality of children and youth involves the power of consumerism as a way of life to school persons into practices focused on commodity acquisition, use and consumption, and disposal that do not remain discretely bounded but come to constitute the wider life context for social relations. Spirituality concerns, among other things, relationships. In consumer-oriented globalized capitalism, even the most intimate of relationships come to be increasingly focused on consumption. Furthermore, from the perspective of adults, within this economic system, relationships and responsibilities toward the young are increasingly figured in relation to their "use value." Such practices place market values of self-interest and utilitarianism in the foreground, and the inviolate humanity of children and youth (apart from any particular benefit they might bestow upon adults) that comes both from their creation in God's image and from their special affirmation by Jesus, falls into obscurity. Put differently, when nurtured under such commodified conditions, young people come to be valued not in and of themselves as human beings, or as it would be put within the Christian tradition, as creatures of God possessing inherent and incomparable worth as bearers of the *imago Dei*. It would be reasonable to expect, though problematic from a Christian perspective, that children nurtured in such a habitus of market-driven (de)valuing of persons would adopt similar practices of treating others in relation to their utilitarian potential for return value to oneself.

YOUNG PEOPLE AS DISPOSABLE

The economic forces that seek to accelerate consumption create a context for the treatment of all kinds of commodities (and other things, such as relationships and commitments) as highly disposable and ever-renewable. When youth and children themselves are commodified, they easily become expendable in a society that values them ambivalently anyway—especially those children who are flawed, defective consumers by virtue of poverty. These and other children come to be seen as disposable entities. Such conditions fly in the face of Christian theological notions that children have a special role among the faithful, not in spite of their smallness, poverty, lack of status, or relative insignificance, but *by virtue of these qualities*. In terms of this theology, those deemed least in stature and significance by the world's measures are the ones who lead all God's people in the creation of a new, inclusive social order.

Christian Theology as Critique

In this chapter, I have suggested that resources exist with a Christian perspective for understanding economic forces and materialism as spiritual matters, insofar as they constitute issues of justice in the lives of children and youth. Using Christian theological understandings of childhood and of economic justice to critique the current situations of children under globalized capitalism, I contended that materialism and contemporary economic forces shape the spiritualities of children by constructing them in identities that suit the agendas of the market. In Christian terms, even though a child like Austin suffers no material want, his humanity undergoes harm and distortion when social practices of consumerism form him into a primary identity as a consumer of commodities, with few opportunities therein for a sense of productive agency or real creativity. Still further harm accrues to him in the commodification of childhood and children rampant in Austin's North American social and cultural context.

Furthermore, I suggest in this chapter that Christian faith brings a critical perspective to the ways economic forces matter in the spiritualities of children as they shape the concrete-material conditions under which children play, work, and make meaning of their experiences. Thus, Christianity critiques the economic systems that harm Ruben by constructing his identity as a low-wage laborer who bears the costs of First World consumerist appetites. And finally, since from the perspective of Christian theology there is no such thing as a "disposable child," given the special welcome of children by Jesus and the role Jesus gave to children like Eva in helping others to glimpse God's reordering of power, Christianity strongly critiques systemic political and economic practices that allow so many children to live on the edge of survival. Much work remains to be done in moving from such resources and critiques, present within Christianity at the level of theological principles or theories, to their enactment in consistent advocacy for children and youth, and for economic justice that can transform the lives of young people today.

References

Andolsen, Barbara H. 1998. *The new job contract: Economic justice in an age of insecurity.* Cleveland, Ohio: Pilgrim Press.

Bounds, Elizabeth M., Pamela K. Brubaker, and Mary E. Hobgood. 1999. *Welfare policy: Feminist critiques.* Cleveland, Ohio: Pilgrim Press.

Schneider, John R. 1994. *Godly materialism: Rethinking money and possessions.* Downers Grove, Ill.: InterVarsity Press.

——. 2002. *The good of affluence: Seeking God in a culture of wealth.* Grand Rapids, Mich.: Eerdmans.

Sheils, William J., and Diana Wood, eds. 1987. *The church and wealth: Papers read at the 1986 summer meeting and the 1987 winter meeting of the Ecclesiastical History Society.* Oxford: Blackwell.

Wilkerson, Bruce. 2000. *The prayer of Jabez: Breaking through to the blessed life.* Sisters, Ore.: Multnomah.

CHAPTER 37

Born with a Knife in Their Hearts: Children and Political Conflict in the Middle East

Arik Ascherman

One day recently I was walking my daughter to kindergarten in Jerusalem and found the entire school waiting outside as a police unit was examining *khefetz khashud*, a suspicious and unidentified object that might have been a bomb. I debated whether I should explain to my daughter what khefetz khashud is. On the one hand, what might be the psychological effects on a little girl to know that somebody might plant a bomb in her school with the intention of blowing up her, her friends, and their teachers? Given how rare it is in recent years for bombs to be used in this way, would I simply be contributing to mass hysteria and even political thought control? On the other hand, this knowledge might save her life. I decided to explain, and she did not have much of a reaction. A few days later she told me about the conversation the kindergarten teacher had held with the children. She matter-of-factly explained how the guards must search the premises every morning and what they did when they actually found something. When I tried to probe as to how this made my daughter feel, she was primarily interested in the robot that the police sent to check the khefetz khashud.

There are two levels of trauma that children and youth in areas of conflict must face. The more horrific is the trauma faced by children who have been directly harmed by violence or who have witnessed violence and its results. The second level is that faced by children who have had their childhood taken away. Beyond the more universal infringements on childhood innocence, such as parental warnings about talking to strangers, a violent reality penetrates their world through restrictions on what they are allowed to do, special instructions on what they must do to protect themselves, and so forth. If parents don't screen them from the media, they hear every day about this reality. It is not something that happens "somewhere else," but rather what is happening next door. As a parent, I see children robbed of the innocence of childhood. As the director of a human rights organization, I witness the trauma of children who are victims of violent action. As a rabbi, I try to see what wisdom our traditional sources have to offer.

Traditional Jewish texts do not devote a great deal of attention to the inner life of children, let alone children in times of conflict. A notable exception is the biblical figure of Isaac as reflected in midrash (plural, *midrashim*), a form of Jewish commentary on the Bible that specializes in "filling in the gaps" created by the sparse nature of the biblical text. In addition, the story of the near sacrifice of Isaac (*Akedat Yitzhak,* literally, "The Binding of Isaac," often referred to simply as "the Akedah" or "the Binding"; Genesis 22) has become symbolic through the ages of Jewish suffering. This significance is reflected in many literary forms, up through modern Hebrew poetry.

One question left unanswered by the biblical text is what precipitated God's command to Abraham to sacrifice his son. The text tells us that God puts Abraham to the test, "After these things . . ." (Genesis 22:1). Rather than understanding that this simply means after the events of the previous chapter, the midrash reads this as referring to other events that bring on the test. (It should also be noted that many commentators argue that Isaac is much older when these events take place. We will assume he is a young child, as the biblical text seems to indicate.) For example, some midrashim imagine a bragging contest between Isaac and his half brother Ishmael. Ishmael claims that he suffered more by being circumcised at age thirteen than did Isaac, who was circumcised when he was eight days old. This suffering indicated Ishmael's greater devotion to God. Isaac responds by saying that he would be willing to sacrifice his life were God to so command. Immediately, God orders Abraham to sacrifice Isaac (see, e.g., Genesis Rabah 55:4). Other midrashim indicate that Satan (in some versions angels) accuses Abraham of not offering sacrifices to God when he held a feast on the day Isaac was weaned. In much of rabbinic literature Satan is more of a prosecuting attorney than a demonic figure. In Hebrew, the word for *incitement* comes from the same root as *Satan.* As in the story of Job, the one place where he appears in the Bible itself, Satan accuses and incites God against various characters.

In this second midrash children are the victims of events beyond their control: it is they who pay for the actions of others. In the first midrash there is an indication that the youthful desire to prove ourselves can wittingly or unwittingly put us in harm's way. If we wish to do midrash on the midrash, we can ask how seriously Isaac meant his words. If he meant what he said, to what extent was he aware of the import of his words, and what would drive a young child to put himself or herself in danger? Both midrashim are indicative of a worldview that life is fraught with hidden dangers. We must be very careful with our actions and cognizant of how God may perceive them.

Certainly, the tragic reality of the Middle East conflict or any other conflict is that countless children are physically, spiritually, and emotionally harmed because of events beyond their control. We must also question what it is that prompts a young Palestinian to risk his life by going out to throw stones at soldiers—or even to agree to give up his life by being a suicide bomber. Why has there developed what Palestinian psychologist Eyad Saraj calls "The Culture of Death" in which the ultimate aspiration of many Palestinian young people is to be a "martyr"? Veteran Israeli peace activist Uri Avneri recalls that at age fifteen he was a child soldier and would have been willing to blow himself up had his commander asked him to do so.

On one level, this willingness is certainly a function of often intentional socialization. Much of the Israeli educational system, especially youth groups, is designed to prepare young people for military service and to motivate them to serve in elite units. This training sometimes includes absorbing stereotypes about Palestinians, who are portrayed as the latest in the long chain of those who have oppressed Jews. The world is against the Jews, and only our military strength can put an end to the history of oppression against us. Negative stereotypes of Jews in Palestinian schools and messages in the official media praising "martyrdom" have also been documented. Sometimes the exploitation of children and youth is even more direct, such as a recent incident in which adults persuaded a developmentally challenged youth to become a suicide bomber. However, the fact that children are born into conflicts they did not create or are socialized to participate in these conflicts does not absolve us of asking which elements of a child's psyche, from the demand for justice to the need to prove oneself, the need to avenge loss, and the need to preserve dignity, make children susceptible to this socialization.

One remarkable midrash attempts to understand the feelings and thoughts of a young person seemingly about to lose his life in a situation not of his own making, but one with which the midrash believes he identifies. Satan wants to ensure that Abraham fails the test before him. He appears to Abraham as an older man, asking why he would destroy all that he has hoped and dreamed for. This ploy fails. Satan then appears to Isaac as a young man, asking why he should allow a crazy old man to kill him when he has his whole life ahead of him. According to this midrash, Isaac is not the unaware potential victim he appears to be in the biblical text. This and other midrashim indicate that Isaac knows what is about to happen and fully identifies with this test of faith. He too rejects Satan's appeal to his inner world (Midrash Tanhuma Vayera 22). This midrash tries to get inside the head of young Isaac and teaches that the prospect of having one's life cut short before being able to live one's dreams is a great challenge to a young person's faith. On the other hand, this midrash teaches that deep faith can give a young person the strength to stay on the path, even when that path is fraught with extreme danger.

The vast majority of Jewish literature up until the modern era views the binding of Isaac as the ultimate and exemplary demonstration of faith. In some classical and many modern Jewish sources, however, we see more varied and even critical understandings of the Akedah. Some sources believe that Abraham's faith is to be measured not by his willingness to sacrifice his son but by his belief that God would not ultimately ask this of him. (We can view Isaac's faith in the same light.) Others see this as God's way of teaching that the practices common among other peoples of the time were not the correct ways of serving God, who does not wish us to sacrifice our children. Some would even suggest that Abraham failed this test (Genesis Rabah 56:8; see also Driver [1904], 222; Hertz [1981], 201; Plaut [1981], 149–54, 169–89). However, the classical midrash also understood that Isaac did not leave this encounter unscathed.

According to the biblical narrative, Isaac is nearly blind in his old age (Genesis 27:1). According to the midrash, this condition is a result of the fact that, when Isaac lay bound on the altar with his face toward the heavens, the tears of angels weeping over his imminent sacrifice fell into his upturned eyes (e.g., Genesis Rabah 65:9). Permitting ourselves to create midrash on midrash, the text is recognizing that faith can enable us to face trauma, but that the impact of this traumatic event affected Isaac permanently. If we note that Isaac's blindness figures prominently when Jacob tricks Isaac into giving him Esau's blessing and that God has already told Isaac's wife Rebecca that it is Jacob who is destined to be the recipient of the physical, and perhaps spiritual, inheritance, then perhaps Isaac's traumatic childhood experience makes him blind to certain aspects of his own children.

Akedat Yitzhak deals with the traumatic experience of one family, as opposed to a context of warfare or general conflict. In the medieval and modern periods, however, Akedat Yitzhak becomes the prism through which Jews understood Jewish suffering and persecution. For example Efraim of Bonn (1132–1200) wrote a long poem retelling the Akedah, *Et Avotai Ani Mazkir* (I remember my ancestors). This poem includes many of the midrashim mentioned earlier and includes a tradition that says Isaac was in fact sacrificed and resurrected. The second-to-last stanza reads:

> Remember, in our favour, how many have been slaughtered—pious men and women murdered for Your sake. Oh, reward the martyrs of Judah, slain in righteousness, and the bound of Jacob. (Carmi 1981, 384; see also Spiegel 1979)

The modern poem "Isaac," by Amir Gilboa, continues this theme with a reflection on the Holocaust invoking the Akedah. Only here, it is the father who is sacrificed (Gilboa's own father was murdered in the Holocaust). The boy's feelings turn from fear for his own life to terror and horror to a sense of powerlessness.

A theme that only a poet would dare broach is the question of what the relationship could be between Isaac and his father after Abraham seemed so willing to sacrifice his son. The trauma of violent conflict can shake a child's faith in his or her parents, the most immediate symbol engendering hope and trust in the world. They prove incapable of protecting, and possibly even share some responsibility for endangering, the child.

Perhaps the most powerful and best-known expression of this theme is the poem "Heritage," by Hayim Gouri, which retells the story of the Akedah and concludes that Isaac was not sacrificed. Ironically recalling the traditional midrash, Gouri writes that Isaac lived for many years and "saw" pleasure until his eyesight failed. "But he bequeathed that hour to his offspring. They are born with a knife in their hearts" (Carmi 1981, 565).

Today many Israeli parents remember the Akedah when they accompany their children to their mandatory induction into the Israeli army. For all of the socialization in Israeli society discussed earlier, one can only wonder whether at some level youth feel sacrificed by their parents, who have raised them in Israel, who have not managed to achieve peace, and/or who have chosen to live in settlements deep in the Occupied Territories surrounded by hostile and angry Palestinians. A popular song written after the Yom Kippur War in 1973 tells of the promise of a soldier to his young daughter that the war will be the last war ("HaMilkhama HaAkharona," words and music by Yehoram Gaon). The reply of youth was conveyed in another popular song, "Winter of '73," by Shmuel Hasafari and Uri Vidislavsky, in which youth identify themselves as the "children of the winter of seventy-three," born after soldiers returned from the Yom Kippur War. They were conceived to find comfort and make up for the losses of war; but for all the parents' sincere vows to bring peace and prevent their children from needing to go to war, "We have grown and are now in the army, armed and helmeted." These youth both understand the pain of their parents and ask that their parents understand what it means for them to go off to war, potentially never to have their dreams fulfilled, because their parents were not able to keep their promises:

Therefore we won't press and we won't demand. It therefore isn't pleasant
When we were young you said: Promises must be kept
If you need it we will give strength, we won't hold back, we just wanted to whisper
We are the children of that winter, seventy-three.

The message evoked by Isaac and the message of this song have important common elements. Isaac has a quiet, strong faith, in some ways stronger than the faith of his more dynamic father or of his son Jacob. He is blinded by his traumatic experience, however. Israel has an extensively developed youth culture, with a large percentage of youth active in a variety of largely self-run youth movements educating for social involvement. In a sense, our difficult reality has forced children and youth to develop their inner spiritual resources. The percentage of youth involved in youth movements has dropped significantly, however, and among secular Israelis the once dominant ideological movements are now dwarfed by the much more conformist and less dynamic Scout movement. Secular youth diligently enter the army and defend their country (although there are growing numbers openly or surreptitiously getting out of reserve duty, if not compulsory service as well). Many are deeply cynical and look to "escape" on long trips abroad soon after finishing compulsory army service. In the Orthodox religious community (non-Orthodox religious movements in Israel tend to represent a small minority), there is less cynicism because children and youth are socialized into a powerful and problematic mixture of extreme nationalism and extreme particularism dedicated to "redeeming" the entire land of Israel by any means necessary. Although I do not wish to oversimplify, this fundamentalism is remarkably similar to Islamic fundamentalism, which is the most powerful religious force today in Palestinian society.

At the heart of this dark reality is a spiritual crisis born of long years of conflict and the resulting despair. The solution must include a restoration of hope, an essentially spiritual concept. Others can do a much better job than I both of detailing the history of the Middle East conflict and of elucidating theories of spiritual development. Let me simply indicate that I accept the basic concept of stage theories of development along with the critique of excessively linear and uniform models. Thus, the successful resolution of Erik Erikson's infancy stage leading to basic hope and trust does not guarantee that events later in life will not require us to work through this need again. As long as hope and basic trust and faith remain, adversity can produce a dynamic youth culture such as the predominantly secular but very spiritual Israeli youth culture, which has been incredibly involved, mature, responsible, and optimistic. When long years of seemingly endless conflict begin to extinguish hope, and there is no faith system to help make sense, give meaning, and guide the way to potential change, cynicism takes over. Alternative meaning systems and spiritual directions are too often fundamentalist, offering nationalistic, particularistic, and simplistic worldviews and suggestions. Some of these systems of belief offer cataclysmic hope for redemption; others remain essentially pessimistic.

What is needed are meaning systems that offer hope and meaning through conflict resolution. Judaism, like any other ancient and varied tradition, contains many voices. Often they can be in tension. The Torah teaches both to love the stranger and to fight wars without pity. One of the guiding principles in my life is the basic teaching found in the first verses of the Torah that all human beings are created *b'tselem elohim* (in God's image). We are not told that only men or only women are created in God's image, nor does this concept differentiate between rich or poor, Jews or non-Jews. As the midrash elucidates, an attack on a fellow human being is an attack against God, in whose image we are created. It is analogous to defacing coins, statues, and other objects that bear the image of an earthly ruler (Mekhilta D'Rabi Ishmael, B'Khodesh 8). Based on this teaching in the Book of Genesis, the midrash tells us that "one who destroys a single life, it is as if he or she has destroyed an entire world. One who saves a single life, it is as if he or she has saved an entire world" (Mishna Sanhedrin 4:5). Many Israelis blink because they know a different version. In the Middle Ages, this text was amended to read, "One who saves or destroys a single *Jewish* life . . ." (see Urbach 1987, 561–77; cited in Zohar 1991).

Much of our educational work in Rabbis for Human Rights (RHR) is teaching the human rights messages in Judaism, Islam, and Christianity, both to introduce to students the often neglected hopeful and more universalistic readings of their own tradition, as well as to break down stereotypes of the religion of the "other." For the same reasons, we have created, along with Palestinian Muslim and Christian clergy, an "Interfaith Declaration of Faith." In our region and much of the world, those advocating nationalistic-particularistic versions of our respective traditions have been much more diligent than we in creating frameworks, institutions, and mechanisms for teaching their outlook. We have much to do.

While it is theoretically possible to strengthen hope by cutting through the Gordian knot and jump-starting a peace agreement or imposing it from without, clearly a restoration of hope would make that peace process more possible. Studies have consistently demonstrated that there is a sane majority of both Israelis and Palestinians who want a compromise, negotiated agreement but that an even larger majority believe nobody on the other side thinks the same way. Combined with the strange fact of human nature that people tend to harden their positions when being shot at, is it any wonder that people are reluctant to take risks for peace when they have no hope that doing so will improve the situation?

Hope thus begins with breaking down stereotypes that Israelis and Palestinians hold of each other. This is not a simple thing. I am hesitant to speak in parallelisms when the power relationship between Israelis and Palestinians is so asymmetrical. However, we all have created seamless, closed worldviews in which the other is evil, sometimes even demonic. We are all so convinced we are the victims that we cannot conceive of the fact that we can be both victims and victimizers at the same time. The early Zionist and pacifist Rabbi Aaron Samuel Tamares of Lithuania (1869–1931) wrote that God ordered the Children of Israel to stay in their homes the night God slew the firstborn of the Egyptians because, even when one's cause is just, any contact with violence can turn a victim into a victimizer. Just as Isaac's victimhood blinded him, so do acts of vengeance. In the human rights work that RHR engages in, I often feel that, as important as it may be that we sometimes succeed in preventing or rectifying human rights abuses, our very presence creates cognitive dissonance leading to some small chink in those seamless worldviews. If we can't truly restore basic trust in a world that is so fundamentally harsh and oppressive, at least we may rekindle hope that there is somebody on the other side to talk to and that things can one day be different. This also empowers those Palestinians advocating for nonviolent cooperation with Israelis. Palestinians who went against the flow of what was happening on their street at the outbreak of the second intifada report that, as more Palestinians heard of some of our joint activities, they received newfound support.

It is children and youth who most deeply suffer the traumas produced by the conflict. It is at these stages in life that it is most difficult to grasp a more complex worldview in which not all Jews or Palestinians are enemies. Just recently an RHR delegation completed a day of olive harvesting with Palestinian families and returned to the home of one of the villagers for coffee. Since some of us were religious and wearing *kippot* (religious headcovering; RHR has many nonrabbinic and nonreligious volunteers, so not all were wearing kippot), the Palestinian children knew that at least some of us were Jews. The parents had a difficult time explaining to the children that we were Jews but not enemies or oppressors. A few years ago, RHR, along with the Israeli Committee Against Home Demolitions, rebuilt the home of a Palestinian family that had been demolished because of a catch-22 policy in which Palestinians find it almost impossible to get legal building permits. At the end of the day, the family was horrified to discover that a tape player was missing from the car of one of the Israeli volunteers. After asking around, the father of the family discovered that a six-year-old boy had stolen it. When asked why, the boy replied that he had thought he was doing a praiseworthy act. "These are the Jews who demolished your home."

These stereotypes are all too often reinforced in our children's literature and in our educational systems. Unfortunately, these reinforcements build upon the fact that every Palestinian child age two and older is deeply aware from personal experience that Jewish soldiers and settlers wreak death and destruction on them. There is no family without a *shaheed* (martyr). Having worked with many families whose homes have been demolished, I know the pattern very well. Homelessness causes great strain on marriages and sometimes leads to family violence. Children's grades plummet, while nightmares and bedwetting skyrocket. The sight of a soldier or sound of a helicopter can lead to frenzy, temporary paralysis, or collapse. Basic trust no longer exists. In one case I am aware of, a teenage daughter went into a trembling fit upon seeing missiles being fired in the distance. She could no longer stand. The father held his distraught daughter and tried to reassure her: "The missiles are far away, and in any case I am here to protect you." She answered: "You can't protect me. I saw how the soldiers beat you when they came to demolish our home." All youth must eventually learn that their parents cannot protect them from the world, but, like the helmeted Israeli youth, Palestinian youth learn this brutally and wrenchingly at an all too early age.

Israeli children not living in the Occupied Territories may have a better chance of being shielded for a few more years. Nonetheless, every Israeli family knows someone who knows someone who has been personally affected by the violence. In Israel there are various organizations running summer camps and providing outings for children who have been injured and/or lost loved ones in acts of terror. On the one hand, they need relief from family life in a home struck by violence. On the other hand, only among others who have experienced the same pain and loss can they find someone who "understands."

No personal history, however tragic, can justify the use of terror and aggressive violence. We must grapple with the fact, however, that these childhood traumas often cause blind hatred and leave people unable to move beyond stark and fundamentalist worldviews. In the story of almost every Palestinian terrorist is a background of loss and trauma. I recently heard from a Palestinian friend that his seven-year-old son still keeps the broken pieces of his tricycle, which soldiers broke when he was three years old and they invaded his home. From that time on, all he wants when visiting toy stores is a model gun so that he can kill Jews.

It is thus children and youth who are most in need of having hope introduced into their world. As important as it may be that RHR prevents or ends human rights violations, it is at least as important that we create a space in children's hearts where hope can survive. Almost every time we rebuild a demolished home a scene repeats itself. Parents insist that their children meet us. The explanation is often the same: "Our ten-year-old son has seen his home demolished in front of his eyes. He has seen his parents humiliated in front of his eyes. What do we tell our son when he says, 'I want to grow up and be a terrorist'? We want our son to know that not every Israeli comes with guns to demolish our home. There are also Israelis who are willing to stand shoulder to shoulder with us to rebuild our home."

I was in the Palestinian village of Bidu, one of the eight villages that participated in the landmark appeal to the Israeli High Court leading to the decision on June 30, 2004, that we Israelis had a right to build a separation barrier in order to defend ourselves from terror, but that the planned route disproportionately and unnecessarily violated Palestinian human rights and international law by separating Palestinians from their land. A demonstration had just ended that day when I received a phone call to come quickly to another neighborhood in the village because a thirteen-year-old boy had been caught by the border police and was being beaten. Tear gas was shot at me as I approached the police jeeps, and then I was taken into custody by the commanding officer, handcuffed, and put in front of one of the jeeps along with a Palestinian man whom the worried parents had also sent. A third individual was soon similarly handcuffed. The young boy was strapped to the windshield of a second jeep, shivering with fear and unsuccessfully trying to hold back tears. Other Palestinian youth began to throw stones, hitting the jeeps we were positioned in front of. Repeated appeals on my part that it was illegal to use us as human shields and that the boy's medical condition had to be looked after were met with threats or simply laughter and derision. I know that this young boy woke up every night with nightmares for at least a month after this incident. Who knows what psychological scars and blind spots that child will now carry with him for the rest of his life. Who knows what he now thinks about Israelis, if not all Jews. However, after describing in an affidavit all the horrific things that happened to him, he concluded by noting, "And then a tall man in a *kippah* came to my rescue and told me not to be afraid." If I wasn't able to prevent the trauma, I at least hope that my presence will leave a chink in a potentially seamless and stark worldview.

One day an RHR delegation was helping to protect Palestinians who were attempting to harvest their olives near a particularly violent settlement. The family could not believe that we had coordinated with the Israeli security forces, which they feared and hated, to be in the settlement to ensure that we were not attacked. I was rather surprised to find out that the young man working next to me was taking time off from his usual job to help his family with the harvest. He was a member of the Palestinian Presidential Guard. If I was somewhat surprised, he was ten times more surprised to find out that I was working with an Israeli rabbi. At a certain point he couldn't contain himself any longer, and he burst out: "Why are you here? I just don't understand. Explain it to me." I proceeded to explain the Jewish tradition of justice and so forth. He replied, "For us Palestinians there is no justice." Although this was a few months before the Jewish holiday of Hanukkah, I answered with one of the central lessons of the festival: "When all is dark, you have to start by lighting that first candle." He went to repeat this to all of his family. I am not naive. I don't know what that young man did the next time he was confronted with an ethical choice. I do know, however, that, as a result of our encounter, there is a much greater chance he will choose the path of nonviolence.

Why is it that we Israelis get upset when we hear about hatred toward Israelis being taught in Palestinian schools? It is because we know that, even if we sign the perfect peace treaty tomorrow, that treaty cannot last if we continue to teach hatred about each other and reinforce stark worldviews without hope. Some choose to curse the darkness. In my opinion, we must be lighting candles of hope for all of our children and youth.

Midrash Pesikta Rabati Piska 8 on Hanukkah teaches that when one of the lights went out on one of the branches of the menorah (candelabrum) that once stood in the Temple in Jerusalem, it could only be rekindled with fire from another branch of the menorah. The midrash then gives an exegesis on the verse from Proverbs, "The human soul is the lamp of God" (Proverbs 20:27), and describes how the human being must do God's work in this world. We have not yet eliminated violence and conflict from our world. When the lack of hope dims the light of the human soul, our youth find it difficult to discover and develop their inner spiritual resources. Only we can help them do this. We help when we create and strengthen frameworks that pass on the spiritual wisdom of both our religious and secular traditions. We do so when, recognizing that we cannot protect our children as we or they desire, we can maintain through our beliefs and actions the light of hope for them, and they for us. When our souls provide light, their souls will find the way.

References

Carmi, T., ed. and trans. 1981. *The Penguin book of Hebrew verse.* New York: Penguin.

Driver, S. R. 1904. *Genesis.* New York: Edwin S. Gorham.

Hertz, J. H., ed. 1981. *Pentateuch and Haftorahs.* 2nd ed. London: Soncino.

Interfaith declaration of faith. Cowritten and signed by Israeli and Palestinian Muslim, Jewish, Christian, and Druze clergy. www.rhr.israel.net/projects/index.shtml.

Plaut, Gunther, ed. 1981. *The Torah: A modern commentary.* New York: Union of American Hebrew Congregations.

Spiegel, Shalom. 1979. *The last trial.* Translated by Judah Goldin. New York: Behrman House,.

Urbach, Efraim. 1987. *The world of the sages* (in Hebrew). Jerusalem: n.p.

Zohar, Noam J., edited For Rabbis for Human Rights. 1991. *Life, liberty and equality in the Jewish tradition* (in Hebrew; currently being translated).

POSTSCRIPT

Expanding the Conversation

The conversation begun in this volume makes a significant contribution to the scholarship regarding the spiritual lives of children and adolescents and the ways those lives are nurtured and shaped by the world's religious traditions. However, there is much more to explore, critique, discuss, and envision. These chapters offer important information and evocative insights, but they also tease us with their necessary brevity. We are left with further questions even as we acknowledge an increase in understanding. We need to go deeper within each tradition, looking at a wider range of beliefs and themes within each tradition as well as the subtle—and sometimes dramatic—differences and accents in intratradition interpretations and practices. We need to encourage thorough critical analysis of the relationship between foundational beliefs about childhood and concrete religious practices with young people. We also need to examine these foundational beliefs in the light of emerging interdisciplinary understandings about children and adolescents. We need to identify dissident voices, marginalized perspectives, and emerging experiments within traditions, highlighting the variegated viewpoints obscured when only a few voices try to speak—however carefully—for large and diverse religious communities.

Furthermore, for every religious perspective that has been given voice in these pages, many others remain unheard. We can only surmise what practitioners of the Australian Arrarnta religion believe about children's spirituality, what Sikhs claim as essential for nurturing adolescent spiritual formation, what Santeria teaches about inward and outward movements of the spiritual life, what Syrian or Russian Orthodoxy identifies as the pressing cultural issues challenging children and the Church, how Pentecostal Christians view social responsibility for children on the margins, why Wiccan practices attract growing numbers of American and European adolescent girls. We wonder what Taoism, Confucianism, Jainism, the followers of Native American traditions, and many, many others might contribute to the discussion. Our table full of ideas from persons within Islam, Buddhism, Judaism, Hinduism, and Christianity requires more leaves so that a larger group of scholars can crowd around and add their contributions to the intellectual feast.

Additional expansion also requires us to acknowledge that the book only begins to delve into the rich diversity both within and across traditions when culture and context are added to the mix. Although we have been able to hear from at least one scholar on each of five continents, each continent (and regions within each continent) merits focused attention. How are religious traditions coping with the nurture of the young in a highly secularized European context or amid the geopolitical changes in Asia? What is the place of child and adolescent spiritual formation in the rise of Pentecostal Christianity in South America? How have spiritual practices among children in Africa developed in ways that integrate indigenous religious traditions with Christianity and Islam? One quickly becomes overwhelmed—and stimulated—by the complexity and breadth of the possible conversation.

Delving Deeply into Specific Traditions

One response to the breadth of the agenda before us is to spend more focused time in dialogue and discovery within a particular religious tradition. Indeed, one measure of this volume's success will be whether it provokes individual scholars and groups of theologians, historians, philosophers, and other religious scholars to reexamine their knowledge, traditions, and beliefs for insights into the spiritual lives of children and adolescents. If, for example, a tradition has not yet clearly surfaced its core beliefs and practices related to child and adolescent spirituality, a worthy task is for scholars within that tradition to undertake that work (as modeled by the authors in this volume),

There are, of course, already efforts under way (outlined in the introduction to this book) to engage in these faith-specific conversations. However, the ongoing task is to examine sacred texts, historical sources, contemporary practices, and other resources to articulate more fully the ways the tradition has and has not taken spirituality seriously in childhood and adolescence.

Creating Space for Interreligious Dialogue

As this volume illustrates, limiting the conversations to within a tradition—though more comfortable—risks missing the stimulating opportunity for exploration and learning across and among religious traditions. Such interreligious engagement is vital, not only for its intellectual value, but also as an antidote to the mistrust and misperceptions that tend to flourish when people of faith remain isolated from one another.

However, this deeper and broader conversation will not occur without careful attention to how we continually create and maintain safe and hospitable space for interreligious dialogue. A collection of individual essays is helpful for generating conversation, but we know that personal relationships and face-to-face dialogue (rather than just coauthoring a book) will be essential if we are to move to a deeper level of trust and discourse. Few of us are used to interreligious exchanges. We typically talk with persons in our own traditions or those most closely aligned with ours. We know our own religious vocabulary and are comfortable with the conventions of our tradition's discussion and debate; we often are not knowledgeable about or prepared for the different hermeneutics practiced by other religious groups and cultures. We live with the danger of "talking past" rather than "communicating with" each other. Diana Eck's (1993) distinction between types of interreligious relationships may be useful here. She suggests that *inclusivism* recognizes the partial truth of other religions, but sees one's own as the best or the most comprehensive. *Pluralism,* on the other hand, celebrates one particular tradition, but understands it as one of many valid representations of reality or truth: "If we are pluralists, we recognize the limits of the world we already know and we seek to understand others in their own terms, not just in ours" (Eck 1993, 169). The inevitable tension between inclusivism and pluralism in the type of deep and broad interreligious dialogue we are encouraging demands scrupulous honesty with ourselves and great sensitivity in expressing ourselves to others. For us to become true colleagues in an ongoing exploration of childhood and adolescent spirituality, we will need to spend time listening carefully to one another as we describe our tradition's core concerns and passionate commitments, historic missteps and contemporary fears, and internal struggles to remain faithful and relevant with and for children and youth in the twenty-first century. We will need to remain open to what we have to learn from one another as well as what we have to offer as insights and ideas from our own beliefs and practices.

Such candor also demands that each tradition hone its own understanding of the theological and philosophical roots that inform how its adherents understand and address spirituality with its young people. Several of the essays in this volume point to conversations about these matters that are already under way in the world's major religious traditions. It is not always clear, however, that spiritual nurture—rather than the simple transmission of religious doctrines and practices for institutional survival—is the primary goal of these discussions. The relationship between spirituality and religious identity is defined differently by traditions; to tease out the distinctive aspects of each may not always appear in the best interests of some traditions. Minority or marginalized traditions may feel a more compelling need to transmit their histories, rituals, beliefs, and stories than their widely accepted religious kin precisely because their survival as traditions depends on how well they continue to convince their young people to remain within the fold as adults. Furthermore, scholars within these traditions may be inclined to "protect" their tradition from ridicule or criticism in interreligious discussions by withholding information about internal disagreements and stressing their religious ideals. Our ongoing conversation needs to be patient with such hesitancy while it continues to develop a shared language and comfort level that invites risk taking and respectful challenge.

Expanding the Cross-Cultural Conversation

The need to expand the conversation cross-culturally also merits careful development of hospitable ways and means of talking with (and not at) one another. Our social locations as well as our traditional histories significantly frame the questions we ask about spirituality, children, and youth as well as the answers we are willing to consider and accept. African Anglicans bring different cultural concerns and narratives to the table than do their British counterparts. Israeli Jews sending their youth into mandatory military service in a nation plagued with terrorist violence talk about spirituality and religious identity in some different ways than do Midwesterners trying to raise their children in the Jewish tradition in the context of the Christianized civil religion of the United States. Tibetan Buddhists bring a particular social and cultural history and struggle to the table. We need to enrich the perspectives offered by the authors in this book by drawing in more voices from around the world who can address the issues identified and others not yet imagined through their particular sociocultural lenses.

Engaging with Social Scientists

There is a third risky turn that the conversation needs to take as well, and that is toward greater interaction between scholars of religion and scholars within the social science disciplines. Since the Age of Enlightenment in the Western world, religious traditions steeped in rationalism have struggled with the process of developing a uniquely "theological" voice that can hold its own ground in conversation with the "developmental" voice of the social sciences. Too often, the latter voice has drowned out theological perspective, or even silenced it altogether. This book has sought to call forth the theological voice in a separate "room" from the social sciences conversation being held next door (i.e., published in a separate volume). Nonetheless, the editors believe that a mutual conversation would enhance the understanding of scholars across these usually separate disciplines. Social scientists might help religious traditions better interpret some of their experiences of and insights into the spiritual life, whereas religious traditions might challenge some of the assumptions or conclusions held by developmentalists and others engaged in scientific inquiry regarding the human spirit.

One of the places we might begin such a cross-disciplinary dialogue is in relation to definitions of spirituality. In this volume, our working definition (as stated in the introduction) has been:

> Spirituality is the intrinsic human capacity for self-transcendence in which the individual participates in the sacred—something greater than the self. It propels the search for connectedness, meaning, purpose, and ethical responsibility. It is experienced, formed, shaped, and expressed through a wide range of religious narratives, beliefs, and practices, and is shaped by many influences in family, community, society, culture, and nature.

Although grounded in the priorities and language of theology and religious philosophy, this definition was intentionally developed to be consistent with the working definition being proposed through the social science accent of Search Institute's initiative:

> Spiritual development is the process of growing the intrinsic human capacity for self-transcendence, in which the self is embedded in something greater than the self, including the sacred. It is the developmental "engine" that propels the search for connectedness, meaning, purpose and contribution. It is shaped both within and outside of religious traditions, beliefs and practices. (Benson, Roehlkepartain, and Rude 2003, 205–6) (Also see Roehlkepartain et al. 2006.)

There are both subtle and important differences between these definitions that will, we hope, continue to stimulate exploration, dialogue, and clarification. Some are more a matter of emphasis and extension, such as the deeper explication of religious practices in the working definition for this book. In other cases, the differences are more substantial, such as the use of the term *spirituality* in the religious perspectives definition versus *spiritual development* in the social sciences definition, as well as the articulation of the importance of broad social forces in the former versus the potential separation of spirituality from religion in the latter.

The point is not to critique or select one definition or another, any more than the point of interreligious or cross-cultural dialogue is to compare and elevate one traditional form of spiritual expression over another. What is valuable in both these boundary-crossing conversations is the potential for increased scholarly insight into the spiritual lives of children and youth and for the development of more effective social and religious processes of spiritual nurture in the first two decades of human life. These are laudable goals shared (albeit in varying degrees) by social scientists and most, if not all, of the world's religious traditions. It seems only fitting that we might pursue them in conversation with one another as well as within our own intellectual and religious arenas.

BUILDING BRIDGES TO PRACTICE

To this point, the conversation has remained fairly academic, focusing on theoretical, philosophical, and theological issues, questions, and challenges. Although these dialogues have intrinsic merit, we believe they need to be strengthened and enriched by also engaging in sustained dialogue with young people themselves as well as their leaders, educators, and parents. How do they understand spirituality and its nurture? What rituals and practices do they find to be meaningful and transformative? How do they connect their inner life with the daily choices and challenges they face in a complex world? And how does the historic wisdom of their tradition inform, strengthen, and reshape their approach to spirituality today?

These questions move the discussion from "how do we teach them what we know?" toward "how do we learn from each other?" By opening a dialogue, those of us with primarily theological, philosophical, textual, or historical perspectives in academia can listen for the issues, questions, and realities of twenty-first-century life that call for reexamining the sources within the tradition for insight and application. At the same time, our active engagement with practitioners—both within the religious traditions as well as in other settings and places that are concerned with the spiritual lives of children and adolescents—can help us bring the wisdom of the tradition to bear in the lives and issues that religious leaders seek to nurture and shape.

AUTHENTIC ENGAGEMENT ON BEHALF OF YOUNG PEOPLE

In sum, this volume suggests the need for more theological and philosophical reflection within and among religious traditions about the intersection of children's lives and their spirituality with the broader context of society and the world around them. It calls for dialogue across religious and social science disciplines and perspectives in ways that bring new light to understanding the spiritual nurture of the young in an increasingly diverse, complex, and interconnected world. Underlying this challenge is the need for faith communities and scholars around the globe to find and maintain an authentic and yet respectful and bridge-building voice to contribute to the conversation, so that the world's children may have rich and challenging spiritual lives that allow them to build a more just and beautiful future for the world.

References

Benson, Peter L., Eugene C. Roehlkepartain, and Stacey P. Rude. 2003. Spiritual development in childhood and adolescence: Toward a field of inquiry. *Applied Developmental Science, 7,* 204–212.

Eck, Diana L. 1993. *Encountering God: A spiritual journey from Bozeman to Banares.* Boston: Beacon Press.

Roehlkepartain, Eugene C., Pamela E. King, Linda M. Wagener, and Peter L. Benson, eds. 2006. *The handbook of spiritual development in childhood and adolescence.* Thousand Oaks, Calif.: Sage.

About the Editors

Karen Marie Yust, Th.D., is associate professor of Christian education at Union Theological Seminary and Presbyterian School of Christian Education. She is the author of *Real Kids, Real Faith: Practices for Nurturing Children's Spiritual Lives* and a regular participant in the International Conference on Children's Spirituality. She directed the Faith Formation in Children's Ministries project, funded by Lilly Endowment, Inc., which studied efforts to nurture children's spirituality in American Protestant congregations. She is an ordained clergywoman with standing in the United Church of Christ and the Christian Church (Disciples of Christ), and the mother of three children. She holds a bachelor of arts from Trinity University, a master's of divinity from Texas Christian University, and doctor of theology degree from Harvard University.

Aostre N. Johnson, Ed.D., is associate professor of education at Saint Michael's College, where she teaches curriculum and pedagogy courses and directs the master's program in curriculum. She focuses on spirituality and education through teaching courses and co-coordinating the Center for Spirituality and Education and the Committee for Spirituality and the Intellectual Life, which sponsor programs for college faculty and staff as well as area pre-K through high school teachers. In addition, she was instrumental as a consultant in launching a graduate-level master's program on contemplative education at Naropa University, the nation's leading Buddhist institute of higher education. Her research interests include spirituality, spiritual development and education, drawing on both Eastern and Western religious traditions, as well as academic literature in psychology, ethics, creativity, and postmodernity. She has written numerous articles relating to these topics. She holds a bachelor of arts from Harvard University, a master's in education from the Harvard Graduate School of Education, and a doctorate in education from the University of North Carolina at Greensboro.

Sandy Eisenberg Sasso, D.D., received her bachelor of arts and master of arts degrees from Temple University, was ordained from the Reconstructionist Rabbinical College, and received her doctor of ministry degree from Christian Theological Seminary. She has been rabbi of Congregation Beth-El Zedeck since 1977. She lectures at Christian Theological Seminary and Butler University. She is the author of many articles and children's books dealing with issues of spirituality, including *God's Paintbrush* and *In God's Name*. Two of her books have been named Best Book of the Year by *Publishers Weekly*. She is also the editor of *Urban Tapestry, Indianapolis Stories* (Indiana University Press, 2002). Her latest book, *Abuelita's Secret Matzahs*, was published in March 2005. She is the 2004 recipient of the Helen Keating Ott Award for Outstanding Contribution to Children's Literature from the Church and Synagogue Library Association.

Eugene C. Roehlkepartain is senior advisor, Office of the President, and director of Family and Congregation Initiatives for Search Institute, Minneapolis. He serves as co-director for the institute's initiative on spiritual development in childhood and adolescence, funded by the John Templeton Foundation. He is lead editor for *The Handbook of Spiritual Development in Childhood and Adolescence* (Sage Publications) and has written more than twenty books and numerous articles on youth development, families, community building, religious and spiritual development, and related issues. He holds a B.A. in religion and journalism from Baylor University.

Contributors

Vishal Agarwal is engaged in the collection of electronic versions of Hindu texts and their translation for lay readers. As the director of the Voice of Dharma project of the Bharatvani Institute, he seeks to present a Hindu perspective on socioreligious issues.

Rabbi Arik Ascherman has served since 1998 as executive director of Rabbis for Human Rights in Jerusalem. He was ordained by Hebrew Union College—Jewish Institute of Religion in New York in 1989.

Sherry H. Blumberg is director of education at Congregation Shalom in Milwaukee, Wisconsin. She is coeditor, with Roberta Louis Goodman, of *Teaching about God and Spirituality: A Resource for Jewish Settings.*

Richard C. Brown has taught in and administered various Buddhist-inspired educational programs at all levels from pre-K to university since 1980. In 1990 he founded the Department of Contemplative Education at Naropa University, where he teaches graduate and undergraduate students.

Marcia J. Bunge is professor of theology and humanities, Christ College, Valparaiso University; editor of *The Child in Christian Thought;* cochair of the Childhood Studies and Religion Consultation of the American Academy of Religion; and director of the Child in Religion and Ethics Project.

Rev. Dr. Elizabeth F. Caldwell is the Harold Blake Walker Professor of Pastoral Theology at McCormick Theological Seminary in Chicago, where she teaches courses in religious education. She is a Minister of Word and Sacrament of the Presbyterian Church (U.S.A.). Among her publications are *Come Unto Me: Rethinking the Sacraments for Children; Making a Home for Faith: Nurturing the Spiritual Life of Children;* and *Leaving Home with Faith: Nurturing the Spiritual Life of Youth.*

Ellen T. Charry is associate professor of systematic and historical theology at Princeton Theological Seminary and editor of *Theology Today.* Her most recent essays appear in

Theology Today, Anglican Theological Review, and *Sewanee Theological Review,* among other publications. She is currently working on a book on theology as knowledge seeking wisdom and researching a book on the Christian doctrine of happiness.

Kathy L. Dawson is assistant professor of Christian education at Columbia Theological Seminary in Decatur, Georgia, where she teaches courses in children's ministry, curriculum theory and design, historical dimensions of Christian education, and human development. She is an ordained minister and certified Christian educator in the Presbyterian Church (U.S.A.).

David C. Dollahite is a professor of family life and Eliza R. Snow Fellow at Brigham Young University. He has been a visiting scholar at the University of Massachusetts-Amherst and Dominican University of California. He has published widely on fathering, faith, and family life, and is editor of *Strengthening Our Families* (2000) and *Helping and Healing Our Families* (2005), both on LDS families.

The Dzogchen Ponlop Rinpoche is one of the foremost scholars and educators of his generation in the Nyingma and Kagyu schools of Tibetan Buddhism. An accomplished meditation master, calligrapher, visual artist, and poet, Rinpoche is also fluent in Western culture and technology. Nalanda West, located in Seattle, Washington, is the primary seat of his educational and spiritual activities in North America.

Adrian Gellel is a lecturer in catechetics at the Faculty of Theology and in religious education at the Faculty of Education at the University of Malta. He is particularly interested in research on how individuals and the believing community perceive God's pedagogy in their salvation history. He is also actively involved in the planning and preparation of catechesis and youth ministry in the Catholic Archdiocese of Malta.

Roberta Louis Goodman is the director for distance learning and assistant professor of Jewish Education for Siegal College of Judaic Studies located in Cleveland. From her office in Chicago, Goodman oversees the program that offers master degrees in Judaic studies and Jewish education through two-way interactive videoconferencing currently in eight communities in the United States. Her books include *Teaching about God and Spirituality,* coedited with Sherry Blumberg, and *The Adult Jewish Education Handbook: Planning, Practice, and Theory.*

Rita M. Gross is a scholar-practitioner who has studied and practiced Buddhism for most of her adult life. She is an expert on gender and religion in cross-cultural perspectives and has also participated widely in interreligious exchanges, in addition to teaching undergraduate students for many years. Her most influential books include *Buddhism after Patriarchy: A Feminist History, Analysis, and Reconstruction of Buddhism* and *Feminism and Religion: An Introduction.*

Marcia Hermansen is professor of theology at Loyola University Chicago, where she teaches courses in Islamic studies and world religions. She has lived for extended periods in Egypt, Jordan, India, Iran, and Pakistan, and she conducts research in Arabic, Persian, and Urdu, as well as the major European languages. She is coeditor of the *Encyclopedia of Islam and the Muslim World*.

Monte Joffee is a cofounder and principal of the Renaissance Charter School in New York City. He is a doctoral student at Teachers College, Columbia University. He is also the vice director of the SGI-USA Educators Division, a group of approximately one thousand Buddhist educators in the pre-K–12 private and public sectors.

Ilmee Hwansoo Kim is a doctoral candidate at Harvard University.

Ruqayya Yasmine Khan teaches in the Department of Religion at Trinity University in San Antonio, Texas. Among her areas of expertise are Judaism, Christianity, and Islam; Islamic tradition; and Arabic literature.

Débora Barbosa Agra Junker is professor of Christian education at the Methodist Theological Seminary of the Methodist University of São Paulo, Brazil. Her areas of interest include children, youth, gender issues, and social justice.

Kevin E. Lawson serves as director of the Ph.D. and Ed.D. programs in educational studies at Talbot School of Theology, Biola University, in La Mirada, California. He also chairs the Children's Spirituality Conference: Christian Perspectives planning team, which held its first conference in Chicago in 2003 and has another scheduled for 2006.

Benny Liow is with the Kota Kemuning Buddhist Center in Shah Alam, Selangor, Malaysia. He is also editor of the Buddhist magazine *Eastern Horizon*.

Sumi Loundon has an M.T.S. from Harvard Divinity School in the study of Buddhism and Sanskrit. She is editor of *Blue Jean Buddha: Voices of Young Buddhists*.

Robin Maas is the founder and director of the Women's Apostolate to Youth, a community of Catholic laywomen exercising spiritual leadership with children and youth in the Diocese of Arlington, Virginia. Retired from the faculty at the John Paul II Institute for Studies in Marriage and Family in Washington, D.C., Dr. Maas is the author of *Living Hope: Baptism and the Cost of Christian Commitment*. Her work has also appeared in *Anthropotes, Theology Today, Magnificat, Spiritual Life, The Catholic Faith*, and *Living Light*.

Loren D. Marks is assistant professor of family, child, and consumer sciences in the School of Human Ecology at Louisiana State University. In collaboration with Dave Dollahite, he has conducted extensive qualitative research with more than 100 Christian, Jewish, Mormon, and Muslim families from around the United States and has authored or coauthored about twenty articles or chapters addressing religion in connection with parenting, marriage, and individual development.

Joyce Ann Mercer is associate professor of practical theology and Christian education at San Francisco Theological Seminary in San Anselmo, California, where she teaches and conducts research on children and youth in Christian congregations, education for transformation, and feminist theology. She has published widely on Christian children's spirituality and is currently working on a book on Christian faith and adolescent girls, tentatively titled *GirlTalk on Families and Faith: The Religious Lives of Adolescent Girls.*

Shabana Mir is a doctoral candidate in education policy studies and anthropology at Indiana University. She has lived, worked, and studied in the United Kingdom, Pakistan, and the United States. Her research interests are religion, gender, and pluralism in education.

Yoshiharu Nakagawa is a professor at Ritsumeikan University in Kyoto, Japan. He is the author of *Education for Awakening: An Eastern Approach to Holistic Education* and the coeditor of *Nurturing Our Wholeness: Perspectives on Spirituality in Education.* He has published a number of books on holistic education and spirituality in Japanese.

Dr. Lori M. Noguchi is president of the Badi Foundation, a nonprofit, nongovernmental organization based in Macau. Since 1990, she has been involved in the development of human resources in China through training and other activities to promote social and economic development. As a member of the Continental Board of Counselors of the Bahá'ís of Asia, Dr. Noguchi helps to promote the spiritual, intellectual, and social aspects of Bahá'í life, including the development and implementation of programs for children and youth.

A former Benedictine monk, **Nicholas Otieno** studied at the Consolata Institute of Philosophy. He also has served as editor of an ecumenical newspaper in Kenya and as head of the Ecumenical Documentation and Information Centre in Zimbabwe. He is a recipient of the Martin Luther King Jr. Leadership Award and currently works as a consultant for the World Council of Churches and All Africa Conference of Churches.

Shin-Kyung Park is associate professor of Christian education at Youngnam Theological College and Seminary in Kyungsan, Korea. Her research focuses mostly on young childhood and educational ministry. She teaches courses in educational ministry for children, introduction to education, youth ministry, and human development.

Evelyn L. Parker is associate professor of Christian education at Perkins School of Theology at Southern Methodist University in Dallas, Texas. Her interests include African American adolescent spirituality and sociocultural, socioeconomic, and sociopolitical issues of race, class, and gender. She is the author of *Trouble Don't Last Always: Emancipatory Hope among African American Adolescents.*

Nusaybah Ritchie is a coordinator of the Peace Leaders Program at the Al-Fatith Academy and a consultant with schools on conflict resolution from an Islamic perspective.

Jeffrey K. Salkin has been the senior rabbi of The Temple in Atlanta since August 2003. He is best known as the author, among other publications, of *Putting God on the Guest List: How to Reclaim The Spiritual Meaning of Your Child's Bar or Bat Mitzvah*, which won the 1992 Benjamin Franklin Award for best religion book of the year.

Venkatakrishna B. V. Sastry is a member of the resident faculty at Hindu University of America. A language technologist, he pioneered the enterprise mission "Culture through Computer" by bringing out the Indian philosophical classic Bhagavad-Gita as a CD-ROM Multimedia Book in the year 1995. He is the founder-director of International Sanskrit Research Academy.

Howard Schwartz is professor of English at the University of Missouri-St. Louis. In addition to publishing three books of poetry and several books of fiction, he has edited a four-volume set of Jewish folktales: *Elijah's Violin and Other Jewish Fairy Tales, Miriam's Tambourine: Jewish Folktales from Around the World, Lilith's Cave: Jewish Tales of the Supernatural,* and, most recently, *Gabriel's Palace: Jewish Mystical Tales.* His book *Reimagining the Bible: The Storytelling of the Rabbis* was a finalist for the National Jewish Book Award for 1999.

Rabbi Dr. Michael Shire is the vice-principal of Leo Baeck College-Centre for Jewish Education in London. He received his doctorate from Hebrew Union College, Los Angeles, in Jewish Education. He is the author of four books of creative liturgy incorporating medieval illuminated manuscripts.

Among **Shoshana Silberman**'s publications are *The Jewish World Family Haggadah, A Family Haggadah I & II, The Whole Megillah (Almost), Tiku Shofar: A High Holiday Mahzor,* and *Siddur Shema Yisrael: A Shabbat Family Prayerbook.* A Jewish educator for more than forty years, she has been a teacher, principal, and facilitator who has led workshops across North America on numerous topics, including children's spiritual development.

Melukote K. Sridhar is a member of the resident faculty at Hindu University of America. He has been a professor of Sanskrit, with twenty-four years' teaching experience at National College Bangalore, India. He is the chief editor of the *Kannada-English Concise Dictionary* and an assistant editor for the *Encyclopedia of Hinduism*. Dr. Sridhar also serves as the director of the Indological Research Foundation in Bangalore.

Catherine Stonehouse is professor of Christian education at Asbury Theological Seminary, teaching in the area of Christian discipleship with an emphasis on ministry with children. The focus of her current research is the spirituality of children. Engaging children through their drawings and in conversation, she listens for insights into their understanding of God and their relationship with God. She is the author of *Joining Children on the Spiritual Journey: Nurturing a Life of Faith.*

Afeefa Syeed is founding director of Al-Fatih Academy in Herndon, Virginia, and co-director of the Muslim Education Resource Council, Inc.

Pamela K. Taylor is the publications officer for the Islamic Writers Alliance and Board Member of the Progressive Muslim Union. Her writing has appeared in various magazines and newspapers, including *Islamic Horizons, The Minaret,* and *Mirror International.*

Michael Warren's pastoral experience includes eight years teaching high school religion followed by three years of full-time adult catechetical ministry as part of a catechetical team working in clusters of eight parishes in Virginia and Brooklyn. Since 1975 he has been professor of religious education and catechetical ministry in the Department of Theology at St. John's University, New York City. His recent books are *Seeing through the Media: A Religious View of Communications and Cultural Analysis* and *At This Time in This Place: The Spirit Embodied in the Local Assembly.*

Yetkin Yildirim is the faculty interfaith coordinator at the Peace and Conflict Studies Clinic at the University of Texas at Austin. The founding member and vice-president of the Institute of Interfaith Dialog, he was on the organizing committee for the "Preventing Another September 11" conference in 2002 and the "Peaceful Heroes" conference at UT Austin. His recent publications include "Peace and Conflict Resolution Concepts in the Medina Charter" and "The Golden Generation: Integration of Muslim Identity with the World through Education."

Index

'Abdu'l-Bahá, 287, 288

Adi Shankaracharya, 28

African Christian communities: the African view of children, 122–23; how children become part of the community, 126–27; the naming of children in African societies, 124–26; and singing as a practice for spiritual formation, 264–65; and the spiritual crisis of the HIV/AIDS pandemic, 128–30; and the spiritual matrix of Africa, 123–24; the spiritual passage to adulthood, 127–28

After Heaven (Wuthnow), 2

Ahmad, Mirza Ghulam, 435n14

Ahmed, Leila, 427

Akiva, 50, 147

Al-Ghazali, 136

American Academy of Religion, Childhood Studies and Religion consultation, 4, 56

American Society of Church History, 56

Anandamayi Ma, 25

Aquinas, Thomas, 85, 88

Arndt, Johann, 59

Augustine, 113

Avneri, Uri, 473

Aydinli, Hasan, 74

Bagby, Ihsan, 426

Bahá'í, 285; Badíʿ as exemplar of the faith, 286; conceptual framework of, 287–92; early Bahá'í community in Iran, 285–87; emerging challenges and research implications, 293–94; recent developments in, 292–93; Rúhu'lláh as exemplar of the faith, 286; and the Universal House of Justice, 287

Barlas, Asma, 427

Barna, George, 116

Bass, Dorothy, 245

Beginning Well (G. Smith), 112

"Being 'Amreekan'" (Hasnat), 140

Bell, William Yancy, 268

Berman, Samuel, 276

Berryman, Jerome, 103

Beshir, Ekram, 362

Beshir, Mohamed, 362

Bharati, Uma, 31n33

Blackwell Companion to Christian Ethics, The, 256

Bourdieu, Pierre, 256

Brazil, Methodist Church in, 450–53

Brown, Steven M., 148

Brueggemann, Walter, 449–50

Buber, Martin, 380

Buddhism, 33; the Buddha and his son (Rahula), 33–34; Buddhahood, 34; Buddhist Sunday Schools, 338–45, 349–50; children and adolescents as compassionate bodhisattvas, 39; children and adolescents as spiritual seekers, 40–41; children and adolescents at Buddhist monasteries, 34–35; on dependent origination, 310; and the dharma, 176, 350n1; the Five Precepts for Laypeople, 351n3; the Four Immeasurable Minds, 35, 39; the Four Noble Truths,

495

Buddhism (*continued*)
35–36, 179; gendered paths for boys and girls in, 414–17; important narratives of, 181; and karma and rebirth, 36–37, 177, 341, 412–13, 414; Korean and Korean American Buddhism, 343–46; Kukai's ten-stage scheme of the human mind, 38–39; lay Buddhist practice, 417–18; in Malaysia, 339–43; and meditation, 34, 35, 186, 342, 350; metaphorical images of children, 37–39; the Noble Eightfold Path, 36; perspectives on sexuality, 418–21; and sangha (community), 35; teachings on buddha nature, 189n1; *Ten Oxherding Pictures,* 40–41; the Three Jewels, 180; the Three Refuges, 351n3; the Three Wheels, 176; valuing of celibate monastic life, 411, 415; in the West, 176, 181, 346–49, 351nn5, 6. *See also* Nichiren Buddhism; Shambhala Buddhism; Theravada (Path of the Elders) Buddhism; Tibetan Buddhism
Buddhist Churches of America, 350
Bunge, Marcia, 98–99
Bushnell, Horace, 60, 117, 329

Cahill, Lisa Sowle, 336
Calvin, John, 59, 60, 236, 439
capitalism, "late," 466; and accelerated consumption, 466–67; Christian theological critique of, 470–71; and commodified relationships, 469–70; and flexible accumulation, 466; and the importance of financial markets, 467; and materialism, 468; and postmodern cultural forms, 467; and the utilitarian value of children, 468–69; and the "war against the poor," 469; and young people as disposable, 470
Carroll, James, 261n5
Catholicism, 83–84; and the canonization of children as saints, 86, 87–88; children as ministers, 89–90; Confraternities of Christian Doctrine, 86; importance of family and parish in, 88–89; lay movements in, 89; in Malta, 91–93; and participation in the liturgy, 90–91; and participation through the sacraments, 84–87; and prayer, 213–22; spirituality

in, 83, 88, 90, 253–60; and youth ministry, 260. *See also* Vatican Council II
Cavalletti, Sofia, 103, 222n1
Chaudhry, Lubna, 140
Child Evangelism Fellowship, 113
Children and Conversion (Ingle), 114
Children and WorldViews project, 64n7
Children in the Muslim Middle East (E. Fernea), 141
Children of Deh Koh (Friedl), 134
Children of Islam (Giladi), 133–34
Children's Spirituality—Christian Perspectives conference, 5, 64n7
ChildSpirit conference, 5
Chinmaya Mission, 27
Christian Methodist Episcopal Church (CME), 264–65; central values of, 271; Christian Youth Fellowship (CYF) in, 268, 272; in the twenty-first century, 271–73; and youth choirs, 268, 272–73
Christian Nurture (Bushnell), 60, 117
Christian perspectives on children and adolescents, 58, 62–63; as developing beings who need instruction and guidance, 60; as fully human and made in the image of God, 60–61; as gifts of God and sources of joy, 58–59; as models of faith and sources of revelation, 61–62; as orphans, neighbors, and strangers in need of justice and compassion, 62; as sinful creatures and moral agents, 59–60
Christianity: and baptism, 113, 446; consumerism's influence on, 468–70; critique of unjust economic systems, 464–65; and the doctrine of creation, 444–45, 446; and the doctrine of original sin, 440; and the doctrine of redemption, 445–46; dominance of in European culture, 448n3; ethic of care for the vulnerable, 463–64; and foot washing, 447; and formation of a theological identity, 438–39, 443–44, 447; hegemony of religious beliefs and practices in religious studies circles, 11; influence of Western culture on, 439–43; lack of complex thinking about children and adolescents, 53–55; mistake of being more interested in religious thought than in religious practice and way of life,

261–62n11; research on children and adolescents in religious studies and theology, 55–58; view of children and adolescents, 462–63. *See also* African Christian communities; Brazil, Methodist Church in; Catholicism; Christian Methodist Episcopal Church (CME); Christian perspectives on children and adolescents; evangelical church, the; Presbyterian preschools in South Korea; Presbyterian preschools in the United States; Protestantism

Chrysostom, John, 60, 85

Church of Jesus Christ of Latter-day Saints (LDS), 394; age of accountability, 407n2; Church-produced media, 401–2; Church service callings, 403–5; and the Family Home Evening, 400–401; and the Law of Chastity, 400; LDS missionaries, 403; LDS spirituality, 395–96; LDS Standard Works, 407n4; official LDS Church sources, 397; programs for children and youth, 402–3; religious practices of, 399–401; spiritual beliefs of, 397–99; and the Word of Wisdom, 400. *See also* Smith, Joseph

Clashing Worlds of Economics and Faith, The (Haltemann), 459

Clinton, Hillary Rodham, 389

Club 25, 345

Coles, Robert, 2, 51, 333

Committee on Evangelical Unity in the Gospel, 110–11

Conde, Maria, 450

Confirmation (Osmer), 119

conscientization, 451

conversos, 383

Council of Vienna (1311–12), 85

Courage to Teach, The (Parker), 5

creation, doctrine of, 444–45

cross-cultural dialogue, 483–84

cross-disciplinary dialogue, 484–85

Crow, Stan, 390

Cunningham, Hugh, 65n14

Cushing, Lesleigh, 134–35

Cyprian, 61

Dean, Kenda C., 406, 407

Deen Intensives, 433

DeVries, Dawn, 58

Dewey, John, 275, 281

Dhammananda, Dr. K. Sri, 341

Dharmakirti, 189n2

Dialectical Behavior Therapy, 351n13

Dignaga, 189n2

discipleship, 255, 261n3

Discourse on the Origin and Foundations of Inequality (Rousseau), 440

Dolan, John P., 262n11

Dorsey, Thomas A., 265

Duffy, Regis, 260

Duke, James T., 403

Dykstra, Craig, 245, 332, 333–34, 335

Easum Bill, 2–3

Eck, Diana, 327, 483

Ecumenical Child Care Network, 239

Education as Transformation conference, 5

"Education of the Warrior, The" (Trungpa), 157

Edwards, Jonathan, 59

Efraim of Bonn, 475

Eisenstein, Judith Kaplan, 149, 384

Eliade, Mircea, 391, 393n7

emancipatory hope, 265–66

Émile (Rousseau), 440

Erikson, Erik, 144, 150, 153, 154, 279, 437, 476

Estatuto da Criança e Adolescente (ECA), 451–52

Et Avotai Ani Mazkir (I remember my ancestors) (Efraim of Bonn), 475

evangelical church, the: basic ministry approaches to children and adolescents, 115; distinctives of, 109; emphasis on the proclamation of the gospel, 110–11; spirituality in, 109–10; understanding of conversion, 112–19

Fahs, Sophia, 329

"faithing," 153

Faruqi, Ismail, 426

Faure, Bernard, 419

Fernea, Elizabeth, 133, 134, 135–36, 137, 139, 141

Fernea, Robert, 135

Fine Young Man, A (Gurian), 390

Finke, Roger, 405

Fiorenza, Elisabeth Schüssler, 269–70
Fischer, Norman, 348
Fitzpatrick, Jean Grasso, 328
Fleming, Cynthia, 269
Foucault, Michel, 442
Fourth Lateran Council (1215), 85
Fowler, James W., 144, 145–46, 150, 153, 155, 260, 437
Francke, August Hermann, 57, 62
Freire, Paulo, 451
Freud, Sigmund, 134, 437, 442
Friedl, Erika, 133, 134, 141

Gebert, Andrew, 313
Gellman, Marc, 332
Geneva Declaration of the Rights of the Child (1924), 283n2
Geography of Human Life, A (Makiguchi), 312
George, Anthony, 313
Giladi, Avner, 133–34, 135, 136
Gilboa, Amir, 475
Godly Materialism (Schneider), 459
Godly Play, 103
Golden Generation model of education, 78
Goldling, William, 440
Gouri, Hayim, 475
Greven, Philip, 64n12
Gülen, Fethullah, 77–78. *See also* Golden Generation model of education
Gurian, Michael, 390
Gutiérrez, Gustavo, 254, 261n3

Hakeda, Yoshito, 38–39
Haltemann, John, 459
Hanson, Hamza Yusuf, 425, 432
Hartman, Thomas, 332
Harvey, David, 460
Harvey, Peter, 34–35
Hasafari, Shmuel, 475–76
Hasnat, Naheed, 140
Hassan, Riffat, 427
Hay, David, 97, 309
Hayward, Jeremy, 158
heart, the, in Scripture, 215–16; a forgiving heart, 211–12; a new heart, 211; an obedient heart, 212–13; a whole heart, 213
Heitzenrater, Richard, 452

"Heritage" (Gouri), 475
Hermansen, Marcia, 432
Herrmann, Ulrich, 64n13
Heschel, Abraham Joshua, 208, 450, 454
High School Survey of Student Engagement (Indiana University School of Education), 318
Hindu festivals, 223–24, 233–34; the birthdays of Rama and Krishna, 20, 229; the birthdays of spiritual teachers, 230; Diwali (the festival of lights), 231–33; Ganesha festival, 229–30; Gita Jayanti, 233; Holi, 228; Makara Sankranti or Pongal, 227; Navaratri, 231; Raksha Bandhan, 231; Shivaratri, 227–28; significance of, 225–27; Vijayadashmi, 26; Yugadi, 228–29
Hinduism, 19; *artha shastra* discipline, 378–79; assumption of latent spirituality in children and adolescents, 22–25; Ballal as exemplar of true devotion, 21; and the Bhagvadgita (the Gita), 233; Bhakti Yoga, 27–28; and birth, 370–71; caste system and, 374; classical four stages of life, 29; and dharma, 26, 366, 368; Dharmapada and the temple of Konarka, 22; Dhruva as exemplar of true devotion, 20–21; ear piercing (*karna vedha* rite), 372–73; family prayers, 374–75; festivities in the home, 375–76; first union (*nisheka* rite), 370; the Fourfold Values of Life, 234; Ganapatya (worshipping Ganesha/Ganapati, the son of Parvati and Shiva), 21; and the guru, 24–25; the Hindu calendar, 223; the Hindu Diaspora, 27, 31n32; Hindu medical (Ayurvedic) texts on embryology and parturition, 23–24; Hindu sacred texts, 19, 25–26; initiation into the formal learning of language (*aksharabhyasa* ritual), 374; initiation into the study of sacred lore (*upanayana* ritual), 24, 225, 377, 379; Jabala as exemplar of true devotion, 27, 30–31b27; Jnana Yoga, 28–29; and karma and rebirth, 22–23, 366, 368; Karma Yoga, 29; Kaumaara (worshipping Skanda or Kumara, son of Shiva), 21–22; marriage vows, 369–70; name identity of children, 371; *nishkramana* rite, 372; other Hindu religious traditions (Ayyappan and

Harkrishan), 22; and pilgrimages, 26; practical ways of engaging children and adolescents in religion and spirituality, 25–27; Prahlada as exemplar of true devotion, 20; and pregnancy, 270; Raja Yoga, 29, 31n38; respect for elders, 29; and *rina*, 366, 368–69; rites of passage (samskaras), 24, 30n18, 224–25, 379 (*see also* specific rites); Saura, 22; Shaakta (worshipping the divine mother [Devi]), 19–20; Shaiva (worshipping Shiva and his wife Parvati), 21; Shaivite saint Jnanasambandhar, 21; Shaivite saint Markandeya, 21; sixteen services offered to beloved guests, 226; sources of wisdom, 367–68; tonsuring of the hair (*chudakarma* ritual), 224–25, 373; Vaishnava (worshipping Lord Vishnu [Rama, Krishna] and his consort Lakshmi), 20–21; weaning (*anna prashna* ritual), 372; the yogin Ashtavakra, 28. *See also* Hindu festivals

Hippolytus, 260
Hirsch, Samson Raphael, 50
History of the Reformation (Dolan), 262n11
Hoffman, Lawrence, 393n4
Holy Childhood Association, 90
Hossein Nasr, Seyyed, 426
Hoyt, Thomas, 272
Hussein, Taha, 139–40

Ibn Kathir, 432
Ibn Taimiyya, 432
Ikeda, Daisaku, 311, 314–17
image of God (*imago Dei*), 60–61, 83, 95–96, 146, 463, 470, 477
Inchley, John, 114
inclusivism, 483
Infants, Parents and Wet Nurses (Giladi), 136
Ingle, Clifford, 114
Innocent III, 85
International Conference on Children's Spirituality, 5
interreligious dialogue, 482–83
Iraeneus, 263n11
Islam, 296; the age of maturity, 354–56; the Ahmadiyya movement, 435n14; and Arabic, 301; "bearing witness" during childhood, 137–39; childhood in,

298–99; the college experience for Muslim youth, 428–33; and cultural variations, 305–7; denial of original sin, 298; and *dhikr*, 357–58, 427; distinction between the idea of childhood and the realities of children, 133–36; education of children, 360–63; the ethics of breastfeeding, 136; and *fiqh*, 427; and *fitrah*, 353–54; and the hadith, 364n3; and *halaqas*, 431–32; "identity" Islam, 426; identity issues of children and adolescents, 140–41; and *ijtihad*, 427; importance of the family in, 424; and the "inoculation" of children against moral dangers of society, 424; and *juma'*, 431; major sects of, 296; the nature of Islamic scholarship, 132–33; and *qiyam al-lail*, 431; and the Qur'an, 69, 70, 76, 79, 296, 298, 300, 301, 356–57, 361, 362; Qur'anic schooling, 139–40; and Ramadan, 304, 359; Salafism, 432; Shi'a Muslims, 435n13; spirituality in, 70–71, 297–98, 356–60; spirituality of childhood and adolescence in, 70, 71–79, 423–28; Sufism, 427, 431, 432–33; and the Sunnah, 69, 296, 298, 301; and *taqwa*, 298, 354, 360; *tarbiyya* model of, 428; and *tauheed*, 353; traditionalism, 426–27; in the West, 424, 427, 433–34. *See also* Islam, Five Pillars of; Prophet Muhammad
Islam, Five Pillars of (*Arkan al-Islam*), 137, 296, 299–300; the Hajj (pilgrimage), 304–5, 359, 360; *salat* (prayer or supplication), 137, 301–3, 358, 359, 360; *sawm* (fasting), 303–4, 359, 360, 431; the *shahada* (declaration of belief in Islam), 300–301, 358; *zakat* (sharing one's wealth) and *sadaqa* (voluntary charity), 303, 358–59, 360
"Islamic Bill of Rights for Women in the Mosque," 428
Islamic Society of North America (ISNA), 426, 430, 432
"Isaac" (Gilboa), 475
Israel, and the Palestinians, 475–80

Jarvis, John, 398
Jesus: interactions with women, 269–70; treatment of children, 57, 84, 96–97, 115, 455, 462–63

Jewish holy days, 204, 207; Haggadah, 51; Hanukkah, 149, 207; Passover, 206; Shabbat (Sabbath), 204–5, 280–81; Shavuot, 206–7; Sukkot (Tabernacles), 47, 205; Yom Kippur, 205

Jewish life cycle rituals, 143, 151–56, 208; becoming Jewishly responsible (bar/bat mitzvah), 47, 149–51, 152, 154–55, 380–92; beginning Jewish schooling (Torah study), 146–49, 152; confirmation ceremony, 148, 206–7, 384–86, 392n1; covenantal naming rituals (*brit milah* and *brit habat*), 144–46, 152, 382–83, 387–88

John Paul II, 90

Joseph Hayyim ben Elijah of Iraq, 384

Josephus, 382

Joy, Donald, 113

Judah ben Tema, 48, 381

Judaism, 44; and Abraham, 194–95, 196–97; and *avoda* (ritual and prayer of the community), 44; and the Binding of Isaac (the Akedah), 196–97, 472–73, 474–75; blessings that children bestow, 46; children as blessings, 44–46; children as pure beings, 195–97; children as symbolic of God's relationship with the children of Israel, 50–51; children's deeply spiritual nature, 199–201; children's ritual and moral obligations, 46–48; the everyday as a means for spiritual growth, 207–8; the Four Questions, 206; and *gemilut hasadim* (deeds of mercy), 44, 277; and Hebrew, 202; Jewish religious experience, 277; and Jewishness, 388; and junior congregations, 202; liberalism, 427–28, 433; and mitzvot, 275–76, 277, 278–81, 381, 383; prayer as a means for spiritual growth, 201–4, 208; and the patriarchs, 193–94; on the purity of the soul, 191–92; the role of texts and storytelling in, 191–97; and the sacredness of the family unit, 193; and self-reflection, 282–83; and the Shekhinah, 192–93; and the Shema, 47, 201–2, 326; study and learning as quintessential childhood activities, 48–50; the Talmud and, 147–48; and *tikkun olam* (repair of the world), 152, 277, 281–82, 284n6; the Torah and, 44, 50, 51, 146–47, 152, 200, 204, 208, 382; and *tzedakah*, 278; and the *Zohar*, 192, 193. *See also* Jewish holy days; Jewish life cycle rituals

justice, 289, 449–50

Kabbani, Shaykh Hisham, 432

Kaplan, Mordecai, 149, 384

Kavanagh, John, 261n4

Keleman, Lawrence, 279–80

Keller, Shaykh Nuh Ha Mim, 432–33

Khan, Inayat, 427

Kids and the Kingdom (Inchley), 114

Kintz, Anisa, 292

Knox, John, 236

Kohlberg, Lawrence, 437

Kohler, Kaufman, 385

Korean Youth Leader Association, 344

Kukai, 38

Lambs to the Slaughter (Hanson), 425

Lamport, Mark A., 116

Lang, Jeffrey, 299, 362

Lapdron, Machig, 417

Leonard, Karen Isaksen, 31n32

Lerner, Michael, 1

Levinson, Daniel, 257–58

Linehan, Marsha, 351n13

Linsey, Nathaniel, 268

Little Buddha, 36

Locke, John, 57, 440

Loder, James, 100

Lord of the Flies (Golding), 440

"Lord Will Make a Way Somehow, The" (Dorsey), 264

Losing My Religion (Lang), 362

Luther, Martin, 60, 62, 95

Mahzor, Sephardi, 191

Maimonides, 47–48, 50, 201

Makiguchi, Tsunesaburo, 312–13

Marcia, James, 100–101

Marcus, Ivan, 387

Marty, Martin, 328, 330, 336

May, Scottie, 116–17

Mbiti, John S., 124

McDannell, Colleen, 2

McNeal, James, 468

Melanchthon, Phillip, 62

Meno (Plato), 440

Meyer, Michael, 385
Milarepa, 178–79, 184, 185, 186
Miller, G. D., 314–15
Miller, T., 315
Miller-McLemore, Bonnie, 58, 330
Mindfulness Based Stress Reduction Clinic, 351n13
Mirgeler, Albert, 262n11
Moore, Mary Elizabeth, 46
moralistic therapeutic deism, 5
Mormons. *See* Church of Jesus Christ of Latter-day Saints
Mulder, John M., 117
Muslim American Society, 426
Muslim Brotherhood, 430
Muslim Student Association (MSA), 428, 430
Muslim Teens (Beshir and Beshir), 362
Muslimwakeup.com, 428
Mutations of Western Christianity (Mirgeler), 262n11

Nalanda University, 184, 189–90n7
Naqshbandi Haqqani Sufi Order, 432
National Association for the Education of Young Children, 239
National Center for Early Development and Learning, 244
National Survey of Youth and Religion (NSYR), 5, 13n4
Nazim, Shaikh, 432
Nelson, Larry J., 405
Nennolina, 88, 90
Newbury Center for Childhood Education, 245–46
Nichiren, 311–12
Nichiren Buddhism: and the development of Soka education, 314–17; spirituality in (the Nine Consciousnesses), 310–14. *See also* Nichiren; The Renaissance Charter School (TRCS)
Niebuhr, Hulda, 329
Novak, David, 144
Novak, Michael, 458–59
Nursi, Said, 69, 70, 71, 77
Nurturing Child and Adolescent Spirituality, 6; core questions for exploration, 10; goals of, 7–8; similarities and differences in contributors' perspectives, 11–12; working definition of spirituality, 8–10

Nye, Rebecca, 44, 97, 309

Origen of Alexandria, 84, 259
Osiek, Carolyn, 254
Osmer, Richard, 119
Overholtzer, J. Irvin, 113

Padmasambhava, 416, 417
Pagan, Iris Teresa, 312, 314
Palestinians, and Israel, 475–80
Palmer, Parker, 5
Peirce, C. S., 260
Perry, William, 154
Piaget, Jean, 144, 146, 150, 221, 275
Pieris, Aloysius, 253–54, 261n7, 261–62n11
Pipher, Mary, 329
Pius X, 86
Pius XII, 88
Plato, 440
pluralism, 483
Poling, James, 454
Prayer from Where We Are (Carroll), 261n5
Prayer of Jabez, The (Wilkerson), 458
Precious Key to the Secret Treasury, The (Kukai), 38
Presbyterian preschools in South Korea, 237–38, 241; holy days and celebrations and, 241–42; narratives or stories and, 242; new models of, 242–43; rituals and practices and, 241
Presbyterian preschools in the United States, 238–40; holy days and celebrations and, 244; rituals and, 244; spiritual practices and prayer and, 243
Projeto Sombra e Aacutegua Fresca, 456
Prophet Muhammad, 69–70, 72–73, 74–75, 77, 299, 300–301, 302, 304, 354, 356, 357, 360, 362, 423
Protestantism: and the authority of the Bible, 95; and baptism, 330; emphasis on God's initiative, 99; foundational biblical assumptions, 95–98; importance of community, 104–5; increased interest in studying childhood and adolescent spirituality, 105–6; loss of majority status in the United States, 327; model of religious education, 327; overemphasis on programs and technology for nurturing faith, 106; and the process of spiritual

Protestantism (*continued*)
    growth, 99–101; spiritual formation in
    the home, 329–36; and the study of
    Scripture, 102–3; teaching children and
    adolescents the language of faith, 102;
    tendency toward age segregation, 106;
    understanding of sin, 98–99. *See also*
    African Christian communities; Brazil,
    Methodist Church in; Christian
    Methodist Episcopal Church (CME);
    evangelical church, the; Presbyterian
    preschools in South Korea; Presbyterian
    preschools in the United States
Psychology of Religion (Starbuck), 115

Quam Singulari (Pius X), 86
Qutb, Sayyid, 432

Rabbis for Human Rights (RHR), 477, 478,
    479
Rahman, Fazlur, 427
Rahner, Karl, 61
Ramseth, Pam, 240
Rashi, 192
Ratcliff, Donald, 309
redemption, doctrine of, 445–46
Reformation, the, 440
Religion, Culture, and the Family project,
    64n2
religious traditions, 3–4; delving more deeply
    into, 482; erosion of by cultural
    influences, 323; and inspired texts, 11. *See
    also* Bahá'í; Buddhism; Christianity;
    Church of Jesus Christ of Latter-day
    Saints; Hinduism; Islam; Judaism
Remembering Childhood in the Middle East (E.
    Fernea), 134
Richter, Don, 245
Rinpoche, Sogyal, 36
Robinson, Edward, 277
Rome, David, 158
Rose, Rosetta, 269
Rosenak, Michael, 51
Rousseau, Jean-Jacques, 440, 441
Rush, Vincent, 261n7

St. John's Children's Center, 240
Sakyong Mipham, 158
Samuel, Michael, 279

Sant Jnaneshvar, 28
Saraj, Eyad, 473
Saraswati, Dayanand, 31n37
Schechter, Solomon, 44
Schleiermacher, Friedrich, 58, 62
Schmidt, Garbi, 429–30
Schneider, John R., 459
Search Institute, 6, 54–55
Second Vatican Council. *See* Vatican II
Shalom of Belz, 380
Shambhala Buddhism, 157–58; Children's
    Welcoming Ceremony in, 163–64;
    essential teachings related to spiritual
    development, 158–60; Great Easter Sun
    symbol, 168; the practice of meditation,
    161; Rite of Warriorship in, 167; rites of
    passage, 161–68; and "weapons," 166
Simon ben Shetah, 147
Smith, B. Julian, 268
Smith, Christian, 5, 405–6, 407
Smith, Gordon, 112
Smith, Joseph, 395, 396, 397
Smith, Ruby Doris, 265, 266–71
Society for Christian Doctrine, 92
Society of Christian Ethics, 56
Socrates, 315
Soka education, 314–17
Soka Gakkai International (SGI), 311, 350
Soka Kyoiku Gakkai ("Educational Value
    Creation Society"), 312, 313
Some Thoughts concerning Education (Locke),
    440
spiritual development, 9, 484
spiritual growth, 275
spirituality, 97; of children and adolescents,
    2–3, 4–6; Christian spirituality, 255–56,
    259–60, 328; consumerist spirituality,
    253, 254–55, 256; contemporary search
    for, 1–2; and the inner life, 171; and life
    structure, 257–59; "lowercase" spirituality,
    254–55; mistaken approaches to, 253–54,
    256; multiple definitions of, 253;
    spirituality of resistance, 454–57;
    traditional three stages of the spiritual life,
    261n1; "uppercase" spirituality, 255
Spirituality in Education event, 5
Starbuck, Edwin Diller, 115–16
Stark, Rodney, 394, 405
Stemley, Carol, 268

Stewart, Sonja, 103
Stonehouse, Catherine, 115
Strassfeld, Michael, 154–55
Sun Camp, 166
System of Value-Creating Pedagogy, The (Makiguchi), 312

Tablighi Jamaat, 432
Tai Situpa, 158
Taizé, 332
Tamares, Aaron Samuel, 477
Ten Stages of the Development of Mind, The (Kukai), 38
Teresa of Ávila, 214–15, 216–17, 218, 220–21, 222n3
Tertullian, 85
The Child in Law, Religion, and Society project, 64n11
The Child in Religion and Ethics project, 64n11
The Days—Taha Hussein (Hussein), 139–40
The Renaissance Charter School (TRCS), 309–10, 317–18
Theravada (Path of the Elders) Buddhism, 35, 339, 340
Theresa of Lisieux, 84
Thich Nhat Hanh, 350
Thompson, Marjorie, 329
"Thoughts on the Aims of Education" (Ikeda), 316
Tibetan Buddhism: continuing its lineage in modern society, 188–89; early training of children, 179–81; the Four Reminders, or the Four Thoughts, 414; and karma, 178–79; and kindness to all beings, 413; and the Losar festival, 181; Mahayana (Great Vehicle) Buddhism, 37, 40, 339, 350n2; and meditation, 176, 178, 184; and *prajna*, 176; ritual and practice, 175–76; and Saka Dawa Duchen, 181; and "spiritual friends" (elders, masters, and gurus), 181–83; the Three Wheels of the Path, 183–88; and *tulkus*, 416; view of reality, 177–78
T'ien-t'ai, 311

Toda, Josei, 312, 314
Top, Brent, 401
Trungpa, Chogyam, 158, 161, 163, 164, 167
Tsogyel, Yeshe, 416–17

United Nations, 317; United Nations Declaration of the Rights of the Child (1959), 283n2

Valparaiso project, 245
Vatican II, 87, 89, 90–91, 253
Vidislavsky, Uri, 475–76

Wadud, Amina, 427
Wangerin, Walter, Jr., 99, 102
Way of Youth, The (Ikeda), 311
"We Are Graceful Swans Who Can Also Be Crows" (Chaudhry), 140
We Drink from Our Own Wells (Gutiérrez), 254, 261n3
Wehrman, Carol, 333
Wesley, John, 62, 95, 99, 452
Westerhoff, John, 118, 329
What Do You Believe? American Teenagers, Spirituality and Freedom of Religion, 13n3
Whitmore, Todd David, 64n1
Wilkerson, Bruce, 458
Willard, Dallas, 96
Wilmore, Gayraud, 266
Winnicott, David, 136
"Winter of '73" (Hasafari and Vidislavsky), 475–76
Wulfstan II, 85
Wuthnow, Robert, 2, 334

Yehoshua ben Gamla, 49
Young, Donna, 240
Young Children and Worship (Stewart and Berryman), 103
Youth and Family Institute, 54–55
Youth Ministry and Spirituality project, 256–57
Yust, Karen Marie, 244, 329–30

Zunz, Leopold, 385